DEMOCRACY AND HIGHER EDUCATION

Transformations in Higher Education:
The Scholarship of Engagement

Democracy and Higher Education

Traditions and Stories of Civic Engagement

SCOTT J. PETERS

WITH THEODORE R. ALTER AND NEIL SCHWARTZBACH

Michigan State University Press • *East Lansing*

Michigan State University Press
East Lansing, Michigan 48823-5245

Printed and bound in the United States of America.

16   15   14   13   12   11   10   1 2 3 4 5 6 7 8 9 10

LIBRARY OF CONGRESS CATALOGING-IN-PUBLICATION DATA

Peters, Scott J.
Democracy and higher education : traditions and stories of civic engagement / Scott J. Peters; with Theodore R. Alter and
Neil Schwartzbach.
p. cm. — (Transformations in Higher Education: The Scholarship of Engagement)
Includes bibliographical references and index.
ISBN 978-0-87013-976-5 (pbk. : alk. paper) 1. Democracy and education—United States. 2. Education, Higher—United States—
Administration. 3. Equality—United States. 4. Education, Humanistic—Philosophy. 5. United States—Politics and government. I. Alter,
Theodore R. II. Schwartzbach,
Neil. III. Title.
LB875.D5P48 2010
378'.015—dc22
2010003521

Cover design by Erin Kirk New
Book design by Aptara

Michigan State University Press is a member of the Green Press Initiative and is committed to developing
and encouraging ecologically responsible publishing practices. For more information about the Green Press
Initiative and the use of recycled paper in book publishing, please visit www.greenpressinitiative.org.

Visit Michigan State University Press on the World Wide Web at: www.msupress.msu.edu

Transformations in Higher Education: Scholarship of Engagement

The *Transformations in Higher Education: Scholarship of Engagement* book series is designed to provide a forum where scholars can address the diverse issues provoked by community-campus partnerships that are directed toward creating innovative solutions to societal problems. Numerous social critics and key national commissions have drawn attention to the pervasive and burgeoning problems of individuals, families, communities, economies, health services, and education in American society. Such issues as child and youth development, economic competitiveness, environmental quality, and health and health care require creative research and the design, deployment, and evaluation of innovative public policies and intervention programs. Similar problems and initiatives have been articulated in many other countries, apart from the devastating consequences of poverty that burdens economic and social change. As a consequence, there has been increasing societal pressure on universities to partner with communities to design and deliver knowledge applications that address these issues, and to co-create novel approaches to effect system changes that can lead to sustainable and evidence-based solutions. Knowledge generation and knowledge application are critical parts of the engagement process, but so too are knowledge dissemination and preservation. The *Transformations in Higher Education: Scholarship of Engagement* series was designed to meet one aspect of the dissemination/ preservation dyad.

This series is sponsored by the National Collaborative for the Study of University Engagement (NCSUE) and is published in partnership with the Michigan State University Press. An external board of editors supports the NCSUE editorial staff in order to insure that all volumes in the series are peer reviewed throughout the publication process. Manuscripts embracing campus-community partnerships are invited from authors regardless of discipline, geographic place, or type of transformational change accomplished. Similarly, the series embraces all methodological approaches from rigorous randomized trials to narrative and ethnographic studies. Analyses may span the qualitative to quantitative continuum, with particular emphasis on mixed-model approaches. However, all manuscripts must attend to detailing critical aspects of partnership development, community involvement, and evidence of program changes or impacts. Monographs and books provide ample space for authors to address all facets of engaged scholarship thereby building a compendium of praxis that will facilitate replication and generalization, two of the cornerstones of evidence-based programs, practices, and policies. We invite you to submit your work for publication review and to fully participate in our effort to assist higher education to renew its covenant with society through engaged scholarship.

Hiram E. Fitzgerald
Burton Bargerstock
Laurie Van Egeren

The first and most essential charge upon higher education is that at all its levels and in all its fields of specialization it shall be the carrier of democratic values, ideals, and processes. . . . Its role in a democratic society is that of critic and leader as well as servant; its task is not merely to meet the demands of the present but to alter those demands if necessary, so as to keep them always suited to democratic ideals. Perhaps its most important role is to serve as an instrument of social transition, and its responsibilities are defined in terms of the kind of civilization society hopes to build.

—The President's Commission on Higher Education, 1948

Contents

Acknowledgments

This book is based on a lot of listening. I want to acknowledge two main kinds.

First, it's based on a great deal of listening over the past decade or so to the conversation that has been taking place—both in meetings and conferences and in a newly emerging literature—about the status and future of higher education's public mission, purposes, and work. I've listened as participants in this conversation have raised and wrestled with questions and puzzles, debated ideas and theories, expressed their hopes and concerns, and called for a movement for change and renewal. In my listening, I've been especially inspired, instructed, and provoked by Harry Boyte, Liz Hollander, David Mathews, Ted Alter, Janet Ayres, Don Wyse, Julie Ellison, Peter Levine, Dwight Giles, Ira Harkavy, Noelle McAfee, Hiram Fitzgerald, Maria Avila, Byron White, Matt Hartley, KerryAnn O'Meara, Frank Fear, Lorilee Sandmann, John Recchiuti, Nick Longo, John Saltmarsh, Claire Synder, David Brown, Carol Colbeck, Jeremy Cohen, Barbara Jacoby, Al Dzur, and William Sullivan.

While I've learned a lot from listening in on this conversation, I've also felt that something important was missing. To date, much of the conversation has focused on what should or could be. Not much (or at least, in my judgment, not enough) of the conversation has focused on the lived—and storied—experience of academic professionals who are already engaged in civic life. This feeling led me to engage in a second kind of listening.

With several colleagues and students I've spent a considerable amount of time during the past several years listening to more than 40 Cornell University faculty members tell candid, detailed stories about their experience and work as academic professionals in civic life. The core of this book is composed of practitioner profiles that are based on edited transcripts of interviews with twelve of these faculty members. I want to thank all of them for their willingness to share their life and work stories with us. I've learned a great deal from them about the promise and challenge of public work in the academic profession. I've also been deeply inspired and heartened by their passionate commitment to civic ideals and ends, and the sense of hope, joy, and enthusiasm I so often heard in their voices. Listening to them has been a refreshing change from the cynical culture of pessimism, criticism, and complaint I've all too often experienced, inside and outside the academy.

In conducting the research for this book, Neil Schwartzbach and I also had the opportunity to listen and learn from a focus group of faculty members from Cornell's College of Agriculture and Life Sciences. We convened this group four times over a three-year period (2003–2005). In sessions that were recorded and transcribed, we asked them to share their views about Cornell's public mission, and their stories and experiences of pursuing it in their off-campus engagement in New York State communities. Our focus group included several of the faculty members who are profiled in this book. It also included Angela Gonzales, Tom Hirschl, Margaret Smith, Nelson Bills, Tony Shelton, Don Rutz, Allan Bell, Quirine Ketterings, Cliff Craft, Norm Scott, Robin Bellinder, Cliff Scherer, and Kai Schafft. I want to thank all of them for making time to speak with us. More importantly, I want to thank and acknowledge them for their exemplary work as engaged scholars.

I've chosen to place the main focus of this book on the political roles of academic professionals, and their engagement in the public work of democracy. By "political," I do not mean politics in a narrow, government-centered sense as the activities of politicians and political parties. Rather, I mean politics in a broader, community-centered sense that has to do with the relations and interactions of people who are engaged in public work in many everyday settings and contexts. With respect to this focus, I want to offer another acknowledgment. Most of the faculty members who were interviewed for this book did not explicitly name, describe, or interpret their off-campus work as being political, or as having anything to do with democracy. In fact, many were (and likely still are) skeptical about whether it makes sense to name and interpret their work as being political, and what might be gained by doing so. This reflects a number of legitimate worries and concerns that need and deserve a great deal more—and better—attention than they typically receive.

In my view and experience, the question of the political roles and work of academic professionals in a democratic society has been either off the map entirely as a topic of research, discussion, and reflection, or approached with the polarized (and polarizing) exhortations of ideological soap-boxing. Neither tack is helpful. We need to break the silence about this question. We need to challenge ideological exhortations that leave no space for ambiguity, diversity, contingency, and complexity. And we need to challenge the still prevalent view that academic work is or should always be *apolitical*, and that academic professionals and institutions do or should—following a fixed, universal principle—stand apart from or above the messy and contentious work of democracy. While there are legitimate reasons to worry about the consequences of exposing and illuminating the ways academic work is political, there are also reasons to worry about the consequences of ignoring them.

In essence, the whole point of this book is to provoke and contribute to a constructive examination of and conversation about the positive potential of academic professionals' engagement in what Harry Boyte refers to as the "everyday politics" of public work—not as a volunteer afterthought, but as a foundational element of their core work as civic professionals. To avoid misunderstanding, I don't argue—nor do I believe—that all academic professionals all of the time, in every stage of their careers, should be directly and deeply engaged in the everyday politics of off-campus public work. I'm a pluralist. I believe in and value diversity. The pursuit of public purposes in the academic profession comes in many forms. The profiles in this book illuminate a particular form, one that is often overlooked, or framed and interpreted in ways that miss its full academic and civic significance. It may well be that it is also endangered. If so, we need to make an effort to understand and support it, before it's too late.

Many readers may be unfamiliar with narrative inquiry as an approach to qualitative research, and with practitioner profiles, which are a product of the kind of narrative inquiry that I pursue. Therefore, I want to acknowledge something I repeat several times in this book. The kind of narrative inquiry I pursue, and on which this book is based, is not aimed at establishing relationships between variables in order to inform people's attempts to predict and control for particular ends. It's not aimed at discovering or establishing "The Truth" about democracy and higher education (or anything else). Rather, it's aimed at contributing to a conversation about the nature, meaning, significance, and value of higher education's public purposes and work, in and for a democratic society. By illuminating the subjective truths of academic professionals' public work experiences in first-person practice stories, practitioner profiles can contribute to this conversation in critically important ways. Of course, profiles and the practice stories they contain are inherently partial and subjective. While they include many things, they also leave many things out. They are open to multiple— even irreconcilable—interpretations. Rather than being a problem, this is one of the reasons why they are valuable. Not only can they teach us things we wouldn't and couldn't otherwise know; they can also provoke, inspire, and move us to think and act in new ways. In short, richly told stories have a great and vastly underutilized power as resources for learning. While this is hardly a new insight, it's only been in the last twenty years or so that scholars from academic fields and disciples beyond the humanities have begun to take them seriously.

Another acknowledgment I want to make has to do with the way the chapters in parts 1 and 3 are written. I use the collective term *we* in these chapters, even though I am the one who wrote them. I do so to reflect the fact that the project that led to this book was not solitary, but collaborative in nature. Ted Alter and Neil Schwartzbach, my two main collaborators, helped with and contributed to this book in many ways. I couldn't and wouldn't have written it without them. Neil conducted many interviews with Cornell faculty, and also helped organize and facilitate the collective reflection sessions we held with our focus group. Both Ted and Neil helped me to edit, analyze, and interpret the profiles, and to think through what we can learn from them and how they should be framed and situated. Margo Hittleman and two students from Penn State University, Jordan Humphrey and Kathleen A. Schramm, also helped edit some of the profiles. I thank them for their efforts.

I was in nearly daily conversation with Ted as I wrote the chapters in parts 1 and 3. He provided many excellent critical comments and suggestions for my drafts of these chapters, and—drawing from his deep well of experience as a scholar and administrator—helped keep me on track. I owe him a great deal, and I look forward to our continuing collaborations. Despite my collaborations with both Ted and Neil, I must accept full blame for whatever misunderstandings and shortcomings the chapters I wrote might contain.

This book also reflects a collaboration with many Cornell University students. Students not only read early drafts of the profiles in classes they took with me; they also conducted and transcribed interviews and edited them into profiles. Fully half of the profiles in this book were edited from the transcripts of interviews that were conducted by students. I want to thank Tanya Mooza Zwahlen, Leah Mayor, Lael Gerhart, Milt Kogan, Dan O'Connell, and Allison Jack for their superb interviewing and transcribing skills, and for the time and effort they put into the profiles they helped to edit. It was a pleasure to learn and work with them. They were not only my students; they were my teachers and co-researchers who instructed and inspired me in many ways.

I received a great deal of help from the Kettering Foundation during the time I was working on this book. I offer my profound thanks to the Kettering staff, particularly John Dedrick, David Mathews, Debi Witte, Derek Barker, and Alice Diebel. They inspired, encouraged, challenged, and supported me every step of the way.

The profiles in this book include a great many detailed and often highly intimate passages about the lives, experience, work, and views of a dozen faculty members from my own college: Cornell's College of Agriculture and Life Sciences. We took each of the profiles through a lengthy editing process, during which both the interviewers and our interviewees carefully attended to ethical and political issues related to the potential consequences of making such passages public. As part of this process, I also asked the Dean's office to review the profiles. Barbara Knuth, Senior Associate Dean for the college, organized a review process that included several of her colleagues. The critical comments she provided from their review were helpful in many ways. I thank her for them, and for her willingness to add an extra task to her already extremely busy schedule.

I owe my biggest intellectual debts to Harry Boyte, John Forester, David Mathews, and William Sullivan. I've learned more than I can say from them, and more than I've yet been able to successfully absorb and use. In many ways I'm simply following their lead.

I need to add an acknowledgment about language. The introduction and chapter 1 include many lengthy quotations from historical writings. Several of them include offensive, gender-exclusive language. Instead of noting this each time such language is used, I've chosen to note it here.

Finally, I want to acknowledge and thank my best friend Donna Lupardo (who also happens to be my wife) for her patience, support, encouragement, wisdom, humor, and love during the time when I was working on this book. Among other things, we share a love of politics—both the everyday and electoral kinds. While I might teach politics at Cornell, she has actually practiced it longer and in more ways than me: first as a community organizer and educator, and now as an elected representative in the New York State Legislature. I'm guided and grounded by her wisdom, friendship, and love in both my personal and professional life. For that I am profoundly grateful.

Foreword

Harry C. Boyte

The report by President Harry Truman's Commission on Higher Education with which Scott Peters frames this book defines democracy as the fundamental purpose of higher education. But the democratic dimensions of higher education have eroded sharply since World War II. Though there have been many civic engagement efforts in higher education in recent years, they have not made much of a dent in the forces that are turning higher education into a private good, a system with a few winners and many losers. The 2009 *US News and World Report* special issue on "Solving the College Crisis" defines our institutions as "like other industries" and students "as customers voting with their feet." How many students are turned away—rejection rates—are a basic metric for the magazine's rankings of "the best universities."[1] In a similar vein, when Minnesota Public Radio sponsored statewide discussions in 2001 on "the future of the University of Minnesota," it called the series *Access Versus Excellence*.

Higher education faces a critical moment. The challenge we face calls for civic boldness with parallels to other times when intellectuals helped to change the course of history. Just as intellectuals in the Eastern bloc in 1989 sounded the death knell of Communism, we need to help change the meritocratic culture of American society, which devalues the talents and intelligence of the great majority of people. Rather than objective observers, we need to become political in the older sense of the word, learning to work with people of diverse backgrounds and interests on the basis of equality and respect.[2]

Scott Peters's *Democracy and Higher Education* responds to this challenge. He retrieves the political dimensions and democratic purposes of the work of faculty, showing the richness and continuing presence of the public work tradition in higher education. He presents complex and also wonderful stories of scholars who carry it on, who learn to respect and help to unleash the talents and agency of fellow citizens, and who deepen collective civic power in the process.

In a time of enormous change, *Democracy and Higher Education* contributes to the realization that we in higher education can be agents of change, not objects of change. By renewing the democratic identity of our institutions, we can contribute to the future of our democracies.

A Silent Civic Disease

Major obstacles are in the way. "Politics," in conventional use, is viewed as something that occurs "out there," in elections and government, not in everyday lives and work. In the academy we lack even a language to use in thinking of ourselves as political actors—as relational, interactive, and productive citizens, involved in the messy, often uncomfortable work of solving problems, dealing with people who are different, and co-creating public things with citizens outside of our disciplines and subdisciplines. A political understanding of our work means learning new habits of thought as well as action. It involves coming to see each person in our institutions and beyond them as complex, dynamic, and unique, not mainly as a representative of the abstract categories that are the stock in trade of academic discourse. Most fundamentally, politics in a democratic sense requires learning respect for the intelligence and knowledge-making of all citizens, nonacademics as well as those in the academy.

In this book, Peters recalls important histories to build on, such as the founding land-grant mission of public colleges and universities. Land-grants were established to educate rural, working-class, and low-income students. With a philosophy reaching back to ancient Athens, they held that excellence is the product of inclusive cultures of learning and knowledge-making—of access—not the opposite. But today this philosophy is deeply countercultural. As Josiah Ober observes in *Democracy and Knowledge: Innovation and Learning in Classical Athens,* Athens's relative success was based in practices and methods of interaction between experts and amateurs that aggregated many kinds of knowledge making. In contrast, "Contemporary practice often treats free citizens as passive subjects by discounting the value of what they know. . . . Willful ignorance is practiced by the parties of the right and left alike."[3]

We heard many faculty members express a sharp sense of loss resulting from the philosophy of detachment that has replaced a philosophy of relationship, when the Kellogg Foundation asked the Center for Democracy and Citizenship in 1997 to make a judgment about whether the land-grant mission of the University of Minnesota could be revived. As the late Charles Backstrom, a professor of political science who retired after forty years in the university, put it,

> When I came to the University of Minnesota in 1959, the Political Science department gave students credit for working in the community and on political campaigns. We had what some said was the finest internship program in the country. I thought of my job description as including work with communities. I believed in the "Wisconsin idea'" of public universities: the borders of the University were the borders of the state. I felt pressure to focus only on publications. But I also had examples of rising stars like John Bochert in Geography, who was working with communities to think through what factors make a small community grow and flourish or fail.

Over the years, he said, such public engagement was seen as less and less legitimate. In dozens of interviews, we found similar feelings of powerlessness, detachment, and loss of public purpose in the everyday practices and norms of the university. These were hard even to name. At the end of interviews, senior faculty members would say, "I could never talk to my colleagues about this."

While the stance of detachment in university cultures depoliticizes the worlds of academics, it also undermines the standing of those who are not credentialed. Infused with good intensions, the assumption that "experts know best" substitutes the agency of experts for the agency of everyone else. For instance, Donna Shalala, chancellor of the University of Wisconsin who later served as secretary of Health and Human Services for President Clinton, called for renewal of research universities' mission to serve society in her major 1989 address, "Mandate for a New Century." She championed higher education's pursuit of social justice, peace, and environmentalism, and its engagement in struggles against racism, sexism, and homophobia.[4] But her ideal agent was "a disinterested technocratic elite" fired by the moral mission of "society's best and brightest in service to its most needy." She called on social scientists to "solve social problems as doctors once cured rickets," leaving most people little to do except express thanks or complain if they don't like the results.

Detachment from and condescension toward nonacademics are shaped by the lingering presence of the theory of positivism, based on a view of science as the discovery of permanent, atemporal standards of rationality that can be found and then applied. Scientific method is purported to be pure, its aim to find abstract, universal truths "out there" that can be brought back to enlighten the masses, like the philosopher king returning to Plato's cave. Positivism assumes the detached, rational, apolitical observer as the highest judge of truth and the most effective problem solver.[5] Though it has been significantly discredited intellectually, positivism continues to structure our research, our disciplines, and our teaching, even among its sharpest critics. It is like a genie that academia let loose long ago, now lurking below the surface and threatening our destruction. Faculty members undergo an insidious socialization, especially in graduate school. We learn a stance of ironic detachment from our fellow citizens, seeing ourselves outside what Jane Addams called "the common lot." We embody such aloofness in multiple ways. The image of the detached, objective, apolitical scholar and teacher leads to the expert stance of fixing problems, discovering truths, and dispensing knowledge.

To turn this around requires reconceiving both higher education and ourselves. It means seeing our institutions not as granite mountains or static bureaucracies but rather as living and dynamic *communities*, cultures that have norms, values, practices, and identities that can be changed. It means thinking of change not in terms of reports, studies, or findings, but rather as a political process, in the older meaning of politics: building public relationships across sharp differences. It involves understanding ourselves, our colleagues, and our partners in communities as meaning-making creators of our environments.

These ideas are all largely foreign to academic institutions and the professional networks anchored in them. The cultural norms of higher education are highly privatized, individualistic, meritocratic, and infused with a stance of detachment. Decades of cultural evolution have detached faculty members, their pedagogies and scholarship, from the civic life of living places, as Thomas Bender, among others, has documented.[6]

Yet the Center for Democracy and Citizenship had seen possibilities for change in higher education cultures in early partnerships, preeminently in the work of Nan Kari and her colleagues at the College of St. Catherine in the early 1990s. The Center, an interdisciplinary research and civic engagement institute then at the University of Minnesota, now at Augsburg College, sought to translate lessons from what is called "broad based community organizing" to other institutions through a variety of partnerships. Kari organized a "citizen politics" group of faculty that met weekly and thought strategically to create a more public culture at the College of St. Catherine. They generated many changes. During these years, we also began to develop a more extensive theory of public work, a concept that differs sharply from the dominant conceptions of civic engagement as off-hours and apolitical service or voluntarism.

I met Scott Peters in 1993, when he joined the staff of the Center. He was interested in the civic history of the extension service. Noting that not much of substance had been written about that topic, I encouraged him to develop the field. He quickly emerged as the leading architect of the civic history of extension, bringing this history from the shadows of pedestrian and unexceptional scholarship into a central object for study, discussion, and debate.

Before Peters, scholarship on extension overlooked or denied its democratic roles and significance. Most scholars focused on extension's role in providing technical assistance and transferring scientific information and technologies for economic development purposes, uninformed by larger theoretical discussions and debates about democracy and education, and the dynamics of power embedded in the purportedly "neutral and objective" practices of scientists and educators. Or they viewed the Country Life Commission and key historical figures from extension's founding period (most notably Cornell's Liberty Hyde Bailey) as antidemocratic exemplars of the environmentally destructive and culturally oppressive technocratic temper of the Progressive Era.

Scott's work challenges these views of extension. Using a public work lens, his research illuminates traditions of respectful, collaborative public relationships between land-grant colleges and communities, especially before World War II, that were heretofore largely unexplored and obscured. He unearthed the history of public work in land-grants, and in recent years has engaged in an intensive process of "listening" to faculty members who continue this tradition. His use of a public-work lens highlighted the public dimensions of faculty work. He learned about the public dimensions of professions, disciplines, and individual faculty experiences, and the erosion of those dimensions. He asked: How did experiences that make work more public—more visible, more interactive with communities, more political—enhance the capacities of individuals and groups to be agents of their own lives and shapers of their environments? Such questions are on full display throughout *Democracy and Higher Education*.

In an interesting riff on what might be called the Bailey tradition of civic science as an alternative to positivist science, six of the twelve profiles that are included in *Democracy and Higher Education* are of academic professionals from natural science disciplines. Their stories reveal how and why they have learned to act in sustained, interactive, and public partnerships with communities. Peters has often noted that natural scientists who learn to create public relationships with citizens are often more "civic" than social scientists. This reflects ironies of the politics of knowledge, in which lower-status human sciences seek to prove their mettle in the regnant hierarchy based on detachment and meritocratic success.

In *Democracy and Higher Education*, Peters not only issues a call for public colleges and universities to take their earlier purposes and identities as "democracy colleges" seriously. His narrative research also illuminates the work and experiences of a group of academic professionals who are embodying and reworking these purposes and identities in our time, developing the power, or civic agency, of themselves and their fellow citizens in the process. Peters speaks, writes, studies, and utilizes practitioner profiles, or what could also be called public narratives—in-depth, carefully crafted accounts of individuals' public work—in ways that are themselves examples of a kind of public work. He invites discussion, additional insights, and practical uses. Readers *experience* a democratic politics taking shape by engaging these stories, especially if the stories are used in conversation with others.

I want to draw attention to several aspects of this democratic politics of public work that are powerfully illustrated in the profiles in this book:

- *The politics of public work has a practical, everyday, down-to-earth quality.* As Peters puts it, "Academic professionals can make meaningful contributions to the public work of democracy with grass—or winter squash varieties (Molly Jahn), or gardens (Marcia Eames-Sheavly), or weeds (Antono DiTommaso), or any number of ordinary things." Stories like Frank Rossi's, whose scholarship in the field of turfgrass science led him to productive relationships that helped to bridge bitter conflicts between industry and environmentalists, vividly make this point.

- *It cultivates respect for diverse talents and capacities of nonacademics and the richness and importance of local knowledge.* In her profile, Molly Jahn, a plant geneticist, describes the importance of learning to listen. "I get on the phone, and I talk to people, and I say, 'Here's what we know and what we can do, what do you think? How do we fit? From where you sit, what do things look like?" In a similar vein, Antonio DiTommaso, an associate professor in Cornell's Department of Crop and Soil Science, describes how he learned not to "speak above or below [people's] heads. Don't treat them as though they might not know anything, or use terminology or jargon that we might use in science." The profiles in this book are full of such lessons. They illuminate a process of learning respect that is deeply important, and yet rarely named.

- *Public work is about collective action.* Peters describes the process of organizing collective action as "making I we," using the story of Marcia Eames-Sheavly, who resisted efforts to have her talk about her individual action. "We want to talk with people to make sure that people are on board, that there's a sense of ownership," she says in her profile. "I organized this effort, but I kept pulling in people at various points along the way to own it, to move it forward in their own fashion." Marcia Eames-Sheavly puts vividly what all of the scholars who are profiled in this book have learned: relational skills are indispensable to public work. They often also involve *unlearning* the individualist patterns of action cultivated and reinforced in higher education and graduate school. Collective action is another way to describe civic agency, the power of citizens to meet challenges and shape their worlds.

- *It is infused with large meaning, knowledge, and purpose.* The stories of change and growth on the part of academics that we find in the profiles in this book illustrate what faculty members can sometimes bring to community efforts—not only through the introduction of ideas and knowledge from their academic fields, but also through the pursuit of their civic ends, ideals, and commitments. Marvin Pritts, who specializes in berry crops, describes how he works in ways that "will not only help growers with some immediate problems, but maybe push their thinking a little bit in terms of . . . sustainability, and get them thinking a bit broader than how they thought in the past." Paula Horrigan says that her goals "are to create wonderful and meaningful places *with* communities," in ways that help people develop their sense of power and connection to place. Ken Reardon, who brings an extensive knowledge of community organizing to his work with communities, is explicit about the ways his public work aims at developing people's confidence and sense of agency. "The first lesson . . . is about the importance of helping people appreciate the richness of their own experience and knowledge and commitment and passion," he says, describing what he believes is a key value in participatory action research. He describes the second lesson as addressing "the biggest obstacle . . . the notion that trend is destiny, that there's nothing you can do." Public work, in the deepest sense, is about building hope grounded in real experience of changing the world.

Democracy and Higher Education does more than document and interpret a set of stories of the continuing, usually invisible, democratic tradition of public work and politics in the land-grant system. It also suggests the potential for cultural change in all of our institutions. What would it look like if teaching across colleges and universities were a public activity? What are the public conditions and effects of scholarship? What happens if the norms of higher education encourage faculty and staff learn to see themselves as public people, in sustained partnership and collaborative work with other citizens? What new resources might be tapped and cultivated? What new energies can be unleashed by more public cultures in which the whole is more than the sum of the parts?

The public work approach illustrated in this book holds potential to bring back questions of the larger public purposes of our institutions. Beyond the administrative power of modern bureaucracies or the communicative power urged by theorists of deliberation such as Jürgen Habermas,[7] public work focuses on what can be called "constructive power." It sees every institution as a work in progress. It asks how publics and public cultures surrounding and sustaining civic action can be revived and regrown in a modern, technological society. How might change in the culture of higher education help transform the dominant consumer, meritocratic culture of "me first" and "winning at any cost"?

In *Democracy and Higher Education*, Peters breaks a silence. He puts front and center the struggles and stories of a remarkable group of faculty members who have chosen to break out of the "iron cage" of technical rationality described long ago by Max Weber. He also issues a call for all of us to be involved in the work of transforming the academy, and with it, our world. This is a book to be used, as part of a tool kit for public work. It will have many uses and multiple audiences in the development of a democracy movement for civic empowerment in higher education, contributing to the larger civic movement for democratic revitalization in society as a whole.

DEMOCRACY AND HIGHER EDUCATION

Introduction and Overview

Wе begin with a story.

Molly Jahn was puzzled. A representative of a relatively new seed company had just told her that the company was going to drop its license to grow and sell seeds of a variety of winter squash she had developed. To Molly, a plant geneticist and tenured professor in the Department of Plant Breeding and Genetics at Cornell University, the company's decision didn't make sense. The variety had sold exceptionally well and was widely regarded as the best of its type. Because it was an open-pollinated variety instead of a hybrid, the seeds were inexpensive to produce at commercial scale. It outperformed the best hybrids, thanks to its superior eating quality and disease resistance. Despite its strengths, the company was going to drop it. When Molly asked why, the representative from the company told her they were dropping it because the company had decided to drop all open-pollinated varieties worldwide. But this was precisely the feature that made her variety so profitable for the company in markets that were willing to pay premium prices. Molly and those who knew the seed business argued that farmers in many Northern and Western countries considered the cost of high-quality commercial seed an investment in their success, and would not shift to trying to grow their own seed while they were also trying to produce a commercial crop. But there was no point in arguing. "It's a global management decision," the company representative told her. "We're dropping all open-pollinated varieties."

Molly didn't view this experience as just a private or personal disappointment. She saw it as a matter of public significance. It was a consequence of the globalization and consolidation of the seed industry—an industry that was previously defined by old, small, and regionally focused businesses that knew their customers personally, and knew their products like

1

their children. By 2000, the year the incident recounted above happened, many of those local companies with their long history of commitment and service to farmers had become brands of some of the largest seed companies in the world.[1]

For Molly and others, the company's decision to drop all of its open-pollinated varieties was troubling. This decision—and similar decisions being made by other large multinational seed companies—meant that important low-volume markets would be underserved. It also carried potentially negative implications and consequences for the genetic diversity of crop varieties, for the security and sustainability of the food system, and for the viability and well-being of small-scale agricultural and horticultural enterprises and the families, businesses, and communities that depend on them.

Instead of simply shaking her head or wringing her hands over all this, Molly decided to do something. Together with a remarkably diverse set of people and groups, including the Northeast Organic Farming Association (NOFA) and the USDA Agricultural Research Service, she conceived and organized what became known as the Public Seed Initiative (PSI). In essence, PSI is a web of public relationships between seed companies, university research-ers, Cooperative Extension personnel, nonprofit organizations, government agencies, and small-scale seed producers. Molly and her collaborators created it to address the decline in the availability of varieties of vegetable crops that perform well in the ecology and climate of the Northeast—a decline that had been partly if not largely caused by the consolidation and globalization of the seed industry and the industrialization of the food system. Sup-ported by funds from the "outreach" component of a plant genomics research grant Molly received from the USDA, PSI's original goal was to reverse this decline by increasing the number and quality of seed varieties available in underserved northeast markets, including organic production regimes. PSI grew to have a national reach, with additional short- and long-term goals aimed at increasing the knowledge, skills, dispositions, and capacity of growers, small-scale seed companies, university faculty, staff, and students, community organizations, and others to work together in ways that not only further their self-interests and common interests, but also larger public interests.[2]

There is much more to tell of this story (see chapter 4 for Molly's own account of it). We'll stop here for now and ask a few questions. How are we to understand its meaning and significance? And what, if anything, can we learn from it?

Our understanding of the meaning and significance of Molly's story—and therefore what we stand to learn from it—depends on our own particular perspectives. But it also depends on the context in which we choose to situate it. Interestingly, the context we choose to place it in also shifts our view of who Molly is in the story, and what she is doing.

We might choose to situate Molly's story in the context of the economic crisis our nation and world are now facing. By doing so, we would understand its meaning and significance mainly in economic terms. We would see Molly as a technical expert who serves both the growers and consumers of food (that would be all of us), meeting a need by developing and transferring valuable technologies (i.e., varieties of vegetable crops) that help to advance economic development in the Northeast, and beyond.

But we also might choose to situate her story in the context of the period of civic decline and renewal we're in the midst of in American society. Here we would understand its meaning and significance in political rather than economic terms. We would see Molly as more than a technical expert who serves a clientele, meets a need, and advances economic development by developing and transferring technologies from her area of technical expertise. We would see her as someone who *leads* as well as serves. We would see her as a proactive agent of civic renewal who is helping to revitalize democracy by recognizing a public problem, building public relationships among diverse interests, and organizing a platform for public work (i.e., the Public Seed Initiative) that calls on and enables a diverse group of people to create things together that have real public value.

There is a third context in which we could choose to situate Molly's story: the context of the growing conversation about the nature, meaning, significance, and value of American higher education's public purposes and work—particularly in relation to its opportunities and responsibilities for off-campus civic or public engagement, in and for a democratic society. Our purpose in this book is to contribute to this conversation, with Molly and eleven of her Cornell University colleagues as our main teachers. We have a great deal to learn from their public engagement stories and experiences, and from their larger life stories and experiences. We document some of these stories and experiences in this book in edited transcripts of in-depth narrative interviews that we refer to as "practitioner profiles." These profiles work like windows that provide us with rich, nuanced, and often highly provocative, first-person views of the off-campus work and experiences of academic professionals, and the roles and contributions they strive to play and make in and for democracy. As we will learn in this book, these roles and contributions are many-sided. Their positive potential is only partly realized. And they are presently at risk.

There have been many conversations and discussions in many places over the past two decades or so about "public service," "outreach," and "engagement" in American higher education. Such conversations and discussions often center on normative views about or theoretical models of what faculty members and other academic professionals "should" (or should not) be doing in their off-campus engagement in civic life. While normative views and theoretical models are important, we firmly believe that our conversations about and discussions of higher education's public purposes and work will be of limited or even negative value if they fail to include more than idealized, theoretical talk about what should or could be. We need discussions that offer academic professionals opportunities to tell stories of what they already have done and are doing and experiencing in their off-campus engagement in civic life, and how and why they became engaged. And we need to take the time to listen to and make sense of what such stories and experiences have to teach us, not only about the nature, meaning, significance, and value of higher education's public purposes and work, but also about what we can and should do to improve, support, and defend such purposes and work at this critical moment in our nation's—and the world's—history. This is precisely what we attempt to do in this book.

Before we provide an overview of the approach, audiences, and contents of this book, we take a moment to recall an important event in the history of American higher education: the creation in 1946 of the President's Commission on Higher Education. We use this event as a key reference point in our work of situating, interpreting, and analyzing the stories and experiences Molly and her eleven colleagues share with us in their profiles.

"The First and Most Essential Charge upon Higher Education"

"It seems particularly important," President Harry S. Truman wrote on July 13, 1946, "that we should now reexamine our system of higher education in terms of its objectives, methods, and facilities; and in the light of the social role it has to play." Proclaiming that these matters were of "far-reaching national importance," he created a President's Commission on Higher Education composed of "outstanding civic and educational leaders." His charge to the commission was to examine "the functions of higher education in our democracy and the means by which they can best be performed."[3]

The sense of urgency in the president's words was partly a reflection of the fact that by 1946, over a million veterans had flooded the nation's campuses, taking advantage of benefits provided by the Servicemen's Readjustment Act of 1944 (the "G.I. Bill of Rights"). But it was also—and even more importantly—a reflection of the nature of the historical moment. As the commission put it in the first volume of its report to the president, submitted on December 11, 1947, it was "a decisive moment in world history" marked by a "world-wide crisis of mankind." For the United States in particular, the commission noted four serious challenges that needed to be addressed. First, technological progress brought about by science and invention had "altered in radical ways the interpersonal and intergroup relations of Americans in their work, in their play, and in their duties as citizens." Second, "drawn from the peoples of the entire world," Americans had become increasingly diverse with respect to their faiths, cultural backgrounds, occupations, and interests. Third, the Second World War had wrenched the country out of its relatively isolationist past, giving it a larger role and deeper responsibility in world affairs. Finally, the dawn of the "atomic age" had brought an "ambivalent promise of tremendous good or tremendous evil for mankind."[4]

The commission charged America's colleges and universities with the task of helping the nation meet these challenges. In doing so, they were to teach Americans new skills and develop in them a greater maturity and a deeper understanding of social processes and problems. They were to create a "dynamic unity" out of the nation's rich diversity by making "the national life one continuous process of interpersonal, intervocational, and intercultural cooperation." They were to help citizens gain knowledge of the political and economic systems and social and cultural institutions of other countries. They were to anticipate and prepare the country for the social and economic changes that would come with the application of atomic energy to industrial uses. And they were to conduct research and provide education for the "self-protection of our democracy."[5]

Democracy, above all else, was the keynote theme of the commission's report. According to the commission, "education for a fuller realization of democracy in every phase of living" was to be the principal goal for American higher education in the postwar years. In articulating this goal, it embraced an expansive, participatory view of democracy. Democracy "is much more than a set of political processes," the commission wrote. "It formulates and implements a philosophy of human relations. It is a way of life—a way of thinking, feeling, and acting in regard to the associations of men and of groups, one with another." The commission called for the integration of democratic principles into the active life of the American people, noting that such an integration "is not to be achieved merely by studying or discussing democracy." In its view, democracy "must be lived to be thoroughly understood. It must become an established attitude and activity, not just a body of remote and abstract doctrine—a way for men to live and work harmoniously together, not just words in a text-book or a series of slogans."[6]

Far from being self-congratulatory, there was a sharp, critical edge to the tone the commission used in discussing American democracy. It pointed to democracy's "unfinished business" and imperfections. "The discrepancies between America's democratic creed and how Americans live are still many and serious," the commission declared. Society was plagued with inequalities, poverty, disease, and hunger. Freedom of conscience and expression was often denied to "those who do not agree with the majority opinion of the moment." And while the commission noted that democracy "sets up reason as the final arbiter in human relations," in its view, the cold fact was that the "appeal to emotion and prejudice is more common and often more effective among us than the appeal to reason."[7]

In striking passages on the connections between education and social responsibility in a democratic society, the commission found more unfinished business, and more imperfections. "All too often," it declared, "the benefits of education have been sought and used for personal and private profit, to the neglect of public and social service. Yet individual freedom entails communal responsibility. The democratic way of life can endure only as private careers and social obligations are made to mesh, as personal ambition is reconciled with public responsibility." No group in American society, the commission wrote, should "pursue purely private ends and seek to promote its own welfare without regard to the social consequences of its activities. . . . Business, industry, labor, agriculture, medicine, law, engineering, education . . . all these modes of association call for the voluntary development of codes of conduct, or the revision of such codes as already exist, to harmonize the special interests of the group with the general welfare."[8]

The commission did not assign all the blame for this situation on individuals and groups outside the academy. In its view, higher education itself was partly—if not largely—to blame. "Today's college graduate may have gained technical or professional training in one field of work or another," it noted, "but it is only incidentally, if at all, made ready for performing his duties as a man, a parent, and a citizen. Too often he is 'educated' in that he has acquired competence in some particular occupation, yet falls short of that human wholeness and civic conscience which the cooperative activities of citizenship require."[9]

The commission's critique of college graduates carried implications for the curriculum: namely, that it must include more than technical training for the professions. It also had profound implications for higher education's social role beyond the campus. The "limited concept that higher education still holds of its role in a free and democratic society," the commission wrote, must be broadened. "It must cease to be campus-bound. It must take the university to the people wherever they are to be found." Further, the commission proclaimed that higher education "will not play its social role in American democracy and in international affairs successfully unless it assumes the responsibility for a program of adult education reaching far beyond the campus and the classroom."[10]

As President Truman had written, the commission's reexamination of America's higher education system was supposed to be conducted "in the light of the social role it has to play." But this begged an important question: What is higher education's social role? On this question, the commission expressed strong views. "The first and most essential charge upon higher education is that at all its levels and in all its fields of specialization it shall be the carrier of democratic values, ideals, and processes," it proclaimed.

> Its role in a democratic society is that of critic and leader as well as servant; its task is not merely to meet the demands of the present but to alter those demands if necessary, so as to keep them always suited to democratic ideals. Perhaps its most important role is to serve as an instrument of social transition, and its responsibilities are defined in terms of the kind of civilization society hopes to build. If its adjustments to present needs are not to be mere fortuitous improvisations, those who formulate its policies and programs must have a vision of the nation and the world we want—to give a sense of direction to their choices among alternatives.[11]

A Feeling of Déjà Vu

Reading the commission's report sixty years after it was published, we have a strong feeling of déjà vu. As we were working on this book, President George W. Bush signed a "21st century G.I. Bill" into law. The law provides veterans who have served in Iraq and Afghanistan since September 11, 2001, with educational benefits similar to those that were provided to veterans of the Second World War. Also as we were working on this book, we found ourselves in what may well be another decisive moment in world history. This is a moment that holds an array of deep challenges for the United States, including determining and pursuing the nation's roles, responsibilities, and security in the post-9/11 world, as well as dealing at home and abroad with a host of serious economic, environmental, and social problems. And it is a moment in which there is a renewed call, to use President Truman's words, for a reexamination of "the functions of higher education in our democracy and the means by which they can best be performed."

On July 4, 1999, a group of fifty-one college and university presidents affiliated with Campus Compact signed a document entitled the "Presidents' Declaration on the Civic Responsibility of Higher Education." "As presidents of colleges and universities, both private and public, large and small, two-year and four-year," the group wrote, "we challenge higher education to re-examine its public purposes and its commitments to the democratic ideal. We also challenge higher education to become engaged, through actions and teaching, with its communities. We have a fundamental task to renew our role as agents of our democracy." There is no nobler task, the group declared, "than committing ourselves to helping catalyze and lead a national movement to reinvigorate the public purposes and civic mission of higher education. We believe that now and through the next century, our institutions must be vital agents and architects of a flourishing democracy."[12]

The Presidents' Declaration, which by 2009 had been signed by more than 500 college and university presidents, echoes and reaffirms the view expressed in the report by President Truman's commission that the "first and most essential charge upon higher education is that at all its levels and in all its fields of specialization it shall be the carrier of democratic values, ideals, and processes." But behind and beyond the lofty rhetoric about democracy and civic responsibility in both documents, there is an important down-to-earth reality: *American higher education's social role, its function in a democracy and its civic mission, its public purposes and its public work, are not straightforward empirical facts. They are complex normative and political questions. They are not merely matters of record. They are matters of debate and disagreement.*

The Public Purposes and Work Question

Higher education's social roles and civic mission reflect and are determined by its public purposes. In turn, its public purposes are pursued by academic professionals, students, and their nonuniversity partners in and through their academic and public work. But higher education's public purposes and work are not automatic and unproblematic givens. Rather, they are assigned, chosen, interpreted, reproduced, and contested on the basis of particular values and interests. They are therefore inherently normative and political in nature. This means that the issue of public purpose and work in American higher education is a *question*. And the question is not simply that of figuring out the best ways to pursue public purposes. It is also a question of determining what these purposes are or should be—not in general, but *in a democracy*.

Today, the public purposes and work question is often posed and answered in relation to a single metric: bottom-line economics. Many elected officials and many in the general public speak and act at times as if higher education's main if not only public purpose is to advance economic growth and competitiveness. In this view, higher education's public purpose is to "serve" communities, states, and the nation as a whole by functioning as an "economic engine." The work of pursuing this purpose includes training workers and professionals for the new economy, producing and transferring "useful" (i.e., profitable) knowledge and technological innovations, and providing jobs for the community or region that immediately surrounds a college or university.

Writing during a time of deep economic trouble, we are well aware of the critical importance of a public purpose for American higher education that is focused on economic growth and development. But we are also convinced that economics is not the only metric we should be using in posing and answering the public purposes and work question. We believe it should be posed and answered in relation to values, principles, interests, and ideals that reach well beyond bottom-line economics to the broader metrics of democratic culture and politics, and of environmental sustainability. When we pose and answer it this way, other purposes come into view, including those of educating students to be morally, ethically, and environmentally responsible citizens, leaders, and professionals, advancing the frontiers of knowledge through free inquiry and research, and advancing public interests and cultural and political ideals through technical and social problem-solving, social criticism, and a variety of forms of public work—whether or not any of these efforts ever produce economic returns as a result. President Truman's commission drew on the broader metrics that are reflected in these kinds of public purposes when it declared that higher education's role in a democratic society "is that of critic and leader as well as a servant." It also drew on these broader metrics when it wrote that higher education's function in a democratic society is not simply to strive to meet society's demands, but to alter them to keep them suited to democratic ideals, in pursuit of "the kind of civilization society hopes to build."

Instead of democratic ideals and a long-term view of "the kind of civilization society hopes to build," today higher education's social roles and "function" are being increasingly defined and shaped by society's demand for help in addressing immediate economic realities and problems. Government and industry leaders are pressuring academic institutions—both public and private—to increase and accelerate their contributions to economic growth and development. Reflecting the privileging of bottom-line economics over democratic ideals, this pressure is often accompanied by calls to commercialize the American academy by transforming it from a social institution that produces public goods and advances public interests into an "industry" that produces private goods for the marketplace.[13]

For some academic professionals, students, and concerned citizens, this situation is deeply troubling. In response, they are joining and giving new life to a long-standing conversation about higher education's public purposes and work. As we see it, there are three main threads in this conversation.

First, there is a thread about loss and renewal. Here, the view is that higher education's connections with and contributions to democracy have been seriously eroded, if not lost entirely. Participants in this thread of the conversation are not only trying to understand how and why this has happened; they are also trying to change it by calling for and organizing a renewal of higher education's civic mission. Much if not most of the attention in this thread of the conversation is being placed on liberal and civic education for undergraduates, especially in and through service-learning courses and pedagogies.[14]

Second, there is a thread in the conversation about the expert and critic roles that "intellectuals"—a category of people that includes academic professionals—have taken up in civic life. Participants in this thread of the conversation are exploring two main things. First, they are exploring how intellectuals have served the interests of dominant social classes, groups, or powers by reproducing or legitimizing an oppressive status quo, or facilitating and legitimizing oppressive social engineering and change projects and agendas. Second, they have explored how intellectuals have served the interests of oppressed or marginalized social classes by resisting, subverting, undermining, and delegitimizing oppressive status quos and social change projects and agendas, or by facilitating and legitimizing emancipatory social change projects and agendas, including the project of creating and defending a public sphere that is devoted to open, free, and rational public debate. Much if not most of the attention in this thread of the conversation is being placed on high-profile academic stars in the humanities and social sciences who function as "public intellectuals."[15]

Third, there is a thread about the "proper" mission and work of academic institutions and professionals. Participants in this thread of the conversation are either reasserting or criticizing the conservative view that higher education should not be seeking to contribute to democracy at all, at least not through intentional and direct engagement in off-campus civic life. Stanley Fish, the Davidson-Kahn Distinguished Professor and Professor of Law at Florida International University, has articulated an extreme version of the conservative view in his recent book, *Save the World on Your Own Time*. In this book, Fish proclaims that academic professionals "are in the education business, not the democracy business. Democracy, we must remember, is a political not an educational project." In answer to the question of what politics and democracy have to do with scholarship and teaching, he answers: "absolutely nothing." While it is an open question how many others in American higher education share Fish's view, there are certainly many skeptics who doubt the appropriateness and value of direct forms of off-campus civic engagement by academic professionals and institutions.[16]

In our view, there is something to be learned in each of these threads of the conversation. But we also think that something important is being missed: namely, stories about the off-campus work and experiences of ordinary academic professionals (as opposed to academic stars) in every discipline and field (as opposed to only the humanities and social sciences) who have been and are engaged in civic life in ways that do not necessarily have anything to do with undergraduate education. Stories, for example, like the one we opened this chapter with. Our purpose in this book is to help open a new thread in the conversation in which such stories are not only told and documented, but also situated, interpreted, and analyzed in ways that challenge, complicate, and ultimately enlarge our understanding of the nature, meaning, significance, and value of higher education's public purposes and work, in and for a democratic society.

Approach and Audiences

In this book, we interweave methods, theoretical frameworks, and conceptual tools from narrative inquiry, political and educational philosophy, and democratic theory. While we approach our work as scholars who seek to learn, discover, interpret, and analyze in ways that are trustworthy, we are not—and do not attempt to be—disinterested, neutral, or unbiased. We have particular interests, biases, ideals, commitments, hopes, and values with respect to the question of higher education's public purposes and work, and they guide and are reflected in the approach we take. Here, we want to identify the four main elements of our approach, and also address the question of who our intended audiences are.

Democracy

First, and most fundamentally, our approach is guided by a particular view of higher education's connections with, roles in, and contributions to democracy. The connection between higher education and democracy is often viewed as being about access. In this view, America's institutions of higher learning are understood to advance democracy by providing everyone, rather than just a narrow elite, with access to a college education, to the results of faculty members' research, and to the resources and services of academic institutions. It is also commonly viewed as being about the provision of a liberal education for undergraduate students, which is supposed to contribute to democracy by developing students' civic knowledge, skills, and habits.

Expanding and "democratizing" access and providing undergraduates with a liberal education are important. Access, in particular, was one of the central themes President Truman's Commission on Higher Education stressed in its final report, published by Harper & Brothers in 1948 under the title *Higher Education for American Democracy*. But the connection between higher education and democracy is about much more than providing access and undergraduate liberal education—particularly but not only in the nation's state and land-grant university system, where those who are profiled in this book are situated. It is about more than doing things *for* democracy. As Molly Jahn and many others have taught us, it is also about engaging *in* democracy. It is about the work of academic professionals as active participants in and contributors to civic life, beyond and off their campuses. Such work is not only responsive, but also proactive; it is not only technical, but also social, cultural, and political; it is not only about identifying, framing, and solving problems, but also about creating public goods, furthering values and ideals, and building and exercising power to advance people's self-interests and common interests, as well as larger public interests. In our view, the multidimensional nature of public work in a democratic society calls on the American academy to take up a multidimensional role in civic life. President Truman's commission characterized this multidimensional role as "that of critic and leader as well as servant." We use this characterization as a conceptual and theoretical tool in analyzing and interpreting academic professionals' subjective accounts of their civic engagement work and experiences.[17]

Given all this, in our approach to opening a new thread in the conversation about higher education's public purposes and work, our focus of attention is higher education *in as well as for* democracy. By democracy, we do not mean voting. Like President Truman's Commission on Higher Education, we embrace an expansive view of democracy as not only a formal system and method of governance but also a way of life and a philosophy of human relations. Reflecting our populist political values and convictions, we also view democracy as public work: "sustained effort by a mix of people who solve public problems or create goods, material or cultural, of general benefit," as Harry Boyte defines it.[18]

When we speak in this book of the "public work of democracy," we are referring to the process and means by which individuals and groups develop and exercise power in neighborhood and community settings as they seek to understand and address technical and social problems, stand for and further key normative ideals and values, and promote, consider, deliberate about, negotiate, and take action to pursue their self-interests, their common interests, and larger public interests. Broadly speaking, the public work of democracy has four main interrelated elements that typically play out in unpredictable, overlapping cycles rather than a linear sequence:

- the work of naming, setting, and framing a problem, and/or a positive goal (not everything is a problem—sometimes the point of public work is to pursue a positive possibility);
- the work of identifying options for what *can* be done, and the consequences of each;
- the work of deciding what *should* be done, in light of particular interests, values, and commitments; and
- acting to implement solutions and create something of public significance, and evaluating, reflecting on, and learning from experience.

By seeking to illuminate and interpret academic professionals' engagement in the public work of democracy, we are by definition seeking to illuminate and interpret their engagement in *politics*. To be clear, we do not mean politics in a narrow, government-centered sense as the activities of politicians and political parties engaged in winning elections and passing or fighting against legislation. Rather, we mean politics in a broad sense as the activities of citizens engaged in public work in many everyday settings and contexts.

Civic Professionalism

In relation to our focus on academic professionals as active participants in and contributors to the public work of democracy, the second element of our approach reflects and is guided by our commitment to contribute to the task of strengthening both the theory and practice of civic professionalism in the academic profession. As Steven Brint notes, there are two main aspects of professional practice: a technical aspect having to do with the competent performance of skilled work, and a social aspect that grounds and guides professionals in an appreciation of the larger public ends they serve. Those professionals that William Sullivan refers to as "civic professionals" attend in equal ways to both of these aspects by making a "public pledge to deploy technical expertise and judgment not only skillfully but also for public-regarding ends and in a public-regarding way." Taking this pledge seriously requires academic professionals to perceive and work through what Thomas Bender has referred to as the "dilemma of the relation of expertise and democracy." The dilemma is to decide, among various options, how and for what purposes they should contribute their specialized knowledge and skills to the everyday politics of public work. The ways academic professionals perceive and work through this dilemma is not just a reflection of "what works." It is also a reflection of their interests and values, their situations and locations, their normative views about democracy and politics, and their views about their identities, roles, and responsibilities as professionals in a democratic society.[19]

Stories, not Variables

Third, the approach we take in this book is not designed to pursue the goal of establishing statistically significant relationships between variables in order to inform attempts by administrators, policymakers, or others to predict, control, and intervene for some specific end. Rather, it is designed to open up and contribute to conversations within and beyond the academy about the nature, meaning, significance, and value of higher education's public purposes and work, in and for a democratic society. In line with this design, our approach is centered on the construction, interpretation, and analysis of first-person practice stories (or, to use a more academic term, narratives) of academic professionals' public work and experiences, off and beyond their campuses. As we will explain in detail in chapter 3, we document these stories in practitioner profiles. Practitioner profiles are edited transcripts of narrative interviews. They serve as windows onto academic professionals' practices and experiences by providing us with their subjective accounts of what they do in specific examples of their public engagement work, including the challenges they encounter and how they deal with them, and the roles they play. They provide us with accounts of how their life experiences, interests, values, commitments, and purposes have propelled or compelled them to become engaged in the public work of democracy. And they help us to see and understand what it involves, means, and looks like for academic professionals to work for public-regarding ends in public-regarding ways. Or, to borrow language from the report authored by President Truman's commission, they help us to see and understand how academic professionals strive to "mesh" private careers and social obligations and "reconcile" personal ambition with public responsibility.[20]

In relation to our narrative orientation, we also take an approach that is grounded in a particular institution (Cornell University) within a particular sector of American higher education (the land-grant system). While the practitioner profiles in part 2 of this book (chapters 4–15) include academic professionals from several disciplines and fields, all of them are (or were) affiliated with Cornell University's College of Agriculture and Life Sciences. Cornell is New York State's land-grant institution. Our decision to ground our approach in a particular land-grant college of agriculture reflects our view that the public purposes and work question must be taken up in ways that are sensitive to local, contextual, situational, and institutional differences, realities, and dynamics. No single set of answers to the question does or can fit all times and places, and all institutional types. This does not mean that answers that are sensitive to particular situational and institutional realities are of no value to a broader audience. They can be, as we hope we successfully demonstrate in this book. What it does mean is that we should seek to contribute both to *a broad conversation* about higher education's public purposes and work across the whole of American higher education, and to *localized conversations* within particular institutions and institutional types. It is our goal, therefore, to open up and contribute to conversations not only at the national level, but also within the land-grant system, and at Cornell University.

Our decision to ground our approach in a land-grant university also reflects another one of our goals, which is to provide a much-needed reinterpretation of the nature and significance of the Cooperative Extension work of the land-grant university system. As noted above, President Truman's commission declared that higher education needed to "cease to be campus-bound," that it would "not play its social role in American democracy and in international affairs successfully unless it assumes the responsibility for a program of adult education reaching far beyond the campus and the classroom." When the commission wrote these words, such a program wasn't a mere dream for those who worked in land-grant colleges and universities; it already existed. Congress formally established it in 1914 when it passed the Smith-Lever Act, which created the national Cooperative Extension System. This system was and is the official institutionalized means for land-grant faculty, staff, and students to reach beyond the campus and classroom. However, Cooperative Extension's "social role in American democracy"—past and present—has been largely obscured by a narrowly technical and apolitical view of the nature and significance of Extension work. The profiles that are included in this book contradict this view. By illuminating political dimensions of practice that are typically ignored or even denied, they help us to imagine what it looks like and means for academic professionals in the land-grant system to take up a social role in American democracy in and through their Extension work.

Practical Theory Building

The fourth and final element in our approach includes what we refer to (following Kurt Lewin) as *practical theory building*. In brief, a practical theory has three closely related components: (1) an understanding of "the way things are," and why and how they came to be the way they are; (2) a view of "the way things should be," given the values and ideals we embrace, the ends we think are worth striving for, and the interests we want to advance; and (3) a strategy that identifies what we can and should do to move from the way things are to the way things should be.[21]

In our experience, we have found that academic professionals are rarely expected or invited to acknowledge, explain, and question the practical theories that ground and guide their answers to the public purposes and work question, and their own civic engagement work. This is a huge problem. As we will demonstrate in chapter 2, while there are appealing aspects of the practical theories that are reflected in the main normative traditions of civic engagement in the American academic profession, there are also highly troubling aspects that need to be critically questioned and examined. Efforts to improve our understanding of and conversations about higher education's public purposes and work must include attention to the task of building, testing, and refining sound and effective practical theories.

Audiences

Given our location in the land-grant system, we seek as one of our audiences those who care about or have an interest in the status and future of its public purposes and work. We also seek a much broader and more diverse audience that includes those who are concerned about the status and future of American higher education's public purposes and work more generally. As we write, we are both imagining and hoping to open a new thread in the conversation on this critically important issue that includes not only academic professionals, students, and administrators, but also university trustees, elected officials, business owners and leaders, and people from all walks of life.

There is one last point we want to make about the approach we take in this book, a point that reflects our practical theory and has implications for the question of who our audiences are. We are deliberately choosing not to approach our work as a critical exposé in which we try to show how bad or oppressive higher education's roles in civic life are. Instead, we choose to take a prophetic, imaginative approach that is focused on rethinking presumptions about the politics of academic work in order to discover new—or rediscover old— meanings and possibilities with respect to higher education's positive roles in the public work of democracy. We therefore seek audiences that are hungering not only for inspiration, but also for reasons to be hopeful about the prospects for improving and sustaining a robust set of public purposes and work in American higher education, while also being mindful of the trends, challenges, and obstacles that stand in the way. Because we hope for active rather than passive audiences, we seek to reach those who will take responsibility—in their own contexts and ways—for responding to and building on our work and ideas, just as we have responded to and built on the work of others.

Overview of Contents

We divide this book into three parts. Part 1 consists of three chapters. As we noted above, higher education's social roles, civic mission, and public purposes and work are not straightforward empirical facts. Rather, they are complex normative and political questions, and matters of debate and disagreement. In chapter 1, we identify and sketch out the main elements of four distinct normative traditions in American higher education, each of which represents a different answer to the question of whether academic professionals should be engaged in the public work of democracy, and if so, what public purposes they should pursue, what roles they should play, and what contributions they should seek to make. In chapter 2, we review the answers to this question that we find in the normative traditions, and their underlying practical theories. We briefly identify and discuss some of the appealing and problematic aspects of each tradition, as well as some of the reasons why we think their usefulness is limited.

In light of the problems with and limitations of the normative traditions we sketch and question in chapters 1 and 2, we devote chapter 3 to a discussion of the usefulness and limits of practitioner profiles as resources and tools in our conversations about higher education's public purposes and work. We also explain why and how we created the profiles that are included in part 2 of this book, and offer readers suggestions for how to read and use them. To avoid confusion and misunderstanding, we want to stress that practitioner profiles are not "case studies." Nor are they "interview vignettes." Rather, they are first-person oral histories of faculty members' lives and work. This is an entirely different thing than a case study or an interview vignette. We say much more about this distinction in chapter 3.

The chapters that make up part 2 consist of twelve practitioner profiles of faculty members from Cornell University's College of Agriculture and Life Sciences. The profiles include faculty members from a variety of disciplines and fields in a range of tenured, tenure-track, and non-tenure-line appointments. As part of a research initiative that was conducted in collaboration with the Kettering Foundation, we constructed these profiles from the edited transcripts of in-depth narrative interviews. Our interview protocol consisted of three sections of open-ended questions. The first section focused on participants' personal and professional backgrounds, the second on specific practice stories of their public work in addressing social issues and problems, and the third on their interpretations of the meaning and significance of their civic engagement work and experiences. The practice stories cover a range of social issues and problems related to sustainable development, agriculture and the food system, the use and regulation of pesticides and genetically modified organisms (GMOs), natural resource and wildlife management, community disputes related to migrant labor, community and neighborhood planning, economic decline and the loss of a sense of place and community, and public policies related to student achievement in public schools.

Part 3 of the book consists of a single chapter. In chapter 16, we provide an appreciative interpretation of the practitioner profiles that are included in part 2. The main purpose of this chapter is to illuminate and discuss positive and instructive lessons we have drawn from our reading of the profiles about the nature, meaning, value, and significance of American higher education's public purposes and work, in and for a democratic society.

In the conclusion to the book we argue that the project of reconstructing a democratic-minded civic professionalism will be of central importance in meeting the challenge of improving and protecting the public purposes and work academic professionals take up and pursue in American society. We name and briefly discuss three things we can and must do to improve, support, and defend a variety of civic professionalism in American higher education that includes direct, face-to-face, off-campus engagement in the public work of democracy.

Concluding Note

Before we move on we want to be clear about the meaning of a key term we use a lot in this book: *academic professionals*. When we refer to academic professionals, we are not just referring to professors in tenured or tenure-track appointments. Rather, we are referring to a larger set of professional positions in the academy that also include faculty members who do not hold tenure-track appointments. Both historically with respect to land-grant institutions, and more recently in other sectors of American higher education, faculty members in a variety of non-tenure-line appointments and positions have played key roles in building working relationships between the academy and communities. We should not overlook them in our view of who is included as an academic professional. While this is relatively uncontroversial, we take an additional step that many may disagree with: we also include community-based Extension educators in the land-grant system in our conception of the category of academic professional. We think this is not only warranted by the fact that most of these people are hired and supervised by universities, and receive their paychecks and benefits from them, but also because most have a full array of professional criteria and activities, including training and credentialing in specific fields of expertise, standards and codes of conduct, membership in professional associations, and the like.

This is a big, long book. While we have designed it to be read as a whole, each section can be read independently of the others. Part 1 can be read as an overview of the appeal and limits of the main normative traditions of civic engagement that have been established in American higher education over the past century or so, and of our method of developing narratives of academic professionals' contemporary civic engagement work and experiences. As oral histories of faculty members' lives and work, the profiles that are included in part 2 have a value on their own, separate from our framing and interpretation. We see them as both contributions to the historical record, and as resources for individual and collective reflection and discussion. One or more of them can be read and discussed independently of the rest of the book. In fact, we hope readers will choose to do so as a means of provoking individual and collective reflection about higher education's public purposes and work in their own contexts and institutional settings. While part 3 and the conclusion can be read independently of the chapters in part 2, we hope they provoke and inspire people to read and interpret the profiles for themselves. By including the full texts of these profiles instead of just our own interpretations of them, we are intentionally leaving space for readers to interpret them for themselves, and with others. There is a great deal to discover in and learn from them, far more than we had space to note in this book.

PART 1

The Public Purposes and Work Question in American Higher Education

Answering the Public Purposes
and Work Question

There are, of course, many different answers to the question of whether academic professionals should be engaged off their campuses in the public work of democracy, and if so, what public purposes they should pursue, what roles they should play, and what contributions they should seek to make. This question is effectively answered every day—even if it is never explicitly posed—as academic professionals make practical judgments in particular situations (either alone or with others) about what they should and should not do to address public issues and problems. The best answer to this question, therefore, is "It depends." It depends on the context—on the specific details, dynamics, and politics of a given time, place, and situation. It depends not only on academic professionals' practical theories, abilities, skills, dispositions, interests, agendas, commitments, values, ideals, and political views and theories, but also on those of their external partners. It depends on institutional, disciplinary, and community missions, cultures, identities, norms, and realities. It depends—in highly complex ways—on the development and exercise of power. It depends on the availability of time, money, and institutional and community support. And more.

Despite the wisdom of the "It depends" response, some people have provided general answers that reflect distinctly different normative positions about the roles, contributions, and ends academic professionals should and should not take up, make, and pursue in their off-campus civic engagement work. In this chapter, we name and explore four such positions that have been staked out in American higher education since the late nineteenth century. We situate each of these positions within a different normative "tradition" in the American academic profession. There are three traditions that represent positive answers to the engagement in public work question: the service intellectual, public intellectual, and action researcher / public scholar / educational organizer traditions. A fourth tradition is what we characterize as the "antitradition" of the detached and disengaged scholar. It is important that we not overlook this tradition, as it has been and still is defended as a valid if not essential means of pursuing and protecting one conception of higher education's core public purposes.

Before we begin, we want to note three things. First, with respect to the way we name and characterize the four positions and traditions we discuss, some or even many of our readers may accuse us of creating so-called straw men. In anticipation of such an accusation, we want to say that what we have constructed are not straw men, but normative types. Just as we should be wary of straw men, we should be wary of normative types. While both can be found in academic (and other) literatures and rhetoric, neither exists in pure form in practice, and neither allows for the contingencies, ambiguities, messiness, surprises, diversity, inconsistencies, and contradictions of "real" life. It was our desire to get beyond the limited and ultimately misleading confines of normative types that led us to invite academic professionals to tell stories of their civic engagement work and experiences.

Second, we want to point out that each of the positions and traditions we identify in this chapter reflects or implies a practical theory about the way things are and the way things should be, and how academic professionals can and should (or should not) help to close the gap between them. If we wish to improve the conversation about higher education's public purposes and work, in and for a democratic society, these practical theories—and the presumptions, assumptions, and bets that are included in them—must be both illuminated and questioned. We will turn to that task in chapter 2. In this chapter, our aim is limited to that of identifying and briefly sketching the positions and traditions mentioned above.

Finally, we use key works from the discipline of sociology to sketch the details of two of the traditions we identify in this chapter: the service intellectual and public intellectual traditions. We want to make it clear that these traditions—and the positions and practical theories on which they are based—are not limited to sociology or the social sciences. On the contrary, in varying degrees and situations they have been and continue to be espoused and embraced by academic professionals from every discipline and field, including the arts and humanities, engineering, law, and the social, natural, and biological sciences.

Professionalizing the Academic Calling in American Higher Education

The idea—and reality—of scholars as active participants in and contributors to the public work of democracy was a key component of the "academic revolution" of the late nineteenth and early twentieth centuries. According to Richard Hofstadter, at the start of the twentieth century, "the academic man was beginning to overcome his traditional civic passivity and take an active part in the shaping of political events." Armed with "empirical specialized skills," Hofstadter writes, "academic men had not only prestige but some real marketable advice to bring to public life." For the first time, "the profession developed the capacity both for large-scale innovative work in scholarship and for social criticism and practical contribution to the political dialogue of American society."[1]

Also for the first time, the academic profession developed a quasi-official normative statement of scholars' main roles in and contributions to civic life, and the protections scholars needed in order to pursue them. This statement was the "Report of the Committee on Academic Freedom and Tenure," published in 1915 by the American Association of University Professors (AAUP). Because this statement provided the first authoritative and influential articulation of professional scholars' civic roles and contributions, it is worth examining in detail.

During the late nineteenth and early twentieth centuries, a number of corporate and industrial leaders, most of whom served on university boards of trustees, successfully pressured colleges and universities to terminate the employment of several accomplished scholars who had become vocal in expressing their (relatively) radical political views. The publication in 1915 of the AAUP's report on the topic of academic freedom was prompted in large part by a desire to protect against such meddling. As historian Thomas Haskell interprets it, the report was the "capstone" of reformers' attempts to professionalize the academic calling. Its central aim in this regard was to justify the granting to scholars of collegial autonomy and self-governance, two of the most basic components of professionalism. Importantly, the report grounded the justification of these professional privileges in a particular view of the nature and value of the civic roles and contributions of scholars and their institutions.[2]

Two accomplished scholars drafted the AAUP's 1915 report: E.R.A. Seligman, an economist from Columbia University, and Arthur Lovejoy, a philosopher from Johns Hopkins University. The report includes sections on the "basis of academic authority," the "nature of the academic calling," and the "function of the academic institutions." In the section on authority, the authors made a distinction between "proprietary" and "ordinary" institutions of learning. The former were to be understood as constituting a "private trust," while the latter constituted a "public trust." Proprietary institutions are established on behalf of religious institutions or wealthy individuals in order to further certain predetermined doctrines and opinions, while "ordinary" institutions are established on behalf of the public in order to "advance knowledge by the unrestricted research and unfettered discussion of impartial investigators." The authors argued that a clear understanding among boards of trustees of the distinction between proprietary and "ordinary" institutions is a crucial "prerequisite" to the realization of academic freedom as a means for upholding the public trust.[3]

In the section on the nature of the academic calling, the authors argued that the mistaken view of the university as "an ordinary business venture" and of teaching as "a purely private employment" manifested a "radical failure to apprehend the nature of the social function discharged by the professional scholar." This failure, the authors wrote, required a restatement of the reasons why it is in the public interest that the "professional office" of the scholar be one of "both dignity and of independence." Noting that the academic profession offers no promise of great financial rewards, the authors argued that its rewards must lie elsewhere: namely, in achieving an honorable and secure position that offers scholars the "freedom to perform honestly and according to their own consciences the distinctive and important function which the nature of the profession lays upon them." This function, the authors went on to spell out,

> is to deal at first hand, after prolonged and specialized technical training, with the sources of knowledge; and to impart the results of their own and of their fellow-specialists' investigations and reflection, both to students and to the general public, without fear or favor. The proper discharge of this function requires (among other things) that the university teacher shall be exempt

from any pecuniary motive or inducement to hold, or express, any conclusion which is not the genuine and uncolored product of his own study or that of fellow-specialists. Indeed, the proper fulfillment of the work of the professorate requires that our universities shall be so free that no fair-minded person shall find any excuse for even a suspicion that the utterances of university teachers are shaped or restricted by the judgment, not of professional scholars, but of inexpert and possibly not wholly disinterested persons outside their ranks.[4]

In continuing their statement of the function of the academic profession, the authors were careful to point out that the "lay public is under no compulsion to accept or act upon the opinions of the scientific experts whom, through the universities, it employs." In other words, the proper public function of scholars is not to control or dominate the public but to serve and inform it. The value of scholars' service to the public is bound up in the trustworthiness of their opinions and knowledge. For such a function to be successfully carried out in a manner that gains (and deserves) the public trust, the authors wrote,

it is highly needful, in the interest of society at large, that what purport to be the conclusions of men trained for, and dedicated to, the quest for truth, shall in fact be the conclusions of such men, and not echoes of the opinions of the lay public, or of the individuals who endow or manage universities. To the degree that professional scholars, in the formation and promulgation of their opinions, are, or by the character of their tenure appear to be, subject to any motive other than their own scientific conscience and a desire for the respect of their fellow-experts, to that degree the university teaching profession is corrupted; its proper influence upon public opinion is diminished and vitiated; and society at large fails to get from its scholars, in an unadulterated form, the peculiar and necessary service which it is the office of the professional scholar to furnish.[5]

Following their discussion of the academic calling, the authors turned their attention to what they took to be the three main functions of academic institutions: to promote inquiry that advances knowledge, to provide instruction, and to develop experts for various branches of public service. The latter of these the authors tied to one of the "recent developments of democracy," which in their view was "the recognition by legislators of the inherent complexities of economic, social, and political life, and the difficulty of solving problems of technical adjustment without technical knowledge." The authors noted that professors—many of whom were technical experts with something to contribute to "solving problems of technical adjustment"—were being "drafted to an increasing extent into more or less unofficial participation in the public service." In performing this service, they wrote, "the scholar must be absolutely free not only to pursue his investigations but to declare the results of his researches, no matter where they may lead him or to what extent they may come into conflict with accepted opinion. To be of use to the legislator or the administrator, he must enjoy their complete confidence in the disinterestedness of his conclusions."[6]

Infringements on and threats to academic freedom in the contemporary university, the authors argued, were being caused not so much by religious institutions as by three other sources: business interests, governments and politicians, and the "tyranny of public opinion." The latter of these fostered a tendency for people to think, feel, and speak alike, threatening the liberty of individuals to dissent from conventional views and opinions. To protect against this threat to academic freedom, the authors declared, the university must be seen as an "inviolable refuge from such tyranny." It must serve as an "intellectual experiment station" where new ideas can germinate, ripen, and bear fruit. But the university must also exercise a conservative influence, both by protecting past thought that is "not in the fashion of the moment" and by checking the "hasty and unconsidered impulses of popular feeling." By its very nature, the authors wrote, the university

> is committed to the principle that knowledge should precede action, to the caution (by no means synonymous with intellectual timidity) which is an essential part of the scientific method, to a sense of the complexity of social problems, to the practice of taking long views into the future, and to a reasonable regard for the teachings of experience. One of its most characteristic functions in a democratic society is to help make public opinion more self-critical and more circumspect, to check the more hasty and unconsidered impulses of popular feeling, to train the democracy to the habit of looking before and after. It is precisely this function of the university which is most injured by any restriction upon academic freedom; and it is precisely those who most value this aspect of the university's work who should most earnestly protest against such restriction. For the public may respect, and be influenced by, the counsels of prudence and of moderation which are given by men of science, if it believes those counsels to be the disinterested expression of the scientific temper and of unbiased inquiry.[7]

It is important not to miss the fact that the authors of the AAUP's statement on academic freedom made a distinction between scholars' public functions as professional "men of science" and their "extra-mural" public functions as citizens. While functioning as professionals, scholars were expected to limit their public functions to the provision of "counsels of prudence and moderation," the "disinterested expression of the scientific temper and of unbiased inquiry." While functioning as citizens, however, scholars could enjoy the full freedom other citizens enjoyed of joining or supporting movements or causes of their choice, and of stating their opinions and judgments on matters outside their specialties. By way of reinforcing the distinction between professional and "extra-mural" conduct, the authors took pains to point out that it is "not the absolute freedom of utterance of the individual scholar, but the absolute freedom of thought, of inquiry, of discussion and of teaching, of the academic profession, that is asserted by this declaration of principles."[8]

In summary, according to the authors of the AAUP's 1915 report on academic freedom, professional scholars have two main functions in civic life:

- to provide the public with trustworthy knowledge, judgment, and opinion, based on objective, disinterested, and unbiased inquiry and scientific study;
- to make public opinion more self-critical by checking the "more hasty and unconsidered impulses of popular feeling" and training in the "habit of looking before and after."

Three Positions and Traditions

Reading the AAUP report, one gets the impression that the normative issue of academic professionals' roles in the public work of democracy was a settled matter of agreement. It was not. As Mark C. Smith shows in his study of the debate over objectivity and purpose in the American social sciences during the period between 1918 and 1941, professional scholars were divided by their answers to a set of related questions:

> What is the proper role of the social scientist in relation to his or her knowledge of society? In other words, how should social scientists use their knowledge, and indeed, should they have any say at all in its utilization? Should the correct role of the social scientist be that of a technical expert who provides information and advice to whomever requests it? Or should the social scientist go beyond understanding and analyzing society and use scientifically derived information consciously and personally to help create a better society more suited to humankind's basic needs and desires?[9]

In our judgment, Smith's questions are relevant well beyond the social sciences. Academic professionals in every discipline and field face the challenge of determining which social roles are and are not proper for them to play, particularly when one adds the qualifier, *in a democracy.* At the heart of this challenge is the question of whether they should carry their knowledge and expertise into the public work of democracy, and if so, how and for what purposes. In his book, Smith divides the schools of thought on this challenge into two opposing camps: "service intellectuals" and "purposivists." Drawing on Smith's study, as well as works by several other scholars, in what follows we provide brief descriptions of three normative traditions in the academic profession: the service intellectual tradition, and two distinctly different purposivist traditions: the public intellectual, who writes and speaks to and for the general public, and the action researcher / public scholar / educational organizer, who writes, speaks, educates, organizes, and works with and for specific (rather than general) publics and interests in specific contexts.

The Service Intellectual Tradition

The service intellectual tradition reflects an embrace of only one of the main functions of scholars in civic life that was articulated in the AAUP's 1915 statement: namely, "to impart the results of their own and of their fellow-specialists' investigations and reflections." In brief, scholars who work in the service intellectual tradition are supposed to provide external constituencies and clients—including individuals and families as well as businesses and corporations, nonprofit organizations, and all levels of government—with scientific knowledge, technical expertise, and technologies in order to inform their decision making and help them solve technical and social problems. Service intellectuals are supposed to maintain a strict stance of unbiased, disinterested neutrality about what ought to be done about personal and social issues and problems. Their role is to be restricted to the one-way provision of knowledge, theory, technologies, and expertise to external constituencies and clients to use (or not) as they see fit.[10]

One of the boldest articulations of a positivist variety of the service intellectual tradition can be found in George A. Lundberg's book, *Can Science Save Us?* Lundberg (1895–1966) was a professor of sociology at the University of Washington. In 1943 and 1944, he served as president of the American Sociological Society. *Can Science Save Us?* was published first in 1947, and again in revised form in 1961.[11]

Lundberg opens his book with glowing praise for the physical and natural sciences. According to him, these sciences have "released us from some age-long fears and insecurities."

The "mere possession of scientific knowledge and scientific habits of thought regarding the natural universe," he writes, "relieves us of a world of fears, rages and other unpleasant dissipations of energy." Utilizing a medical metaphor, he proclaims that scientific knowledge "operates as a sort of mental hygiene in the fields where it is applied."[12]

In light of the great powers of the natural and physical sciences, Lundberg notes that it is not surprising that "man should have become increasingly interested in the question of whether this same tool called science might not be useful to him also in his social predicaments." Lundberg's main purpose in this book is to argue in favor of an affirmative answer to this question. The most promising tool for solving social problems, he declares, is the method of "modern natural science applied fully to human society, including man's thoughts, feelings, and 'spiritual' characteristics." As a method, Lundberg writes, science "is a form of human behavior," consisting of

(a) asking clear, answerable questions in order to direct one's (b) observations, which are then (c) reported as accurately as possible and in such a way as to answer the questions that were asked to begin with, after which (d) any pertinent beliefs or assumptions that were held before the observations were made are revised in light of the observations made and answers obtained.[13]

Lundberg calls on the nation to commit itself to this method in the realm of social problems by developing and employing a body of scientific knowledge about human behavior "which will be comparable to that which underlies engineering, navigation, and medicine." He asks: "Shall we or shall we not assume that we can formulate laws of human behavior which are comparable to the laws of gravity, thermodynamics, and bacteriology?" While he notes that these "latter laws do not of themselves create engineering wonders or cure disease," he proclaims that they nevertheless "constitute knowledge of a kind which is indispensable."[14]

The scientific knowledge that is indispensable in addressing social problems is to be discovered by professional social scientists, following "valid principles and methods of sampling, correlation, probability, computation, and logical inference." According to Lundberg, social scientists should devote themselves to three main tasks:

First and foremost, they should devote themselves to developing reliable knowledge of what alternatives of action exist under given conditions and the probable consequences of each. Secondly, social scientists should, as a legitimate part of their technology as well as for its practical uses, be able to gauge reliably what the masses of men want under given circumstances. Finally, they should, in the applied aspects of their science, develop the administrative or engineering techniques of satisfying most efficiently and economically these wants, regardless of how they may change from time to time, and regardless of the scientists' own preferences.[15]

Utilizing a meteorological analogy, he provides an example of what this looks like in practice:

Broadly speaking, it is the business of social scientists to be able to predict with high probability the social weather, just as meteorologists predict sunshine and storm. More specifically, social scientists should be able to say what is likely to happen socially under stated conditions. A competent economist or political scientist should be able to devise, for example, a tax program for a

25

given country which will yield with high probability a certain revenue and which will fall in whatever desired degrees upon each of the income groups of the area concerned. Social scientists should be able to state also what will be the effect of the application of this program upon income, investments, consumption, production, and the outcome of the next election.[16]

Elaborating on the qualifier he provided in his more general statement about the tasks of social scientists that we quoted above—namely, that they should develop techniques for satisfying people's wants "regardless of the scientists' own preferences"—Lundberg goes on to write the following:

> Having devised such a tax program and clearly specified what it will do, it is not the business of the social scientists any more than it is the business of any other citizens to secure the adoption or defeat of such a program. In the same way, competent sociologists, educators, or psychologists should be able to advise a parent as to the most convenient way of converting a son into an Al Capone or into an approved citizen, according to what is desired.[17]

Here Lundberg is stating his normative view that social scientists must maintain a strict stance of unbiased, disinterested neutrality. This stance reflects his view of their main function, which (he claims) is also the main function of the physical sciences. He writes:

> As *science*, both physical and social sciences have a common function, namely, to answer scientific questions. These answers will always be of an impersonal, conditional type: "*If* the temperature falls to 32°F., *then* water (H_2O) will freeze." "*If* a certain type of tax is adopted, *then* certain types of industrial activity will decrease." Neither of these statements carries any implications as to whether or how the knowledge should be used. Far from being a weakness, this characteristic of scientific knowledge is its greatest strength. The wants of men will change with changing conditions through the ages. The value of scientific knowledge lies precisely in this impersonal, neutral, general validity for whatever purposes man desires to use it.[18]

According to Lundberg, then, the only proper function of the social sciences in the public work of democracy is to answer scientific questions with scientific knowledge. The value of such knowledge is that it is reliable, positive, objective, and generalizable. With respect to the question of whether scientists have a "special function or obligation in determining the ends for which scientific knowledge is to be used," he emphatically answers in the negative. Like the authors of the AAUP's 1915 report on academic freedom, Lundberg makes a crucial distinction between scientists' function as scientists and their function as citizens. "As scientists," he writes, "*it is their business to determine reliably the immediate and remote costs and consequences of alternate possible courses of action, and to make these known to the public.* Scientists may then *in their capacity as citizens* join with others in advocating one alternative rather than another, as they prefer." He elaborates by arguing that social scientists

> should first agree that the sole function of scientific work is to grind out and publish systematically related and significant "if . . . then" propositions which are demonstrably probable to a certain degree under given circumstances. Under this definition "to say what one knows," i.e., to publish one's findings is certainly a clear imperative. Any advocacy or attempt on the part of a scientist in his capacity of scientist to specify what scientific knowledge is to be used for is equally

clearly outside the scientific sphere as defined. In his capacity as citizen, the scientist may of course advocate anything his heart desires with all the passion and resources at his command. If we do not rigorously insist on this distinction between scientific knowledge as contrasted with all other forms of knowledge whatsoever, we invite the corruption of science by injecting into it the biases of human preferences, tastes, and values which is precisely the charge today laid at the door of the social sciences.[19]

For Lundberg, the "ideal scientist, in his role as scientist, has allegiance to only one belief, namely, that the presently developing methods of modern scientific inquiry are more likely than any other methods to yield useful warranted assertions for the guidance of men in society." In one of his more provocative statements, he writes that the "services of *real* social scientists would be as indispensable to Fascists as to Communists and Democrats, just as are the services of physicists and physicians." The special skill of the social scientist, he writes, is "the ability to draw relatively valid, unbiased, and demonstrable conclusions from observed data of social behavior. *That* technique is the same, regardless of social objectives. No regime can get along without this technology."[20]

In laying out his vision of the proper tasks and roles of social scientists, Lundberg briefly mentions the issue of academic freedom. According to him, "the only foundation upon which academic freedom can ever be maintained in the long run" is "the demonstrated capacity of its possessors to make valid and impersonal analyses and predictions of social events." To maintain this capacity, and therefore, be worthy of academic freedom, social scientists, when they are functioning as social scientists, must refrain from all attempts to pursue their "private" preferences as citizens. He notes that this is sometimes difficult:

> The temptation is admittedly considerable to bolster one's favorite "movement" by posing as a disinterested appraiser of the truth while actually engaging in special pleading. It is also tempting in this way to seek the right of sanctuary in the form of academic freedom to escape the ordinary consequences of pressure group activity as visited on less clever and less privileged people.[21]

Functioning as "a disinterested appraiser of the truth" while resisting all temptations to pursue and advance one's own beliefs and preferences is the essence of the service intellectual tradition. As a normative ideal (which, we must not forget, is not the same thing as actual practice), the service intellectual tradition was and still is espoused, both in the social science methods literature and in the nation's state and land-grant colleges and universities. It also was and still is espoused in private research universities. A notable historical example of this can be found in the so-called Chicago School of sociology at the University of Chicago during the 1920s.[22]

It is important to stress that the service intellectual tradition has not historically been—and is not today—limited to the social sciences. Its core elements—unbiased, disinterested neutrality, the strict separation of scholars' identities and roles as scientists from their identities and roles as citizens, the provision of scientific knowledge and technical expertise and assistance without any attempt to persuade—have been embraced by academic professionals across the full range of academic fields and disciplines, including the arts and humanities, engineering, law, and the social, natural, and biological sciences. They also have long been and continue to be embraced in articulations of the proper social roles and stances of scholars, both in the classroom and in off-campus civic life. For example, they were force-fully laid out in 1919 in Max Weber's essay "Science as a Vocation," and more recently in Stanley Fish's book *Save the World on Your Own Time.*[23]

Two Purposivist Traditions

According to those who espouse the views that make up the service intellectual tradition, academic professionals should connect and relate their professional work to the public work of democracy in a responsive manner, when—and only when—they are asked for help. Their professional role is to be limited to that of serving as an unbiased, disinterested, and neutral technician—a cruncher of numbers, an "expert on tap," a provider of facts. Their public purpose is to inform decision making by providing reliable, positive, unbiased, objective, and generalizable knowledge (i.e., "the truth")—and nothing more.

In contrast to service intellectuals, those scholars whom Mark C. Smith calls "purposivists" reject the normative position of strictly separating their identity and roles as a professional scientist or scholar from their identity and roles as a citizen. While the service intellectual tradition calls on scholars to draw a clear line between academic work and politics that is not to be crossed while they are functioning as professionals, in purposivist traditions scholars commit themselves to merging their professional and civic identities and roles by functioning in both realms simultaneously. In our view, there are two distinct normative traditions in which purposivist scholars have situated themselves: the public intellectual tradition, and the action researcher / public scholar / educational organizer tradition.

Before we sketch the elements in these traditions, we look closely at an early statement of the purposivist position: an article by Albion W. Small (1854–1926) entitled "Scholarship and Social Agitation," published in 1896 in the *American Journal of Sociology.* Small was an instrumental figure in the formative years of sociology as a discipline in the United States. After receiving a Ph.D. from Johns Hopkins University, he served as president of Colby College from 1889 to 1892. He accepted a position as professor of sociology at the University of Chicago in 1892, where he founded the nation's first department of sociology. He founded the *Journal of American Sociology* in 1895, and like George A. Lundberg, he also served as president of the American Sociological Society (1912–13).[24]

Small's primary purpose in "Scholarship and Social Agitation" was, in his words, "to challenge the claims of that type of scholarship which assumes superiority because it deals only with facts." The type of scholarship that deals "only with facts" while strictly avoiding taking action to pursue scholars' views of what should be done about social problems is the type of scholarship that is espoused in the service intellectual tradition. It is the type of scholarship that George Lundberg would later proclaim is not only the best kind, but also the only legitimate kind for social scientists to practice. Writing many decades before the publication of *Can Science Save Us?*, Small asserted that such a scholarship was actually inferior:

> I would have American scholars, especially in the social sciences, declare their independence of
> do-nothing traditions. I would have them repeal the law of custom which bars marriage of thought

with action. I would have them become more profoundly and sympathetically scholarly by enriching the wisdom which comes from knowing with the larger wisdom which comes from doing. I would have them advance from knowledge of facts to knowledge of forces, and from knowledge of forces to control of forces in the interest of more complete social and personal life.[25]

In our view, the final sentence in the passage just quoted clearly positions Small in a different normative tradition than that of the service intellectuals. To advance from knowledge of facts and forces into the realm of the "control of forces," social scientists would have to walk on both sides of the line between academic work and politics. They would have to reject the service intellectuals' categorical restraint on acting to pursue their views of what should be done about social problems. In Small's view, such pursuits were not a problem. Rather, the problem rested with that type of scholarship that deals only with knowledge of facts. The problem with such scholarship, he wrote, is that it

is likely to become retrospective, and so not conservative but obstructive, in proportion to its insistence that nothing belongs in its province except demonstrative evidence. The only things which to our minds are absolutely certain are accomplished facts. Scholarship which would guard against becoming speculation and adventure, dreads departure from this sure region of the has-been, for exploration of the somewhat conjectural realm of the more reasonable and possible and desirable which is to be.[26]

For Small, social criticism was a key function scholars were supposed to take up in the realm of the "possible and desirable which is to be." In doing so, they would be supplying the public with something he believed it wanted. While "Men's minds once yearned for the one sedative of authority," he wrote, "they now thirst for the thousand stimulants of criticism." He went on to proclaim that "Scholarship must either abandon claims to the function of leadership, and accept the purely clerical role of recording and classifying the facts of the past, or scholarship must accept the responsibility of prevision and prophecy and progress."[27]

Small self-consciously wrote his article in the context of a period of significant transformation and transition in American history that he believed had profound implications for the social sciences. "The paramount duty of social scholarship at this moment," he wrote, "is to reckon with the epoch making fact that today's men have gradually cut the moorings of ethical and social tradition after tradition, and that society is today adrift, without definite purpose to shape its course, and without a supreme conviction to give it motion." There was in Small's view a "radical fact" that people had yet to admit: namely, "that the words around which our civilization has rallied no longer convey our ultimate ideas; or rather they stop short of notions which we will accept as ultimate." He elaborated:

Thus we declaim of "liberty," but men are wondering whether we have begun to know wherein liberty consists. We have boasted of "rights" but the suspicion is rife that the majority of men have never understood a tithe of their rights, and that the rights which our institutions assure are possibly not more than a tithe of the goods upon which complete men will insist. We have appealed to "ethics," but at this late day there is no more open question than, What is ethical? We declare the sacredness of life, but men are asking, What is life? What does life presume? What does life involve? What should life contain? To whom does the prerogative of life belong?[28]

For Small, uncertainty about the answers to these questions constituted "the setting of the urgent problems that confront today's men." It was in relation to this setting that Small articulated his normative position about the role and function of professional scholars. "Scholars are shirkers," he argued,

> unless they grapple with these problems. It is for this that society supports us. We are presumed to be exponents of the higher excellencies of thought and action. We are expected to hold up ideals of the best, to guide the endeavors of the masses of men. It is squandering money to put more endowments into the keeping of educational institutions that are not devoting their energies in larger and larger proportion to search for solution of these moral problems, together with the solution of the physical problems, through both of which the larger welfare of men is to be secured.[29]

According to Small, scholars should work "in either or both of two ways: first, in clarifying fundamental or general conceptions; second, in perfecting and applying subordinate devices and plans." In other words, scholars' roles and functions in society were to include not only "clarifying" the meaning of concepts like liberty, rights, and ethics, but also developing and implementing action plans to address social problems that relate to liberty, rights, and ethics. He devoted much of his paper to an illustration of these roles from his own work of clarifying the meaning of the concept of private property, and asserting and advocating for public policies that he believed flowed from it. He argued that whenever an existing concept or institution was in question, as the concept of private property and its regulation was in the Gilded Age of the late nineteenth century, "it is the scholar's duty to hold his services at the disposal of his fellows, for the purpose of reaching permanent and convincing conclusions. . . . Our relation to the people creates a demand upon us to do this work for the people. . . ." Referring to an assertion by the French anarchist Pierre-Joseph Proudhon that "property is robbery," which Small viewed as "more picturesque than precise," he argued that "it is the scholar's duty to search out the fraction of truth in such wholesale error, to show that some property has been robbery, and to assist in refining principles by which we may guard against permitting any man to call his own what should be partly the franchise of others."[30]

The reason why he provided a detailed example from his own work, Small wrote, was

> to illustrate what I mean when I claim that all scholarship within the field of the social sciences ought to be made to converge at last upon criticism of capital positions in our social order. I have no sympathy with nor confidence in any conception of sociology which is satisfied with abstractions, or which does not keep well in mind the relation of all research to the living interests of living men. Scholars, and especially sociological scholars, are either wrong or wronged when they are said to endorse and support the presumption that whatever *is* in society is *right,* or if not right at least unavoidable. I plead for that creditable and worthy agitation by scholars, which is not hysterical fuss and pother with symptoms and specifics, but rather calm and patient exploration of conditions and causes and principles.[31]

He went on to emphasize that his normative view of scholars' roles and functions in society would enable them to combine their identity and work as scholars with their identity and work as citizens. In a passage that is sharply at odds with the normative position in the service intellectual tradition, that scholars should maintain a stance of strict neutrality about what should be done about social problems by staying on the academic side of the line between academics and politics, Small wrote:

> I content myself with saying that scholars might exalt both their scholarship and their citizenship by claiming an active share in the work of perfecting and applying plans and devices for social improvement and amelioration. It is not only betrayal of his social trust, it is surrender of the best elements of his professional opportunity, for the sociologist scholar to withdraw from affairs, and attempt to grow wise by rearranging the contents of his personal consciousness. The most impressive lesson which I have learned in the vast sociological laboratory which the city of Chicago constitutes is that action, not speculation, is the supreme teacher. If men will be the most productive scholars in any department of the social sciences, let them gain time and material by cooperating in the social work of their community.[32]

In cooperating in the social work of their community, Small wrote, every sociological scholar should "share constantly in some concrete work of two specific kinds: first, work which the thoughtful and careful prosecute for the benefit of the thoughtless and the careless; second, work which the enterprising and efficient organize for the better security of their own social interests." He concluded his article with an assertion and a call, punctuated with an exclamation point. "There is better work for scholars than criticism of men and measures from a distance," he asserted. "It is timely to proclaim a different ideal for American scholars from that which has dominated the learned world for the last fifty years. May American scholarship never so narrow itself to the interests of scholars that it shall forfeit its primacy among the interests of men!"[33]

Like the service intellectual tradition, the normative view of the roles and functions scholars are supposed to play in civic life that Small articulated in his article includes one of the two main functions that were articulated in the AAUP's 1915 statement: that of imparting the results of research. But in a break from the service intellectual tradition, Small also embraced the second main function that was articulated in the AAUP statement: namely, "to help make public opinion more self-critical and more circumspect, to check the more hasty and unconsidered impulses of popular feeling, to train the democracy to the habit of looking before and after." However, he did so in a way that reflects a rejection of a key normative position we find in both the AAUP statement and in George Lundberg's book: the position that academic professionals should stay on the academic side of the line between academics and politics by strictly separating their identity and roles as a scientist or scholar from their identity and roles as a citizen.[34]

The views Albion Small articulated in "Scholarship and Social Agitation" are consistent with two normative traditions of purposivist scholarship: the public intellectual tradition, and what we call the action researcher / public scholar / educational organizer tradition. Before we sketch the main elements in these two traditions, we want to emphasize that they are not necessarily mutually exclusive. While the normative stance of the service intellectual tradition is fundamentally at odds with the normative stances of both purposivist traditions, the normative stances taken in the purposivist traditions are not necessarily at odds with each other. Both purposivist traditions embrace the view that academic professionals should participate *as professionals* in the public work of democracy. As we see it (others may well disagree), the key difference between them has to do with the nature of the relationship between academic professionals and external audiences, and the roles each group is supposed to play. In the public intellectual tradition, academic professionals write and speak as experts, critics, and civic educators *to* the general public, which plays the roles of audience and student. In the action researcher / public scholar / educational organizer tradition, academic professionals educate, learn, deliberate, conduct research, and organize and conduct public work directly *with* specific (and typically localized) groups of people that function not as audiences, but rather as collaborators and participants.

The Public Intellectual Tradition

Consistent with the views Albion Small articulated in "Scholarship and Social Agitation," the public intellectual tradition breaks the normative line between academic work and politics by legitimatizing the work of engaging in conscious acts of political intervention aimed at advancing particular interests and ends—including especially scholars' personal, subjective views of what does and does not constitute "the public interest." To use George Lundberg's language, through their acts of political intervention public intellectuals seek to "bolster their favorite 'movement'" by engaging in "special pleading." The way they do so, as Richard Posner put it in his book *Public Intellectuals,* is by writing and speaking about public issues to general public audiences "by means of books, magazine articles, op-ed pieces, open letters, public lectures, and appearances on radio or television."[35]

The central functions or roles public intellectuals are to play in civic life are those of expert, civic educator, and social critic. As political theorist and current University of Pennsylvania president Amy Gutmann argues in her book *Democratic Education,* it is through their role as social critics that public intellectuals make their most distinctive contribution to democracy. According to Gutmann, the university's "primary democratic purpose" is protecting against the threat of tyranny. Using a line of argument that is similar to the one the authors of the AAUP's 1915 report used, she writes that universities protect against tyranny by safeguarding the freedom for scholars to function as autonomous social critics. "As communities of critics," Gutmann says, "universities make it more difficult for public officials, professionals, and ordinary citizens to disregard their own standards when it happens to be convenient." Under the privilege of academic freedom, scholars are granted control over the creation of ideas without fear of retribution by the state or other interests, allowing them to "assess existing theories, established institutions, and widely held beliefs . . . [and] follow their autonomous judgment wherever it leads them, provided that they remain within the bounds of scholarly standards of inquiry."[36]

According to Gutmann,

> universities have not only a right to relative autonomy from external political control but also an obligation to create an environment this is conducive to the exercise of scholarly autonomy. When they live up to that obligation (by securing for scholars an intellectual realm free from improper pressures), universities provide an institutional sanctuary against repression, which prevents majorities or coalitions of minorities from controlling the creation of politically relevant ideas. The sanctuary protects democracy not only against its own excesses but also against non-democratic tyranny.[37]

C. Wright Mills (1916–1962), a professor of sociology at Columbia University, provided one of the most detailed articulations of the public intellectual tradition in American higher education in his 1959 book, *The Sociological Imagination*. Rejecting the normative line between academics and politics drawn in the service intellectual tradition, Mills wrote that "the most admirable thinkers within the scholarly community . . . do not split their work from their lives. They seem to take both too seriously to allow such dissociation, and they want to use each for the enrichment of the other." By "their lives," Mills was referring to scholars' identities, experiences, and responsibilities as citizens of a particular milieu (i.e., place and time). In Mills's view, scholars should associate their work and their lives by consciously and deliberately intervening in the politics of their place and time. With one important exception, which we will note in our discussion below of the action research / public scholarship / educational organizing tradition, his view of the roles of academic professionals in the public work of democracy was consistent with those that were articulated by Albion Small in 1898.[38]

Mills believed that most "ordinary" people lacked the capacity to "grasp the interplay of man and society, of biography and history, of self and world." In his view, the main purpose of social scientists as participants in the public work of democracy was to attend to this problem. In pursuing this purpose, they were not only to function as experts and critics, but also as civic educators. As civic educators, they were to do more than simply provide people with facts and information. They were to teach and help develop in people "a quality of mind that will help them to use information and to develop reason in order to achieve lucid summations of what is going on in the world and of what may be happening within themselves." This quality of mind is the essence of "the sociological imagination." Its promise, Mills wrote, is that it enables people "to grasp history and biography and the relations between the two within society." The development of the sociological imagination in ordinary people would provide them with "the capacity to range from the most impersonal and remote transformations to the most intimate features of the human self—and to see the relations between the two." It would help them, as he put it, to connect the private matter of their "personal troubles" with the "public issues of social structure."[39]

According to Mills, social scientists should center their scholarly work on the formulation of personal troubles and public issues, in the context of their particular milieu. They should begin by asking: "What are the major issues for publics and the key troubles of private individuals in our time? To formulate issues and troubles, we must ask what values are cherished yet threatened, and what values are cherished and supported, by the characterizing trends of our period." Interweaving scholarship and politics, Mills wrote: "It is now the social scientist's foremost political and intellectual task—for here the two coincide—to make clear the elements of contemporary uneasiness and indifference."[40]

Mills argued that his normative view of the public roles and work of social scientists was consistent with what he called the "classic" tradition in the social sciences of the late nineteenth century. The essential features of that tradition, he wrote, were a concern with historical social structures and a focus on problems that "are of direct relevance to urgent public issues and insistent human troubles." Practitioners of classic social science, Mills claimed, were directly linked to reform movements and betterment activities. They "sought to turn the troubles of lower-class people into issues for middle-class publics." But in his own milieu, that of mid-twentieth-century America, Mills wrote, "there are now great obstacles in the way of this tradition's continuing—both within the social sciences and in their academic and political settings." Within the social sciences, the obstacles in the way took the form of two trends: those of "grand theory" and "abstracted empiricism."[41]

In grand theory, scholars suffered from what Mills labeled a "fetishism of the Concept." They were lost in the Olympian heights, examining and theorizing the meaning of large concepts like "the social system." He argued that the problem with grand theorists—his prime example was Talcott Parsons, who wrote a major book on the concept of "the social system"—was their "choice of a level of thinking so general that its practitioners cannot logically get down to observation. They never, as grand theorists, get down from the higher generalities to problems in their historical and structural contexts."[42]

In abstracted empiricism, Mills claimed that scholars make a fetish of methods instead of concepts. They suffer from an epistemological bias that leads them to be obsessed with getting a certain kind of data: namely, data that can be quantified. Their "most cherished professional self-image," Mills wrote, "is that of the natural scientist." Through surveys conducted with rigorously defined sampling procedures, they produce results that are put in the form of statistical assertions, piling up details with insufficient attention to historical social structures. The problem with this, Mills wrote, is that the "details, no matter how numerous, do not convince us of anything worth having convictions about."[43]

Mills was of course not opposed to conceptual and theoretical work, nor was he against empirical methods and statistics. In his view, the problem was that practitioners of grand theory and abstracted empiricism were "stuck," either in the high level of generalization, or in debates over the epistemological problems of method. Both grand theory and abstract empiricism "ought to be pauses in the working process of social science," Mills wrote. "But in them what ought to be a little pause has become, if I may put it so, the entrance into fruitlessness." For Mills, the way they were being practiced marked an intellectual "abdication" of classic social science. "The vehicle of their abdication," he declared, "is the pretentious over-elaboration of 'method' and 'theory'; the main reason for it is their lack of firm connection with substantive problems."[44]

From Mills's perspective, the older classical social science tradition that (Mills claims) was intentionally pursued for democratic purposes had become overshadowed by what he referred to as "The New Social Science," which corporate and government elites were using to manage and manipulate the masses. By joining the technique of abstracted empiricism with its bureaucratic use, social science had become both bureaucratic and "illiberal." Instead of advancing the liberal, public (and democratic) purpose or end of teaching the sociological imagination, it was advancing the interests of elites by serving "to increase the efficiency and the reputation—and to that extent, the prevalence—of bureaucratic forms of domination in modern society." In Mills's view, the new social science featured the development of two new types of academic professionals: the intellectual administrator and the research technician. Utilizing expensive statistical techniques that only large institutions could afford, these academic professionals were especially helpful in meeting the advertising, promotion, and public relations needs of corporations. As "applied" sociologists, they offered their services for hire. "The sociologist of applied social research," he wrote, "does not usually address 'the public'; he has specific clients with particular interests and perplexities."[45]

As Mills moves from a discussion of the obstacles in the way of the continuation of his view of classic social science, he provides his articulation of what we are calling the public intellectual tradition. He noted that the work of all social scientists has political meaning and uses. Instead of denying them or leaving them to chance, he wrote, social scientists should decide the political meaning and uses of their work as a matter of their own policy. He argued that they should do so in ways that exhibit an embrace of three political values. First is the "value of truth, of fact." To practice social science, Mills wrote, should be "to practice the politics of truth." Because truth and facts are not enough, the second political value Mills believed that social scientists must embrace is the value of the role of reason in human affairs. Social scientists embrace reason when they work to show whether and how the truth of their findings may or may not be relevant to human affairs. Mills declared: "If human reason is to play a larger and more explicit role in the making of history, social scientists must surely be among its major carriers. For in their work they represent the use of reason in the understanding of human affairs; that is what they are about." The third value, which Mills positioned in close relationship with the second, was "human freedom, in all the ambiguity of its meaning."[46]

In general, Mills noted, there are three main political roles social scientists might play in society. First, given their "superior" knowledge and intellectual capacities, they could play the role of the "philosopher king." In Mills' view, this was not only foolish and antidemocratic, it was also unrealistic, given structural realities of power. The second role is to be "an advisor to the king," or, in the case of the United States, government officials and corporate elites. While this role could be performed in admirable ways, Mills noted, it was most frequently performed in ways that served manipulative and antidemocratic purposes. The third political role, the one Mills clearly favored, is for scholars "to remain independent, to do one's own work, to select one's own problems, but to direct this work *at* kings as well as *to* 'publics.'" This third role, he wrote, "prompts us to imagine social science as a sort of public intelligence apparatus, concerned with public issues and private troubles and with the structural trends of our time underlying them both—and to imagine individual social scientists as rational members of a self-controlled association, which we call the social sciences."[47]

In advocating the third political role, Mills claimed that his academic colleagues were failing to practice it. "Where is the intelligentsia," he asked, "that is carrying on the big discourse of the Western world *and* whose work as intellectuals is influential among parties and publics and relevant to the great decisions of our time?" According to Mills, they were not to be found. In the United States today, he argued, intellectuals "neither raise demands on the powerful for alternative politics, nor set forth such alternatives before publics. They do not try to put responsible content into the politics of the United States; they help to empty politics and to keep it empty."[48]

Against this reality, Mills called upon social scientists to become "explicitly political" by addressing their work to three different audiences. First, social scientists should address their work to those who are aware that they have power by imputing "varying measures of responsibility for such structural consequences as he finds by his work to be decisively influenced by their decisions and their lack of decisions." Second, he called upon social scientists to educate and impute responsibility to those who have power but are not aware of it. Third, he called upon them to direct their work to those who do not have power, and whose "awareness is confined to their everyday milieux." The social scientist "reveals by his work the meaning of structural trends and decisions for these milieux, the ways in which personal troubles are connected with public issues; in the course of these efforts, he states what he has found out concerning the actions of the more powerful." These are the major public and educational tasks of the social scientist, Mills declares, "when he speaks to any larger audience."[49]

Working out of his favored conception of the political and public role of the social scientist, Mills writes that the social scientist has two main goals. First, "What he ought to do for the individual is to turn personal troubles and concerns into social issues and problems open to reason—his aim is to help the individual become a self-educating man, who only then would be reasonable and free." Second, "What he ought to do for society is to combat all those forces which are destroying genuine publics and creating a mass society—or put as a positive goal, his aim is to help build and to strengthen self-cultivating publics. Only then might society be reasonable and free."[50]

Here we see Mills's view of the social scientist as a *civic* educator, *in and for a democracy.* As a civic educator, Mills wrote, the social scientist

> must try to develop men and women who can and who will by themselves continue what he has begun: the end product of any liberating education is simply the self-educating, self-cultivating man and woman; in short, the free and rational individual. A society in which such individuals are ascendant is, by one major meaning of the word, democratic. Such a society may also be defined as one in which genuine publics rather than masses prevail. . . . It is the political task of the social scientist—as of any liberal educator—continually to translate personal troubles into public issues, and public issues into the terms of their human meaning for a variety of individuals. It is his task to display in his work—and, as an educator, in his life as well—this kind of sociological imagination. And it is his purpose to cultivate such habits of mind among the men and women who are publicly exposed to him. To secure these ends is to secure reason and individuality, and to make these the predominant values of a democratic society.[51]

In describing what social scientists are doing when they take up the political role he advocates, Mills uses language that echoes that which was used by President Truman's Commission on Higher Education. In taking up the "role of reason, the autonomous role," Mills writes, "we are trying to act in a democratic manner in a society that is not altogether democratic. But we are acting as if we were in a fully democratic society, and by doing so, we are attempting to remove the 'as if.' We are trying to make the society more democratic." The pursuit of this end, he writes, "requires that we deliberately present controversial theories and facts, and actively encourage controversy. In the absence of political debate that is wide and open and informed, people can get into touch neither with the effective realities of their world nor with the realities of themselves." In a phrase that captures the essence of the public intellectual tradition, he writes that the "educational and political role of social science in a democracy is to help cultivate and sustain publics and individuals that are able to develop, to live with, and to act upon adequate definitions of personal and social realities."[52]

Like the service intellectual tradition that George Lundberg espoused, the public intellectual tradition that Mills articulated is not confined or limited to the social sciences. It has been and continues to be embraced and espoused in many academic disciplines and fields. A contemporary example of someone who works in the public intellectual tradition is Paul Krugman, a professor of economics at Princeton University. As we write, his most recent book, *The Return of Depression Economics and the Crisis of 2008*, is listed on the *New York Times* best sellers list. He writes two weekly columns for the *New York Times*, maintains an active blog, and is a frequent commentator and guest on television talk shows. In a recent article about him that appeared in *Newsweek* magazine, one of Krugman's Princeton colleagues referred to him as a "public intellectual."[53]

The Action Researcher / Public Scholar / Educational Organizer Tradition

Near the end of *The Sociological Imagination*, C. Wright Mills wrote the following:

> The role of reason I have been outlining neither means nor requires that one hit the pavement, take the next plane to the scene of the current crisis, run for Congress, buy a newspaper plant, go among the poor, set up a soap box. Such actions are often admirable, and I can readily imagine occasions when I should personally find it impossible not to want to do them myself. But for the social scientist to take them to be his normal activities is merely to abdicate his role, and to display by his action a disbelief in the promise of social science and in the role of reason in human affairs. This role requires only that the social scientist get on with the work of social science and that he avoid furthering the bureaucratization of reason and of discourse.[54]

In this passage, Mills's view of the roles academic professionals should play in the public work of democracy departs in one significant way from the view Albion Small articulated in 1898. The passage suggests that Mills thought scholars should not directly collaborate with nonacademic citizens in localized public work. Indeed, in the appendix of *The Sociological Imagination*, Mills described the "craft" of social science as a solitary endeavor, conducted by lone scholars who deliberately stand apart and detached from contemporary, on-the-ground civic work. In contrast, Small clearly believed that academic professionals should not remain in isolation. Scholars "might exalt both their scholarship and their citizenship," he wrote, "by claiming an active share in the work of perfecting and applying plans and devices for social improvement and amelioration."[55]

In our reading of Small's argument, we find an embrace not only of the public intellectual tradition, but also of a second purposivist tradition, one in which academic professionals do "hit the pavement" and "go among the poor" as part of their "normal" activities. This second purposivist tradition goes by a wide variety of names, including action research, participatory action research, community-based research, emancipatory research, activist scholarship, the scholarship of engagement, engaged scholarship, public scholarship, and educational organizing. In this book, we choose to call it the *action researcher / public scholar / educational organizer* (AR/PS/EO) tradition. We obviously do not do so for the sake of elegance, but rather because we think that each of these three terms captures an important dimension of the normative ideals of this tradition. While different in some respects, they are complementary. We believe they fit together in ways that justify including them all in our naming of this tradition.[56]

As with all normative traditions that have long histories in a variety of cultural and political contexts, terms like *action research*, *public scholarship*, and *educational organizing* have no single "correct" meaning. While acknowledging that people understand and define these terms in different ways (sometimes quite radically so), in this book we use them in ways that reflect the following specific meanings:

- With respect to *action research*, we accept Davydd Greenwood and Morten Levin's definition: "Action research is social research carried out by a team that encompasses a professional action researcher and the members of an organization, community, or network ('stakeholders') who are seeking to improve participants' situation. AR promotes broad participation in the research process and supports action leading to a more just, sustainable, or satisfying situation for the stakeholders."[57]

- We view *public scholarship* as creative intellectual work that is conducted in the context of public settings and relationships, facilitating social learning and producing knowledge, theory, technologies, and other kinds of products that advance both public and academic interests and ends. Its results are communicated to, and validated by, peers, including but not limited to peers in scholars' academic fields. Scholars who practice public scholarship seek to advance the academy's teaching and research missions in ways that hold both academic and public value.[58]

- *Educational organizing* is a type of organizing at the community level in which organizers deliberately function as educators. Rather than only or mainly seeking to mobilize people in protests to win specific short-term battles, educational organizers seek to develop local leadership, facilitate learning, and tap and build various forms of agency and power that will enable people to understand and pursue their self-interests, their common interests, and larger public interests.[59]

Like the public intellectual tradition, the AR/PS/EO tradition positions academic professionals as playing proactive and formative roles in civic life. But unlike the public intellectual tradition, academic professionals in the AR/PS/EO tradition are supposed to educate, learn, deliberate, conduct research, and organize and conduct public work directly *with* specific (and typically localized) groups of people that function not as audiences and students, but rather as collaborators and participants. In and through their direct engagement in on-the-ground civic life, academic professionals who work in the AR/PS/EO tradition contribute knowledge, theory, technical expertise and assistance, social criticism, and civic education and leadership. The products of their work include papers, books, and reports for both academic and public audiences, a variety of material and cultural goods, and organized relationships and platforms for public work.

In American higher education, the AR/PS/EO tradition has historically been (and still is) espoused and followed in many different disciplines, fields, and institutional types. It is important not to miss the fact that the nature and purposes of this tradition are not inherently "democratic." It has been and still is espoused and followed in relatively technocratic ways that serve particular interests and agendas, including those of the state and various industries.

Given the institutional location of the practitioner profiles that are included in this book, as well as our own interests, goals, and locations, we want to provide a brief overview of the historical foundations of a democratic variety of this tradition in land-grant colleges of agriculture. We expect that many readers will be quite skeptical of our overview. In most of the academic literature, as well as in informal culture, the public purposes and work of land-grant colleges of agriculture are portrayed in one of two ways: either as being consistent with those of the service intellectual tradition, or with those of a highly technocratic—even oppressive—variety of the purposivist AR/PS/EO tradition. While both the service intellectual tradition and a technocratic variety of the AR/PS/EO tradition were (and still are) implicitly and explicitly espoused and embraced by many in the land-grant system, our own work and experience has led us to see that a democratic variety of the purposivist AR/PS/EO tradition was and still is espoused and embraced as well.[60]

The land-grant system consists of 109 institutions located in all fifty states, Washington, D.C., and several U.S. territories. It includes thirty-three tribal colleges that were given land-grant status through the Equity in Educational Land-Grant Status Act of 1994. The system was originally created through the Morrill Acts of 1862 and 1890. Two additional federal acts created official, ongoing mechanisms for connecting and relating the work of academic professionals and students in this system to the needs, interests, and problems of individuals, communities, groups, governments, and businesses. The Hatch Act of 1887 established a national system of agricultural experiment stations, and the Smith-Lever Act of 1914 nationalized land-grant institutions' agricultural extension work by establishing the Cooperative Extension System, which eventually placed a new kind of academic professional called an *extension agent* in nearly every county in the nation. Together, these two acts institutionalized an obligation in the land-grant system to directly connect the work of academic professionals to the work and interests of local constituencies and communities, individual states, and the nation as a whole. Broadly cast to include but also reach well beyond agriculture, this obligation is often referred to as the "land-grant mission."[61]

The creation of the national land-grant system institutionalized a particular configuration of the broad academic reform movement that took shape in American higher education in the latter half of the nineteenth century. As it developed in the land-grant system, the reform movement embraced the view that academic professionals should play active roles not only in addressing technical and social problems and challenges, but also in promoting and advancing particular interests, cultural values, and civic ideals. They were to do so not as altruistic volunteers, but as professional scholars, educators, and scientists in a host of newly established disciplines, offering their specialized skills and knowledge and expert judgment to industries, governments, communities, families, and individuals.

In the field of agriculture alone, more than two dozen new disciplines were created in land-grant institutions during the period between 1890 and 1915, including horticulture, plant pathology, farm management, entomology, animal husbandry, farm mechanics, agricultural chemistry, agricultural economics, home economics, rural sociology, and landscape art. Scientists, scholars, and community-based extension agents not only extended and applied the knowledge and expertise that were developed in these disciplines to farms and rural communities, and to policymakers at all levels of government; they also worked with nonuniversity people and organizations to develop, test, and use local, nonacademic knowledge and expertise. Importantly, extension agents were not (and are not today) charged with the exclusive and narrow task of handing out scientific facts and information. As originally conceived, they were to function as both teachers and organizers, bringing land-grant faculty and community members together in public work projects that included but also ranged well beyond technical problem-solving. The extension work of land-grant colleges and universities was not supposed to be aimed only at informing people of the findings of scientific research, in ways that were consistent with the service intellectual tradition. Rather, it was supposed to be aimed at encouraging and organizing specific behavioral, social, and cultural changes, in ways that were consistent with the AR/PS/EO tradition.[62]

Both technocratic and democratic varieties of the purposivist AR/PS/EO tradition were espoused in land-grant colleges of agriculture in the late nineteenth and early twentieth centuries. Perhaps the most important figure in articulating and establishing the latter of these varieties was Liberty Hyde Bailey. A graduate of Michigan Agricultural College (now Michigan State University), Bailey was a highly productive and accomplished horticultural scientist who served as a professor of horticulture at Cornell University from 1888 to 1903, and then as the founding dean of the New York State College of Agriculture at Cornell from 1903 to 1913. In addition to being a superb scientist, Bailey was an eloquent educational philosopher, visionary, and prophet.[63]

Bailey's prophecy was, in his own words, of "a new day coming" in American country life. The "new day" was not only to be one of enhanced agricultural productivity, economic prosperity and material comfort, but also of deep civic, cultural, moral, environmental, and spiritual vitality and integrity. It was to be the outgrowth of a new rural civilization "worthy of the best American ideals," and the colleges of agriculture in the nation's system of land-grant universities were to be the central means for bringing it about. "We are now beginning to be consciously concerned in the development of a thoroughly good and sound rural civilization," Bailey announced in 1909. "The colleges of agriculture will be the most important agencies in this evolution."[64]

Bailey's interpretation of the mission of land-grant institutions—particularly their colleges of agriculture—was extraordinarily broad and ambitious. He placed this interpretation at the center of his 1907 speech given at the dedication of the buildings for the New York State College of Agriculture, established under his leadership on May 9, 1904. While noting that the "main or central business of a college of agriculture is to teach the science and the practice of farming," Bailey proclaimed that

> such an institution really stands for the whole open country beyond the bounds of cities, taking this field because it is indivisible and also because other institutions have passed it by. There are whole universities that have a lesser scope than these leading colleges of agriculture. These institutions mean not one iota less than the redirecting of the practices and ideals of country life.[65]

Land-grant colleges of agriculture, in Bailey's view, "contribute to the public welfare in a very broad way, extending their influence far beyond the technique of agricultural trades."

Revealing his strong purposivist leanings, Bailey said: "Out of all our facts and discoveries we must now begin to formulate a new social economy." "In twenty-five years," he prophesied, "there will be a new political and social philosophy of the open country born out of these institutions."[66]

On February 26, 1909, almost two years after his speech at the dedication of the new buildings, Bailey delivered an address before an audience gathered on the Cornell campus for Farmers' Week. Bailey used the address, titled "The College of Agriculture and the State," to lay out a detailed description of the work of the college. Just as he had done in 1907, he placed the same broad, ambitious educational vision at the center of his speech. "While the College of Agriculture is concerned directly with increasing the producing power of land," he said, "its activities cannot be limited narrowly to this field. It must stand broadly for rural civilization. It must include within its activities such a range of subjects as will enable it to develop an entire philosophy or scheme of country life." He continued:

> All civilization develops out of industries and occupations; and so it comes that agriculture is properly a civilization rather than a congeries of crafts. The colleges of agriculture represent this civilization, in its material, business and human relations. Therefore, they are not class institutions, representing merely trades and occupations. The task before the colleges of agriculture is nothing less than to direct and to aid in developing the entire rural civilization; and this task places them within the realm of statesmanship.[67]

Bailey's broad-gauge vision of the mission and work of land-grant colleges of agriculture marked an embrace of a democratic-minded variety of the purposivist AR/PS/EO tradition in the land-grant system. Until the Second World War, this tradition found many supporters and advocates. It can be clearly seen, for example, in Kenyon Butterfield's presidential address before the Association of American Agricultural Colleges and Experiment Stations in 1917, which he titled "The Morrill Act Institutions and the New Epoch." Butterfield, a pioneering rural sociologist who was serving as president of both the Association of American Agricultural Colleges and Experiment Stations and the Massachusetts Agricultural College at the time he delivered his speech, proclaimed that the "imperative obligation" of land-grant colleges was to "seek the highest welfare of the great industrial classes in terms of their own prosperity and development, as well as a part of the common, national prosperity and welfare. We must not merely sympathize with the aims of democracy, we must deliberately choose to serve the complete democracy." While he noted that fundamental research was crucial in pursuing this obligation, he proclaimed that

> the people demand more than that. They crave also light and leading with respect to those political, economic and social adjustments which they feel are essential to their full welfare. Gentlemen, our programs are still too small and narrow. We can serve democracy only as we study all the problems of democracy. In our investigations we still stress too much the goal of increased productivity as our great task. We still have too much faith in knowledge of the physical and biological facts and principles as all sufficing. There should be searchings of heart as to our policies and programs. Are they adequate to meet the needs of the new epoch?[68]

Butterfield went on to say that the major democratic contribution of land-grant colleges to date had been the training of experts "on whom reliance must be placed for leadership."

The leadership he envisioned for these experts was supposed to be democratic in its nature and purposes. He wrote:

> The trained expert serves democracy only as he does the work of democracy, advances its interests, works its will. The expert must be a real democrat. His obligation is to the great society, not to any small or exclusive group of society; or if he work with such a group, always as the ambassador of the mass, the protagonist of the common weal.[69]

"Here at last is the key to the relation of the Morrill Act institutions and the new democratic era," Butterfield concluded:

> To socialize as well as train experts; to give men and women a vision of the new social order; to equip them with the tools that they may forge for the common man a new freedom out of the shackles of ignorance as well as out of the chains of injustice; to send them forth as persons who know the meaning of life and its toil as well as they know the technique of their chosen calling—these are the very secrets of power for our Land-Grant Colleges and Universities in the new day.[70]

The democratic-minded experts the land-grant system was supposed to socialize and train included a new generation of academic professionals who took up positions as faculty in land-grant colleges or as educators in community-based extension offices. The Cooperative Extension System (CES) became the organized vehicle for their civic engagement work. Established through the Smith-Lever Act that was signed into law by President Woodrow Wilson on May 8, 1914, CES launched an ambitious experiment in higher education through the creation of a system of partnerships between a federal government agency (the United States Department of Agriculture), land-grant institutions, state and local governments, and the general citizenry.[71]

The text of the Smith-Lever Act states that the Cooperative Extension System was to "aid in diffusing among the people of the United States useful and practical information on subjects relating to agriculture and home economics, and to encourage the application of the same." Its work was to "consist of the giving of instruction and practical demonstrations in agriculture and home economics to persons not attending or resident in [land-grant] colleges in the several communities, and imparting to such persons information on said subjects through field demonstrations, publications, and otherwise." While the bland language of the act suggests that the educators and faculty who engaged in extension work should adopt a service intellectual view of their proper public functions, the espoused theory presented in much of CES's official literature reflected an embrace of a democratic-minded variety of the purposivist, AR/PS/EO tradition. Nowhere was this more clearly articulated than in *The Agricultural Extension System of the United States*, the first major text that detailed the official view of the philosophy and work of the extension system.[72]

Published in 1930, *The Agricultural Extension System of the United States* was authored by two national extension leaders, C.B. Smith and M.C. Wilson. Smith and Wilson opened their book with a dramatic paragraph that set the democratic-minded purposivist tone of their book:

> There is a new leaven at work in rural America. It is stimulating to better endeavor in farming and home making, bringing rural people together in groups for social intercourse and study,

solving community and neighborhood problems, fostering better relations and common endeavor between town and country, bringing recreation, debate, pageantry, the drama and art into the rural community, developing cooperation and enriching the life and broadening the vision of rural men and women. This new leaven is the cooperative extension work of the state agricultural colleges and the federal Department of Agriculture, which is being carried on in cooperation with the counties and rural people throughout the United States.[73]

Smith and Wilson wrote that while extension work was "essentially that of teaching," it was a teaching to be based "not so much out of books and printed matter" as on "living things." They wrote that the "end sought is a more efficient and profitable agriculture, an adequate supply of food and clothing for the nation, a wholesome rural life, and an intelligent, alert, progressive rural people." The deeper significance of extension work, they believed, was its results in developing people, in drawing them out and enlarging their vision through engaging them in cooperative work. Involvement in such work would result in "a larger social and recreational life, . . . pride of occupation, growth in education and culture, and a satisfying feeling of greater responsibility and power." It would also result, they believed, in a deeper spiritual life.[74]

As for the work of the county extension agents, Smith and Wilson believed that they should not only be "carriers and efficient teachers of technical information, but must also be students of local conditions." Furthermore, their work was not only to educate themselves and others, but also to spark the great organizing task of bringing people together for cooperative action. In this work, an important role for agents was to help establish respectful relationships between people in local communities, and between these people and the experts and specialists of the USDA and the land-grant colleges. In doing this, agents were pursuing what Smith and Wilson believed was one of the most significant and distinguishing principles of cooperative extension work: the principle of a full partnership between government and the people. They wrote that Cooperative Extension had "begun a new experiment in government, where federal, state, and county government and local people all cooperate in financing, planning, and carrying out a great constructive movement in rural education and progress."[75]

The principle of a full partnership meant that in extension work, the knowledge, experience, ideas, and desires of local people were to count as much as those of the staff, specialists, and administrators employed by the government. Smith and Wilson wrote:

> important and helpful knowledge is resident in every community that, if generally applied, would greatly improve agriculture there. This local knowledge may be as significant for the up-building of the community as anything the government may bring in from the outside. The county agent and other extension forces find out and spread this local knowledge.[76]

Smith and Wilson described a process in which local citizens and the "agents of government" met around a "common council table" to discuss important problems and needs. In such meetings, specialists "bring to the conference their technical knowledge . . . , while the farmers and their wives bring their experiences of the years in the community and knowledge of what has succeeded, what is likely to succeed and what may fail." Out of these meetings there would arise a "common plan of work for the benefit of the community."[77]

The serious attention Smith and Wilson give to the importance of local knowledge and the possibilities of partnerships between citizens and government workers brings out the deep civic mission and spirit of Cooperative Extension work. Extension was to be a kind of public work, aimed at creating and tapping diverse resources for the development of people and communities. In closing their chapter on the importance of partnerships between people and government, Smith and Wilson wrote:

> it is desired to leave the thought that the agent of the government does not come to the farmer with a program or plan all worked out in advance but that he or she and the people, working as partners, develop the plan together and carry it out together. The government contributes technical knowledge, based on its continuing researches; the farming people contribute from their local knowledge and experiences, each supplementing the knowledge of the other and both the stronger for the association.[78]

The "agent of the government" Smith and Wilson is referring to here includes both locally based extension educators and campus-based scientists and scholars. The passage just quoted reveals these agents to be performing as more than service intellectuals, but as purposivists who are directly engaged as active players in civic life, "guiding" social change by using their knowledge and expertise to help to bring about certain normative ideals and aims.

In a key chapter, Smith and Wilson argued that the approach to extension programming had undergone an "evolutionary process" which included three phases:

(1) The phase when the government or its extension agent assumed to know what was needed on the individual farm and in the community. . . .

(2) The phase when the farming people themselves, in council with the extension agent, were made to feel largely responsible for the work and the extension program became what was called a "self-determined" program and was largely based on local information and conditions.

(3) The phase when agents of government and the people concerned together made the analysis of conditions, together selected the outstanding needs, and together made a program to meet these needs.[79]

The third phase was put forward as ideally embodying the "cooperative" principle. Instead of dismissing local knowledge and insight, as agents in the first phase did, or treating the work as purely local, as in the second phase, the third phase had the advantage of facilitating a "pooling of knowledge" from both inside and outside of the community. The key principle that must always be followed in developing extension work, they stressed, was the "principle of participation by the people."[80]

To facilitate local participation, Smith and Wilson wrote, it was the extension agent's responsibility to call people to public work. They suggested that boards of agriculture be created in each county, each of which would be comprised of about thirty or forty men and women elected by their local townships. They noted that such organizations would be "official, public, [and] democratic." The "public" dimension was especially important for Smith and Wilson. They stressed that "Any extension organization must be an educational organization that all the people can support, hence it must be public in origin and conduct." Cooperative Extension, they wrote, is a "distinct public service, supported wholly by public funds and wholly in the public interest." Therefore, "extension work is public in character, being carried on for the benefit of all people."[81]

This stressing of both the "public" and the "constructive" nature of extension work is important. One of the characteristics of public work is its view of all people as potential "producers" of common resources, of what was once understood as the "commonwealth." Smith and Wilson's book is rife with praise of the untapped capabilities of rural people, and of the productive possibilities of both adults and youth. They believed that by engaging people in public work on small or individual problems, Extension could help spark a community spirit that would lead to larger work. In language that reflects the spirit of democratic public work, but which today sounds quite sexist and condescending, they vividly described the way they saw this working with women:

> When farm women have learned to work together to solve individual problems like hat making or canning, serving a meal, garden planning, cutting out patterns, singing, playing games, their active minds seek larger expression and they may be found interesting themselves in the establishment of a playground for the children, the improvement of the school, a community picnic, development of a play or community pageant, starting a club or club market, meeting together in camps for a week's vacation and recreation, and undertaking other like matters. And in this work all women, rich and poor, high and low, meet without distinction on a common level of service and helpfulness.[82]

This same vision was put forward for work with men and youth, as well as for work that involved all rural citizens together. In each case, Smith and Wilson paint a portrait of Extension that brings out its public work dimensions, and the extent to which it was engaging people in an effort to link their work with their education and their practice of citizenship in a democracy.

In summary, what Smith and Wilson offered in their book was a democratic purposivist vision of extension work as public work: visible, creative efforts of a mix of people, producing things of lasting importance to their communities. Increasing the productiveness of agriculture or the health of livestock counted as public work just as did building a community center or improving schools. Each was understood to add to the resources of the community (i.e., the commonwealth), and each involved the visible efforts of a mix of people. Each developed capacities for leadership, while also feeding the fire of a community spirit that could be tapped for future work. The participation of people in extension work, Smith and Wilson declared, "is unquestionably making for broader-visioned men and women who are seeing the large problems of the community and county and are insisting that their solution be undertaken." Such a result, they believed, was Extension's "largest hope," and pursuing it was its "major work."[83]

During the period between 1914 and the Second World War, many—but decidedly not all—men and women in the land-grant system not only embraced the view of extension work that Smith and Wilson espoused, but also tried to put it into practice. For example, in 1933, Gertrude Humphreys, a home demonstration agent from Randolph County, West Virginia, organized local citizens in a planning process that gave them, in her words, "an opportunity to visualize their own community with its existing conditions and problems, to study these problems, and to discuss as a group the steps which need to be taken to improve unsatisfactory conditions." The citizens designed and conducted their own survey research of conditions in their county, and then held a two-day farm and home economic conference where people from all parts of the county joined with a small group of state and national extension staff to discuss and analyze the data. They then divided into committees to discuss a number of issues the data revealed and possible strategies for dealing with them. Out of this work, which took several months, specific objectives for the next several years were identified, and groups of citizens rolled up their sleeves and developed projects and initiatives to pursue them. Humphreys noted that the organizing approach the county agents used for this effort "meant a great deal of work," but that it was worth it "because of the interest created among the farm men and women of the county in working out a long-time program which these people themselves recognize as a product of their own efforts and thought."[84]

Smith and Wilson's book—and the writings of many other faculty members, extension agents, and administrators—offers evidence of an embrace of a democratic variety of the purposivist AR/PS/EO tradition in the land-grant system's extension work by at least some people during its formative, pre–World War II period. The institutionalization of extension work in land-grant colleges of agriculture during this period led to the creation of new and unique kinds of academic professional positions that are not found elsewhere in American higher education: the campus-based faculty member whose official job description includes a blend of research and extension responsibilities; the campus-based extension specialist; and the community-based extension agent. According to those who espoused views that are consistent with a democratic variety of the AR/PS/EO tradition, the people who held these positions were supposed to directly connect or ground their scholarship and teaching in off-campus civic life by engaging with others in the public work of democracy. Whether or not academic professionals who have held these positions in the past practiced what early proponents of the AR/PS/EO tradition preached is, of course, an open question. These positions still exist in the land-grant system today. Several of the profiles that are included in part 2 of this book are of contemporary faculty who hold such positions at Cornell University.[85]

The Antitradition

We want to close this chapter by acknowledging that there is a fourth normative tradition in American higher education that represents a negative position on the question of whether academic professionals should be engaged in the public work of democracy. This is what we think of as the "antitradition" of rejecting direct forms of civic engagement altogether. Stanley Fish embraces an extreme version of the antitradition in his recently published book, *Save the World on Your Own Time*. Fish is currently Davidson-Kahn Distinguished Professor and Professor of Law at Florida International University. He is the former dean of the College of Liberal Arts and Sciences at the University of Illinois at Chicago.

Fish opens his book by raising what he refers to as a "simple" question: "What exactly is the job of higher education and what is it that those who teach in colleges and universities are trained and paid to do?" To this "simple" question, Fish provides a "simple" answer:

College and university teachers can (legitimately) do two things: (1) introduce students to bodies of knowledge and traditions of inquiry that had not previously been part of their experience; and (2) equip those same students with the analytical skills—of argument, statistical modeling, laboratory procedure—that will enable them to move confidently within those traditions and to engage in independent research after a course is over.[86]

The university's "point," Fish claims, is "to produce and disseminate (through teaching and publications) academic knowledge and to train those who will take up that task in the future." According to him, academic professionals "teach materials and confer skills, and therefore don't or shouldn't do a lot of other things—like produce active citizens, inculcate the virtues of tolerance, redress injustices, and bring about political change." While he acknowledges that "a teacher might produce some of these effects—or their opposites— along the way," he insists that "they will be, or should be, contingent and not what is aimed at." For Fish, there is and should be a clear line that separates academic work from politics. Once academic professionals cross this line, he argues, "we are guilty both of practicing without a license and of defaulting on our professional responsibilities."[87]

As both this latter passage and the title of his book suggest, Fish's views of the university's "point" hinge on a conception of the work and responsibilities of the academic profession that rejects any connection whatsoever to the public work of democracy (i.e., "saving the world"). On this point, he leaves no room for misunderstanding. Using the word *we* to signify academic professionals, he writes that "we are in the education business, not the democracy business. Democracy, we must remember, is a political not an educational project." In answer to the question of what politics and democracy have to do with scholarship and teaching, he answers: "absolutely nothing." The public work of democracy, in his view, is someone else's job. If academic professionals wish to engage in it, they can. But they are not to do so "on-the-clock" as professionals, but rather "on their own time" as "private" citizens.[88]

Fish's views reflect the embrace of a deliberately narrow and idealistic view of the nature and functions of the university, and with it, the nature and functions of the academic profession. Such a view has historical roots. It was expressed in Max Weber's 1919 essay, "Science as a Vocation." It was also expressed in Abraham Flexner's 1930 book, *Universities: American, English, German*. In that book, Flexner asked: "suppose we could smash our universities to bits, suppose we could remake them to conform to our heart's desire, what sort of institutions should we set up?" In answering this question, he sounds a lot like Stanley Fish. "Whatever allowances we might make for national tradition or temperament," Flexner wrote, "we should see to it somehow that in appropriate ways scholars and scientists would be conscious of four major concerns: the conservation of knowledge and ideas; the interpretation of knowledge and ideas; the search for truth; the training of students who will practice and 'carry on.'"[89]

The four major "concerns" Flexner names are, in essence, his view of higher education's four major purposes and functions. While most people outside the academic profession would likely view these purposes and functions as being merely academic, many if not most academic professionals would likely view them as being both academic and "public." In all but the most extreme versions of the antitradition, an embrace of Flexner's (or Fish's) purposes and functions and a corresponding rejection of active and direct engagement in the public work of democracy does not constitute a rejection of public purposes and work. Rather, it reflects a view that the conservation of knowledge and ideas, the interpretation of knowledge and ideas, the search for truth, and the training of students for the academic profession *are* public purposes, and that they have inherent public value. If one holds Fish's and Flexner's narrow view of the university, these purposes and functions also have *sufficient* public value. In other words, they are enough. They rightfully account for *the whole* of the university's public purposes and work. Not only is nothing else required, but also, anything else is inappropriate. In the most extreme version of the antitradition, going beyond these purposes and functions by becoming engaged in the public work of democracy is both a distraction from and a *violation of* the academy's "real" work. To use Fish's words, civic engagement is equivalent to practicing without a license and defaulting on professional responsibilities.

Journalist and philosopher Walter Lippmann (1889–1974) presented a defense of the antitradition in his Phi Beta Kappa Oration delivered at Columbia University's commencement exercises in 1932, entitled "The Scholar in a Troubled World." His defense is worth noting because it highlights a key element in the antitradition: namely, the view that academic professionals should not only reject civic engagement because it does not fit with the "proper" view of the university's purposes and functions, but also because scholars lack the skills that are needed for effective political work.

In his address, which was given in the midst of the Great Depression, Lippmann described scholars as being torn between two different consciences: a "civic conscience" that tells a scholar that he or she "ought to be doing something about the world's troubles," and the "conscience of the scholar, which tells him that as one whose business it is to examine the nature of things, to imagine how they work, and to test continually the proposals of his imagination, he must preserve a quiet indifference to the immediate." By "the immediate," Lippmann was referring to the messy, contentious world of civic life. The main point of his speech was to argue in favor of *detachment* from civic life as the right and proper stance of the scholar.[90]

Lippmann acknowledged that if scholars remained "cloistered and aloof," they would suffer "in the estimation of the public, which asks impatiently to know what all this theorizing is good for anyway if it does not show a way out of all the trouble." Yet he also argued that if scholars became engaged in civic life, they would also suffer. It would "quickly be revealed that the scholar has no magic of his own, and to the making of present decisions he may have less to contribute than many who have studied his subject far less than he." Lippmann noted that there was "an insistent presumption that prolonged study should have produced immediate practical wisdom, that from the professors should issue knowledge of how to decide the current controversies." There was also a "notion that the contemplative life is a preparation for immediate participation in the solution of current problems." But Lippmann argued that "the traditions of human wisdom" stand against these views. "The art of practical decision, the art of determining which of several ends to pursue, which of many means to employ, when to strike and when to recoil," he claimed, "comes from intuitions that are more unconscious than the analytical judgment."[91]

Lippmann's argument about why scholars have nothing useful to contribute to civic affairs and life was based on a particular view of academic professionals' proper work and functions. "The true scholar," Lippmann wrote,

> is preoccupied with presumptions, with antecedents and probabilities; he moves at a level of reality under that of the immediate moment, in a world where the choices are more numerous and the possibilities more varied than they are at the level of practical decisions. At the level of affairs the choices are narrow, because prejudice has become set. At the level of thought, in the empire of reason, the choices are wide, because there is no compulsion of events or of self-interest. The immediate has never been the realm of the scholar. His provinces are the past, from which he distills understanding, and the future, for which he prepares insight. The immediate is for his purpose a mere fragment of the past, to be observed and remembered rather than to be dealt with and managed.[92]

Lippmann acknowledged that his "view of the scholar's life will seem to many a mere elegy to a fugitive and cloistered virtue." But for him, maintaining a cloistered position of detachment and disengagement was necessary if scholars were to remain undistracted in their pursuit of their proper purposes and functions, which for Lippmann, were identical to Flexner's four concerns. "I doubt whether the scholar can do a greater work for his nation in this grave moment of its history," Lippmann proclaimed, "than to detach himself from its preoccupations, refusing to let himself be absorbed by distractions about which, as a scholar, he can do almost nothing."[93]

Fish, Flexner, and Lippmann articulated similar versions of the antitradition. At its most extreme, there is not even any room for two of higher education's most recognizable public functions: the provision of a liberal education for undergraduates in preparation for their future roles as citizens, and the training of public-minded experts in a wide variety of professions. While Fish and Flexner effectively rejected both of these functions, others who work out of the antitradition have embraced them with great enthusiasm. Of course, these functions have been and are being pursued in civically engaged ways, through community service-learning courses and a variety of other means. But in the antitradition, they are to be pursued in ways that preserve civic detachment and disengagement, keeping the focus on the past and an imagined and distant future rather than the actual and immediate present.

By way of illustration, consider how Yale University president Arthur T. Hadley described higher education's contribution to the community in an address he delivered in 1900 on the topic of "The Relation Between Higher Education and the Welfare of the Country":

> I think that there are three distinct ways in which higher education helps the community, and by which it proves its right to exist. First, it makes our people better workers in their several occupations. Second, it makes them better members of the body politic. Third, it makes them better men morally and spiritually.[94]

According to Hadley, higher education makes better workers by providing students with technical and scientific training in campus classrooms and laboratories. It makes students better people—civically, morally, and spiritually—by providing them with courses in the liberal arts.

Today, when community service-learning has been embraced across the whole of American higher education, Hadley's views may seem antiquated. We don't think they are. Many in the academic profession continue to hold the view that higher education's public purposes not only can but also should be and are best pursued in civically disengaged ways.

Conclusion

Our purpose in this chapter was to name and briefly sketch several normative traditions in American higher education that represent different ways of answering the question of whether academic professionals should be engaged in the public work of democracy, and if so, what public purposes they should pursue, what roles they should play, and what contributions they should seek to make. We are well aware of the fact that a great deal is missing from what we have written here. We have only provided rough sketches of the positions and traditions we named. What we have written should not be considered in any way to be definitive. There are many other ways to name and characterize how the public purposes and work question has been framed and answered in American higher education, in and through the writings and rhetoric of academic professionals and various people outside the academy (e.g., elected officials). Nevertheless, we think the positions and traditions we have named and sketched in this chapter are useful as reference points in conversations about the nature, meaning, significance, and value of higher education's public purposes and work, in and for a democratic society. In using them as reference points, we need to take two additional steps. First, we need to illuminate and question their underlying practical theories. Second, we need to place them in tension with stories of the public work and experiences of academic professionals who have been and are engaged in civic life. We will turn to the latter of these steps in parts 2 and 3 of this book. It is to the former of these steps that we now turn.

Questioning the Answers

In chapter 1, we identified four general answers to the question of whether academic professionals should be engaged in the public work of democracy, and if so, what public purposes they should pursue, what roles they should play, and what contributions they should seek to make. We related each answer to a different normative tradition (or type) in American higher education: the service intellectual, the public intellectual, the action researcher / public scholar / educational organizer, and the "antitradition" of the detached and disengaged scholar. All of the general answers and their related normative traditions are appealing in some ways, and they are all useful as reference points and theoretical tools in conversations about higher education's public purposes and work. But all of them are also problematic, and their usefulness is limited. They must therefore be questioned.

In this chapter, we briefly identify and discuss some of the appealing and problematic aspects of each of the four normative traditions, as well as some of the reasons why we think their usefulness is limited. Before we begin, we want to note that normative traditions are informed and shaped by practical theories about the way things are and the way things should be, and how academic professionals can and should (or should not) help to close the gap between them. In turn, these practical theories are informed and shaped by professional and cultural identities and norms, bets and assumptions about what works, and academic professionals' (and others') public philosophies and political theories—that is, their conceptions about the nature and meaning of democracy, politics, civic agency, citizenship, freedom, and public life.[1]

In our experience, these things are rarely illuminated and questioned in direct and sustained ways. Yet we must attend to them if we are to improve our understanding of and conversations about the nature, meaning, significance, and value of higher education's public purposes and work, in and for a democratic society. We do so in this book only in a preliminary, partial, and highly simplified way. We think the majority (and most important part) of the attending must take place in collective, face-to-face deliberation and reflection. It is both our hope and intention that this book will be useful as a resource in such efforts.

The Four Normative Traditions

In identifying and discussing the main appeal of and problems with the four normative traditions we sketched in chapter 1, we are in essence questioning the general answers that have been provided in American higher education since the late nineteenth century to the question of whether academic professionals should be engaged in the public work of democracy, and if so, in what ways and for what purposes. As we noted in the introduction, our view of the public work of democracy includes four main interrelated elements:

- the work of naming, setting, and framing a problem or a positive goal (not everything is a problem—sometimes the point of public work is to pursue a positive possibility);
- the work of identifying options for what *can* be done, and the consequences of each;
- the work of deciding what *should* be done, in light of particular interests, values, and commitments; and
- acting to implement solutions and create something of public significance, and evaluating, reflecting on, and learning from experience.

Ironically, the main appeal of each of the normative traditions with respect to the public work of democracy turns out to be the main thing that is also problematic.

The Service Intellectual Tradition

As we sketched it in chapter 1, the service intellectual tradition positions academic professionals in a responsive, nonpolitical stance of unbiased and disinterested objectivity. They are to limit their engagement in the public work of democracy to the first two of the four elements named above. They are to be responsive to requests for help and assistance with the work of naming and setting public problems and goals, and the work of identifying alternatives and consequences for what *can* be done to address or pursue them. But they are to strictly avoid—as professionals—playing any direct role in the latter two elements of democracy: the work of deciding what *should* be done, and taking action to implement solutions. Their roles in the public work of democracy are thereby limited to the provision of facts, knowledge, technical assistance, and technologies. The main public purpose they are to pursue in and through these roles is that of helping individuals and groups to understand and address a public issue or problem in ways that enable them to advance their own freely chosen ends, values, and interests. Setting aside or "bracketing" their own personal ends, values, and interests, academic professionals who work in the service intellectual tradition are supposed to serve and assist whoever asks for help, without prejudice or bias.

The practical theory of the service intellectual tradition is based on three related assumptions or bets: first, that individuals and groups need a neutral, unbiased, disinterested, and nonpolitical source of knowledge, information, and expertise in order to decide how they can and should address public problems (partly because interested parties often provide uninformed and self-serving opinions or propaganda, when what is really needed are scientifically established and verified facts); second, that it is in fact possible to produce and provide knowledge and expertise from an actually or at least relatively neutral and nonpolitical stance of disinterested objectivity; and third, that what academic professionals provide from such a stance will—if done well—be more than just trustworthy. It will also be trusted and utilized by people beyond the academy, as well as effective in helping them understand and address the problems they face.

The main appeal of the service intellectual tradition is that it offers the public a neutral, unbiased, disinterested, and nonpolitical source of scientific knowledge, information, and expertise. There is a multidimensional promise in such an offer. First, it makes sense to believe that the complex nature and dynamics of many public problems simply can't be understood without a level and quality of scientific knowledge and expertise that most people just don't have. Second, in order to further their own agendas and ends, vested interest groups routinely try to influence and control not only views and decisions about what can and should be done about a public problem, but also understandings of what the problem is (or whether there even is a problem). In this context, a neutral, unbiased, disinterested, and nonpolitical source of knowledge and expertise has a dual appeal: it appears to offer a means of settling what is true and what is not, and it also serves as a means of looking out for the broad public good or interest instead of narrow special interests. Third, by refusing direct roles in the work of deciding what *should* be done about public problems, as well as in acting to implement solutions, academic professionals in the service intellectual tradition resist the temptation to use their expertise in elitist, antidemocratic ways. They thereby protect democracy and avoid the danger of technocracy. They do so in a way that fits quite comfortably with what Michael Sandel refers to as America's prevailing public philosophy, which is grounded in a "minimalist" version of liberal political theory. Minimalist liberalism gives priority to individual rights, views people as freely choosing, unencumbered selves, and professes neutrality towards the values citizens hold and the ends they pursue.[2]

In essence, service intellectuals are supposed to resolve the dilemma of the relation of democracy and expertise by staying out of the normative decision-making and action-taking phases of democratic politics. They are supposed to separate their identities and roles as professionals from their identities and roles as citizens, never letting their "private" interests, views, and ends interfere with or "contaminate" their professional work. They can be viewed in this sense as democratic-minded civic professionals who deploy their technical expertise and judgment not only skillfully but also for public-regarding ends and in a public-regarding way. Their central public-regarding end is to equip individuals and groups with the facts, skills, and technologies they need to pursue their own freely chosen interests, values, and ends. The way service intellectuals are supposed to do this is "public regarding" in that it is responsive to requests for help and assistance without prejudice or bias, and it leaves the crucial task of determining interests and ends and deciding what should be done about social problems in the hands of individuals and groups outside the academy. For academic professionals, part of the appeal of the service intellectual tradition is that it insulates and removes them from two of the most contentious, difficult, and time-consuming elements of the public work of democracy, thereby relieving them from expectations that they should have anything beyond their knowledge and technical skills to contribute to it.

However appealing the underlying practical theory of the service intellectual tradition may be to some people, there are multiple reasons to question its main assumptions, its view of professional identity, its way of resolving the dilemma of the relation of democracy and expertise, and its political theory. Among the questions we should ask are the following: Is there really such a thing as even a *relatively* neutral, unbiased, disinterested, objective, and nonpolitical source of knowledge, information, and expertise? To what extent and in what ways do people who are engaged in the public work of democracy really need such a thing? Is it reasonable to assume that what academic professionals produce and provide from such a stance will be trustworthy, trusted, utilized, and effective? Is it possible—and does it make sense—for academic professionals to "bracket" their own views, values, interests, and ends? Can they really resolve the dilemma of the relation of democracy and expertise by removing themselves from taking part in deciding what should be done about public problems? And is that always and automatically a good thing? Does it really protect democracy against technocracy? Can academic professionals serve everyone without prejudice and bias, even if one of the interested parties provides them with funding?

There are numerous studies, books, and articles in various academic literatures—including those in the fields of science and technology studies, philosophy, political theory, education, sociology, and anthropology—that offer doubtful if not flatly negative answers to the above questions. According to these works, there is no such thing as a neutral, unbiased, disinterested, objective, and nonpolitical source of knowledge, information, and expertise. It simply isn't humanly possible. Academic work is inherently and inescapably nonneutral, biased, interested, subjective, and political, in ways that are often—but not always or automatically—bad (i.e., oppressive, destructive, deceptive). Like everyone else, academic professionals simply can't bracket or set aside their own views, values, interests, and ends. Furthermore, there are reasons and times why it would be unwise for them to attempt to do so. Finally, not only do individuals and groups outside the academy often distrust, refuse or fail to utilize, or find ineffective the information and expertise academic professionals provide; academic professionals disagree among themselves about the trustworthiness, effectiveness, and value of what they have to offer. They are supposed to "legislate" what is and is not trustworthy knowledge through processes of peer review. But this process rarely if ever produces a consensus. Rather, it often produces dueling and conflicting "facts," and dueling and conflicting theories about and interpretations of the significance of "facts."[3]

In light of all this, the service intellectual tradition looks less like a form of democratic-minded civic professionalism than like a dishonest, deceptive, incoherent, and even dangerous myth. From one critical perspective, service intellectuals are what Antonio Gramsci referred to as "traditional" intellectuals—that is, intellectuals who view themselves as standing apart from the interests of any particular class or group, whose only nonneutral interest and commitment is that of pursuing the truth on behalf of humanity as a whole. According to Gramsci and many others, such a view is nothing more than a delusion or smokescreen. It can—and many say, often does—function to hide the self-serving and elite-power-serving dimensions and consequences (both intended and unintended) of academic discourse and work, including research, teaching, and "service." For example, particularly but not only in the social sciences (see our review of C. Wright Mills's views in chapter 1), the stance service intellectuals are supposed to take and the public purposes they are supposed to pursue effectively restrict their roles and contributions to those that fit the cultural and political project of prediction and control, mainly for economic ends. While such a project has value, it can also be highly problematic. It may well be approached in ways that are intended to support democracy. But as C. Wright Mills, Jürgen Habermas, Michel Foucault, Frank Fischer, and many others have demonstrated, it can end up corrupting democracy by supplying government experts and corporate and other elites with the knowledge and tools they need to pursue an oppressive technocratic program of social engineering, and of discipline and control.[4]

In highly simplified terms, these are a few of the ways and reasons the service intellectual tradition has been—and we think should be—called into question. Ironically, the main appeal of the service intellectual tradition—its stance of unbiased, disinterested, nonpolitical neutrality—is also the main thing that is problematic about it. It is not only problematic because it is doubtful whether and to what extent such a stance is even possible, but also and more importantly because its underlying practical theory restricts academic professionals' epistemology, pedagogy, and methods, as well as their political identity, agency, and roles, in ways that are in some contexts and situations both unnecessary and undesirable. In order to see how and why this is so, we need to move on to an examination of the purposivist traditions of the public intellectual and the action researcher / public scholar / educational organizer.

The Public Intellectual Tradition

As we sketched it in chapter 1, the public intellectual tradition positions academic professionals in an independent, inherently political and nonneutral stance of biased commitment that is *interested* in the sense that it openly professes values and ideals, but "disinterested" in the sense that it declines to partake in partisan politics and pursue financial gain. Instead of being *responsive* to requests for help and assistance, public intellectuals *proactively intervene* in civic life. Unlike service intellectuals, academic professionals working in the public intellectual tradition are not supposed to try to serve everyone in equal and unbiased ways. Rather, they can serve those they want to serve in ways that reflect their own biases. Also unlike service intellectuals, public intellectuals are not supposed to avoid becoming involved in the work of deciding what *should* be done about public problems. Rather, they actively seek such involvement. But they are to do so mainly if not entirely from a distance, by speaking to and writing for general public audiences through various forms of media. Through their primary role as critics and their secondary roles as experts, civic educators, provocateurs, and even subversives, they provide the general public with criticism, knowledge, expertise, and ideas that are meant to influence how public issues and problems are discussed, framed, understood, and addressed. The three main public purposes they pursue in and through their roles and contributions are to fight tyranny and the oppressive workings of power, to help construct and defend an open, free, and rational public sphere, and to cultivate civic-minded individuals and active publics. These purposes are pursued in ways that are meant to advance particular interests, ideals, values, and ends: namely, ones that reflect public intellectuals' own biases and commitments.

The underlying practical theory of the public intellectual tradition includes several assumptions. It assumes that in the world as it is, the workings of power tend toward various forms of corruption, oppression, and tyranny. It assumes that most people lack a clear and "correct" understanding of the workings of power, the nature, causes, and meanings of social problems, and the ways in which their "private" situations are linked to larger public problems. Its view of the world as it should be is centered on the positive project of constructing an open, free, and rational public sphere, and of the cultivation of individuals and publics capable of participating in civic life in smart and effective ways. It assumes that academic professionals can and should adopt an independent stance of "detached attachment" that is interested, in a values and ideals sense, but also disinterested, in a financial and partisan politics sense. As such it is nonneutral, but in a way that is supposed to be free from the seductions of money and partisanship. It assumes that it is precisely this kind of stance that enables public intellectuals to contribute something of value to civic life. It assumes that academic professionals have not only the right (protected by academic freedom) but also the obligation in a free and democratic society to use their knowledge and expertise to fight against tyranny and the oppressive workings of power, to defend and advance interests, values, and ends they agree with and support, to cultivate civic-minded individuals and active publics, and to contribute to the construction of an open, free, and rational public sphere. It further assumes that the roles public intellectuals take up and the contributions they make can and will be useful and effective in pursuing these ends.[5]

Several of its features lend great appeal to the public intellectual tradition. There is a real and persistent threat of tyranny in all societies. The workings of power often do tend toward corruption and oppression, and must therefore be called out and held accountable. The positive projects of constructing and defending an open, free, and rational public sphere and cultivating civically active, conscious, and effective individuals and publics are both compelling and important. In relation to these things, there is a strong case to be made for the importance, value, and efficacy of a protected, autonomous source of criticism, knowledge, expertise, and ideas that works from an interested but also disinterested stance of "detached attachment." Part of the appeal of the public intellectual tradition in this regard is that its epistemology, pedagogy, and methods are much less restrictive than are those of the service intellectual tradition. The latter focuses exclusively on prediction and control via the production of technical knowledge, the facilitation of instrumental learning, and the application of technical skills. In contrast, the public intellectual tradition centers on understanding and meaning making via the production of practical knowledge about what should be done about a public issue or problem in a cultural, political, and moral sense; the facilitation of communicative learning that includes an examination of values, interests, and ideals; and the development and application of political dispositions and skills related to public deliberation and action.

In terms of political theory, the appeal of the public intellectual tradition—particularly the variety of the tradition that C. Wright Mills favored—is quite different from that of the service intellectual tradition. The appeal is that it does *not* fit comfortably with America's prevailing public philosophy of "minimalist" liberalism. It fits instead with a formative, deliberative politics in the tradition of civic republicanism, and/or an activist protest politics of social movements. With respect to politics, it is important to note that public intellectuals are not all of the same type. Some are "left wing" or "right wing" radicals, while others are more moderate liberals or conservatives. Instead of functioning as "traditional" intellectuals who claim to stand apart from any class or group, academic professionals in the public intellectual tradition are supposed to function in a Gramscian sense as "organic" intellectuals. As such, they are supposed to support and promote the interests and popular movements of a particular class or group to which, or with which, they belong or identify, mainly by offering criticism, ideas, and knowledge from their position of "detached attachment."[6]

Unlike service intellectuals, public intellectuals aren't supposed to "resolve" the dilemma of the relation of democracy and expertise by staying out of the work of deciding what should be done about public problems. They are supposed to integrate rather than radically separate their identities and roles as professionals from their identities and roles as citizens. They are to ground their work in the particular interests, views, and ends that they are personally as well as professionally committed to and biased in favor of—including their personal views of what constitutes "the public interest," and how it should be pursued and protected. They are not burdened by worries about neutrality. The whole point is to avoid neutrality by taking sides and making a stand—particularly when something of value is under attack or threatened. Of course, they are not to do so as ideological demagogues. Rather, they are to do so in ways that are both academically excellent and civically responsible. In this sense, they function as democratic-minded civic professionals who deploy their expertise in a public-regarding way and for public-regarding ends. Their main public-regarding ends are to protect against tyranny, to help construct and defend a free and open public sphere, and to cultivate civic-minded individuals and active publics. The public-regarding way public intellectuals pursue these ends does not involve a resolution of or escape from the dilemma of the relation of democracy and expertise, as it (allegedly) does for service intellectuals. Rather, it involves and requires a negotiation of the dilemma and its various tensions and trade-offs.

We should note one way in which public intellectuals do resolve or escape the dilemma of the relation of democracy and expertise. They are supposed to absolve themselves of taking part in the fourth element of the public work of democracy: the face to face, on-the-ground work of acting to implement solutions or create something of value. It is of course true that speaking, writing, and publishing do constitute important civic or political actions. But as C. Wright Mills argued in *The Sociological Imagination*, academic professionals "abdicate" their proper political roles when they choose as a normal part of their work to "hit the pavement" and become directly involved in action to address public problems. This is one of the meanings of "detached attachment." Public intellectuals are *attached* in their engagement in the work of public discussion and deliberation (through their writings and speeches), but *detached* in their passive, onlooker stance with respect to action (beyond speaking, writing, and publishing) to address public issues and problems.[7]

However appealing the public intellectual tradition may be to many, its underlying practical theory, its view of professional identity, its way of resolving the dilemma of the relation of democracy and expertise, and its political theory are in many ways questionable. For starters, we might ask the following: In actual practice, how useful and effective are the roles and contributions public intellectuals take up and make in the public work of democracy? Are there any downsides to the integration of their professional and civic identities and roles, particularly with respect to the trustworthiness of their knowledge claims? How do scholars working in the public intellectual tradition deal with the complex issue of "objectivity" or "trustworthiness" in their research? How do they avoid the temptation to produce knowledge and theory that fits and advances their political views and interests, while ignoring evidence they don't agree with or like? Exactly how should public intellectuals negotiate the dilemma of the relation of democracy and expertise? As experts and critics, how do they avoid succumbing to technocratic, elitist, and authoritarian temptations and tendencies? And how—if at all—do they manage to maintain a stance of "detached attachment" that is both interested, in a values and ideals sense, but disinterested, in a financial gain and partisan politics sense?[8]

As with the service intellectual tradition, the main appeal of the public intellectual tradition—social criticism delivered from an independent stance of "detached attachment"—is also the main thing that is problematic about it. While independent social criticism is of great value in a democratic society, it can be condescending and elitist—ironically so, when it is done, as it often is, on behalf of the oppressed and marginalized. It tends to privilege a political theory of protest and mobilization politics at mass national and international levels over a more localized democratic populist politics of public work. And it limits the work of academic professionals to research, writing, and speaking *about* public issues and problems *to* the general public, thereby missing or rejecting reciprocal relations of inquiry, learning, and work *in public and with publics*. It is in relation to these limitations and problems that the second purposivist tradition of the action researcher / public scholar / educational organizer (AR/PS/EO) is both appealing and—in its own particular ways—problematic.

The AR/PS/EO Tradition

As we sketched it in chapter 1, the normative AR/PS/EO tradition positions academic professionals in a stance that is similar to the public intellectual tradition, but also different in a few key ways. Like the public intellectual tradition, the AR/PS/EO tradition positions academic professionals in an inherently political and nonneutral stance of biased commitment that is *interested* in the sense of advocating values and ideals sense, but "disinterested" in the sense of avoiding partisan politics and financial gain. But in the AR/PS/EO tradition, academic professionals are not only proactive, but also responsive. And they are not independent, at least not in the same way public intellectuals are supposed to be. Instead of being engaged indirectly at a distance by taking up a fiercely independent posture of "detached attachment," academic professionals in the AR/PS/EO tradition are supposed to be *directly* engaged in *interdependent* ways with their external partners.

In the democratic variety of the AR/PS/EO tradition, academic professionals are supposed to form direct, close, reciprocal, and highly collaborative public relationships with their external partners. They are allowed to engage in all four elements of the public work of democracy, including taking action. Their roles in such work include not only those of expert, critic, and civic educator, but also leader, organizer, and facilitator of face-to-face, locally contextualized inquiry, learning, problem setting, deliberation, and action. Additionally, academic professionals are supposed to take up an active role as hands-on, locally situated change agents. Their contributions to democracy include not only knowledge, criticism, ideas, and expertise, but also organized opportunities and platforms for collaborative public work. As in the public intellectual tradition, the public purposes they pursue in and through their contributions include fighting tyranny and the oppressive workings of power, helping to construct and defend an open, free, and rational public sphere, and cultivating civic-minded individuals and active publics. But unlike the public intellectual tradition, academic professionals in the AR/PS/EO tradition also pursue the public purposes of co-creating and utilizing knowledge in action and change projects that are meant to advance not only the self-interests and common interests of particular individuals and groups, but also larger public interests.

The underlying practical theory of the democratic variety of the AR/PS/EO tradition is in some ways similar to that of the public intellectual tradition. But its view of the world as it is includes not only a negative assumption about the oppressive workings of power, but also a positive assumption that there are untapped creative and constructive resources, power, and potential—intellectual, political, economic, cultural, and even spiritual—in so-called ordinary people and places. And while its view of the world as it should be is much the same as that in the public intellectual tradition, it is more sharply focused on the fulfillment of the full potential of people as leaders and producers of their communities and culture. It assumes that academic professionals can and should be fully engaged in all four elements of public work in ways that position not only themselves but also ordinary people as leaders and organizers. It assumes not only that academic professionals should have the *skills and dispositions* to function in effective and productive ways as organizers and facilitators of public inquiry, learning, and work, but also that they should, can, and will have both the *support and time* to do so.

As with the other normative traditions discussed above, aspects of the AR/PS/EO tradition are appealing. Its main appeal has to do with organizing: specifically, the promise and value of a variety of organizing that is relational, educational, developmental, democratic, and productive. This kind of organizing is not only about achieving instrumental or material ends. It is also aimed at facilitating inquiry, learning, and growth; at developing people's knowledge, relational power, leadership potential, civic skills, spirit, and capacities; at advancing common and public interests; and at creating things that are of cultural as well as economic value for specific people and places as well as the larger public. Historically, as we discussed in chapter 1, the idea of academic professionals as interdependent organizers and change agents in local, face-to-face public work initiatives was particularly appealing to some (but not all) of the pioneers of the Cooperative Extension work of the nation's land-grant colleges and universities. Many academic professionals who participated in the early decades of this work functioned as organic intellectuals from rural communities who sought to advance the self and common interests of farmers and other rural citizens in ways that also advanced the larger public interest.

Both historically and in contemporary society, the AR/PS/EO tradition also was and is appealing for two other reasons. First, it enables academic professionals to work with a broad range of epistemologies and methods, including those that require nontrivial participation of external groups in knowledge construction and theory building in ways that value and draw upon people's experience. Second, it enables academic professionals to ground their work in a political theory that departs from minimalist liberalism and includes but also goes beyond civic republicanism and mass-protest politics to a localized, face-to-face democratic populist politics of public work. As active participants in such work, academic professionals function in ways that are both academically excellent and civically responsible. In other words, they are to function as democratic-minded civic professionals who deploy their expertise in a public-regarding way and for public-regarding ends. While their main public-regarding ends are like those of the public intellectual tradition, but with greater emphasis on the development of local leadership and public goods, their public-regarding ways are markedly different. They include the establishment of direct, interdependent public relationships with localized external groups, the organizing and development of platforms for collaborative inquiry and public work, and taking part in all four elements of democracy. Like public intellectuals, the public-regarding way academic professionals in the AR/PS/EO tradition are supposed to pursue public ends requires a negotiation rather than resolution of the dilemma of the relation of democracy and expertise and its various tensions and trade-offs.

However appealing the AR/PS/EO tradition may be, its underlying practical theory, its view of professional identity, its way of resolving the dilemma of the relation of democracy and expertise, and its political theory are in many ways questionable or problematic. Among the questions we should ask are the following: How useful and effective are the roles and contributions academic professionals in the AR/PS/EO tradition take up and make in the public work of democracy? Aren't there serious limits to a localized, democratic populist politics, particularly in a highly mobile and globalized world? Exactly how do and should academic professionals in the AR/PS/EO tradition negotiate the dilemma of the relation of democracy and expertise? As experts, critics, leaders, and organizers, how do they avoid succumbing to technocratic, elitist, and authoritarian temptations and tendencies? Does the loss of independence that comes with taking an interdependent stance have any negative consequences or implications with respect to the trustworthiness of their work, particularly their research? Do or can academic professionals actually have not only the skills and dispositions but also the time and institutional support they need to function in effective and productive ways as organizers and facilitators of public inquiry, learning, and work? Doesn't this require a level of time commitment and types of skills and dispositions that are not normally part of the training and culture of the academic profession and academic institutions?

As with the other two normative traditions, the main appeal of the AR/PS/EO tradition—namely, the promise and value of organizing—is also the main problem with it. Organizing is incredibly difficult and time consuming. And while a variety of organizing in the tradition of democratic populist politics is historically rooted in the extension work of the land-grant system, it has always been and still is in tension with a technocratic variety of the tradition that has managed to gain the upper hand. Most importantly, perhaps, a democratic and developmental variety of organizing is deeply counter to the academic culture. It is not only up against a technocratic model of organizing, but also an old but still powerful model of the academic profession and academic institutions that is represented in the "antitradition" of the detached and disengaged scholar.

The Antitradition

We will be much more concise in questioning the normative antitradition of the detached and disengaged scholar. In short, this tradition assumes that academic professionals should not be directly engaged *as professionals* in any of the four elements of the public work of democracy. As Stanley Fish argues in *Save the World on Your Own Time*, academic professionals "are in the education business, not the democracy business. Democracy, we must remember, is a political not an educational project." By making a distinction between education and politics, and by building a wall between them that is not to be crossed, the antitradition positions academic professionals in a stance that is similar to but also distinctly different from that of service intellectuals. Both are to take the posture of Gramsci's traditional independent and classless intellectual. But in the extreme variety of the antitradition, not even responsive service is allowed. The only legitimate work in the extreme variety of the antitradition is research that is not directly motivated by or closely linked to the current affairs of civic life, and teaching that is to be conducted on-campus in laboratories and classrooms. The former is to be focused on expanding the frontiers of knowledge, and the latter on training the next generation of scholars. In less extreme versions of the antitradition, an allowance is made for undergraduate liberal education and graduate education for other professions beyond that of the scholar.[9]

The central appeal of the antitradition is that it (allegedly) protects the academy as a source of objective, trustworthy, autonomous, and disinterested knowledge. It also has the benefit of excusing scholars from having to be engaged in the present, thereby enabling them to focus on the past or the future—the two realms Walter Lippmann declared were the only legitimate ones for scholars to attend to. By being granted the privilege of being "irresponsible,' as Abraham Flexner put it, for the off-campus public work of democracy, and by maintaining what Lippmann referred to as a "quiet indifference to the immediate," academic professionals in the antitradition pursue a particular conception of higher education's public purposes that does have value and is appealing in some ways. Freed from the responsibility to be engaged in messy, difficult, and time-consuming public work—work that academic professionals are not trained for and are understood to have little to offer to—academic professionals have the time and energy to pursue research and other forms of creative scholarship at levels that those who are engaged in civic life cannot. While such work may have no immediate payoff or usefulness, it does have public value in the long term for humanity as a whole simply by passing on existing knowledge, and by contributing new knowledge. In this sense, academic professionals in the antitradition can be seen as civic professionals who deploy their expertise in a public-regarding way and for public-regarding ends. They do so by focusing only on what they can do best: namely, advancing the frontiers of knowledge and training the next generation of scholars (and also, perhaps, providing undergraduate liberal education and graduate training in other professions). They thereby avoid the dilemma of the relation of democracy and expertise altogether by staying out of democracy.[10]

Despite its appeal to some, the antitradition is also highly problematic. It reflects and privileges the elite research university model of higher education and marginalizes or dismisses altogether other institutional types and cultures. By placing scholars outside of civic life, it cuts off epistemological and methodological avenues that can be highly productive in both an intellectual and civic sense. Most importantly, *when it is seen as the only legitimate tradition*, as people like Stanley Fish apparently see it, it radically and unnecessarily constrains the civic roles of the academic profession, and robs society of the positive benefits of other traditions.

The Limitations

The four normative traditions we have briefly sketched and discussed have considerable value as reference points and theoretical tools in conversations about the nature, meaning, significance, and value of higher education's public purposes and work, in and for a democratic society. We have only scratched the surface of these traditions. Others could say—and have already said—a great deal more than we have about their complex, fine-grained details, nuances, and variations in their theoretical and idealized form. Many articles and books could usefully be written about their historical origins and evolution as normative ideals, and their philosophical, epistemological, methodological, pedagogical, political, and cultural dimensions.

However valuable deeper and more sophisticated studies of and conversations about the theoretical dimensions of these normative traditions may be, their limitations with respect to the task of improving our understanding of higher education's public purposes and work will remain. There are three main reasons why their usefulness is limited.

First, while they may reliably capture academic professionals' general opinions, by themselves these traditions cannot reliably tell us anything about academic professionals' inherently situational work and experience. Normative traditions in their idealized form are in essence representations of normative types. In this sense, they can rightfully be viewed (and critiqued) as being little more than "straw men." Like straw men, while normative types can be found in academic (and other) literatures and rhetoric, they don't exist in pure form in practice, and they don't allow for or help us to understand the ambiguities, contingencies, and contradictions of "real" life.

Second, an *exclusive* focus on normative traditions in conversations about higher education's public purposes and work opens participants to two risks: the risk of becoming stuck or paralyzed in unending, hair-splitting theoretical distinctions, and the risk of becoming polarized in ideological battles over which tradition is "correct." Both are unproductive.

Third, conversations that focus *only* on normative traditions offer academic professionals and their external partners little opportunity to engage in critical reflection about their own work and experience. A key source of learning and knowledge about the meaning and value of higher education's public purposes and work is therefore missed.

There are several ways these and other limitations might be addressed. For example, we could conduct ethnographic studies of academic professionals' civic engagement work, and incorporate what we learn into our conversations about the public purposes and work question. We could develop case studies. Or we could invite academic professionals to tell detailed, first-person stories about their civic engagement experiences. These could be recorded, transcribed, and edited into *practitioner profiles*, and then interpreted for their implications. While each of these approaches has value, we have chosen to do the latter in this book. We turn now to a brief discussion of what practitioner profiles are, how we construct them, and how we understand their usefulness and limits.

Developing and Using Practitioner Profiles

The four normative traditions we sketched and questioned in the previous two chapters represent general answers that have been provided in American higher education since the late nineteenth century to the question of whether academic professionals should be engaged in the public work of democracy, and if so, in what ways and for what purposes. Questioning these answers is one important step we must take in the task of improving our conversations about the nature and value of higher education's public work, in and for a democratic society. But if we are to avoid becoming stuck in theoretical debates over what should or could be, we need to take an additional step. We need to listen to and interpret firsthand stories of the experiences of academic professionals who have been engaged as active participants in civic life. In this chapter, we discuss how practitioner profiles can be used for this purpose. We note not only their appeal and usefulness, but also their limitations. We then explain why and how we created the profiles that are included in this book, and offer readers suggestions for how to use them.

Constructing Practitioner Profiles

Practitioner profiles are a particular kind of text produced from a particular kind of interview, one that is markedly different from the kind that some scholars in the social sciences tend to favor. Social scientists typically conduct individual or group interviews that survey people's views and opinions about a particular topic or problem. The results of such interviews are typically aggregated and reported in the form of statistics that are analyzed in order to identify patterns and relationships in and between thematic "codes" and demographic variables such as gender, race, and age.[1]

In contrast, practitioner profiles are constructed from the edited transcripts of *narrative interviews*. Narrative interviews are not focused on eliciting people's views and opinions, although they may include such elements. Instead, they are focused on drawing out *stories* of practitioners' experiences. Stories are not simply chronicles or reports of events. Stories have plots. They have a beginning, middle, and end, or some kind of resolution. They have characters who have interests and goals, face challenges or problems, and act and respond and feel in particular ways. They are contextually specific. Things *happen* in stories that are surprising, tragic, funny, troubling, inspiring. Stories *matter*. They have—or more accurately, are interpreted as having—importance and meaning.

In narrative interviews of practitioners from a particular profession, or of a particular activity, interviewers draw out first-person stories of practitioners' work and experience. Practitioner profiles are edited transcripts of this kind of narrative interview, with the interviewer's voice edited out. They are not "written" texts. Nor are they, in an academic sense, "papers" or "case studies." Rather, they are *spoken* texts. They are oral histories of practitioners' experiences that are deeply personal and inherently subjective and partial. The centerpiece of a practitioner profile is a first-person "practice story." In practice stories, practitioners speak of what they did and learned in particular moments of their work and lives.

In highly simplified terms, our approach to constructing and using practitioner profiles includes the following five steps.[2]

We begin by assessing our interests and purposes. We ask ourselves what the main issues, problems, puzzles, and questions are that we're interested in exploring through storied accounts of practitioners' experiences. (For example: How do academic professionals negotiate the dilemma of the relation of expertise and democracy?) We also ask ourselves how we intend to use the profiles we construct, and what we hope they will help us accomplish.

Guided by the interests and purposes identified in the first step, we next find and approach potential interviewees. While we may use several different criteria to select our interviewees, depending on our interests and purposes, the main thing we look for are practitioners who have first-person stories to tell about their work and experiences that show promise of being instructive in helping us learn about the issues, problems, puzzles, or questions we identified in step 1. The selection process involves not only identifying potential interviewees, but also doing "preinterviews" with them. During our preinterviews, we explain our project to our potential interviewees, and give them a chance to ask questions. We determine if they are interested in being interviewed. If so, we identify specific practice stories to place at the center of their interviews. We secure their written approval to be interviewed by having them sign a permission form that follows academic "human subjects" protocols. Finally, we arrange the times and places to conduct the interviews.

The third step in the process is to conduct and record the interviews. The length of each interview is variable. For us, they can last anywhere from 45 to 120 minutes. Instead of using an "instrument" with a list of predetermined questions, we generally conduct our interviews as structured conversations that have three distinct sections. In the first section, we ask practitioners' to tell us about their personal and professional interests and backgrounds, including where they grew up and what it was like, how they came to hold the job they have, and how they became interested in the work they do. In the second section, we draw out the details of a specific practice story. In the third section, we invite practitioners to reflect on the meaning of their practice story and to draw lessons from it. To elicit stories rather than reports, chronicles, or explanations, we generally avoid asking too many "what" and "why" questions. Instead, we mainly ask "how" questions. For example, we ask how (rather than why) they came to be engaged as academic professionals in civic life, and how they came to be involved in the public work projects that their practice stories are about. We ask them what kinds of challenges they encountered and how they dealt with them. We ask them who the main actors were in their projects, what they did, and how they interacted with and responded to them. We ask them to identify the key moments and turning points in their projects. We ask them how their projects evolved and turned out in the end. We ask them how they assess the meaning and significance of their experience in their practice stories, and of their own work, roles, and contributions as participants in them. Usually near the very end of our interviews, we ask practitioners to give us their views on a few specific issues, and how the experiences they described in their practice stories have influenced their views.

The fourth step in the process is to transcribe and edit the recorded interviews. We begin by transcribing the exact words that were spoken, adding only basic punctuation (e.g., periods, commas, colons, semi-colons, exclamation points, question marks, dashes, and perhaps italics or bold or all capital letters to signal changes in tone of voice). We save a copy of this first draft as the original unedited text. We then make a duplicate copy and begin a fairly long and difficult process of editing. During this step of the process, we remove all of our words from the transcript, correct grammar, and shape what is left into paragraphs that make sense and flow well from beginning to end. The editing process usually involves removing some parts of the text, and moving other parts around. It involves listening to the recording of the interview several times in order to catch changes in tone of voice, laughter, pauses, and other verbal cues that we may want to capture in the profile. It also involves checking back with our interviewees. We ask our interviewees to fix mistakes and fill in missing details, and we give them an opportunity to rephrase or remove passages or words they are not comfortable with. We also secure their approval of the final edited drafts, and their permission to use them.

The last step in the process is to work with the completed profiles as "data" for studies, articles, and books, or as resources in classes we teach and collective reflection sessions we facilitate with practitioners.

The Usefulness and Limits of Practitioner Profiles

The goal of mainstream social science as it is commonly pursued is to document "facts" and a certain kind of "truth" (i.e., "objective" truth) in order to build theory about the social world and people's behaviors in it. It involves the establishment of statistically significant relationships between variables through the use of rigorous scientific and scholarly methods of data collection and analysis. The results of this kind of work are supposed to inform attempts by administrators, policymakers, or others to predict, control, or intervene in the world for some specific end. While this kind of social science has value, it is not the kind we practice.

The use of practitioner profiles does not fit the "mainstream" model of social science. Rather, it is part of what is referred to as "narrative inquiry." As one variety of "interpretivist" research, narrative inquiry reflects the so-called narrative turn in the social sciences. This "turn" has involved the development of a robust set of methods and tools—including practitioner profiles—that scholars use to draw out, document, or construct stories, and to illuminate, analyze, and interpret their meaning. The variety of narrative inquiry that includes narrative interviews enables scholars to document and interpret a kind of truth different from that of mainstream social science: namely, the subjective truths of people's life and work experiences.[3]

As we have stated several times, our project in this book is to improve our understanding of and conversations about the nature, meaning, significance, and value of higher education's public purposes and work, in and for a democratic society. Conversations about this issue are occurring in several settings: in academic and other literatures, in academic fields and disciplines, at conferences and meetings, in the classrooms, conference rooms, and offices of particular institutions, and in deliberations about public policies at local, state, and national levels. As resources, data, tools, and reference points in these conversations, practitioner profiles are both appealing and useful in five main ways.

First, practitioner profiles provide us with windows onto the situational and contextual work and experiences of academic professionals who are engaged civic life. These windows can help us avoid becoming stuck in abstract theoretical debates over what should or could be. By shifting our attention from the abstract, theoretical, and general to the concrete and specific, these profiles can help us reassess our presumptions and assumptions about the nature and value of academic professionals' engagement in the public work of democracy. In doing so, they can provoke us to rethink the trustworthiness of normative positions and traditions.

Second, practitioner profiles can open up our imagination to unforeseen possibilities. They can give us insights into how academic professionals and their civic partners might be more successful in navigating key dilemmas, challenges, and obstacles, such as the dilemma of the relation of expertise and democracy. They can also expand our sense of what academic professionals and their external partners might accomplish together through their engagement in the public work of democracy.

Third, practitioner profiles don't just offer windows onto successful work and positive experiences. They often include stories of failure and disappointment. This means that they can offer us a means of learning from others' mistakes. They can help raise our awareness of false roads, of what doesn't work, as well as what does.

Fourth, profiles can offer two kinds of opportunities for practitioners. They can offer an opportunity to engage in critical reflection about their work and experiences, both in the interview experience, and by discussing their profiles with others. They can also offer an opportunity to teach, gain visibility, and exert agency by taking part in a particular kind of social action: that of making practitioners' stories public. Here we need to understand that profiles are not only appealing and useful because of *what* practitioners tell us—namely, their stories. They are also appealing and useful because of *how* practitioners tell, and make meaning of, their stories. Profiles don't just illuminate practice and experience. They also reveal what Susan Chase calls the "narrative strategies" people use to position themselves and others in their stories, and to make sense of their work and life experiences. We can learn as much from how people tell and make sense of their stories as we can from what their stories contain.[4]

Finally, as we have already hinted, but now want to state more directly, practitioner profiles that are constructed from narrative interviews are useful because they can help us to discover or make meaning. As the environmental historian William Cronon has argued, narrative is "our best and most compelling tool for searching out meaning in a conflicted and contradictory world." The meaning we discover or make from the narratives that are contained in practitioner profiles flows from a particular kind of truth: the subjective truths of people's life and work experiences.[5]

Of course, practitioner profiles aren't just appealing and useful. They also have four main problems and limitations.

First, we don't and can't learn what practitioners "actually" did or do by constructing and reading practitioner profiles. Nor can we learn what the "actual" results and outcomes of their work were. This doesn't mean that we should expect that people simply make their stories up. Rather, it means that we can't, using practitioner profiles, make firm and settled knowledge claims about what "really" happened, no matter what we do to ensure that practitioners are honest when they tell their stories. In short, we don't get "the Truth" from profiles. Rather, we get small-t truths of practitioners' lives and experiences.

Second, we don't and can't learn "how to do it" by reading practitioner profiles. Profiles do not provide us with recipes, blueprints, or bullet-pointed lists. That's not their nature, or their purpose. They provide us with stories that can help us discover and make meaning, not instructions for how to conduct specific kinds of work.

Third, there are many difficulties in interpreting the significance of practitioner profiles. The meanings of profiles are not self-evident. Meaning and significance must be *interpreted*. Interpretation is a subjective rather than objective activity. There can never be just one "correct" interpretation of the meaning and significance of a practice story, or a practitioner profile. Meanings can be contested, and stories can be "restoried," both by situating them in the context of larger stories, and by telling them from a different perspective. A fundamental task in narrative inquiry is to see the world as being storied, in multiple, overlapping, and often contradictory ways. Because the act of storying or restorying the world is a form of social action that is inherently political in nature, it must be viewed critically. Thus, we not only need to critically examine and interpret stories, but also the way stories are told. (It's worth noting here that this third problem or limitation can also be viewed as a strength. Profiles and practice stories can be appealing and useful precisely because different people can discover and make different meanings of them.)

Finally, the construction and use of practitioner profiles takes a lot of time and effort. It not only takes time (and skill) to conduct narrative interviews, and to transcribe and edit them into profiles. It also takes time to read, discuss, and interpret them. Not everyone is willing to spend the time and effort it takes to construct, read, or work with profiles. Busy institutional settings—including research universities—tend to offer little space and time for collective, reflective storytelling; they also tend to discourage it as a waste of time.

The Practitioner Profiles in This Book

Part 2 of this book consists of a dozen practitioner profiles we constructed as part of a research project we began to conceptualize and pursue in 2001. In the remainder of this chapter, we explain why and how we created these profiles. We also offer readers suggestions for how to read and use them.

All of the practitioner profiles that are included in this book are of academic professionals who are or were situated in New York State. With just under 20 million residents, New York is the nation's third most populous state. More than 90 percent of its population lives in urban areas, well over half of which is in the downstate, New York City metropolitan area. The rest of the urban population resides in upstate metropolitan areas, including Buffalo / Niagara Falls, Rochester, Albany and the Capital District, Poughkeepsie and the Hudson Valley, Syracuse, Utica/Rome, and Binghamton. Upstate New York also includes Adirondack Park. At 6.1 million acres, it is the nation's largest National Historic Landmark, and the largest single area protected by any state. About a quarter of the New York's land area is farmland. There are just under 35,000 farms. While top farm commodities include dairy products and apples, New York's farmers and horticulturalists produce many other commodities for local, national, and international markets.

There are more than 150 colleges and universities in New York State. Cornell University, the home institution of the academic professionals who are profiled in this book, is the state's only land-grant institution. Founded as a public-private hybrid in 1865, Cornell is also a member of the Ivy League. With a budget of almost $2.5 billion (in 2007–8), it is one of the world's top research universities. Its main campus is located in the small town of Ithaca, which is in the Finger Lakes region of upstate New York. It also has a medical college with campuses in New York City and Doha, Qatar. Cornell employs almost 3,000 faculty and just over 12,000 staff. It has more than 13,000 undergraduate and 6,000 graduate students.[6]

All of the academic professionals we profiled for this book have (or did have) academic appointments in Cornell's College of Agriculture and Life Sciences (CALS). CALS is composed of twenty-six academic departments that include disciplines and fields in the natural, biological, and social sciences, architecture and design, and engineering. With an annual budget of $257 million (in 2005–6), it has more than 350 faculty members and more than 3,000 undergraduate and 1,000 graduate students. Cornell Cooperative Extension (CCE) is CALS' official "outreach" system. CCE has an annual budget of more than $125 million, two-thirds of which comes from county, state, and federal government appropriations. It employs over 500 extension educators in fifty-seven county-based associations, plus New York City. CCE offers educational programs in five broad areas: Agriculture and Food Systems; Children, Youth, and Families; Community and Economic Vitality; Environment and Natural Resources; and Nutrition and Health.[7]

The technical and social problems New Yorkers are trying to understand and address in and through the public work of democracy include nearly everything imaginable. Like their colleagues from other colleges and universities in New York State, Cornell's academic professionals—including those who are employed in its College of Agriculture and Life Sciences—face the question of whether they should be engaged in off-campus civic life in efforts to deal with such problems, and if so, what public purposes they should pursue, what roles they should play, and what contributions they should seek to make. While those who have chosen to become engaged as academic professionals in civic life have stories to tell of their work and experiences, they are rarely if ever asked to tell them in detail, especially in ways that closely attend to the public purposes and work question.

We can trace our decision to interview faculty members in Cornell's College of Agriculture and Life Sciences about their civic engagement work and experiences back to an offhand remark by Cornell University's former president, Hunter Rawlings III. In his 2001 "State of the University" speech, President Rawlings referred to Cornell as "a great private university with a public mission." While there was nothing particularly remarkable about the president's claim that Cornell has a public mission—who would say that their college or university doesn't?—it set us to thinking in a way we hadn't before. It's one thing to say that Cornell *has* a public mission, we thought. But it's quite another thing to say *what that mission is*. President Rawlings didn't say what it is in his speech. Not saying what it is, in our minds, implied not only that we're all supposed to know what it is, but also that we would all agree on what it is. But the more we thought about it, the more we doubted that we—or anyone else—could articulate just what that mission is in a way that is both clear and uncontestable.[8]

Instead of taking President Rawlings's offhand remark for granted, we decided to take it seriously. We wanted to know how we were supposed to understand the *meaning* of the claim that Cornell has a public mission. We were not interested in determining or debating what Cornell's public mission is in general, abstract terms. Rather, we were interested in figuring out how, when, where, by whom, and for what purposes it is pursued. More specifically, we were interested in how we might learn about its nature, meaning, significance, and value as it is pursued by Cornell's faculty and staff in their off-campus engagement in civic life. Instead of viewing Cornell's public mission as a "fact" to be documented and explained, we saw it as a question to be understood, examined, and interpreted, in and through stories of practice and experience.

Taking up this question across the whole of the university would have been quite literally an impossible task, given the size and diversity of the institution. Instead, we chose to take it up in just one of Cornell's colleges, the College of Agriculture and Life Sciences (CALS). We chose this college because we knew that it included many faculty members who are engaged in off-campus civic life across New York State. We also chose it because it was about to mark a key historical moment: the centennial of its official establishment in 1904 by the state legislature as the "New York State College of Agriculture." The nature of this historical moment raised both the interest in and the stakes for illuminating and examining the college's public mission, purposes, and work. We conducted several exploratory interviews of CALS faculty members in 2001 and 2002 (profiles from a few of these interviews appear in this book). Based on what we learned from these initial interviews, we wrote a proposal for a research project, and submitted it to the Kettering Foundation. Our plan was to identify and interview a diverse set of practitioners of civic engagement in the college, and to edit the interviews into practitioner profiles. We would also convene a focus group of interested faculty members from the college and facilitate a process of collective reflection with them about CALS' public mission. The Kettering Foundation supported our proposal, and we began to implement it in the fall of 2003.[9]

In selecting faculty members from CALS to interview, we looked for people who are directly engaged off campus in addressing public issues with nonacademic audiences in ways that both their peers and college administrators viewed as being extensive and exemplary. We also sought a measure of diversity in terms of academic discipline and field, type of academic appointment, gender, and stage of career. Through discussions with administrators, department chairs, and others, we identified 149 potential interviewees. Using the above two criteria, we narrowed the list down to fifty-six. We ended up interviewing forty-four faculty members. Thirty-five were in tenure-line positions (twenty-three full, nine associate, and three assistant professors), and nine were in non-tenure-line extension positions. Twenty-three were from natural science disciples, eighteen from social science disciplines, two from an engineering discipline, and one from the field of landscape architecture and design. Thirty-one were male and thirteen female. We followed the steps we outlined above in conducting the interviews and editing the transcripts into practitioner profiles.

During the summer and fall of 2003 we recruited a focus group that consisted of fifteen CALS faculty members, including eight from the natural sciences, six from the social sciences, and one from engineering. From December 2003 through December 2005, we conducted four interviews with this group, lasting 90 to 120 minutes each. We recorded and transcribed all of these interviews. The first two were designed to stimulate dialogue and collective reflection on the nature and meaning of CALS' public mission, purposes, and work. In these interviews, we made a concerted effort to press faculty members to illustrate their views with examples and practice stories from their own work and experience. The third and fourth focus group interviews were designed to elicit collective interpretations of excerpts from two of the practitioner profiles we constructed. We made an effort during these focus group interviews to probe for areas of agreement, disagreement, and uncertainty.

We ended up with massive amount of data, over 2,000 pages of 10-point, single-spaced type. In working through our data, we conceptualized and began working on this book. We selected a dozen profiles to be published in full in the book. The ones we chose represent some diversity in terms of academic discipline, type of position, gender, and age. But they are not meant to be representative of any of these categories. Rather, they are meant to be both instructive and provocative with respect to our central aim of improving our understanding of and conversations about the nature, meaning, significance, and value of higher education's public purposes and work, in and for a democratic society.

While there are many ways to read and use the profiles that are included in this book, we want to offer the following suggestions.

First, we urge readers to restrain from leaping immediately to the project of trying to figure out what's wrong with them. Instead, we suggest that they make a concerted effort to discover positive possibilities, meanings, and lessons in the profiles with respect to these academics' public purposes and work. The academic impulse to find fault above all else must be restrained if we are to be open to positive potential and meanings.

Second, while we urge readers to make an effort to discover the positive, we also want to warn against glossing over the troubling and the ambiguous. One of the reasons why profiles are valuable is that they have not had all the rough edges shaved off. All of the profiles in this book have passages in them that should be questioned with a critical eye. So while our readings should be appreciative in nature, they should also be critical. (Here, we want to acknowledge that we do not provide a critical reading of the profiles in this book. This reflects a deliberate strategy on our part that we will explain in chapter 16.)

Third, pay attention not only to the stories faculty members' tell in their profiles, but also how they tell them. Ask not only what we can learn from their stories, but also what we can learn from how they narrate them. How do they position themselves in their stories, and how do they position other characters or actors? How do they interpret the meaning and significance of their own work and experiences?

Fourth, we suggest that readers not gloss over the beginning parts of the profiles, where faculty members are talking about their life stories. While some of these are quite lengthy, and may seem at first to be irrelevant, in most every case they turn out to be quite useful in helping us to understand faculty members' practice stories and experiences. The personal and professional are interwoven in many interesting ways in these profiles. If we miss that, we lose something vitally important to our task of understanding their significance.

Fifth, we want to note that interpreting the meaning of the stories should not be exclusively a solitary endeavor. It should also be a collective, social endeavor. Therefore, it is our intention and hope that one or more of these profiles will be read and discussed by groups as well as by individuals, in classrooms and other settings. Group readings and reflections can be of particular value in determining how the lessons drawn from the profiles might be relevant to readers' own situations.

Sixth, we want to warn against the temptation of trying to fit the academic professionals we profiled into one or another of the normative traditions we sketched in chapter 1. We did not select these profiles because we thought they illustrate or exemplify these normative traditions. We selected them because we think they can provoke us to look beyond debates about what should or could be, in a theoretical or normative sense. People are much more interesting and complicated than normative traditions and types, as their stories almost always reveal.

Finally, while we offer our own deliberately appreciative reading of these profiles in chapter 16 of this book, we want to emphasize that what we offer is *only* our reading. By including the full text of the profiles, we leave space for others to do their own readings, make their own interpretations, and draw their own lessons.

Practitioner Profiles

Reaching Outside the Compartmentalized Structure

A Profile of Molly Jahn

Professor, Department of Plant Breeding and Genetics, Cornell University

Interviews conducted by Neil Schwartzbach, May 27 and August 16, 2004

In this profile, Molly Jahn tells us how and why, as a plant geneticist, she became engaged in civic life. As the title of the profile suggests, the goals she has decided to pursue in her academic and public work have required her to reach outside the compartmentalized organizational structure of the land-grant, research university. The stories and experiences she shares about her development and work as a publicly engaged scientist and scholar help us to see and imagine the civic possibilities of the natural and biological sciences. She turns our attention to a problem she has observed of people "muddling" the distinction between academic priorities, obligations, and measures of success and what she refers to as "societal missions and accomplishments." This distinction is of the highest importance for all those who wish to practice and support civic professionalism in the academy. In August 2006, Molly left Cornell to take up a new position as dean of the College of Agricultural and Life Sciences at the University of Wisconsin–Madison. In the fall of 2009, she took a leave from her position as dean in order to accept a new appointment in Washington, D.C., as deputy undersecretary of research, education, and economics for USDA.

I arrived at Cornell in 1983 as a graduate student, so I've been here twenty-one years. I started in a tenure-track job in January of '91 in the Department of Plant Breeding. I also have a joint appointment in the Department of Plant Biology, which came about two years ago. We have a big lab, with between twenty and thirty people that I support on soft money. We just brought in two or three million dollars worth of grants in the last couple of months.

I have a twenty-year-long project exploring both fundamental, cutting-edge research and areas that have application. I believe with the kind of conviction akin to missionary zeal that fundamental and applied science are not even close to being mutually incompatible. Properly conceived—and not everything is amenable to this—they are highly synergistic ways of

75

viewing the world. Actually, I feel like my professional history has really borne that out, because we publish in heavy-hitting journals and we release commercially successful crop varieties. Within the last year, I was invited to sit on the editorial board of *Plant Cell*, the premiere plant biology journal. But I still spend plenty of time out in the field messing around with very practical things.

I'm really serious about getting work done that fulfills Cornell's public mission. There have been certain barriers to delivering the impact of my work in the real world, and I've had to find some unconventional ways to work around them. I tend to think a little bit outside the box, and I tend to be very focused on delivering a specific impact, and then being sure that that impact is what I meant it to be. As for meeting grower, consumer, and environmental needs, I've realized that a partnership of the public, private, and nonprofit sectors is essential. I'm in close touch with the seed industry, and their job is to know what growers need. So I've made a practice of going directly to people within seed companies, within the private sector, who would tell me their opinion. I've discovered that nonprofits are very energetic if they're serving a specialized interest like organic agriculture. So between the conventional seed business, nonprofits, and a nascent seed industry for organics, I've got everything I need. And I know in New York State and around the world, we've had some positive impact.

I started out as one of those kids where school was really an outlet for me, but I also was really connected to the natural world. I spent a lot of time outside growing up, and knew a lot about what I'd now call field biology. When I was thirteen, I got extremely sick and wound up in University Hospital in Ann Arbor, Michigan, for a long time. It was a life-threatening situation. When I got out, I knew that what I wanted to study was biology. That obviously might have led to a career in medicine. But after thinking about things really quite seriously for a thirteen- to fourteen-year-old, I decided that I wanted to move in a direction that would make a difference in the interactions of humans with their environment, and environmental quality. This was the mid to late '70s, and the environment was a big deal. I came from the Great Lakes area, and saw both their beauty and the danger they were in.

I was a pretty serious student in high school. I applied to college and wound up at as the Midwest Scholar at Swarthmore College. I placed out of Intro Bio, took a genetics class as a freshman, and promptly flunked my first genetics test (I always tell my genetics students this). My professor called everybody in who had gotten a C, D, or F, which was most of the class. When I showed up, he said, "Did you study?" And I said, "I studied so hard, I studied so hard! I *studied, studied, studied!*" And he said, "Well, there are two possibilities. Either you're not very bright, or you don't know how to study. Let's hope it's the latter." He said I could come in and see him once a week, with a list of questions. And I did, very faithfully. Pretty soon he offered me a job doing lab preparation.

At the end of my four years, he said, "I've done you a lot of favors, now you do me one. I want you to apply for a National Science Foundation (NSF) fellowship, and I don't care where, but you've got to apply to graduate school." Well, I didn't really want to go to graduate school. I had no real idea about graduate school. I'd worked at the Natural History Museum in Philadelphia during summers, and also at Woods Hole, but always as a technician, not aiming to be any kind of academic star.

There was a part of me that was really attracted to hardcore research. I loved genetics, and I loved molecular biology. But my real focus was the environment. I suppose now you'd call it sustainability. So I decided that I would write my essay for NSF on an organism that was ecologically important, both in terms of straight ecology, but also in terms of environmental quality. I picked blue-green algae: Cyanobacteria. Nobody had done very much genetics on it, although genetics of microorganisms was possible. It's got some really amazing metabolisms, in that it fixes atmospheric nitrogen. But it's also photosynthetic. And it has had some remarkable adaptations, having two mutually incompatible pathways: one involves oxygen, and one needs to be protected from oxygen. And so I thought, "Well, that's an awful lot going on in a little thing." It also has a lot of implications, both positive and negative, for the environment and for humans.

I looked around, being very naive, and picked a graduate program based at MIT that had a biological oceanography component. I applied and was accepted to the Department of Biology at MIT, and got my NSF fellowship. I was really young, and I had these very particular ideas, which in fact are the same ideas that are very evident in the research I do today. The Department of Biology at MIT at that time was the number one ranked graduate department in the country, or at least that's what we were told. And they tended to select very intense, young, highly ambitious people. I had some of those qualities, but sorely lacked in others.

The traditional academic trajectory was just not, in and of itself, attractive to me at all. It became less so once I saw the world at MIT and what was identified as our targets. In fact, on a personal level, I found some of the human values exemplified in that community at least not attractive, and in some cases, even really objectionable. Nevertheless, the intellectual values—the way science was done there—was really thrilling. I mean, *really* thrilling. I found a couple of people there who really understood what it was I was trying to do, and they were very encouraging. But if I was going to hold my vision for the integration of great science and its application outside the biomedical field, there really wasn't a way to fit my own funny ideas into that graduate program. Of course, it was preposterous to even have those ideas at that stage of my career. This level of training is so much along the lines of medieval apprenticeship.

In the spring of that year, a close of friend of mine from undergraduate school, a brilliant, very motivated, and talented guy who was here at Cornell committed suicide in his third year of graduate school. When he disappeared from Ithaca—I was in Cambridge at the time—we got a call right away, and we thought, "Well, he'll be showing up shortly." We don't quite know exactly what happened, but apparently he turned up in a parking lot close by the university with cyanide.

At that point I thought, "You know, I really don't know what I'm doing in graduate school. I'm not very happy on a personal level. I don't think this is worth dying for. This just isn't that important. I have this vision, and the more I hang around here . . ." I did find one lab in civil engineering that was interested in issues related to water quality and biology, but molecular stuff wasn't addressed there. So I thought, "I'm going to take some time off and think about what the right thing to do is." I could do that because I was on an NSF fellowship.

I went home to my parents' house, and I picked up this book about my great-grandfather's generation. My great-grandfather had four brothers, each of whom became a bit legendary.

They were Canadians, and they all had a very joyful spirit of inquiry. Most of them became scientists. I have a picture of one of them right over there. The oldest became one of the leading naturalists of Canada, and a prominent spokesman for conservation and ornithology. The next one became a musician.

Here's where the plant breeding comes in. He and his father—my great-great-grandfather—bred a hard red winter wheat for the short seasons of the western plains, opening up the western plains in Canada for settlement. In fact, my great-great-grandfather, when he got the idea that practical science could make the world a better place, visited the New York State Agricultural Experiment Station in Geneva in the early 1880s. He then went home and founded the central experimental farm in Ottawa. I have a Canadian postage stamp here with his picture on it, and another Canadian postage stamp with a rose named after my great-great-grandmother, the "Agnes."

My great-grandfather was the youngest of the five, and in a sense, he was the black sheep, because he didn't do plant breeding. He was very involved in natural history and ornithology and music. He was a physicist at Harvard, and he was very instrumental in founding the study of acoustics. He was also a stringed instrument musician. He was used to blending personal interests and pleasures with academic pursuits. Then another one of the brothers was a peony breeder. I still have remnants of his collection at my house. He wound up being a chemistry professor at Hamilton College. But what he's extremely famous for are his peonies. As a hobby, he had revolutionized peony breeding. These guys had a lot of music in their lives, and this intense involvement in natural history, especially ornithology and entomology. They had this bent towards academia combined with this kind of unbridled, joyful way of moving out into whatever it was they did.

So I read this book about my great-grandfather's generation, and I thought, "Plant breeding, plant breeding . . . There must be plant breeders!" And I thought, "Maybe that's what I want to do." At MIT, we had no books on this. So I went down the road to Harvard. By this time, I knew I also really loved botany. So I would go look at the glass flower exhibits on my lunch hours, which were these amazing botanical models made of glass—absolutely staggering artwork. And I'd go to the Harvard library and try to find books on the subject.

Meanwhile, that spring I decided to take at least a hiatus from grad school. My professors told me I was ruining my life. They said that nothing good would ever happen to me, that I had destroyed my career. And I thought, "You know what? I'm twenty years old. What career? I'm a great technician. No one can take that away from me. What are you talking about?" Of course, their feeling was that MIT is the pinnacle, the ultimate pinnacle, so leaving there would be by definition some kind of failure. I suppose I thought that too, but that didn't matter so much to me, that kind of failure. So I told them, "I'm twenty years old. I just lost this person that was important to me, who was a very serious scientist. I'm not sure I'm on the right track here." And they said, "What do you mean? You're doing fine."

A couple professors understood what I was saying, so as soon as I made it clear I was quitting, I was hired to run a lab that did all the electron microscope work for an institute that was staffed by about half Nobel laureates or Nobel laureates-to-be. I wasn't remotely qualified for the job, but there I was, twenty-one years old, I had my own lab, two beautiful microscopes, two darkrooms, my own office, and a wet lab. I was the lab head, and I was working with these incredible scientists, these Nobel laureates, including Salvadore Luria, and my immediate boss, Phil Sharp. Phil Sharp used viruses to tell about the hosts they lived in—a very accessible thing on a molecular level, a very simple thing genetically, but it lives in this cell we would like to know more about. And I liked that approach.

I worked at MIT for two years without losing my NSF funding. I had a really wonderful experience. I discovered that I liked running the lab but that I was going to need to do something else. I did all these fun things like winter botany classes and this and that, and I thought, "You know, there's more to what I want to do with my life than this. This is probably as good as it gets in this category of job, and I need to do something more." So I thought about plants and everything else, and thought, "What am I going to do?" And I decided that I wanted to work on disease resistance, because that would address issues of pesticides and human health as well as environmental safety. So I looked around for departments of plant breeding, and there's exactly one in the U.S., and this one here at Cornell is it. So I applied. I think they had no idea what to do with my application. But I had my own funding, so I came.

This was back in 1983. Plant breeders didn't really have labs as a standard thing then. I was stupefied at the challenge I faced learning the genetics vocabulary plant breeders use. I really couldn't understand what people were saying here for several months. Fortunately, one of my fellow students translated for me for several weeks until I began to understand the language. The cultures were profoundly different. But despite the fact that I was a woman in science, which had been a huge issue at MIT, I was welcomed by these very traditional people, absolutely without a backward glance.

One guy in particular, Henry Munger, who just turned eighty-eight this spring, let me follow him around holding his note cards and writing down what he said for weeks that fall. He'd look at plants and say, "Clearly this is going on." And I'd look, and the plants all looked the same, or they all looked different. I couldn't see anything clearly at all. But I followed him around. And at one point he said, "Would you like to try to make some evaluations over here without me?" Oh, my goodness, it took me a full Saturday. But I was outside, and I was working on crop plants, and I felt like I'd arrived.

In this department, "application" was not a dirty word. In fact, clearly this was a department that had a long history of service and engagement, both in the U.S. and in the developing world. There was a breadth of focus, but an integration also, that I found very attractive. I found that it was not an elite, snobby environment. I know many people feel it's that way, but considering where I was coming from—MIT—Cornell was so down-to-earth. I was in heaven, I really was.

Here's a little story that shows what I mean about "down-to-earth." We breed food plants in this department. When I started as a faculty member here, we never bred pumpkins, because pumpkins aren't food. Pumpkins are decoration. Well, it turns out if you look at the way farmers work locally, pumpkins could be the largest cash crop they could grow in some years, because for whatever reason, people pay insane prices for pumpkins, especially if what the farmer does is open up his field and let them cart pumpkins out of the field for fifteen dollars apiece. In the last fifteen years, we've had a lot of people who have saved their farming operations because of this special holiday kind of thing with pumpkins.

So we started looking at pumpkins. There's a disease that's very prevalent in pumpkins called powdery mildew. Well, my predecessor had spent thirty years bringing resistance to powdery mildew from this wild gourd in Florida. He had all sorts of things in the right species, wrong shape—like acorn squash—that had this resistance. And then we happened by accident to hear an extension person telling us about how they make aerial applications of this horrible fungicide to control this disease. We had no idea people were out applying carcinogens aerially to control it. And we thought, "Why don't we put powdery mildew resistance in pumpkins?" So we did it. And the variety we bred is now in seed catalogs. Some say "Cornell" and some don't, because a lot of that germplasm went out before we had that identity.

This issue came to our attention because we talk to people, especially farmers. When I talk to people, and see where they can make the most money, then I'd better pay attention to that. As a plant breeder serving New York, that's probably relevant information. I live out in a little town called Lansing. I never aimed at an academic background, so my peer group is not the people who have the same job as me. The people that I run into—my neighbors, people I go to church with, and a guy that sells vegetables up at the top of my hill—they're people who tell me things like, "Goll-darnit, these pumpkins have rotten handles!" If there's a major disease problem that accounts for 60 percent of their production costs, and I have the solution sitting on my shelf, well that's not a very hard one to figure out, is it?

One of the crops we work on is pepper. When you expand out the value of that crop for pharmaceutical and processed food uses, it becomes a significant plant in our portfolio of plants. We just won a big NSF grant to study the biochemistry that's responsible for pungency in pepper. We've been using it medicinally for probably thousands of years, but that biochemistry is not yet known. It represents an example in plant biology that's of acute interest to many people, because plants have this trick of developing these novel biochemistries, these very specialized biochemistries that are limited to a very narrow swath of diversity. The only organism with that particular set of compounds that makes pepper is so pungent is in just a few species of peppers.

Where does that capacity come from? We really don't know how these pathways evolve in plants. We know that many plants share genes across an enormous evolutionary gulf. So if all these plants have so many of the same genes, where do these very specialized and important pathways come from? They're important for nutrition, they're important for medicine, they're important for industry. They're important for all sorts of things humans use plants for. That's a question that has a lot of economic significance. But it's also a question that has a lot of biological interest.

What are the modifications in a particular gene that mean that the function of that gene produces changes, such as the changes in a plant that make these pathways appear? That's a really fundamental biological question. What are the specific shifts in that chromosome sequence that account for the acquisition of this whole new trait? It's a neat trait ecologically. It's meant to deter mammals with crushing molars, and attract birds that like bright-colored fruit like pepper has, and lack the pain receptor that this molecule interacts with. So mammals don't like it, except us. It's a twist that peppers didn't figure out. Birds have no ability to perceive the burning sensation. Birds like the bright-colored fruit. Birds eat the fruit, and after they eat the fruit, birds roost in trees under which wild peppers grow really well.

So there's some interesting ecology. Pretty tricky. The one little thing that peppers didn't count on, which relates to humans, is that the capsaicin molecule mimics a precursor of dopamine. *Newsweek* recently listed the twenty most important questions of our age. And it turns out that the nineteenth most important scientific question of our age on their list was, "Why do people eat hot peppers?" The answer is perhaps that this molecule mimics dopamine in the brain. So it really does "hurt so good." We're learning about the genes that are part of this pathway. The other thing is, capsaicin is an important pest deterrent in organic agriculture.

We're doing very fundamental studies that are leading us to learn a lot more about the chemical diversity that's out there. We've gone back in and reexamined what you can extract from pepper fruit. We found a range of related molecules that had previously only been found at very, very low levels, but nobody had done what a geneticist would do right away and look at a whole bunch of related peppers from different environments. Well, guess what? The low levels are not genetically fixed. You can find peppers that are very highly enriched for these interesting compounds that were considered very rare.

Very quickly we can move to a lot of industrial, pharmaceutical, and food applications. Some of these variants clearly have somewhat different biological properties. We may come up with a more effective organic pesticide. We have been contacted by Frito-Lay. We are starting a collaboration with an ecologist who's interested in a variation of these molecules with respect to some of the diversity he's interested in. That's an example where work that's funded by NSF's metabolic biochemistry panel—one of the hardcore NSF panels—is instantly linked to applied work, work where there's this intersection between application, interesting population-level biology, and really important molecular biology and biochemistry. And it all comes together in a system that tends to be regarded as marginal, because if it's crop-oriented, it's not seen as a system in which you would do important work in a fundamental sense.

One of my students just came back from the meeting of the American Society for Plant Biology and said his feeling is that the focus on experimental systems is having a dangerous effect, narrowing the number of biological organisms that are being studied intensively. In fact, that's potentially very detrimental, because the whole point of investing in these model systems is to apply them. But if what it does is suck all the talent into these species that really nobody cares about for any practical reason, then you've just really defeated the purpose.

That's a place where the land-grant universities should be stepping up and saying, "We are where you take those model systems." Hundreds of millions of dollars have been invested in my particular subarea. We have the capacity to take the results from that investment and apply them in an innovative, creative way. And we don't do that. And yet, we have the perfect structural reason why investing in the kind of science that land-grants do is critical, especially now when we have the capacity that's developed as far as it has in these systems in which a lot of fundamental progress is possible very fast.

The public-sector, land-grant domain has a historical commitment to working on seeds. I happen to deal in seeds. We had a number of private-sector players that were taking our varieties in a way that fits the Cornell Research Foundation model. Everything was going fine until those large corporations ran into ownership problems and other tough conditions. By the end of the 1990s, we were engaged with only a very few companies that were the product of rounds of consolidation. They were very large and moved tons and tons of seed, and that made us very vulnerable to whatever affected the health of the companies. We ran into some severe bottlenecks when our major players ran into trouble. That was a very difficult time for commodity agriculture in general, worldwide.

When I went to the research meeting of one of these companies a few years ago to tell them what we were doing, they gave me bad news over the dinner table: they were going to drop their license for the winter squash variety they had gotten from us. And I said, "What do you mean you're not interested in it? You just produced five tons of the seed. What do you mean you're not interested?" Well, they're globalizing. Their markets have changed. The guy I dealt with about pepper varieties is now making a decision about winter squash. And he said, "Well, it's an open-pollinated variety." And I said, "That's exactly why you took it! You took it because it's on open-pollinated variety." That means you grow the seed in an isolated field, and that's all you have to do. It breeds true. This variety outperformed the best hybrid. With hybrids, you have to make a very specific cross between a male and a female, and there are seed purity issues, and you have to control the pollinations. Hybrid seed is way more expensive to produce, and therefore way more expensive to buy.

This company took the winter squash variety we developed because they could produce the seed cheaply and sell it at hybrid prices, and because it outperformed the best hybrid on the market, partly because it had a lot of disease resistance in it. But now they were saying they were dropping it because it's open pollinated. They said, "Farmers can grow their own seeds." And I said, "Virtually no major commercial growers in the developed world grow their own seed. That would be ridiculous. I mean, the risk of doing that in most regions in the U.S. is so high, you'd never do that." But they said, "Nope, it's open pollinated, it's a command from on high. We're dropping all open-pollinated varieties." So I began to think: this company is a new beast. It's a consolidation of a bunch of great North American companies, and now it's owned outside the U.S., and they're starting to make decisions that don't make sense for them.

This little incident at that research meeting led to the birth of the Public Seed Initiative (PSI). PSI is a mechanism for connecting smaller seed companies and growers with public-sector germplasm. It's a very simple idea. In many ways it's traditional. It's really what we did in the days when Cornell didn't have a lot of fancy research farms, so of course they relied on grower input. They probably did have extension agents that knew their growers, but in our case, our extension agents are often dealing with only the largest growers. In this case, we wanted to be sure we also included organic agriculture. It's not focused at all exclusively on organic agriculture, but we wanted to make sure we didn't exclude organic either. I had noticed in a number of mainstream assessments of North American agriculture that organic agriculture was growing 10 to 30 percent a year, and conventional, commodity-based agriculture is not in a very strong position right now. It's being squeezed every which way.

If you're in the public sector, you should be looking at what's growing, even if it's starting from something very small. Organic food is making ingresses in all kinds of places nobody would have thought, and a lot of very mainstream science is supporting its value—not only its environmental value, but also its health value. We just saw a very credible study showing that pesticide levels in children's urine in Seattle comes way down when you put them on a diet of organic fruits and vegetables. And if you think about rural economic viability in this region, it's not going to be beating the Midwest at commodity production. If you're a relatively small operation, chances are you're going to be really diversified. So the idea from my point of view is to contribute as much value as possible to what it is a farmer can grow. I'm not an economist, but that makes sense to me.

Once the winter squash license I was talking about was dropped and it became clear that I was depending on just these few very large companies to deliver the impact of my work, I had a summer undergrad scour the Internet to identify everyone working in the public sector in a range of vegetable crops. She traced down people that sold seed all over the country, and we tried to figure out who had a serious commercial catalog and where they got their varieties. Maybe they weren't breeding new material, but they were at least trialing materials for their customer base. That's what that private sector is supposed to do in the classical pipeline model, and that is what Extension used to do: test out these innovations in some market, pick the best, and then advocate for those products.

We whittled the list down by looking at their catalogs and talking with people. If we found a public-sector breeder, we would ask, "Are there any small companies in your region that you think we should know about?" So it was a relatively unbiased attempt to identify all the possible players we should be serving, and then going after relationships with them as their capacity and our capacity allowed. That's how we came up with our private-sector group of partners. Of course, a number of those companies were serving markets we didn't know a lot about, including the organic agriculture market. That's been an adventure, and continues to be an adventure—to overcome all of the issues involved in having a dialogue with a community whose values are quite different.

I'll give you an example. In January of 2000, I was invited to attend the annual meeting in Syracuse of the Northeastern Organic Farming Association (NOFA). It was a total accident I was invited. I had never talked to this group of farmers, and had no contact with them. They didn't know who I was, and I didn't know who they were. So I went up with my new little baby and my husband and sat in for an hour on a variety roundtable session with growers. There were only about fifteen people there.

I said, "So, what varieties are you growing in these crops?" And they said they're growing fifty-year-old varieties with no disease resistance. And I said, "Why are you growing these?" They said, "Well, they're just standard cucumbers, aren't they?" So I told them, "Yeah, from like 1940! Why are you growing them?" And they said, "Well, that's what our companies are selling." So I said, "What companies do you buy from?" They listed off a string of companies— I'd never heard of any of them. I hadn't even heard of a small seed company in Syracuse, New York, less than an hour from my house! I'm thinking this doesn't make any sense at all. We have maybe twenty to thirty seed companies that support vegetable breeding here from all over the world—India, all over Europe, South America—and I've never heard of this seed company in Syracuse. So I asked, "What is it that you'd really like in varieties?" And they start naming off all this stuff *we* work on. And I'm thinking this really doesn't make any sense. I began to realize that we had a profound disconnect between one element of my local agriculture and me. They didn't know who I was, what type of resource I was, and that

83

I was available to them. And I had no clue who they were, or how to get my product to them.

Later I called up some of those seed companies that they listed, and I said, "We have some material that you might be interested in." And they said, "Who are *you?*" They were very, very suspicious of me, coming from Cornell. That's when I encountered this thing I had no idea about, which is that Cornell has this major image issue in some communities about being a service to corporations. I had never encountered that. I didn't understand it clearly. At the time I really just kind of ignored it. Well, that spring we got a call about a large USDA program that was going to fund genomics. The trendy thing in this large genomics money from NSF and USDA is outreach, and the trendy outreach is K-12 curriculum development. And I thought, "I want one of those big grants to do my basic research. But I want my outreach to address this issue, because this is the kind of outreach I do. I have varieties in some catalogs; why not get varieties into these catalogs?"

I called up NOFA and said, "I have this idea, what do you think?" And the woman who was there says, "Well, that's a very, very interesting idea." But she said, "I'm not sure you really understand the context. Let me send you some things to look at." So she sent me some of the NOFA newsletters, folded open to articles about Cornell. I'm a really busy guy. I glanced at them and they didn't seem to have anything to do with vegetables or with me, so I didn't really get it. In essence what those articles said was, "Why doesn't Cornell pay attention to us? We've been knocking on Cornell's doors for a decade. They ignore us. We're not their clientele." I honestly didn't even read the articles closely enough to really get it, other than I could detect they were sort of negative, and they weren't about me. So I just forged ahead. We submitted this big genomics grant to NSF with NOFA as a partner for outreach, and it got funded.

We wound up having a very funny experience related to this. After this project had gotten started, we were invited to speak up at Wells College as the keynote speakers for a daylong symposium on activism in the academy. When we got up there, I said to the NOFA employee, "I'll talk about the PSI, but you do the activism part, okay?" And he said, "Sure." So he got up after me, and he said, "Let me give you a little perspective on this. We've been trying to get Cornell to do this for fifteen years, and we were so frustrated. Their attitude was totally corporate." All this bad stuff. So my guys, who are in the field most of the time and not operating within the political realm of Cornell, all start to look at this guy, thinking, "Where is he going?" and "We didn't know this!" Then he said, "Five years ago, we were so frustrated with Cornell we'd given up all hope. We really hated Cornell." By this time, we're all going, "You hated us? What do you mean you hated us?"

Suddenly, sitting up on that stage, it flashed on me what my friend Sarah was trying to tell me with those NOFA newsletters. Like a year and a half later, you know? I suddenly thought, "Ooh, *that's* what she was trying to tell me!" It's pretty funny. Now we're trying break down those kinds of stereotypes in a very conscious way. People have a lot of attitudes that don't necessarily serve them well. I can understand where they come from, but I think it's our job to go out and be available to provide alternative information. We don't have to convert people or anything like that. But I think it is where participation is important in reaching the end point we set our eyes on. I think we need to go out and be present, and if that means me, then it's me, or one of the guys on our team.

One of the ideas we put in the genomics grant was a mobile seed-processing unit, because when I talked to these seed companies, I said, "Let's say we give you a bunch of varieties that look good. Do you have everything you would need to put those across as products?" And they said, "Actually, we're really struggling in a number of areas, one of which is we don't have growers that really know how to grow good, commercial-quality seed, as opposed to the vegetable itself. And the other thing is, you have to isolate these things, so you need a kind network of people all over the place." We thought, "Okay, that'll be our outreach. We'll aim at helping people grow good-quality seed. That's something land-grant colleges know how to do. And we'll come up with something clever to address the decentralized production issue." Well, that clever thing we actually stole from international development, where when you have a problem like this, you put the infrastructure you need on the back of something that moves and you move it around as the season and need dictates. And that's exactly what we did. We put a bunch of seed-cleaning equipment on the back of a trailer, funded by this genomics grant. That was an important element. The trailer goes on farms. It's booked ahead, so growers know when it's coming to their neighborhood. That's been really, really fun, and very successful in the community. It addressed a real need that I would have never known about if I hadn't gotten on the phone and called these seed companies and asked them, "If I hand you a small packet of seed, what are the issues?" I really had no idea.

Complicating the process was that growers had problems with the seed companies. Some of these small companies did not have a lot of experience with contract growers, and we would hear problems about seed growers being unreliable from the company's point of view, in terms of delivering the products the companies were after. So in the case of the contract growers, I said, "Do you have a contract? How does that work?" We looked at the contracts these little companies were asking their seed growers to sign, and they were ridiculous. So we looked at sample contracts, and we asked one of the big companies for a template of their seed grower contracts. We showed the small companies this template, which is a much more reasonable document, and said, "Why don't you try something like this, where you don't ask the grower to assume all the risk, and should things go the grower's way, you cut them a break: they get some of the extra. If there's extra benefit, you share that extra benefit." Well, the ironic thing is the tradition some of these smaller companies come out of is more like a "back to the land" thing, so you'd think they'd be sensitive to the needs of small partners. But if you compared the seed grower contracts between the large multinationals and these smaller, more alternative companies, the big multinational companies had more grower-friendly contracts. So we just did a little communicating, and my understanding is a lot of the contracts now offered by the smaller, more alternative companies have become much more reasonable for their contract seed growers.

Now it's not my job to mess with seed contracts. I really didn't know anything about them. I'm not a lawyer. But I do know that link has to be in place for my products to get out, and if there seems to be a problem with a link in the chain to deliver my impact, I will try to figure it out. Not that I have any particular expertise, but at least I will try to figure out the nature of the issue and then look for a simple way to solve it. It's not my job, formally speaking, but it's critical for our success, if we measure success by making a difference in real life.

Those smaller companies couldn't go to each other, because they all had the same problems. And they certainly couldn't go to the large multinationals, because there are very few healthy channels for dialogue between these small companies and the large companies, even though they're all in the same business. A lot of times in the Northeast our growers are smaller, and especially with a new item and a new market like this, they're not well connected. For the large commodities in New York State—potatoes, alfalfa, wheat—there are commodity organizations and people talk to each other. We don't have that in the smaller sectors that I deal with.

Another thing I came to understand as a result of thinking I did on a sabbatical was that the company-farmer link was less direct than it was previously. We could no longer rely on what had hitherto been very trustworthy informants: that is, the companies. So we also set out to identify farmers' needs—independent of the seed companies' perceptions—with respect to our work. We used a combination of farmers and extension educators. We set up a network of on-farm trials of varieties that we thought might do well in the environments in which those farms were operating. In this case it was a direct link between the farmer and me. Those components were part of PSI in its original conception. Now there are plenty of farmers that just can't manage this kind of interaction on top of their businesses. The way we identified the right farmers was through NOFA, in the case of organic farmers, and through extension educators and word-of-mouth, in the case of farmers with conventional production regimes.

So PSI involved these farm-based trials of varieties that we managed. We managed the network here, and we went out and connected with extension educators, and got them onto farms. Some of the organic growers said it was the first time they'd seen a Cooperative Extension person on their farm. And then the other thing we did, especially in the area of organics, was to get extension educators who were interested and able to conduct organic and conventional trials on their ground. We handed the educator packets of seed and said, "Take a look at these. We're breeding this for this, and that for that. What are your problems? What are your interests? What are your opportunities?" And we'd try to get back and select from our warehouse things that fit that, and handed it directly to them.

PSI was a consequence of my feeling that however it's supposed to work, there was nobody doing that function of identifying farmers' needs for me, and I needed to do it if I wanted to have an impact. So it's really three different directions that we moved, recognizing that the pipeline model of faculty research handed off to Extension was not working for us. The Public Seed Initiative was invented to fill in that pipeline for the Northeast.

We stay in touch with the seed companies, NOFA, and others through field days. We bring people onto campus to look at what we're doing and comment on it, so we have what we now call "stakeholder input." It's all just common sense—keeping channels open. I get on the phone and I talk to people, and I say, "Here's what we know and what we can do, what do you think? How do we fit? From where you sit, what do things look like? What are your problems?" That seed mill we use in PSI was NOFA's idea.

The annual field day, which will be two weeks from today, is also designed to create better communication between the large companies and the small companies. We're asking the smaller companies to join a group, which they can do by a $250 donation that contributes to setting research directions here at Cornell. We've got Seminis, we've got Syngenta, we've got all the big multinational seed companies. We now have Turtle Tree Biodynamic Seed Company, and Fedco, one of the oldest organic companies in Maine, and we've always had Johnny's, which is a kind of in-between company. So PSI is broadening the network here, and is an example of what could be done in other parts of the nation. It was funded at a high level thanks to the links with basic science. USDA has been absolutely thrilled with it. It's been showcased in reports about these large investments in plant genomics for Congress. This has been highlighted both by USDA alone and in interagency publications that also go with NSF.

In September, when we start our next major grant, we're exporting the PSI model nationally. We're not making it one centralized thing; it's kind of a federation of activities. We have people in the Northwest, and then we have several schools that are in minority areas with linkages to minority farmers. I can't wait to see what happens. We've got one in the center of New Mexico, which is a Hispanic-serving institution with a lot of Native American presence, one in central Mississippi at Alcorn State, which is an 1890 school, and one at West Virginia State, which is also an 1890 school. I can't wait! This is going to be really interesting from a human point of view—*really* interesting.

We're also putting in a grant to USDA for a new organic crossover proposal to make a similar unit on the west coast. Again, we've created a university-nonprofit partnership. Not just Cornell—it's going to be several universities, USDA, and public sources of germplasm connecting to nonprofits. Cornell says it wants to be "the land-grant to the world." Well, that's not entirely possible by ourselves. But what we can do is federate across land-grants, and provide that kind of service, regionally oriented. That's been the concept of PSI: do a better job of local networks, and stay tuned-in across pretty different environments.

PSI reflects our priority of working on things that are relevant to the public. Unfortunately, the priority in academics often has been, "I want to work on a disease that's interesting to me, and I'm going to make up a story about why you should care." It's not that it's untrue, but if you step back and state it objectively based on actual importance in agriculture, chances are that wouldn't be the disease you'd pick. But you pick it because you really love this particular category of organism, and then you write the story around it. In general, we haven't done business that way in my program, at least not very much. We have maybe a little bit here and there focused on extra-interesting pathogens just because they're interesting. But again, it's been an intersection; the conversation doesn't start one place or the other. What we pick to move forward with are places we see opportunity on both sides. And there's no shortage of opportunity.

A lot of programs like mine will say, "Oh, funding is so hard to get. We're really constrained because the land-grant system isn't supported very well by public money anymore, and we don't have state money to do this work." Well, I argue if it's worth doing, and you intersect with strong science and the private sector, you'll be able to find resources. Now maybe my experience is just unbelievably unique. I really don't see why it should be. We've built a pretty significant endowment, partly through research assessments that companies pay us and now through a very healthy royalty stream from the use of our varieties. But a lot of the endowment is to the credit of my predecessor. Companies were willing to honor the value they received from him through the years with some very large gifts. I've saved those gifts in an endowment. I haven't used them for operating money. I've used the funds as a war chest. It helped us last through the time when applied research wasn't so fashionable in crop and plant genetics. Land-grants have lost a lot of their infrastructure and a lot of their capacity. Cornell's lucky—we've kept it here. Many universities haven't. So we're starting to think much more along the lines of federated, regional approaches.

What's the value of investing private and public money in us? We need to enhance the visibility of the consequences and benefits of investment in the public sector. One of our tried-and-true indicators of success is the open-pollinated squash we developed at Cornell, which the organic people all say they want. The company that sold and publicized seeds for it is actually the largest multinational vegetable seed company. One of my academic colleagues recently said to me, "Public plant breeding is irrelevant." And I thought, "I don't think so."

We get a lot of publicity all over the world in seed catalogs. Here's an example [pointing to pictures of her team's Delicata squash in a seed catalog]: "Cornell University: this exciting new disease tolerant, award-winning sweet potato squash is simply superb." Here's another example from the 2004 commercial catalog from Johnny's Selected Seed: "Cornell's Bush Delicata. Hats off to Dr. Molly Jahn and George Moriarty at Cornell University for this nice Delicata." If that isn't outreach, I don't know what is. It's in commercial catalogs, and right there it's clear what their taxes support. [Reading from another catalog:] "New squash varieties with powdery mildew tolerance, featuring Cornell genetics." Here's another catalog with our seeds, mentioning our name, and bragging about the fact that they pay us research assessments. How do you like that? It says, "A portion of the profits support vegetable breeding programs at Cornell University." companies didn't used to brag about having to return dollars to us. But they see it as a marketing scheme. These are open-pollinated varieties, which is kind of a groovy thing. We've always bred open-pollinated varieties, because if we can equal a hybrid, then we're doing our part for the grower, to give them some lower-cost alternatives to expensive hybrid seed.

I believe if people are going to value what we do at land-grant universities, we have to show them what the benefits are in places they're going to see them, not just in reports we write for ourselves to read. These catalogs with our varieties in them are what we have to show people who pay taxes. They're what I want to show my dean. They're what I want to show my president. They're what I want to show my mom. It means I've finished the job. It's what we should be doing. This is how it's supposed to work: we see our product all the way through.

Simply put, my understanding of the land-grant mission is to build a public-sector research and education capacity. What's become very clear to me, especially as I've worked in the system for a while, is that the public sector is positioned to do things no one else is positioned to do. Since the land-grant system was invented, the private sector has grown by leaps and bounds in many areas to the point of absolute dominance. But what's still clear to me is that it's not a duplicative function. The private sector does not do what the public sector does. The functions are fundamentally different. For many hundreds of years, from the very earliest university, there was recognition that an objective center of learning was critical and precious, and clearly a public good. I see no private-sector model that can cover that base, and I don't see any private-sector activities trying to perform that function, except for perhaps some private foundations that set up institutes. So the public sector has a unique mission and a set of responsibilities to society as a whole, and that's what we're all about in the land-grant system. There are private universities that certainly contribute to that mission in many different ways, but they don't have the obligation that we have here.

It's true that in agriculture, you can't compete with the private sector on corn in Iowa. I'll give you that. That would be stupid. But I would argue that most markets in the U.S. for seed are now underserved. Now you don't hear people say that. But with the consolidation of the seed companies, they necessarily have to focus on the markets that make them the most money. There are these enormous multinational operations. They just can't care about summer squash in upstate New York. Most all of them have pulled out of the Northeast completely in terms of any kind of research presence. In this and many other crops, the public sector has not just an opportunity, but—I'd argue—a *responsibility*. The paradigm that everything's going to be perfectly served by the private sector isn't valid. It just doesn't work. It's nobody's fault, it's just the way it is.

We have a lot of very sobering issues in North American agriculture to face right now. But it's been really invigorating for me to encounter a lot of these smaller operations. One of our varieties—Hannah's Choice, named after my melon-loving daughter, Hannah—was picked up by a breeder in Hall, New York. He's on a farm that has a long history of being a seed company research farm. That company was bought by a larger company. He worked for the larger company for quite some time, and then they laid off many, many, many of their senior breeders, including him. They let him buy that farm, and he began his own operation called Seneca Vegetable Seed. He's a sophisticated plant breeder. He's serving local companies. He's perfect for us. It's important for us to stay tuned to these kinds of developments. Clearly, on one level you could say he's a casualty of corporate consolidation. But he's bounced back from the loss of his job, and now he represents an opportunity for growers to receive diversified products.

Hannah's Choice is a hybrid eastern cantaloupe. You can't ship this thing to supermarkets 3,000 miles away and expect it to hold six weeks. It holds ten days at full ripeness, which is plenty long enough for local and regional markets. And its eating quality is really, really good. The flesh is soft, and it's very sweet. But you can't treat this thing like a western shipper. We're very proud of this melon. You have to have somebody who's got an interest in selling to eastern markets, and now we found that company. The private sector's been incredibly important to success in my story in terms of really having the kinds of impacts that I wanted. I work directly with the private sector and/or nonprofits that manage decentralized networks of growers. And we take grower feedback back to the private sector.

Both the private and public sectors had a big issue to solve: we had no mechanism to release new seed effectively from this campus, aside from just giving it away. That was fine until the intellectual property laws changed, and giving it away meant that you left everybody who received it vulnerable to a preemptive move by any one of the parties that received the unprotected intellectual property that seed represented. So if you fail to protect the public domain, anybody who received it can move to preempt everyone else's access to it.

We're not a seed company. It's got to go to a seed company to be blown up to a scale where it's available for production. If we don't have a way to not only transfer the seed packet, but to protect that company's assets in terms of what's in the seed packet, then we're cheated and they're cheated, and the public's cheated. Everybody's cheated.

I became militant about some of these novel approaches because I really can't and don't want to handle anything more complicated than it needs to be. I can't stand dealing with licenses that are twenty-five-page legalese documents I can't understand. But we clearly had walked into a situation where we needed to address the management of intellectual property if we were going to be responsible partners. This is one of the achievements we're proudest of. It sounds basically like an administrative challenge, but it turned out to be very important to figure out a way to get new varieties out of here for commercial use, because after all, that's what a success is going to look like. This is not my training, but it became clear that it was going to be essential. And again, I know a lot of other people with my job who say, "That's not my job. That's the licensing office for the university." We tried that, and we got nowhere. We just got nowhere. Relative to the stuff that they're doing for engineering, the vet school, human health, medical textiles, and all of that, it just doesn't make sense to put the next acorn squash variety high on their priority list. They've got vaccines to deliver.

So we figured out a one-page document that allows us to send materials out for anybody to do whatever with. Should they choose to commercialize, I don't care if you're in Pakistan or if you're at the largest multinational seed company, you get a two-page license that lays out terms that are important to us. The paradigm is that we don't litigate to resolve disputes over things like a squash variety. I'm very upfront with that. That's a personal value. I don't have time to litigate, and it's not in the university's best interest to litigate. Therefore, we say we reserve the right to terminate our formal relationship upon written notice. Should you act inconsistently with this understanding we'll alert you to the fact that that's our perception, give you eighteen months to deal with your seed, and we won't deal with you again. Should you cheat, all we'll do is not work with you anymore. This is really a very different paradigm from the way that world has evolved in the private sector. I feel like we've actually provided some leadership to the private sector. We've been able to help to calm down this hysteria over patenting vegetable varieties. Not single-handedly, of course, but we offer an alternative way of doing business. This isn't anything I knew how to do. It's not my job, but it's really important to assure public access to our materials. So I feel very proud of this piece. I don't know if anybody, short of the guys that work with me, really appreciates the importance of this. But we know that it was the difference between getting things out and not. It reflects our integrated view of the land-grant system.

Fundamentally, we view the components of the land-grant system as being highly integrated and functionally diverse, which means if you compartmentalize the functions, you run the risk of disconnect. I think in a lot of ways that's what our relatively advanced state of development has led to. And I think that's a hazard in any number of organizations, public and private. I think what we've done in the land-grant system is try to define different functions, and then we separate those functions organizationally and institutionalize those functions in such a way that the natural linkages are broken, or fail to function. Then we have this structure in place where all the boxes are checked off. But in our experience, for relatively subtle reasons what's actually supposed to happen doesn't always happen the way it should.

I can certainly cite examples on this campus where those functions work extremely well together. We have people working on potatoes right next door, and that's a case where we've got a really well-integrated group of people who have very different sets of expertise, and it all seems to work very, very well. We weren't a part of a group like that, and despite every effort, I couldn't make it happen here for what we're doing. So we fell back on this alternative view, which involved engaging people off-campus far more than we ever had before. It was a big breakthrough for us to begin to realize that just as you would in a developing country, you need to look at the nonprofits, the NGOs. You wouldn't think about doing a serious development project in a developing country without figuring out what your NGO landscape looked like, and yet we did that all the time here. I really had no idea who we were relying on. Now, some of the nonprofits are not a good match. Others have been completely essential to our success for a whole bunch of reasons, not the least of which is that they have advocated for us in communities that were skeptical of us, and have assisted us in learning vocabulary that we didn't necessarily know that was essential for communicating with our target audience. That nonprofit piece was really important for us, as was direct contact with the right farmers. So it really was a matter of reaching outside the compartmentalized structure that was handed to me when I took my job here.

A larger systemic reconfiguration is implicit in the emphasis Cornell's president, Jeffrey Lehman, is putting on engagement. It's a very different kind of impact. Not that publications don't have impact sometimes. They do. But I think we've confused societal impact—land-grant-type impact—with academic impact. I think we've got some things confounded in our institution, where we've got academic priorities, academic obligations, academic measures of success, and then we've got social ones, or ones that pertain to society—societal missions and accomplishments. And we've muddled those, I think, in ways that are very difficult for people to sort through and identify clearly.

How can we un-muddle them? I think by getting a clear view of what societal impacts are desired. A relatively straightforward way to think about that is to focus on rural economic vigor. There's something you can measure there, where things are not the way we might hope them to be as a society. What are the impediments there? Here we are really dependent on social scientists. I can come up with a really naive argument that more profitable agricultural enterprises will be good. But I recognize it's probably a lot more complicated than that.

I think about an educated citizenry, and why that's important. And a healthy citizenry—I think about that a lot, too. I live a little bit out of town, and a lot of people around me aren't very healthy, and they're poor. I run into dire situations all the time, right in my backyard. There's a big tension in my life that I'm anticipating as I get closer to age fifty between local and global issues. There are plenty of local issues that are within ten miles of here that we as a land-grant are not out in front on. And that might be something we'd like to ask ourselves as a college of agriculture. Actually, I had a former student at Minnesota who really wanted to come back here and do a thesis that asks, "What would it take to eradicate hunger in Tompkins County?" He couldn't get funding to come back and do that as a master's project.

I think as an institution, we could start small. We want to be the land-grant to the world, and that's great, but I think we might learn some lessons very near home about respecting the dimension of these kinds of tasks, and distinguishing them from our academic accomplishments. It's something I think about personally. That might be a way to help us as an institution struggle with this. We really do a lot locally. But if we're asking, can we discern impact of the type we're hoping for, I'm not sure that we even have the metrics, locally, to do that. I don't know. It's something that I know others are thinking about, too. Better metrics is an important issue. I watched a lot of large, multimillion-dollar projects in the developing world fail without anybody being called to task about it. Maybe there's not a way to address that in a global sense. There are a lot of interested parties who benefit, whether the thing fails or succeeds. I get my million and a half for my lab, I'm happy. I get my publications, I'm happy. And whoever goes to the country of Mali anyway? There are disconnects that allow some of us to hide out from failing to deliver on a grand scale.

There's a lot about doing science these days that isn't really very nice, especially the harder-core, higher-tech science. A close friend of mine on an editorial board said, "You know, really anything becomes a treadmill. You start publishing in *Science* and *Nature*, you've got to keep that up or else you've just slipped." And he said, "At some point, you're trapped by your success. You can't explore." But what I've found is, I'm *not* trapped by our success, partly because I don't feel obligated to deliver that type of, or any single type of, success. That's one of the wonderful things about the land-grant environment: there's flexibility in terms of what it is I generate.

I think it's very important, from the point of view of maintaining the vitality of this discipline, to present to students an environment that's stimulating and invigorated, as opposed to browbeaten and driven by thoughtless productivity: "Have to have more of this, more of that, more of this, more of that. Bigger of that, bigger of this." We've tried hard in this lab to remain thoughtful, which may mean we don't have as many papers. But maybe we have more interesting papers. It's been interesting to me to see the impact of some of our papers that didn't require very much work, but simply presented an important view, an important analysis of a problem that others who have been very involved in racing each other for the detail have just missed.

I've had a lot of constraints to the way I can approach an academic career, in terms of my own personal life. So we *can't* work faster and harder. We just won't survive in those rat races, and besides, they're no fun. I have a lot of friends that wind up trapped in them. So we try to stay out of them. Working on crops is a good way to do that. Pepper happens to be one of the things we've really had a riot with. It's a tough thing to work on, and that makes things difficult. We've been able to compete very successfully without having to win rat races, because I really can't win rat races. I can't do breeding and this kind of high-profile, high-technology lab work and win rat races. I just can't. So we don't even try, and that's been a good approach. I've watched careers ruined, I've watched tenure lost because of not getting out of rat races in time.

When money for genomics went up in scale, there was a lot of talk about doing "big science." I was on sabbatical at the time, and I thought, "You know what that is, it's industrial biology. That will have its benefits, but it will also have its costs, just the way industrializing anything has its costs and benefits." And I thought, "We in my lab can't afford and don't want to become a factory. That's certainly not why I went into this." But many of my friends saw these large pots of money and went after them. A lot of those funds come with a lot of oversight. You hand somebody a five- to seven-million-dollar grant, and you're going to get a lot of oversight. And they wind up feeling like, "Who's running this lab, anyway? Me or you?" We've avoided that on purpose. That was a strategic decision. It meant we didn't go for some of the large pots of money. We tried to be careful about where we put our effort, to make sure that we're doing things that wouldn't necessarily be done otherwise. We're trying to set good examples in terms of the principles that I bring to this job, and not just chasing trends because that's where the dollars are, or that's where glory might be. And it's turned out that after all that, we're extremely well funded via competitive grants. We didn't lose a thing I care about by staying out of the fray around early genomics.

So it's relatively new in my understanding that I don't feel like I've lost any ground in the hardcore science and high-tech world. For whatever reason, we've been able to keep our hand in the hardcore science, so that I'm routinely asked to sit on big NSF panels, and I'm serving on the *Plant Cell* editorial board. So I don't feel like I've been marginalized in any way by this perspective.

Hundreds of millions of dollars in the U.S. has been invested in plant genomics, and the impact on agriculture outside of just a few crops has been very limited—*very* limited. That will change, I'm sure, but even NSF is getting worried about this, and it's not even NSF's mission. I don't know why so many scientists are perfectly happy to take that money—my colleagues and me, we all do it—and then fail to notice that they didn't deliver on the promise they made in that first paragraph. Of course, the promise is *only* in the first paragraph. And the concept, which is absolutely widespread, is that somehow research publications are as good as—or are equal to—impact on agriculture.

For whatever reason, and I think it's partly history, here at Cornell there was a culture of following your product out. There was a culture of interacting with the private sector. There was a culture of doing whatever it took to get what you needed to make a difference in the field. So it wasn't good enough to check the box off. You had to be able to go look at a large field of your variety. You had to be able to see it in a catalog. And *then* you were done. So I don't know what it was, but I have been shocked to discover that we're almost unique in this attitude. I don't know why. I can't figure it out, because from my point of view, that's a thrill. That's really fun. We've got a dozen varieties now in over a dozen catalogs. We've got probably thirty commercial licenses now. I mean, that's great. That feels really good to me.

I realize that getting publications in top journals is the way Cornell is defining my job, more and more. In order to succeed the way this institution defines success, my job is putting out heavy-hitting publications. The Public Seed Initiative ain't it, right? So I'm sure I don't have the kind of publication record that I should have had if all I did was generate publications. The interesting thing is, that hasn't hurt me at all. I'm amazed. I mean, if you'd talked to me a year ago, I wouldn't have said this. But I am finding myself invited into circles that typically are only earned by a steady stream of *Science* and *Nature* articles. I *don't have* a steady stream of *Science* and *Nature* articles, although I do publish in some other very esteemed journals. And we've done some interesting work that wouldn't have been done otherwise—partly because we're encountering interesting biology in uncommon places, and partly because everything we do is kind of a commonsense, "Let's not get on the bandwagon, let's be smart about this" kind of attitude. It was not my ambition to end up in the *Science* and *Nature* circle. And yet that's where I'm finding myself, over and over again these days—for straight science, not for my outreach work. Go figure.

Still, I may not hit the really big time, whatever that means. I could give you a few examples. Getting elected to the National Academy of Sciences would clearly be a criterion of success. But I didn't walk in here with that as my goal, and when I look at people who do walk into Cornell with that kind of recognition as their goal, I don't necessarily want lives like that or careers like that or labs like that—or marriages like that. And of course many of those people don't reach that goal, and some get quite bitter and disappointed. And some people who just love their work are the ones that in the long run get recognized by their peers—or maybe not, but throughout their careers they're much happier. For whatever reason, we've been able to find middle ground, which is actually proving to be more than middle ground. That's what I was trying to say had surprised me. I don't feel that I've compromised very much I care about by putting that other hat on. We just brought in $3 million or so worth of grants in the last couple months. I don't see a lot of damage. So why not?

When I look at people who have set their sights on that kind of basic science pinnacle, even when they sometimes get up there, they're not all that thrilled about what it's really like to *be* there. I've watched that pretty carefully and don't want to wind up having sacrificed a great deal to get somewhere that turns out not to be very great—not very *meaningful* is really the right word. We do play the conventional game reasonably well. We have a big lab, with twenty to thirty people I support on soft money. Some years we don't have as many publications as I think we should have. Nobody's ever said that to me, but I feel that way. This year is a big year for publications. I think if you smooth us out, we're okay. So when I say "lack" of publications, it just means I haven't gotten where I could imagine getting. That's been an important process of maturing: to realize that just because I can imagine that I could be there doesn't mean I have any right in reasonable life to get there.

The most important thing for me has been to realize that I can't play this bigger, faster, harder, better game. I can't do that. For whatever reason, we in the more fundamental research part of academia believe that's what we're supposed to do. There's a very unthinking adherence to that model that kind of blows my mind. And people become very strategic about where the high-impact contribution is going to be. But typically, there are multiple labs racing to that point, and there's going to be only one winner. I'm sure there's a place for that, and we have people here who've been phenomenally successful to the great benefit of the institution, and to me. *But I can't do that.* I have too many constraints on the way I can approach this job to win those games.

The next chapter of PSI is going to be doing a better job of reaching beyond the agricultural producer. We have a lot of specific ideas about how that happens. We've done it a little bit at county fairs and through Community Supported Agriculture operations. Fairly often, I get calls from people who want to be a part of what we're doing. To me, that's great! That's very consistent with what it is I'm supposed to be doing—it's education writ large, in a sense. I can't always handle every single interaction, but I have wonderful people who work with me to turn that interest over to. I am extremely close to the people who work me, whose lives are as involved with this enterprise as mine is, and whose commitments to it are as great as mine. Maybe they don't each one necessarily have the full picture, but for the sections of the operation they take care of, their degree of devotion and familiarity and their ability to represent us is equal to mine, and sometimes better.

Like George Moriarty, for example, whose name is all over the seed catalogs. He started work in Geneva at the New York State Agricultural Experiment Station in the boiler plant as an eighteen–year-old. He has no college degree. He taught me to do my first squash pollination when I was twenty-three and he was twenty-four. We've worked together on and off for more than twenty years. This is his career, and it's mine, too. We have a partnership that really works. That degree of partnership is really essential in a program like this. I think the land-grant system, because of its relative stability, makes that more possible. But I've had to do some unusual personnel moves, and I know when I came here, you didn't treat your research support specialists like this. I've been really aggressive about promoting people and paying them properly and putting their name where their name belonged. In the old days the system was very hierarchical. Everybody had a "George," but he didn't get treated like a co-breeder. I feel very strongly that that's exactly what he is. George doesn't sit at the computer and write papers, but his name is on them because he's led lots of the work. He's traveled all over the country and the world to represent this program. Together we've been to so many amazing places all over the world.

I have this vision about partnerships, even within my little unit, that's made us able to do way more, and a much broader range of activities, than I think is normal. For me, this is almost a spiritual principle. It's that fundamental in terms of my beliefs about the way people can interact. It's one of the reasons I do all right with these communities that are locked into preconceived notions like, "We hate you because you do genetic engineering. Monsanto does genetic engineering, therefore we hate Monsanto, and you and Monsanto are best friends, and so we hate you." We're really building teams, not defined by some sort of compartmentalized function, but by looking at the capacities we have on the table at that moment, and figuring out the best way to get from point A to point B. A lot of the way I approach things is to say, "We're here, we're not there. We want to get there. How do we get there?" A lot of people go there the way they think they're supposed to go there. My experience, now that I'm forty-five years old, is very frequently you really *don't* get there. Sometimes you get to other good places, but you don't necessarily get where you set out to go.

Universities impose hierarchies, pretty much like any organization. Hierarchy certainly has its advantages in terms of chain of command and all of those sorts of things. But when it comes to getting things done, that hierarchy can be very dangerous. No matter where you sit in it, it has some real perils. Our team operates with a different view. Each function that's performed in this integrated team is as important as the next, because any break in the pipeline means the whole pipeline is useless. So whether you're washing dishes in the lab or making our next multimillion-dollar-budget, or whatever, any of those functions are critical for our success, and we need to communicate what those functions are as a group. It does require personal chemistry that's hard for us to describe and manage and quantify and discuss. It involves taking a little time to build common vision.

I've done some of those exercises you're supposed to use in forming groups, and they don't always work very well. I think our success has to do with being organized around getting from point A to point B. Point B is what people really care about. That seems to work, in my opinion. You need an ability to pull together the different interested parties who have trouble with each other. It's a personal value, but it's one that I have found resonates remarkably broadly, regardless of ethnicity, religious background, whatever. People respond as if they're starving for this. All around me I see groups of people not working well together, and I think a lot of it is, they haven't identified point B. What is point B? Where are we going?

We continue to experiment and make adjustments when things don't work well. We're just coming in now to a wonderful time after two years of really having to work hard on that. But again, I think a lot of us just pretend that level's not there, and try to manage groups of people or institutions as if that doesn't matter. And of course it matters tremendously. It probably matters more than most things like salary—the degree to which we've defined point B, and are actually in a noncynical sense really working to get there. I get fabulous students because they love this approach. We're much better than we could ever be by ourselves. We have much more fun here, and that's important to us. We have the deep satisfaction of seeing real-life things show up in real places. It's not just a publication. (Not that I mind publications. I like publications lot. Probably more than a lot!)

Conversely, in any human enterprise, fearful people don't behave very well. When I see fear in others' behavior, then I know what slot to put that ridiculous email or behavior in, and then I have some tools to address that. I think we as an institution, as any level of organization, probably don't know how to do that very well. As humans we're not good at detecting fear in bossy superiors who are acting in ways that strike us as really unfair, or in subordinates who are not acting the way we think they should act. I've learned that a lot in hard ways, and now I see it very quickly and clearly. But I don't think it's how we're trained. We're not trained well in this area at all, to see fear. I think it's not so hard to learn, and incredibly helpful in terms of putting together a human system that'll work well.

I see a lot of people who spend decades in academia but don't have something real to look at that matters to them. I mean, obviously, you define your terms, so what matters to me may not matter to you, and vice versa. I think academics tend to get confused by their institution's priorities for them, and their own personal priorities. I see that a lot. Most of us come into this business for very wonderful, interesting, important reasons. But we don't always hold ourselves carefully to task for following those ideals through. We're willing to say, "I've got some publications this year, brought in a couple million dollars, so I'm doing fine." And we forget what our original motivations were. Or we write them at the beginning and the end of our grant proposals, and we talk to our students about them, but we never call ourselves to task for really assessing impact.

I understand now how hard it is to do, to really assess impact. It's probably easier in my business than it is in many areas here at the university that are very important, because I can say, "X percentage of the crop" when I have a market-leader variety. That's an easy way to document my impact, whereas, for example, creating an educated citizenry, that's a much more difficult thing to quantify. I think most of us rely on others to assess the value of what we're delivering, and we don't necessarily step back and think, "How am I doing according to what I thought when I was twenty-five? When I went in here, I was going to save the environment. Have I done that?"

I was giving one of those glossy fund-raising speeches for Cornell recently, and I made a passing allusion to the fact that global warming was clearly having an impact on crop production and the environment. I briefly said that we were breeding for heat tolerance in the developing world, particularly in this one environment where it was going to be important in beans. And this medical doctor in the audience, one of the alums visiting for the weekend, stood up and said, "So why aren't you doing more about global warming? If global warming is a fact like all you academics tell me it is, why aren't you doing something about it?"

I've thought about his question a lot, because my immediate thought was to excuse myself by saying, "That's not my academic specialty." But his point is absolutely well taken. I'm a citizen of the world and a parent. Global warming's *clearly* my thing. I keep telling my husband, "When I'm fifty, watch out!" I'm going to reconsider everything. Five more years, and then I'm really taking a good, hard look at all of my premises about the way I'm working and what its impact is. From an agricultural point of view, I'm doing what I wanted to do when I started out. This is what I wanted. And to some extent, it's what Cornell was doing, but we didn't get acknowledged. People didn't know. The seed companies knew. No one else did.

I keep saying to my students, "The most important thing is that you get your own sense of direction and your own criteria for success." We are so rich and lucky here compared to lots of people I live and work with and am related to. I think we just don't always get how much flexibility we have. We joke a lot that I'm the only squash breeder on the board of *Plant Cell*. It is what it is. But it's been fun. I keep in touch with some of my friends from MIT, and if the truth be told, I've had just a great run since I jumped the fence. I would do it all over again just this way.

It Isn't Rocket Science

A Profile of Ken Reardon

Associate Professor, Department of City and Regional Planning, Cornell University

Interview conducted by Tanya Mooza Zwahlen, October 7, 2002

As a professor with a background in community organizing, Ken Reardon has not only been a leading scholar and change agent in his academic field; he's also been on the front lines of the larger civic engagement and service-learning movements in American higher education. In addition to sharing part of his life story with us in this profile, Ken also tells a highly provocative and instructive practice story about a public work project he and his students helped to organize in New York City with a group of small merchants who were in danger of losing their livelihoods. His practice story is rich with lessons about the perils and promise of community-university partnerships, particularly those that openly take sides in against-the-odds battles. Instead of being "rocket science," he tells us, the work of fighting and winning such battles involves "helping people appreciate the richness of their own experience and knowledge and commitment and passion." Ken left Cornell in 2008 to become director of the Graduate Program in City and Regional Planning at the University of Memphis.

I'm an associate professor in the Department of City and Regional Planning. I have a joint appointment. Half of my time is in a research-teaching, tenure-track faculty position where I'm expected to teach two courses a year in the area of community development, do advising, and secure funding for external research related to collaborative planning. The other half of my appointment is to promote campus-wide public service activities. It's jointly paid for by the College of Human Ecology, the College of Agriculture and Life Sciences, and the College of Architecture, Art, and Planning.

I've been to Cornell several times. In this latest incarnation, I came in 1999 as a sabbatic visitor, as a visiting associate professor from the University of Illinois, in order to work on a book related to a long-term project I had in East St. Louis. In 2000, I was offered a tenured associate professor position in City and Regional Planning. I'm now in my third year of the appointment.

I'm motivated by a deep and profound sense of rage. I grew up in a strong Irish Catholic family that was second-generation American. My grandparents were very involved in the labor movement. My parents were very involved both in the settlement house community and in various civic activities, motivated by a deep sense of the Social Gospel. Growing up in the 1950s and 60s, I had the good fortune of being alive and impressionable at the height of the civil rights movement, the antiwar movement, the student movement, and the feminist movement. Through the New Deal politics of my parents, which was a natural outgrowth of their own sense of ethics and the political activity of an older sister, who was very progressive, I got involved at a young age in volunteering at a settlement house, working in an after-school program in a public housing complex in Patterson. I did this during the summer of the '67 riots, which made an enormous impact on me. I got to work in 1968 for a renegade democratic presidential candidate, Eugene McCarthy, who was the antiwar candidate, against a somewhat popular sitting vice president, Hubert Humphrey. I joined the "Get Clean for Gene" campaign.

I was influenced by my grandparents, who had a very deep sense of justice, having been forced to leave Ireland because of the neocolonial situation there. Coming to the U.S., they were deeply disappointed that the streets were not paved with gold for hardworking immigrant families. Both of them got involved in the labor movement, and then my parents continued that tradition. I think that my siblings and I very much know that, as they say, "The acorn doesn't fall far from the tree." We've all been active in some form of civil rights and social justice work.

My primary goal as an educator is to seek a just society where people have opportunity for all the basic resources needed to thrive as individuals and as part of families. Unfortunately, that's not the situation today in America. It's deeply upsetting and it fills me with rage. The rage comes from the unique opportunity I've had for a middle-class white guy to see the consequences of gross inequality in terms of children who live without, who live in fear, of women trying to raise children in very unsafe neighborhoods, of visiting lots of public schools that don't have the minimum expected resources to send young people on their way, and of volunteering at the New Jersey State Correctional System, at the Yardville Youth Correctional Facility, and Trenton State Prison. They have buildings filled with eight and ten thousand people, mostly of color, many of them illiterate, many of them drug addicted, who spend their entire day outside of the context of any program.

I just think we can do better, and there are countries with much more modest resources that *are* doing better. If you look at the global system in which our nation really dominates, the elites in our country have thousands of times more than what they need to survive. What kind of pain and misery does that inflict upon people in developing countries? The oppression is intense. I don't wish to collaborate in that kind of system.

On the flip side, there are moments where you can bring people together across race and class lines to address factors that are causing inequality, or to address the lack of response to it. You can make something happen that really makes a difference in the lives of people. I've had a chance throughout my whole career to be involved in such efforts. It really is transformative. It gives you a glimpse of what the "City on a Hill" could be like—what life in America and on the planet could be like if we were a bit more responsible to our fellow human beings, if we had keener sense of justice. That keeps me going. I've been blessed.

On my birth certificate, it says "New York, New York." Ever since I was a little boy my father told me how special it was to have that on my birth certificate—that New York was a special place. I lived until I was three in the Bronx. I have no memory of it. My dad's company moved out of New York, as part of the great suburbanization move, to a place called Morristown, New Jersey, which was one of the cradles of the Revolution. It's where George Washington hung out in the winters while his men froze their asses off in Valley Forge. He lived in a twenty-two-room mansion. So we had a little problem with equity right from the beginning, I guess.

I grew up in Morristown, which was an integrated community. We lived in the first residential block next to a public housing complex. My father, because he had been a professional athlete, got tapped to be the Commissioner of Recreation. I remember hearing about his struggles to try to get basic recreational services and youth development services into "The Projects," which was a euphemism for the black ghetto. My father made a lot of effort to do that, and I really admired him for it. As a result, I got a chance to meet neighbors. In my community, it was a violation to go over and hang out in the projects, to go over as a white person to what was called "The Nabe"—the neighborhood house. My sister and brother and I were among a small number of white kids who went there. My father was one of the few board members who spent time there outside of the board meetings, because he was a former New York Knick and was a bit of a local celeb. He did a lot of coaching and fund-raising, and it was a wonderful experience.

My best friend when I was a little kid was an African American kid named Albie. His brother Marcus and I spent a lot of time in their house. I was loved by their mother and I think on some subliminal level I understood that their lives and mine were very different. I went to a much better school than they did. I didn't have to worry about getting recreational services in my neighborhood. They did. They often had the same large casserole meals. We didn't do that in our house. And so I became aware.

I lived most of my youth in Morristown and then Denville, New Jersey. And then I had the great fortune (I didn't think so at the time) of going to a Catholic high school. The religion department of the school was captured by followers of Dan Berrigan. Dan Berrigan was one of the most important antiwar priests. He was an important figure in the social justice movement of the 1960s. He was the Cornell chaplain. He founded the Center for Religion, Ethics, and Social Policy (CRESP) at Cornell, which I'm now on the board of, ironically. He had a big influence on me. Going to high school, I got involved in many volunteer activities, as my sister, who is a little bit older than me, had, because of the effort to live those values of these Jesuit men. They also introduced us to the antiwar movement early on.

I went through the conscientious objector process, refusing to register for the war, with the encouragement of my school, with the discouragement of my own conservative Catholic parish, and with the support of my family. That was a great experience. I also got to be involved a little bit in outreach work to migrant camps around my affluent town, which were busy during the summer, because New Jersey is "the Garden State." In fact, my hometown

101

still hosts several hundred farmworkers every summer who come up as part of the harvest. That was all pretty formative.

I then left there to go to college. I went to a business school for two years—Rider College—on a track scholarship. I was the slowest runner in the history of the NCAA. I won't go into that any further, because it was a painful period in my life. I went there because my dad was unemployed and ill, and that was the only way I could get away to college, really. If it hadn't come along, I would have gone to the community college, and who knows, I would have worked at UPS. Then I was able to transfer from there after two years to UMass-Amherst, which was like dying and going to heaven. UMass had a very good sociology department. One of my advisors was Peter Rossi, one of the most significant figures in twentieth-century American sociology. I minored in African American studies, where I met a bunch of folks who were really influential in my thinking.

I finished up at UMass and decided along the way that I wanted to be a community organizer. I read all of Saul Alinsky's books and then, upon graduation, looked for an organizing job. I found it back in New Jersey, working for a group of labor retirees funded by the Catholic Church called the North Jersey Federation of Senior Citizens. I did that for four years, 1975–78, three of them as the executive director, which may sound like I was brilliant, but I went in as a staff person. Everyone else who was there was a priest, and the executive director got sick. So I was the last man standing.

It was a very remarkable group. The organization was responsible for passing some fourteen laws in the state legislature, largely because of the brilliance of the board, which was dominated by labor retirees who in their early years had actually created the American labor movement in New Jersey. A guy named Gene Zoppo, whose picture hangs on my wall, was president of the organization. He had been an international rep for the United Automobile Workers Union for forty-two years, one of the most militant unions during the Congress of Industrial Organization (CIO) period. Gene had an enormous influence on me. I actually thought I was training him to be a community organizer! I now realize what patience he had in slowly training an arrogant young man how to be effective in dealing with these kinds of people's troubles.

I then went to work for Ralph Nader. I worked in Connecticut for Ralph for three years, 1978–1981, and then I sort of ran out of gas. I had worked for two state-level organizations: the New Jersey Federation, and then the Connecticut Citizen Action Group. I drove a lot, didn't sleep much, smoked a lot of cigars, drank a little bit of beer, and it caught up on me. It was very exciting work. We did some really innovative stuff in terms of energy conservation, antihighway fights, water quality, workers' right to know—it was really exciting. I learned a lot working on that staff. I was the organizing director.

It felt like I needed both better analytical skills and a break, so to make a long story short, I took what was going to be nine months off to get a master of science in urban affairs at Hunter College. I went there because I heard Paul Davidoff speak about advocacy planning and I said, "Gee, this might actually be a profession where I could get paid to do the work I'm doing." I didn't want to change my activity. So I went to New York and quickly found that the planning curriculum was a bit more exciting than the urban affairs curriculum. So I switched majors.

At the end of my second year of study, I was just beginning to get into planning theory and methods and it was over, and I felt that maybe it would be worthwhile to get a Ph.D. I was totally naive. I had no idea what the hell that would mean. I thought if I ever wanted, after my useful life, to teach, perhaps I should acquire a Ph.D. That was my view. And I guess that didn't come through in my applications because I applied to a bunch of Ph.D. programs, and I got accepted. My advisor was from Cornell, and Cornell gave me a very substantial financial aid package. I got accepted, was going to come, and then in the spring before I was going to enter, I got cold feet. Being a working-class kid from the Bronx, I felt, "Gee, was I smart enough? Could I jump high enough? Could I run fast enough for the Ivy League?" So for a moment I thought I would go back to City College of New York and get a Ph.D. in sociology.

My advisor, Don Sullivan, who was a very influential man in my life, called me up on spring break and said, "I've got a hotel room. You get the car, we're going to Ithaca. If after meeting Cornell faculty, you think they're rocket scientists, then you don't have to go. I won't be mad at you. But I think after fifteen minutes, you'll realize that they can't find a bleeding elephant in a snowstorm. Even though they're brilliant men and can teach you a lot, I think you'll be perfectly comfortable." So I came up at spring break, met all the faculty, met the staff, and met a bunch of students, whom I really liked. Barclay Jones made a huge impression on me. He was a different kind of scholar than I'd worked with before. That was interesting to me. I really enjoyed meeting the faculty.

So I came, and did my Ph.D. at Cornell in city and regional planning. Near the end of it, I got married. I was starving, financially, so I took a second T.A. job up in the College of Human Ecology, which turned out to be a marvelous experience. I was a T.A. for the Urban Sociology course in the housing program for a brilliant woman named Ann Schlay, who is now the dean of urban affairs at Temple. I guess I did an okay job, because at the end of it, they asked me if I would want to teach in their New York City urban internship program, called the Field Study Program. Since I didn't have my degree—I was "A.B.D."—it was very nice of them to hire me, given that they had many other Ph.D.s to look at. I taught there for six years. Loved it.

When I finally finished my dissertation after six years of ignoring it, Pierre Clavel, who was my Ph.D. advisor, and others said it was now time to look at getting a planning faculty position. There was an opening at Illinois. Since I had done my dissertation on a very famous Chicago mayor, Harold Washington, I looked like I was an Illinois-able product. They offered me the job. I thought it was at the University of Illinois at Chicago. I would have never have gone to the interview if I had known it was in Champaign-Urbana. But I went and taught there for ten years.

The most significant thing I did while I was at Illinois was to get involved in the East St. Louis Project, which we're not going talk about much. It was interdisciplinary urban research and technical assistance that was focused on community development. It started out with just eleven students in my class in 1990. Last year, the project probably involved three or four hundred students from ten different departments at Illinois. It's produced nearly $40 million in new development in the city's poorest neighborhood. It's among the work that I'm most proud of in my life. It was a collective effort, but I did play an important role, and I'm still connected. I'm going out next month to give the keynote speech for the St. Louis Federal Reserve Bank on local economic development. What's most exciting is not that I'm the speaker, but that it's being held in East St. Louis, in the neighborhood that twelve or thirteen years ago everyone said had no future, but now is the shining example for the Federal Reserve Bank in St. Louis of dramatic revitalization.

So why would you leave a project like that? I had no interest in leaving, but in 1998 and 1999, both my mother and my mother-in-law became ill. We needed to come back to New York, and I was fortunate that Cornell was willing to patch together an appointment for me, this bizarre appointment that I have, which gave me a chance to come back to a university that I really do love, and a department that I'm very proud of, despite its moles. It tries to do things that very few other departments attempt. And it allowed us to be near our mothers during a very difficult time. My mother-in-law has since passed on, and we miss her. So that's the story.

Now I want to tell the story about our Essex Street project. There was a group of ethnic merchants on Essex Street representing some sixteen different nationality groups from the Lower East Side of Manhattan who operated small retail businesses in a publicly owned market that had been created by Mayor Fiorello La Guardia in 1938. Every five years they renewed their lease on the space as a cooperative. In 1980, the City of New York, under then Mayor Koch, informed the merchants that they would not be renewing the lease and that instead they would be opening up the lease for the entire market facility—four buildings on the Lower East Side, in the center of the most dense immigrant community in the country—for national bids. They further told the merchants, "Don't apply because we don't think you have the capacity to manage this resource," even though they had been managing it cooperatively for twenty-five years!

The merchants were stunned. They wanted help putting together a bid so that they could try to compete for the right to manage what they had put their lifeblood into creating and maintaining, some of them for three generations. They asked the then borough president of Manhattan, David Dinkins, for help. The city had a very modest budget. Because Dinkins was viewed as a very likely candidate for mayor, his budget was squeezed further by Koch, so there weren't a lot of resources around. A staff member there was a classmate of mine at Hunter College. He called me up and said, "I understand you have a group of smart Cornell undergraduates in New York City. Would it be possible for them to spend a portion of their time here helping this poor merchant group out, as part of their class work?"

I was a lecturer in the College of Human Ecology, running their urban internship program in New York City, which was called the Field and International Study Program. It brought twenty to thirty students a semester down to New York to work Monday through Thursday in high-powered internships in the public and private sectors—everything from American Express to Merrill Lynch to Gotham Advertising Agency to Koos Van Denakker to Donna Karan. I placed the students in all these places, and then on Fridays we would have a seminar about what they were learning.

The borough president's office was basically suggesting that there could be value in the students learning about the city more intimately if they were involved in a struggle over a critical public resource. They were aware of us because we placed interns in their office that represented many disciplines. They imagined that this project, if done well, would require students with backgrounds in economics, marketing, merchandising, advertising, consumer education, and physical design.

I thought about it, and I decided to take it on. We reduced the amount of time that students were at their placement from four days to three and a half days. We also contracted what was a daylong seminar into a half a day, on Thursdays. Then we told the students that they would be required to do a day-a-week internship, focused on a community-based research project in a low-income community with a nonprofit partner, using action research methods. They didn't know what the hell that meant, except that they were going have one day a week less at Nicole Miller and Donna Karan, and Governor Cuomo's office. They were less than happy about it. But that's how we got started.

So the story is about a community-university partnership involving the poorest, newest immigrants in the city and some of the most privileged men and women in Western civilization. It focused on an effort to see if there was a way to preserve a seventy-year-old public resource—i.e., the public market—at a time when Wall Street was exploding. All of a sudden the land just north of Wall Street was the gold coast, and everyone knew it. There was a grab for public resources, because the private sector knew that private land values were skyrocketing, and they could cut a cheap deal with a city that was probusiness.

The way the story began, as I already mentioned, was with a call I got from my Hunter College classmate, who now had a job as the planning director of the Manhattan borough president's office. He said that they had a request from a group called the Essex Street Merchants Association that represented all the merchants in the market. I was aware of the public market system, which are these small auditorium-like buildings around the city. I remember as a kid my mother used to take me to the Arthur Avenue Market in the Bronx to shop for my grandparents. In these big auditorium-like buildings were these tiny eight- by four-foot stands where ethnic merchants would have goods from the old country, regardless of what your old country was. I was vaguely aware of them, but I had never actually in my adult life been in one of these markets. And I had never heard of the Essex Street Merchants Association. I knew very little about the Lower East Side.

So I called up the Essex Street Merchants Association. The president was a guy named Alan Ruhalter, who was the big butcher, the anchor vendor in the market. He was a third-generation vendor. His grandfather had been one of the men who sold ethnic food products on Delancey Street in the Lower East Side. As a Jew, at that time, most of the jobs were in manufacturing. You had to work six days a week, which meant Saturday, so you couldn't observe your religion. So many of these folks started selling small items, rags (they're called *schmattes*), and then food products. Alan's grandfather had been one of these men.

Alan was desperate to talk to me, which made me nervous. It sounded like they really needed help. This sounded like a very complex issue. I wasn't quite sure the students and I could figure it out in a semester and be all that helpful. I didn't want to waste a lot of their time meeting with us if we couldn't be of assistance. The first rule of planning consultants is, "Do no harm by wasting your clients' time, money, and energy."

So anyway, I went down and met with Mr. Ruhalter. I met him at his stand. He was behind what looked like to be half of a cow. He had blood all over his apron. Soon as I walked in the door, he said, "Professor Reardon, I presume?" Then he came over and he gave me a big bear hug. And I now had shit all over my pants and my loafers, and my lovely buttondown shirt was now full of chicken shit and guts. He attempted to wipe it off, and I went out to lunch with him and his son, who was the fourth-generation merchant.

Over lunch, they described to me how their master lease for the market had not been renewed ten years ago, and how they had been operating on a year-to-year lease. The city had stopped making improvements in the building and maintaining it, which was part of their obligation under the lease. The building was really run down. It looked like four turn-of-the-century high school gyms that hadn't seen a coat of paint in forty years, connected to each other like a series of freight cars lined up along Essex Street. He took me on a tour before we went to lunch, and it was, to be blunt, a hellhole.

If you could look beyond the peeling paint, the broken windows, the lack of sanitation, and the rodents, there were some beautiful, beautiful stands. There were Indian women selling hand-dyed materials from India, very reasonably priced. There was the world's largest wholesale candy store, Julius the Candy King. The women behind the stand had three-foot-high hair. They had piles of all the kids' candies that I grew up with in the city—Jujubes and things like that. There was a phenomenal fish stand, six counters long, with beautiful fish, lot of species I had never seen before. The fish man explained to me that because they had such a diverse ethnic market, they had to get very specialized items. They went everyday down to the fish market at 2:00 am just to get the stuff that his low-income ethnic customers needed. So there were remarkable businesses that were managing to hold on in a building that was falling apart, in an environment that most people would say you couldn't do business in. That intrigued me. It really caught my attention.

When I went to lunch, I heard the story about how as long as the Lower East Side had low property values and there wasn't much demand for the land, the city was willing to allow the merchants to stay. But now that the property values were heating up, they no longer were committed to this form of public entrepreneurship. One of the most exciting things was the long list of businesses that had started in the protected, almost incubator-like space of the public market, which after three to five years were successful enough that they moved off onto Delancey Street, Essex Street, and Houston Street. They included some very, very famous New York City businesses—landmark businesses like Ratner's Dairy Bar, which had started as a stand in the Essex Street Market.

So obviously I was smitten by the story, and by Alan Ruhalter, who I got the sense didn't need to be coming in from Long Island every day at four o'clock in the morning to run this business. It was an obligation to honor a family tradition, and his son was there. I could tell that he really loved this place and loved the neighborhood. While we had lunch, everyone was banging on the window, saying hello to Alan—black folks, Latino folks, old people, young people. He's like the mayor of Essex Street. So I thought the project would be interesting. That's how we got started.

We began our work by collecting the basic information: the story, the history of the market. I went to the New York Historical Society, and they gave me some materials that they had on the evolution of the market. They told me that the Smithsonian had a whole division of ethnographers, two or three of whom had been very interested in public markets going back to the turn of the century, and they had tapes of the calls that public market merchants used. You know, there might be six fish men. So how do you get the customer to stop at your stand and not another? You use the popular tunes of the day—jazz tunes, and later on, bebop and hip-hop tunes to get people to come to your stand.

To introduce my students, I had Alan and his son come to my class. I had taken slides of the market. They told the history. It's pretty interesting that many of the students' grandparents or great-grandparents came through Lower East Side as new immigrants, so there was some real interest in the topic. Then I showed them the slides of the markets and you could hear oohs and ahhs and gasps. "Jesus, close it!"—you could just feel that was their sense. And then I invited these guys from the Smithsonian ethnography division to come and share some of their tapes. They played tapes of these calls and talked about the social and cultural importance of the market. The students were mildly curious. I wouldn't say they were hooked.

The next week, we organized a trip down to the market. There were sixty-five businesses operating, so we thought a good thing to do was to inventory the number of businesses—the names and what they were selling—and then ask a couple questions: When did you come? What's the best thing about being at the market? What's the biggest challenge? If you could say one thing to Mayor Koch, what would it be? We thought this was great. It *seemed* great. Except one little problem was, we discovered that in forty of the sixty-five businesses, the proprietors didn't speak English. We thought this was a big economic development problem, that they couldn't speak to their customers. And then Alan helped us appreciate that in the Lower East Side, it was more important to speak the language of the growing number of immigrant residents. The Lower East Side has never been a more popular immigrant destination than it is now. It has the highest percentage of immigrants since the end of the nineteenth century. The diversity of languages meant that they were really able to serve the increasingly diverse new immigrant population. The folks that had a problem weren't the merchants: they were the students, who were monolingual. So we realized that if we were going to do anything in the market, we had to get partners to do the translation and to help us get the story of the people.

We talked to Alan and we decided that we needed to hook up with a local church coalition, which represented different foreign language churches. Instead of having the normal geographic organization, these were churches that spoke the language of each of these immigrant groups that were in the Lower East Side. There was an association of these immigrant churches called the Inter-Faith Community Coalition (ICC). It was an organizing project. We invited the pastors from the churches to the market one night for a late-night meal, and they agreed to help us, to be the intermediaries between our single language-only students, the multilanguage merchants, and their customers.

With translation assistance from the churches, we were then able to begin to think about what kind of data we would need to collect in order to prepare what would have to be a very compelling proposal. It would have to show how this market could meet its expenses, provide a modest return to the city, and serve, in a better way, the dramatically changing ethnic population of the area. So we went back with the representatives of the church coalition. We surveyed the merchants with a short questionnaire. We found out that many of them had been there a long time. We found out how many full-time jobs the merchants provided. There were 300 full-time jobs. Many of them were well above living wage, many of them with benefits that one would have never imagined, looking at this filthy dirty market space. In completing these interviews, we realized what an important resource this institution was to the community. Even if the city got a little more rent from someone else, the impact of displacing 300 heads of households, who were making eight to ten bucks in a neighborhood where the average wage in the garment industry was five or six, would be devastating. So we really got to appreciate what a critical role the market people played in the economy of the Lower East Side.

The other thing we found out, which we realized was probably even more compelling, was that these small businesses were paying modest rents. They were making a lot of money because they had very low overheads. They had a low-cost business infrastructure. With just a modest amount of sales they could do well. We realized that one of the secrets of the public market was that it was a place that you could operate a business cheaply. And then in interviewing some of the new merchants, we realized that they were folks who weren't in the United States more than a year. They were able, in this very supportive immigrant culture of the market, to find people who knew what kind of goods would sell well, who could hook them up with a wholesaler and help them with their bookkeeping. A lot of that was provided by the Merchant's Association. In essence, it functioned as a small business incubator. The city was trying to create incubators in other parts of the city, and here they had one functioning, and they were ready to toss it out the window because they didn't appreciate how remarkably well it ran. So that was our first set of "Ahas!" and we got it by interviewing the merchants.

The next thing was that we realized that some of the businesses were barely holding on. They weren't really capturing this teeming immigrant population. So we decided to do a price-quality survey. We designed a survey instrument and set up at the market and at the competing supermarkets, to find out why some immigrant families went to supermarkets instead of Essex Street, or vice versa. As we got into this, one of our students, who was placed at Merrill Lynch's retail group, got interested in helping us design the instrument. We took the whole class down to the Merrill Lynch headquarters in the World Financial Center, into their conference room, their Partners room, which used to be the old Lehman Brothers inner sanctum, the center of capitalism maybe seventy-five years before. Over a sixty-five-dollar salmon lunch, which finished up with cigars from Cuba, which our women students relished taking and lighting up, we designed the instrument for the Essex Street Market with the guys from Merrill Lynch.

We then went out the next week and tried to use it. It was six pages long. Trying to get people to stop for six pages of questions, no matter how energetic you were, wasn't easy. The next week, we were supposed to come back to Merrill Lynch. They were ready to crunch all the numbers. They had all the software ready. They had their whole staff. We came back and they said, "Where are the surveys? We'll show you how to enter them and we'll get the analysis done by five o'clock." We said, "We didn't get any of them." And then they starting really trashing Cornell, saying that if only they were at Wharton, where they went, they would have figured out how to do this. One of our students told them that they were full of shit and that they should come down and try to use their instrument, that the instrument was crappy. They laughed and said, "Fine."

So at five o'clock that night, five of them showed up in a stretch limousine, asked me to hold their jackets, took their Merrill Lynch baseball caps and put them on backwards. They were going to use the instruments in order to show us how real researchers did fieldwork. After fifteen minutes, they realized that their instrument did suck. We then had a big laugh over it. The next week, we redesigned the instrument to be very short, very concise. We then got three hundred surveys back in a couple of days, and analyzed them.

Interestingly, we were able to tell the merchants that what they thought were their most positive attributes—cheap food, flexible hours—were not the attributes that residents most valued about their market. What residents most valued was the fact that they could get culturally appropriate foods at a fair price—not a cheap price—and that they could also get knowledgeable information about how to prepare these materials if they were younger immigrant families. They could also learn about the cultural ways of other groups. The market was much more viewed as a cultural reproduction institution than a cheap food store. That really had an impact on what the merchants came to believe about what was special about the place. They saw that moving away from ethnic traditional food products into more mainstream American processed food would kill the market, that what was special about it was its rich cultural traditions. This was pretty interesting.

Then the merchants began asking us, "Well, where are there public markets like ours that were suffering but turned around?" We did a quick set of phone calls to people who were involved in public markets, farmers markets, and green markets, and we found out that Washington, D.C., and Baltimore were actually using healthy public markets that they had invested in as anchor institutions in working-class neighborhoods. So we got on a bus, the students and the merchants, and we went down to Washington, D.C., to the Sixth Avenue Market, which is right behind the Capitol. We interviewed the merchants, and a dramatic role reversal took place, because the merchants understood how to do business in these vendor market environments. They were the ones who knew what questions to ask. They were the ones who knew how to probe and get the definition of what the D.C. and Baltimore merchants meant by practice X or Y. It was really wonderful to see working class people who were being viewed initially by our students as the recipient of expert knowledge begin to realize that they had a lot to learn about this environment from the very people they were hoping to help. We also interviewed merchants at six public markets in Baltimore.

When we came back, we closed the Essex Street Market for a day, the only time it's ever been closed since 1939, and we invited all the merchants to come to see the basic data we had collected on their market, to identify the problems that had been addressed by the merchants that inhibited good business. Then we showed them slides of what other public markets looked like. And the whole room filled up with noise as people yelled, "We could do that!" "Yeah! Yeah! Yeah! I've been telling the city for years!" "That's exactly what we should be doing!"

The question now was, how do we share this knowledge about the public market with the city before we submit our proposal for the RFP (request for proposal)? It was clear that the city was just looking at this as, "Who is going to give us the most rent?" Period. They needed to understand that there were many other values that were part of this deal, that it was not just an economic project, but a socioeconomic and cultural institution. They would miss the real value of the market if they failed to take in a broader perspective.

So we tried to get Mario Cuomo, who was running for office, to come to the market. At that time, he was the most popular Democratic politician in the United States. Everyone thought he was a shoe-in to become the next president. As a result, his schedule was a little busy. But we were persistent. Finally we got a wonderful woman who didn't quite know what she was getting into, from the Queens office, which was Mario's home borough. She was the local constituent respondent for the governor's office. She answered the phone. She had no power or standing. We got her to say that she was going to come to the market, and we used the fact that she was coming to say that the governor's office was going to be there, which led some people to jump wildly to the conclusion that the governor himself was going to be there. It was pretty remarkable. As soon as we had, quote-unquote, "Mario Cuomo" coming, every state and local neighborhood politician called up the Essex Street Merchants office, asking if they could come in on the motorcade from Kennedy Airport with the governor.

Twenty-seven elected officials showed up for the public information hearing, which my students and the merchants organized in the middle of the Essex Street Market. We did it on what we claimed was the sixtieth birthday of the market. It actually wasn't quite the sixtieth birthday. We gave a very organized presentation of what the market could look like. Meanwhile, we hooked up with Pratt Institute graduate program in planning, and the Pratt students helped us quantify the cost for renovation and develop some renderings that would show what a dramatic improvement in the market would look like. At this public officials' tour, the students from Cornell and the Pratt students presented, and the merchants got up and said this is what they wanted. We then pressed every elected official there—we had a scoreboard, "YES or NO: Do you support the Essex Street Merchants?" Channel 4 was there, NBC TV, the *New York Times* was there, and the *Boston Globe* was there, because an AP story had gone out on it ahead of time. And in front of the lights and in front of the reporters, a very large number of politicians said that they were with the merchants.

We then finished the proposal. We submitted it to the city's Department of Ports and Terminals on behalf of the merchants. We had a big party. Three days after the party, I was notified by Al Ruhalter that the city had given away the market to a private developer. The developer was somebody who had been unsuccessful three other times in doing commercial development in more favorable locations, so we didn't think he had the know-how to make the market work. But he was a well-connected New York developer.

So what did we do? We went to a law firm, called Strock, Strock & Lavan, who I had heard did some pro bono work on commercial leases, to see if we could challenge the process that the city used. Did they skip over any steps? Did they mess up with citizen participation, as required by the city charter? Strock, Strock & Lavan was a very big, highly regarded New York law firm. They were Donald Trump's law firm. Remarkably, they took our case. So we went down with the merchants and showed up at the law firm at Eight Hanover Square. They held twelve of sixteen stories in the building. They had five hundred lawyers. We showed up in the partners' room, filled with orchids, and we were introduced by Mr. Strock to the staff who would work on this. We met two attorneys, and they asked us to tell the story. We told them.

They said, "Well, we need to challenge this decision." And Mr. Strock got on the phone to Mayor Koch.

By this time, we were in the middle of the primary season, and this issue was featured in the first *New York Times* mayoral debate. The first question asked from the floor was, "What is your position on the Cornell University study of the Essex Street Market?" They had articles in the *New York Times, Newsday, El Diario,* and the *Boston Globe,* which was great fun. To make a long story short, Strock, Strock & Lavan was a very well-known entity. Mayor Koch knew them. So Koch gave us a meeting with the commissioner of Ports and Terminals, which managed the market.

Meanwhile, Strock, Strock & Lavan, with our help, documented how thoroughly the city had failed to meet the requirements for citizen participation and public review for this project, as required by the charter. And the lawyers and the press created enough hoopla about this issue that I think they decided beforehand that they needed to cut a deal. So a couple weeks later, we were invited to meet with the commissioner of Ports and Terminals on the Essex Street project. We thought that was encouraging, because why would they give us a meeting unless they were going to give us something? So we expected crumbs from the table, that they would give us five years, which would be the time the developer would need to do the architectural drawings and the land review. They would give us five years of continued use of the space, maybe even rent-free, but the sixth year we'd be out on our asses. That's what we expected.

We prepared a whole set of demands with the help of Strock, Strock & Lavan, and we prepared the merchants to very pointedly press, "Yes or No? Will you or will you not?!" We had one woman, Alan Ruhalter's wife Gloria, whose only job was to press the commissioner: "Yes, no, or maybe?" We called her "The Pinner." The demands went from wildly optimistic, ridiculous demands down to what we really wanted. And somewhere in the middle we hoped to settle. We didn't really expect very much. We really had Alan's wife all pumped up to press the commissioner. She was a tough small-businesswoman herself, and she was ready to give the commissioner hell. People were very angry at having been jerked around and see their market that had been so critical to the uplift of so many immigrant families be turned over to a private developer for another boutique shop.

Well, we went in there, and we presented our case, and then the first issue was, "Will you or will you not give us a ten-year lease at our current rent?" To our utter shock, the commissioner said yes. But Gloria, having been trained to press the commissioner, said, "*Yes or no? Will you or will you not?*" She really pinned his ears back, and he was sort of surprised because he had said yes to our most outrageous demand. We went down the list and she kept doing this. And it got more and more uncomfortable. He would say, "Yes, I'll do it. I agree to your demand." He would try to explain it, and she, because we had only practiced boxing his ears in, would say, "*YES OR NO!? YES OR NO!?*"

Finally, halfway through the meeting—and the fellows from Strock, Strock & Lavan were really quite enjoying this, it was really sort of a Fellini movie—I suggested that we take a break, that we needed to caucus. I asked them if they would they please leave the room, which was fun because it was their conference room. We sat there, and as soon as they all left, Alan said to his wife, "Gloria, what the hell are you doing?" We all laughed. She said,

"Well you told me this was my job. I'm taking this very seriously." And we said, "But the poor guy is falling over dead." She says, "Well, I didn't know what else to do. We didn't practice what happens if he says yes!" So we all laughed like hell. We spent about twenty minutes ordering Chinese food for back at the market, so when we got done with the meeting we could have lunch, basically keeping the commissioner waiting in the hallway. Because we had waited for so many months for their response, we thought that was appropriate. Plus we were having a good time. We wanted to savor the moment.

They came back in, we basically cut a deal, and what happened was remarkable. The city took two of the four buildings and gave them to the private developer. On the one hand, that was really a terrible setback. But the truth was, only half of the buildings were occupied by merchants. What we got out of it was a commitment from the city for two of the four buildings for merchant use and five million dollars in renovation—immediately—and a ten-year lease for the merchants at current rent levels, with like a 3 to 5 percent escalator, which was unbelievable. They basically agreed to all the demands that we had.

For a year or so after this, not much happened. As it turned out, the private developer went bankrupt on another project. So that part of the project never moved forward. But the merchants worked through the process with a year of our assistance, fall and spring semester. The merchants also worked with Pratt and some other people, coming up with really attractive designs, many of them reflective of what we had learned about what worked in Baltimore and Washington, and also Pike Place Market in Seattle. And the story is that the market did receive a dramatic upgrade—five million dollars of improvements. Today, it's drop-dead beautiful, and it's a thriving market that now has more ethnic merchants in it than it's had since 1945.

So we participated in a joint effort that saved fifty small businesses serving the city's poorest residents. We helped save an institution that somehow managed to generate three hundred better-than-living-wage jobs. We managed to save one of the few democratic public spaces in New York, where immigrants from a variety of cultures, often coming from very repressive environments, where they weren't allowed to even think about the culture of others—that was viewed as a disloyalty—could learn about the remarkable diversity of America in this space, and learn about the ways and means and language and cultural symbols and resources of other peoples. We helped create a coalition of merchants with their local religious communities that hadn't existed before. And in the end, we also brought in a local development corporation, which was run by radical young Puerto Ricans, called Pueblo Nuevo. Never would these people have gotten to know each other.

We also brought together two universities, Cornell and Pratt, which even though they had strong community-planning histories, hadn't done a lot of work together. That was a really good thing. They had some technical skills that we didn't have. We had some other skills that I don't think they had. And that was quite nice. I think we demonstrated the possibility for respectful community-university collaboration on a critical economic development issue.

The last thing is that I think it was transformative for many of the students. They realized through the project that doing this kind of research for folks like the ethnic merchants, who were being squeezed out of our economy, and in some ways our political life, that working with them was an enormously powerful experience. One of the students early on said,

"No one works harder than these people. In my education I've been told that if you work hard, you'll get ahead. We have a liberal mayor, a liberal governor, a president who says he cares about entrepreneurship and business and the American dream. These folks really embody that. They came to America to participate in that, and they're getting screwed." I think the students felt real satisfaction in trying to help extend to these ethnic merchants the kind of opportunities they and their family had.

The other thing that was remarkable was that many of the students' families had histories in the Lower East Side. And the project gave a way for them to connect with their grandparents and great-uncles, and learn the story of their own family's journey. For example, a young woman, her name is Alena Tepper, who ended up working as a buyer at Macy's, her father met her mother while working in a rag business across the street from Essex Street. Her grandparents actually bought a stand in Essex Street back in the thirties, and yet that had never been taught to her, this period in her own neighborhood's history. The family's effort to move ahead had largely left behind these really powerful stories of how they made it in America. The fact that Alena worked on this project gave her a chance to talk to her grandmother about difficult and challenging issues that helped her better understand the making of America in a way that I think most students can't appreciate.

When they came back to campus, the students were so excited about the project. They wanted to show other faculty and fellow students how meaningful this part of their experience was. So they organized a presentation of their project on campus. In the College of Human Ecology, about thirty faculty came, and forty or fifty students came. They were packed in the faculty lounge. The students were in the middle of the presentation, and Dean Jerry Zigler, who is now retired but still teaches, was leaning over so far in his chair during the presentation listening to every word, that about halfway through, his knee gave out and he fell, almost on the floor, disrupting things a bit. Anyway, afterwards I went over to him and said, "You seemed really riveted by this." And then he told me the story of his own family. His grandfather had sold potatoes on Delancey Street, and as Jew, that was the best job he could get. He said that he knew about the importance of these kinds of markets, and that as the dean of this college, he was never prouder that his students were making a contribution by trying to guarantee that this pathway to a better life wasn't closed.

This project went on from '84 to '86. We made a videotape of it that keeps it alive in some way. It's used a lot by other schools looking at service learning. Obviously this was a meaningful experience for me as a teacher.

Several years ago, I had the chance to go back to the Lower East Side to attend a national planning conference in Brooklyn. They asked me if I would do a tour of the Lower East Side. Thirty people signed up, we went on the train, we got off, we went to Ratner's, we went to Gus's Pickles, we went to the Henry Street Settlement House, we went to the Jewish Daily Forward Building. Everything was going great. We're a block away from Essex Street and my wife Kathleen, who was with me at the conference, said, "You know, if anyone sees you in this neighborhood and you don't go to the market, they're going to be really mad at you." I had been in Illinois for more than ten years by then, and it just didn't occur to me that I should go. So anyway, I took the whole group one block out of the way to the Essex Street Market. And of course, it looked drop-dead beautiful, and my heart just raced. I went in, and there's Alan Ruhalter, coming out of a refrigerator with a half a side of beef, just like I saw him when we first met. He threw the goddamn cow on the ground, came over, and gave me a huge bear hug, and asked me if I got tenure yet. I said yes. He said, "Where are the kiddies?" And I said, "Well, I have some people outside." He said, "Bring them in!" And I brought the whole thirty-person walking tour in. And then Alan Ruhalter regaled them for thirty minutes about how the merchants working with these local churches and this radical group of Puerto Ricans, with the help of the students from Cornell, had saved their market, and how grateful they were. Then he took us on a tour of the market, and every merchant that I knew came and showed me all their goods. It was one of those days where I thought it was a pretty good thing to be a teacher of planning.

I don't think anything we did in the Essex Street project was rocket science. There were some basic problem-solving and research techniques that many of us in our own lives use, but not in an intentional and organized fashion. I guess one of the qualities I have is to remind people that they know more than they think they know, particularly poor and working-class people, who are told every day that they're where they are in their station in life because they don't have something that someone else has, and that's why they're poor, and that's why they're working class. So I think the first lesson from this story is about the importance of helping people appreciate the richness of their own experience and knowledge and commitment and passion, and to value that. I think that's really done well in the participatory action research field. So I think bringing to people that appreciation and giving them some sense of the techniques that are available that extend their own thoughtful commonsense approach to problem solving, I think that's one lesson.

The second lesson has to do with the biggest obstacle we have in changing the socioeconomic landscape: the notion that trend is destiny, that there's nothing you can do. I think part of what I do well is to tell the stories from other places where I've been privileged to work, in order to remind people that many of these things that they take for granted as immutable and unchangeable structures are only the inventions of mere men and women, and that thoughtful men and women can change them. So I think it's bringing out those stories through storytelling. I think that has a value.

Think about when people have been moved into action. Often it's been because of the wisdom of the community or culture that has been shared with them in the form of a story. Being able to share the experiences of other successful communities that have turned things around, through sort of storytelling, I think that's an important thing. In the Irish tradition, there is the *seanchaí*, who is the keeper of village wisdom, who is the storyteller, and it's often tales of heroic accomplishments by very common people. It seems to me that that's probably helped the Irish survive through very tough times. The African American community has the same kind of thing—the role of the elder storyteller.

The third lesson is about organizing principles. I know something about an undervalued profession called community organizing, which is a rigorous approach to addressing issues of power and inequality. And I've had training and experience participatory action research (PAR), which is, in many ways, the people's science. Other than that, nothing that I think I've learned is that unique. And I think all these things are teachable and learnable by anyone who has a heartbeat left. It isn't rocket science.

When I left my work as a community organizer and came to the university, I got very interested and excited about learning something new, which was basic research methods. I had the good fortune of meeting Bill Whyte and Davydd Greenwood. I realized that this alternative approach to research—participatory research—really fit my instincts and skills. I got so excited about learning about that. When I left the university, I thought that was all you really needed to know how to do. So when we started working on the Essex Street Market, I really thought that participatory research was going to be able to carry the day. So we involved people in defining the problem, collecting the data, etc., and we did a hellaciously good report that has been copied and mimeographed and sent all over the country to places where people are struggling to keep public market places alive. More and more of that's happening, which is exciting. We played a small role in helping to ignite that prairie storm. But we lost—at least at first we did. We had a great report and the mayor turned around and gave the market to a guy who should have been locked up, let alone given a public trust of a market founded by Fiorello La Guardia. I mean, talk about a horrible reality.

I came to realize that I was so eager to learn the new pedagogy, the new problem-solving approach of PAR, that I left behind at the door something of value that I had learned previously, and that was the need to address issues of power through community organizing. So really it was Essex Street that, for me, put together the idea that PAR was necessary but insufficient to address most of the most critical human needs of poor people who lacked power. You had to modify PAR to not only use it as a data collection and analysis technique, but also to use the PAR process as a way to invite people who had fallen out of contact and relationship with institutions representing their class interests to reconnect, so that you'd not only be building a good plan or a good proposal, an innovative design, but you'd be building the political power necessary to counter the very strong influence in New York City of major developers, real estate interests, their attorneys, and their planning consultants.

I put those two things together in what I began to call—to distinguish it from the advocacy model of planning—the *empowerment* approach to planning. It isn't doing *for*, it's doing *with*. It's focused on building the capacity of grassroots organizations to effect change. I think that was a useful contribution to the field. It hadn't been spoken about very much. It had gotten hinted at in some work that John Freedman, the Berkeley planning theorist, had done, in a book called *Planning and the Public Domain*. He had hinted at this, but he didn't specify it enough to be able to know it if you saw it.

The other two people who had done some work (I found out later) in a similar vein of putting these two things together, were Marie Kennedy at UMass-Boston, who called it "transformational" planning, and Lisa Peattie from MIT, who had been one of the leading advocates of advocacy planning. After twenty years, she said, "This clearly ain't working, ain't doing it for people—participatory planning and proposal making without dealing with power." So she called for something that she called "insurgent" planning. So I think the three of us—you know, everyone likes to use their own term so they get credit for being the inventor. But I think it's really the same thing.

Later on, when my practice evolved in East St. Louis, I basically thought I had gotten these two things working together in an integrated approach to planning in poor neighborhoods. It really seemed to be working. In East St. Louis, we began to generate quite a lot of

115

investment in very poor neighborhoods using this method. That's when the leaders called us down to this church basement and said, "Your approach to this work is unconsciously racist, classist, and sexist. By not taking into consideration the historical exclusion of poor people from the training needed to really be full-fledged partners, you're reproducing highly uneven partnerships, even if those partnerships are improving conditions in low-income communities. The day you move away, we lose the capacity."

That's where, in my thought, the third leg of the stool—popular education, based upon the work of Paulo Freire and Miles Horton and bell hooks (who's not really recognized as being in that genre, but I think she really is)—entered my thinking. And that's my current thought, that in very, very poor rural and urban areas, you have to have an approach that hits on all three of those cylinders, because of the unique problems in those areas. And community education—you know, there's a high-end theory, John Dewey and others, and then there's people who do how-to, nuts-and-bolts books. But there's very little work that's been done in this intermediate area, connecting theory to specific pedagogies that would then allow you to thoughtfully choose particular practices in a community to effect change.

I think this idea of empowerment planning, which integrates PAR, community organizing and popular education, is a contribution to building the middle-range theory which is, I think, critical. And it's ongoing. I think, if anything, that's where my contribution has been. But like many practitioner-oriented scholars, I, too, am guilty of not reserving enough time to write about the work, so that much of what I just explained doesn't really appear in a very articulate and accessible way in anything I've written. The most commonly cited article that I have on empowerment planning is an unpublished mimeographed paper that was accepted for publication, but I haven't had time to go back and rewrite it. I think that's a problem. And the work that we did for ten years in East St. Louis—I had the book three-quarters of the way done for three years. It would take three hours a day for six months to finish it.

My lack of discipline has meant that those materials aren't available. And that's bad, in two ways. One, the experience of another community or communities that have struggled and done some things isn't accessible to other communities. But the flip side is, by not writing it down, these ideas haven't been criticized and reviewed and analyzed and deconstructed by people whose experience is much broader, who are smarter, who have read different literature. So these ideas are not crystallizing as well as they might, which means that we continue to be plagued by inadequate theory and canon in the area of community education, because we're not producing enough of the literature in a timely manner for it to be reviewed.

Many of us are spending an enormous amount of time writing political tomes to try to maintain our steepled place in the academy to continue to do this work. The most important thing to me right now is finishing the East St. Louis book, which is the most detailed articulation of empowerment planning. I'm feeling a little pressure to get it done, because a couple of the folks whose work as organic intellectuals, as Gramsci calls them, who are really the civic leaders, people like Dorothy Cotton and others, people who have always been at the forefront of change, they're getting quite elderly. The main person in the East St. Louis work, her health isn't well. It's not good. And I would just be very saddened if they don't have a chance to see their work recognized in the form of a book. So that's the most important thing. And secondly, we've now mumbled our way through ten or fifteen neighborhood planning projects from around the country, and there's an enormous upswing of interest in this, and there isn't a decent book that explains even *bad* practice in this area. So I think doing that's pretty important.

I also think, in the midst of this enormous upswing of interest in community-university partnerships, that most of the leadership is pretty weak. The current generation of community-university partnerships are efforts that, under the guise of empowerment and redevelopment and community renewal, are largely the university using interest in declining areas to reaffirm its political position by appearing to be responsive. But the day that the COPC (Community Outreach Partnerships Centers) money ends, many universities often walk away from the commitment to low-income communities. There are exceptions. There are places that are really using this movement to transform their practices. But there's not a place to go, really, to exchange ideas with others who are trying to do the same thing.

There's not a lot of documentation of these truly transformative community-university development partnerships. They're articulated or at least described in brief in Dick Schramm and Nancy Nye's book, *Building Higher Education-Community Development Corporation Partnerships*, which I think is a really nifty tome. And there may be an opportunity to create a national institute to get young scholars and their community partners and older scholars who are interested in rethinking their work to come together and be trained in this new method, to carry out evaluation studies to see under what conditions these methods are effective, and to identify new emergent forms of empowerment-oriented practice, which right now are hard to find.

If you go on the Campus Compact web page, many of the most exciting projects that I'm aware of aren't even listed. They're not at big schools, the places where outreach has really resulted in transforming the university. It's sometimes a bit threatening to middle–of-the-road university presidents who want to see this be an extra jewel in their crown, in terms of their work, but who don't really see how community outreach can transform the core nature of what it means to be a well-educated man or woman from a liberal arts tradition.

It's happening in some institutions that have taken this really seriously, who understand that the university is in as much of a desperate need of salvation from mediocrity by engaging their community in real-life problems as the community may be in need of the support of the university. Both are in trouble. They're members of a family in which its not just one member of the family who has suffered. There really is very little understanding that the current wave of community-university partnerships is as much a resurrection project for the university—a renewal project for universities' hearts, minds, souls, pedagogy, and intellectual life—as it is just helping the poor. You have an image of men and women with white gloves coming down from the hill at Cornell, lifting up the poor ethnic and minority neighborhoods. But it's the leaders of those communities who are doing the heroic work, doing really interesting data collection, analysis, and problem solving on the cutting edge. Those folks have much to offer students in our Department of City and Regional Planning, in Education, etc. That's not often acknowledged, and yet I think it needs to be. So I'd like a center that celebrates such work. That would be cool. I don't know if any foundation in America is ready to fund it. But hope springs eternal. I'd like to think so.

I've been very influenced by the rural poet, essayist, thinker, and philosopher Wendell Berry. I'm almost fifty, and I've been doing this work for more than thirty years. One of the things Berry talks about as one of the hallmarks of American higher education is this notion that you go to the university, you're transformed, and you're elevated above your humble origins. There's a value added that really makes you a new man or woman in a cosmopolitan, global world. You're now a leading, cutting-edge thinker, etc. There's this whole notion of graduating to a different world, a different plane. And Wendell Berry suggests that leaders who have gone through this process have very little loyalty to place or community, and that they've done horrific things, and that there is something wrong with the moral and ethical formation process at the university such that people could sit in Wall Street or they could sit in the Federal Reserve Bank of St. Louis and make decisions without imagining the consequences for communities, including communities that nurtured them and raised them up.

So Wendell Berry's been calling, particularly among land-grant universities, for a program that he calls "Homecoming." Graduation should really be a moment at which you come to appreciate the richness of your place of origin, and feel an obligation through your own educational journey to see how and in what way you could strengthen those communities. A larger and larger share of our students would go back, if not to the community that they came from, to a community that's similar, in which they may be uniquely situated to provide civic leadership, because they come from that experience.

As I get to fifty, I'm feeling the tug to go back to New York City, which is the area that I come from. It's a place that I really love, and I think that in some small way I may be better prepared to contribute. And it's also maybe modeling for my own students a sense of responsibility to the community that made it possible for me to have the really remarkably privileged and blessed and special life that I've been able to have. So I'm feeling little tugs. Either the community that my grandparents and parents came from, the Bronx, or the community that I married into, Greenpoint-Williamsburg in Brooklyn, where I'm currently working with a couple of our students on some rezoning issues.

It feels really terrific to be among my extended family, and my wife's extended family, using the skills that, in some ways, I only had a chance to develop because a community like that took care of me. They sent me food boxes when I was in college, rooted for me when I came home, encouraged me in activities that they couldn't even imagine, having been denied a chance to even finish high school. They couldn't imagine what a university education would be like, but yet they had faith that it would be a good thing. There's something really good about being back in a place that I have a long history doing work in that I think is honorable. So I'm looking at that.

The Making Is the Learning

A Profile of Paula Horrigan

Associate Professor, Department of Landscape Architecture, Cornell University

Interview Conducted by Leah Mayor, November 1, 2002

The practice story Paula Horrigan tells in this profile shows us how she uses service learning and action research in ways that engage neighborhood residents and students in participatory planning processes. As her practice story reveals, this can require faculty, students, and community members to undergo fundamental reconfigurations in attitudes, identities, and practices, each of which can generate significant resistance. Emphasizing an epistemological insight, "The making is the learning," she helps us see that collaborative public work can be a means not only of creating things of public value but also of knowing and learning.

I come from art, and I've always been an artist. I come out of the conceptual era of art of the seventies, and thinking about challenging systems like the museum, which is very much a privileged place of engagement. I'm interested in earth art and art for social change, a lot of those motivations—that you can create things that are meaningful and expressive but you can also create them in ways that construct new dynamics between people and places. So that just translates right away into landscape architecture. A lot of the stuff that I try to teach is, "Yes, we can create meaningful and wonderful places, but that is not at the expense of the dynamics of interacting with community." I feel like our discipline has fostered a separation of people and places. Changing that is part of what motivates me.

I love the individual practice of art. I find that I've done a lot more of that kind of teaching, where art is a personal exploration. That's very important, too—a personal passion—because that's really what turns you on. I find that the more I get into this, or the older or more mature I get, that teaching doesn't have a lot of significance unless it is tied to place and people. It's not just throwing the design out into the world. The gift of the design has to come out of a set of relationships that are created with the design and through the design process. The process very much dictates or propels the product. They are integrated. If the process is critical and reflective and thoughtful and dynamic, the theory is that the product will be that way. If the process is static and individual and separated from community, and the studio is this isolated place and the academy is this hallowed place, then chances are the design is going to be as precious as the methods that made it. That's the theory, I guess.

A lot of my engagement at the University in terms of my community work involves learning. The way I teach is with a service-learning pedagogy. I think, at heart, I am somewhat subversive. I am interested in challenging the institution of learning, and also challenging institutions of design.

My field comes out of a modernist approach, with a lot of bias towards form and aesthetics. Beyond form and aesthetics are the dynamics of design as a power construct having to do with human relationships: relationships between people and each other, people and places, and people and their environments. I'm interested in challenging modes of thinking that have separated people from places. I think design has to have a lot of accountability around that, because it's really been focused more around aesthetics and form than on the dynamics of people-place interactions.

Education in the design field has focused on the cultivation of the designer as the elite individual: Designer with a capital *D*, or Artist with a capital *A*. It has fostered that through the way it educates people. Part of that is that education has been very much situated here at the academy, and a lot of the learning is in isolation. It's reflective to the extent of individual and personal reflection, but it's not reflective in a more community-situated way. It's like looking at your belly button, I guess; you continue to look at yourself to find the answers as opposed to really looking at the larger citizenry and context.

We have done, in our department, a lot of community work. However, it has been mostly work *on* the community as opposed to work *with* the community. And that's one of my interests. There's a bit of an interest in challenging the status quo. There's an interest in subverting those systems that support that.

My goals are to create wonderful and meaningful places *with* communities, to reinvigorate the relationship between people and their places and empower them through that process. Another goal is to empower my students to recognize that their work has the potential to change the world. They can be leaders in that respect. I want to motivate them at that level so that their work is situated in a meaningful way. I want to connect them at that place where they can embrace the spectrum of power that they can have in helping to motivate the relationships between people and places that are empowering to people and sustaining. I want the education experience to set up an opportunity for them to engage at that level, so that they can see that their work has ethics and values associated with it. When they make a place, it goes out into the world. Our field is about making space that directly impacts relationships. I want them to be accountable and sensitive to that and responsible to it, and combine that with all their other motivations—poetry, art, or whatever. Those things aren't exclusive of one another. That's what motivates me with my students.

Having been educated here in the landscape architecture program at Cornell, I have a desire to change it. A lot of my colleagues have gone back to teach at places they were educated in. I think a lot of us are interested in offering a critique of the way we were taught. I was definitely taught in the modernist way, so I feel like some part of me is trying to change the culture here, to get Cornell's Department of Landscape Architecture to step up to the plate.

There is some collision of the cosmic forces that got me here, which happens to a lot of us. I started working in the late eighties, and the economy really changed a lot and practice was really low; there wasn't a lot of opportunity in practice. It was cheap labor and expensive living. Generally, wanting to teach over practice was a big thing for me. I had practiced for several years and found that practice was very much driven by the economy. There is a lot of selling without promoting what you really believe in. I feel like a better place for me to be is in education to help students frame how they are going to be in the world, and also to help them realize that they have choices as to how they are going to practice. They can take a stand. It's possible to be that kind of practitioner and not just take anything that comes into the office. They can have choices as to the methods they use to practice design, so that the methods are a critical process. They are not just a given.

This is a weird field because we're an accredited program. The landscape architecture profession accredits us. The profession has very much, in the past, dictated the kind of education that we have. There is a practice-based pedagogy—you have to teach *these* courses. It's been more oriented toward having to teach basic courses than to really create thinkers. I think our department suffered from that. The way that the curriculum was designed wasn't so much focused on thinking as it was on the technical and practical and functional aspects of design. You have to have that, too, in order to make something, but there is dialectic between theory and practice. We've tried to become more theoretical here.

I'm very conscious of the way that I'm teaching. I think adult learning is really important in how you empower people. I try to break down those hierarchies of the classroom, too, so that there is more mutual engagement and so that we can all co-learn. I think that's really important. Many Cornell colleagues are still the kind of teachers who stand up in front of the room and just talk, talk, talk at the students. The students are either falling asleep, or they're hanging on every word they say. I'm just not interested in that kind of teaching or learning. I'm interested in fostering in the classroom democratic practices and engagement, and co-learning.

The dynamics that are happening in the classroom, we're all responsible for them. I'm very conscious of that. And the way I approach the courses I teach is setting the stage for that. It's a challenge because I have to think about how I do something that isn't just telling. How can I do something that is going to reveal knowledge to people in a way that they have their own revelations? So you put them in a situation where revelation comes to them because of the experience, not because you tell them. And that is why I do service learning.

I can tell students forever, "This is what it's like to work with communities." But I want them to *feel* that. I want them to feel their heart beating and to have the experience of thinking about how, in the moment, they're going to respond, or think of what to do next. And to reflect on what happened, so that all the things in between become important: the stuff they know and the stuff they don't know. And it happens all at the same time. The students will say, "All this time I thought I was doing the design for the professor, but I'm doing the design for people, or for Joe in the community. And suddenly I feel differently about what I'm doing. We're really going to impact people's lives!" It seems like a fairly ordinary revelation, but to really *feel* that isn't so ordinary.

I think the same thing of the classroom. I am more interested in rhetorical learning: questioning and delving through discourse and really trying to reveal answers through dialogue, and figuring out how we set up those dynamics. It is challenging for students. We have too much telling in our teaching: "These are the rules, this is how you do it."

I grew up in Connecticut. My first five years were in New York, in Flushing. I went to Catholic school until third grade. There is no doubt that a lot of my ethics and service agenda comes from my religious upbringing. I was very involved, even when I was a teenager, in spiritual engagement that was both personal and social: getting the spiritual message to young people, myself being one of them, and making it meaningful. That was a big thing.

I came from parents who definitely had a service mission. My mother is an educator. She went back and got her master's and started her twenty-three-year teaching career at age forty. I definitely come from a matriarchy. My grandmother (my mother's mother) worked all the way through until she died. She could not stand not working or doing something. She worked in the Department of Agriculture. Even after her husband died she continued to work and drive and do everything. She just did it to the end. She was not nostalgic and she was very independent. She put my mother through grad school. There was much matriarchy on my mother's side of the family, and even on my father's side there were working women. His mother was a nurse. I think both parents very much focused on independent thinking and not so much being part of the group. They were focused on being passionate about what you did, and also on education and learning. My dad studied philosophy and theology, even though he wound up in corporate America.

Growing up I got very involved with service. I lived in the suburbs. I was a counselor at an intercommunity camp in the inner city. I ran a tutoring program when I was in high school, taking kids from my school to tutor in the city next door—Bridgeport, Connecticut— the opposite of suburban Westport. Then I also worked with the Youth-Adult Council, which was about creating better relationships between young people and adults. We did a lot of programs through that. I also did training in human relations, when I was in high school, through the Drug Dependence Institute at Yale. We were trained over this intense period and we ran human relations groups. It was all about convening groups where people would really share who they were and what they were doing. Those are some of the things I was doing in high school.

Of course, I was doing my artistic practice, too. There was certainly a lot of engaging with social things, and education and personal meaning, reidentifying who you are. It all probably adds up. I wasn't into sports; I was into art and social things. It was during the Vietnam War, which was certainly a dynamic time. I was kind of at the young end of that, but I remember going to march in Washington. There was a lot of asserting our independence. I think our parents were going through the same thing, which was interesting because that was the era of parents who had started raising their kids in the fifties, and then they went through the sixties, too.

Going to Brown University was really important to me because I wanted a school that was small and liberal. I was advised by my high school art professor, who I was very close to, that I shouldn't go to a school that was just art but I should go to a liberal arts school where I could really embrace why you make art and how you make art in the larger context. You make art out of who you are, not just as a technical solution. He always underscored that. So I chose to go to a school that had a really good art department but also had a really good liberal arts school. It was also a school that had a liberal curriculum. There was tremendous focus on the individual and learning in smaller classrooms. When I came here to Cornell the classes were huge. I didn't take any classes like that at Brown. It was mostly an experience of direct engagement between the teachers and the learners. So Brown was pretty important. I'm actually fonder of it now that I'm gone. In hindsight I think that it was a really good experience.

Definitely my high school art teacher was a mentor. His name was Jim Wheeler, and he was very important in my life. A lot of *who* he was was important. One of his big messages was that you don't need drugs or anything to get in the way of your own inner self. By probing that inner self, you find your expression, that expression of where the creative person comes from. That was a pretty heavy-duty message about the level of commitment and the level of engagement to probing the depths. He had a really big following. We used to take courses with him in the summers. He was a pretty interesting person. I actually had a boyfriend in high school that was a couple of years older than me who had had a really hard time in high school and gotten into drugs, and then he discovered art. Then he came back to high school to study with this person for two years. Jim Wheeler was sort of our guru. I remember writing my college essay about Rodin and Jim Wheeler. He was definitely a really important mentor.

I have had lots of pivotal experiences. I really got involved with "living history" museums. When I went to college I took a year off, and I was interested in art as being socially dynamic. I took a trip with my parents. We went to Plimoth Plantation at Plymouth, Massachusetts. And I really loved it because you walked into this living theater of history, the pilgrim's settlement, and they were challenging the notion of representing it as a set of objects or artifacts. They were showing it as a *living* place. Everyone was in costume and in character, but they were actively building, cooking, gardening, and making it come to life. You could sit on things, you could smell, it was multisensory. The seventies was a pivotal moment when a lot of museums were changing to living history museums. I actually took a year off and worked there in 1976. Brown's anthropology department was a part of Plimoth too. There was an emerging interest in the environment. There was an emerging interest in living theater. There was an interest in education and how you do it: you can either tell somebody something or you can immerse them directly in it and they experience it.

In combination with Plimoth, I took part of my year off and spent time at a biodynamic farm in Covelo, California. Alan Chadwick, who was an important teacher for a lot of people, was there. He was a gardener from England who was really involved in biodynamics, and he was very elderly at the time. There was a large following of people. I wanted to just quit college and be a part of that. I got very involved with the earth. I remember spending time on that journey across the country and starting to find out about the environment. Biodynamic gardening is really about how you garden: the dynamics of the biology of the earth and doing that in ways that foster and sustain plants and people. Permaculture, biodynamics, those all became important things to me.

Then I went back to college and got really involved in my artwork, and a lot of my artwork became things that related to plants. After I graduated from college I became a resident farmer of a living history farm for two years called Coggeshall Farm Museum. I lived in a farmhouse and ran this farm, a forty-acre farm with an 1810 house. I did programs on the weekend, and basically the way it was all run was with students. Every morning there I was, twenty-two or twenty-three years old. I would have, in the summer, twenty kids show up. Everything that we did was developing this place as though it was an early-nineteenth-century working farm. We were planting all the gardens and we were building the fences, and everything had to be done with the tools of 1810. So I did all this stuff with kids, and it was definitely engaged teaching and learning. Of course, I was learning a lot of the stuff myself. And during the weekend I was running programs like how to make herbal salves, using things from the garden. I also ran education programs with kids from the elementary schools during the spring and fall.

Then I got really interested in "interpretation." That's what a lot of this was about: interpreting the landscape and doing it with a living history aspect to it, and all the multiple dimensions of that. I had known about landscape architecture because I had taken a course in college at Rhode Island School of Design. I began to think that landscape architecture might help me to look at this stuff in a holistic way. That was an emerging interest.

Then, after I left Coggeshall Farm, I ran a solar energy barn called Earthwise Energy Education Center in Smithfield, Rhode Island. I was a leader of a crew of young people through the Youth Conservation Corps. Here I was, delving into all these parts of the world that I hadn't had a lot of experience in. The great thing about being in your early twenties is that you can do anything. But I felt that I needed this other level of knowledge to do all this stuff, to embrace a holistic way. In a place like Earthwise you are involved with the interpretation, the education, the whole thing—and the design, too. That *is* the design; it is the whole thing. I didn't have a lot of design tools, and that's why I decided to go back to graduate school. It would give me an opportunity to design and interpret what you are trying to represent through the built place and how to communicate that to people. I was doing all these things and touching on all these things and thought, is there a discipline that would pull all that stuff together? So that is when I went to graduate school in landscape architecture.

There was a set of forces that brought me to Cornell. I was looking at schools and I came here in the summer of 1982 and they accepted me immediately. They said, "If you want to come this year, you are welcome to come." So I changed my life and came here. That again was one of those collisions of the moment.

When I got here and started studying landscape architecture, it was neither as challenging as my art undergraduate degree nor as challenging in what it might address in terms of human-plant and human-human interactions. None of that was in the program. It was about form and composition. Even my art undergraduate hadn't been just about that. So it was pretty disappointing.

I learned a lot and I tried to bring a lot of what I already knew into it. I remember a professor saying, "You need to get rid of some of your background," as opposed to saying that my background should be something upon which I build. He didn't really say, "Get rid of it," but you know, basically, he said, "Get back to the basics." That's why I'm here teaching too, offering a critique of that. I don't believe in that approach at all.

The department has changed a lot since then. When I was going through it, there was a lot of disappointment in this field because it was so professionally based and practice based. I mean, practice is important—how you make stuff—but it wasn't more situated. The field seemed very uncritical of itself. In the last decade and a half there's been an increasing view that theory is important and that what informs how you practice is important. But when I went through graduate school, there wasn't a lot of theory at all. There was history; you learned what was happening but you didn't criticize it. You just take it all and put it into your data bank.

Anyway, that's how I got here, through living history and my interest in the environment and my interest in art and expression, and a lot of work in education. I don't think I would have called it that then, but that's really what it was. It was all about education and interpretation, and interpretation was what I was calling it way back when I was on Plimoth Plantation, Coggeshall Farm, and Earthwise. You get trained, but you were an interpreter of the place, so you were a participant in interpreting it.

I teach an undergraduate course called Senior Studio, and it's a community design studio. Basically, I teach the terminal studio, the last studio that students have in their sequence of studios. Studios are the core courses students are supposed to practice landscape architecture in. They're five-credit courses, so they're very intense. They're structured a lot like how I learned as an artist: a lot of time spent in the studio practicing what you are learning. A lot of time we do projects through our curriculum where you are given a problem and the students do it. Or they are given a problem in a community or with a client as an example, and then the community might come in at the end and look at it. It's a client relationship, really. The client has something they want, you do it, give it back to them, and they review it.

What I teach is a service-learning-based studio that is on community design, so I'm teaching them the theory of community design and teaching it through an experiential, service-learning studio. So what I do is immerse them in a community project. I have already done preliminary work in the communities where I've set up what that project is going to be, set up an understanding of the community's needs and what we can offer them. We start building a relationship and then we move into a project.

The project I'm going to talk about is on the North Side of Binghamton, New York, and it's interesting because it has a few other dimensions. One of them is that I am working with a colleague at the State University of New York College of Environmental Science and Forestry (SUNY-ESF) up at Syracuse University. Her name is Cheryl Doble, and we're part of something called the SUNY Network. This is something we have just established through the state of New York with five SUNY schools that teach design and planning. We're engaged with the state in trying to help communities. There are twelve designated communities this year. They're part of the Quality Communities Initiative. They happen to be small, medium, and large cities in New York that are in particular need of economic development and help. They've had a lot of problems. Cheryl and I are working as a part of the SUNY Network and the QCI. We both share an interest in the way that we teach. She teaches a visioning studio in community design at SUNY-ESF, and I teach the community design studio here at Cornell. The two of us got together and said, "Let's work together." In our first pilot project we decided to combine our two classes and work in the same place over the duration of a semester. It made it even a little more difficult in terms of the choreography.

We met with the elected officials and staff of the City of Binghamton, and with a lot of state agencies, and they told us what was going on with the city and its needs. They're working on a comprehensive plan. One of the areas that's crucial to the health of Binghamton is the North Side neighborhood. Economically, a lot of disinvestment has happened there. It's had every possible modernist planning strategy applied to it—transportation planning and urban renewal, tearing down whole neighborhoods and putting in highways. And it's had a lot of deterioration over time. And yet it's adjacent to downtown, so conceivably, it should be a very healthy neighborhood. But a lot of the community's dynamics are very disturbed by bad planning decisions, by economics, and by land use issues.

As a result of these initial meetings, the city connected us to a community group called the Communities of Shalom. This is a consortium of leaders from the churches in the North Side neighborhood. They had just been going through a training called the "Shalom Community," a national program of the Methodist Church that trains community leaders to understand community needs and undertake grassroots planning. So these folks from the North Side had been going through the Shalom training, and they were beginning to identify and develop a vision statement and mission for their neighborhood. They were at this pivotal moment in their work. There was a group of them. We connected with them and told them who we were. We told them that we would be interested in helping them shape some of their community visions and do a participatory planning and design process with them. And they were very receptive.

It's funny because we just did this presentation last week at the QCI conference in Albany with two of the folks from the North Side Shalom group. I interviewed them a few weeks ago, just reflecting on some of the process, and one of the things that the Methodist minister, Gary Doupe, said was that initially they were a little skeptical of us. But when we said that we were interested in working *with* them instead of *on* them, they realized that that was really important. They were really scoping us out. They didn't want to work with somebody who was going to work *on* them. But *with* them was different. They recognized that there was a sympathy we shared, a way of thinking about how to undertake a project that was consistent with what they had been doing with Shalom.

We shaped a process working with the North Side Shalom group over the duration of the semester. A lot of the terms for that process were very much set by them, like where the meetings were going to happen. We had a lot of community meetings. They always had to include dinners. They were held at area churches, so that they were not associated with any one specific place. They were basically a sharing of food and dialogue. They were always on Sunday nights. The churches made sure that people got there.

In terms of how we were teaching this, we were giving our students a lot of tools here on campus, and preparing them, setting up the project. The project was unfolding through the whole semester, and it was a reflective process. We were doing something and there was a response that happened, and then we designed what the next response was going to be. We were shepherding our students through this process, and both of us were doing things at this end, too. For example, I have a reader and I give students readings. We do a lot of practicing and developing the methods here, and they are also connecting with community people at the same time, and then they are connecting with the students at SUNY-ESF. So there are a lot of dynamics.

The students think it is very messy, and it is, because it is unpredictable what is going to happen and who all the players are. We had two sessions between just our two schools to do some team building; because that is the other thing we are dealing with—students who have worked more autonomously. They have worked in groups but not really in groups in this sense; there is a lot of accountability on this level. So there is a lot of team building that's necessary. Then there are all the dynamics of a lot of people being involved. Things just don't go as predictably as you would want.

Our students went down to Binghamton five times for these informal sessions. What happened was that we had had an initial visioning session with the community and our students, and then out of that came an identifying of realms of the neighborhood that needed work. And then there were four groups that formed. One was called the Visioning Group, one was called the Neighborhood Group, one the Riverfront Group, and finally the Marketplace Group. All those groups had different students and community members in them, and they worked on particular areas.

As a result of the process, some of the areas started to come together. For example, you couldn't really look at the marketplace without looking at the riverfront. So they started to work together over the duration of the semester. And they did a lot of different things in terms of their methods. Storytelling was a very important method for disclosing personal histories and feelings about the communities. There was a lot of participatory modeling where people could move movable parts around and try new ideas out. We created a matrix vision, which emerged from the Visioning Group. It was a whole wall of places in the community, and the dynamics that the community wanted to start to see happen there, and then ideas for how that might occur. That group built the matrix as the tool. That was neat because they didn't know what they were getting into, and then they realized that everything is connected to everything else. What came out of this was a set of vision concepts and ideas for the community that this smaller group of community folks shared with the larger group at the end. And what happened as a result was that it allowed them (the Shalom group) to see that they could be empowered much more. They had no real relationship with city hall. They had to create a relationship with city hall. Suddenly, they were on city hall's radar screen.

During the summer we wrote a follow-up grant with the Department of State to undertake a much longer process for a longer duration, which would have more community members involved. The city helped us write it, and the city's community planners are involved with it now. So this is a huge shift. It also made the Shalom group think in different levels. They can think small *and* big. They don't need to think of those things as separate. They can think small and big at the same time—like to think globally and act locally. They can think that way in their communities. That's very empowering to them. And also gaining the vocabulary, because so often they feel like they are so totally divorced from the planning process that they don't understand the vocabulary around it. They can't speak the same language, and the planners aren't thinking of how to educate them to do that. They got a lot of that vocabulary, so they have a more common ground. So it was a very effective process.

The students were helping to manage the group. They were developing ways of working that would be participatory. If you do something, it has to be participatory. It's got to engage people. They've got to see the knowledge disclosed *through* the learning process. You're not here to just *tell* them, you're here to *invent* ways that knowledge gets *disclosed*. And it's also for you to see differently, because you can't see those dimensions of the community from the outside. You have to become an insider. A lot of the things you hear "in between" are where you learn. So that's really important.

But again, like so many who have done a lot of these things, it's messy. It's not linear. Students are often asking, "What are we doing next?" They don't have the exact syllabus. One student said, "I learned how much you've got to think by the seat of your pants." It's emergent. It's reflective. You need to be able to improvise. That is one of the things that you are learning: when you're involved with somebody, you realize that when you're in a dialogue, there's a response. It isn't just linear. You can go in circles and backwards and forwards at the same time.

The way I think of myself has shifted a lot. I'm not "professing." I'm mentoring students and community members. That's the other part of it that's messy. All of these relationships are built. I met with the Shalom group a lot this past summer. Some of them are local leaders from churches; others are members of the community or members of the churches. Because of the nature of this whole project, because they are committed to their communities, they are very much a part of that place.

It was interesting recently because we were at city hall. Phil Stanton shows up. He's very active in this community. He doesn't have a car. He had a stroke. He doesn't have any front teeth. And he shows up to our meeting at city hall. And it's like you can hear people thinking, "*He* doesn't belong here!" But Phil Stanton is willing to step into that scene because he wants to make sure that they're going to get what they need for the North Side. He is extremely bright and extremely committed, and he's a very important part of the community. He presents himself as who he is. He cannot afford to get his teeth fixed. He's not that old. He's probably in his late fifties. He's been married twice. He apparently was very athletic, and he was a Vietnam vet, and he had a stroke at a pretty young age. He has probably had a pretty hard life. The stroke left him with one arm that is numb and he can't use it, and with a limp. He can move around and he has somewhat slurred speech. He has to wear a sling all the time. And he walks strangely because he had a stroke.

So this guy shows up and he's like a representation of the community just physically. He's a local person and he represents all that the North Side is—people who have been around awhile who don't have a lot of economic flexibility and don't have a lot of mobility, either. They don't have cars. This is a big issue there. They don't even have a supermarket. The closest place that people can walk to is Kmart. A lot of people are getting their food, their nutrition, at Kmart. They are not getting fresh vegetables and things like that.

Then you get to know Phil Stanton, and he's an incredibly committed social person with incredible consciousness. He's very involved with the Methodist Church because they are very liberal and accept gays and lesbians. His best friend is Sheila, who is a gay woman who is very much engaged with the community, too. He's got an incredible open mind. He's very critical of city government. He's going to peace marches in Washington now. He's got a very definite social agenda. He's very bright. He was very involved with our meetings to make sure that there was local representation there. After one of the first meetings, when he realized that there wasn't any one from the Muslim community there, and there are a lot of Muslims in the North Side, he went out of his way to get a couple of people to come to the meetings. He called me and told me about a young woman who he thought we should invite. Basically, he made sure that she got there. He asked me to call her, too, and invite her. And then he made sure that she got picked up and driven home so that she could participate. He also wanted to make sure that there were young people there, representing high school kids in the community. So he's very much engaged.

He just wrote me an email the other day. It said something like, "The Burger King has closed, the bowling lane is gone. *Help!*" Everyone is leaving the community, economically, so he's really very much engaged with what is going on there. And he has no fear. That's what is amazing to me. He's not afraid of how he looks or who he is. He's ready to step up to the plate and do what it takes. He came to Albany last week and comes to all the meetings. He's very sensitive to who is involved and how to involve them. That's why I'm interested in doing these projects, for people like Phil Stanton and Sheila.

There is another character, Bob. I'm always surprised that he's still around. He must be about seventy and he's still trying to finish his high school education. He had a learning disability when he was young. No one understood it. He never got to finish high school. He has an incredible memory. But apparently he's had a hard time with reading and writing. But he's very committed to finishing this. Physically he's kind of a wreck, too. He comes to all the meetings. It is hard to work with people like Bob, but it's important that they are there and that the students experience them. It's one thing to find out that there's a neighborhood of people who don't have a grocery store and don't have cars. It's another thing to be in the same room with them.

The students are very respectful, and they're very careful. The community tells us that they feel like the students are not pushing their ideas on them, that they are respectful, and that they really appreciate the students' freshness—that they bring a certain enthusiasm and freshness and hope. We do a lot of talking about how to be together and how to *be* a listener, not just listening. It's all a big dance.

The Methodist church on the North Side is very liberal, and they are very engaged. It's really neat to go into these churches and realize that they really are the hubs of the community. Everybody in the city is thinking that there isn't much going on in the community because the economy is falling apart, but there are five churches on the main street that have been there forever. And when you go to the Methodist church for a meeting, there's also an AA meeting upstairs, and there's choir practice, and there are all these things happening. They're providing things for the community which are not evident anywhere else. So that was pretty neat.

In a project like this, there's a compressed time frame. You're just running every minute. The whole thing is trying to keep some momentum and keep all these dynamics in balance—student dynamics, community dynamics, teaching and learning dimensions. Also, working with students who have never done this before, you're trying to teach them to do it and get them to do things that they say they are going to do. For Cheryl and me, we realized that it was difficult for the students because of the team-building part; we hadn't spent enough attention on that.

The project came to us late in December, and we didn't have a lot of time to think about how we would plan. I don't think we really anticipated what some of the problems would be. One of the things we thought about was doing an immersion before the process to do more basic team-building. So there were frustrating moments when we were throwing our hands up and saying, "Can we do this?" And students weren't communicating very well with each other. There were people complaining that someone is not doing anything, or not doing enough.

There were a couple turning points. One of them was the summer when we wrote the grant, because until that moment I don't think the City believed that the North Side was doing this. One of them was that we were asked to comment on a comprehensive plan that the city was doing with an outside landscape architecture firm consultant. We put together a comment on it, which ended up being about twenty pages. Then the whole North Side group and I went to the city council meeting, and all the press was there, and so were the consultants. We presented our findings of the comprehensive plan. That was an "aha" moment for city hall. They finally realized the North Side has really gotten a lot done. The councilman from that neighborhood was getting a lot of congratulations. It made city hall look really good because there was this project going on. They came up to us afterwards and said, "We couldn't have done that level of thinking because we just can't look at that neighborhood that well."

That was a pivotal moment for the North Side to be taken seriously. They were so proud of themselves and the whole process. They said they felt that it allowed them to prove that they were not a wacko group. They used that phrase, a "wacko group." They were really there for the community to see. Also, the press was there, so that was important. That really led to getting enough attention to write this grant. The city dedicated a grant writer for a week, and she worked with us and the North Side to develop a grant. So I think that was a pivotal moment. The students by then were gone.

There are always surprising things that happen. I guess I'm used to the surprising. The surprises are often the inventions. Like the matrix; that wasn't something that we planned. That's part of the teaching and learning, too. That becomes part of the cadre of tools. You share that and possibly use that again. Cheryl and I got together and came up with the matrix idea. We gave it to the students, and the students then used it to invent. They tried it out and it worked. Then there's some innovation that happened from doing it. That's how things go in trying to teach the participatory design process. There are things that are part of the literature and things that we have tried before. Then there is the flexibility to look at other groups. Each group had different things they were working on. The Neighborhood Group decided to focus on one particular part of their community called the Liberty Street neighborhood. Each group had very different dynamics and each group was designed differently.

I think there's definitely resistance to the whole participatory dynamic. It isn't as predictable, and therefore the view is that it's not as good or as valid or as organized. Students are definitely used to these linear processes: the faculty gives them a brief, and they follow the rules. But in this setting, they're also designing some methodology. There's some preconception, obviously, because people like Cheryl and me are helping to facilitate the process. But they have to design and invent the methodology, and the process is as important as the product. Students are very product oriented. They're used to developing their beautiful drawings that they author. But here somebody is saying that's not as important as the process, or that it's as important—that it's not going to be a persuasive drawing unless it has been informed by their engagement. There's a lot of resistance to that.

How I think of this is that *the space of learning has shifted from the academy to the community*. When the space of learning changes, who is the teacher and who is the learner changes. There's a huge difference in terms of dynamics. The spatial shift in terms of the physical geography also corresponds to the psychological space as well as the space that interchanges everything. So everything changes, because the space of the academy constructs its own system of learning—you do *this,* you get a grade. That's one of the tensions that provokes resistance.

There's also the challenge of working in groups. I had a student in here one time in tears saying, "I'm a really good student, I've always gotten A's and I'm working with so-and-so, and she and I work totally differently, and I don't want it to affect my grade." Suddenly, the terms of measurement are different, because we're not focused on individuals for grades. And they're really nervous because if the group is going down, they're going down with them. They're all totally concerned with grades here at Cornell. And then you've got the opposite person who is self-consumed, and they're very resistant to working in a group because it's beneath them. Then there's resistance to having to spend your whole Sunday night going down to Binghamton, and they want to go to a concert or a wedding.

It takes a lot of active faith to engage in something like this, from everybody. I have to have faith that the students can do this. I have to have faith that they aren't going to fall apart. I have to have faith that the community really is going to be involved. Or that Cheryl and I can do this together, given the realities that get in the way in terms of scheduling. It is a big act of faith because you don't really know what is going to happen. So it requires a lot of belief. And that's what is great about working with the community, because generally they have been in situations where they've been so disempowered and they haven't had any help. They're just really excited about it.

I worked for three years with school communities on landscapes for learning. I really like that because it's pretty much designed around the belief that you can do something with nothing. You have parents and teachers. And the teachers are really dedicated. The kids are enthusiastic. They're really used to thinking about the design of their courses in terms of, "How can we build this? We can do it! It doesn't matter if we don't have any money." The Shalom group is like that, too: "We can do it. We got the people, the resources, we know how to make food, we know how to pick people. We can do this." Whereas municipal governments tend to be very cynical: "We can't do it unless we have the money." Their cynicism has driven me away from them a lot of the time. I find there is a lot more empowerment in groups that are more nested in the social dynamics of the place. And they're not politically driven.

The biggest failing in projects like this is the fact that it's a huge liability to create so much momentum, to shift the dynamics and then not be able to sustain it. That's a huge problem with this process. You have all these students come in, they do all this work, and then the project comes to an end. It hasn't ended, but it comes to an end in terms of that level of engagement. Then you're back to real time. There aren't as many people at your disposal. It makes me feel like there's a level of responsibility. You get people excited and then you can't be there. You can only do so much. That's a big problem. In Binghamton, that was a big problem: keeping momentum.

In terms of other failings, Cheryl and I wouldn't characterize it as failing, but the interaction between our two schools, we would like it to be more effective. The team building I described was about trying to structure the interactions. As much as we talk about community, we have to make and shape and build community everywhere. And it's amongst your students. A lot of conscious effort has to go into that. Sometimes I don't think we pay enough attention to that, or we just don't have the time or energy to do it. It really wears me out. It's wearing. It's *really* wearing.

It's hard to keep and be invested at that level, to care about it at that level. You get invested with all of these people that you build relationships with—the Phil Stantons and the Gary Doupes. Another failing is that there is still dependence. I really see that there's a lot of dependence on us being a conduit or a voice for them. So that's a failing, too. How long does it take and how do you get them to have a voice? They need an advocate. They need somebody who can connect them, somebody who can be in both worlds. I can walk into city hall and be critical of that world, and I can walk into their world and be part of their world and also be critical of it. I can be in both worlds, but it's much harder for them. So that's hard. Then the rewards are all the things that have to do with the liability. The rewards are, obviously, if you can motivate some real significant change in the dynamic, then that's great.

The thing about the North Side is that it's a disturbed site. It actually has all the components of what would constitute a neighborhood. But they're all out of whack. If you could actually get those into a healthy place, you would have a healthy neighborhood. Could you get a grocery store in the neighborhood? Could you actually build some sidewalks to get to and from there? Could you design a bus system so that people could get back and forth more easily? One of the things the Shalom group wants to do is start a computer center and some teaching and learning for young people and some job training and things like that. If you can get all those things started and going, you can have a healthy neighborhood and then be engaged at another level. Can you get the housing programs going? Can you get rid of the drug dealers? Can you redesign the zoning?

What happens in the dynamics of a real community is that there's a lot of overlap. The more complex it is, the more stable it is. If something goes wrong, there are enough dynamics in place to reassociate with one another. They are spatially close enough. If you can start to mix that stuff up physically and spatially, you could get more overlap between areas. That's what I'm trying to do, to help shape healthy systems where these dynamics are in play. That's what gets me excited about it, to help initiate some change. I don't like the idea of going in and giving somebody a bunch of plans that end up on a shelf.

Part of being in the North Side is asking, "How can we facilitate this change?" You're up against a lot of the realities of time. One of my grad students did her thesis on ecological dynamics, and she found that the level of disturbance of a system is consistent with the level of time that it takes for it to reclaim itself. So you have to really speed up time, or change time just to get things rolling again. A lot of what I see in the North Side is that it's pretty comparable to a disturbed ecological existence. It's had quite a bit of disturbance. The kinds of things that disturbed it, like urban renewal and the roads that got built in the sixties and seventies, destroyed a lot of interaction. The zoning fosters separation. City-planning initiatives have cut off the North Side. There's a lot of disturbance there, so I feel lucky that these churches are hanging on. It's like the vital thread that remains, the connectivity. You just wonder how long it's going to take to change these dynamics.

I continue to learn how difficult it is to do this stuff. It's difficult to embrace complexity. That's very hard. As much as you believe in all this stuff theoretically, it's hard to do it all and be with all those players and understand all those things and continually engage at that level. That's one of those huge things I continue to learn from. Part of my reaction is to continually address how to be more effective. The other reaction is just to pull out. It's like, "This is too hard, and I can do something a lot easier." Like I could just go back to another way of doing things and it would be a lot easier. There would be a lot less dimension to it.

I think with something like our North Side project, a lot of things get upped in terms of the ante. There was the state and SUNY-ESF working in a bigger urban area than I generally work in. Now the time frame, that's clearly going to be extended. So it's a little scary. There's a lot of learning with each one of these projects that relates to the specific place. Obviously, I've learned a lot about the North Side as a place. And I think I've learned a lot about the dynamics of this place and what is out of whack. I've learned it through the experience of engagement. I didn't know anything about the North Side when I got there. I've learned about the North Side, I've learned about the city. I've learned a lot about neighborhoods like that in general.

There's always a lot of learning from the students—what gets them excited, what gets them frustrated. It continues to challenge me to figure out ways to be more effective. It also does this other thing where there are certain things I cannot take care of. I'm never going to be able to take care of the fact that this is messy. That's just how it is. So I say, "This is a messy process. That's how it works." And generally, that's really how design works. And it's very difficult to have people see that *the design process itself is the process, the process that actually reveals both the questions and the answers.* Because sometimes you don't know what the questions are until you start to probe them. The design process raises this question and answers it at the same time, simultaneously. It's not only about answering questions, because sometimes the wrong question has been posed. That's the hardest thing about teaching studio in general, is that you are leading somebody through this inquiry.

It's like painting. You don't sit around and read about making a painting. You really learn about making a painting through the painting itself, and then that painting is going to be the embodiment of everything you know, and you are going to take it to the next painting. *You have to keep making to keep knowing, to keep finding out.* That's what keeps it fun and exciting. You're going through this journey of making and knowing and wondering. I think of that with everything. It's part of what drives everyone crazy around here. *The product is not that important.* I can actually let go of some of the product. I'm not that attached to what the product is going to look like. I'm becoming less attached. Maybe that's part of my learning, too. For somebody who is coming from art, it seems like it's a bit of a contradiction. I'm actually becoming less and less attached to the product. As long as it actually is producing, maybe it's not so important what it looks like and what the aesthetics are. It's more important how we interact—the dynamics. There's actually a lot of ways it could look. It doesn't really matter. What are important are the relationships it creates, rather than what it looks like.

That's really hard for young designers to get, because they are so immersed in trying to get the product. I find this increasing detachment from caring what it looks like. It comes from my art background. You make to know. That is the revelation. That to me is the integration of theory and practice. The practice is the making, and we theorize *through* the making. In the making we are revealing knowledge. It's interesting how there's a way that you go on to do something, and that's the embodiment of everything that you know, and so it's kind of a good thing to get detached from those things. It's hard, also, because you get very fond of your objects.

The North Side is very much in process. One of the things is to keep on deepening the level of inquiry and engagement, so that more people are involved and so that we really get something out of this project design and reshaping. It's the identity of the North Side that we want to represent and set in motion. That's always a big dilemma. People are afraid of change that is going to change *them.* But change that is going to help *sustain* them is hard to see. People assume you are going to redo or undo something they value. But really what you want to do is deepen it and make it better, but in a way that keeps everything in it while doing the next layer. It's difficult.

In doing this design project, for example, we will redo the sidewalks. It's going to be new, because everything old is going to get dug up. It's going to look new and sparkly. And that's scary to people, too. Even though the newness is going to make it better for everybody, it's still going to *look* new. We need to make the new somehow not look so new that it's disengaged from the place. It's a difficult task, and there's a lot of reaction to the task—that we might overdo it and change the psycho-dimension of the place that people see as being home and authentic and quirky and different and original, and not like anywhere else. That's the hardest thing about design.

Design is very much driven by aesthetics, and the view that the aesthetics have to be coherent, that everything should match, and it should be balanced. That's horrible. It makes me cringe. When I'm mentoring the project and students are doing the drawings, they often come back with stuff that is so generic. They're just applying a lot of generic things. It's a big dilemma. The goals of how it gets redesigned have to fit the neighborhood and the place. It doesn't want to drive away the community; it wants to compel them be part of it. It also has to be designed. The city has to understand that the city as an organism is a multiplicity of places, and those multiplicities of places all have ways of expressing themselves. I think that's one of the learning dimensions of this we tried to make evident to the city. They were thinking about the waterfront as a walkway with fancy lighting. And this community does not want the waterfront that way. They want to think of it as a place where they might have playground equipment and get community members out to, and be a community place and a civic place, not just a city place that is chichi and fancy. It's sort of striking that middle ground where it feels like design is situated and thoughtful and really constructs new relationships that are also wonderful and experientially rich and imbued with memory.

It's hard. I'm definitely at a moment in my career and my life where I'm asking, "Why do I want to be doing this stuff?" Don't think that I don't think about it every day. You spend a lot of time on the literature and the meaning, and you are learning new languages. I guess I go back to that thing about faith—faith that something is going to happen, and that it's going to lead somewhere. Because you may have asked a question from the outset that isn't really the question you discover in the process. There are a lot of different layers. And maybe the question that you asked is not at the core of the problem. And that leads you in another direction.

One of the things that we've discovered and learned in the North Side is that zoning is one of the limiting factors. The whole way the city thought about zoning the neighborhood has led to a lot of these problems, the way that it has produced itself spatially. So it's cut off a lot of potential for overlap. So now we've got to go redesign the zoning. You can't redesign the physical place unless you redesign the legal structure. That leads us to a whole new series of questions and a whole other level of work. That's generally how all design processes are.

The design process itself is the inquiry. It answers and asks the questions that it surfaces. Now all of these questions have surfaced. And now all of the community people who are negative are coming out of the woodwork. It's kind of like they got the implications of the change and they finally can see it and can understand it, and they're scared. All this stuff is coming up, and it's all coming out now. There's a reaction that you should be acting *against* something, but what you are really doing is reacting *to* something that you can finally see. The real questions have finally surfaced. The design process is exactly where it should be. It led us to this. But then the people want to blame the very design process that got you there!

The design process is the revelatory knowledge process. It's just like art, like the artistic process. The artist is doing something. You make to know. You are making something to learn something. You make a painting not just to do it, but every time you use the paint or make a shadow or whatever you do, that's how you are learning. That's how you learn about color. You learn about color or light in the making. The making is the learning.

Every Interaction Is an Educational Opportunity

A Profile of Daniel J. Decker

Professor, Department of Natural Resources, Cornell University

Interview conducted by Scott Peters, April 11, 2002

In this profile, Dan Decker recounts why and how he helped to establish a new research unit at Cornell University on the human dimensions of wildlife and natural resource management. In telling his story, which involves the development of public relationships with government agencies, professional associations, and community groups, he refers to himself and his colleagues as "change agents, in the old-fashioned sense." The change Dan and his colleagues have sought to catalyze has to do not only with the way wildlife and natural resources management is conducted, but also with the way it is taught and studied in academic institutions. As a publicly engaged academic professional who works as a critic, leader, and servant, Dan seeks to seamlessly integrate community-based research and teaching. One of his guiding principles, "Every interaction is an educational opportunity," has a two-way, reciprocal meaning. It includes as learners academic professionals and students as well as management professionals and community members.

Currently I'm serving as director of the Cornell University Agriculture Experiment Station, and associate dean of the College of Agriculture and Life Sciences (CALS). I've been in this administrative role for almost exactly one year. The emphasis of the role is on how to improve the relation of applied research and Extension across the college. I was associate director of the Experiment Station prior to this. At that time, it was combined with the Office of Research, so I was the associate director for Research for CALS as well. I'm also a professor in the Department of Natural Resources. I started as a tenure-track professor in 1988 with a split of 70 percent Extension and 30 percent research.

In my work as a faculty member I'm interested in how one integrates what we refer to as the human, sociological dimensions of natural resource management into management decision-making, and eventually policy and practice. I focus on wildlife management; that's my specialty. My central focus as the director of the Experiment Station is to promote and facilitate applied research that falls within the purview of the Experiment Station, which will have an impact on people, particularly in New York State.

I grew up in downstate New York in the Catskills, in a rural area outside of the small town of Port Jervis, New York. In high school, I became involved in conservation issues by organizing people at school as well as in the community to clean up a stream that ran through the school grounds. I got into my first extension education effort that way, with a slide show projected on the wall of the city hall meeting room where the town council met, to convince them there was a problem and they should support the effort that was going on amongst the students at the school. I organized the students, got that done, and got an award.

At the time, I had a wonderful mentor who was a Cornell University graduate, Phil Chase. He was my physics teacher. He was also a conservation columnist for a regional newspaper in downstate New York called the *Times Herald Record*. I ended up following him around during my junior and senior year, going to various meetings that were related to natural resources and the environment. He was covering the stories. I watched the information exchange that was occurring. I became interested in the process of how people who were experts communicated—and miscommunicated—with laypeople.

I have a personal love, because of my family tradition, of the outdoors, of hunting and fishing. I was involved as a youngster, while I was still in high school, in representing a local rod and gun club to the county-level affiliate of a group called the New York State Conservation Council that has representation from regions at the local level. I was elected as a sixteen- or seventeen-year-old. I couldn't even drive at night to represent the local club at the county level. I was also engaged in seeing natural resource managers, and fish and wildlife people in particular, interacting with stakeholders. (They didn't use the term *stakeholders* then, of course.) I was seeing the same things there: the struggles of people who are well-educated specialists trying to deal with stakeholders and just butting heads. I was becoming impressed with the difficulty of that interaction.

It was isolated where I grew up. It was rural and beautiful. It was what a kid with my interests wanted. I could walk out my door and go fishing or hunting. I was outdoors all the time. I was not interested in group stuff at school. It made my involvement in the effort to clean up the stream that ran through the school grounds—which was very public—quite a challenge. My family still has the front-page news clippings of me in front of the common council. It was big-time press back in those days, because that was also during the days when kids were generally problems. We're talking 1969–70. Drugs were happening. Armed students took over Willard Straight Hall at Cornell. There was a lot of turmoil. The war in Vietnam was going on. Young people were usually seen as, "You're protesting, you're on drugs, and you're causing some kind of trouble." But here we had a group of high school students trying to do something positive in the community.

Growing up in an isolated community, the furthest west I ever traveled independently, except when I was on a trip with the Scouts, was when I came to Cornell for an interview to see if I could get in. I didn't really know what Cornell was. When I was accepted, I had some people oohing and aahing all around me back in Port Jervis. I was just going to some state college, for all I knew. I didn't think it was a big deal.

I was the first member of my family to go to college, even a community college. My father did not complete high school. That was the highest level that anybody in my family completed. I was an oddball in that respect. Family members were impressed at some level, but they didn't know what it meant. I didn't either. I came here and had to learn what a term and a semester was. I didn't know what those words meant, because we didn't have them in high school.

I decided to apply to Cornell because my mentor was a Cornellian, and so was the guidance counselor who took me out of the hands of another guidance counselor who was trying to put everybody into our local community college to get high placement ratings. I was put with a young fellow who was a Cornell graduate from the education department. Between the two of them, both graduates of CALS, somehow—miraculously—I got into Cornell. That's how I got here. It was the only place that I applied. If I hadn't gone to Cornell, I was signed up to go into the marines, which is stupid when you think about it, since it was 1970.

Cornell was absolutely, unbelievably overwhelming, because I was not worldly at all. I ended up in the worst rowdy dormitory. I tried to be a student and absolutely hated it. I wanted to leave my whole freshman year. My mentors back home, including another gentleman who was my high school chemistry teacher and was like family, were persistent that I was going to stay at Cornell. My own parents were actually indifferent about it. It was up to me.

At any rate, Cornell was overwhelming. There was a huge dichotomy at Cornell in those days between being in the "Ag school," as it was called then, versus being in Arts and Sciences. You have to remember that as a freshman you're thrown in with people in these other colleges, and your courses were in those other colleges. You were treated like a second-class citizen. It was very uncomfortable territory. Plus, you go from working moderately hard and being in the top of your class in high school, to working your buns off at Cornell because everybody else was in the top of their class. The academic pressure was like nothing I ever experienced before.

I was a natural resources major, which was entirely biologically oriented in those days. The kind of things that I do today with the human dimensions of wildlife management weren't even discussed then. There's another fellow, Gary Goff, who still works at Cornell in the Department of Natural Resources, who I met during orientation week on a trip out to Arnot Forest. He was equally a hick from the sticks. I was a Catskill hick, and he was an Adirondacks hick. We gravitated towards one another and kept each other going. He was bright and was somewhat overwhelmed by Cornell also. He came from a smaller place than I did. There were a dozen and a half kids in his graduating class. We sort of buoyed each other up to get through, and finally were able to become roommates. Life started to get better. We tried to support one another, and that's how I made it.

About the time I was in my junior year, I started to see another arena in the nonbiological side of natural resource management. I found myself able to take electives where I went from hating courses to loving courses. I found myself not memorizing but problem solving, thinking, and being creative. I went from a 2.5 average to a 3.7 in those final semesters. I was flourishing. I was also more responsible, probably.

I came to Cornell thinking I was going to be trained as a wildlife biologist. But an instructor can change your life. I took a course that was offered at that time in public relations and communication in natural resource management. I was exposed there to ideas of extension education and communication that we didn't get in traditional biological types of courses. I looked around and said, "Hmm, this is an area nobody's doing anything in." There was no such thing in our field then as the human dimensions of wildlife management, and no courses on that specifically. I did an independent study as a senior on issues relating to deer management in the Adirondacks.

In the course and the independent study I took with Professor Dickson, who was an extension forester in the Department of Natural Resources, I became exposed to Cooperative Extension. In his course, he used extension examples. I became intrigued with what this whole extension system was like and its role of educating people so they could be better informed. It harkened back to all the problems I saw, even before college, with "experts" trying to communicate with laypeople. My independent study project looked at issues related to how managers interact with stakeholders, and the possible role of educational communication in natural resource management. I ended up applying for graduate school with this gentleman. He'd never had a grad student before. He took me on as a master's student, probably with great pain to himself to get me in, I'll never know for sure. I did a project continuing my work in the Adirondacks. I finished it off in a year and a half. (I actually wrote a thesis I wouldn't let one my own students get by with, but you live and learn.)

I started a relationship with the New York State Department of Environmental Conservation's Bureau of Wildlife at that point in time. They funded my master's research when I started it in 1974. I've had a continuous, contractual working relationship with them ever since. It's gone from fifteen thousand to a quarter of a million per year in that time. I've tried to use New York State as my laboratory, if you will. I've stayed engaged with rural people, on the ground. I grew up professionally with people who became regional wildlife managers and bureau chiefs in the Department of Environmental Conservation (DEC) by the time I was in a position to work with them.

My minor in my master's degree was in adult and extension education with Paul Leagans in Cornell's Department of Education. He's gone now. I took two courses with him, which opened my eyes up to how an educator can take broad concepts and help you to apply them to your specific context. He was teaching fifteen very different people from different parts of the world and having us all gain from it. I was amazed. I'd never seen that before. I was quite taken by the concepts I learned, which I still use today. They involve program development, ideas about situation analysis, about understanding who you're trying to teach, about accommodating how adults learn, which is one of the biggest problems with communication between natural resource professionals and their constituents.

When I finished my master's degree I stayed on in the Department of Natural Resources as a research support specialist. I quickly moved to research associate, but part of my time was devoted to Extension. I was an extension fish and wildlife specialist for several years as a research associate on soft money. Along the way, I got an offer to be an extension specialist from Sea Grant, which is a nationwide network of university-based programs that work on coastal issues. It was solid money, but I didn't take it. I caught hell for not taking it from a fellow that I worked with as a grad student as his teaching assistant in a wildlife course. I didn't take the job because I actually loved what I was doing. I took the risk that even though I was in a soft-money job, that things were going well and I could keep it going. Later a policy analysis job, which was all natural-resource-oriented, came up with the Tug Hill Commission out of Watertown. I interviewed and was offered that job for a huge increase in pay. For reasons in my family and my personal life, I didn't take it, either.

Here's where another mentor comes in. When I was making the decision not to take the job with the Tug Hill Commission, the same individual who I caught hell from, Dr. Jim Caslick, who was a full-time extension wildlife specialist in the department (he wasn't just my professor, we were partners on wildlife extension work), told me that if I decided not to take that job, I was not welcome in his office unless I walked in with a letter of recommendation form for him to fill out for me to go to grad school here at Cornell in the employee degree program. So the next time I saw Jim I asked for a reference letter for graduate school for the doctoral program in the Department of Education in Extension and Adult Education. Four years later, I had my Ph.D.

In my doctoral program, I wanted to focus on evaluation. I wanted to improve the extension system. The program focused on evaluation methodology and theory, but I also took course work in extension administration as well as natural resources. I had a great experience with Dr. Bruce from Education, who's since passed on. He's another great mentor. Not that we had an everyday relationship, like my weekly meetings with my own students now. But we had a professional relationship. Every minute with him was valuable. He gave me guidance and the freedom I needed. At that point in time, I had already been a professional for a good number of years. I was able to take course work again, which I loved. It was a nice break from work. I had to add it on to my workload to do it.

One semester before I finished my Ph.D., a job opened up for state program leader for natural resources at the University of Minnesota. I interviewed for it. I was about ten years younger than everyone else who was interviewed. It was an assistant director job. I left thinking I didn't have a chance in the world. I got a little irked because they didn't give me a minute on the schedule to ask any questions about the job. They filled up the schedule with "assigned" items.

I was supposed to do a presentation to the search committee. It was not a huge group, only about a dozen people. By the time I got to that part of the interview process, realizing it was toward the end, I just flat out said I wasn't going to do it. I had my slide tray (in those days that's what we had) and presentation ready to go, but I said, "Here's what I was going to talk about, and I'm going to cover that without all this stuff in just a couple of minutes and give you my ideas about what's needed in program development in natural resources. Then I want to use the rest of the time to ask you questions about this place, and your perspective on what you want out of the job." And I did that. A lot of harrumphing went on around the room, but it was courteous.

My wife had gone out to the interview with me, and when we left I told her I didn't stand a chance of getting that job. To my surprise, the phone was ringing with a call from Minnesota soon after we got back to Ithaca. I was asked to return for a second interview. The interview was only with one person, and that was the director of extension. He said he heard I'd

141

caused quite a stir, but they thought they might take a chance on me and offered me the job on the spot. A 50 percent pay increase, including an appointment in the Department of Fish and Wildlife. It was absolutely amazing. I came back home from the second interview, and soon had another call, from David Call, the dean of Cornell's College of Agriculture and Life Sciences. He called me in to his office and said, "What's this I hear about you interviewing at Minnesota? What is it you're looking for?" I said, "Well, I need some security, I need some more money and I'd like to try administration. That's what I did my dissertation work in." He said, "Well, here's what we're going to do. We're going to give you the same amount of money Minnesota is offering you, and we're going to give you security." It wasn't a job as a professor, it was as a senior extension associate. He said, "We're going to give you a new position in a new unit in Extension, the Office of Program Development and Evaluation. Cindy Noble (she was the director of Cornell Cooperative Extension at the time) wants you and a couple others to come over and work on that with her. Take what you did in your dissertation work and put it to use in the system here. Are you willing to do that?" I said, "Sure."

So I did that for a year and a half. I still kept my research program going, and did this new job half-time. It was one of the best jobs I ever had in my life. I was essentially an evaluation consultant to the system. I had an office in Martha Van Rensselaer Hall, and I worked with a whole bunch of new people, wonderful people in the counties and on campus. I learned about how to take evaluation ideas, just like my professors in education showed me how to do, independent of specific technical subject matters, and show people how to apply them. I actually got some publications in evaluation out of that. It was a great experience. I loved it. Cindy gave me a free hand, and I had some good mentoring from Carol Anderson, who was an associate director of Extension at the time.

I was there a year and half and I got another phone call, and I'm sure Cindy Noble, the director of Extension, set this up. The next thing I know, I find myself as an assistant professor and the department extension leader (DEL) in the Department of Natural Resources. That was in '88. That's when I became a professor.

There were only two administrative jobs in the department at that point, chair and DEL. In those days, the DEL had responsibility for program and budget. It was good administrative experience. Many chairs came out of the DEL ranks in the college; it was a training ground. I had a mandate to do what I loved to do in extension administration. I supervised several people. Our department had a large group of extension faculty and extension associates: probably twelve people, between support specialists, associates, and faculty, some of whom had been my professors when I was a student. I was able to keep my own research going in the area of the human dimensions of wildlife management. I was coleader of the Human Dimensions Research Unit (HDRU).

I want to tell you the story of how we established the HDRU. The story started for me with my master's program. I got a grant to look at the image of the DEC deer management program among the stakeholders in the Adirondacks. It was a huge controversy up there, a major contentious issue. The then chief of the Bureau of Wildlife, a Cornell grad, had said, "Our problem is not our biology but our image, our communication. We need you to go up there and look at that. You've been interested in it, go do it." So I did that piece of work, and when I finished, Tommy Brown kept me on. He was a research associate, and he had a couple projects he asked me to work on. He was a mentor for me as well. He's been the most consistent person I've worked with over my whole career. Tom does not have a Ph.D. He started in '70 in areas of research that would become the research unit, and I started working with him in '74 as a grad student. It wasn't a unit then, it was only Tom and an assistant working on a couple projects.

One day I came in and I said to Tommy, "We really ought to name this thing." So we called it the Outdoor Recreation Research Unit. I said, "We ought to have a logo." So we did that. "We ought to have a consistent report format." We did that. I ended up taking on some projects, expanding my portfolio, and gradually had staff working with me. We magnified the effort, drew in more money and grew from a couple people to a unit that focuses on the human aspects of natural resource management. That was an area that, believe it or not, was just not being studied. It wasn't looked into except from a recreational standpoint—as users, what do recreationists want. Soon, though, we were looking at how you do management, not just for recreation, but across the whole spectrum of natural resources, for the benefit of society.

Cornell is a land-grant institution. We're supposed to be doing work that's applied. The truth of the matter is, the biological work doesn't get you anywhere in the real world of natural resource management unless society is supportive of it. The top-down expert model was going by the wayside quickly. If it ever worked at all, it wasn't working by the late 1970s. I learned that from failure after failure of natural resource agencies, as a result essentially of revolutions by stakeholders where they used political means to take away authority from natural resource agencies. In the Adirondacks of New York, for example, the political folks got together because of the pressure from the constituents up there, and one-third of the state became off-limits for the New York State Bureau of Wildlife to do any deer management. That was a bit of a problem. It's not a success story.

We had some Bureau leaders who were very insightful about this, and they came to us saying, "You guys seem to know something about this." We were focusing originally on the recreational aspects. I wasn't, but Tom Brown came from an outdoor recreation background. I come from a wildlife management background, which is a little different. We started asking, "Why do you manage wildlife?" This is a fundamental question. It's not to make jobs for wildlife managers. It's to meet the needs of society. With that perspective, the number of stakeholders interested in wildlife management expanded from just the recreationists (i.e., hunters) to landowners, farmers, and forest owners. The managers in the Bureau knew little about what those folks wanted. They didn't deal with them much directly, at least not systematically, but they made assumptions about their attitudes and expectations. So we came in and did social science to try to identify who these stakeholders were and characterize them. What were the nature of the problems that they were having with wildlife and the nature of concerns they had with management technology? What did they want to see in terms of benefits from the wildlife resource, and how could that inform decision making so you could apply the biology to get those effects? The tradition had always been, and still is in many places, that agencies start from what they want to do on the biology side, and somehow it all works out. Well, often it doesn't.

We were so lucky to be in New York, where the DEC folks were willing to take chances and risks to learn about the systems they manage. We ended up being able to develop this specialization of human dimensions in wildlife management, in large part because of our relationship and work with the DEC. We've dealt with all sorts of issues. The neat thing was both Tom and I had extension appointments. We were able to take our research-based knowledge out to communities. More importantly, initially, we could bring it out to the wildlife professionals, who we saw as our audience for education efforts. New York was our specific case, but eventually other states were following New York's lead. The DEC in New York kept supporting us, and we kept them positioned as the lead agency in the country in this arena. Everybody looked to them regarding the human dimensions of wildlife management. We brought knowledge of what the real needs were of stakeholders to agencies charged with managing wildlife resources.

We've been through phases. In the first phase, we did survey research to help the agencies and the whole wildlife management profession go from a top-down, "We know what's best for you" approach to an inquisitive stance where they would realize, "We've got to learn what people want." We were instrumental in moving the profession out of a top-down approach and into what is called the "transactional phase" of wildlife management. (We wrote a paper on this.) New York State was a leader in that, through the collaboration between the DEC and our research unit. There was a point in time—I didn't know if I had my research hat on or my extension hat on—where I helped design, implement, and evaluate a citizen task force system for deer management, which became standard operating procedure for deer management in New York State. We studied this stakeholder engagement process to improve it as it was implemented across the state.

In the second phase of our work, we studied community-based approaches to wildlife management. It was revolutionary to go from the expert not being the only one who knows what's best to actually inquiring and using the input from stakeholders, even if it was remote through surveys. It was another revolution to go from survey research to transactional work where stakeholders interacted with one another. Still, the DEC staff members were the ones who did the work and took the risks associated with the change in approach. Now we've moved beyond that to a third stage, and the next revolution: comanagement, where communities accept some of the responsibilities with agencies, so it's a collaborative effort to get management done. We're in that revolution right now. It's been exciting to observe, study, and evaluate.

You can see there have been two levels of inquiry and education going on. One is for the professionals to understand how you do this work, to accept it and become comfortable with it (I don't want to make it sound like everybody's adopted this—that's not the case, but progress is being made). The second is for local communities to be able to be informed in their engagement, and sometimes to go from being informed to having the capacity to actually engage in comanagement. There's a transformation occurring here both for the professionals and the stakeholders. That's why I get excited about it. We have some wonderful staff and grad students in the Human Dimensions Research Unit who keep pushing this envelope.

My own work in the development of the Human Dimensions Research Unit has changed over time. At one point, I was a person who did surveys. With experience, I became a person who has a vision of where this whole thing might go, working with others in the design of studies. Nowadays I work with people who are trained to do surveys. I'm about to be the president of The Wildlife Society, the professional organization for wildlife managers. I hope to use this recognition to get us over the next hump and to gain global acceptance of these ideas about the human dimensions of wildlife management.

There are specific things our research unit has done that have made a difference. During the midseventies to mideighties we conducted studies of agriculturalists in New York State that demonstrated a threshold of tolerance for deer damage to their crops. This had great implications for management objectives. That was back in the inquisitive stage of wildlife agencies' approach to considering stakeholder input. We engaged farmers in discussions and did empirical studies. Around that same time, we were doing similar work on black bear management in the Catskills in New York that essentially upset the apple cart of assumptions in the theory and practice of bear management at the time.

If there's one thing that we have learned, it's the value of testing assumptions of wildlife management. We've often shown them to be wrong. For example, it used to be that deer managers would use the "principle of least complaints," where the level of complaints indicated that managers needed to minimize interactions of people with wildlife. Yet that's not what many people reporting interactions with wildlife valued at all. They needed to maintain some tolerable level of interaction. Same thing with the black bear issue.

A major watershed event was when we moved into piloting citizen task forces for deer management, in five different areas. Most of the people in the state agency here did not want to do that. Fortunately, we had a regional wildlife manager who was a respected risk-taker and a chief of the Bureau of Wildlife who supported him. I'd worked with the regional manager since I was an undergraduate. He trusted us. That individual showed that it could be done. Our research unit helped guide the design of the citizen task forces and evaluated the pilot implementation of the process. There were positive outcomes that came from it, not only in terms of getting stakeholder agreement on management objectives but also in improving the agency's image. The experience for a couple of skeptical wildlife managers was transformative. Afterward they stood up in front of their peers and said, "For the first time in my twenty-five years in this agency, I feel like a professional." These were watershed moments that just turned the whole tide. A lot of it was luck. We had a leader in the chief of the Bureau of Wildlife who had encouraged change. We had movers and shakers, innovators if you will, risk takers at the local level who we worked with intimately. They made it happen.

My relationship with the New York State Department of Environmental Conservation started when I was an undergraduate doing an independent study that was focused on a problem they had. I went to them with my study idea, and they said, "Sure, we'll let you do it." I interviewed leaders of that organization, and that's how they got to know me before I was even a colleague. The thing one has to remember is these things don't work unless people accept it. We were blessed and are blessed with some fine thinkers and innovators in the agency, and that's been my good fortune. That's also why I've been reluctant to leave New York from a research standpoint, because it is a fine laboratory. There's no other state that will be as good as this for the work I want to do.

In all of this, I'm not saying enough about Extension. We used extension educators as facilitators of all the citizen task forces during the pilot phase. I was giving training with my extension hat on for those people. I worked with the local extension people, who became key actors in this effort, and that helped to increase the interaction between the wildlife agency and local extension people. It was quite rewarding to me to get that interaction, when it really hadn't happened before. Now it's happened all over the state. There have been somewhere around 120 citizen task forces that have been formed since the first few pilots. Most of them have worked with extension educators.

Another landmark in this work was with The Wildlife Society. You have to understand, wildlife professionals specializing in human dimensions went from a feeling of being outcasts in professional wildlife management conferences to the fact that I'm going to be the next president of the Wildlife Society. One of the very few books that the Wildlife Society has ever published is the *Human Dimensions of Wildlife Management.* It is the first textbook of its type, and Tom Brown, Bill Siemer, and I were the editors and primary writers for the volume. It's a transition that twenty years ago you could never imagine would occur, because the wildlife management profession did not recognize at that time that this was an area of serious inquiry and application. Conventional thought was, "We know what's best for everybody. We just have to keep going to the biologists. We know more about the critters and the ecology, and if we know that, then we can do management."

Through our extension positions, Tom Brown and I disseminated knowledge to communities and professionals who work with communities in natural resource management. If we were going to get change and improvement in the management system, we had to deal with these professionals. Extension provided leadership for all that—leadership for change. We're change agents, in the old-fashioned sense: changing the perspective, philosophy, and approach of a profession across the country, starting in New York. In New York we helped lead a process of change in how the wildlife management profession interacts with communities, and how it builds the capacity of communities to deal with management problems. We helped lead that effort through research and education.

When I was department extension leader, our staff often thought the only audience they had was a landowner. I tried to emphasize through our extension educators that in the area of natural resource management, and it's probably true in other areas as well, we also need to be working with those professionals who are dealing with landowners, especially the ones who are implementing and interpreting natural resource management policy. Every interaction that we have with those folks is an educational opportunity: every single one of them. You should plan it that way. You should treat it that way. That's how I built my extension program. In large part, I directed it toward changing that set of people. That's still what I do. Part of my work is consulting and advising wildlife managers in nonformal situations, trying to help folks learn about how to do their work differently and more effectively.

I had an opportunity to do that when I went on sabbatical recently. I didn't take what might be a normal sabbatical. I went to work in Colorado with the Colorado Division of Wildlife as a human dimensions consultant to the agency. They asked me, "Can you help us build our human dimensions philosophy and capacity?" Those people didn't know me personally. I went out to Colorado, a dude from the east in their mind, and ended up helping them develop a human dimensions section of the Division through a relationship with

Colorado State University, a partnership that they didn't have before, but was contractual by the time I left. I learned that you can transport certain concepts from your research and extension experience from one place to other places, and with a strategy even accelerate their adoption. I undertook that whole assignment as an inquiry and educational effort. I applied an adoption model, which I wrote out and shared with the group. Essentially, I practiced extension education with them—adult education—and it worked.

In Colorado, they expected me to be this effete Cornell professor. I was going to come in and tell them what to do. Over the years they'd been through a whole series of hot-shot consultants coming in and telling them what to do, but who didn't really care a hoot about them. Instead of taking the stance of "I know what's best for you," I went in and asked them, "What do you need? What are the problems you're having? How can this organization respond to that?" I used that approach, starting where they're at, to bring them around and help them to see more clearly the human dimensions issues that were impeding their success. One has to take the initiative to go and do that. Isn't that how we should do it in extension education? It's like falling off a log for some of us. Yet in some disciplines there is a top-down tradition in Extension. I don't want my story to be interpreted quite that way. I don't think that's the way you do business effectively.

In terms of how I got tenure at Cornell, it was a combination of productivity, impact, and demonstration. The scholarly work I've done has involved identifying general themes, theory, and concepts that can be applied across all sorts of wildlife management arenas. I originated ideas, like a concept called "wildlife acceptance capacity," and published an article on it in an applied journal for managers. This and other concepts we have developed often are not the result of one study. We often do studies for agencies that need to make a decision today. But the thing we're always mentoring and training students and staff about is to keep in mind that we also have a scholarly, knowledge development, and conceptual development agenda as an academic institution. Every time we do an applied study to help meet a need out there, we must also keep in mind how we do that in a way that enables us to contribute to and keep improving our knowledge base and conceptual frameworks. Then we're doing our direct land-grant mission and our academic mission simultaneously.

I always try to integrate these two agendas in my work. There's the practical agenda of research for agencies, and then there's our own agenda as scholars. It took twenty studies to get where I felt comfortable with the wildlife acceptance capacity idea. I think it took literally eighteen studies to develop something we called the "wildlife attitudes and values scale," which has been widely used. It's a method for measuring people's wildlife attitudes and values. It's conceptual. A lot went into that. Eighteen practical studies went into developing a reliable measure for that concept.

I have interpreted the land-grant mission through my years of being an extension wildlife specialist as helping agencies and others to address societal needs as they relate to wildlife resources. Other people were doing that through understanding biology better. I felt that where I could make my contribution was through improving management by paying attention to people, to the human dimensions of management, which is a component that had long been ignored. The folks who pay taxes—not just for the agencies but also for the land-grant universities—were having real problems or were seeking real benefits from a wildlife resource. A public agency that was mandated to address those problems wasn't always doing so very well with the tools it had. As a partner in all this, which I think the land-grant institution is, the questions we asked were, "How do I bring research, the scholarship of discovery, to bear to improve the situation? How do I bring or integrate scholarship across disciplines to bear on the issue?" We have a relationship with many different kinds of stakeholders in the state around wildlife. I try to bring science and the knowledge that we were developing to help guide wildlife management policy and practice.

The essence of the land-grant mission is to help improve the lives of people. It is to help them meet their goals and objectives and to articulate and understand what those are. I don't mean us *telling* them what their goals should be, but rather helping people understand and realize what is possible or appropriate in their situation. Then they can communicate that to people who are supposed to help deliver those services. That's why the transition in wildlife management that I described, to transactional and comanagement approaches, was so important. We're accountable for having the results of management benefit people, putting it in the simplest terms. We're one player in that. Just like in agriculture, the university isn't the only player; it's one player.

Something that concerns me today is that I sense we're losing people in the institution (Cornell University) who are really concerned about the impact of their work on society. The work of academics, and its worth, often is judged not by the impact it's having on people, but on how peers in their field, doing similar kinds of work, judge their science. That scares me. People do great science. That's not the problem. The problem is maintaining their orientation, motivations, and willingness to benefit society, and not just their peer scientists. You hear folks say, "I do my science because it interests me, and the rewards are that I get publications." What in the dickens does that mean? You can count publications, but what does that mean? People have trouble articulating the impacts of their work without talking about publications or grants. If anything, grants and publications are a means to something. But what are the ends? What are the real fundamental objectives you're shooting for? At a land-grant university we need to keep our societal-benefits mission—our "prime objective"—out front.

In all fairness, I find that while some of my academic colleagues have difficulty articulating their social objectives, ultimately, they're very dedicated to trying to improve something in society. For example, they might say, "I may be working on some fundamental mechanism in biology, but ultimately the reason I'm doing that is because I hope that I can contribute to the cure for cancer." You might have to dig before you get them to say that, because that's not what counts in the world that they think that they're operating in. At least they perceive it that way. I find that to be very distressing. They should be able to articulate clearly the societal impact they hope to make, and feel good about it and be rewarded for it. This reinforces a sense of mission for the whole institution. It's pretty cold to say, "All I want to do is improve science."

There are threats to the land-grant mission. The dichotomy of basic and applied research is problematic. It sets up the impression that there are "better" and "lesser" kinds of research, almost like a caste system. What I like is when I talk to a department chair and he or she says, "We have people working over here in genomics, but the work that these people are doing is answering some fundamental questions that the people in the applied side of my department have to have answered, because they're stymied on this or that issue. If Jane can do this one piece, then Joe can move ahead on what he's doing, and the extension folks are getting the practical implications of the body of work out into the field." That's a conceptualization of how we work as a *system*, as opposed to individuals. That's good, but I fear that if we're not careful, we could lose a culture of this mission orientation. We have to reward the right kinds of things. I'm not saying we shouldn't do basic work, but rather, we need to be able to see how it fits. Folks have to feel like they're contributing to the whole mission. They have to understand the value of their scholarship for society, and that *that's* what's valued, not just that they do science for its own sake. It's the difference that I hold between a land-grant and some research institute, between doing fundamental work with an understanding of how it fits into creating an impact out in the world, versus you're just here because you want to win a Nobel Prize for your work someday.

To Be in There, in the Thick of It

A Profile of Marcia Eames-Sheavly

Senior Extension Associate, Department of Horticulture, Cornell University

Interview conducted by Lael Gerhart, April 2, 2004

The practice story Marcia Eames-Sheavly tells in this profile centers on her work of organizing a community garden project at an elementary school in Freeville, New York. Her story is instructive and deeply moving, on several levels. Working as a mother and community volunteer as well as an academic professional with expertise in horticulture, Marcia helps us to see how academic and public work can be integrated in mutually beneficial ways. She tells us how and why she aimed to facilitate a collective process of creating a community garden in a way that was "as *inef*ficient as possible." By being "in the thick of" a messy, time-consuming public work project, she shows us what it can mean for academic professionals to negotiate the dilemma of the relation of expertise and democracy in a public-regarding way.

My title is senior extension associate in the Department of Horticulture. I'm half-time youth development, and then another almost quarter-time teaching in the department. So I'm not quite three-quarter time. I've been in this system since 1987. I started out in Cornell Cooperative Extension in Saratoga County, came here, and my position has evolved. I have had the title that I have now for about four or five years.

The piece that I think is most relevant for what we're going to be talking about today is that I am the 4-H garden-based learning program leader. All of my energies are spent doing youth development extension work. I coordinate and develop resources for a statewide garden-based learning effort through Extension. I also work a lot nationally with folks to find out what's happening in our garden-based learning arena nationwide. I work very closely with the American Horticultural Society, for example. But primarily here in New York State, it's the coordination and leadership for the garden-based learning effort.

In our department, everyone loves plants. It's neat that we're all crazy about plants, and we garden at home. For many people in the department, it's both their vocation and avocation. What gets me excited is not so much the plants, but the plants as an avenue through which we can cultivate human and community well-being. I mean that just really thrills me. It's accessible, it's inexpensive, it's time honored. It's amazing the change that plants and gardens can make in a community and in an individual's life. That's what gets me going. It's not just the plants but how they have an impact on us, on a number of levels. My goal is to see that impact happen with young people and with adults, cradle to grave. Babies can interact with plants, preschoolers can have an experience with gardens, right on up through older folks who can be impacted by the garden. I like to see it across the life span.

In terms of the kinds of impacts that plants and gardens have on us, often we think about food—for example, in this department, healthy food. Or we'll talk about the act of growing plants as being healthy for us, and I think that's important. But it's just so much more. Plants have an impact on our well-being just by virtue of being beautiful. Sometimes I think we are almost embarrassed about that as a community of horticulturists. We think it's kind of a fluffy thing. I don't think it is. I think it's huge. We need now, more than ever, beauty in our lives. And plants can provide that.

I love to see kids get out of the house and interact with plants. More and more, I think people are concerned about the disconnect that people have from nature and their surroundings. The garden can be an avenue through which we reconnect—even just digging around in the soil, or whatever the experience is. I love to see kids moving outdoors again, and adults, too, for that matter.

In conversations about gardening these days, it seems like we're moving from seeing it as a deeply personal thing to more of a community experience. This can happen across the age and life span, and it can be multifaceted. So if a person can experience beauty and joy and healthy living and activity and a sense of well-being outdoors, and get exercise and all of these kinds of things on a very personal level, that same thing can happen on a community level, too. So there are so many layers. My goal is to see that happen more and more with folks in communities.

What led me to my work at Cornell? That's a question I think about a lot. I grew up in a very active gardening family, and I'm sure that has a lot to do with it. I grew up in Vine Valley, New York, which no one has ever heard of. It's a tiny little settlement on Canandaigua Lake in the Finger Lakes. We moved to the village of Canandaigua later on. I think, like many people in this discipline, my love of community horticulture sort of came around to me later. I was a horticulture major, so intellectually I fell in love with this discipline. But this stuff that I've been talking about that's important to me came later on. In my early thirties, it really just hit me. It all started to coalesce and come together. I had a family experience with gardens, I had a university experience, and now I have it at home. I can see the impact in the community, and I think that all started to pull together and gel when I was in my late twenties or early thirties. I think when you start gardening in your own home, it comes together. I grew up in a family that participated in gardening, but I don't think I had my own until I was in my maybe twenties or so. I had my own as a child, but there's something about coming back around to it later. It really grabs you.

When I was little we grew strawberries, and my mother had a monstrous perennial garden. We lived in a tiny little rural home, but the garden was a showstopper. What I think is really interesting, and I think about it a lot, is that I have two older brothers, and they were forced to work in the garden. We had a huge garden and a huge strawberry crop, and they had to work on it, whereas, as I recall, I didn't. I think because I was much younger and a little off to the side, they sort of forgot about me when they'd all go out and work in the garden. But now my brothers don't garden much, and I do.

I think that for me, gardening was like a backdrop against which my childhood played out. I can remember playing in the flowers. I can remember hiding in the lilac hedgerow and eating strawberries, and that sort of thing. But I didn't work as hard as they did. For me, it was not a work experience. It was more of this sort of background of my childhood. I think that's one reason that I've come back around to it, whereas they have not. We talk in our department at Cornell about people who are forced to work in the garden in their childhood. But that was not my experience. And I think it's not a coincidence that I came to it on my own later. I had a very rural upbringing, a lot of gardens and strawberries, and a massive vegetable garden. But I didn't associate it with anything negative, like, "Oh man, I have to spend all weekend out there!"

When I was an undergraduate, I did a total about-face, which I think happens to many people. I was a biology major, probably because I thought my biology teacher was incredible. If he had taught history, I might have been a history major. I was in a small women's college that I applied to because my guidance counselor suggested that I do it. It was Russell Sage College. I wasn't fond of it. I didn't enjoy it there. It was in a city. It was not an environment I was comfortable with.

I remember taking a walk one day and thinking, "I'm going to figure out what I'm going to do on this walk." I walked into a little shop called Of Growing Concern, and it was packed with plants. I took one look around, walked back, and made an appointment to talk about applying elsewhere. My biology professor said, "I think you should apply to Cornell, and I think you should go into botany." Later he was a little bit disappointed that I chose horticulture, because he viewed botany as being more science oriented. You know, we see these moments as being pivotal, as if they happen overnight. But then you look back and you realize that it was all leading up to that point.

So I came to Cornell and majored in horticulture. I loved it, absolutely loved it. I loved this department. I mean, I'm still here! Every once in a while my husband and I will joke around, we'll be walking around campus and say, "Oh, there's a lifer; there's somebody who never left!" And then we realize, "Oh yeah, we're that same kind of person!" When I was an undergraduate, it was a small and very nurturing department. Folks will talk about Cornell as being a big and kind of scary experience, but for me it was like being in a little village in the city. It was very supportive, a really good experience.

I think growing up with a gardening experience, going to university, and then having my own garden at home is what led me to the work I'm doing today. My position in Extension and here at Cornell is a 4-H and home-gardening kind of position. I don't know how to explain it, but for me, having that thing that we talk about at work—the plants and human well-being focus—reiterated at home in our own lives really makes it a powerful thing, rather than just being an intellectual thing that you've read about.

153

I think that my mother, who is a really passionate and total plant nut, is one of the people who influenced me. She's eighty now, and we'll be on the phone talking about what we are planting, and planning our excursions to where we're going to go scrounge up plants. She'll come to my home with a trunk load of plants. She still prunes my grapes for me. A lot of our relationship is around that, which is really fun.

In high school, I experienced my first truly passionate teacher—you know, the teacher who is so into what he or she is doing that it rubs off. And that was my high school biology teacher. He was an absolutely extraordinary person. I had this sense that biology is something that I really like, and horticulture wasn't a stretch after that. I mean it's almost more of a fine-tuning. And then I had this professor at Russell Sage who was kind enough—I would think it's difficult for a professor at a college to say perhaps you don't belong here, I mean to care that much that they can say to you, "I think you're not happy here and you would be happier elsewhere. I think there's a better fit for you." So those are three people along the way who just made me turn a corner a little bit and head in a slightly different direction, to focus in a different way.

Steve Austin was my biology teacher in high school. He was a passionate teacher. Sadly, I'm not so sure that we experience that as we're going through school, somebody who is wild about what they're teaching about, and they want you to be, too. He was warm and humorous. In high school, I was a terribly shy student, which now I find sort of hard to believe. I was *terribly* shy. He understood somehow that it was difficult for me to talk in front of people, and he would just sort of gently draw me out.

I think for me, the combination of really liking the subject matter, working with somebody who was passionate and caring and warm and funny, and clearly tuning into each student and how to work with them, was a really nice combination at that time. It's neat because he later on came to a keynote speech that I was giving, and I got to say in front of everyone there, "You know, at times in our life there's this person, this incredibly special person. He's right there today." He has since passed away. It was wonderful to have that opportunity to let him know, "You were the one who set me on this path," or one of them.

I think that there are probably a lot of small experiences that led me here, too many maybe to talk about in this conversation. I am not a narrowly focused person. I am not somebody who has my eye on this really focused thing that I want. For me, it's more about breadth. I love art; I'm a watercolor artist. I love gardening. I love working with people. I love to cook. This job really integrates a lot of that stuff. It integrates working with young people, and the people who work with young people and communities, and this greater appreciation of growing and loving the food and the plants in our lives. I think it's not any one thing. I think it's that this position allows me to pull all of that stuff together, all of those experiences, all of those little pivotal things that make me realize that I'm more about breadth than I am depth. It's definitely not that I have my eye on this one thing, and I'm working on a straight line to get there. It's richer and broader somehow.

Before I got my current job, I had a couple of really wonderful experiences. I worked as an intern in Minns Gardens at the Plant Science building on the Cornell campus, and at the Cornell Orchards. I was a technician for a couple of years. That was not viewed as a very lofty position by a lot of people. But I felt I needed it because if I was going to be involved in the plant world, I wanted to know how to grow them. So working in an ornamental and a food-related setting, I really know how to grow plants now. That's very important to me, that I am not just able to talk about it from a, "Well, I've read that this is the case . . ." *I really know about it.* I really have done it with my hands in a public garden and a working orchard setting. Those are two really pivotal experiences that were very grounding for me.

What I'll be talking with you about today is my work in a school garden program in a school that my children attended, and how that has become the framework on which a lot of my youth development work here at Cornell hangs. Even though it was a volunteer experience, it's become pivotal in helping me understand the realities, theories, and conceptual framework I now use in my extension work. It was a very exciting thing for me.

At one point, and this would have been quite a few years ago now, maybe eight or nine years ago, it seemed as if several things came together. I was working here in the department. My position had changed. I was doing all youth development, all programs and projects and creating resources around a notion of children and gardening. My husband and I have two children. One was in a little daycare center right across the street from an elementary school where my older son was going. The school asked me to be a part of a site-based team, which in New York State are these groups that engage in decision making. It's a way of New York State putting some of the decision making back into the community. So, there was this site-based decision-making team, and as a parent, I was involved in it.

This was a local school that was having some difficulties. From my perspective, many of the teachers seemed frustrated and even outright demoralized. It was at a difficult point in this school's life. We were talking about what would be a project that we could engage in that would rally people around something that we could master, feel good about and do, and feel a sense of accomplishment. It seemed to me that a garden might be a really wonderful way to go. I must say, looking back on it, we—I mean it sounds sort of trite to say we did everything right—but we really did a great job with this.

I didn't want it to be mine, or something that just I was doing, so I threw it out to this committee, "What do you think about this idea?" The idea I suggested was to create a very small, manageable school garden for students in grades K-4 that would create a sense of success and excitement, that would help pull this school community together to feel good about what we had done. It would connect to the curriculum, so it wouldn't be just an exercise in creating a garden. It would be created by a team of parents and teachers and community members working together.

This site-based decision-making team that I mentioned was the avenue through which this effort began. And then, there was a groundswell and others came to be involved in it. I was the parent on that team that brought the idea to the floor. My role in the project was as catalyst, cheerleader, and organizer. Eventually it was to step back and allow the movement of the thing to go on without me, because we eventually moved from this school.

What we did first was, we batted the idea around: "What do you think about a garden?" And people said, "It makes a lot of sense. We have a lot of room; we don't have anything like that. It could offer experiential learning for our students. We can do this. It's manageable. We'll do something really small, and we'll do well at it."

What often happens is people get excited about the idea of creating a garden and they get out the rototiller. But this committee took a year to plan it before ever digging up the ground. We talked about our approach, we planned what kind of a garden we wanted, and we met with each grade level to see what kind of theme might work with what the students were learning. We were very thoughtful about the process. We spoke with the principal, the custodian, with parents, with the groundskeeper. We talked to everyone who would possibly have an opinion about this before moving forward.

What I did was . . . You know, I have a hard time saying "I." In a community-based project, you want it to be *we*. So at the same time that I was initiating this and moving it forward, it was very important that "I" be a "we." What I did was bring up the idea and suggest a process. I said, "If you like these ideas, then we need to think about these things. We can't just get out the rototiller. We want to talk with people to make sure that people are on board, that there's a sense of ownership. We can't over-plan." I organized this effort, but I kept pulling in people at various points along the way to own it, to move it forward in their own fashion.

We began with a series of meetings, and I asked if there might be people that would like to be on a subcommittee, the site decision-making group that would be more like a garden planning committee. I identified another parent in the school that I knew was really crazy about plants. She actually works at the Cornell Plantations in youth education. She and I had similar roles. I asked if there could be two of us sort of leading the charge. We then began talking with other teachers to get a sense of their excitement around the project. It was a process that involved speaking with teachers, with parents, and with the principal. I remember lining up a meeting with the groundskeeper.

This may not sound earth-shattering, but often when people do a community-based project, they'll just *do* it. I spent a year *not* doing it, trying to think of everybody that needed to know or needed to be involved. With this kind of project, it's almost like we think in terms of efficiency. But for this type of job, I think of making it as *in*efficient as possible, because you want to pull in so many people. It's almost like a backward way of thinking. Instead of making a straight line to the garden, you want to think of all the different people that you can pull in. It may make it a little bit unwieldy at first, but it's a way of making sure that everyone is involved.

One teacher, for example, was most excited about the plants. I have a picture of her in my mind. She really embraced the idea that this was going to be a really good thing for the kids to learn about plants. I began talking with her about the kinds of plants that we might have in the garden. The other parent from the Plantations was all over the idea of this being a really good thing for her to be involved in as a volunteer, and she was really excited about her kids partaking in this. So she and I worked together to make contacts in the community, to begin lining up activities, to begin planning for the actual garden itself.

This teacher was much respected among the other teachers. The garden would be right outside of her window, which may not seem like a big deal, but she'd be looking at it every day. She was not what I would call an effusive, bubbly, warm person. She was very serious minded and would only embrace those things that she knew were going to work out. She didn't have a lot of time to mess around. But I talked with her, and asked, "Are you on board with this? Do you like this idea? Are you really going for this?" She was all over it. She then became the connection for the other teachers.

You have to understand that in a small rural community, a "Cornell person," as they're called, they're maybe not trusted much. So I really put myself in the role of Jake's and Will's mother in this project, and approached it as a parent. I really didn't want to step in and start telling the teachers, "Here's how this is going to be done." I worked with a teacher and she in turn, in team meetings, would talk to the other teachers about communicating what the project was about, getting their ideas for the plants they wanted in the garden and how it connected with their curriculum.

I only attended one of the main teacher meetings and did a slide presentation about children's gardens and the impacts that they can have on a community. It was full of beautiful slides and kids working in the garden and that sort of thing. It was as a catalyst; it was to get them excited. Then this teacher stepped in, and I asked her if she would feel comfortable being the one to communicate with the teachers.

I remember it was from September to April that we spent planning all the facets of the garden. I wasn't so much wrapped up with what plants were going to go into it as I was wanting it to be really, really well organized. I was more at the helm with the "who" part. I was asking, "Who are we going to involve? Who will be doing the maintenance for this program? Who needs to know? How do we get people excited about it? How do we guarantee that people are going to care for this, that it won't be vandalized, that people are going to own it? How do we create excitement among the students?" When someone got excited and said, "I'd like to do that, I'd like to be the one to communicate with the teachers, I'd like to be the one that helps organize the planting day," then I very quickly shifted out of that role.

Let me tell you about how this garden came about, and I think that will help you understand what I'm talking about. To the committee, I said, "You know, we could easily do this ourselves. We could do this ourselves. We could go out on a Saturday morning. The garden is small, we could do it easily. But let's think of how to be as *inefficient* as we possibly can. How can we involve so many people with this that people will feel that it's their garden?"

And so we planned a big bed-building day. We decided to have square raised beds. That's not an ideal children's garden design, but we knew that we could maintain it. I felt that in this case, for this site, it's not going to be what we know as ideal and having hiding places and water and all sorts of children-friendly things. We wanted to make a garden that would last and be well maintained. The other parent and I came up with a very simple design for beds that would be built. This was another place where someone said, "Let me take care of getting all the materials together for the beds." And someone else said, "And I will be the one that has the tools." And so on and so forth.

We asked the school to send a note home to every child in the elementary grades, saying that we're having a big bed-building and we want everyone there. We invited all the children. I remember asking the McDonalds and the Dunkin Donuts to contribute food. I sent a notice to the police and fire departments, letting them know we were doing this and please join us. I think I even sent a note to all the service groups, like the Rotary. Imagine taking this simple garden and making it into a three-ring circus! We wanted everyone in town there.

So on a Saturday morning there were 120 people that showed up in the rain. It was a day just like this in April, in the forties and raining. Tons of children. The school principal was there, and the groundskeeper. We mixed soil and compost in the parking lot and a couple hundred yards away we had people building the beds. I invited someone from the Department of Horticulture at Cornell to come and just be an extra, to oversee the whole thing. I knew I would be so wrapped up and involved that I might not see the forest for the trees.

And so we built the beds. We mixed the soil. Rather than take a backhoe and put the soil into the garden, which would take about five minutes, we lined all 120 people up from the parking lot to the beds and they passed the soil in fifty small buckets for an hour and a half. And the kids all year would point to the spot where they dumped the soil from their buckets and say, "That's mine! That's my spot! *I did that!*"

Because we had 120 people there, 120 people owned that garden that day. It was a very, very simple bed structure, but a heck of a lot of people made it. The principal, she was just circulating and talking to people, and there were people in the school bringing out coffee and sandwiches and donuts to the people who were working all morning.

When we left, we had done this really incredible community thing. And I had initiated this whole process and organized it. But, I realized later that summer that my deep-seated goal of wanting to disappear, of not wanting to be seen as a foreman, came true when someone came up to me and said, "Did you see what they did here?" And my inner reaction was, "*They?!?*" She said, "Come here, I want to show you something," and brought me over to this garden which was in full bloom and was just extraordinary.

She said, "Look what they did," and then explained this whole process to me. "There was this day, and all these people came together in the community and they created this thing, and it's amazing. And my child was the one that put the footing in, right there!" I stood there talking to her and I realized that it's a community thing. It isn't identified as one person's project, which was really important to me. Everyone, *everyone* owned it. It was an incredible thing, and I look back on that as being an ideal experience, because we moved away and it's still thriving.

Reflecting back on it, I feel as if I spent that whole first year sort of putting on the brakes, saying, "No we don't want to get the rototiller yet. Just wait." I was trying to help people understand the significance of this yearlong process of bringing people in, that it would totally minimize problems that could happen later on. I think the only problem that I remember is that this was a school where the teachers didn't feel that they had the authority to do this incredible, huge, community wide thing. Getting over the sense of feeling beaten down was difficult.

I do remember something about this teacher that I mentioned earlier, who was really almost stern at times. She wasn't warm and effusive. She was an excellent teacher, and that's where she put her energy. But after we did this, she said, "I don't ever remember such a successful event in the school or such a successful program. *This is the greatest thing we have ever done.* And there are so many people involved." She said that later she would go in her classroom in the summer, and the garden became a destination point for grandparents and their children who would go there. In later years they added on to it. They built a deck, they built benches, and it expanded. And she said that it was becoming a community focal point. Never a thing vandalized. It was sacred ground. There were too many people involved. It was loved by too many people to ever have anything messed with, despite the fact that it was in a very public place.

Back to the feeling of being beaten down and kind of coming out of that, one thing that I quickly realized was that these teachers were working so hard. I remember a meeting where the project was raised and the superintendent was in the room. I just noticed a change in the behavior of the teachers. I remember asking him questions about coming and visiting the school, spending time in the classroom. It was clear that he didn't. The teachers just seemed, I don't know, there was like a weight over them or something. One of their concerns was, "We're already so overwhelmed, this is going to overwhelm us further." So I suggested that we form a partnership, and that the parents make the commitment to oversee the care of the garden, and the teachers make the commitment to take advantage educationally of the garden. I said, "This won't be burdensome for you."

An example that comes to mind is planting day. We suggested that rather than have a few kids in the school do the planting, that every child participate in planting by way of a relay; eight kids come out from a class, eight kids go back in. Eight more, they go back in. Eight more, they go back in, until we end up with four or five or how many hundred kids. I said, "We'll organize that. The parents will take care of that." I called other parents, I had them at stations out there, each was assigned a grade level, and each oversaw the relay of kids who would come out to plant.

When the teachers realized, some of them who were worried about this overwhelming them, that we had an incredibly well-organized planting day, in which every child in the school participated, it evolved into events where we'd have other activities out there for them. They realized all of this was going to happen and that they'd be able to take advantage educationally of this amazing event. And we said, "Trust us, we're going to organize this well." Then, I think, there were some that really turned the tide and said, "This is cool, we can do this, this is great. We trust you now."

The parents are the ones that said to the teachers, "Let us organize the planting and everything, you do the teaching, you take advantage of this in your curriculum, that's your job." So there became a real division of labor. And I think the teachers came to see parents as these capable people who could do an incredible educational program outside and not just pour Kool-Aid or serve brownies. The parents that we brought on board were hardcore gardeners who contributed plants from their gardens. There was a real turning of the tide when the teachers realized, "This isn't going to flatten us; in fact we're going to look out our window and see this riot of color all spring and fall." So it was really exciting. It was a real crucial point.

There were people who were so worried about this being one more thing on their plate. Without this yearlong organization ahead of time, I think it may have not been successful, but anything that could have been thought out in advance was. I remember that feeling of having so many people start to realize that this is really quite amazing. It doesn't cost much. It takes a little time, but with planning that's minimized. And it was really an incredible project.

Summer maintenance is a real problem for school gardens. This teacher that I mentioned, I talked with her and said, "How about if you were to take a calendar to all the teachers, and I were to take that calendar to the parents and everyone were to sign up for a several-day period in the summer to adopt the garden? People would get a certificate of adoption, and that means that they need to water, they need to weed, but most importantly they have to go every day. Even if they don't have anything to do there, they have to be there every day." And she said, "I think that's a great idea."

She and I worked together to make the calendar. What it meant was that all summer, every day, there were people in the garden. It's really pretty remarkable when you think about it, for a small community in the summertime. Of course, what does that lead to: picnics in the garden, activities in the garden, playing on the school playground, games out on the lawn. All summer long there's somebody there. It solved the problem of summer maintenance, and once again, it was also an opportunity for people to buy in, to own it, to be there, to be present. There was not a weed in that garden when people came back in the fall, and it was a knockout—absolute knockout! So again, I felt that anything we could do to go from "I" to "we," to the "big" we, was so important.

Bringing it back to my position here, I tell people all the time how to go about these projects. Most of what people will do is focus on what to plant, or what kids like. But for me, now I feel that I have this framework in my head of this whole process of bringing parents on board, teachers on board, community members on board, thinking about what plants do grow well, how it connects to the curriculum, who never to leave out of the loop, what community members to approach for donations. The fund-raising around this was a whole other thing. It really became a great learning experience. We said, "We can do this, we can make money, and it's not going to be that big a deal." And we did; we made lots of money.

Everything that I do in this job with respect to youth development hangs on the framework of that one volunteer effort. People will ask me, "How would you suggest doing this?" And you know how you have a map in your head, this conceptual framework that you hang theory on? It all gets tucked there. *Everything for me gets hung on the conceptual framework of this one community project.* For me that's so important because it's not just something I've read about. It's not just something I've dabbled in or that I've witnessed. To be in there, in the thick of it, is a much more meaningful way than, here in Extension, telling people statewide how you go about this. Well, *I know how to go about it.* That's why, although it was a volunteer thing, it's just so deep in my heart as such a formative experience. It's the thing on which everything sits for me.

I would say—and this is my experience, maybe other people would say something else—but here at Cornell it seems to me that there's a lot of ego and a lot of authority and a lot of expertise. But in community projects, you have to think of a way to get yourself out of it, like how do you pull back your person? How do you quickly become a member of a greater team and gently be moving a movement forward in a way that people don't realize you're doing it? That for me is the goal. What are all the ways that you can get people to step in and own it? You can still be the catalyst, the organizer, the coordinator that's moving it forward, but if somebody asks whose project is this, and everyone points at you, that's not the goal for me.

What is the goal? It's to have *this* group that is doing this, and *this other group* that is in charge of fund-raising, and *these teachers* excited about this butterfly garden. In the process, you begin to step back and watch things happen, or be gently moving them along, but not so flat-out yourself that you're doing everything. I think that our model in the university is often that we have to be in the limelight, and we have to get credit for it, and we have to be the experts. This—what I have described—is like a totally different way of thinking about these things.

If I could have done something differently in the project, one thing that we realized a year or two into it was that it was dominated by adults. If I were to do it all over again, that first year of planning I would have pulled, for example, a child from each grade level to be on the planning team, or maybe turned to the fourth-graders and said, "You're the oldest in your school community, we would like some advisors from your group to serve on this committee." Or maybe work them into a different approach, so that they don't have to sit through dry committee meetings, but that they're doing something concurrent. As it was, we involved the kids: they named the garden, and they were involved in all the activities. But if I were to do it again now, eight years later, I would involve them much more in decision making.

There was a phase 2 to the project. It involved the kids in decision making. We interviewed them afterwards, and they said—this came from each of them—that one of the most exciting things for them in the second part of the project was that adults cared about what they thought. They weren't used to that. We didn't do that in the first phase. I don't know that I was as in tune with youth voice and with young people's participation at that point as I am now. I was much more into just the organization of it from more of an adult and community perspective. I do think that the single biggest problem in the children's gardening movement is that you have these passionate, caring, earnest adults who do the project, and then the children participate in it. But they could be involved much more in the decision making. I would have done that differently now.

One thing that I learned was that not everyone has to buy in at the same time, or at the same rate. There are people who are early. There are the people who jump into an idea, other people who hang back to see if it works, and other people who may never embrace it. I learned that some of the people who hang back and watch to see what's happening, but then embrace it, may be your greatest supporters over the long haul. People who don't just jump into anything new but really want to see how it's going to go are often the ones that stay with it the longest. They're not just jumping on the newest idea and moving on to the next thing. I learned a lot about different learning styles and how people work together, and understanding that someone with a different approach, you can maybe learn from them. It's really exciting when you're working with a community of people, taking advantage of all those different approaches. If we all did everything the same way, it wouldn't work out.

In terms of what I think we accomplished in this project, we showed people that if we all work together toward a common vision, we can do something extraordinary. Something extraordinary in this case may not seem like much—a small garden. But for a community of folks who were feeling that they couldn't achieve or maybe hadn't had a success in a while, it was a really big deal. Also, we learned that many hands make light work. Often I'll see that people will get involved in a community project and they want to run the show. But if you want it to last, that's probably not the best approach.

Some of the key contributions I would say I made were balancing the need for organization with understanding plant needs. It was huge; I don't know how to sum that up. It wouldn't be there, there would not be a garden, if I hadn't been involved. So the garden itself could be a key contribution. It enlivens the school landscape. It's a gathering point. It's beautiful. Kids love it. There are birds that visit the garden. I mean the garden itself is a key contribution. But the sense that "we can" is a key contribution, too, that people feel that they can achieve something.

The kinds of skills I would say are necessary to achieve a project like this include recognizing different abilities in people, and that there is a role for everyone—understanding the need for creating ownership, and understanding the need for creating a sense of identity around a project. Certainly, there's a whole group of folks who need skills in planting, in knowing what plants need, what plants are going to thrive, and the full kind of horticultural skills arena. There are two pots of skills: one around horticulture, and one around organizing.

We had people who would come and say, "I really don't know anything about plants." Well, it doesn't matter. There's a role for everyone. I think that's probably the main thing, understanding that we can all find a place. I think it's one of the biggest skills, understanding not that there's a certain type of person who can rally around a project like this, but that there's a role for everyone, that everyone can be welcome. Everyone can come to the table. Everyone has something to contribute, and everyone can gain from it. Obviously, something like this isn't just for children because it's in a school. It benefits anyone who interacts with it in any way. So everyone can contribute, everyone can gain.

Where do I think I learned how to do this? That's a really good question. Of course, we read about it here at the university, and we have an understanding of it intellectually. But I think the roots of that understanding are around my father who was very much about not calling attention to yourself when you are involved with a group. He was very involved in the community, but I remember him being very happy in the role of worker bee. Part of it was that he had a very deep faith, a very deep spirituality, and he had this belief that you don't do things to call attention to yourself. I think maybe that's where the roots of that are. If you're working in a community setting, you're one of many, and it's not desirable to put yourself in any sort of a spotlight for things to be a success. I think maybe that's where some of that comes from. I feel as if I should quote, you know, great philosophers and educational theorists. But no, I think I learned this from my father.

If you ask what the benefits of gardening are in terms of community education and development, I would say there are several. There's the whole benefit of the product, the amazing appearance of a garden and what it can do for people's souls. Just the garden itself is a benefit. It looks extraordinary. Food comes out of it. There are educational things we can learn from it. We can celebrate it, and have celebration and events around it. Our children can reconnect with nature, see a butterfly and watch a bird feed. There's a lot we can learn from a garden.

The benefits are also from participating in the process, what we can learn about that, about each other and how we all have a role. Projects on a grander scale can catalyze support, new initiatives, and community. Even this project brought in funding. We did fundraising, and we made money and became very sustainable. It can bring support into the school or the community that wasn't there before, and expertise and people, folks who are enthusiastic about the project. It can be a catalyst through which other good things happen in the community as a direct result.

Even though it's a garden, the horticultural knowledge is probably the least of the worry. We know you have to work with the soil and find a right site and all that business. But I think the real challenges are moving this giant body of people forward and helping people to see how critical it is to move slowly, to involve others and to think of everyone that ought to be involved, to ask people's opinion. The whole process of moving a group of people forward is challenging—and also, understanding that not everybody's going to buy in all at once.

I think this kind of work is great, I really do. And I just absolutely *love* it. I get really excited when people call and say, "We're thinking about starting a community garden or a nature trail or a school garden or an adopt-a-plot. We're thinking of doing this in our community. How do you suggest we begin?" When I get these calls, this whole experience pops up in my mind, this whole process, and overlaid on that is everything that I've read and learned.

I think gardening is a way of bringing people back together. It's really odd when you think about it, that we have a setup in our communities where children are completely isolated from the rest of folks in town. From a very early age, they go to schools on their own, they come home, they're with their families, they're in structured activities with kids their own ages. There are few opportunities for lots of people of diverse ages and abilities to come together. And that's something important that happens in this kind of work. A child may be working alongside an older person in the community who loves composting. That's where it happens, and what it's all about. I really believe there are fewer and fewer opportunities for that sort of thing to happen.

What's got me really jazzed right now is this whole garden-based learning part of my job. I have another completely separate part of my job, teaching art and horticulture. I want those worlds to come together. I haven't been to a professional development opportunity in a long time, and I'm so excited that at the end of April there is an international symposium in Vancouver, Canada—Art, the Environment, Community Activism, and Youth. I'm so excited. I would like to start pulling the arts into this notion of plants and gardens as an avenue through which we pursue human and community well-being. I'm not quite sure what it looks like yet, but I'd like to be doing that more, pulling those pieces together. That's my goal for the next few years. I'm hoping to come back really charged from that symposium with ideas to incorporate art more explicitly. With this project I have been telling you about, might there have been some evening mini-theater opportunities or musical performances, taking advantage of the garden as a backdrop through which those types of things happen? As I recall, we may have done a little of that, but to do that more explicitly would be exciting. I'm eager to see what that looks like.

I Never Set Myself Up as Somebody Special

A Profile of Antonio DiTommaso

Associate Professor, Department of Crop and Soil Sciences, Cornell University

Interview conducted by Milt Kogan, April 9, 2007

"Someone has to be responsible to society for the long term," Antonio DiTommaso points out. "Who's it going to be?" As we learn from reading his profile, Antonio assigns a share of this responsibility to publicly funded faculty members such as himself. He pursues it in practice through his research on, and teaching about, weeds. As a participant in the public work of pursuing sustainability, he often travels beyond the campus to farms and towns in New York State, and to neighborhood gardens in New York City. While he holds a tenured faculty position in an elite research university, he tells us that he never sets himself up as somebody special. Rather, he sets himself up as a learner, both with his students and with the farmers and community members that he works with. We can learn a lot about the significance and value of higher education's public purposes from his views, stories, and experiences.

I'm an associate professor in the Department of Crop and Soil Sciences at Cornell University. My official appointment is 55 percent research and 45 percent teaching. I've been at Cornell for eight years, since 1999.

I was born on June 11, 1962, in a small village south of Salerno in southwestern Italy. The town was called Piaggine, and it had a population of about 3,000 folks, mostly agriculturists and farmers. I learned what subsistence agriculture was like there. This was in the late 1960s, and the southern part of Italy still wasn't very industrialized, certainly relative to northern Italy. We had about thirty dairy cattle that were free-roaming during the spring and summer months. I spent time working with my dad. When I was nine, my parents decided to emigrate to Canada, where they had family. The main reason was economics. My father had worked ten years in Germany, so he knew what it was like to be elsewhere. They loved the land and the culture in Italy, but economically farmers were down the totem pole in that part of the country at that time. My dad just didn't want to see us languish and not get anywhere with all this hard work. There was also a societal hierarchy back then in that part of Italy where if you weren't the son or daughter of a lawyer, engineer, or medical doctor, you had little chance of making progress in life. He didn't want that for us.

In 1971 my parents decided to move to Montreal in Quebec, French Canada. I remember it clearly. We moved on May 15. My older brother, named Enrico, was eleven at the time, and I was nine. We were the only two kids in the family. It was tough leaving the homeland because the cherry trees already had small fruit at that time, whereas when we arrived in Montreal, snow from the winter was still piled up in the city parks. We were devastated. But we did have family. My father had a sister and brother in Montreal and lots of relatives, so we had a fairly strong community of folks to help us. Still, we didn't understand a word of English or French and really felt displaced. We cried some, and we asked, "Why are we doing this?" It took us about a year to adjust, to learn to play hockey and baseball and settle in. So I grew up in Montreal and lived there for about thirty years. I completed my undergraduate degree majoring in environmental biology at McGill (Macdonald Campus) in Montreal.

My dad had several jobs when we first arrived, but mostly he worked as a custodian in a local hospital. He also was an assistant chef in Italian banquet halls. He would help serve two or three hundred folks. He was, and still is, a great cook. My mom, on the other hand, was a seamstress. She worked in the textile industry in the seventies and eighties. This is before all of the textile work was shipped elsewhere in the world, especially to developing countries. Mom was a great cook, as well, by the way.

My dad loved gardening. We had a small yard—no bigger than twenty by ten feet—in the middle of a city of about three million people. He wasn't afraid to plant anything. At one point I counted that he had about thirty different plant species in our garden, including a fig tree. He planted tomatoes, grapes, plums, eggplants—anything you could name, he planted it. He raised and used every part of the plant. The green tissue would be used for composting; nothing was wasted. Seeds were kept for the next year. It was almost like the old country, except that now we had more freedom to do it without worrying about having enough food. In our family that was never an issue. We didn't come over, as many of our relatives did, in the early part of the twentieth century, or even after World War II. We were relatively well off economically. We didn't come with only a suitcase in hand. I want to make that clear. We flew in. We didn't take a boat. That was already different. We were one of the last families in our village to emigrate. We have relatives all over the world because of the economic hardships people faced in our region of Italy.

My dad had a real passion for plants. He couldn't wait to get his hands into the ground. I would help him out every step of the way. My brother didn't enjoy that part. He's now a psychology professor at the University of New Brunswick in Canada. He enjoyed reading and listening to music much more than working in the garden. He was more of a homebody type, but we both loved sports. We quickly learned to play on organized and pickup baseball and hockey teams, which helped us to strengthen our language skills and allowed us to integrate into the Quebecois/Canadian culture relatively quickly.

I mentioned that my father planted a fig tree in our yard. I think it was his attachment to the homeland. He didn't want to forget about it. Each year, he'd bury this fig tree because it couldn't survive in the Canadian winters. Anything below twenty degrees Fahrenheit would basically kill a fig plant. So he would bury the whole tree, roots and all. He would bend it. The one thing about fig trees is that their trunk and branches are relatively flexible. They bend almost like willows. Basically the front and the back end of the root system were cut so that just the horizontal roots remained in the earth. He would toggle it down, and dig a trench of two or three feet. Then he'd bend the whole tree in. He would tie up the branches so they wouldn't be springing, because it was a pretty big plant. Then he would cover the tree with old carpets, straw, and leaves. This was sometime in October, and the tree wouldn't come out of the ground until late April the next spring. The whole fig tree! It would be pulled back up—straight up. The plant was kept alive by its horizontal roots, because the front and back ends were basically cut. The plant obviously never achieved maximal growth. But it was a rite of spring in our household. It was amazing the amount of time we spent on that tree, and how we looked forward to seeing if it would survive from year to year. It was a "coming to life" that really struck me as a young kid growing up. I said, "Boy, that's interesting." I think that's where some of my passion for plants and then weeds began, and why I decided to pursue a formal education in agriculture and the environmental sciences.

My undergraduate and graduate degrees were all completed in Canada. As I mentioned, I completed my bachelor's degree at McGill University in environmental biology. I always had a passion for plants, so I completed a master's degree in plant ecology at Queen's University, which is in Kingston, Ontario, right across Lake Ontario from Watertown, New York. Queen's was a good school, and I enjoyed my time there. Then I went back to McGill University to complete my Ph.D. in biological weed control.

My brother's and my advanced degrees certainly proved and confirmed to my parents that their move to Canada was a good one. The decision was tough, having to leave the old country and what they knew. My mom had six siblings at home in Italy, and to leave like that—boy, I admired her courage. It wasn't easy. I think they were delighted that we both went on to be professors at universities. My dad gets a real kick out of the fact that I'm in agriculture, or at least a field related to plants. He's still alive. Both of my parents are. My dad is seventy-three, and my mom is seventy. They remain some of the best cooks I've ever experienced. A characteristic of that generation, whether they are Italian, Spaniard, or from somewhere else, is that they made use of every piece of meat, and everything that came out of the garden. They still do. They make their own salami and *soppressata* and an array of cakes and biscuits. They still make their own tomato sauce and homemade wine. They make things with eggplants and vinaigrettes, and they ship stuff to us to this day. My brother gets stuff, too. He lives in New Brunswick, which is a Canadian province in the Maritimes, just north of Maine. It's neat to see when all the goodies arrive. It's amazing that they keep doing that. I think it reflects their attachment to family, the land, and how they were raised.

Although my parents had family here, being culturally cut off from Italy was pretty hard. Today, whenever I meet Italian citizens, graduate students, or folks from Italy, when I speak to them in Italian, I speak a dialect that their grandparents spoke. They don't hear that dialect any longer, because basically the Italian language has evolved since the early 1970s. I had picked up whatever my parents knew, which was Neapolitan. Although I'm fluent in Italian, when I get into the Neapolitan dialect, Italian strangers' eyes open up. Here's a forty-year-old guy—me—who speaks this form of Italian!

My grandfather, who passed away at ninety, would always tell me that he loved that I was in a discipline of science and admired that I "knew what I was doing." He would say that I was doing exactly what he used to do in his life, except I had twenty years of university to back it up. He admired that I knew what manure did for the soil. "Much better than I knew it," he would say. "I just threw it on and prayed to God. You, though, understand what manure may mean for soil fertility or weed control."

Those are my major influences in a nutshell. I had a love for the land. I also enjoyed being outdoors. I could not be indoors. Every moment that I could I would be out in nature, even a city park would do. I just loved nature in general, so it was great when I was offered the position here at Cornell, doing the very things that I love.

Cornell is really the second university I've taught at. When I finished my Ph.D. at McGill in Montreal in '95, it happened to be in August. By September, I was helping to manage the lab of my major professor for my Ph.D., Professor Alan Watson. Alan was "seconded" at that time. For five-year time spans, he would be in the Philippines, at the International Rice Research Institute (referred to as IRRI), to help develop and implement biological weed control programs in rice systems. He would spend half the year in the Philippines, so I was asked if I could manage his lab during his absence. There were easily fifteen people in that lab when I started. I was also asked to teach some of Alan's courses, even though I had no postdoc experience. I had served as a teaching assistant many times during my Ph.D. preparation years, and I also guest-taught a course in plant ecology for a professor who was on sabbatical. So the McGill administrators knew what they were getting, in a sense. They recognized my passion and interest in teaching. That's how I began at McGill. I taught there in a nontenured position and carried out research in the Biopesticide Laboratory at McGill for four years. So I worked in Canada from '95 to '99.

I came to Cornell in August of '99 because the McGill position was a temporary and nontenured position. I was on soft money. I was looking for long-term stability. By then, I'd been at McGill for so many years. I did my undergrad, my Ph.D., and had filled other positions that came up there. It was time for a change. We couldn't have found a better location than Cornell or Ithaca. Cornell is such a world-renowned place. In fact, several of my professors from McGill had obtained at least one degree from Cornell. It wasn't far from home, and most important, I knew the agriculture. Northeast agriculture was similar to what I had experienced in southwestern Quebec. Also, my wife was an ornithologist and the Cornell Lab of Ornithology was here. It just worked out really well for us.

I remember as soon as I arrived at Cornell, in mid-August, I began teaching. Typically, most faculty don't teach right away. Professors need time to get their courses together, but I came in running because I had taught the previous spring in Canada. As soon as I arrived, I was teaching my introductory weed science course, which had about twenty students. It was the only weed science course that was available to most of our ag students. I taught the course my first semester and repeated it the following year. I've been teaching that course every fall since. I picked up a course three or four years ago called Integrated Pest Management, or IPM. I co-teach that course with John Losey, an entomologist colleague from the

Department of Entomology. Also, I now teach a graduate-level course every other year called Weed Ecology and Management. This spring I'm teaching it again. I have about fifteen students in the course.

People ask me if I get tired of teaching the same course all the time, but I always mention to them that teaching was the reason I came to Cornell in the first place. It was important to me then that my appointment had a teaching component. At McGill, it was 60 percent research, 40 percent teaching. I had been offered a couple of positions in my area of expertise, which is weed ecology, in Canada that involved 100 percent research. I turned them down, because I needed to be in touch and in contact with students. It was a passion that I had. I still have it. It's probably been instilled in me from when I was a student.

I was influenced by a number of professors who were stellar in terms of what they did—their research and their ability to communicate information to students. There are few people who can do that really well. In my mind, I said, "I want to be like that. I don't want to be like these professors that are stellar or outstanding researchers, but who never turn around from looking at the board or the screen to look at their students, to see if they understand the material or not." I wanted to really be connected to my students and make them see the excitement that I saw in the course material that I presented. I always told myself that if ever I get to a position where I'm actually on the other side of the blackboard or the desk, I want to convey my passion and interest to my students. Because they have it, too, and it's just my responsibility to pull it out of some of them. In my view, it doesn't matter if a teacher or researcher brings in a million dollars worth of grants. If he or she can't communicate that information to students and the public in general, then I think we're all missing something.

I enjoyed my original field of plant ecology. That's the discipline I received my training in at a master's level. As I was going through that program, I realized that it was fairly strong on the theoretical. I didn't want to spend my time working on models of what might be, and what happens with *this* population if *this* happens. I needed to *apply* my knowledge. As I was completing work on the effects of soil fertility on plant competition in an old field, I asked myself, "How do I apply this?" As I began reading weed science articles in some of the scientific journals while I was doing my master's, I said to myself, "This is exactly what I'm looking for!" Weed science is really a field of applied plant ecology. You're applying plant ecological principles in agro-ecosystems. You're having an impact on growers and other people who need help. Weeds are frequently a major constraint in most agricultural systems, whether you're in industrialized or developing countries. It's often the number one issue, or maybe second to fertility.

I'm interested in the sustainable management of agricultural systems, and trying to move us as much as possible away from our sole dependence on herbicides and pesticides to manage pests. I feel that economic and environmental sustainability should be the major impetus for weed science practitioners such as myself. When I look back at my youth in Italy, what I see is that the land had small landowners. My folks didn't have a hundred acres or two thousand acres—it was maybe five acres. They just got the most out of the land, primarily because they had diversified crop systems. They grew a lot of different things, including potatoes, corn, fava and dry beans, and beets. Crop rotation and intercropping were integral

169

parts of their cropping system, with lettuce, for instance, planted in between rows, or inter-cropped with tomatoes. Things always came in and came out; the soil only rarely had no vegetation on it. However, I also knew how difficult it was sometimes to manage weeds, because we didn't have any herbicides at our disposal. Everything had to be hand-weeded. I'm certainly not saying this type of approach was great. We were happy and had plenty of food, but it was a difficult life and it was physically tough.

Today the use of herbicides and pesticides is a touchy issue. There is no doubt about it. People are always pointing out that chemical pesticides affect health. I talk about it in class, though I try not to bring out my personal view in my teaching. I try to provide students with perspectives on both sides. For instance, I ask, "Why do we need herbicides in certain situations? Why don't we in others, but we spray anyway?" I treat herbicides like any pesticides. They're chemicals. They should be used judiciously and according to label directions. Some of these products may be more problematic than others. My general feeling, and this is a personal opinion, is that there generally is no need for the use of herbicides or pesticides in urban areas, certainly related to landscaping. Given the way our agriculture is practiced at this stage, it's difficult to ask growers to stop using herbicides when they have to manage one thousand or one hundred acres of cropland. And they are aware that a fair number of urban and suburban people are using herbicides on their lawns! I can't expect farmers with one thousand acres to transition out of using herbicides on their land when they need to make a profit from their growing activities. I say that mainly because we don't have any easy or quick alternatives right now. It's difficult. The problem lies in the way we practice the agriculture. Industrial agriculture makes it very difficult to wean ourselves off the use of pesticides.

There are two sides to this issue, and I can see the merits on both sides. Certainly, I'm not comfortable with the direction that agriculture is going, with relatively few multinational companies dominating the agribusiness sector. In many ways, power and decision-making is taken away from the growers. In today's agricultural and economic environment, you have to be a large grower, buying up smaller local farms, to make it. I have issues with that. I don't think it's sustainable long-term when 99.5 percent of our population has little clue as to how their food is produced and where. I don't say that with any disrespect, but basically, most urban dwellers are not working the land. They're depending on 0.5 percent of the population to grow their food. This is why we run into the issues of agrochemicals. Part of it is that we have this urbanization of the American population. How do we get these folks to get in touch with the land once again? I don't think urban people would do that voluntarily. The truth is that if there is a famine one day, those who can get back to the land and grow something are going to make it and the others are not. As I mentioned, we have a large sector of the U.S. population that has little clue as to where their food comes from. That's scary! What I'm saying is that, in a sense, we cannot blame these large agribusinesses. They're giving people what they want. So who is to blame? What came first?

Folks are going to have to reassess. Consumers are going to have to reassess. Ninety-nine percent of Americans may decide to live in urban areas, but we all have to figure out if we really want to depend on the 0.1 percent or the 0.5 percent of the population to feed us. If we have issues with farmers or agribusinesses, we can't just blame them. Today farmers need to farm two thousand acres or more, and that generally means that operations have to be mechanized and likely be dependent on synthetic inputs such as fertilizers and pesticides, because there is little chance that we can feed our population in any other way using this model of agricultural production. Some people say we should just let other countries feed us. "Let *them* be the farmers," they say. But just look at what's happening to us, with our dependency on foreign oil and energy supplies. Depending on other countries seems almost ridiculous when one appreciates that America has such great farmland and farmers. I don't want us to depend on foreign food production. These countries need the food themselves. Is it right for us to import food that we can grow right here from developing or emerging countries when they need their own food? Their own people don't have enough to eat!

Let's acknowledge that we have lots of fertile land and a great climate. Growing up in Canada, I was always envious of people in the U.S., because they had California and Florida to feed them during the winter. Canada had no such thing. We had to store carrots and potatoes, just like folks in the Northeast and Northwest. The U.S. has this valuable land, and what are we doing? We're building homes over it! Our best land is being covered with houses and shopping malls! I just don't think that's a sustainable program for the future of our country. The only way to do it seems to be sustainability and self-sufficiency. We need to get people—young people in particular—interested again in economically and environmentally sustainable agricultural production.

In the U.K. and in some Scandinavian countries, governments are interested in helping people to live and grow food on the land. They pay farmers just to stay and be "stewards of the land." That's one solution. America has many of those laws in place in certain states, where they are trying to protect farmland by providing funds to farm families to keep the land in agriculture. They're trying to protect good land from being developed for housing, etc. You can imagine that it's difficult for many of our farmers when they see the sums of money being offered to them by land developers and land speculators. They've worked that land for so many years. Then a developer's money is swinging before their eyes. Can we say, "Forget about your retirement money and don't sell your land?" What incentives or rewards are there for farmers to keep their land in production?

In certain regions of the country, favorable laws are being implemented to protect farmland and stimulate rural development. But it's not happening fast enough. In fact, the government is doing the same for wetlands, trying to keep some of the wetlands on people's farms. Farmers get paid not to farm that part, and to leave it for wildlife. There's a recognition that we need to do more of that if we are to be more sustainable stewards of the land.

The truth is that despite the large proportion of the U.S. population living in urban areas and away from farms and agriculture, there are an increasing number of citizens who love the land. One can see it in the increasing number of students that we have here at Cornell interested in agriculture, from a sustainable production, business, or rural development perspective. Many are here almost on a mission. Monetary wealth is not the driving force for their lives. They could do much better financially by pursuing careers in other disciplines. In my own case, I knew I wasn't going to make a lot of money doing what I wanted to do, but money never was the driver. I just wanted enough money to live right.

There are enough young people interested in the land who are also filled with the optimism of youth and a sense of the difference that they can make. I'm seeing this more and more. I'm encouraged almost daily to see young people being aware of issues like climate change, sustainability, recycling, etc. They put pressure on their parents and neighbors to become more active citizens on these issues. I see it in some of our young farmers whose parents are farmers. They go back home and bring their new ideas. I've had a number of students introduce new, more niche-oriented crops on their farms. One student helped revert an old family farm to an organic production system. This is tremendously encouraging to see firsthand. At this stage, many farmers can still get some premium prices for their organic produce. It wasn't a choice for many farmers. They had to do something drastic or they risked losing their farm. College students are young enough and maybe foolish enough to take these chances. We need more of that. Money, though, is not going to be a major motivator for folks to return to the land; it's just a different approach or way of life that they have chosen.

Despite anything that government might do to help, we're going to have to do more to ensure a sustainable future for the United States. For instance, I think we need to recognize that grassroots movements are critical. You need that. You need involved citizens who are invested in the cause. Some people have to pressure the legislators, too. I grew up in Canada and have experience with more of a social government structure. Universal medical care and general welfare were key pillars of Canadian society. Legislation was often put in place at the government level grounded in the concept of the "common good." It was good for the nation. If that meant saving some farmland, it was done. So I have more of that kind of a background. In my view, governments can make a substantial difference; it's their duty to do it. Perhaps growing up in Canada taught me that government's role is to make sure that these grassroots issues are brought to the higher level. Grassroots are critical. You can do a lot if you have them, but you need a spokesperson. You need somebody at the higher level, a Hillary Clinton, a Barack Obama, or a George Bush, whoever it is that takes up the cause. Otherwise, it's not going to happen at this higher level. The country is too large and too diversified. You need the help of influential people at the higher levels of government.

I realize you could stir things up for twenty years and never get anywhere. But I just heard that San Francisco is now banning the use of plastic grocery bags! I had been thinking about that for years, telling people, "Why do you need so many bags?" I grew up in southern Italy in the 1960s where resources were scarce. Water was prized. You didn't take a long shower or wash your car and leave the hose running. That didn't happen. Everything was recycled. You brought the same bag to the grocery store back and forth maybe ten times before it was recycled or discarded.

People ask if I consider myself a spokesman for scientists. I answer, "In the true sense, probably not." I'm a scientist in terms of my degrees, but I consider myself an individual, a person, and a part of the whole community. I never set myself up as somebody special. I'm like that with my students. I consider myself one of them. I understand where they are coming from. But in terms of being able to produce information that could be useful to people— yes, I can do that. I publish in peer-reviewed journals and am just as pleased to pass on information to citizens through the popular media. Yes, sure, I'm a scientist. But what I really want to be known for is that I'm someone who can get information into the hands of people who really need it, people who may not have access to it. I do this by going to grower meetings.

I get involved with them, even though I don't have any formal extension responsibilities. I tell that to the young students in my class, that Extension is just a responsibility to work with your stakeholders. If they're going to be weed scientists, like in my case, then they should go to grower meetings. They're the links between the university and agronomy groups, and they need to pass on what's relevant out of their studies that could be useful to folks.

One of the things I've noticed is that your educational title does make a difference to some of these growers. They'll listen to you. They'll listen to you even more if you start speaking their language. Don't speak above or below their heads. Don't treat them as though they might not know anything, or use terminology or jargon that we might use in science. I think that's a skill some of the extension folks here at Cornell have. Some of them have gone out to farmer groups for twenty or thirty years. I sit there and absorb all the stories of their work and how they interact with growers—how they put to rest some of their fears, how they address growers to get information. This is a real skill. Growers appreciate that, even if they may disagree with something you said.

I recall one time telling some growers that once a weed is under a crop canopy, such as common lambsquarters or velvetleaf, those weeds are not going to impact their yields. Some of these growers were still worried that these plants would produce seed, so they would go back and spray herbicide despite what I had just told them, and despite the extra cost. I was trying to tell some of them that my applied research is being motivated by their questions. For example, I was focusing my research on velvetleaf, which is a real troublesome agronomic weed. It's an annual weed whose seeds can last a long time in the soil. It has a very hard seed coat. However, seeds growing under a corn canopy have different traits than seeds produced by velvetleaf plants that break through the corn canopy and are exposed to sunlight. Weeds that break through to sunlight are the tough ones in terms of seed dormancy (i.e., their ability to survive in soil). Their dormancy potential is formidable. They're alive, but they can stay dormant in the soil for many years, or even decades! Those are the ones that we need to watch. However, those that are under the canopy don't present the same kind of danger. Some of the work that I was doing was showing that their dormancy wasn't strong. I admitted that maybe the next year these seeds might be alive and germinate. But the growers could go in and clean them out with an herbicide or tillage operation.

Having said all that, I think part of the problem was that I was relatively young. A few years back, they were saying, "What's this hotshot Cornell weed scientist telling us?" We'd been working with this weed, and we knew it was a weed that we could handle. So I then engaged them more by saying, "Why don't we do some field trials? Why don't we work some small plots for you? You can continue to do what you are doing, but let's see if we can show you if what we're saying is true or not."

I wasn't just coming to give a talk. This provided them some confidence, some reassurance, that I was invested. I made sure I could give them evidence! I let them know that I understood what they were getting at. I didn't just dismiss what they were getting at or say, "You guys don't know what you're talking about." I understood totally what they were talking about, and I learned more from them than I could ever have learned from any textbook.

Often, I have to explain what a weed is. A weed for most people is a plant that grows where one doesn't want it to grow. The word *weed* is an anthropogenic term. The whole concept is human-related terminology, because in a sense all plants have a role. Yes, a weed can be a plant that interferes with human activities, or that affects our health or our agriculture. I admit that's the standard agronomic definition, but there's a second way to define what a weed is. There's a plant ecology definition of a weed, and that's what we call a *pioneer species*. This is a plant or a species that grows in an area that has been disturbed, say after tillage or after there has been a storm or hurricane. Those plants have a critical role in trying to colonize the denuded land, to protect the land, to keep it hospitable for other species that might not be able to handle those harsh conditions early on. We can't disregard the importance of this role.

A good example is a weed like common ragweed—*Ambrosia artemisiifolia* is the scientific name. Common ragweed is an annual. It lives just one year. It regenerates from seed each year. It's also native to North America. It doesn't stay there for many years. It's always a different individual. It's a plant that appears any time you have housing developments or a vacant lot. It will occupy harsh conditions, such as roadsides or land that has been devastated by de-icing salts or snow plows in winter. It will grow there. The problem is, it's an important agronomic weed, and it also causes hay fever. Most of our hay fever issues are due to common ragweed. Some people have issues with that, but you can see that it has a very important ecological role. So that role is another definition that folks have to think about.

A third definition is that a weed is a plant whose virtues are yet to be found. For example, somewhere in the future, we might find a medicinal use for it, as we're finding in the tropical rain forest with many of the species we don't know much about. That same ragweed, for instance, can be food for insects. So a weed definition depends on who you talk to.

The dandelion is another example. Most folks are aware that dandelions grow easily in urban areas. To my dad, a dandelion is the worst thing you can have in your lawn. He'll do whatever it takes to knock it out, whereas I have beekeeper friends who love to have it. I have friends who love the aesthetics of the flower (maybe they don't like it when it's in seed). There are folks who eat the tender young shoots in salads. People make dandelion wine. It depends on who you talk to. These are referred to as "conflict of interest" issues. That's important. As a weed scientist, you always need to be aware. It's not just a weed to me, but what is it to the people I'm talking to? Do other people see it as just a weed? That's critical. Some farmers let their animals utilize ragweed. Sheep eat the fresh leaves.

Weeds can create animosity in some people. The question "What is a weed?" is very important. A lot of my work, in the agronomic sense, is about how to deal with the problem of weeds. Not all weeds are a problem, though. Take lawns, for example. Why do they have to spray for creeping Charlie or ground ivy or white clover, when it's the only thing that can possibly survive in that specific ground without constant human intervention? One of those plants is actually a legume. It fixes atmospheric nitrogen into useful forms and has advantages for our environment. Often I get into this argument with folks, mostly landscapers, when I ask them why they have to spray the commercial herbicide 2,4-D on landscapes. Asking these type of questions can create some tension. Taking a stand on 2,4-D is a personal thing. I don't do it in my teaching. The whole urban herbicides use issue is one that I obviously get into, because I feel somewhat strongly about it. I understand that white clover or creeping Charlie can take over your bluegrass lawn. But what's wrong with having white clover or other "weeds"? There is no question that people have strong feelings about that one way or the other.

I'm certain that one could probably find neighbors that disagree strongly on this issue of herbicide use in lawns. New York State appears to be slowly moving away from allowing the use of pesticides in urban areas. There are certainly individuals who will say, "I spent a lot of money to have this turf and I need to protect this investment!" But in my view, this landscape approach is so artificial and nonsustainable. You have to keep up a lawn. You have to mow it and water it. Nothing is sustainable in that "perfect lawn." People should be able to tolerate some weeds, unless they are a threat to health—for example poison ivy, stinging nettle, or common ragweed. Apply herbicides if you have to in that case. But when white clover takes over ground areas, it's low to the ground and requires no fertilization, since it fixes its own nitrogen. You hardly have to do anything to it. It's a perennial that remains green during droughts.

The whole debate about GMOs (genetically modified organisms) is another issue. It's biotechnologically amazing to have developed such products. For example, Bt corn and Roundup Ready technologies have been great tools for managing pests. Sometimes I see them as helpful. The widely used nonselective herbicide glyphosate (Roundup) typically kills all plants regardless of whether they are crops or weeds. With the introduction of glyphosate-tolerant corn and soybeans in the 1990s, weeds could be killed by using this herbicide. But the transgenically modified crops that had a tolerant gene introduced into them protected the crops from being killed. The adoption rate for GMOs has been astounding for some crops. For example, above 90 percent of the soybeans planted in the U.S. are GMOs.

The use of GMOs continues to be a hotly debated topic, especially between organic and conventional growers and agrobusinesses. My main concern with this technology is with the way that it's being implemented. For instance, I see Roundup Ready technology as a valuable tool in our weed control toolbox, but the way it's being promoted to growers by the agrochemical industry is somewhat disheartening. The reason I say that is that growers have now resorted to spraying glyphosate for most of their major cash crops. They have Roundup Ready corn, soybeans, cotton, alfalfa, etc. In my view, this is one of the "don'ts" in weed or pest management. One should stay away from using such products over and over and over again. Some in the agrochemical sector are thinking only in the short term, trying to maximize profits rather than promoting the judicious and sustainable use of this very valuable technology. That a high percentage of growers have adopted this technology is not surprising. It's very effective, relatively cheap, and allows greater flexibility to growers as to when this herbicide can be sprayed on their fields. Part of the concern is that growers are tied into this technology once they adopt it because they often have to buy the crop seed from the same company that will supply the herbicide. However, there's been increasing pressure on some of these agrobusinesses to encourage a more judicious use of these products, so that the long-term sustainability and success of growers can be achieved.

Part of the problem is that by relying too often on the same herbicide to control weeds, one is favoring the development of weeds that will be resistant to such a valuable herbicide as glyphosate, and we're starting to see this happen. That makes many of us as scientists say, "We told you so!" Where is the public good in this approach to weed management?

Fortunately, there is a call even in the chemical agribusiness sector to use this technology more effectively and sustainably. Using herbicides with different modes of action will delay the development of resistance in weeds. Of course, eventually some resistant weeds can develop to any type of herbicide one may use, but at least it's a more sensible approach to herbicide use and resistance problems.

Some industry representatives counter that resistance is occurring because growers are improperly applying GMO technologies, or they say that resistance shouldn't happen if the growers do what they're supposed to do. But many weed scientists do not agree with this view. We're all very concerned. As scientists, we should be speaking out more—particularly those of us who are state-funded or publicly funded faculty members. We have a duty to be responsible to our stakeholders, especially farmers. Stakeholders can certainly understand private industry's need for profit, but they must realize that they can't only look at the bottom line. Someone has to be responsible to society for the long term. Someone must look out for farmers' long-term sustainability. Who's it going to be?

In our privileged position, it's critical that we provide objective views. I certainly also defend private industry in some ways. When people tell us we should get away from herbicides altogether, I tell them there are no alternatives right now, or that the current alternatives don't make any sense. I try to provide information for our students and stakeholders, but I also try not to drive their decisions—except when, like this issue with the poor use of a new valuable technology, I feel that I should. I will say that it will not be sustainable if we are constantly using one herbicide.

Every time I tell people about what I do or explain my profession, I have to say I'm a weed scientist. First, they get the word *weed* mixed up with *wheat*. Then I have to tell them it's not wheat, its *weed*. Then they have this funny look on their faces. *Weed*, for some odd reason, has an illegal connotation. But then, right away, as soon as I tell them exactly what I do, they'll take me to their backyards. They'll immediately talk to me about a plant or an issue that has come up. It's amazing. It's like the weather. Everybody has an opinion about weeds. What a great conversation starter! Anywhere I go, I can just say that I am a weed scientist, and I know that I'm going to get into a conversation.

Presently, I'm heavily involved in a project that is part of a larger project called Garden Mosaics. It's a National Science Foundation project that's led by one of my colleagues at Cornell, Dr. Marianne Krasny in the Natural Resources department. The project is about bringing together kids in some inner cities, particularly underrepresented minorities, and giving them some exposure to and encouraging their interest in science. We want to encourage them to go to school, and hopefully on to graduate school. We also want to bring different generations of people together, to get grandparents talking to their grandkids about where they came from, like I was telling you about my dad and my grandfather. We want kids to listen to what elders have done with their lives. We're particularly focusing on those kids who are born in the U.S. and who don't know much about where their parents or grandparents came from. This is a project to bring them together. We're looking at community gardens, and one of the issues that always comes up in community gardens is, how do you control weeds?

In Garden Mosaics, Dr. Krasny asked me whether I would be interested in developing a project that looks at weeds as a way to get these kids interested in plants and science. We're looking for ways for these kids—a lot of them are Hispanic and African American—to interact with a scientist. There are few opportunities for them to have that experience. Garden Mosaics is a program where these kids can work with their elders and with community leaders throughout the growing season and the year. They all collect data together, and then send that data over the Internet to Cornell—to us—where we interpret the numbers and give them some information about why a weed was there. I say what this weed means or what that term meant. I put it into context. The kids ask, "Can you eat these weeds?" We help them understand that a lot of the weeds were closely related to the crops they're growing, and that's why they are there. That's why you have mustards growing in with the broccoli and the arugula, for example.

There are ten or fifteen cities where Garden Mosaics projects are going on. The initiative seems to be achieving its goals. I met with some of these kids at a recent national weed science meeting. We talked about weeds and related issues. I enjoy coming back to the question of what a weed is. I tell these kids that weeds are important and have a role. I say, "You go into the Bronx and all you have is buildings. Then you have this plot of land. How do weeds get there? How did these weeds get into your area?" I explain that some of them are edible. I ask, "Why do some ethnic groups eat these? Why don't you or your parents eat them?" I also speak about the use of pesticides. For the first time, some of these kids are talking to their grandparents about what the family did back in Puerto Rico, or other places they came from. And for the first time, they're thinking about going into science.

After these meetings, many of these kids go home and talk to their parents about the fact that they want to become scientists. What a pleasure for me. The kids and their parents had never talked about that before! The kids might be eight- or nine-year-olds. Of course things can change, but this kind of interrelationship impacts kids. One of the things we're going to try to do is to bring these kids up to Cornell in the summer. We'll have them see our work. They'll observe some farmers and growers on their farms. These are the kind of kids that would, otherwise, never even know where their food comes from.

I think it's critical that kids know where their food comes from. I think the more that our society moves away from knowing how food is produced and where it comes from, the more we are in danger of major issues happening and losing control. Ultimately, it comes down to the fact that we need to eat, we need to drink, and we can't just depend on the grocery store. Food is not suddenly just there.

I'm not saying that we should all be in agriculture. Farming is not easy or predictable. It's hard. You can understand why. I tell my students, "Would any of you want to gamble every spring with maybe getting a salary or not in the coming year?" That's what most growers do. They're gambling against the possibility that if something happens, there will be problems. Yes, there is crop insurance, but that may not be enough to cover losses. What's more important is that we need to have folks thinking about and investing in agriculture for the common good, the greater good. We must develop people who want to do that, who want to serve others. Students need to hear that the world is not just about them. We need to have young people that want to do things to help sustainability.

Our job at Cornell as teachers is to foster that flame. You do it by being excited about what you do; at least that's how I do it. Every day that I come to work, despite any problems and obstacles I may be facing at the time, I tell the students that I want to be in this class-room with them. I remind them that our togetherness is worth something. I impress the personal aspect of it. I also explain to them how important it all is at this particular time, because the world is changing. It's "globalizing." Yes, we computerize things, and we get this and that, but ultimately what it comes down to is fundamental. Are we going to have a meal or not? Although I did not grow up experiencing famine, I have heard much about it, espe-cially from my grandparents who made it through the Great Depression of the 1930s and World War II.

This is where I think government has a major role to play. Government has to think small scale as well as globally. New York State should, for example, encourage communities to buy local food. Why, when New York has a great apple industry, do we have to import apples all the way from Washington State and California? Oranges are a different story. Now I still have issues with that, too. Should we be eating bananas twelve months a year? I love bananas, but there are deeper issues about what kind of society we need to be, even locally. We need to help our local farmers. Helping them will impact transportation, sustainability, and the local community. Those are things that government can do.

We also have to think about what we need for a democracy. Where I see democracy in this situation is that we need our government to be responsive to the people. We need them to do things for the common good. I know that's sometimes a problem. I see Canada doing more of that than in the U.S. "We are free to do whatever we want," Americans say. "This is America, and you do what you want." Sometimes that thinking goes against the larger good. Of course, defining the larger good is an issue. A lot of people can agree that having safe food and making sure that agriculture is sustainable should be respected—not just for farmers, but for all of us.

New York State has some of America's best cropland and microclimates. It's one of the most diverse states in terms of its agriculture. You can have maple syrup, eat peaches, grapes, or apples, or drink fresh milk that's produced in this state, all in one day's drive. That's what's amazing about the state. You look at its agricultural production in most categories, and it's in the top five nationally. We represent diversity in people and in agriculture. We're not like some of the Midwestern states, which have corn and soybeans growing over the entire area. We have forestland. If there is any state that folks should envy, this is the one. It has diversity. Our agriculture feeds New York State, and a lot of New York City, one of the nation's largest metropolitan centers. We've debated how far food has to travel. The food that New York produces travels about a hundred miles. Food from Midwestern states travels close to 2,200 miles. Most of what is produced in Midwestern states is shipped elsewhere. So New York, as a state, is pretty self-sufficient, and we could do more. There are marginal lands that we should be doing more with. Should we make state parks? We have that flexibility, especially upstate. But we must always remember where food comes from.

How can we help rural people live day to day? For example, we must help protect all our water that is coming from upstate. We must remain vigilant about the watershed. That fits in with how we work locally, and how we make sure that food is provided. Locally grown foods affect many parts of society. They sustain rural communities in particular. If we think about globalization over time, we're going to realize that in order to survive, we need to strengthen local communities. We're seeing it now with fossil fuels. New York is well placed to support ethanol and biofuels because it has productive land. These are issues that recognize the importance of agriculture, and like I said, I came from a place in Europe where things were scarce.

I do some work with invasive species. Invasive species, like climate change, are kind of the "in" thing now. People are asking, "Is this issue real, or is it just scientists getting together trying to create hoopla for funding?" We have had some of these plants here for a hundred years. Why are they all of a sudden "invasive" and causing problems and costing so much time and money? Being someone who does work with invasive plants, I don't think this issue came out of nowhere. There's a reason why things have been here a hundred years and we haven't seen them. Something is going on right now with some of our land issues. Why are these plants becoming invasive? A very small percentage of what comes to this country actually becomes invasive. People think that whatever comes to this country takes over. It's not true. Only about 0.1 percent of what comes in becomes invasive. Most other things that come into the U.S. can't handle the weather or the climate; they die off.

Some groups are trying to ban certain plants. They say, "You can't plant this thing. It's invasive! It'll take over!" Opponents argue, "It's been here. What's the big deal?" Kudzu, for example, was planted in the fifties and sixties. Now we have a better understanding of the plant. It became "The weed that ate the South." It's a legume that has taken over. I have images from all over the South. Anybody from the South knows about this plant. It's a controversial issue and it's causing havoc, just like climate change.

Some people might say invasive species are not a big deal. But I know some landowners up in Jefferson County, near Watertown, just south of Lake Ontario. They had a forest area, one or two hundred acres that in the last five years has become infested with a weed that I'm working with called swallow-wort. It's a climbing vine that was brought in about a hundred years ago as an ornamental. It got away and has taken over. It basically excludes everything else from the forest floor and open field. It's poisonous. Deer don't eat it. It's toxic to goats. It's in the milkweed family, and it's recently been placed in the closely related periwinkle family. It's causing monarch butterflies to die. For some reason, some monarchs mistake the vines for native milkweed plants, and they lay their eggs on it. The eggs hatch, but the larvae, the little guys, don't make it. It's a dead end. It's a trap. Ecologically, this plant may have some big repercussions not only for the monarchs, but other plant and animal species as well.

When somebody comes to tell me that invasive species are not a big issue, I say talk to that rural grower, that agricultural producer. What has that rural grower changed in the last five years? Has he or she reasoned why all of a sudden there are two hundred acres of this weed that's taken over? Why there is depreciation of land value because of the weed's presence now? Why the owner is having a hard time selling because people are aware of this weed? Those are the sort of things that are part of my work, and this is just a simple example.

Historically, before agriculture, ten thousand years ago, we didn't have weeds that are adapted to disturbance. We weren't tilling. We were nomads before agriculture started. So where were these weeds when we didn't have these tracts of land that were disturbed? If you look at some of the history, these plants were there, in small areas, say in the bison pads, or deer pads, or where there were other disturbances to the land. They just hung around those areas and continued. But they never expanded because there was plant competition. But as soon as agriculture got going and we tilled up the land, then they were able to expand. So these weeds, these annual weeds in agriculture, are just plants fighting to do their job.

I guess thinking about these things has my Italian arms flailing. I seem to be making gestures up and down. Forgive me. But, that's a piece of information that's real history.

So, again, what's a weed?

Is It Your Problem, or Is It a Social Problem?

A Profile of Tom Lyson

Professor, Department of Development Sociology, Cornell University

Interview conducted by Daniel O'Connell, October 21, 2005

As a publicly engaged scholar, Tom Lyson—who unfortunately died in 2006—was an outspoken critic of industrial agriculture and, at times, his own academic institution and discipline. He was also a leading theorist and advocate of what he called "civic agriculture." The main practice story he tells in this profile is about his experience fighting a school consolidation initiative in Freeville, New York, a small town near Cornell University that he not only lived in but also served as mayor. Tom viewed the school consolidation initiative as more than just his problem as a Freeville resident. In the spirit of one of his main sociological heroes, C. Wright Mills, he saw it as a social problem that he felt compelled to work on as an academic professional. The story of what he did and learned in fighting the initiative is highly provocative. From some vantage points, it's also quite troubling and problematic. A few of the people we asked to review Tom's profile were deeply troubled by and highly critical of the way he relates his experiences. They were also highly critical of the way he worked when he was a Cornell faculty member. In light of their criticisms, we want to remind readers that the stories and views that are expressed in the profiles that are included in this book are inherently subjective and partial. While we think they all merit appreciative readings, including Tom's, they must all be read with a critical eye as well. Instead of searching for capital letter *T* "Truth" in Tom's profile, we urge readers to look for the small letter *t* truths of his experience, and to remember that what some people view as inspiring and true, others may have reason to see as troubling and misleading.[1]

I'm a professor in the Department of Development Sociology. I came to Cornell in 1987 as an assistant professor. I was promoted to associate in 1988 and full professor in 1991. That's the trajectory. I have a teaching-research appointment. which means that I teach two to three courses a year in the area of development, food systems, and research methods, in addition to having an active research program in the area of community development, agriculture, and food systems.

I've always known that I wanted to be a sociologist from the time I went to college. I knew that this was something that really excites me. There are a lot of interesting issues that need to be explored. The world needs more sociologists. If you can understand the forces that lead to constructive change in society, then by investigating and presenting those in a coherent fashion that's accessible to the public in general, it's the best hope that we've got to have a rational analysis of society. I hope that people find my work useful, that it can be used by practitioners in the field, that it leads to a better problem-solving in communities.

I was born outside of Chicago and grew up there and in West Virginia. I grew up in an immigrant household—Polish on my father's side, Irish on my mother's. I was an only child. My father passed away when I was in the second grade. My mother had to raise a son with the resources she had. She was in retailing and took a bunch of retailing jobs. We had one of the first laundromats in Chicago in a Polish neighborhood. Then my father died as we were opening up another one. My mother did that for about a year. I was in about the second or third grade, and I was emptying coins out of the laundry. I'm probably the last generation that is going to do that. Anyway, then we moved all around Chicago, where my mom was doing those retailing jobs. We moved because she was getting better jobs—not better jobs, but at least good jobs. I went to about eight or nine different schools before I graduated from high school. In 1963, we eventually ended up in West Virginia, and I stayed there.

It was kind of rough, but we always had food and clothing. One thing is that the government was really helpful because my father was a veteran. I got Social Security and Veteran's money. It's that supplemental stuff, that safety net that Roosevelt put in, that helped me. My mom and I still talk about that. It's not like we were rich, but a check would come every month. This is that thing that Bush wants to take apart, and that's just pure bullshit, because I'm living proof. When I was falling, the safety net was there and caught me.

I didn't know if I would go to college. I was either very, very smart, or very, very dumb. I failed eighth grade. I was in Catholic school, and apparently I took a test and they said, "He's not ready for eighth grade. He has to repeat eighth grade, or, if he goes, he'll be put in with all the retarded people, the lower group." I could go to summer school, and if I could get past summer school, they may let me in. So I went to summer school. I was with really dumb people. Who knows why I screwed up there. I did okay, and I think they put me in the average class. We moved around. The thing about when you move around is you have a new slate. I ended up in Atlanta. I graduated from a high school in Atlanta, with all accelerated classes. I accelerated in math, economics, and English.

I never studied much. School always seemed to come easy to me. I think a lot of it is just genetics. I never studied much and always seemed to do okay. I only decided to work hard in graduate school. In undergrad, it was party and protest, basically. The good old days, '66 to '70 in West Virginia, and there was plenty of activity. I was a member of SDS (Students for a Democratic Society). I did antipoverty work in the War on Poverty. As a student I was actively involved in the antiwar movement. I kept a B average. A lot of classes, I would sign up, take the test and that was it. I was a fool for doing it. I'm not saying, "Look at me, wasn't this great!" I look back now, and somebody should have had a big boot and kicked me all over the campus, because the opportunities at a major state university were all there. But this is when you have no guidance, and you're going to a big state university. You don't have parents who really tell you what to do or guide you. I became my own advisor. I would forge the signature. I wouldn't go and even see my advisor, because they would try to make me take eight o'clock classes in the morning.

I was going to be drafted, so I considered going to go to law school. It was in the summer of '70. I went for my preinduction physical, and I failed it because I had flat feet. I turned eighteen in Atlanta—that's where they wanted me to have my physical. I said, "I can't go from Atlanta to West Virginia!" And they said, "Okay, well, we'll transfer you up to Pittsburgh, that's were you'll take it." This is really interesting; I haven't thought about this in a long time. I didn't do my physical until like July, and so when they were filling up their quotas, they were sending draftees and recruits in from March, April, and May, getting them processed, all the graduates of 1970, even into June. They had this huge quota, so the group I went with, 50 percent of us failed. They didn't need us, so they were just trying to find reasons not to put us in the queue. This was during the draft lottery, and I had a low number. I was set to go to Canada, by the way. I was working with the Quakers.

So then it was the end of July. I didn't know what I was going to do. You can't do a whole lot with a bachelor's in sociology. The first week in August, I went back to West Virginia. I thought I was still going to go to law school, but a year of graduate school in sociology would probably enhance my chances, because I was a graduate from the program and had a B average. I had a good average in sociology, but had a B average overall.

They let me in, and I got an assistantship, just like that. It was a very, very small program. That's where I met Harry Swartzweller. He's from Brooklyn. He was a very good mentor, an intellectual father figure. He's a graduate of our program at Cornell. He went to the University of Kentucky after he graduated from Cornell in the late 1950s. Then he went to West Virginia University as a chaired professor. He's the one who really told me I should go to graduate school in sociology, that I was really suited for it. He's the one who also got me interested in education. He had been looking at various issues in the sociology of education. So I did both my master's thesis and doctoral dissertation broadly in the area of education. He was very smart and he took an interest in me. He gave me insights into sociology, the sociological imagination, and basically the potential of sociology to be a source for change and good. He took me aside after the first semester and said, "You know I have an RA, and I am wondering who I should give it to." I thought he was asking me about my colleagues. I said, "You should give it to Frank, he's really smart. Or you should give it to Jim." He just looked at me and wanted to slap me and says, "No, I meant you!" I said, "You want to work with me?" And he said "Yes." And from that day on I thought, here is this famous—and he really is well known—professor who wants to work with me.

That's when I became serious. I had a girlfriend, and she would say, "Why are you doing this, going to the library? Why are you doing all this work? You're at the computer center all the time." I taught myself SPSS. I taught myself Fortran programming. I was like the whirling dervish, and I was just absorbing this stuff. Then Harry calls me in the next year and says, "By the way, I'm leaving West Virginia and going to Michigan State. Do you want to go with me as my RA?" And I had never thought about graduate school, and there I am, floored.

"Yeah! Of course, I want to come!" So I went with him to Michigan State. I mean he sort of adopted me. I became part of his family. Even to this day.

He had a tremendous influence on me. I try to spend as much time with my students as he spent with me. Get this: I saw him *every day* from the day I started to work with him. If he was in town, I saw him. I would stick my head in just to say "Hi." A lot of times we would have lunch together or have long talks, but every day I would go and see him. It became this really close relationship. He told me, "When you become a professor, I want you to spend time with your students, because it's valuable." I've really taken that to heart. I have a lot of meetings, but I can always see anybody anytime. I enjoy it, because you can see it. Now I've been putting out Ph.D.s for fourteen years—training, "put them out" is not correct. I've had really good relations with them. I go to professional meetings now and when I see them, it's like family.

In 1976, after graduating from Michigan State, I went to work for the Migrant Labor Commission for the State of Michigan, and found out that state government and I were not a good match. The Migrant Labor Commission—get this: "migrant" "labor" "commission"—you would think would be composed of migrant laborers. There were eight big growers and one migrant laborer on the commission regulating migrant labor. So there were a lot of issues that needed to be addressed, and they clearly were not going to be addressed from labor's perspective. Rather than getting fired, I actually quit.

Then I went down to Clemson University in the Department of Agricultural Economics and Rural Sociology, and we were like thirty-two agricultural economists and two rural sociologists. That's where I learned my economics. It was fun. Clemson is in the rural South. That's America's Third World. It was there that I got interested in regional development and community development, and wrote a couple of books on development in the South, on the uneven development that is going on—how some areas benefited and a lot of the poor areas didn't. I spent nine years there, and then a position opened up at Cornell for somebody doing rural development. I applied and got the job. Then my interests began to change and move into the agriculture and food area.

I had worked a bit in agriculture when I was down at Clemson. I arrived at Cornell and began working in the mid-1980s, during the farm crisis. In 1985, the state of New York created FarmNet to help ease farmers out of farming. As dairy farming was undergoing a crisis, it was a way to put up a little extra money to help farmers. The State Assembly in Albany said we should put some money into keeping these farmers in business if we can, or let them look for alternatives. So they put money into something called the Farming Alternatives Program—alternatives to dairy farming. It was housed in Cornell's Department of Agricultural Economics in the farm business management section.

When I got here, they were putting together an advisory committee, and they asked me to sit on it because I had some expertise in agriculture. While I sat on it, the state of New York went into fiscal crisis, and budgets were cut. The money was pulled from the Farming Alternatives Program. Agricultural Economics said, "Well, if there's no money, then we aren't going to have a program." But Joanna Green, who was the program coordinator for it, said, "No, we can't let this go." She asked me to consider being director. I don't think she had any authority to do this for a basically nonexistent program. So we arranged for her to get into graduate school and support her with an assistantship.

We met with groups out in the state. You just go out into the state and start talking with farmers. Go into rural communities and the issues are all there. They just pop up at you. Groups were forming. We had a newsletter. When they initially cut us to the bone with no program, and no program staff, the only thing we had was a newsletter. We sent it out to about 7,000 people. We put every penny into that, and that became basically the storefront. There was nothing behind it. We were going to push this. We went in and said, "Hey look, we have 7,000 people out there who want this." And they go, "7,000 people!" We go, "Yeah, 7,000. Here's our mailing list." That's how you build it. We got enough people interested at Cornell. When you're a professor at Cornell, there are all sorts of opportunities that are open to you. People call me up. Some people had known that I had done some surveys of farmers. So I started working with animal scientists, and we went out to western New York. We started talking to dairy farmers out there.

You get out into the farm community, and then other people ask you to come and do things. When the opportunities come, you take them. We got money from the Aspen Institute—which is Ford Foundation money—to study livelihood strategies of low-income farmers in the Northeast. We just sort of parlayed all this stuff. You make it up as you go along. I can't tell you what I'm going to doing next year or even six months ahead. It's whatever just comes along. I would have never guessed that a year ahead. When you're a sociologist, as C. Wright Mills said, you're taking personal troubles and linking them to social problems. If one farmer goes out of business, or has trouble making it, that's his problem; if half the farm community is not making any money, that's a social problem. There's an issue there, and so sociologically, you don't deal with those individuals, you've got to figure out what that problem is.

We ran the Farming Alternatives Program for at least a semester or two from out of a graduate student office. We found another vacant office, and we moved into that. By then the college had put a little bit of money in to support it. We grew it from basically nothing into a nationally recognized program. The name changed to the Community, Food, and Agricultural Program. We moved it from alternatives to farming, which was a farm management program, to a community-based agricultural development program. I'm the one who changed it. Other people took up farm management, which included emu farming, deer farming, agri-tourism, petting zoos, anything to keep things going. Not us. I said that sociologists just don't look at individuals; economists do. We look at the broader picture.

We began looking at agriculture and food as engines of community and economic development. It was the only program of its kind in the country. This was the time when sustainable agriculture was emerging. The dominant discourse around sustainable agriculture was that it rested on three legs: economics, environment, and community. It had to be economically profitable, good for the environment, and enhance the community. Everyone jumped on either the environment or the economics bandwagon, and nobody knew how to do the community piece. So we, meaning Cornell and the staff of the Farming Alternatives Program, took on that task and tried to figure it out. I thought it was interesting, and nobody was doing anything like this.

We became known as a quite radical group. We were not touting the conventional agriculture line. The organic farm movement was starting. Cornell was doing nothing in that

185

area, and didn't have a program at that time. There were a lot of programs starting then, like the Leopold Center at Iowa State, the Agroecology Program at UC Santa Cruz, and the Minnesota Institute for Sustainable Agriculture. Wisconsin had a program. We thought Cornell should have a program. But the line from the administration here was, "Everything we do is sustainable." As a sociologist, you know that's not true. We may be doing some things that are sustainable, but we're certainly not doing everything sustainably. We went and got outside funding. There are all sorts of funders like SARE, the Sustainable Agriculture and Research and Education Program. USDA is where most funding came from. We also had money from Wallace Genetics, which is a big NGO.

Our work faced resistance. This is the famous story: when the Kellogg Foundation was putting a bunch of money into sustainable agriculture and food systems, Joanna Green, Louise Buck, and I put together a proposal to Kellogg. They liked it. We ran it through Cooperative Extension, the Agricultural Experiment Station, and the associate dean. They all thought it was good. We had a site visit. Kellogg sent people down. I think we asked for $650,000 to run the program and to bring together all of these emerging groups who were in the state working with sustainable agriculture. There were a lot of local groups, and we were going to form this interesting network, funnel money out to them, and basically build problem-solving capacity. We went out for dinner the last night of their visit. They said, "Hey look, if we give you more money, can you do more?" They were going to give us three-quarters of a million dollars! It was basically a done deal. I went down to a meeting in Newark the next morning. The last thing that they had to do was have an exit interview with the dean. Joanna and Louise Buck were there. So the dean says, "I don't agree with this!" He said to the Kellogg staff, "If you want to support me, do something with manure management on large dairy farms." So Kellogg took the money and went down to Penn State, and started a big center down there. Joanna and Louisa were in tears calling me. I was as mad as I'd ever been. And I thought, "Okay, I can get mad or I can get even." The dean should never have done that, and so it really galvanized us.

That story is known throughout Cornell, and it's not the only story like it. Once you get hammered like that in the social sciences, all of a sudden people will start talking with you off the record. I found out at the same time that there were professors like me at the Hotel School. They wanted to go out and work with homeless people, to feed the homeless by using the resources of the Hotel School. They garnered about a half a million dollar grant. The dean said, "Homeless people? We aren't dealing with that." The dean passed up a half a million bucks. This is a lesson in power: what runs Cornell and Cornell's image. There were other stories like that, where Cornell will pass on money that will not make them look good. We were not going to be critical of them. They just didn't want to work in the sustainable agriculture area. The dean said, "Look, the future of agriculture is not with these small farms that you guys are dealing with. They're just a drop in the bucket. I've got to worry about the state, and the future is big dairy farming. We have real crisis with big dairies. We've got to do new management."

We talked to everyone else in the administration who all had egg on their face—the director of Cooperative Extension, the head of the Agricultural Experiment Station. They had all endorsed it. They loved us afterward, because they knew we were on the cutting edge. They did not dislike the dean, but they then started supporting the program because they knew that it was important. We had some supporters in the administration, and we built a program up. Shortly after that the organic farmers had gotten wind of this. The farmers' groups were just furious. We had all of these grassroots groups on our side. They were part of some of the groups that we were working with and they demanded a meeting with the dean. They wanted to know what Cornell was doing for organic farmers, and why they had done what they did. The dean got so mad, he started pounding on the table and stormed out of the room. They didn't go away. They kept coming back, demanding to meet with him. Eventually, the reason we have all of this organic stuff now going on is because of the movements that we generated. I thought, "Okay, you're going to eat your lunch. We're going to do this because I know something about power, too. I can mobilize and build a social movement." And we did it.

I want to tell you another story. My family and I moved to Freeville in 1987. From probably 1989 on, I had been involved in village politics. I was asked to join the Planning Board in 1989, which I did, and I served for several years. Then I went over to the Zoning Board of Appeals, and became chair of that for several more years. A vacancy opened up on the village trustees, and I was appointed to fill out a term there. I ran for a term, and then we had a village controversy over parking, and the trustees split three to two. I was in the two, the minority, but the village split 99 percent with the two of us and 1 percent with the three others. So I was encouraged to run for mayor, and basically we ousted the other three trustees. I became mayor. This was in 2000.

At that time we had a new school superintendent, and there were rumblings that the Freeville School was going to be closed. The school is just vital to the community. All of a sudden I become the Freeville mayor, and the key institution of the community may be going down. A school has integral meaning to a community. Broader than that, this situation is about what civic institutions mean to a communities. They are just critical to the survival of rural communities, and even urban neighborhoods. This is where you can take the work that you do at Cornell, this grand and abstract theory, and actually apply it.

One of my sociological heroes is C. Wright Mills. He did a study in the 1940s where he looked at the effects of big business and small business on community life. What he found was that communities whose economic base rested on small business, on the economically independent middle class, were much more viable, vital, and sustainable than big-business communities. He talked about the economically independent middle class being the "civic class" that provided the leadership for school boards, local planning boards, zoning and other municipal organizations, because they have a vested interest in the communities. In corporate communities, the leaders are upward looking. The corporate class is always looking outward at their competition; they're not looking at the community that they are in. What you want are communities where the leadership is looking *inward*. Then you have to have a set of institutions—schools, fire departments, churches—where problem solving can take place.

There were a group of residents in the village who became concerned about what was going on at the schools. It included Rachel Dickinson, who is the wife of Tim Gallagher from the Cornell Laboratory of Ornithology; Lin Chic Lee, she's an architect; my wife Loretta

Correo; Gree Wildenstien, a veterinarian; Karen Lamont, a farmer; and Andy Young, who lives in the district and is a professor at SUNY Cortland. I didn't take the lead in it—we found each other. Everyone had a role to play. Rachel was like the quarterback. Gree Wildenstien is from Denmark, and she would just go to the school board meetings and ask the most inopportune questions and just nail them during comment period. She would tell them, "Why are you doing this?" and "Can you answer me why this?" and "Give me the research." Andy Young, who is a professor, he would take them apart when they would trot out their statistics. He would say, "You've got an N of 20 and you're generalizing 20 cases to several thousand. Statistically, you can't do that." Every time they would try something, we would have someone who would block them. My role was to be mayor of Freeville and to do basic research: to be the sociologist, to sit back and make sure we were covering the bases. I would ask, "Do we need to get a lawyer? What do we do about the State Environmental Quality Review? Who do I have to contact nationally? How do we raise funds for this?" I was thinking about it in broad way.

We called a meeting at the village hall with some of the teachers and concerned citizens. I think Rachel is the one who organized it. Maybe we had thirty people show up, and from that, we built something called the Community Based Schools (CBS) Committee. Rachel became the nominal head of it. It was loosely organized. We did all of our business on email. I probably have more than a thousand emails. We shadowed the school board. We went to every school board meeting.

We never knew we were going to win. We were closed; we had closed email. We didn't put it out publicly at all. We would exchange tons of emails, just tons of them. It was collective problem-solving. It wasn't just one individual figuring it out. It was a group of seven of us. We would meet regularly at somebody's house, and we would have wine and cheese and figure out our next strategy. We would ask who we needed to meet with. Would the Rural Schools Program at Cornell help us? They didn't, because Mike Joseph, who was head of it, was good friends with a person who was on the school board. I went and talked with Joseph. He knew in his heart that we were right, but he could not go against his good friend.

The closing of the school was a stealth threat. Pat Archinball was the superintendent of the schools, and a person who works at Cornell was the president of the school board. I knew the person who works at Cornell through church. I'd sat on some committees with him. When I heard this, he and I had lunch here. I said, "Look, I think you're making a mistake. You don't really want to close these schools." He hemmed and hawed and said maybe they weren't going to. But they kept moving. It was stealth. It was moving, but they didn't want to ruffle feathers. They wanted one big school in Dryden, and to get rid of these outlying schools. Then I had another talk with the person who works at Cornell. After that, the friendship just disintegrated. He was going to push it. It divided the community.

Over a period of two years they slowly, slowly built the case to close the school. And it was as dirty and underhanded as you can imagine. The superintendent of schools took the school board on a trip to Canandaigua, which is a very affluent community, to show them what a big consolidated school can look like. They came back, and it was written up in the paper, "Oh, Canandaigua, what a beautiful school. They have this. They have that. We can have this in Dryden. This is what we should have." The superintendent did things like constituting the "Team South Committee" with her cronies of old superintendents that she knew. And she got other officials who clearly supported consolidation to come in as "independent" consultants. There were reports that said, "Oh yeah, you should consolidate." They did things like have tours of the school, and then have school board members say things like, "These are dumps. These are embarrassments. They're falling down." Then they had the buildings appraised. Freeville's was appraised at $60,000. McLain's was appraised at $50,000 or $70,000. We found the insurance policy, and we said, "Well, if that's what they are appraised at, why are you insured at $1.8 million?" It was that kind of scummy stuff.

Meanwhile, we built up this huge research base to show how small community schools were advantageous. I could not find one study that showed that consolidation improved student performance. Not one. It doesn't exist out there. We had voluminous material and we would go and we would present it to them. They would just get furious. We even got the schools on the New York State Historical Register, which meant they could not tear them down. Rachel thought of that. Anything we could do to trip them up, we did.

We were using the Internet. We were trying to find people around the country that could help us, people who support rural communities and rural schools. People who had heard this story before and were sympathetic. Marty Strange, the director and founder of the Center for the Center for Rural Affairs in Walthill, Nebraska, became an expert on rural education. He since left that job and now is connected with the Rural School Community Trust. He and I had several email exchanges. He said we shouldn't close. We had petitions with 600 names. The school board discounted that. Then we gave them 1,000 names. They said, "No, we aren't going to pay any attention." We knew we had this base. So Marty Strange said, "That's your political lifeline. Enter all of that into a computer database, and mobilize them when votes come up."

So we got volunteers and we entered all 1,500 names. And when the vote came up, they all got postcards, a lot of them got phone calls, and it went down two to one, because we had mobilized our base. They were astounded. Then we booted them all off of the board. The new board came in, and the superintendent quit. I was still mayor. I took the village newsletter, and I used it as a political organ, much like I did with the Farming Alternatives Program. I've learned how to use publicity. We talked about how closing the school would drop the property values through the floor, and our taxes will go down because property values will go down, but everyone else's taxes will go up. As soon as that newsletter hit, it was all over the superintendent's and district's offices.

This all culminated in a referendum. We started electing people to the school board who were favorable to us, and we had a couple of our people on the board. It was two to five—two clearly favored us, and five were against us. We started trying to elect people who would be against consolidation. Meanwhile, they moved forward toward a referendum. We organized a whole social movement against it. The school board had to do a SEQR study before they could take it to a referendum. They voted, as the lead agency, that there was to be no environmental impact. Their lawyer said the same thing. They hired a high-priced lawyer out of Syracuse or Rochester.

We have something in New York called the State Environmental Quality Review (SEQR). It meant that we had to show that we were losing the school because they were consolidating it, that we weren't going to lose the school because enrollments were declining or the building was bad, in which case they can close the school. They were closing it simply because they wanted to build a new school. According to the SEQR, if a community loses its school, it has to be compensated for its loss. As part of the ammunition for our side, I wanted to show what a school means to a community. So I wrote a paper to show that small, rural schools are vital to communities, and we had to be remediated. Well, they didn't like that at all, and we were getting ready to go to court to challenge them.

Now to take it all the way around, the paper I wrote was eventually published in the *Journal of Research on Rural Education*, and it's become somewhat of a cult classic. I've heard from people all across the country—from Maine to California, and everywhere in between—who were losing their schools and kind of stumbled on this paper, because it's on the Web. It's read into minutes of school boards who are trying to consolidate. There's one in California where you Google me, put in "education" and you find school board minutes where the whole paper is read in. It's a "How to save your school" paper. It's gotten out there.

There was a school in Sidney, New York, that the Sidney district just arbitrarily closed. People were furious about it. They'd read my paper, and they had contacted the head of the SEQR. They said, "Lyson, who is in New York, says that you have to do this." So the woman who is head of the SEQR sends me a note saying, "What are you saying? We don't understand." So I send her the paper. Three months later she said, "We're going to read your paper into the next SEQR so that the state will have to mandate that communities will have to be compensated." So there's a real positive effect. I mean, we're changing state law and really making it explicit. She was delighted with the work.

We saved the schools. They're being renovated now. They're going to be beautiful. They're architectural gems. The Freeville School is a gem of a school. It was built as a WPA project. They said that it was the one outstanding design. It's got a slate roof, which the school board had said, "Oh, it's crumbling, that slate roof has to be pulled off." We got architects out there and they said, "That slate roof is going to last longer than your kids are." It was like "big hat, no horse," the school board. They would just say things and people would believe them. We would just call them on everything. It was all smoke and mirrors on their part.

Afterward, we had a lot of community healing to do, because this really became class warfare. The scars are still there. There is a tremendous animosity against what we did among the business class in Dryden. They will never quite forgive us for denying their kids that education in that big school. It was the upper middle class. I don't even know if that's the right word. Engineers and businessmen and their spouses in Dryden wanted this. There were maybe half a dozen families, not on the school board, who wanted this. They wanted one big school, with a big gym, and a big cafeteria, and a music room and really shiny new stuff. They wanted that in their community, and they did not want to support these rural schools in the rural communities. They thought they were a drag. It's where all the poor kids went, and they just did not want that at all. It was in their class interest to have that big school in Dryden, to close these punky ones out in the district and make us modern. We're arguing, "No, the schools are vital to the community." Not only is Freeville's, but the one in McLain is right across from a trailer park. I've talked to the superintendent, and he said that if that school wasn't there, there would be nothing in that community for those poor kids. They do a lot of activities there where they bring in after-school, weekend, and summer programs. They have pizza parties and do reading nights. It's clearly the center of the community. If you're living in Dryden, you've got your SUV, and you want to have soccer practice. They think, "What do we care about those hicks out there."

A couple of school board meetings really got out of hand. When it looked like the proponents of consolidation were going down, they got really mad. They started name-calling. I remember sitting out in the hall at the Dryden Intermediate School and just shaking my head. I was sitting next to somebody else who supported what we were doing. The upper middle class was furious. One of the school board members had been passing us information, and it had become clear that there was a traitor on their board. He was called names. They tried to oust him. It was the "Jerry Springer" meeting. I was sitting out in the hall, and I tried to block that out. There were only a few of those.

I keep thinking about how could it have been different. They were so committed. It's like the people who believe in intelligent design. You can't change them. They just do what they want. They were incapable of seeing the bigger issue about what the welfare of the entire district should be. In a way, they were selfish. They really were selfish. They bought into this political rhetoric in the United States that it's your money and you should do with it what you want. "Government is not the answer; it's the problem." It's that whole Reagan stuff. They were overwhelmingly Republican. It's just real selfishness. "Cut the taxes. I want for me and screw everybody else." The interesting thing is that most of them don't live in communities. They live in these subdivisions out in the rural areas where you get a string of houses. They don't actually understand what community is, where you walk across the street to your school, where you go across the street to the grocery store, where you know your neighbors.

The lessons of this story are, if you want to effect change, you need some core leadership. You can't do it alone. You need to build a social movement. Those are the real lessons. You create social movements because there is a felt need that there is something wrong out there. Going back to C. Wright Mills, he asks, "Is it your problem, or is it a social problem? Who's affected?" Is it me who is affected when the school closes, or is it my whole community? With my community, that's a social problem. As soon as people see that, it becomes a social problem. That's how we got a thousand signatures. People were dying to sign it. We went to different festivals. We sat out in front of the local grocery store. We sat in front of post offices on Saturdays. We would put it in businesses. I would say that ninety-five out of one hundred people supported us. We really had them. We had organizational skills. Those supporting consolidation came with a petition of twenty names. It was all their friends. They wouldn't go to Dairy Days in Dryden or the Freeville Harvest Festival or sit out in front of Clark's like we did and gather these names and build this social movement. They just thought, "No, we want a new school, and we are going to get it."

You can effect change. I've worked on a lot of national, regional, statewide issues, in big social movements, but this was the most local one that I've ever worked on. It takes a lot of work! We won, but you don't know what you're signing up for. I have a family that I love and want to spend time with, but this was taking a lot of time. Both my daughters would say,

"All you and mom ever talk about is the school. That's all you ever talk about." That's right, that's all we ever talked about. Rachel and Tim would come over, and we would sit and drink wine until all hours of the morning talking about this. Andy and Mary, his wife, would come over. All six of us would get together, or other permutations of these groups. Once we were at Andy's, and we had to get another school board member there, so he calls and says, "I'm in the bunker right now." I don't think the school board knew what we were doing, that we were that organized. If you looked at it, you had an architect, you had two professors, you had Rachel, you had a farmer, you had a really well-educated and politically savvy group of people that were head and shoulders smarter than the school board. If you saw the school board, it was like Curly, Moe, and Larry. That's not to make disparaging remarks, but there were a couple of them who were home-schooler types. They were on the school board, but they won't send their kids to the school.

Community education and problem solving is where people get together. It isn't like there is a manual, though actually we did put together a toolbox afterward. You figure it out with your friends in the community. You could read the material, but you would benefit a lot more from the discussion. It's collective problem-solving, a perspective that I don't think we spend enough time developing and thinking about at Cornell. We adopt these economic, off-the-shelf answers that the market will solve things, or take a reductionist biology solution. But in point of fact, you want to take a solution that is a process that involves everybody. We had community forums, and we invited the school board to come. We held them at the church. We did a lot of things where we tried to educate the community. We were not hostile or disrespectful to them, but we wanted to get them out there to make them justify what they were doing.

Community problem-solving could also be used to try to relocalize the food system to have more local foods. We could do that by supporting smaller farms, CSAs (Community Supported Agriculture enterprises), and farmers markets: subsidize them like we are subsidizing the big farms and stop the industrialization of agriculture, which doesn't make any sense. I want to look at agriculture, food, and health issues. I think health is going to be the big touchstone in the coming years—how our food supply is really not leading to healthy outcomes. I don't know how it's going to play out locally. You need to have a national movement against industrial agriculture and for the workers. People still don't know how bad farmwork is. They still don't know where their food comes from, and how many chemicals are used. They don't understand the biotechnology.

You have to build regional community problem-solving, community by community, until you reach a tipping point. Get people really connected. I don't know if it's going to happen. First of all, you have to build community. I mean you can't do community problem-solving around any issue without *having* community, and we're still in a period where we're going against community. We're taking *apart* communities. We're diminishing the problem-solving capacity of the country. We're told to do three things: work really hard, come home and watch TV or sit behind a computer, and go shopping. There's no benefit from breaking down community. You create fascism. And that's what we're getting.

Communities are being broken down to make money, and for political control. I do think we're slipping into fascism. I know that may not be popular with some people. But I can make the case where corporations are ruling the world in a lot of ways and really setting the tune. The inequalities are growing. Let's just think about what happened in Germany in the interwar years. When the Nazis were emerging, and the people were incredibly poor, what they played on was nationalism: wave the flag, you're persecuted. They gave them political propaganda. That's what Hitler did. We can look at the analogy and it's not too hard to see that that is what's happening here.

My Path Has Been Different from My Predecessors'

A Profile of Marvin Pritts

Professor, Department of Horticulture, Cornell University

Interview conducted by Scott Peters, October 16, 2001

Marvin Pritts hated picking berries when he was growing up in rural Pennsylvania. It's ironic, because his position as a professor at Cornell University is focused on berry crops. In this profile, he recounts how he ended up at Cornell, and why and how he has built long-term public relationships with berry growers and others across the Northeast (and beyond) in his work as an academic professional. The brief practice stories he tells along the way reflect a path that is different from his predecessors'. Instead of framing his academic and public work narrowly as responsive service aimed solely at helping growers make more money, we see that he integrates responsive service and proactive change agent roles by gently pushing growers to think about larger issues related to environmental sustainability and responsibility. What we end up seeing in his profile is a scientist and educator who listens as much as (or perhaps even more than) he speaks, and who has a great deal of respect for the growers he works with, a profound sense of humility about his own knowledge and roles, and a strong sense of public purpose.

I'm a professor in the Department of Horticulture at Cornell University. My official appointment is 55 percent Extension, 35 percent research, and 10 percent teaching in the area of berry crops. I've been here seventeen years as of last week. I remember the date because someone just asked me, "How long have you been here?" It happened to be my seventeenth anniversary, so I said, "Oh, seventeen years today!"

The focus of my research, teaching, and Extension is not specifically defined. The subject matter area is berry crops: things like strawberries, raspberries, blueberries, currants, gooseberries, which are minor crops that people love in the Northeast. The intention of my research and extension responsibilities is that I work with growers in an applied research program focusing on things that they can take and use on their farms. As for my teaching,

195

I have a course in berry crop production every other year in the fall semester. It's a three-credit course. I also participate in teaching many other courses, giving lectures here or there. Cornell Orchards, located right off campus, is a real popular place. Plant pathology and entomology classes take field trips there, and often times I'm the one who gives the orchard tour. All week long the lab sessions go out there, walk around the orchard, and talk about whatever they're interested in related to fruit crops.

My interest in berry crops started way back in high school, when I was interested in biology, and continued when I was an undergraduate and a biology major. I was always interested in nature, so biology seemed like a natural to study. Ever since I was very young I collected bees. I loved collecting bees and butterflies in jars and identifying trees.

I grew up in southwestern Pennsylvania, in a rural community down near West Virginia. We lived out in the country. We had a three-quarter-acre plot of land, and we had a small garden. You could go miles and miles behind my house and never hit a road. It was very rural. When I was only six years old, I would take off all day with my seven-year-old neighbor. My mom never knew where we were, but we always showed up about suppertime. I have a five-year-old and an eight-year-old now, and when I think of them running around the places I ran around, it scares me. My mom must have bit her tongue a lot.

My grandmother, who lived about a quarter mile away, had more land. We would grow strawberries and vegetables there. I remember picking wild strawberries and blueberries from surrounding meadows when I was younger. My mom would make jelly. We would go out with this bucket, and we had to pick until the bucket was full. I hated it. The berries were so small it took forever. I'd rather be playing softball or running around the woods.

Berries were interesting to me, but working with them wasn't something I envisioned doing. I never really thought there was actually science behind the cultivation of these crops. I guess, like a lot of people who don't think about it, I assumed they were just there. You plant them and they grow. That's it.

I went to Bucknell, which is a small liberal arts college in central Pennsylvania. It wasn't such a good experience at first. There were a lot of culture shocks, because I left a community where nobody goes anywhere. In fact, if somebody lived more than about fifty miles away, you could tell they weren't from around my community by the way they talked. We were so insulated. We had a very large school district, maybe the largest area-wise in Pennsylvania. I had to ride the bus for an hour just to get to school. Most of my friends were long-distance phone calls. Then I went to college "out east." There were all these New Yorkers and people from Jersey. Some had gone to prep school. It was tough for me to fit into that crowd, that culture.

The biology major at Bucknell turned out to be a little factory for doctors. It was very heavily animal focused. I did okay with it, but it wasn't turning me on because it was a premed-focused curriculum. The intention really was to weed out the weakest students. I almost flunked out my freshman year. I didn't do very well at all. It took me a while to get my act together and figure out how to study. Then once I did, by my junior year, I did fine. I didn't like animal systems and models; cutting open the rats wasn't my thing. My senior year, I took a course in plant ecology and systematics, and I really liked it. When I graduated, I didn't know what I wanted to do, so I thought, "Well, I'll go into graduate school and learn some more about this," because I found it fascinating.

After I graduated I went to the University of South Carolina in Columbia, which is one of the few places that would accept me because my grade point average wasn't that good due to the poor grades I had my freshman year. Things worked out. It was a turning point in my life, a chance to start off with a clean slate. I was a teaching assistant, and I liked teaching. I met a lot of people there.

I met a professor—not my major professor but another one—who was hired to teach a course in plant genetics and taxonomy. The person he was to replace refused to retire and brought a lawsuit against the university. It was one of the first cases where tenure protected the professor from retirement at sixty-five. The older professor stuck around, and the guy they hired didn't have anyplace to go. He didn't feel comfortable there, so he applied for jobs at Cornell and at Michigan State as a blueberry and strawberry breeder. He had worked with a real famous breeder in California and had a genetics background.

He took the job at Michigan State. We kept in contact, and when I finished my master's degree working in plant ecology, he asked, "Why don't you come work with me on blueberries at Michigan? There's work that needs to be done on wild species of blueberries. You can run around the state of Michigan and pick these wild plants and do some studies on these wild populations of blueberries." It was in the Horticulture Department, but he was essentially doing ecological work at the same time. I decided to accept his offer because it seemed as good as anything. You're on an assistantship, so you're not costing your folks a lot of money. I moved into that work and got to know the field of horticulture, while doing this project on wild species of blueberries.

It was absolutely the turning point of my life, because Jim Hancock, the professor I followed to Michigan State, changed my direction. I found an area I was comfortable in. I thrived in the horticulture field. For the first time, everyday people could relate to what I was doing. When I told people I was working on breeding better varieties of blueberries, they would light up. They would relate their childhood experiences. Everybody has a story. Prior to that people couldn't relate to what I was doing. It was too academic, and they were kind of stymied. I found this sense that I was doing something that mattered and that people liked it. It was reinforcing, and I kept pursuing it.

Despite the fact they're native to North America, blueberries have only been cultivated for about a hundred years. In fact, blueberries are one of only five food crops that are only found in North America. Most of the other foods we eat come from other places around the world. We have a wild population of blueberries. People have taken some good plants from the wild and crossed them, and taken those offspring and crossed them, and then crossed those varieties again.

Four wild selections accounted for the original germplasm of all these varieties of blueberries. When breeders were starting to make crosses, they were basically crossing brothers and sisters, because everything was so closely related. There was little diversity in the germplasm. You get more diversity by going out and bringing in more wild plants. But our idea was not, "Let's just go out and grab a plant because it's wild and it looks good." Maybe natural selection has already identified traits that we'd be interested in, but if we could identify populations or environments that gave us certain things, we could go to those environments and make our selections, as opposed to just picking a plant willy-nilly. We could let nature do some of the work for us.

Indeed, that was a successful strategy. We found habitats that were awful; they were dry and shaded and so forth. If you could find a blueberry plant growing there and you brought it into a good environment, it would outperform on average anything that looked good in the field, because it was now growing in a moist site with lots of sun. Then we would take those plants and cross them into the germplasm and start the process of improving it.

I traveled throughout the state of Michigan. The first step was to find wild populations of blueberries and characterize the environments in which they grew. We looked at what the plants are doing in those environments, transplanted them into a common environment to see how they would do under conditions that were more favorable, and then checked back to see what were the characteristics of those environments that were common in those plants that performed well.

I spent four years at Michigan State completing my Ph.D. working on blueberries. I was out in the state a lot, and got connected with Extension, which was something I had no previous contact with from my master's. There were a number of opportunities to meet growers at field days, when they would come to campus or when graduate students were asked to give talks and presentations. Because my research wasn't directly applicable to growers, often I would volunteer to give a talk on fertilization and nutrition. I would read about it, put together a talk, and then go in front of the growers. That was a real fun thing to do. I also participated in events such as pruning demonstrations. I would go to those and learn how to do some of these horticultural techniques that I didn't have any prior experience with. So I learned a little bit about how horticulture is done.

Five academic jobs in berry crops opened up just at the end of my Ph.D. In 1984, several people who worked in the berry world retired. Those of us graduating about the same time were applying and being interviewed for these jobs. We all ended up getting hired, because there aren't that many people studying berries, as you can imagine. I ended up at Cornell, while others got jobs at Penn State, Iowa State, Rutgers, and Michigan State. I interviewed in August, was offered the job in September, and came here in October.

When I came to Cornell, the expectations surrounding my work were not clear. I don't think the process of conveying what was important was done well. After the interview, Warren Stiles, an old time pomologist (a specialist in apples), called me up at Michigan State. I answered the phone and he said, "I just want to know, are you willing to do Extension?" And I said, "Yeah, I wouldn't have interviewed for the job if I wasn't." And he goes, "That's all we wanted to know," and hung up. That was it. So I came here, and he said, "I hope you like to travel." "Why is that?" I asked. He said, "Your predecessor drove 40,000 miles year to see growers." I thought, "I don't know if I want to spend my life in a car."

My first year, I said, "I have to find out what I should be doing." One of the first things I did was meet with all the extension agents that worked with fruits at an in-service that they have in November. Right here in this room where we're sitting, I stood up and I asked, "What are some of the problems out there? What might someone like me be working on?" People gave their opinions, and I took notes and thought about things that they suggested.

During my first year I visited 179 farms. I called up extension agents and said, "I'm a new guy. Do you have any berry growers you'd be willing to take me out and visit with?" Everybody said yes. We'd set a time, and I'd go out and visit four or five farms. I got to visit a huge part of the state. During that process, I found out that because of my predecessor, everybody had the expectation that I would be coming to their farms on a regular basis. I found that unworkable, because there was no time left to do any programming and research. The message I got from growers was they expected to see me out there in the field, and the extension agents were the same way. My mentor, Warren Stiles, did the same thing. He spent a lot of his time out on the road, and never published much of his work in scientific journals. He did research, but it was usually on grower's farms, and I think the expectation was I'd follow in his footsteps.

My path has been different from my predecessors'. I see my role as trying to identify some key areas of research that I can work in that will not only help growers with some immediate problems, but maybe push their thinking a little bit in terms of issues that might involve sustainability, and get them thinking a little bit broader than how they thought in the past. I do this because I feel not only a commitment to them, but a commitment to society, to people who pay my salary, to New York State residents. My work should not be focused exclusively on the grower community. I have an obligation to the greater part of society, too, and if I can help growers produce high-quality fruit in a way that is more environmentally sustainable, everybody wins.

For example, about the time I was starting here at Cornell, there was a new type of strawberry that was coming out that was insensitive to day length. Most strawberries are day and night sensitive. They form their flower buds in the fall, and then they flower in the spring. You pick the fruit in June, and then the cycle repeats. This new strawberry, because it was insensitive to day length, produced flowers and potentially fruit all summer long, into the fall. There's potential to expand the season from three weeks to five months. It seemed like an opportunity to figure out how to grow these plants. They were developed and bred by the USDA, but no one figured out how to grow them. I thought, "Here's something I can work on right away. I can figure out how to grow these things and get some publications out, and it will be something that will be useful to growers." That was one of the things I worked on.

As for tenure expectations, when I would ask my chairman, "Do you have any advice on the tenure process?" I'd hear, "Oh, you're doing just fine. Keep it up." I never had annual performance reviews. It was always, "You're doing a good job. Keep it up. You're working really hard. We're happy with what you're doing." That was it. It was mostly intuitive, how I thought about what needed to be done. We had an external department review with faculty from other departments and a USDA representative the year I was to go up for tenure. My chairman took stuff from that review document and made a tenure package for me, and sent it off. I never did a thing for it, believe it or not. I got word one day that I got tenure. It's unbelievable. The world worked differently then, and it wasn't that long ago.

Anyway, with respect to how I developed my program of work, it was clear to me that visiting 200 farms a year wasn't a sustainable way to maintain connections with growers, let alone to do something proactive and productive for them. In 1987, three years after I came here, I called a bunch of growers and invited them to come to Ithaca to discuss the possibility of organizing a berry grower association. The idea came from looking at how the grape and apple growers were able to call all the shots in New York State when it came to anything political, anything with funding, and anything with government. Berry growers weren't on the radar screen. They weren't organized. They were never invited to the table, because there was no one to invite to represent them. So I said to myself, "Berry growers need to have a presence at the table. Their voices aren't being heard."

I called maybe twenty or thirty different berry growers from all around the state, and invited them to come to Ithaca and talk about the desirability of forming an association or some sort of body, so we could have representation with the New York State Department of Environment Conservation, the Department of Agriculture and Markets, and whoever else they needed to have a presence with. There was enthusiasm for that idea. I think berry growers had an inferiority complex. Things were happening that they weren't involved with, and this was an opportunity to have a place at the table. It almost spontaneously took off.

In New York State, there are probably six or seven hundred fruit growers. Probably two hundred of those are apple growers, and maybe two hundred are grape growers. They're organized. New York is the second or third biggest apple-growing state in the country. It's also the second or third biggest grape-growing state in the country, depending on what Michigan and Washington bring in—it goes back and forth, but New York's big. Then there are probably three hundred or more berry growers. Berries are scattered all over the state, in every county. Apples are primarily limited to a few major production regions in the state. Those regions have regional specialists in Extension that work just with those apple growers. The situation is the same with grapes. Two big grape-growing regions—actually three now—have specialists that work with grapes. Berries, since they're scattered all over the state with no concentrated region, don't have many specialists. All they have is me at the university, and then extension staff in the field who having interests in berries. There's someone in the Hudson Valley who has an official berry crop responsibility, somebody in northeastern New York where 30 percent of their job is berry crops, and a fruit team in western New York.

So that's the landscape. There are two very organized groups that are very powerful economically and very well connected with the state legislators and Cornell. And then there are many more berry growers—a lot more—but with smaller operations. I would say there are three hundred. It depends on where you draw the line between someone who's a commercial grower and others who don't make their living from berries.

That's the other problem. There are few people—very few people—who make their living exclusively from berries. Most of those people that do grow just berries also have a job off the farm, because berries are very seasonal. You harvest strawberries for three weeks in June. You harvest raspberries the next four weeks, and you then harvest blueberries, and that's it. So most people have to have another job, or they supplement the berries with vegetables or something else to extend their cash flow, whereas almost every grape grower is just a grape grower, and almost every apple grower is just an apple grower. But berries are scattered into part of a larger crop mix.

After I suggested the idea of a berry growers' association, I solicited the help of a couple of extension educators who thought having an association would be a good idea. They would bring some growers with them whenever they came to Ithaca. We first talked about the desirability of having a presence. For three years, I had been around and visited people a couple of times. I knew most of the movers and shakers, the people who felt the need and would get behind such an effort. Then we sent a letter followed by a phone call. At the first meeting we had, there was a lot of energy in the room. It really surprised me. People stood up and gave their opinion. Every single person thought it would be a good idea to have some sort of an informal association.

At some point during the meeting, they said, "Well, where do we go from here?" Somebody then volunteered to serve as president of the group for a couple of years. It was a young fellow who said, "I'd be happy to serve as president to start things moving forward." Everybody voted him in, and it just snowballed. One of the first things they did was to let deans and directors at Cornell know that whenever discussions were going to take place about the fruit industry, they were going to be part of it, and they wanted to be at the table. A couple of the extension educators offered some support. They said, "If you need some secretarial support or getting some letters out, let us know. We can help you." Things came together.

The first thing the organization did, as I recall, was to compile a list of names of berry growers around New York State. We talked to the extension educators and said, "If you have any growers that grow berries, will you send us their names and addresses?" From list we compiled, we produced a newsletter letting people know what we were doing, and that there's an opportunity to join the New York Small Fruit Growers Association—that's what they ended up naming it at first—for fifteen dollars. Three years later they changed the name to the New York Berry Growers Association, because *small fruit* has a pejorative connotation; they didn't like the word *small*. They developed a logo, a letterhead, and a newsletter. Over the years, they've evolved into doing different activities. We've written grants, done IPM labeling, held annual meetings, and produced calendars and marketing materials—everything you would expect an organization to do.

In the early years, I served an important role, I believe, as an advisor. Eventually there was a board of directors that was selected from the various regions of the state. They decided they would meet three or four times a year. This group had no understanding of how you interact with Cornell, of who you need to talk to, and when you need to be at the table. A lot of my early advice was, "Okay, the dean is meeting with such and such, one of you needs to request to be there." And, "Here's an issue you need to talk about with Jim Hunter because he's the director of the Experiment Station. Here's an issue you need to talk about with Hugh Price, because he's the chair of the Horticulture department." I helped them understand the politics of Cornell, the DEC (Department of Environment Conservation), and anyone else, because they really weren't aware of the political landscape. I would do this advisory work both through meetings of the whole group and often just with the president or the executive director. We would talk a lot, at least initially. After the first three years, they got a different president, and an executive secretary who happened to be a retired extension agent. He already knew the landscape around Cornell, which was great. He knew how to work the system and who was who.

Then my role changed. It evolved to identifying issues that the group would have to deal with in the future. We had this organization, but we weren't able to leverage any research. We can beg people, saying, "This is a problem, we can work on that, but it would be really nice to have some funding to put toward projects." We put a research kitty together and talked about how that might work. I had experience as a grant manager for the North American Strawberry Growers Association, a much bigger continental organization. We modified their grants program for the berry growers, identified research topics that would be a priority, and set up the whole grant system. That got it started. The grant program provided some money. It was based on donations.

There was a six-year process of weaning this whole initiative away from Cornell. When people first came together, they met in Cornell buildings, where there was no cost. All the mailing and distribution of materials was done through Oswego County Cooperative Extension, which printed the newsletters and mailed them out. Then the organization would reimburse them. In fact, there was a lot of hand-holding and help initially to get this thing going. Once they had enough money, the office moved from the Cooperative Extension office to a farmer's home office. He was given enough money to hire a part-time secretary to help with the mailings, printings, and administration. There was also money for him to travel to trade shows and set up a booth to promote the berry growers around the state. The association filed with the IRS and got nonprofit status about six years after forming, because the newsletter list was getting large and they had to be a nonprofit in order to send out the newsletter using bulk mail privileges and to collect money for research. Now the association is not subject to tax, and contributions are tax-deductible.

One of the main things that Cornell does in response to an organized group like this is hire people to work in particular areas. Job descriptions are written based on perceived needs. For example, the Entomology department gets permission from the dean to hire an entomologist to work on fruit crops. They write the job description based on what we say we want this person to work on. If the only people who participate in that process are apple growers and grape growers, then that's what you're going to get. You're going to get an entomologist who works on apples and grapes. But if you have a berry crops person at the table too, you might get two positions, because the need is perceived as being broader. Then the berry growers can have their needs addressed. They also can have an influence with extension educators in terms of who is hired, what the jobs are, and how responsibilities are split up. Cornell contributes in response to the needs of organized groups.

I try to maintain connections and relationships through the old, standard way of doing things—going out and making farm visits with some extension agents. I find you can't do all your scholarly work through the Berry Growers Association because it's not set up to do that. It's set up to fulfill these other goals of being at the table and networking, which have to happen, I believe, through the extension system. It's not suited to the programs that I deliver. I would use this group, if I wanted to, to survey berry growers and find out their needs. I also learn a great deal from going out and talking to people, listening to what people are saying. They meet and come up with research priorities for their funding. They have a committee that decides the priorities, and sometimes they ask my opinion.

At this point right now, they're perfectly happy to have meetings without me being present, and this is the first year that's probably happened. Part of why they have wanted me there is that I provide the history, continuity, and connection to Cornell. There was no one else at Cornell up until two years ago whose full-time responsibility was berry crops. Everybody else has their work in another area. Berries might be part of their responsibility, as in entomology where there's someone who has responsibility for that, but the rest of their job would be with tree fruits. When you split between tree fruits and berries, tree fruits win out.

A main function the New York State Berry Growers Association serves is that they're involved in the education meetings hosted by Cornell. I almost always give a talk at those meetings. They also meet alongside other fruit growers and with the deans and directors. They're participants in the statewide program committees. They're *active* participants. If there's a program review that involves fruit, they're at the table involved with that program. Sometimes they have special programs, like the integrated pest management (IPM) labeling program they did for a couple of years.

The New York State Berry Growers Association was able to obtain a grant from USDA to develop standards for certification of IPM-produced fruit. It was this case that may be the best example of working with a group to deliberate over a problem. I was heavily involved with that because of the apple growers. Wegmans, a large regional supermarket chain, came in and met with some of the folks at the Geneva Experiment Station, and said, "We want to sell our apples as IPM grown. What do we need to tell the growers to do?" They worked out some guidelines, and then Wegmans told the growers, "This is how we want you to grow the apples." But the growers were left out of the process. Needless to say, the apple growers weren't very happy about that, and we didn't want that to happen with berries.

So before anybody dictated to us what IPM was, we thought, "Let's get together and determine our own reasonable criteria for IPM-produced berries." The growers, myself, the director of IPM at Cornell, and the coordinator of the Association all sat down and went A through Z and came up with a system that we could use to certify products as being IPM grown. The process probably took six months. I was pleased with those meetings. Everyone was on the same wavelength. Everybody knew what should be done, so the discussion came down to how many points should be awarded for these particular practices—if a particular practice was possible, how much it should be point-valued.

We were more or less weighting the various practices, because the idea was that there would be a hundred points total, and if you can get eighty of the hundred, we all thought you were definitely on the track towards IPM. The question became how many accumulated points would be given for some practices over others. No one argued about the specifics of something being a good thing to do—everyone agreed on that. The growers came away from that feeling, "Wow, I learned a lot. I learned how close I am. I'm going to go back and change a couple of my practices so I can get the eighty points."

I think the whole thing turned out to be a good educational experience, because no one was forcing growers to do it. If they didn't want to do it, they didn't have to do it. It's a voluntary program you can participate in, and you can get a stamp for your produce and a poster to hang up at your farm. It educated growers. They could look and say, "If I do this, this is a good thing." My role was developing the standards and negotiating over the weighting system, because I was most familiar with growers' constraints and IPM philosophy. I was the liaison between the two groups. If there were differences between the growers and the IPM perspective, because the fruit people were focused on apples and grapes, and IPM folks weren't as familiar with the berry production system, I was there to explain and bridge those differences.

I was around the table with everybody, but I wasn't the chair of the group. The person leading the discussion and calling the meetings was the fruit coordinator for the IPM program at the Geneva Experiment Station. He called the meeting in response to growers, who were saying, "Let's go ahead and develop our own standards before somebody else tells us what they should be." I could best understand both sides if there was controversy. I had worked with the growers and knew their constraints and limitations, and what they were up against. I had experience growing the crops. Plus, I was familiar with the IPM philosophy. The IPM folks were the ones that actually own the trademark "IPM Grown." They could certify it, but they had no experience with berry production systems.

I've come to know the growers and what they're up against by visiting farms, talking to them, asking what their problems are and how they try to solve those problems. You have to grow the crops yourself in order to do any research on the crops, so you find out quickly that weeds are an incredible challenge in growing strawberries. You find out that birds are an incredible problem in trying to grow blueberries, and that some soil diseases are terribly problematic for raspberries. Those problems have to be addressed to have any yield to harvest. That's the same thing the growers are doing. They have a crop to harvest to sell.

The case of Roundup Ready strawberries gives a good example of how I try to educate growers. As I mentioned earlier, growers have this terrible weed problem with strawberries, and most growers would like nothing better than to go out and spray the inexpensive and powerful herbicide Roundup on their strawberry field to kill all the weeds and still have their strawberries. The soybean and cotton growers are doing it now, and strawberry growers are thinking, "Boy, wouldn't this be lovely."

Well, there are issues that involve Roundup Ready strawberries that most growers don't consider. One is consumer acceptance. Right now strawberries have a wholesome image. People come and pick strawberries. How would people feel if they went and picked their own strawberries, and then they find out, "Oh, these are Roundup Ready, and you didn't tell me? I don't trust you anymore." There are environmental issues about Roundup-resistant genes getting into wild strawberries that grow abundantly all around. In fact, there are about ten different issues that impact the Roundup Ready strawberry that most growers haven't thought about, other than the fact that it will kill those weeds.

So last year, at the New York State Berry Growers Association meeting in Oswego, I gave a talk about Roundup Ready strawberries. I talked about the advantages and the disadvantages they hadn't thought of regarding this issue. Then I passed out a survey and asked them to rate their feelings on a number of different issues. How concerned were they? I got the survey results back, and shared them widely with the people who were at the meeting. It educated growers about the broader set of issues that are involved in this matter. It's not only, "This will help me in the immediate term." This is also going to cost money to label and license. You have to buy the Roundup, too, and you're not going to make every variety of strawberry Roundup resistant. You're only going to do it to one or two, and everyone's going to be growing those one or two varieties, and it's going to increase the risk of all sorts of things. With just one or two varieties, you won't have the season extended, and you'd have susceptibility to various insects and diseases.

There are a large number of issues that are involved with Roundup Ready strawberries. I tried to bring those out. I was intentionally not being biased. I gave the advantages and some of the concerns. After they had a chance to hear the concerns, they felt as a group they weren't ready. Afterwards they were saying, "I never really thought about this as an issue, but you're right." On the survey, the very last question was, "Would you grow Roundup Ready strawberries if they were available today?" Most people choose no, we're not ready, despite the fact that two months earlier the New York State Berry Growers Association wrote a letter that they sent to Albany and Washington stating a very pro-GMO strawberry position—*very* pro. Yet the membership, after they heard all the issues, responded differently.

Now they weren't ready to rule it out, either. Hardly anybody said, "I would never under any circumstances ever grow genetically modified strawberries on my farm." Nobody was willing to go that far. But few people were willing to say, "Yeah, if I had it today, I'd do it." And I bet you that if I had asked before I gave a talk, a lot of people would have said, "Sure, bring them on." This was an important thing, because rather than biology, it involved the social and environmental implications, and particularly the marketing, that they hadn't thought of.

The Roundup Ready strawberries story could be seen from a different perspective. You could argue that land-grant universities are big bureaucratic structures that aren't serving our customers well, and if the customers are demanding Roundup Ready strawberries, then we should be giving them to them, that it's the job of the land-grant university to give the growers what they say they want. That group's viewpoint takes the position that the desires and the needs of the growers and the producers trump everything else. If they say, "We want Roundup Ready strawberries," we give it to them. But I'm contrasting that with other people who may have different views of the land-grant university. My approach would be, "Let's see if we can't balance these in some way."

This past winter I had an interesting experience when I was asked to speak at a biotechnology conference in Binghamton. I was asked to take the side of, "Does technology actually move us more towards sustainable agriculture?" Nobody wanted to do it. They were calling around for somebody, and I said, "I'll do it." I think there's possibly a role. It might not be a big role, but let's wipe the slate clean and think about some ways that this technology might help.

What's the main limiting factor to most of the growers in New York State? It's labor. Might there be a way that we could use technology in a way that wouldn't compromise the environment but still allow growers to reduce labor and maybe even herbicide inputs? I talked about an example that wasn't genetically modifying a food crop. If we could genetically modify a cover crop that was potentially more potent as a weed and nematode-suppressant crop, we could grow that crop before we grew our strawberries, and eliminate the need for fumigation or herbicide treatment. The strawberries wouldn't be genetically engineered, but we used the technology. Another example is trees, where pruning is a tremendous sink for labor. Would it help to genetically modify a root stalk that would make the tree dwarf? Then we could try to grow non-GMO apples on it and not have to prune as much, because the tree would have a more desirable growth habit.

I'm not willing to dismiss technology. Our role is to get people to think about the possibilities—pro or con, just think about the possibilities. I wasn't received very well at the conference in Binghamton. I think that most of the people at that conference were polarized between pro- or anti-GMO. In my mind, the process is not the issue; it's how the tool is applied. I see a lot of problems with the way the tool is being applied. It's not the technology,

205

in my mind, that's the problem here; it's the application of the technology. So I was trying to get by that, but clearly most people weren't trying to get by that. Just the mere fact that I tried to come up with some examples where I thought the technology could be used in an environmentally responsible way, in a sustainable way, wasn't well received by that group. I think it would be well received by other people, maybe.

You ask me about my relationship with growers. The growers have known me for years. They trust me. Probably the most important thing in developing that trust is listening. That's the key to everything—really listen to what they're saying. Often growers don't have to hear a particular response from us. That's something that's hard for us: we think we need to do something and react. But I've got more growers thanking me for listening than anything I've ever done in terms of research. For example, there was a fellow who had a hailstorm this spring, and his berries got ripped to shreds. He called me practically in tears. I listened to him for a long time. He said, "What can I do, *what can I do*?" There's not much you *can* do once hail rips your plants, but we talked about a few things. He called me up again and again. I think the fourth time, near the end of the year, he said, "You know things are looking better than they were. I have to tell you, you're a great listener. It was really wonderful you took the time and listened to me. It was the best thing you could have done for me because I was ready to cash in. I was ready to quit farming, on the spot." He said, "To know someone at Cornell is just willing to *listen*, that's really important to me." I felt good, because I had been feeling inadequate. We want to solve problems, and what do you do when hail rips you out? You can't spray for it, you can't change the cultural practices, and you're just a victim of circumstance. Listening was a good thing in that case.

When there's a conflict, and you listen to both sides, it amazes me that there's often a solution that neither side ever thought of. It's surprising to me. That was driven home to me most strongly when I was asked to be on an external review panel for Iowa State University's Department of Horticulture a couple years ago. Being completely removed from the situation, you go into these things and you have no history. You hear the stories, and the solutions are right there. It's just that they never thought of them. Sometimes you're too close; you're too locked into certain ways of thinking. It reinforced my thinking that there's almost always a solution. You just have to be creative, or maybe get away from it to find what that is.

I've learned that it's important to listen. It helps when you see people and ask about how things are going and can remember something specific from your visit. You can ask, "How's that patch up on the hill that wasn't looking so good a couple years ago? Did it ever come around?" Or, "When I was there last time, you had a twelve-year-old boy running around, what's he doing now?" Things like that help. Try to personalize things as much as possible. If they see you have a genuine interest in them, it goes a long way toward building trust. It's trying to be objective whenever you're talking to them, and not trying to come across like you're selling something, or that "My research is going to solve all your problems" as a panacea. I always recommend that people try something in a small area and see how they like it. I say, "This is what we found. Maybe you'll find the same thing."

The other thing I've done, I don't know if it's a hindrance or a help because I haven't "tooted" it a lot, but my wife started a pick-your-own strawberry operation about three years ago. It's not on a huge commercial scale, but she does it, and it's a significant amount of cash flow. I wouldn't say we're making money, because of high costs, but a lot of money comes in. The important thing is that we're actually *doing* it. We're putting things into practice, and I know for a lot of extension educators, it gives them more credibility and trustworthiness because they're actually doing it themselves. It's not anything I stand up and say much about, but there's a network of people that know, and I think that adds some credibility. It's one thing to suggest ideas to people, but it's another thing to put them into practice yourself, and put your own money and time at risk.

The berry growers of the state rely on me for a couple things. One is helping them think through some of their production or pest management problems, sometimes even marketing problems. They often call me, and though they know where they want to go, they say, "What do you think of this? Do you see any red flags?" They relate what they're planning to do. They'll say, "What do you think? Do you think this will work? Do you see any flaws in this reasoning?" And if I do, I tell them. So that's one thing they rely on me for.

They also rely on me to say, "This happened to me, and I just don't have a clue as to what to do next. If you were me, what would you do?" They rely on me to keep coming up with new ideas, and to try new things and keep the new ideas flowing, so they don't get stuck in the same way of doing things all the time. Another thing I do is keep them informed about what's happening around the rest of the country. I travel and give talks all over the place. I hear from other people. The growers rely on me to let them know if somebody is trying something in Ohio that might work here. I meet with my colleagues from around the country that are doing the same thing I'm doing. I sit there, exchange ideas, and come back. So the very rural client relies on me for that. We also produce resources and make recommendations. And I maintain a web site.

You ask if my work is political. Politics for me is maintaining visibility so you don't get lost in the crowd. It would be easy for someone who works with a minor crop to disappear off the radar screen. So I'm very active in terms of publicizing, not so much what I do, but things that involve what I do—small things like the dean gets a nice flat of strawberries in June and certain people get thank-you notes. When I hear people using *apples* and *fruit* as synonyms, I can point out that this is inappropriate. I have to do it all the time. It's making sure that there's a visibility there for berries, that we're not forgotten. Some faculty members that work on some crops, even with the big crops, tend to be overlooked if they're too quiet. They don't promote their programs and what they are doing. You need to maintain visibility. You have to do that actively. You can't just assume that people are going to come looking at what you're doing. That's where I probably play the most politics.

I think I'm fairly influential in what happens in the department, but I do it in a quiet, subtle way. I often make suggestions to the department chair, like "What about trying something this way?" or "This might be a way to approach it." I don't try taking credit for it. I just seed ideas and push and prod in a quiet way. I'm usually pretty quiet. I don't talk a lot at meetings. I try to listen. When you take those personality tests, I come out INTJ: the person who listens and may take a while to synthesize things and formulate ideas, not someone who talks through their ideas as they work them out. INTJ's work them out internally. I do that. That's definitely the way I work. I'll share those ideas with key people in a way that I hope isn't intimidating or comes across as "You should do this" or "I told you so." I just say the ideas and see what happens. Most of the time things happen eventually the way you want them to.

I'm the same way with growers. When we make a farm visit, I try to leave them with one or two, three things at the most, that they should maybe think about or work on. I try not to ever tell them more than two or three things, and it's in the form of suggestions: "Have you tried this?" or "Why not try that?" I would never tell them, "You need to do this." But that's the way a lot of extension agents operate. They say, "Well, the way to get through to the growers is to go in there and tell them what to do." Also, I never make farm visits without going through an extension educator. I don't want to be perceived as working outside the current system. And if I make a farm visit and an extension educator is along, then they would learn something too, and maybe I wouldn't have to go out again to identify something that they really ought to be able to identify and give advice on themselves. I still have that policy. It's educational and political. I rarely go out and visit a grower without informing the agent at least that I'm going to be in their area.

In my mind, the land-grant mission applies to what I do. My job responsibility is multi-faceted. It has several stakeholders in it, and it might be different for each of the stakeholders. In general, it's to work with producers to produce high-quality berries that are nutritious, good to eat, and provide consumers with a healthy source of food. I must do it in a way that's environmentally sustainable, and do it in a way that allows farmers to make a living without exploiting people. That's the land-grant mission as it's applied through what I do.

The land-grant mission in a broader sense, I believe, is to identify problems that are researchable that society faces, and try to conduct research that can help address those problems, and then see if those results can be implemented in some way to help improve a number of things. In general, it would be to improve society and the way we live—improve our environment, improve our relationships with people, the way we're doing business. The land-grant largely originated in agriculture, so a lot of our focus is still on rural communities. There are other agencies and institutions that have evolved to take care of other things, like for example, medicine and health. We really don't play much of a role in those arenas, because there are other institutions that do. But in a pure sense, there's no reason why that couldn't be part of a land-grant mission, because I think we're especially asked to address these kind of problems. But now we're limited to things where there aren't other institutions out there to pick up on those problems.

I don't know if I'm right about the land-grant mission. Nobody ever talked about it when I came here. My understanding is evolving. I'm just sharing my perspective with you, and if you ask other people, there are diverging views about what it means to be a land-grant university. Other people understand the land-grant university as the research and development arm of United States agriculture. The idea is that a lot of other industries, perhaps because they're more centralized and integrated, can afford to do their own research and development. But because agriculture is dispersed widely and because it's so important to our security, it's in the best interest of society to develop a research and development arm to do what each can't do individually.

Collectively, the task is that we serve growers and help them produce food. But I expand this beyond helping growers make money. That might be part of it, but it's broader than that.

It's also teaching people about issues that involve the environment. It's teaching people about how to solve some of the problems in rural communities. It's teaching people about how to be good citizens and be familiar with issues that will be important to them when they vote. And it's teaching them about how to make good food choices when they get into the supermarket. There are a lot of things that go beyond just helping the grower make money. I see that in contrast with the people who feel like our role is to help growers make money, and that's the bottom line.

I've never really thought about where my commitments came from, beyond subject matter, in terms of my scholarship and who it serves. Throughout my life, I guess I've felt a calling to serve. I'm very generous with my time. Not just at work—I do volunteer activities. I feel like that's what we're here on earth to do, to try and make the world a better place. That has influenced my work.

I went to graduate school at Michigan State before there was a lot of talk about sustainable agriculture. The horticulture I learned was still pretty traditional. We weren't talking much about pesticide and fertilizer reduction or growing crops in different ways that have less of an environmental impact. I picked it up, truthfully, from being around other people who were talking about it here at Cornell. There were a few people who were talking about that, even some graduate students. I can think back and name a couple of graduate students at the time who were challenging the current ways of doing things. Ian Merwin was one, for example. He's now a faculty member. I can remember Gay Nicholson, who is now the executive director of the Fingerlakes Land Trust. She was a graduate student in the old Vegetable Crops department. I remember having panel discussions and talking about the need to change the way we do things. What they said made sense. It appealed to my nature, my inclination to work for more than just the growers. On the other hand, there were still the traditional people who viewed the growers as their only clientele.

I think what was pivotal for me was when we got together as a Department of Fruit and Vegetable Science. The dean said, "We're going to merge fruits and vegetables." And we did. We then had to come up with a mission statement, and we had this debate among the faculty regarding our mission—who our clients were, and what we were about. It was polarized. There were a few people I resonated with; my thoughts were the same as theirs. And there were clearly people who felt that we work for the grower and no matter what, they come first. All this other stuff about civil society and good citizens and environmental sustainability was secondary. It wasn't in the ballpark. They thought, "If the New York State fruit and vegetable industry folded, we'd have no reason for being here at Cornell. That's who we're here to serve." There was no sense of a broader context. That didn't sit well with me. It pulled me more and more in the other direction.

In looking at that contrast, one specific example that happens all the time is when growers say, "I have this pest and I want to spray something to kill it." And you say, "Well, here are some options to consider. Spraying is one option, but here are some other options you can consider. Did you ever think about changing the way you mulch or the way you fertilize, to make the plants less susceptible?" They always come back and say, "Oh, we know you know what works against those pests. What works really well?" You can say, "There's nothing that's labeled for use." Berries are so minor. There's hardly any pesticides labeled for use with berry crops. So they say, "Come on, we know you know. Tell me what can I really use to kill this?" It happens all the time, but it's illegal to recommend something that's not labeled to be used on a crop. Some educators try to skirt around it, and they'll say, "Well, you know in Belgium they use this chemical, and in the United States they sell it to corn growers. It's called this over here. In Belgium, they use three ounces per hundred gallons per acre, but we can't do that over here." So you've given them all the information they need to come out and buy the product and use it. But I don't do that. We *can't* do that.

I don't have anything to sell. I have ideas. The private marketplace has to come up with something to sell to the growers. I'm not in the business of developing products, for the most part. I have different approaches, different ways of thinking about marketing. As a private consultant, you could probably go in that business maybe and do your own research somehow. I think that works for some of the bigger producers, like dairy farmers. A lot of them hire private consultants. Some apple growers have their own consultants. But in crops like berries, where it's widely dispersed and no one person has a lot of acreage, they can't afford the types of services I provide one-on-one. It has to be a collective effort. For a private enterprise to be involved, they have to have some cash coming in. They have to have a product to deliver. What I often do doesn't involve a new product. It involves using what farmers currently have, growing things in different ways, adopting different approaches. It's not something we typically think of as currency.

When I think of connecting with constituents beyond growers, like consumers, it's harder to figure out how I can connect. I was meeting recently on this Farm to School program, trying to develop the agriculture side of things as it relates to the school cafeteria. I was helping them think through that issue. I view that as a consumer issue. So when I see those opportunities, I try to work with them. I would certainly view connecting with policymakers as part of my role, but I haven't had much opportunity to work in that area.

The tough things of my position are the demands on time from all different areas. The berry growers see me as their extension guy. Students see me as a professor who teaches classes. There's a research expectation. Other expectations come up, like one of my colleagues asking me to work on small farms, which I'm happy to do because most berry growers are small farmers, and I think there's a future in it. So there are a lot people who ask for input. I'm the only berry guy in Ithaca, so there's not anybody to share that responsibility. There is somebody that we just hired to breed berry crops at the Experiment Station in Geneva. But when you look at the Northeast, there's no other faculty member with a full-time program in berry crops. Canada gutted their extension system last year. They only have twenty-seven extension educators in the whole province of Ontario now. The phone calls and emails I get from all the over the place are difficult to manage. So it's a constant changing of gears. This morning I was up at Geneva for the IPM fruit coordinator search committee meeting, then back down here to meet with you. There's always something, and it's all worthwhile. I think the biggest challenge is to find a block of time I can sit down and work on something for an extended period. That's a challenge.

People are saying that agriculture is in trouble. They're right. The world is going to become more globalized and standardized as time goes on. But that's going to create a tremendous niche for smaller farms and specialty crops, because not everybody wants a McDonald's hamburger all the time. You can't produce variety with standardization. You produce the

McDonald's hamburger, and that might be okay for a lot of people, but there's still going to be a significant segment that's going to want a more diversified product. Berry growers, and actually horticulture in general, have been providing that for a long time.

In my opinion, for horticultural produce anyway, there's a lot of hope. It's a growth area. There are certain segments—like apples right now—that are having a hard time, because some of them are trying to sell a nondifferentiated product. But the apple growers that are *not* playing that game are doing okay. The same thing has happened with the wineries and grapes, and even vegetables. Organic farms growing vegetables are exploding. Berries are doing great. It's really an exciting time, because people are interested in not getting the same old thing anymore. For those clients, it's good. I have of hope for the future.

There are some challenges, though. We're not going to be dealing any longer with people whose *sole* job is farmer. We'll be dealing with people who have a winter job or have a part-time job, and they're growing specialized, differentiated products—horticulture products primarily—the other part of their time. We're going to have to learn how to work with this different group. I see them all the time—people with no experience with farming who want to get into it on a part-time basis.

On a more sobering note, I believe that mainstream production agriculture is going to be in trouble. The small wheat farmer in the Midwest is probably not going to be in business for much longer. A lot of us in agriculture, despite the fact we complain about the big crops, we've been riding on their coattails. There's been money that's flowed to land-grant universities, that's flowed to the state Department of Ag and Markets, because there is this type of agriculture. I worry that if this folds, and it's no longer profitable to grow wheat, there will not be any justification for having some of these programs that we've been able to benefit from in the past, like Extension. There's still a justification, but states may be too small-scale to have it. I think there would still be justification for a northeast extension service, for example. With enough resources, I could probably develop a research program that would address most of the problems in my field in the northeastern United States. But, each state can't afford someone like me. Unless we can regionalize and get past that, that's going to be a problem.

When you consider all the emerging issues, there's a strong future for the land-grant university. There are emerging issues with the environment and with how we are going to manage farms that go out of business, particularly in the Midwest. What are we going to do with that land and those resources? How are we going to keep it in a way that's going to benefit society in the long run? That's going to require some thought. How do we manage the urban-rural growth interface? A lot of the issues are environmental. What do we do in terms of job development in rural communities to at least keep them moderately healthy, so they don't have these tremendous differences between rich and poor? There's an important role just in educating citizenry about where our food comes from. I'm amazed that very smart, intelligent people don't think at all about where their food comes from, and the environmental implications of food choice. It never even enters their mind. But when they think about it, their eyes open up. I don't know how you would do it, because the schools tend not to. It's not in the secondary schools. They don't have to teach it. It's not on the Regents high school exams. But it's an important thing for people to know about. So there's a tremendous role right there for the land-grant university: educating about those issues.

The Expert in the Middle

A Profile of Frank Rossi

Associate Professor, Department of Horticulture, Cornell University

Interviews conducted by Neil Schwartzbach and Scott Peters, July 21, 2004, and August 4, 2005

In the first paragraph of his profile, Frank Rossi tells us that his primary responsibility as a professor in the field of turfgrass science is to extend information from the university to the public. But what we see him doing in the stories he tells about his work and experience in the rest of his profile goes well beyond this. We see him taking bullets and dodging flying bombs (metaphorically speaking, of course) as he challenges the views and behaviors of industry and environmental groups and mediates conflicts in the debate over the use and regulation of pesticides and other chemicals on golf courses and lawns. As an expert who positions himself in the middle of conflicting interests, he challenges our understanding of the public purposes and work of academic professionals in highly technical fields such as turfgrass science.

I'm an associate professor of turfgrass science, and the New York State turfgrass extension specialist. My primary responsibility is to externalize or extend information from the universities (it used to be "the" university, now it's universities) that I interact with to the citizens of New York State. I guess when you get good at that, you not only do it for New York, but for the entire Northeast. And now I do it for the world, because I'm a contributing editor to TurfNet.Com (formerly *Golf Week* magazine). I used to write two columns a month that extend information to the golf industry world. Now I do a column and some multimedia stuff for the Web. So I get commentary from people in Asia and in Europe, as well as Kansas and Oregon and New York. I guess I do extension for the whole world. I do a lot of transfer-of-technology kind of work. What appeals to me is problem-solving work—come across a problem, let's get some really rigorous science after it. And I have an absolutely voracious appetite for information. I absolutely love learning new things that are important to my industry, including environmental issues, management issues on golf courses, unique things on sports fields, and innovations in lawns.

How I got interested in grass is a really long story. I'm a real blue-collar guy. My dad was a railroad engineer. I've always viewed myself as a very blue-collar kind of person, and this is never what I aspired to do. I wanted to be a golf course superintendent when I started out. I was born in the Fordham section of the Bronx, and I grew up in an Italian American neighborhood. My brother-in-law worked for the New York Telephone Company. They went on strike, and he decided he was going to be a landscaper. I started pushing a lawnmower when I was eleven years old. I immediately became fascinated with it. I thought it was the coolest thing to go to these really neat houses and mow their grass and trim the hedges and take care of the flower beds.

I don't know if it was in my blood, because both my grandfathers were landscapers. They came from rural areas in southern Italy, outside of Naples—one from a seafaring community and another from more of an agrarian community, with olive plantations and things like that. I got fascinated with cutting grass at a young age. I remember doing it when all the other kids were playing and going to camp. When I wasn't doing it with my brother-in-law, I was doing it in the neighborhood with a little mower and a Clorox jug filled with gas. I'd go around and for a few bucks mow people's grass. I just thought it was the coolest thing. I got paid to do it, and every week it grew back, and I got to go back and make more money doing it.

My motivation was that I wanted a bike. Everybody else had a bike. My folks said if I wanted a bike, I had to make some money. My parents would tell me when I was a kid, "It builds character to be pushing a lawnmower when everybody else is at the beach. It's going to pay off for you later on." And I was like, "Mom, I want to go to the beach." Or, "Ma, I want to go to the playground," or, "Ma, I want to go play ball." They were like, "No, you've got to go work. And it's going to be worth it for you." I'd be out there sweating when I was a teenager, and I'd see these kids driving by in convertibles in Westchester County, and I'd think, "Hey, how come I'm here and they're there?"

My fascination with grass got me into working with a big landscaping company in Westchester County. They put me on crews when I was a teenager, installing landscapes and providing initial care, not just mowing and maintenance. When they didn't have work for me there, they put me at the local nursery taking care of flowers and shrubs. It was cool learning the names of the plants, but it wasn't as fascinating to me as taking care of the grass.

The landscaping end of the business went under for this large company. The owner didn't have enough work for me, and he got me a job on the local golf course in Westchester County. He was a member of the club, and he went down to the maintenance shop and asked, "Can you hire this kid?" So I worked at the golf course for three summers—sophomore, junior, and senior year of high school. I had a weekend job during the day making sandwiches and cut cold cuts at the local deli. It's the only other job I ever had outside of growing grass.

I remember sitting with my guidance counselor in my all-boys Catholic school in Westchester County, and he said, "What do you want to do?" I said, "I like working outside on golf courses and doing landscaping." He said, "Oh, you ought to be a farmer if you like working outside. We have these SUNY (State University of New York) ag and tech schools that have courses in farming." So I went to a college admissions meeting, and I met this guy, Walter Smith from Cobleskill. He said, "Yeah, we've got dairy farm management." I said, "Great. I'll take that." It never came up that I did grass. It never came up that I wasn't farming. It came up that I was interested in farming, and he never asked me what kind.

So when I left high school, I enrolled my first semester in a dairy farm management program at Cobleskill. And I was just was like a fish out of water. I had shorts on and wore a Yankees hat, and I was going to courses called Feeds and Feeding, Animal Husbandry, and Forage and Feed Crops. One of the advisors at Cobleskill noticed that I was kind of a jokester and maybe a little bit out of place there, and he asked, "Are you from a farm?" I was like, "Noooo . . . I'm from, the metropolitan New York area." "Do you have family in farming?" "No, no!" He said, "Well, why are you taking courses in farming?" I said, "My guidance counselor said that's what I had to do." He said, "You know, we've got turf management here." So they transferred me. They let me be an agronomy major so I wouldn't lose my credits for that semester.

Then I met a guy named Bob Emmons, who's now, just recently, retired from the faculty at Cobleskill. I was one of his first turf students. From then on, all I wanted to be was a golf course superintendent. I finished my junior college degree and had every intention of going on to be a golf superintendent, and Bob said to me, "You know, you're a pretty good student. Why don't you go on to school?" And I said, "Well, fine. Where should I go?" And he said, "The University of Rhode Island's good."

So I finished my bachelor's degree at the University of Rhode Island, and I became the assistant superintendent at the Greenwich Country Club in Greenwich, Connecticut, a really affluent community outside of Westchester County. I was there for two years, and I became very disillusioned. I was *really* disillusioned. I didn't like the standards you got held to. The members didn't care whether the grass died or not, as long as they could get conditions they could brag about to their friends. It was one-upsmanship down there. This was back in the early eighties.

I was planning on leaving, and I went to a field day at the University of Rhode Island, my alma mater. I'm looking around the plots, and I'm on my hands and knees looking at one of these new bent grasses that were coming out, and my old advisor comes up to me and asks, "You're interested in this grass, Frank?" I said, "Yeah, it looks really good." He then asks, "Have you ever thought about graduate school?' I said, "No, I haven't thought about graduate school." He says, "Well, we've got a graduate assistant position." And I said, "Well, do I have to pay for it?' "Well, no. We pay for your school, and we pay a small stipend—$6,000 a year." "Well, I make $33,000 now. What's my wife going to say?" I was married at the time, and I was applying for jobs that were making into the $40,000 range as superintendents. Back in the mideighties that was decent money for a twenty-three-year-old kid.

I decided that this was a chance worth taking, so I went back to graduate school at the University of Rhode Island. Within a year and a half, my wife left me. I finished up my degree, and I applied for jobs. I had no intention of going on for a Ph.D. I wanted to be a USGA agronomist. The USGA—the United States Golf Association—has about fourteen agronomists around the United States. I had a lot of practical experience, so I was a good candidate. But they didn't have an opening at the time, and I couldn't find a job. Then I spoke at a meeting, and I met Joe Neal, who was the weed scientist here at Cornell, and he said the same thing to me: "Have you ever thought about getting a Ph.D.?" And I said, "No." And he said, "I've got this graduate assistant position." I said, "Well . . ."

I literally had nothing better to do, so I came to Cornell. I finished my Ph.D. and tried to do anything else but work in turf. I got very disillusioned when I was here as a graduate student, spraying chemicals all the time. It didn't appeal to me. So I applied to a West African rice development association down at the UN to work with them. And then I interviewed for a job with the Royal Canadian Golf Association, being the director of their greens section in Toronto. At the same time, I interviewed for and got offered a job at Michigan State University as an environmental education specialist. My job was to be an environmental watchdog for the turf industry in Michigan. So off I went.

I was on the faculty at Michigan State for two years, and we were very successful. It wasn't a tenure-track position. The University of Wisconsin in Madison had a tenure-track position, so I applied and got that job, and spent four years on the faculty there doing Extension, teaching, and research. I developed a reputation among my colleagues and in the turf industry as being able to breathe life into a dormant program, and the industry responded enormously. I loved working there.

That's when Cornell came calling. Marty Petrovic called me and said, "Would you think about coming back to Cornell University?" And I said, "Well, I really like it out here." But my wife was from the Finger Lakes region, we loved the area, and we thought the opportunity to raise the kids up there would be a great deal. So we left Wisconsin and came back to Cornell in June of '96.

Before I go on, there's something I'd like to say. When I first got to Michigan State, I had been in recovery from drug addiction for four years. I found the Twelve-Step Program when I was here in Ithaca doing my Ph.D. I had been using drugs pretty much daily for ten to twelve years. I was a functioning addict for most of my teenage and early adult life. I got clean here at Cornell, and began to emerge as a person. So it was important for me to do meaningful work. I really felt like I had let people down by being a drug addict. My first marriage failed, and my family was disappointed, even though I was doing a Ph.D. at Cornell University and I looked like I had all the trappings of success. When I left here and went on to Michigan State, it was really important to me to be successful. I was really fortunate and blessed to be able to work with a really good interdisciplinary team of scientists who, though not knowing my past problems, were genuinely concerned—to the man—about my success. Every one of those guys is a really good friend of mine today, and we have never forgotten our time there together, thirteen years ago now.

When I was working at Michigan State, I became a highly visible member of their turf extension program. I was outspoken. I was in everybody's face about environmental issues. I was engaged in the environmental debate with advocacy groups and regulators and legislators. That's where I got my reputation for working in these kinds of situations, for my willingness to get in there, into that debate. I did it, and I felt very comfortable doing it. I don't know if it was because I always lived this alternative lifestyle that I could appreciate why these people were having problems with what we were doing.

I also realized that the only way I could ever make a difference was to change the turf industry from the inside. I was watching what these advocacy groups were doing. They took an offensive approach. They were saying to the turf industry, "We don't even want to talk to you. We don't like what you're doing with chemicals. We're going to pass laws so you can't use them. We're not going to discuss it. We're going to go to our legislators. We're going start a grassroots movement and get laws passed. And then these regulators are going to regulate you, and you're going to have to change what you're doing." And that put the industry in a defensive mode.

So I really thought my job was to go in and take them off their offensive approach. I went to the environmental advocates and said, "Look, if you want to change the turf industry, your law-based approach will do that. But long term, it's going to make it adversarial. You're going to come to a place where you just can't regulate anymore, and you're going to need some cooperation. And you need to understand why they're doing what they're doing. They're not addicted to spraying chemicals. They're doing it because right now it's the only technology they've got to provide the products people want. This is not a viable long-term strategy. You need to think about their end of this deal." And on the other hand, I said to the turf industry, "You need to knock it off, spending $100,000 a year fighting advocacy groups in the legislature, and open a dialogue with them so they can understand what motivates you. Because right now they think what motivates you is killing stuff—killing insects and killing weeds. They think that ultimately, you're killing them. They view what you're doing as damaging to their health. They don't see the recreational benefit, the quality-of-life benefit, the environmental benefits that might come from having a well-maintained turf. And we've got to do a better job with it."

I was willing to go in there and say to the advocacy groups, "You know what? I can't defend some of the things we do in the turf industry. I can't defend them. I know some of the things are problematic. I know some of the things could be wrong. We're missing a lot of data about health effects, and these guys are lacking alternatives. They have to produce this product, and this is the only way they know how to do it right now. They're a generation of guys who were trained in managing turf a certain way, and they'll fight before they give in to what you're trying to make them do." I said to them, "I think we can change it. Let's work together on this. Let's do a project with zero pesticide use. Let's do a project on reducing fertilizer use. If you have some money, I'll lend the expertise. If you don't have money I'll just give you some advice, and we can get moving along." At the same time, I'd go to the industry and say, "Look, we need to really start moving towards the way these people are talking, or we're going to get regulated back to the Stone Age." And it was hard for them to hear that, too.

I've been really successful at maintaining an interdependent relationship with my constituents—*interdependent*. In other words, they go their separate ways. Advocacy groups do what they do, and when they need my expertise, I get involved. We become dependent on each other, and then we both go and do what we do. Same with the industry. Same with the government agencies. I've been able to not be viewed as a stooge for these groups because I'm willing to criticize and be criticized by everybody.

Now, I get a lot of criticism from my industry. I just finished a twenty-eight-page brochure on lawn care without pesticides. It's going to be published, and the turfgrass industry feels like it undermines their ability to do their job, and people are going to lose money if I keep espousing this. I get letters written to me. Right now it hasn't translated to anything but a concern.

217

They fund our research team here, about $275,000 a year, and I think there is a growing concern about that. But on the other hand, I say to them, "Look, you're spending $40,000 a year on a lobbyist. Why don't we take that money and develop some alternatives? Let's invest that."

I say the same to the advocacy groups. "You guys keep putting these bills in front of the legislature. You're spending money to do that. The industry is spending money to fight it. You put that money together, we have solutions that take our reliance off chemicals, if chemicals are the issue." Sometimes nutrients are the issue, sometimes water is the issue. Together, the advocates and the industry are spending six figures promulgating and fighting regulations, when if they invested in research, we could have answers, and they wouldn't be spending time fighting politically.

From my perspective, ultimately I feel like they all want the same thing. This is the goofiest thing! They want the same thing. But they walk toward each other with their hands up! Now there's motivation on both sides that's problematic. With the industry, there's tradition and comfort. They're comfortable spraying—they spray, the weed goes away. There's a comfort level that they have using chemicals. The industry doesn't subscribe to a precautionary principle: "When in doubt, err on the side of caution." On the other hand, the advocacy side stirs things up to get members. They need members. They need dues. They need issues. Otherwise, why would they exist?

I would say the key to my success in working with people, whether they're a golf course superintendent, athletic field manager, a homeowner, a landscaper, whoever they are, is that I speak their language. I pushed a lawnmower for days on end. I can take a small engine apart and rebuild it. I know just about everything I need to know with regard to the practical aspects of my area. I've been doing it all my life. I know how to ask the right questions, and my personality is such that I try to find out a way to say the right thing so that they'll like me in a professional way. Now, "like" also means they recognize my credibility. If I go in there and start talking about the enzymology involved in carbon fixation, they're going to just think, "Well, that's interesting, but what spreader setting should I put it on to put this fertilizer down?" You have to recognize the people that you're talking to and try to talk to them on a level that they understand. And I do that. I talk to the Brooklyn Landscape Gardeners, and I talk to the highest level of golf course superintendents. I was talking to the superintendent of Oak Hill Country Club the other day. He called me about some research, and he offered to have me come up and do some work on some of his greens. I know how to speak their language, and my credibility is really high.

Now there certainly is a contingent of people who think I'm too judgmental and opinionated. If I think what they're doing is a lot of baloney, I'll write about it without personally attacking anyone. Like right now these consultants are running around our industry, making soil-testing reports for nutrients. I'm not a soil fertility expert, but I'm a fairly knowledgeable guy about this stuff, and it doesn't make any sense. I can't understand it. I sit there as a Ph.D. in turf, and I look at this stuff, and I don't know what they're talking about. So I wrote an article about it recently. I think that this is all a bunch of baloney, and I say it. And it aggravates them. But on the other hand, it endears you to people who don't understand it also, and they're willing to say, "Hey, you know, he's a pretty smart guy, and he says he doesn't understand it. Well, I don't understand it either."

So you've got to speak their language. You need to be willing to ask questions about what it is they're doing. You need to be willing to say you don't understand certain things, and you need to be an expert in the area, both from the research end and education. Now what makes me successful as an educator, I think, is I'm stupid. And when you're a little bit stupid, you have to put things in a simple way. I have to get my arms around something first before I can talk with somebody about it. I think sometimes I struggle getting my arms around things, because I'm stupid. It's like, "No, I don't get that." And I sit and I read, and I chew on it a little bit more, and I say, "Oh, okay. It's like this." I use analogies I understand, and I communicate those analogies to people.

Here in New York, things are pretty volatile. If you can't put up with people being in your face and challenging you openly in a group, and questioning your credibility, if you're really just a data guy, you aren't going to make it in a situation like this. I try to go in and get right at the heart of the matter that I know is on people's minds, or is something that I think they need to know about the person or the subject that they're trying to deal with. By doing that, I think it becomes a meaningful experience to them. Now, whether I make a difference in people's lives, that's a broader question. I think that's too strong maybe, but we certainly are getting people to think about things differently.

If you want a good illustration of how I do my work, I'll talk about the project that I'm working on at a golf course at Bethpage State Park with Jennifer Grant, who is a senior extension associate with Cornell Cooperative Extension's Integrated Pest Management (IPM) Program. We've basically taken all the putting greens on the Bethpage Green Course, and we're doing this large-scale project to see what happens when you stop spraying chemicals to control weeds and pests. We're in the end of our fourth year now. Laws are being passed to ban pesticide use, and there's very little understanding in the legislature, in the industry, or among advocacy groups about what would be the real impacts on the ground of not being able to use pesticides. So Jennifer and I wrote a grant proposal to the United States Golf Association, and we said, "We've got this big problem in New York, and we think you should provide some funding to help us with it." We proposed doing it on our research plots here at Cornell, and they said, "You probably ought to do it on a golf course." And we're thinking, "Who the hell is going to give us a golf course and let up not spray when we know the grass is going to die?"

I approached my friends at Bethpage—I trained a lot of them through short courses— and I said to the park superintendent, Dave Catalano, "Would you let me do this?" Dave is such a visionary that he gave me this speech about how important it was for Bethpage to do this. I was literally choked up by it, that he felt so strongly that it was something that he needed to do. So anyway, the industry funds it, the state park system is in on it, we've got these colleagues at the golf course that are working with us.

So there are two sides: you've got the golf industry, broader scale, and you've got environmental advocates. Day to day, we're trying to get this thing going, to set up the experiment on an eighteen-hole golf course, five hours from Cornell, in the heart of golf world. The project starts the year before the U.S. Open is coming to the Bethpage Black Course, so all eyes are on Bethpage. This is the first time a public course has hosted the Open. And then, September 11 happens. And then it's all a New York thing, and every day I'm getting phone calls about the project: "What's going on? What are you going to do?" Phone calls from the press, phone calls from other members of the golf industry, phone calls from Canada, phone calls from Europe. "How is this going to happen?" and "We're having problems with pesticides!" and *da da da da da da*. They want more information.

Then the bombs start flying. We're about three months into the project. Golf course superintendents were calling me, and taking me aside at meetings when I would talk to them about what we're doing, and they'd say, "Frank, I hope those greens die, so we can prove that we need pesticides." I didn't really have a response to that. I'd just say, "Well, I'm sorry you feel that way." And the environmental advocates we're saying, "You're probably going to let the greens die so that you can keep using pesticides." And I said, "Well, I don't see what the benefit would be in that. I can appreciate why you think that, but that's not what we're doing."

We took bullets from both sides. The industry was saying, "You're giving chemicals a bad name!" The environmental advocates were saying, "You're not really doing the organic approach, and that's why the greens died, because you didn't go far enough." But we had very set criteria; we had a really solid scientific approach to doing it. My dad once said to me, "If they're shooting at you, it's because you're doing something right." Four years later we're still taking bullets.

When we began to release results of the project that were really credible, legislators across the state were starting to look and say, "We have to visit the golf course." They went, and they saw that the six greens that we didn't spray died—drop dead. I have the pictures. They're very dead, from very simple problems that pesticides would have solved. It wasn't unexpected. We tried to keep them alive by doing a number of other practices, including using products that had been shown to work experimentally. But what might have worked in research plots didn't work in the real world. You've got 55,000 golfers a year over that golf course. It is a totally different environment than a research plot, even where you might be simulating golf traffic.

Six greens died the first two years, and it created a lot of problems. Revenue went down on the golf course, and Dave, our park superintendent who said we could use the golf course, said, "You know what? You can't do this a third year. We have to do some mitigation." And we did do some rescue treatments. Now we're in our fourth year, and we've come off nonchemical approaches. Now we're trying to do it based on an environmental impact model. In other words, if we use pesticides, we're using the softest ones available, the most benign ones to the environment. And we've ranked them. Now that's gotten us into another whole area of hot water.

You have a disease. There are seven pesticides that control that disease. They're all efficacious. The question is, which one's the safest on the environment, or the most benign on the environment? Well, heretofore, nobody's asked that. Jennifer Grant and I are plowing new ground here. We're starting to tell people that *this* material is better than *that* one, from an environmental perspective. The chemical companies don't like that. We're starting to get bullets from them now. They're saying, "Oh, it's not valid. You don't have a valid dataset, there's missing data. You can't make broad conclusions like that. These numbers are not accurate." And we say, "Look, it's the best information we have available. If you'd like to give us more information about your products to make this more accurate, we'd be happy to work with it." And that's the end of the conversation.

Probably my credibility is the worst with the chemical companies. They think I'm antichemical. But I write the chemical recommendations for New York State. You ask any golf course superintendent who chats with me about a problem, and I will be—without hesitation—recommending chemicals to control the problem. "Go out and spray Heritage at 4/10 of an ounce per thousand." Or "Go out and do this." I know that they can't be worrying about some of these things when they have to provide a service, right? The chemical companies don't care that I make these recommendations. The advocacy groups are the ones that are most suspicious.

I think the advocacy groups want to keep a controversy going. They don't want it defused. They want it alive and well. For example, a guy like Neil Lewis, who represents Neighborhood Network on Long Island, which is a radical environmental advocacy group that's made a lot of hay with the "1 in 9" group (the breast cancer advocates), he's been the most vocal. He's written letters to the dean of my college. He's written letters to the state that we're not doing the project right. I offered to chat with the guy, and he wouldn't respond to me. Dave Catalano, the park superintendent at Bethpage, helped a lot. Dave brought him in for a meeting, and we sat down and had a conversation. I told him what we were doing, we worked it all out, and now I never hear from him anymore. We send him data, we send him reports, and now he rarely mentions it anymore. It's not mentioned anywhere in his literature now. But he never interacts with me, either.

So that's one example of how I do my work. If it's advocacy groups who are very antichemical, who don't really have an understanding of golf course superintendents and only think these guys spray, I go in and say, "Look, here's the situation. These golf course superintendents, they're in a tough spot. The golfers who pay their six-figure salaries say, 'You produce this surface, or we're going to get somebody else.' The superintendents understand your concern about the environment, and don't believe for a minute they're not concerned, too. They're the ones dealing with the pesticides. You think they don't have wives and kids and concerns themselves? Don't you think they hear the word 'cancer' and get concerned themselves? But, they're in a tough spot. You want to beat on somebody, tell golfers to say, 'Maybe we can accept lower-quality conditions.' But nobody does that."

Because of the industry I work in and the efficiencies that are required to be productive and successful at what I do, I don't usually have a lot of time to spend with people. But because this Bethpage project is something I've been sustaining now with Jennifer for five years, and by the time the second grant ends we will be in our ninth or tenth year, I'm very much involved in their lives personally. I stay at their houses, we go to dinner, we chat about things. They've known about my personal challenges, I know about their personal challenges. But beyond a project, the only way I develop personal relationships with people in my field is if I'm traveling to a meeting and I'm traveling with them, or we're spending a couple of days in a place where we spend time together. My favorite way to develop a relationship is in a car, with no distractions. I've had a lot of excellent relationships with industry and colleagues develop behind the wheel of an automobile.

My work is not the old-fashioned kind of Extension. We can't do that anymore, because that was back in the day when Cornell supplied me an operating budget, and that was how you did it. Now we just have so many more people and so many more needs, and so much less money, that we can't do it that way anymore. But those personal relationships are really vital. Let me put it to you this way. There are times when I travel down to see the project on Long Island. I take a day and half out of my life, fly down—you know, rat-race it and come back, strictly to maintain the personal connection. Not because I'm bringing anything technical to the table. Now, we will have some technical discussions when I am down there taking data or something, but the fact is a lot of times I go down there to maintain the relationship. And that's critical when you're cooperating with people on the scale of work we're trying to do down there. So in a certain sense, I kind of do what extension faculty used to do: you know, sit there with the kids or have a cup of coffee. I do it, but I do it in a different way. But the goals are still the same. We have to have those relationships for successful cooperation and collaboration to meet both our needs. They get good information, and I feel like I get good information that I can then multiply to other people.

I'm concerned that a lot of public funding is going into other areas of state government to do education on fertilization, on phosphorous, and on pesticide-using turf. Money is going to regulators and litigators like the attorney general's office and the New York State Department of Environmental Conservation (DEC), and they're generating these campaigns. People who don't know anything about education are getting money to do educational programs. So what do they do? They call me, and I advise them. They've got all the money, and I only get limited input into the process. Next thing I know, this brochure shows up that's half wrong. If they would have just given us that money, we'd have done it right. They're going off half-cocked, giving money to NYPIRG (the New York Public Interest Research Group) and other environmental groups who write crappy stuff that doesn't help anybody. Or the attorney general writes a brochure on phosphorous fertilization that doesn't help anybody. It just volatilizes the debate even more. Nobody gives the people a practical way to get from point A to point B.

The money that would come to us is going to these other organizations, who then call us. We try to help them, and they push us away. They're the most frustrating part of this job right now. In your wildest dreams, would you ever imagine the attorney general's office educating people about phosphorous fertilization? Oh my God! It's a huge deal. They've got tons of money. We're doing a terrible job accessing these funds. I think some of that is related to a historical or institutional memory that we might be stooges for the turf or golf course industry, and therefore we wouldn't be unbiased, and the only way they're going to get what they want is to give the money to the attorney general's office, or the DEC.

Here's an example. The attorney general's office had been working on a phosphorous fertilization education project for a year. I finally got wind of it. They invited me to a conference call. I looked at everything they'd done so far, and I basically said, "I don't know what you've been doing for a year, but this is way off." "Ohhh," they say. So I say, "Here's what you ought to do." And they say, "Oh, wow! We never really thought about it like that." These are lawyers. What are they doing this for? *They think they can get everything they need to know from a sheet of paper.* They got the money. I don't have the money. And now, I've got to take time out of my schedule to help them fix the mess they created, so they can produce a brochure they got funded to do that will be wrong. That's very frustrating. People want to invest in the things that we're doing in nontraditional agricultural areas, but the money's being invested in a place that is not charged with a mission of doing it.

I have an enormous amount of credibility in my industry as well as in the environmental community. I've got perceived objectivity, even though they will all criticize me about it, and I'm willing to go into dicey areas with the industry because I think my credibility is rock solid. And that apparently is a fairly rare thing among people that I speak with. I'm constantly leveraging that credibility. I feel like that's what I spend most of my time doing.

Coming from Cornell University, they assume you're smart. Everybody assumes you're a smart person or you wouldn't be here, right? That they know, but what people worry about is do you have common sense. Are you smart enough to understand what they're talking about and then smart enough to be able to explain to them a solution that they can under-stand, that doesn't sound like it came out of a textbook. This is the thing, I think more than anything else, which has made my credibility. When I'm out there, I might have read it in a book, but when I say it, it doesn't sound like it's coming out of a book. In other words, you're easy to dismiss from a university when you talk like you just read it out of a textbook, or when you're giving them kind of a pat answer of what science would say.

You have to relay very complex scientific information to them in a way that sounds like you know what *they* have to do with it. I can do that because I've got experience. You got to get out there and get your hands dirty in this business. That's where the credibility comes from. I test my credibility with the industry all the time, and it doesn't seem to be bothered by it.

We're a very practical-minded industry. We mow, and we apply stuff, and we're doing stuff that is centered on biology, ecology, chemistry, physics, and all the basic sciences. I tell my students that it's their job to synthesize the information and deliver it or communicate it in a way that doesn't go over people's heads, but helps them find a way that they can integrate it into what they're doing. That's what our credibility ultimately is all about. Even if I don't know an answer to a question, I'll stand up there in front of a group of superintendents and I'll say, "Listen, here's what I know. I know that when you spray this, this happens. I know when you mow like this, this happens. So it's possible what you're talking about is some kind of interaction between those two things." You know what I mean? I don't know the specific answer to their question, but one of the things that I have a real innate ability to do is to get people to think about what they are doing. That ultimately is what the goal is.

I want turf professionals to question every single practice they're using, because a lot of what we have come to know in our field has been borrowed from other fields, and the major-ity of the guys that are out there in the field today have been educated over the last twenty years. Our science is only about forty years old, right? So probably the majority of guys, in my opinion, are doing things based on research from ten years ago that is no longer valid. We're such a new and evolving industry. I want them to constantly be thinking about the things they're doing.

For example, when they make a decision to use a chemical for a pest, are they chronically using that product because there's an environmental problem at that particular site where there's not good air movement, and it's conducive to creating the pest problem? If that's the case, why don't they fix the inherent problem rather than choosing the technology as the short-term fix? Now, that's not to say that careful, thoughtful use of water, fertilizer, and pesticides is problematic! Careful, thoughtful use of antibiotics, it's not problematic, right? But we've become a society where we don't think about it. We just want to move on to the next technology.

That's the kind of thing I want them thinking about. I want them thinking about efficiency. Gas prices are going up. They use a lot of nonrenewable resources. Are there ways you can stop mowing certain areas? Are there ways you can minimize the amount of water you're using? Are there ways that you can be more efficient with your labor resources? I'm always curious, I'm always thinking. I want *them* to be thinking. If we're thinking, it's going to keep getting better. I tell my students, "Your job, in the time people take to read what you write, listen to what you say, or see what you do, is to get them to *think* about what they're doing."

Is there resistance to what I do within the turf and golf course industry? Of course there is! Absolutely! They get very annoyed with me. They get visibly angry at me. Some guys just get completely distressed and walk out and say, "He doesn't know what he's doing." I've got this under control. I say, "Fine, I don't care!" The worst expression of their distress is complete silence—they don't say anything. The best expression that I love when I give a talk is when they start challenging me. And because I don't hold any position other than what the data says in the limited confines of the study, I don't have any problem with being challenged. If they say, "What about this?" we say, "Well, we didn't test it under those conditions. We tested it under these conditions." And of course, this is a problem I think with society in general: people don't know how to interpret science. I say, "Hey listen, we had it under very controlled circumstances, and I'm trying to tell you, here is what we found. If you have situations similar to this, you can expect similar results. However, if you don't have those situations, I can't draw conclusions beyond my limited study here." Now, people don't understand about statistics, and they don't understand the scientific method. They don't understand any of that stuff. So they read more into the data sometimes than they need to.

I don't know if I've been lucky or what, but when I say something, it starts to get things going. I've been at this for fifteen years now, since I finished graduate school. I think the kind of credibility I have takes time to build. It's not the kind of thing you can do straight away when you start a new job. I don't think about it much because I've been in this industry most of my life. You have to have a huge comfort level in talking to these guys, I don't want to say on their level, but I feel like I've been able to take things that have been really complex, that many of my academic colleagues are not willing to make a decision on or to interpret, and bring it down to something that somebody can understand.

It takes longer to move your more research-oriented faculty colleagues off of their little one-lane highway in the direction you want to go. So what I find myself doing is building on-ramps to their roads, picking up stuff from them, and building off-ramps back out to where I need to work. I'm on the road with the people like Jennifer Grant and Suzanne Snedeker. Suzanne is the associate director for translational research for the Program on Breast Cancer and Environmental Risk Factors (BCERF) at Cornell. They're in the world, not on these one-lane rural roads where these guys can plow along their whole careers in their areas of expertise. But you have to have those guys, too. I need those guys. I maintain an academic life. I do scholarly work as well. I don't do as much as maybe some of my other colleagues. I like doing scholarly work; I like thinking about what I'm doing. And I've had great graduate students over the years that have really done well here, really contributed importantly to the industry scientifically, and have gone on to be good scientists themselves. So in my heart, I like to think I'm a scientist.

When I'm working with my graduate students, the first piece of advice I give them is that they need to be attentive and vigilant on keeping up with what is going on in industry. The next thing I tell them is that as much as possible whenever you interact with people, the first thing you need to do is to listen to what they have to say. That's hard sometimes, when what they're saying is blatantly wrong or just misinformed. There's a difference when what they're saying is not accurate, than when what they are saying is along the lines of being accurate, but just not properly informed.

You ask what my main role is. I think it's to be the expert in the middle. That's my role. And to convey information in a way that effects change, that helps people make change themselves. In this job, we're in the middle. I'm not uncomfortable in that spot. I think the groups I work with all have valid points, and I think it's my job to be in the middle. That's my job because I get state dollars. I'm supposed to be the most knowledgeable guy in turf in New York State. This is an area that I'm an expert in. And I'm not in anybody's pocket. I'm completely objective. I have no hidden agenda. That's my job. I don't know *why* it's my job, I just think it's my job. I think that was what the people who set up the extension service would have wanted it to evolve to.

I had been disillusioned as I progressed toward becoming a golf course superintendent. And then when I went on to graduate work and got my Ph.D., I was disillusioned with becoming an academic in the turf area. I think maybe deep down, I always felt like it really isn't that important. I'd like to contribute to society in a meaningful way, and can I do that with grass? Well, turned out I could.

When I got the job at Michigan State, I got to work in this environmental area, which put me right in the middle of the discussion. I had to go and meet with advocacy groups. I had to go and meet with legislators. I had to go and meet with regulators, and I had to work in a traditional land-grant industry model as well. And I learned early on that a lot of people cared a lot about what I was doing. There were regulations, there were people who had to enforce those regulations, there were people who were pushing for those regulations who were genuinely concerned about their health and well-being, the quality of their water, and then there was a turf industry that was mindful of the whole thing going on, but in the end, they're judged by the product that they put on the ground. It really appealed to me to be in that situation. I was no longer disillusioned. I saw that there was real value to what I did, and everything that I did to get into that place, I could use.

Now I can't imagine doing anything else with my life. I really like what I do. Because I've been doing it for so long, I feel very comfortable working in this environment. I think bottom line is, I've been doing it long enough that I actually believe that I've been able to make a difference in people's lives. That's ultimately what keeps me going. This goes back to my personality as a drug addict. I like instant gratification, and you get that when you do what I do. You don't get that when you're a researcher. What's the gratification? Publish a paper that maybe ten people read, maybe a hundred people. I impact thousands of lives every year, with talks and getting involved in issues. There's a certain amount of instant gratification you get from that.

It's important to point out that education is a very inefficient way to change behavior. It's horribly inefficient. This is a very disheartening thing, and I tell it to my students that work with me. I say, "I have been educating for fifteen years, and for the most part, the most effective way to change behavior is to regulate people." But when you change behavior through regulation, you have to keep regulating it. It's a bad path to get on, but it's the path we're on as a society. We are all about regulations. I think we need *fewer* laws, not more, but I fear that we can't trust ourselves. When you change it through education, it sustains itself.

A number of years ago, I had a huge emphasis on water quality protection around the home lawn. We did a publication, I did some applied research, I gave a lot of talks, I put a lot of information out on the Web, and I did a seminar series. With each of those things, we did immediate surveys, and then we did three- and six-month reflective surveys. And we saw that we were really moving people. We got them to soil-test more. We got them to sweep their driveways after they fertilized, because we made a concerted programmatic effort for change. Now, I don't have hopes of always going in and changing what people are doing. My goal is to go in and present information in a provocative way that gets them to think. And if I've provoked them to think, then I've met my objective.

I almost entirely stay on the technical end of things in my work. And politics—you know, I just stay away from that. But I imagine if you probed me about it, you might find that I am absolutely pushing (in the environmental arena, anyway) the turf industry to be more responsible. But at the same time, I'm pushing the environmental groups by saying, "If you want the industry to be more responsible, stop bashing them, and let's work together." I don't know if that's political, or if I'm just leveraging my technical expertise. I guess I don't view either of those positions as espousing political or ethical feelings or opinions. I think that's a slippery slope for us. The way I look at it, I guess it's political if you think about it with a small *p*. I immediately think of politics as taking a stand on things. But I feel like what I'm doing is facilitating the discussion. A lot of times in my field, you can't even get these people to talk to each other. So one of the things I have to do is find a way to facilitate that discussion. Now, some people might say I'm beholden to science. I think that puts us in a good, neutral position. If I state my ethical or political feelings, then I think that undermines everything. It's the combination of technical knowledge and practical experience that allows us to facilitate the discussion.

What I realize is, there aren't a lot of guys that do what I do. And up until recently, I haven't felt that what I've done here, in academic life, is valued at the university as much as the really hardcore researcher. I don't believe that I'm valued as much as that kind of a scientist, because I don't bring in enough money. But I think the university is finally coming around to the fact that there are a number of intangible aspects of running a university that you can't count in dollars and cents. I generate a fair amount of money to do the work I do. I'm fairly efficient with the money I get. I fund the people that work with me. But I don't bring in a gazillion dollars. I don't make a huge contribution to the indirect cost recovery of the college. I don't fault them for their views. I understand that it's a big operation, and I'm one cog in the wheel. Ultimately, it's a numbers game, and I don't provide a lot of the numbers here—"numbers" being indirect cost recovery for the college or university. I guess most people would consider me to be a drain on the university. But on the other hand, I'd like to think that I bring a certain amount of visibility and credibility to the university itself that you can't measure in dollars and cents. I bring in enough money to pay a lot of the things that I do. I pay my own way around here, except for my salary.

I do feel valued now. I was given tenure, although they did put me through the wringer to get it. Also, I was thinking about leaving, and when they found out, they really made me feel appreciated, financially and support-wise. So I felt the college really does care about what I do, and that it's important. That was very refreshing. But I'm not sure a lot of people have that feeling here.

I tell people that work for me, "You know what? People are going to want you to believe that this is really serious stuff, but it's not. I mean, it's important work, but you know, it's not brain surgery. It's not AIDS research. It's not cancer research. If you start taking yourself too seriously, you're not going to survive in this work. It's absolutely imperative that you maintain a certain level of detachment in the work that we're doing." I tell everybody, "I make a lot of money doing this, but you know, it's only grass. It's just not that big of a deal. I mean the world is going to go on fine if grass wasn't here."

I think the founders of the land-grant extension system wanted the system to help farmers produce cheap food. Well, the fact is, we've got cheap food. But we still have people concerned about human-managed landscapes. Now, I don't manage food crops. The landscapes that I manage are in urban and suburban environments. And people are concerned—it's not so much that they want cheap food as that they want clean water and clean air, and they want to recreate, which is important. That's where we come in. Recreation has become an even more important part of our society than it might have been years ago. People want to make sure what they do to get those recreational services provided doesn't affect their health in other ways. That's the place for me.

I work for the best interest of the state of New York. I feel like I have a high level of ethics. This may seem like a little thing, but you know the companies that make chemicals and equipment are always trying to give me shirts and hats and watches and bags. And I never take them. I say, "I don't wear logoed stuff." I don't think it's appropriate for somebody in a land-grant institution to be wearing that stuff. Now my colleagues nationally don't share that. It's well known among my industry colleagues that I don't accept industry gifts. I've been offered to go to Alaska on salmon-fishing trips. I've been offered a week in Cancún at a junket for a chemical company. And I don't take any of those things. I never, ever do any of that stuff. That's as much as I express my ethics in the industry. But I can tell you, I'm in the minority.

We have to be really careful in our work. If we intend on being able to stay in the middle of discussions about environmental issues, if that's what we think the future role of guys like me is, or twenty years from now when my grad students are in my shoes, if that's the role we think is their future, we have to knock it off with getting the industry to support us like they do now, or at least be clear to them that we need support, but don't think this buys you preferential treatment. But the problem is, there aren't enough public sources of funding for the kind of work that really needs to be done. So we become beholden to the industry we're trying to change.

At the Rothamstead Research Center in England, a research experiment station about thirty miles out of London, they've got these pasture experiments that have been going on for 150 years. They've been applying the same nutrient treatments to these plots for 150 years! What you see there is real. It's not like a small experiment. This thing has been going on for a while. It takes up about forty-five acres of land. Now, it's not necessarily turf. I think it's mowed three times a year for hay, and you can see the role the nutrients have played on weed populations. Where you see certain nutrients applied, you see more weeds. Where you don't see them applied, you see fewer weeds. So I come back and I look in the literature, and I find out that there hasn't been a study in our field in this area in thirty years, since the pesticide 2,4-D was created. Once we got that technology, we stopped thinking about ecology. Pesticides allow us to feed people on small amounts of land. They allow us to have perfect golf courses. The golf course in the desert in Arizona can look like a golf course on Long Island, and look like a golf course in Florida, because of pesticides. I think because we got this technology, nobody is thinking about what they are doing anymore.

The area of alternative pest control is not lucrative. It's cottage industry stuff. There's not a lot of money in it. It's a lot of scraping in the dark. To make that technology work, you've got to know a lot about the system you're introducing it to. Because we are such a young science, we don't have a lot of that baseline information. My colleagues nationally, some of them are exploring some of the basic stuff, and I latch right on to those basic researchers and try to grab information wherever I can. A lot of guys did really good work in these alternative areas, like for example, our Eric Nelson here at Cornell. He did work fifteen years ago about compost, and he developed some naturally suppressive soils for pests. Nobody cared about it fifteen years ago, and now it's all the rage. So you know, he was shunned. People said, "What are you paying attention to this for? We got Chlorothalonil. What do we need compost for?" Now that there is a lot pressure to reduce Chlorothalonil use, people are looking back at that work.

I'm deeply concerned about the future of the land-grant mission. Now that we have a decent food supply and agriculture is less and less a part of our lives, the public is not going to support the kinds of things that we do anymore. And the nontraditional areas that are really expanding—like what I do—will not get supported anymore because the whole thing is going to go away. People just aren't going to see the value. Ultimately, the future of the land-grant institution, I think, revolves around two issues: we have to be more responsive, and we have to be willing to step outside of our own expertise and be willing to engage in things that society cares about if we're going to be viewed as relevant. I think that's the thing we suffer from the most—a lot of us aren't viewed as relevant any longer.

What is the relevance of the university, unless you're willing to go to some of the lengths maybe I go to interact and work with people? Just putting information up on a web site isn't a solution to anything. That confuses people if you don't take them through it. I think the biggest threat is that as long as we remain reliant on public funding, and we rely on the agricultural community lobby for that public funding, we're going to stay beholden, doing things that really don't impact a lot of people, and don't really have broad relevancy. I view it as a huge risk, but one worth taking, to start getting into the urban-suburban areas, making them aware of what it is we do as a land-grant institution, and risking that they'll support us with public funding, and at the same time, not kowtow to the ag industries that lobby for us. We're very much beholden to them. But we need to move some of that interest into the urban-suburban areas and get them to lobby for us for public funding.

I don't see anybody willing to take that risk. It's a risk because you could lose your ag base. And then suburban and urban people might say, "Well, we don't need you anyway." I mean a lot of people in urban-suburban areas don't know a lot about Cooperative Extension. They get their gardening information from the garden center, or from the local landscaper, or the newspaper. They don't get it from Cooperative Extension, or they don't even know what Cooperative Extension is. I don't know how you change that, but I'm deeply concerned about the future of public funding.

We're in a really difficult spot for the future. I'd be hard pressed to tell young people that what I do will be viable over a twenty-year period, because I don't know how it's going to be supported. And the sad part is, without continued public support, it's going to make me like every other researcher doing extension work: I'll have to get money to do projects that other people think are important, and I won't have the flexibility in my program to do the things that benefit the long term. It'll have to be a lot of short-term stuff to get grants. We have to get grants to do projects. We can't do the projects without the money, but I'm sure there are a lot of projects you'd like to do if you had some discretionary money. And that's virtually dried up. I get most of my discretionary money—you'll love this irony—from spraying chemicals. Most of the money I get to run the day-to-day discretionary part of my work in Extension comes from evaluating chemicals for companies. That's the irony.

Leapfrogging Back and Forth

A Profile of John Sipple

Associate Professor, Department of Education, Cornell University

Interviews conducted by Scott Peters, April 21 and April 28, 2004

In this profile, John Sipple gives us a richly detailed account of his work and experience as a graduate student and his efforts to develop and pursue a research agenda as an assistant professor in the field of education. The main practice story he tells helps us to see how scholars who choose to integrate their academic and public work can end up leapfrogging back and forth between scholarly and public worlds. John's reflections on his work and experience in the story also help us to see that civic engagement can have both public and academic value. While John speaks in uncertain terms about his future at Cornell, based on doubts about how his peers will judge his work, his worries turned out to be unfounded. He was promoted to associate professor with tenure in 2005.

I'm an assistant professor in the Department of Education. This is my sixth year. I'm in the learning, teaching, and social policy area of the department. I came into the social foundations program area, but it was shut down about two or three years into my time here. I originally had a 50/40/10 time split: 50 percent teaching, 40 percent research, 10 percent Extension. That was changed a year and half ago, when the decree came down from the college that we're supposed to get rid of those three-way splits. So now I'm 50 percent teaching and 50 percent research.

When I was hired and I came in with my three-way split, it was pretty clear to me what that 10 percent Extension was supposed to go to (10 percent: how, how do you bracket out 10 percent of your time? It's strange). I was supposed to work with the Rural Schools Program, which has since changed its name to the Rural Schools Association of New York State. My 10 percent extension appointment was supposed to be time spent serving the group, working with the group as a liaison from the department to the organization, which is a statewide organization representing approximately three hundred rural school districts. And part of the conception of how that was supposed to work was through my research. I was supposed to be useful to these people. It could work as a nice conduit out to the field. I do my work, I do my research, and then the next step is to disseminate it or diffuse it through the organization. The conduit works both ways. Through my association with the organization, many, many opportunities—consulting opportunities, research opportunities, just interaction opportunities—have come up. It is truly both ways, where I serve them, and I get great benefit out of working with them. There's a two-way flow of information back and forth.

My teaching program was fairly clear when I came in. There were two courses that had been previously taught for decades. One was the Sociology of Education undergraduate course, a large lecture course. I took that over. The second one was Education 661, the Administration of Educational Organizations. It's an organizational behavior class, the first course that brand-new students in the Foundations of Policy graduate program would take. So those two courses were kind of set. I designed a third course called American School Reform, which is a graduate-level seminar. It's still rooted in organization studies, but it's much more about policy than 661. Students certainly can—and I argue, should—take both, because they complement each other nicely. So those are the three main courses that I've been teaching for six years now.

I had also at one point taught an interdisciplinary course with Rolf Pendall from the Department of City and Regional Planning, and Lorraine Maxwell from the Department of Design and Environmental Analysis. We got a grant with a grad student, Kieran Kileen, to create this Clarence Stein lecture series, where we tried, in an interdisciplinary manner, to bring together issues of education, planning, and design, and explore how those various disciplines can speak to school settings and various learning environments. I also taught a seminar that coincided with our Ph.D. administrator certification students. When they went out and did their internships in the field, which were typically yearlong internships in school districts, I would run a monthly seminar to bring them back to campus. We'd do a little debriefing, and then reflection, and they'd talk about their experience. And of course, I also would make observations of the interns out in the field. That has ceased in the last three years or so since we closed our administrator preparation program. Finally, the last portion of my teaching was the capstone seminar for undergraduate majors. We no longer offer that, because we no longer have undergraduate majors. So while there's been a fair amount of flux in my peripheral teaching, the core three courses have remained pretty much the same.

My research program has been very focused and very consistent, right from the get-go. It took me a good year when I first came on campus to really get my head around how I was going to lay this work out. Essentially, I ask a very simple question, which is then enacted in multiple layers. The simple question is, "How do school districts in New York State—I have a specific focus on New York schools, and New York State policy—respond to the dramatic change in graduation requirements that the state has imposed on them?" And of course, this change in requirements is happening all over the country. But in New York State, there's been quite a dramatic shift. So I'm focusing just on New York State as the case. Underneath that applied, simple kind of question are issues ripped straight out of sociology, out of the new institutionalism and organizational studies, which essentially posit that organizations structure themselves and function and control their internal and external tasks not so much to maximize gains in efficiency or productivity, but to maximize their legitimacy in the environment.

Schools have some quirky behaviors and organizational structures. And you say, "Well, that must be very inefficient." And lo and behold, often it is; but that's not the point. The point is for them to pass their budget every year. Organizations such as schools, and oftentimes hospitals and other public service agencies, often don't operate in a highly competitive free market, but much more of an institutional environment where they need to match socially prescribed norms and patterns of behavior in order to earn support from the environment. So I take that theoretical lens and apply that in New York State to school districts, which traditionally have always—and quite successfully—adhered to the socially prescribed forms of what a school is supposed to look like. As long as you have certified teachers, as long as you have a teacher with twenty-five kids, as long as you have your football team and your band and your math and all the rest, by and large you get your budget passed, and you can stay open each year.

What's been interesting in the last five or six years, in New York State and elsewhere across the country, is a huge press for technical inspection of school performance. I argue this is relatively new, in no small part because the technology is now available to do this. Measuring how students perform on these many, many exams and courses and so forth is one version of the technical inspections that are going on inside the classroom. There is much debate about whether that's valid, or whether that's measuring anything of importance. But it's certainly measuring something that goes on in schools. And some schools have had to be publicly held accountable for their performance. All the while they still must adhere to those institutionalized expectations and constraints.

I think what drives me, and what makes this really so fun (I really enjoy the work I do), is that schooling—public or private K-12 schooling—is one of three things that our government makes us do. Every citizen has to pay taxes, males have to register for the selective service, and they have to go to school. Now the government doesn't care if you're home-schooled, or you go to a public school or a private school. But you have to be in school. And that signals something to me. There's something different about this enterprise. For whatever reason and whatever motivation or motivations, it is very important to our society to demand that all kids go to school. Part of it is an economic function where your parents are off working, and they need a place for the kids to go, so it's convenient that kids have to be in school. If you go back in history a little bit to the development of the compulsory attendance laws, they go hand in hand with child labor laws, where you're keeping kids out of factories. They have to be somewhere, so schools step in with a caretaking role.

We have tremendous government intervention in schooling. Over the last ten years, curricular interventions, curricular demands, inspections, and statewide assessments have proliferated. Students will take multiple assessments over the years. What's really intriguing is not that kids are spending hours and hours taking exams, but there are tremendous ramifications for success or failure on those exams for the schools. It's the equity issues that arise with state standards I find quite interesting.

233

I think the main reason these statewide standards of curriculum and accountability have become so popular across the entire country (and in no small part, around the world) is that advocates from the far right and advocates from the far left are all calling for the same thing. That's relatively unique in our history of public education, where you get ultraconservatives and ultraliberals calling for the same thing. Of course, they're calling for it for different reasons, but ultimately the product is the same. The conservative argument is, "We need accountability. We're spending $400 billion dollars a year on our public education system, and we need accountability for that. We have to know if teachers are doing their job, if the schools are doing their job, if the kids are working hard enough." The left-wing view is that it's been well documented forever that many, many kids, based on color of skin, based on gender, based on wealth of their family, based on where they live, have been excluded from any meaningful educational program in schools, and are relegated to lower tracks, and relatively meaningless work in schools. And so creating a system in which we demand that all students are exposed to higher-level curricula and higher-level forms of instruction is one way of ensuring that minority kids are being exposed to the same curricular opportunities as the middle- and upper-class kids.

So there's tremendous state intervention in schools, and now federal reforms and interventions with the No Child Left Behind Act. And what I'm working on in relation to all of this is to decipher, uncover, and analyze to what degree these new interventions and reforms are reducing inequity in our schools, or whether they are reinforcing the traditional inequity. There's great public debate about this. There's great debate amongst academics about this. So that's what the focus of my work is: looking at educational opportunities, how they're shifting, how they're changing, what schools now have to pay attention to which heretofore they didn't have to pay attention to.

Knowing what I know about how schools function (this might sounds elitist), I'm not terribly concerned about how my own kids will do. Every kid is different, but statistically, with two college-educated parents in a stable household, attending a well-funded school, my kids have a great chance of doing quite well. My oldest son now is in first grade, and I see him working through the system, I see what the teachers' priorities are, and how the social interactions are in the school. It personalizes what I've been studying a little bit. I think it will more so as he goes on in years, and my other kids get into school. The sixth through the ninth grades are really make-or-break years for many kids. As a former seventh- and eighth-grade teacher, I witnessed that firsthand from the teaching standpoint. And in some sense, I get nervous about thinking about my kids going through those ages. But it's not a great personal concern that motivates my research. The motivation is more of a broader, societal concern. I look at some of my son's classmates, and statistically, you can see that where some of these kids are, they are not likely to succeed. I'm very curious whether or not we can devise a system in which more and more kids can succeed; we worry about whether all kids have an equal—or at least more equal—chance of success.

I grew up in Dewitt, which is a very middle-class suburb in the first suburban ring out around Syracuse. It's where Shopping Town mall is. It was very, very white. There was some religious diversity in terms of a Jewish population, and Catholics and Protestants. But there was a very small African American population. Of course, growing up, you have no idea that other communities and other districts were very, very different. You grow up with what you know. I had a stable home life and a mother at home, father off working. He was a physician in Syracuse. I was the fifth of six kids, so I had older siblings who had gone through the school system before me. They were successful, which laid the groundwork and opened opportunities for me when I came through. "Oh, here's another Sipple. He must be a good student."

I went to a school that was well funded. I believe 90 percent of the kids from my school went on to some form of higher education. I had a wonderful public school experience. I was involved in a lot of different activities: student government and athletics, academics, and all the rest. Just a good, healthy, happy first twelve years of school. I think that speaks to my desire to go back and teach in the schools. People who have a bad experience in school typically don't want to go back.

The strongest mentors for me growing up, besides my parents and older siblings, were school-related people. They were teachers and coaches. I wasn't involved with a lot of community groups, if any. I wasn't in the Boy Scouts. I didn't do some of those community-based activities. It was pretty much all school-based activities. I explicitly remember a couple eighth-grade teachers who were just fabulous. Not just because of what or how they taught (I'm not even sure I remember how they taught), but for the relationships they had with the students, and particularly myself. And then through high school, the same.

I got on a path right away with the student government—very serendipitous is best way to describe it. I was elected freshman class president for—who knows why? As a freshman you don't have any sense about why you're doing stuff. Once you're in that kind of student government circle in schools, you're typically viewed as someone who can be trusted by the administration and by other teachers, and you get a lot of breaks. I explicitly remember that I'd be late for class sometimes, and it was always assumed that I had a good reason for being late. Generally, I was doing something student government-related. Twice I was a member of the four-person student council, as a sophomore and as a senior. And we actually had a fair amount of, I'm not going to say power, but we were able to actually do things in our high school, which kind of empowered the students, at least some of the students. It wasn't just a title, or a figurehead. We were actually able to do something. So I had a real positive experience. That really made a huge difference for me, being on the student government, and the relationships that helped me form with the principal, the superintendent, and the teachers.

I also had quite a bit of success in athletics. I was captain of the football and basketball teams. I was recruited to play football in college, so my senior year I had a fairly lengthy string of coaches stopping into the school to visit me, and I got out of class a lot. And I think of the irony of—I guess what I'm trying to share here is, now that I study how schools function, and the opportunities afforded kids, equitable and nonequitable opportunities, I see the phenomenal advantages I had through my fairly serendipitous entry into student government, and then through my success in athletics.

There was never any doubt that I was going to go on to college. All my four older siblings went on to college. It was just a matter of which one. And football played a huge role in that. I wanted to play at the college level, and I made a series of visits to different places. At that point I didn't have any great sense of what I wanted to study. I had some sense that engineering was the route I wanted to go. I've always been successful in math and science, and people always said, "You should be an engineer." It's one of those funny things. It's so deeply rooted in our society that if you're good in math and science, you should go on and be a physician or be an engineer. We don't have that same press to be a schoolteacher, or that same press to go out and be an artist. I find that quite interesting.

I remember a recruiting visit up to Dartmouth. They flew me in, I got off the plane, and a coach picked me up and took me to campus. I just couldn't believe how beautiful it was. It matched my mental image of what a college was all about, this small place with a strong commitment to the liberal arts. I ended up going there for my undergraduate degree, and they told us for four straight years that it doesn't matter what you major in. They said, "You'll have a Dartmouth degree and you can go out and do whatever you want. Sure, go be an English major and go off to medical school. That's fine. People do it all the time. Get an engineering degree and then go be an artist." They talk in those terms. And of course there are probably not that many universities in the country you could actually do that. But as a young high school kid looking at the college, as a freshman, you buy into it. Since gaining some distance from it, I can see the real privilege that comes along with this.

I got my acceptance letter to Dartmouth on the same day I got my rejection letter from Cornell. A week later, I got a phone call, and it was from the guy who did my alumni interview for Cornell. I thought, "This is strange, he's calling me." And he said he was so angry that I did not get accepted to Cornell that he called up the admissions office. After a long shouting match, in his words, they agreed to let me in. So he told me, "If you want to go, you can go." He essentially got me by the admission process, and I didn't know this guy from a hole in the wall. And I said, "Well, thanks, but I'm all set." Again, what strikes me about this is that privileges and opportunities are continually heaped on some people, and not others.

Dartmouth was a great experience. God, what a lot of fun. I played football three years (I did not play my senior year). I was a quarterback, and I met some fabulous people. Growing up in Syracuse, we didn't travel hardly at all as kids. And then, look at my roommates. One was from rural Kentucky—Owensboro, Kentucky. And one was from outside of Cleveland. And then down the hallway, there were people from California, Alaska, Colorado, Florida, Utah, and the Philippines—people from all over the country, all around the world. What a fabulous experience to meet all these people with different backgrounds. So the whole social aspect was fun. I wasn't much of a partier, and it struck me how comfortable that was. People didn't have a problem with that.

The academic side of things was quite a—I'm not going to say "rude awakening," but it was an awakening. I'd always been successful in school with some but not a ton of effort. I realized pretty quickly that the degree of effort I had made during high school wasn't going to take me far at the college level, and I was going to have to bear down and work harder if I wanted to succeed. I realized that everybody up there's from the top 10 percent of their class. Everybody had SATs higher than mine. So there was a bit of struggle with that. And the other thing I realized, I figured out after about a year and a half what engineers actually do—they do calculus. And after a year and a half of calculus, I said, "This is not how I want to spend my days." So I tried some different things. I wasn't the least bit panicked or worried, because they kept telling me it doesn't matter what your major is.

I ended up being a religion major, which was very much a philosophical, historical, sociological look at religion in various societies around the world. My interest in that came from a random course I took. Religion in American Society was one of the introductory religion courses. I found it just fascinating to really understand history and contemporary society in ways I never understood before, because I never really thought too much about religion and how it impacts government policy, peer relations, and social relations. It opened up a whole other world I just didn't know existed—a whole other intellectual world, really. I began to explore societies. I had taken an intro sociology class, and I had taken some other social science classes before that. Those didn't have the effect that this religion course did. The teacher was great: Professor Green, I remember him to this day. He ended up opening up an ethics institute at Dartmouth. It was a great course: the reading was good, the discussions, the lectures. It really did awaken me to this whole social construction issue, which I just didn't have any sense of before—the whole social construction of knowledge, and the whole notion of what drives different societies, and the conflicts that can arise between them. I also went to Mexico for a semester, and that was a great experience as well.

A year or so before I was going to graduate, I was sitting around trying to figure out what I was going to do. I had this religion major, which I was really enjoying, but didn't know what I would vocationally do after that. I knew I didn't want to be an engineer, and that whole business-corporate world didn't have any intrigue to me. It had a lot of intrigue to other people up there, the whole investment banking thing. That was what people were gravitating towards—the professional schools, law school, and so forth. I thought, well, maybe I'll teach. I had all these science courses. I had tons and tons of science courses from the time I was in the engineering program, and some biology and chemistry courses. I honestly don't remember where the idea came from to become a teacher, because no one in my family had ever been one. I had an aunt who was a teacher, but no one in my immediate family. No one in my immediate family had worked in a school, or even been on a school board.

What I do distinctly remember is going downstairs in the basement of a building to talk to the director of the teacher ed program. The department was kind of tucked away where people couldn't really see it. I went down, and I met with a woman named Faith Dunn. She was all friendly and excited. She said, "Great. You want to be a teacher." She then asked, "What do you want to teach?" I said, "Oh, I don't know. High school?" And she said, "What have you taken?" I said, "Well, I've got all these science courses." The subject matter wasn't that important to me at the time. But it did make sense. When I told her I played football, she said, "Well, I don't think you can make it through the program then." I said, "What do you mean I can't make it through the program?" And she said, "Well, the time commitment to football and the time commitment to the teacher ed program, typically students can't do both things. You're welcome to try, but I don't think you can make it." Well, I got myself signed up and started taking the courses I needed to begin the process toward certification. The way Dartmouth ran their program is, you did your student teaching after you graduated, so it didn't take so much time in the undergraduate program. So I took whatever required courses I needed to take, while completing the religion major and my other distributive requirements. I really enjoyed the education courses as well.

237

I graduated, and then I went back that next fall to do my student teaching. Once I got into it, I said, "This feels right, this feels good." I had great support from my parents. I don't know inside truly what they thought, but they certainly didn't pose any of the obstacles that I sometimes hear about from many undergraduate students here at Cornell. "We paid all that money to go to Cornell, and you're going to be a teacher?" I've gotten that in a few different settings. Not people talking about me, but people talking about their kids. It's a hard thing for kids to deal with, and it's a hard thing for parents to deal with, too. But I didn't have that obstacle.

I did my student teaching after I graduated in a tiny little 270-student school, grades 7–12, up in Thetford, Vermont—a rural, tiny little place. That was a fascinating experience, to see rural life, with these kids coming from the middle of nowhere. That was my first consistent exposure to kids coming from real rural life, and the issues that face them. I remember them talking about the FFA and the FHA. FFA I'd heard of through other places—Future Farmers of America. FHA—I asked them, "What is that?" "It's Future Homemakers of America," they said. I thought, wow. I come from Dartmouth, where you get shot if you ever talk like that: I mean, literally strung up. The culture shock of the twelve-minute drive between the two places was enormous. But I found it very intriguing, and had some success, and really enjoyed it. And I realized at that point, "Okay, yeah. I'm going to be able to do the whole teaching thing."

I finished my student teaching in December, and then thought, what do I do now, because there are very few teaching jobs open in December. I taught photography two days a week in the Hanover schools, and then substituted the other three days a week in three or four different school districts around the Dartmouth area. I was a kindergarten teacher one day, and high school band teacher the next day, getting the full range of experiences there. And then that spring and summer, I started applying for real jobs.

I got a job teaching seventh grade down in Cape Cod, in Falmouth. I actually was at the beach in July when the time came when I was supposed to call the superintendent to see if I got the job. I said, "Well, this is hard to turn down. This is really quite a deal." And of course, in Cape Cod once you hit October, half the places shut down, and you see a whole different side of the world there, the whole rural thing. Cape Cod is a summer resort area. In the winter, it has all kinds of rural characteristics. And again, in a serendipitous way, because several years later when I applied for the job here at Cornell, right in the posting was this interest in or experience with rural education, rural school systems. Having taught at Cape Cod, with the rural aspects of that (although most people don't think of it as rural) and the little experience I had up in Thetford, I was able to talk about those issues in the job interview.

I taught in Falmouth for two years, though I had every intention of staying for a bunch of years. I never would have thought I'd only be staying two years. The first year I loved it, though I was exhausted. It just drained me trying to figure out how to actually do this job— the sheer number of hours of preparation, grading papers, and all the rest. The second year, I enjoyed the teaching even more. Personally though, as a single guy down in Cape Cod in the winter, it was hard. I wasn't a big social person. I didn't need to be in Boston, but I needed something. All my colleagues were in their forties and fifties and sixties, and I was living with a seventy-six-year-old woman, just renting a basement apartment from her. I just didn't have anything socially going on. I don't know if I'd call it going stir crazy or what, but I realized I needed something to keep myself personally going. While professionally it was fun and interesting, personally I needed some kind of balance.

All the while I was teaching those two years, I was very perplexed as to how the broader system worked. I kind of understood my classroom; I sort of understood my school. But I remember being hired, when I was signing the contract, they said, "Do you want to be a member of the union?" I asked the typical questions: "What are the pros and cons? What do I get? What does it cost?" They said, "Well let's just cut to the chase. If you don't belong, we'll take your dues anyways." And I thought to myself, how legal is that? That can't be right. But I joined the union, and I remember how we worked without a contract that first year. We had several pseudo-picketing sessions at the board meetings to try to publicly make a polite stink about our cause. It was very politely done. And I remember standing on the stairs going up into the board of education office, where all the school board members and superintendent were walking through to go to a meeting, and some senior faculty saying to me, "God! Either you're so brave or you're so stupid for standing there." You know, I was this nontenured person. I thought to myself, "I have a contract. I'm not beating anybody, I'm just standing here." It was a civil disobedience kind of a thing, and I wasn't being obnoxious. I didn't see the big issue, and I wasn't terribly scared of any repercussions. Separately, I knew the state government did something for schools; I didn't know what it was. And the feds were involved in something, and I didn't have any idea what it was. I knew there was this Title I, Chapter I classroom in our school that you couldn't get kids out of or into. The teacher was very isolated. I didn't have any idea what that was all about.

So anyway, I'm teaching in this system, and I have all these questions about the broader environment. With those professional kinds of questions, coupled with my personal dissatisfaction with where I was, I started applying to grad school. I applied to master's programs in a couple of different places. I ended up going to the University of Virginia the next year, and began to study these issues. The program looked to be exactly what I was looking for, and I began to understand how they could take my dues without being a member, and why this Title I, Chapter I room was off-limits: you get federal money coming in and it had to supplement and not supplant the local and state money. I began to understand what the state governments did, and I began to understand a little bit about the broader environment in which my classroom was situated, which in no small way really shaped and constrained what I was doing. I was quite intrigued with that.

When I was done with my master's, I said, "Okay, let's go back and teach again." My goal was to keep teaching, and then become a principal, and then a superintendent. So I got a job teaching eighth grade in Braintree, a suburb right outside of Boston. It was much more homogenous than Falmouth. It was your classic segregated, middle-class, white town, with all of the other issues it had. I was planning to teach there two, three, or four years until I worked out some way to get into a doctoral program. The very first year I was teaching in Braintree I applied to a couple places, one being the University of Michigan. I wasn't that serious about it.

I got a phone call from the Michigan program a month or two after I applied, and they said, "I want to let you know, you've been admitted, and you'll get a letter soon. I also want to know if you want to supervise student teachers as a TA. If you'll do that, we'll waive tuition and pay you a stipend." And I'm thinking, wow! I remember talking to my superintendent about that. I apologized and said, "I'm really sorry." I'd only been there six or eight months at that time. I'd been successful in my teaching, and I enjoyed it. But then I got this offer to go to school for free, plus they'd pay me, and Michigan had a great program. My superintendent said, "You know, do what you want to do. But if I was in your shoes, I would take this chance and go." And so I resigned from my job effective the end of the year, and accepted the slot at Michigan. In the meantime, right before I got that job in Braintree, I got engaged. I got married right at the end of the school year in Braintree. So we were married for a month or so, we packed up all our stuff, and moved out to Michigan.

At Michigan, I continued my study of the broader environment in which schools are set. I focused on organizational process and behavior, and how that interacts with the environment—the constant give and take, what we call in organizational literature the "iron cage" in which individuals in organizations find themselves. You don't see the cage. The cage is kind of invisible strings. That's one explanation of why there's such consistency in schools.

When I went to Michigan, they had recently done a whole reorganization of their program, and really the whole school over the five years preceding the time I got there. When I showed up, I was one of I think twenty-two in my cohort. It was the first real cohort they had, and their explicit goal was they were preparing researchers. They were preparing Ph.D.s who were going to go off and teach at universities or work in policy groups. And I said, "You know, that's all fine and well, but I want to be a superintendent." And they said, "More power to you. That's great. But we are going to train you to be a researcher anyway." And I liked that. I knew from exploring many other administrative preparation programs that what you learn in many of these programs is not very rigorous, not very substantial. And so I thought, well, here's a rigorous, scholarly program. I'll learn how to analyze data and how to understand organizations, the politics and policy. That was my intuitive sense of what superintendents need to know anyways. So I thought, let me go through this program, pick up all these good skills and knowledge, and then I'll go back and be a principal. I'll still get to be a superintendent. And they jokingly said, "Well, we'll brainwash you." And they were joking. If I pursued that path of superintendent, it would have been totally fine with them.

My initial advisor, Carolyn Riehl, was just wonderful. She was relatively new; she was an assistant professor. I got there during her second year. She was trying to get a research program going. We got involved in a project together, and worked on the issue of worker commitment to their organizations. I just had a blast working with her. I had some questions, and in trying to answer them and explore complexities, I read a lot of the industrial organization literature and the educational literature, and tried to tie the two together. I began to think less and less about being a superintendent, and more and more about the possibility of being a university professor.

During my second year, I took a course from the dean of the school, Cecil Miskel, who is an organizations person. He called me into his office after I'd taken his course. I didn't have any idea why he was calling me in. He said he wanted to talk. So I went in and talked to him, and he said he had this opportunity that he wanted to offer a graduate student, and would I be interested. He explained a little bit about what it was. Several faculty members from the business school and the Institute for Public Policy, some government relations people at the university, and two people from the School of Ed had been involved with this group of business leaders at Michigan for about four years. And it had just been a service project. They had been consulting with the business leaders, helping them to understand the school system, helping them to understand how they could impact state policy. And he said, "We want to continue this service work, this consulting work. But I really want to start a research program around this, to study what is going on here with this business group." He said, "I'm not really sure where I want to go with this, but I want to get something started. Are you interested?" So I talked to a couple other people involved in that project, and got quite excited about it, and said, "Sure. Sounds great."

So this opportunity kind of fell in my lap, to be able to work with a couple people that I have a ton of respect for—Cecil the dean and a finance guy named Phil Kearney—on a project that I thought was actually quite interesting, an examination of public policy that affects public schools. And all these big multinational corporations were involved in this—Ford, Chrysler, Upjohn, Dow, Whirlpool. So I got involved, and it allowed me the opportunity not only to get to know these businesspeople, but to design my first real research project without Carolyn. Actually, she designed our earlier work and I helped her with it. Cecil, the dean, was busy doing his dean stuff, and he told me, "I want you to figure something out to do here." I had taken his course, that's the only way I knew him. But he somehow realized that maybe I could do this, or who knows what he was thinking.

So I began to read about interest groups and ended up writing a couple papers—well, one paper, and then a dissertation—on this whole issue with the business group. It's not the stuff that I'm doing now, but in this early work, I was delving into the institutional literature, delving into the whole theoretical notion that organizations within a given sector are bound by very powerful, very similar constraints. And so you get a group of business leaders coming into this education world, and they just start bumbling around, and have a heck of a time getting their feet under them, because they were coming from a very different sector, with a very different set of constraints and expectations.

The approach I took for that work was all qualitative; I did a bunch of interviews. I also had the good fortune to be able to draw on two previous waves of interviews, and an incredible amount of archival data that had been kept in the dean's office. There were notes from the business group's meetings in these files. So from the get-go, from the time I got involved in '95, there was all this data available. And there had been two previous pseudo-studies done: one early in probably '91 or '92, and then one in '93, '94, under the supervision of another faculty member, where they were trying to do what they termed a "gap analysis." In the first one, they interviewed probably twenty people. In the second, they probably interviewed forty people. And I had access to all those transcripts. The data was collected for a different purpose than I was interested in, but it was actually relevant data. I then had access to the files of the executive director of this business roundtable group, and I sat around, spending a couple days just filtering through the files, going to the copy machine. I felt like I was in Watergate or something. And then I said, "Okay, here's all the archival data I have. Here are these two rounds of interviews that were done for different purposes. I need to get more information to really answer the questions." So I designed a research protocol—all qualitative—to meet with as many people as I could get to talk to me, from the CEOs to the state legislators (Republicans and Democrats), the governor, the governor's advisors, some of the school people (mainly statewide school leaders), members of the statewide teachers' union, and the statewide administrators' association.

There were four or five main theoretical lenses I used to understand this business group in terms of the preexisting literature on interest groups. What I found was that while the different theories had some value in shining a light on different aspects of the organization, none of them really hit the nail on the head that would explain what this group was all about. But what struck me as I was going through that was the phenomenal consistency over time in that message. At this point in time, they'd been at it probably six years. And from late in year 2 through the sixth year, the message this group was putting forth—these are business-people, who aren't really known for consistency of message, particularly in terms of policy issues—was consistent. They had a consistent strategy, despite some turnover, and I got a real sense through my interviews that they were phenomenally committed. These are big-time, senior-level VPs, and yet they had a real personal interest in this thing.

I won't go into all this, but they didn't sound like corporate people by the time Michigan faculty had got done with them. And I also heard that from the Republican legislators, who told me point-blank, "These guys have lost their mind. They've forgotten everything that got them into General Motors and Chrysler, because now they're getting soft. They're no longer talking about abolishing the unions and forming charter schools. They're now talking about early childhood education, they're about a common curriculum." I was really intrigued by that, and I remember ending the first publication I ever did solo with a little paragraph at the end, kind of posing questions about the consistency of the organization over time, the consistency of the message. And that led me to the whole institutional literature, which really dominated my dissertation, in terms of really trying to understand how it was this group was able to be at the table long enough to actually effect change. They truly did effect change.

Cecil wanted to continue the relationship with the business group. The U of M folks enjoyed the interaction, they enjoyed the legitimacy of working with this big-time group. It also brought money into the school. Most of the work that was done by the university people for this group was really for the benefit of the business roundtable group. We added on this research layer, this scholarly research layer, as Cecil would call it. But to do the research, we had to secure the permission of the business group, to make very clear that we weren't trying pull a fast one. We said, "Here's what we're going to do. One, do you mind if we conduct the research; two, do you care if we do it; and three, do you want to see what work we do?" And they said, "No, we don't care if you do it. That's fine. We're not too interested in that theo-retical stuff. I mean, who cares."

To broach the topic, Cecil arranged a golf match. Two of the business leaders, Cecil, and myself are out playing golf. One of the business leaders was the executive director of the roundtable group. This was the point in time when we wanted to tell them about our research plans. We decided to just tell these two first, and have them bring it to the next big meeting. And I remember somewhere in the back nine, Cecil brought it up. We talked about it with them, and they said, "Fine, fine, fine." And then to have some fun we said, "We'll give you all the royalties from the publications that come out of it." And the businesspeople, their eyes lit up. "Wow! Really?" You know, they still didn't make any sense out of what this scholarly work was. And then of course they asked, "How much? How much is that?" And we said, "Well, nothing." And then they were just so perplexed. "Why do you do this if you don't get any compensation for it?" To this day, I'm not sure if they've ever read any of the scholarly work we did. I honestly don't know if they ever read it. It was available to them, but I don't know if they read it.

I'd say the School of Education had three motivations to maintain the relationship with the business roundtable. One, they thought they were doing something good, in terms of a service project. Two, they knew they were getting money from it. So that was good. They could fund grad students. And three, it provided a fertile ground for some research that Cecil argued needed to be done. And so I went ahead and did that. They then hired another grad student the year after, so I had a partner in the work.

The research we did contributed to the knowledge base around interest groups, in terms of trying to understand why some interest groups in education are more successful than others. Separately, I think it contributed to the literature and practice of involving business—corporate America—in public education. There's been a real press from the first President Bush on down to get corporate America more involved. Most of the literature that's written on this is very scathing, and I think rightfully so. If you read the studies Ros Mickelson and some others did, the work that's been done in Chicago and down in North Carolina, it's really pretty scathing. The business interests have been forced into the public education system—to the detriment of the educational system, these researchers argue, and I don't disagree with them. I had a very different story, and I think my story ended up being different because the group was in no small way co-opted by the university. *Co-opted* is actually the word the Republican state senators and state house leaders used.

When the business group first got together in 1989 in Michigan, they said, "We've got to abolish the teacher's union. We've got to abolish the bureaucracy around schools, and go to complete school choice. We need to really hold principals' feet to the fire, and impose real strong accountability measures." So that's what their initial agenda was. They then floundered badly. They got nowhere the first year and a half. That's when one of the CEOs, from Whirlpool, I forget his name now, called up a good buddy of theirs; Jim Duderstadt, the president of the University of Michigan. So he called up President Duderstadt and said, "Can you please help us out? We've been struggling for a year now. President Bush asked us to get involved, and we got involved, and we can't make heads or tails of how to change the system—we can't get anywhere with our issues." And the president said, "Well, I can't help you, but I know somebody who can."

So he gave him Cecil's name at the School of Education, and that began a series of conversations with the business school, the Institute of Public Policy, and the School of Education. And I was able to trace the group's message and how it changed, a year after what they called teaching sessions. There were twelve monthly teaching sessions run by the U of M folks, and after they were over, the group had a new message. And it was that message that they stuck to over the next three to four years, including Christmas Eve, 1993, when there was this quirky finance struggle going on in Michigan, where they abolished the use of local property taxes to pay for their public schools. Something had to be done to pay for the schools. So this law was going through. This group was savvy enough to slide a quality package into the bill. And what slid in was almost verbatim what their message had been for three years. I don't know exactly how that worked. It's a little hard to document where those words come from. So the co-opting, you know, I was able to document in my dissertation how that relationship created this new message, what it was based on, and the strategies that the government relations people at the University of Michigan used to impose it. It became the group's talking points for years.

So it's serendipitous how the relationship with the business roundtable came to be. They happened to know President Duderstadt. Duderstadt happened to have a good relationship with Cecil. And I think from the CEOs' point of view, they liked the fact that we're dealing with the dean, and not just a couple of assistant professors. In their words, they were also trying to be good corporate citizens.

In terms of my own development, this project pulled me hook, line, and sinker into the research enterprise. The first bit of research I did with my advisor was very quantitative; it was secondary data analyses of a national dataset. This was very qualitative. It pulled me in a very different direction, with a very different literature and very different methods. When working toward defending my dissertation, I was fully committed to finding an assistant professor position. And I had a broader, mixed-methods point of view as I was going out to look for a job.

While I was looking for a job, I was still finishing up my dissertation. It was clear it was going to be late summer or fall by the time I finished. I missed the main job season that winter before, because I wasn't sure I was going to be anywhere near finishing. Things didn't fall into place until the spring, so by the time I started looking, there were only a few jobs available. I got an offer from Auburn University first. The program was quite intriguing, but my wife and I just could not pull the trigger to move down there. We just couldn't do it. We really wanted to get back east. Then a visiting assistant professor position at Dartmouth was posted the night I returned from Auburn. It was a one-year position, and the contact person was a professor I had as an undergraduate years ago. So I called him up, and I said, "What's this all about, this one-year visiting assistant?" And he explained that they didn't have a tenure-track line for it. They were hoping to some day, but right now it's just one-year position to teach some courses.

So I applied, and I got the job. I was actually their second choice. They offered it to a woman from Harvard first, who turned them down, and then they called me up. It had a terrible salary and a terrible teaching load of six courses. But it gave me a chance to go back to Dartmouth, to get back east, and no other options were available. So I took it. Within a month of starting, I defended my dissertation. We had just gotten up there in September, and I drove back to Michigan and defended. And then another month thereafter, in late October or November, I started looking at job postings for the next year. I viewed that one year as a teaching postdoc, if there is such a thing. I began to learn how to teach at the university level, which I actually found quite helpful. Teaching twenty-year-olds in a university setting is different than teaching seventh-graders. So I didn't mind. It was actually a good, fun experience.

I applied for a number of jobs, I forget how many, all within roughly the same field of education administration and policy. I remember getting an offer from St. John's University in Queens. I could not for the life of me figure out how I could afford to take that job. They were offering $44,000, whatever it was, and I went down to look for housing. I talked to the dean, and I said, "There's no way." He said, "How much more do you need?" I kind of laughed, and I said, "How do you get people to do this?" He didn't give me much of an answer. So I turned that one down.

Then I saw this quirky posting for Cornell. It was exactly what I was looking for: working with David Monk and Ken Strike, taking Emil Haller's position—people I'd read about for years. It was a neat position that had this rural thing to it that I didn't quite understand. I remember having a long conversation on the phone with Ken. I'd never met him before. I said, "Well, what is this rural thing?" And he explained the Rural Schools' Program and how they were hoping the person they hired would be the real liaison between the two, more so than David or Ken had a chance to be. There was also a really interesting position down at Penn State.

To make a long story short, I ended up with two offers, one from Cornell, and one from Penn State. I ended up choosing Cornell, partly because it was Cornell, and partly because it was upstate New York. I think probably the bigger reason was because it was upstate New York. Also I was comfortable with the small department in what I perceived to be a broader liberal arts enterprise. I was just comfortable in that setting. It was a tiny little place here. We had, I think, fifteen people at the time, whereas Penn State had a whole college of education. I was comfortable with Penn State, too. It had great people to work with and nice opportunities, but I opted for Cornell. So I took the job, and I remember the Penn State people saying, "That's fine. You're choosing between two very different kinds of places," which I of course knew. And I said, "Well, we'll keep in touch."

So I took the job at Cornell, and I came to campus in the fall of 1998 and began to figure out what this was all about here. I was charged with growing a little, fledgling school district superintendent certification Ph.D. program that Emil, Ken, and David had got going in '95 or '96. They got approval for it from the state. And so one of my real goals, beyond teaching those courses I talked about earlier, was to recruit and build and grow this school district superintendent certification program. I was intrigued by that. I was really looking forward to that.

That first year, I thought we did a fabulous job. We brought in five people. In my second year, these people started. Those five people right now, one is a superintendent of schools, one's a high school principal in western New York State, one is a principal in the Buffalo City Schools, one was one of two finalists for principalship of ACS, which is an alternative high school in Ithaca, and one is an assistant principal down in the White Plains area. She's returning right now to finish her dissertation. Four of the five have finished their dissertations, one hasn't. It was a good first group. So when I came on board, a lot of my initial time was spent on building that program.

Before coming to Cornell, I had zero experience with the land-grant mission. I was so perplexed when I found out that my appointment was 10 percent Extension, and not 10 percent outreach. Most places use words like *outreach* or *service*. Cornell uses the word *Extension*, with a big *E*. I didn't even know enough to ask questions about what that really meant until I got to campus and started to realize what this whole Cooperative Extension

System meant. I learned early on that much of what I had been doing would not be counted by the college's administration in Roberts Hall as big-*E* Extension. And I just didn't know any better to even ask questions about it. It was all brand new.

In terms of the choice to come here, I felt good about the fact that Cornell is a land-grant institution. That it's a place that—at least in principle—is charged with serving the state of New York. My interpretation of the land-grant mission at the time was that it was applied service to the state of New York—that we're going to help New York State, which is my home state. I was kind of intrigued by that. And I really did like some of the applied work I did at Michigan. We were helping the State of Michigan, and yet we were able to do our scholarly work on top of it. I viewed the chance to prepare future educational leaders as part of the land-grant mission. I think that might have come out in the paperwork that was developed to get that program approved through the university and through the state. There's a lot of that conversation in the paperwork, that this is the way Cornell can serve the state, by preparing highly trained, high-quality leaders. Even if we prepare a small number of them, they're going to be in high-level leadership positions, and can affect a greater area, even to the point where they could then hire Cornell-prepared teachers. So that might have been where it came out, the notion that this is one way to serve. Cooperative Extension is another way to serve the state.

So the land-grant mission was something I could really buy into, and get committed to. Land-grant meant we could serve the state. And we have been. At one level, it gives us some cover in a "Research I" institution to serve the state. You know, there is some institutional legitimacy for doing these types of activities, because that's what we're supposed to do. Now, when I was new here, I didn't know how seriously it was taken. I still don't quite know how seriously it's taken by certain parts of the university. I've come to know many of the extension, outreach, and service type of venues that exist on campus, and how different they are from the University of Michigan, where they don't really exist. The mission at the U of M is not to do outreach. That's not how they view their role. They see themselves as a world leader. They serve the world. But they serve as scholars. The University of Michigan is a state university, but Michigan also has Michigan State University, which is a land-grant. The University of Michigan says, "We do the real scholarly work here," and Michigan State University says, "We do stuff that's useful and scholarly." I think there's an identity issue there, and it's similar to what we see here at Cornell, between the endowed and the statutory colleges.

The story I want to tell about my work today focuses on the implementation of New York State's new learning and graduation standards, and the basic question of how school districts are responding, what pressures they are feeling, who are the key agents involved, and bottom line, where the equity issues are in the implementation. The story really starts in the late fall of 2000 with David Monk, who was department chair at the time. David had been doing a little bit of work for a group called the New York State Educational Finance Research Consortium. This was a relatively new group. I believe they were in their second year of existence at that point in time. They had an interesting notion to try to improve the flow of information to policymakers, and then to policy implementers. That was their goal. The consortium was founded on the belief that there was so much information coming out of the State Education Department and so many decrees from the Board of Regents, it was very unclear what the bases of their decisions were. The EFRC's aim was to improve the flow of information back into the State Education Department.

When the consortium was being set up, the initial conversations were between a couple of key senior state education officials—Jim Kadamus and Deborah Cunningham. Jim is the deputy commissioner. I think it was Jim, the number two person in the State Ed Department, who was really spearheading this. And there were four or five academics involved at the time: Leana Stiefle at NYU, David Monk from Cornell, Jim Wyckoff from SUNY-Albany, and a couple others. They all got together to try to figure out a way that research could be sponsored in a fairly autonomous way, meaning it would be separated from the State Education Department, and yet somewhat be connected to the State Education Department people. So there's this interesting tension of trying to solicit studies that would be relevant to the agenda in the State Education Department and the Board of Regents, but also autonomous from the State Education Department so that they wouldn't be viewed as reflecting the company line. They're actually fairly sophisticated in how they think about this. And of course the academics, this is where they come from, where all their work is reportedly independent and not biased per se by specific political agendas.

So this group got together, and they pulled together a proposal. My understanding is they got State Assembly funding for this. I believe the original source of the dollars was actually federal money for R&D that is kicked out to each state. And so this group got together, and they put together a proposal, and lo and behold, got it funded. Jim Wyckoff, from the Rockefeller School at SUNY-Albany, became the executive director of the group. He's kind of running the show, and then there's what they call a Board of Governors, which includes three State Education Department people and four academics. So you get that kind of balance in this little group of seven people.

They would get together several times a year, and their biggest task was the development of RFPs (requests for proposals) for small studies. The original goal was three or four studies per year, and the original intent was to have the researchers make use of existing state data. The belief was that the existing state data was underused, or not used in a very productive way. So David Monk, while being a member of the Board of Governors, got one of these original grants to do a study. He and a grad student did the first condition study (these studies were called condition studies). At the end of that study they were left with a relatively superficial view of what the state data were telling them. So David went back to this group and said, "Let's try to dig a little deeper." They needed time-series analyses showing the buildup to the new state standards. This is back in 2000. So they did this trend analysis from 1992 up through 1998 or so, and then he wanted to extend that the next year. He came to me and he said, "Would you be interested in going out and doing some case studies to show at the ground level what this actually looks like?" We had the statewide numbers, but we didn't know what was really going on in practice. He offered me $8,000 to do this. It was in November or so of my second year, and this well-connected individual offers me $8,000 to become part of this project. I thought the $8,000 is more or less irrelevant, but the opportunity—the door opening—is the key.

So I agreed, and I assembled a team of eight or nine people to begin conceptualizing this work, and actually go out and do it. The team included Kieran Killen, who was a grad student at the time. He was one of David Monk's grad students. He had an assistantship already, so I didn't have to pay for him. He is now a faculty member at the University of Vermont. Kieran and I began this process with a number of questions. What do we ask? What we do? There are 700 school districts in the state and we have $8,000. What did we do? Now this question of trying to get, as David would put it, behind the numbers and tell some stories of what this looks like in practice, fit very closely with my broader research agenda. This was right on target with what I was trying to accomplish.

I was developing my research agenda, and I had $50,000 of Hatch money (Hatch money is allocated to land-grant universities through USDA formula funds). My research agenda was to go out and explore how in the world school districts are going from their prior models of educating kids, which had the result of less than half the students in the state earning a Regents Diploma. And being phased in through 2005, school districts would have to have 100 percent of their students earning a Regents Diploma. How were they doing this? What programs were put in place? How were dollars being allocated? What were the politics involved between what the local communities wanted and what the state wanted? This has become a real interesting theme for us. The superintendent gets stuck in-between what the local community wants and what the local board wants, and what parents want for their kids and what the state wants. So this new request for these case studies was consistent with my research agenda. I agreed to do it.

After I got Kieran on board, I said "Okay, we need more people." So we talked to some other grad students, and three or four were quite interested in participating. They hadn't done a lot of research, but they were quite interested in school districts in New York State. They'd either been teachers in New York State, or were going to be administrators in New York State. We then realized we needed a real live teacher who's actually in the field right now. And through a stroke of luck, again a lot of serendipity, a prospective student had been in contact with me from the Syracuse area, inquiring about our program. I asked him, "Would you like to be involved in this project as a teacher? Would you be able to take some days off to go with us on these site visits?" He checked with his principal and superintendent, and they were quite pleased that we were going to do this, and he got on board.

The reason we needed to have a teacher involved was partly for legitimacy reasons, and partly because the implementation of policy was changing every single year. The regulations were being phased in, and they change them all the time. The grad students that I had working with me had all left their jobs in the schools either one year before or two years before, and I thought we needed some kind of ongoing local knowledge of what was actually happening. And I thought as we went and interviewed a number of people in these districts, it would be great to get the interpretation of a current practicing teacher, in contrast to myself, who had not been in a real classroom since before grad school. We also needed to have someone on board with some special education expertise and experience. It was very clear that a big part of the process of implementing these new state standards involved special education programs. Through an intern we had down at the Ithaca City School District, we got in touch with the director of special education for the Ithaca City Schools. I met with her for a good hour one day, and she was very interested in this. Being the district-wide director of special education, I presumed she'd be intimately knowledgeable of the regulations and what was involved, and the legal issues throughout special education. She had been in practice for twenty years as a special ed teacher and administrator, and it seemed like she would be a wonderful person to get involved. I had heard very good things about her. So I met with her and she absolutely agreed to be part of this. She checked with her boss, and the superintendent said, "Great, you have my blessing to go be involved in this project."

The State Department of Education's interest or goal in funding these condition studies was to enable more informed decision-making—to get better information to the Board of Regents, who was the ultimate decision maker, as they tried to implement these policies. They have a lot of data, but they don't have the person power to do much with it. And I think they also realized that there is a lot of general skepticism when they do their studies internally. (I have a quick story to tell you later on about a comment about the value of this consortium from a member of the Board of Regents that speaks volumes about why this is going on.)

Our interest as scholars, as I remember from the early days of this, was to have a chance to impact practice. It was a way to contribute to the conversation that was taking place in the state around the raising of standards, around pushing kids and teachers and administrators to higher levels of performance. And as I recall, we all welcomed the opportunity to interact with state policymakers, and to be able to do what we do and have them actually use it in a small way. There were no guarantees it was going to shape practice, but we would contribute to the conversation.

So we got the team together, and Kieran and I kept doing a lot of work behind the scenes, separate from the team, designing the core questions we wanted to address. I remember we had a meeting where we got everyone together and bought everybody lunch—part of our $8,000—and we handed out packets and said, "This is essentially a work in progress. Let's have a conversation about what you see here." In those packets were the overarching goals of the research project, some draft interview protocols and some other kinds of rationales about the need for the study—you know, the typical pieces. We had a really interesting conversation that day and got some interesting feedback. Then we began to schedule the site visits.

There's a process that we went through in selecting the districts. There are 700 districts. Which do we choose? Kieran and I rigged up a fairly sophisticated system, which in hindsight was way too much time to spend on selecting the districts. But we wanted to have some defensible, logical way of selecting them. We had districts that were in one of four categories: hot movers, cold movers, hot stayers, and cold stayers. Hot or cold was, in relation to all of the districts, whether they were above or below average in terms of their recent performance. Movers or stayers was a notion of who had moved an above-average number of kids into the Regents program versus a below-average number before the year 2000—so kind of the early adopters versus what you'd call late adopters. We had a grid with four cells, and we pulled six districts from the four cells.

I should clarify what the Regents program is. This is what I think is relatively unique about New York State. And it's a good-news, bad-news thing. The Board of Regents is a remarkably stable body. There are eighteen members of the Board of Regents, and they're remarkably stable in that they're appointed by the governor, and then they need full approval of both bodies of government, the Assembly and the Senate. So in a joint session they're approved. They have these fairly lengthy terms, and they're fairly immune from local politics. They're not voted on by the public, so it's a fairly stable body. In 1993, they began serious conversations, saying, "Are we preparing all our kids for the new world economy?" And they said, "Well, we don't think so. We need to raise our standards and push more kids to higher levels of learning."

In 1995, they continued these conversations. In 1996 they decided, "Okay, one way that we're going to do this is all kids are going to need to earn a Regents Diploma." Heretofore, local school districts had set their own graduation standards. And through the 1990s, somewhere between 42 and 46 percent of students were earning a Regents Diploma. All the rest were earning the local diploma. Generally speaking, the local diploma was less rigorous. There were probably fifteen districts, most of them down in Westchester County, that opted out of the Regents Program because it wasn't rigorous enough. So they had a more rigorous set of standards, but they're the outliers.

In 1997, the Board of Regents adopted a timeline for this and said, beginning in 2000, and then fully phased in by 2005, every single kid in the state, if they want a high school diploma, will need to follow this set of courses and exams. Coupled with that are brand-new fourth- and eighth-grade exams in several different subject areas. They cover course content over multiple years. There was some revamping of some of the curriculum content standards, revamping of some of the exams. The English exam went from a three-hour, one-day exam at the high school level to a two-day, six-hour exam. That was the first exam really to come online in 2000. So the phase-in began in 2000, and if you wanted to graduate in the spring of 2000, you needed to take and pass the English exam and course. If you wanted to graduate in 2001, you could do English and one math exam, and then they phased in other courses over time. That's essentially what they were doing.

The state does a remarkable job of warehousing all kinds of data. There's just oodles and oodles of data in the state, and most of it's publicly available—not all of it, but most of it. That's what David Monk had been using, and he essentially found—and it was no great surprise—that the number of students participating in the English Regents exam and the math Regents exam was dramatically increasing throughout the late 1990s. But with the initial study he did, the data stopped in 1998, so it was unclear what was happening between '98 and 2000. But not all kids were doing this, and districts were at very different rates of increase in terms of where they were pushing their kids into this program. So questions come out as to why. Why isn't everybody moving towards this? The Regents have been very visible and very vocal that this was going to happen. In one of our cases, when we were sitting on site with them, it was the first year they had made any changes. And we said, "You know, you've known about this for probably six years now. Why haven't you done anything until this year?" And they said, "Oh, we didn't think they were actually serious about it." That was very telling.

Anyway, the original, preexisting state data showed some broad trends that fit roughly with the state expectations, but not precisely. And questions starting coming out. Why would some districts adopt these practices early? Are local communities or are parents pushing this? How are resources playing into this? Is it the wealthy districts that do this, and poor districts are not? So a number of questions were generated that you could not answer with the preexisting state data. And we tried to answer those with our more qualitative work, with our $8,000. It's important to remember that the motivation for this study came from the research consortium and David Monk. There was not a field-based push for this.

Back to the story. So we convened the group over lunch, and everyone bought into the study and said, "Yeah, this is good." They had a few suggestions for language changes and so forth. The language in the interview protocols was mine and Kieran's. We tweaked it a little bit, but realized we just needed to go out and start working with it. We had a few core issues that we really wanted to focus on when we got to the sites, one of which was the question of how resources were being allocated. Were resources being pulled away from art and music and high-level AP classes and moved more towards the lower-level students, or were districts hiring additional personnel? That's a basic question. We were very interested in the types of programmatic strategies that districts were using to enrich their academic programs, arguing that if you only had half your kids earning these diplomas before, you're going to need to substantively do some things differently to ensure more kids can take these courses and pass the exams. And scheduling. How do you schedule these classes? We then got on site and got to our very first district, and some of our questions were answerable. People had the answers, and they understood what we were asking.

We would always tell the schools ahead of time that we're going to be there all day long with between five to eight people that are working with us, and we're going to speak with everyone from the superintendent and any assistant superintendents they had, to building principals and English and math teachers. We gave them generic titles of who we wanted to interview. We wanted three or four English teachers, three or four math teachers, building principals, and department chairs. By in large, the districts were helpful in setting up these interviews. We brought our tape recorders and brought our interview protocols, and we went in and spread out and began the conversations.

I remember that the reallocation-of-resources question confused the heck out of people. They said, "What do you mean by that?" They just didn't know quite know what to say about that. What they did give us an earful about was the pressure they were feeling. We didn't go in to ask about pressure. We went in to ask them about their set of priorities, what's first and foremost on their agenda these days as they're doing their job. The conversation was virtually always dominated by the state standards, so it clearly got the attention of these practitioners, from superintendent down to teachers. I should say we expected this, and we got it.

When we would show up on site the administration was typically fairly enthused about us coming. Principals, when they understood what we were doing, were very welcoming. Superintendents were always very welcoming. We would typically work initially through the superintendent. We needed the superintendent's permission to go do anything, so we got the superintendent's buy-in, and then asked them, "Okay, how best we can do this? Would you like us to contact the individual buildings, or how do we do this?" Almost always the superintendent said, "Let me take care of it, or my secretary will take care of this," or "I've got an administrative team meeting tomorrow, and let me tell everybody what's going on."

In some districts the communication never really got through, and all of a sudden there's Cornell people showing up on their doorstep. They're very busy, and they would say,

"What do you want?" That kind of thing. We had to diffuse some fairly tense situations some-times, which we understood. Here we are intruding in their school day, and for whatever reason, the word that we were coming hadn't gotten through to them. But other times when we showed up on site there would be these agendas for us: at 9:03 you meet with this teacher, 9:37 you meet with this teacher, there's a group of teachers over here at 10:37. We would tell them we could break into two or three different teams, and some places would then have three different schedules for us, and we would go out and everything was remarkably well organized. One district even catered lunch for us.

Once we got in and actually sat down with the teachers and sometimes the administra-tors, we would ask, "Do you have any idea why we're here?' And most times they would say, "No, we have no idea. We were told to show up in this room at this time. We know you're from Cornell, we know you're studying something. Why don't you tell us again what you're studying?" We had this little paragraph we'd read to them so we were consistent. And then of course we'd do the whole human subjects thing, to get their permission to participate in the study and to have the interview be tape recorded. There was a real healthy degree of skepticism, which didn't surprise us, because we'd all been there with busy school days, and the role of research in the public schools—research by and large doesn't have a real good connotation to it. It is irrelevant, it is not helpful, and then it's just very distant. Research is very distant from the lives of current practitioners. And so here's a group of Cornell people coming in. They're doing research, and no one was really very clear about what we were trying to accomplish, so we explained it.

It was really kind of fun on our rides home from these districts to bring up this conversa-tion with the other researchers and talk about the first ten minutes of the interview versus the rest of the interview. The first ten minutes was always like pulling teeth, and the teachers would often say, "I've got about ten minutes here, let's quick get this over with and I'll get out of here." And 98 percent of the time, thirty-five to forty minutes would go by and they're still talking. At the end of the conversation, as we were thanking them, they'd say, "You know, this was really interesting. This was really fun. I never get to have conversations like this." And it was uncanny how often that happened, that the teachers were incredibly suspicious, and then once they realized what our agenda was, once they realized that we wanted to hear from them and they were going to tell us about the implementation of standards and the obstacles and so forth, they really enjoyed it. The bell would ring, which meant they had to go to the next class, and oftentimes they didn't want to stop.

So there was a learning process all around, in terms of us learning how to access teachers to get information, and then teachers learning about what research might look like that would involve them. And it was remarkable how much they enjoyed the twenty minutes or the hour that we spent with them. Our assessment is they were really quite candid with us once they got comfortable. We had 120 interviews across the five districts our study covered. Sometimes they were group interviews, sometimes they were individuals. We had high-need districts, we had wealthy districts, we had urban districts, we had suburban districts, and we had a rural district.

Now there are three interesting points I want to make about what happened with this study. One is the timeline, the time crunch that we were under to get this thing done. The research consortium had a public symposium scheduled for late May of 2001, and we began this in November of 2000. So we had to design the study, find the sites, get access to the sites, conduct the interviews, get them transcribed, conduct the analysis by this date in May. And they wanted the paper a good week or two in advance—they being the consortium. So the time crunch was exceedingly uncomfortable and very hard to do. We literally got our last transcripts back from our transcriber two or three days before we had to get the initial draft off to the state. We developed coding schemes and strategies, and had multiple people code each transcript. I distinctly remember sitting down with the data coming out of the computer, trying to draft up what the heck this report would look like. I had some skeletal parts done and the methods part done and the front part of the paper done, and then tried to do the substantive analyses in a very short time crunch. So that's one issue—trying to merge academic work with the timeline with which this is to go to the policymakers.

The second thing was, we submitted the initial report with big, huge letters: "DRAFT." And within two days, there were these fairly forceful emails being zipped around, which we were then copied on, saying that something had gone awry with our initial report that we had sent to the consortium, this draft report. I'm not sure the word *dangerous* was used, but essentially the emails insinuated that this study is dangerous. They said, "What is going on with this study? What agenda do they have? What are they trying to do? This could have potential ramifications down the road." We got these emails, and I remember it being on a Friday afternoon, and I'm thinking, "Oh God, what'd I write? What'd I do?"

What happened was, I had included a literature review, as if I was presenting this paper at a conference to an academic body. I reviewed the existing literature, and discussed what we know about how school districts respond to state policy, how we know that they rebuff or they rebuke policy. It's exceedingly hard for state policy to infiltrate through a district shell and work its way into the classroom. I reviewed that. Well, that got interpreted by these policymakers that these policies in New York State are never going to work, that we're wasting all this money. Now, it was just a lit review, so we had that disconnect. Also, as with most any research study, at the very end of the paper, in the last paragraph, I raised some concerns and questions for future research. I forget the comment I made, but I lived to regret it. It was something about how the worth and value of the new state standards are being called into question, which was roughly based on some of the comments from our interviewees. And that just scared and then horrified some of the people who read this. And this got up to the highest echelons of the State Ed Department, and the people were in a tizzy.

We got word of this, and we said, "Wait a minute. We're not out to get anybody here. This is just a lit review. We posed a question at the end. Okay, we'll take the question out, we'll take the last sentence out, fine, because it's just a thought-provoking question. It's not a substantive part of the study." I tell this story because it's how I began to learn what pressures practitioners were under, and what role research could play in their jobs. We then altered some of the lit review, toning down some of the language a little bit, making it clear that these were studies from other states, because I had no intention of saying this is what's going on in New York State. And I believe I took out the last line of the paper. We then got word a day or two before the symposium that they were going to add a second discussant to our paper, a woman named Roseanne Defabio. I didn't know who she was. I called Mike Joseph (executive director of the Rural Schools Association) and I said, "Who is Roseanne Defabio? I know we've angered a lot of people at the state already. Who is she?" Mike then explained to me that whenever the state gets in trouble, this woman comes out and she's very politically savvy and is able to kind of beat back opponents of what the state's trying to accomplish. So I'm thinking, "Oh my God, this is savage. We're going to get roasted in front of all these people, and it's the first time I've ever done this kind of work."

So we get to the meeting in Albany and we're not quite sure what's going to happen. We give our paper, the first discussant was positive, and then Roseanne Defabio stands up to critique it. And I'm just kind of sweating at this point, wondering, "What is she going to say?" She went on to say how phenomenally valuable this study was, and here's what it really means. So she took, in a sense, the high road of not discrediting the paper, but saying, "This is the type of work we need to do. This is really interesting, and here's how we interpret this. A lot of progress has been made, but a lot of work needs to be done." She put a fairly positive spin on it. Then she sits down, and everyone was feeling good about it. It really was quite remarkable as I sat there and watched it. Part of me appreciated it, and part of me thought, that's really quite savvy.

Before these papers go on their web site and are disseminated, they go through a revision process to address all the comments readers have made about them. So we revised our paper and completed more of our analyses. It was fairly sketchy at the early draft stage. We learned to take out some of the conjectures, some of the interpretation. What we learned, what we were told explicitly, and what I then began to understand in a much better way, was that the role of these condition studies is to provide information to the state, and then let the state interpret what it really means. They said, "Don't interpret this for us. Let us interpret it." That final paragraph we wrote was our interpretation, and so we took out our interpretation. Now, to their credit, they never pressured us to change any of our findings. They never pressured us to change any text. They never pressured us to hide anything. They said, "Just present it, and let us interpret it."

In terms of academic work, you can't get away with that. You have to interpret what you find in light of theory, and in light of previous empirical literature. Here you just present your findings, and let others interpret them. So I learned how the game was going to be played, and I began to understand the phenomenal pressure the State Department of Education and the Board of Regents were under. I guess I hadn't really thought about it. I wasn't thinking they were just goofballs up there, immune from pressure and immune from politics. I just hadn't really thought about it, which was my fault.

So we revised the study and resubmitted it. It was then put on the web site in December of that year, six months after the public presentation. We were then asked to give a presentation to the Board of Regents, at their monthly meeting in December in Albany. We were given twelve minutes or so to present the study. The other condition studies either had been presented already, or were presented at the same time. Beyond the pressure and the lack of reallocation of resources, one substantive point that we stressed in our presentation was this whole notion of gaming, where principals told us, "This year our dropout rates are 5 percent, next year it's going to be 2 percent. And we're doing this because we're taking kids out of our high school academic program and registering them in a GED program." Given the state definition, the state dropout definition explicitly excludes GED transfers. The practitioners figured this out pretty quick. They were engaged in this and they knew that their community probably wasn't going to pay attention to the GED numbers.

When we talked to the Board of Regents about the GED thing, the deputy commissioner of education asked us, "How prevalent is this?" When we talked about staffing increases, they asked, "How prevalent is this?" When we talked about other programmatic changes and additions with Academic Intervention Services, they asked, "How prevalent is this?" Here we were presenting data from five school districts, and they had a real hard time getting their head around the question of what value this is. They said, "You tell us that this is going on in a very, very minute number of school districts. What are we to do with it?" And so there was somewhat of a tension, somewhat of a disconnect between our qualitative casework and the information they needed in terms of decision making about broad statewide policies.

We looked at them and we said, "We have no idea how prevalent these things are. We don't have the first clue, because we only have data from five school districts." We then talked about the value of what we did, and some of them understood and some did not. And we said, "If you want us to answer those questions, we will. But you need to fund us for that." And the crowd laughed. (Actually, I had already submitted a new proposal for another condition study in August, a few months before our presentation to the Board of Regents.) So I said, "Well, let us go out and survey across the state, because there's no preexisting state data that can answer these questions, and our casework can't answer these questions. We're not going to do casework in 150 school districts; you just can't do that. So let us to do some of the survey work."

The experience of presenting to the Board of Regents was really interesting. It was highly organized, highly structured. You walk in and they are sitting there, and you're given a very short amount of time to give your formal presentation. We had some handouts, and we went a couple minutes long so we were being kind of rushed off the podium. There were just a few questions that they asked, and then the next group was coming in. So it was not nearly as rich a conversation as I had hoped. But it was clear they heard what we had to say. We boiled it down to a couple key points. We said, "What you've done has gotten educators' attention, which is no small feat." Given the lit review that we had taken out, this was at one level unusual, that all these people were scrambling out across 700 school districts, or at least across the five that we looked at, because of the decisions the Regents made. We told them that there is a lot of scrambling, a lot of staffing additions going on, and there's a bit of gaming they need to worry about. And I said to them explicitly, "If you don't care or you don't mind that more and more kids are going to be entering a GED program to circumvent the system, then don't do anything. If that bothers you, you need to do something, because that is going on. We don't know how prevalent it is. We can come back a year from now and tell you how prevalent it is.' So it was a very quick conversation, and who knows what they took away from it. It's hard to say.

It's the juxtaposition of qualitative work and quantitative information from surveys that's relevant to state policymakers. They did see the value of peering into a classroom, peering into a school and seeing what's going on. They actually found that quite interesting, and they said, "Yeah, this actually resonates with what we've heard anecdotally from the field." Much of our first paper was actually quite supportive of the state policies. It's not at all bashing the system, but there are some concerns in there. They found it interesting, but they weren't sure what to do with it. So we then had to go out and do our survey work to address the prevalence question.

There are several lessons I took from this. The first lesson was that there is a logical, plausible explanation for why research and practice—at least practice in a policy sense—can be so distant. It's because of the temporal nature of research versus the temporal nature of what is necessary in the policy community. I found and I still find it exceedingly hard to keep up with the pace at which policymakers need information. I don't have a solution for it, but I've grown to understand it. I've done three condition studies now, and with each one, the initial draft we gave to the consortium, as I look back on it, was very shallow. They're very nonanalytical. They're purely descriptive, which is what they're comfortable with. But they're not as valuable as the papers I wrote for academic journals that were all done literally a year or two after, through much revision and much further analysis, and through much further thought. Now we make these other papers available to the consortium. But what is posted on their web site are the original papers. The second condition study we did, which is going to be published this summer in the *Journal of Educational Policy*, is the most dramatically different. You almost cannot recognize what we gave the state and what we finally published as high-quality scholarly research.

At one level I think it's a shame that given the time crunch, I was not able to deliver a high enough quality analysis that could be considered both scholarly work and work that is useful for policymakers. I find that frustrating. They expressly said, "Give us the findings, and don't interpret them for us." But I think if they read these scholarly papers, outside of a few sentences, and maybe the word *concern* in the title of one paper—"Context, Capacity and Concern"—I think they would actually appreciate them. We weren't saying anything that wasn't supported by our data. As an academic, I've been taught not to overstep what I can say, not to go beyond the data. And I think I've gotten much better at that. I think grad students have a tough time with that, where they try to make broad claims they can't really justify. I was guilty of that early on, but I think I've gotten better at that as a scholar.

A second lesson has to do with academic freedom issues. We can stand by our academic freedom and say, "Look, at all costs we have academic freedom." And I think that's fine, most people would support that, and I support that. But we have to understand that there are implications for other people in how we use our academic freedom. If I stand up and I'm exceedingly critical of something—and I have every right to do that, and I'm not going to lose my job because of that, if I ever get tenure—that doesn't mean it's not going to make people exceedingly uncomfortable in a very different world than I work in, in the policymaking world.

I did a press release a few years ago on some of our survey findings related to this dropout GED issue, and we got scolded by some members of the consortium for being troublemakers, for rabble-rousing and making a big deal out of what they perceived that we did. And I think there are tensions that at some level are healthy. But I think what I've learned is that these people have jobs, they have lives, they operate in an exceedingly politicized environment, and research can play a role in helping them do their work. But research can also make their lives quite miserable. I think as academics we need to understand that. Not that it censors our work, but if I truly want to be party to and contribute to a conversation about practice, I have to understand the constraints practitioners are under. That's an important understanding, and I'm still trying to make sense of how that actually impacts my work. So that's the second lesson I think is really important.

A third lesson—here's where I want to tell you that quick story I mentioned earlier about a comment a member of the Board of Regents made about the value of the consortium. After our third condition study, we gave a presentation at one of these consortium symposia, which would have been September of 2003. We gave our presentation, and it was narrowly focused on academic intervention services. We do not have a scholarly paper out of this one yet. It was arguably the most well received of the three condition studies. The audience was very interested, they had all kinds of questions. And one guy, a longtime staffer at the State Ed Department, gave us a very backhanded kind of a compliment/slap when he said, "You know, you guys have really come a long way with what you've been doing." And then he proceeded to say how this is really interesting and valuable. So I laughed, everyone laughed, and I said, "I'll take that as a compliment." He was good-natured about it, but I think that's absolutely accurate, that there was a learning process that we engaged in about how to do work that other people find useful. When you're trained as an academic, you don't necessary learn how to do that. It's hard to do.

So here's the quick story. There were conversations and rumors that another five years worth of funding for the consortium had not come through yet. I was speaking with Jim Dawson, a member of the Board of Regents who is integrally involved in the Rural Schools Program, who I had gotten to know quite well—he's called "the Rural Regent"—and I said, "Jim, what's going on with the funding for the consortium? Will there be more condition studies? Will be more of this work down the road?" And he said, "Boy, I sure hope so. I think there will. It's not officially decided, but I think there will. I think it's just a matter of time when the Assembly works up their budget. I hope the funding will come through, because we really found it valuable." And I said, "Great." And he said, "You know, the research is good, but the legitimacy it gives us is fabulous." He said this, and I'm thinking, "You know, that's really telling," At one level there's a technical gain to what is going on, but at the other level, there's a great gain of legitimacy for the state to say that they have research that has been ongoing, that more or less documents, if not supports, what the state is doing.

The lesson here is that while the role of research oftentimes can be to help make technical improvements, it can also be for political gain—the fact that it's being done, the fact that it's in the lexicon of government now, that it's evidence-based and so forth. And they absolutely understand this. Now this was a comment from one member of the Board of Regents. I would love some day soon when I get some time to actually design a research project around this consortium and just try to understand how it got started, what it has been doing, and why it has been continued. It's like an interest group kind of thing, and I really am quite intrigued by what motivates the group, what motivates the individuals, and what impact it has had. I would really love to do that work and sit down and have lengthy conversations with all the participants—the Board of Regents, the commissioner, the Assembly leaders, and the other academics who have been involved in this. I think the existence of this group is much more complex than what it may seem on the surface. I'm not denying there has been some technical advantage in that there has been some policy adjustment as a result of some of this work. They're no longer requiring school report cards to define simply completed or Regents diplomas, local diplomas, dropouts—they're no longer doing that. They're talking about high school completers versus others—the others are GEDs and dropouts. So there have been some changes. Whether that's because of our work, who knows, but there have been some changes in the system. There are other condition studies that talk about staffing and quality of teachers and so forth, and I know they have stimulated some fairly important conversations on certification and compensation.

There was a lot of what I call "leapfrogging" in our work. We did our casework, presented it to the policy community in Albany, and they said, "How prevalent is this?" We didn't know, so that motivated the next study, which was all survey data. We then said, "Okay, we now have a much better sense of the prevalence of these practices. How instructionally are things changing?" We needed more detail of what programmatically was changing—what more successful districts we're doing versus not successful districts. So we were going to do a second survey, which would get into instruction, much more into explicit program, much more into explicit scheduling and the other constraints that confine the district. We felt absolutely unprepared to do that after our first survey. So what we did was we revisited our cases, we went back out and we did sixty or seventy, I forget, maybe eighty interviews with the sole expressed purpose of making sure the language we were going to use in the next survey was useful language. We wanted the language to come from the people in the field. The leapfrogging here was between the quantitative work in our first cases on the one hand, and our first survey and more casework on the other, which increased the chances that our survey was going to be meaningful to the people in the field. And then we went back and actually did that survey. What comes next we don't know. We're trying to catch our breath, and I'm trying to get tenure, so I'm trying to write as much as I can at this time.

There was also a leapfrogging back and forth between the scholarly and the policy world. That's been an interesting struggle, to try to take a document that was formatted for the consortium, that was also being constrained by their timeline, taking those manuscripts, the technical reports we give to the state, and then altering them, revising them, enriching them both from the analytic standpoint and from the theoretical standpoint. We inserted theory, inserted lit reviews into these things, leapfrogging back to the scholarly literature. I had to do these academic papers, because I would never survive here on just these technical reports to the consortium.

The academic paper I wrote for the first condition study I did has been under review for two years in *Educational Evaluation and Policy Analysis,* and I still haven't heard if it's accepted. I'm supposed to get word any week now. It took us several revisions to get to the point where we are feeling pretty confident that it will be accepted in a first-rate scholarly journal. The academic paper I wrote from the second condition study has been accepted in the *Journal of Educational Policy.* The third condition study is being published in *Educational Policy Analysis Archives.* It took an extraordinary amount of work to adapt these three papers to another audience. I think time is necessary—thoughtful time—when you leapfrog from the policy world back to the academic world. And again, I do think the consortium would actually like these academic papers we've done. I think they'll find them more valuable than what we originally gave them. But the back and forth leap-frogging really is a challenge. It's not like you can take a technical report from the policy community and then just submit it to a journal. You can't do that.

I made a decision three or four years ago when I was thinking of writing a series of papers off our qualitative work, because we had hundreds and hundreds of pages of transcripts—really interesting questions, really interesting data. We were in the middle of a phase of this thing, the state wants this work done, we have money that's available to do this work. So I said, "Okay, let's work on this one paper, the condition study revised into an academic journal article. But let's go out and collect more data, and do the survey work." I then made a decision after that survey was done, "Okay, we have these two bodies of data now, we could write for another year or two off these." But again, the implementation is continuing, the state has more money available. I can't come back later on and get this data because between 2000 and 2005 is the implementation period, and here we are right in the middle of that. I made a decision that may come back to haunt me to continue to collect data.

Now when you look at my CV, you get this gap—a huge gaping hole. Now part of that is maybe because I'm not smart enough, I'm not good enough, I'm not quick enough, I'm not talented enough to actually juggle all these things at once and collect the new data and write up the old and keep it going. I didn't have a whole cadre of well-trained grad students that could do this work for me. We didn't have enough infrastructure to do that. But I explicitly remember in a series of meetings, having these conversations with grad students and saying, "Okay, my call, we're going to keep collecting data. And if I get fired from here, well, I'll at least be somewhere else where I can write directly off this data." So what I've been scrambling to do of late is to get enough of this work published to keep my job here, because of that decision I made years ago. I think I could have kept my job much easier had I sat down, no longer engaged in the policy community, no longer engaged in the data collection, and gotten four, five, six journal articles out of that initial work. But then I would be sitting here right now and saying, "Okay, now I missed that opportunity to collect the data." So those tensions exist. I was very aware of the tensions and the trade-offs. We'll see next year what happens when I go up for tenure.

So that leapfrogging, there's a—I'm not going to say inefficiency to it, but there's a time-consuming nature to it. But I'm also absolutely convinced that because I kept interacting with the policy community and practitioners in the field, in terms of my data collection and in various forms of survey and casework, right now when I sit down to my work in 2004, I can produce better-quality work than I would have been able to produce had I not engaged in that activity. My CV doesn't look nearly as impressive as it would otherwise, but I think where I am right now, the quality of work I can do, my understanding of what has gone on in New York State has been so enriched that I don't regret what I did. I think if I had sat with that initial survey and tried to work for several years off that, I would not be where I am today in terms of the sophistication of how I understand what's going on in New York State. So I think I'm a better scholar for having done this, and I think my work in the long term—well at least my productivity over the next six years—will be much richer and much better for having made the decisions I made that day. It may not be at Cornell; we'll find out. But I think these next *x* number of years will be more productive for those decisions I made. And I have a much greater appreciation of how to interact with the policymaking community—a much greater appreciation—although I still have not figured out in any great sense how to go out and help actual school districts. I often get into conversations with superintendents, and they often threaten to bring me into a staff meeting and say, "Help us out." I'm actually doing that in another couple weeks in a small district down south of here. But research work for the policy community is very different than research work for practitioners in schools, and I think I haven't yet figured that one out—how to really be useful to a teacher. I'm beginning to get enough guts to try.

I was invited down to do a study for a very small 500-student school district down on Route 17, a little rural, isolated place. The superintendent asked us to come in to study their program in the context of what we're doing in the state. So we followed our site visit protocol from our cases and did our survey down there, and then we were able to compare and contrast what is consistent in their district with what is going on in the state. We were very clear that we're not going to make any judgments by saying, "You should be doing this because most of the state is and you're not." We don't really know what most of the state is doing. So I'm beginning to enter into that realm. I'm also beginning to enter into some work with the Ithaca City Schools in terms of the performance equity issue, and I would not have done this years ago. I'm beginning to take some baby steps. There's actually a meeting I have to go to today over there about this at the Ithaca City Schools.

In my early years here at Cornell, what I thought was extension work—small letter *e* extension, as I understood it—was, in some feedback I got, not really viewed as extension work. I guess it didn't fit the land-grant mission narrowly defined by Cooperative Extension. But the land-grant mission helped us when we went into these school districts. People said, "What is Cornell doing?" And I could say, "We're the land-grant institution for New York State. We're supposed to be serving and studying New York State." We used that line a few times, and I know it helped people understand that this was going to be kind of grounded work that might be useful to them, versus some highfalutin Cornell work.

There's a real dual image of Cornell out there, depending on people's experience with us. And I think we need to remind people or teach people that this is a land-grant institution. I could play that card in certain environments and it was useful to me. I think in terms of Hatch money, I suppose that was useful to me. It paid for some of the graduate students and some of the travel that the $8,000 couldn't cover, or the $32,000 couldn't cover in years 2 or 3. So I think that is a nice fringe benefit of being a land-grant: you get Hatch money that otherwise wouldn't be available.

In my discipline and my field of educational policy and administration, this type of work is not uncommon. So it's like when I go to my professional conferences and I share the nature of my work with the policy community or share my casework or share whatever I'm writing, people do not look at that as being very strange. This is what we do professionally in this area, as opposed to a straight sociologist in a sociology department. It may be looked upon very differently from other professional colleagues, but for my colleagues around the country, this kind of work doesn't surprise them. They like it. I think they appreciate this kind of work. So with respect to the question of the land-grant mission, and what advantage there has been or what value there is in it for my work, there's a few interaction effects, and access to resources helps, and the political advantage within the state. Sometimes you play that card and say that's why we're doing this, and people let their guard down. One thing I've learned is that the practitioners out in the field will very much resist participating in a research project that they don't feel is ever going to impact practice. We were able to explicitly say the results of our work were shared with the consortium, shared with the Board of Regents, and widely disseminated around the state. But you know, if I was at the University of Rochester, if I was at SUNY-Albany, if I was at some other place within New York State, it would not have affected my work. I have to believe that if I was at any number of universities, I could do what I'm doing and it would be acceptable.

As my tenure and promotion decision comes up, I certainly hope that there's an appreciation for the work I have done in New York State, because as a land-grant, we're supposed to serve New York State. But whenever I look at the list of land-grant priorities in my college—the College of Agriculture and Life Sciences—I have to interpret them fairly liberally in terms of creating an umbrella for my work. I think it can be done, but there's an interpretation there, because my work is not as explicitly connected to the land-grant mission as some other people's work in the college is. To this day, I haven't done any work at all in the Cooperative Extension system. And when I look at the priorities of the college, I don't see any explicit mention of public policy for public education. I see rural community development. In rural communities, the school often is a major employer. And in terms of developing better-educated, more productive citizens, people send their kids off to school to do that. So I think it's not a big leap to get to the point where my work ties in. It's not explicitly tied in at this time, and I don't necessarily mind that, as long as I can trust that other people can make those same interpretations. I think as long as you're allowed a more liberal interpretation of the land-grant mission and the priorities of the College of Agriculture and Life Sciences, my work fits in quite nicely.

I Feel Like a Missionary

A Profile of Tom Maloney

Senior Extension Associate, Department of Applied Economics and Management, Cornell University

Interviews conducted by Scott Peters, May 24 and June 3, 2004,
and July 27, 2005

In this profile of Tom Maloney, which is edited from the transcripts of three lengthy interviews, we gain considerable insight into the life story and work of an academic professional who says he often feels like a missionary. We understand the meaning of that term in an old-fashioned, prophetic change agent sense. While Tom tells us that his work is focused on helping managers of agricultural and horticultural enterprises become better leaders and managers, we come to see him as a leader in his own right. We also learn why he sees himself as an educator instead of a servant, and why it is important that we view what Tom and others like him in the land-grant system do as education rather than service.

I'm a senior extension associate in Agricultural Human Resource Management. I've been in the position I'm in now for eighteen years. I started as an extension associate, and I was in that position for probably seven or eight years. And then I went to the chair of my department and asked if it would be possible to continue in the department over the long term, what kind of a career path could I look forward to, and what would my professional progression be. It was through discussions with him that we created a career progression to senior extension associate.

I spend two-thirds of my time on human resource management, including ag labor policy and regulations. I spend a great deal of time teaching seminars and workshops to agricultural and horticultural employers on how to manage people: training, recruiting, motivation, communication, all the traditional things we think of when we talk about human resource management. I spend the other third of my time on some leadership responsibilities in Extension. We just had our farm management retreat last week. I spent three months organizing and getting ready for it. Not the entire three months, but you have to start three months before to get the faculty and field staff team together. There are thirty of us in the farm management field staff/faculty group, and we meet once a year for two days.

I'm half on college funding, and the other half on federal funds that are provided on an annually recurring basis to Cornell (and every other land-grant university) by USDA through the Smith-Lever Act. Since extension administration has gone to an RFP (request for proposals) process for allocating Smith-Lever money, I was off, and now I'm back on. Smith-Lever money now is much softer money than it ever was before. I'm working on two three-year Smith-Lever projects, so that constitutes the half of my job that is not college funded at the moment. I think the writing is on the wall for most of us that Smith-Lever funding is not necessarily intended to continue into the future, and outside grants need to become more a part of our lives, even as extension associates.

There are a couple things that really drive me. One of them is, when you teach management—especially to people who need to learn management because they're growing a farm or small business—it can be remarkably gratifying if somebody goes home and really changes their outlook, changes how they treat people, and changes their human resource strategy. If they go home and say, "I want to have a human resource strategy," then that is remarkably powerful. We have lots of people who just love production. But if you cannot grow your organization and the people in it—train them and grow them and work with them—it may limit how successful you can be in business.

It is not easy to develop and grow a farm business or a horticultural business today. It's a small business in a competitive environment, and we have farms going out of business left and right. Strong, well-managed businesses are important to New York agriculture, and our national agriculture. If agricultural businesses are going to be successful, then I believe they need to place value on being good employers. And that's my challenge every single day: how do we help the people who want to be good employers become better, and how do we help the people who aren't good employers, and never think about it, want to be good employers?

My primary approach to human resource management education is through seminars and workshops. I also write for national magazines. I see two ways to do my work. One is an awareness approach. If I write an article for *Hoard's Dairyman* on management, or I get quoted in national farm or horticultural magazines, that article is going to give somebody the sense that there are some things they ought to be doing. Also, when I go out and talk for an hour on human resource management at a conference, that's awareness. Somebody can pick up a couple of ideas and take them home and put them to work. But it's the multiple-hour seminar where we have a workbook, and we have group activities, and we have written activities where people are really engaged, where I think behavioral change really takes place. It's through these seminars that participants can learn new management skills.

Let me tell you how I ended up working in Cooperative Extension. I was born in Buffalo, and until third grade, we lived in the city. My father was a railroad engineer. My mother was a farm girl and a homemaker. I'm one of eight children. When I was in third grade, we moved from the city. My grandparents (my mother's parents) had passed away, and we moved to the family farm, which at the time was a thirty-five-cow dairy farm located halfway between Orchard Park and East Aurora, in southern Erie County, in the snow belt. My mother's brother was operating the farm with his parents, and after my grandfather died, he decided to sell out, and he got a job with a local feed company. There was an estate involved, and my aunts and uncles who had inherited the farm kept all of the land and sold the farmstead to my parents.

I remember the first week or two we were there. The cows were still there. I was in third grade. They were getting ready for an auction. And I still remember things about the auction. The auctioneers were Harris Wilcox and his son. They wore white Stetsons. It was like all the farm auctions I have ever been to. All of the farm neighbors were there—some to buy and some to check out the auction prices and catch up with their neighbors. After the auction was over, everything was gone. The cows went, all the machinery and everything was sold, and the farmland was rented to the neighbors. We were left with a two-acre farmstead.

After a few years, my brothers and I signed up as individual 4-H members. For a couple years, that really didn't mean a whole lot. We got the regular 4-H newsletters, but we weren't really involved in 4-H. But one day the 4-H newsletter came, and it had an article about a new market hog project they were starting in Erie County. We read it, and we showed it to my mother and father. The article said, "Come to this meeting and we'll tell you what you need to know to buy pigs at a young age, raise them, and show them at the fair and sell them at the fair, and be a part of this new program." And so we went. We weren't a commercial farm, but it really fit, because we had the buildings and the resources we needed to do it. It wasn't a cattle project, where it was year-round and a huge commitment. It was something that could be done in four or five months. For me, that really was a defining moment. It led to the whole world of 4-H, and that influenced me tremendously. In fact, I'm sure that if it weren't for 4-H I would never have had the career that I've had.

At that time, Erie County had a huge extension staff. I think they had fifteen or eighteen people there, not all in 4-H. The lead 4-H guy was Al Lasky. He had two daughters who were my age, and I knew them through 4-H. Then he left to go to Nevada after a few years and Dick Bitterman took his place. But probably my greatest role model and mentor was Walt Halbauer. He retired five or six years ago. He and Dick Bitterman were very involved in all of the agricultural parts of 4-H in Erie County.

The first door that 4-H opened for me was the county fair. To me, 4-H was a social thing, and something that really helped me mature as an individual. I was fourteen, I think, when I went to the fair for the first time to show market hogs. I met a lot of people, and it was remarkably exciting getting to show animals, and just be a part of this. The Erie County Fair was one of the largest county fairs in the country at the time, and probably still is. I met a lot of kids my own age, and I joined 4-H Teen Council on the encouragement of the 4-H agents. I got involved with the square dancing team, and each year we would compete at the state fair. We took a bus to the state fair for the annual competition. I made a lot of friends by participating in those activities.

One of the interesting parts of this is that I graduated from a Catholic grade school and went to a Catholic high school: St. Francis. The high school was ten miles outside of our school district. There were a handful of people that I knew from grade school, but I was there with a whole new group of people. I went to that school for two years, and it really wasn't working out. It was expensive for my parents, and I wasn't doing that well, so they weren't sure that it was really worth the financial sacrifice. So as a junior I went to a public school: Orchard Park High School. Both of those experiences were okay, but I never really developed the friendships in high school that most people do, because I was in two different schools. As I look back on that, it is really interesting, because today, I keep track of some of the people who I met in 4-H, and I don't keep track of anybody who I went to high school with. One of the reasons why 4-H was so influential in my life was that it provided an entire maturing, social, engaging, learning experience. I received a lot of support and mentoring from 4-H agents, and that really influenced me.

When I was a senior, there were four teenagers in the county who were awarded a statewide 4-H educational trip to New York City. It was a competitive application process and I was very excited about being selected. Al Lasky was the county 4-H agent who led the trip. He was originally from the New York area, so he knew how to show us around New York. He took us to the Broadway opening of *Mame*. It was the first time I'd ever been on a plane. We flew down from Buffalo. It was really exciting, and something I probably would not have gotten to do otherwise. It was a big deal for my parents, too. They were as excited about me receiving the award trip as I was.

Let me add one important thing. All the new friends I was making told me that if I really wanted to do something cool in 4-H, I needed to attend 4-H Club Congress. You applied for it, and you got to go to Cornell with the Erie County group. You got to attend all the educational activities, and Cornell was a really cool place. So when I was sixteen or seventeen, I applied, and my friends applied, three or four of us that were really good friends, and we all ended up going. One or two of them had gone previous years, so they knew that this was something exciting and fun to do. And it's not all the educational programs that are emphasized when they're telling you about this. It's all the fun you're going have staying up until three in the morning, and all the new people you're going to meet from other counties. One defining moment that I still remember is driving up Buffalo Street in the Erie County Extension van, and seeing the college students. It's early June 1967, and it's warm outside, and there's college kids in tie-dyed T-shirts and cutoff jeans sitting out on porches on Buffalo street. I thought it was great. That was my first image of Cornell, and I never forgot it.

I went twice to Club Congress, and it was great fun. They had music and talent shows, and education. Professor Jim Mass was a regular speaker. He was always a big hit. He was a psychology professor at Cornell who taught Psychology 101 for many years. As part of his research, he did *Candid Camera* type videos showing how people reacted in certain situations. He interpreted their behavior from a psychological point of view. Some of the videos were very funny.

All of these 4-H activities put together created a social network that really had a lot of influence on me. In addition, Walt Hallbauer was a great mentor and encourager. I was a member of Teen Council, and I was an officer on Teen Council, so I had to learn how to run a meeting. I had to learn how to be an officer. I had to learn how to interact for the good of the group. We did lots of activities, we had to do them as a group, and we had to be respectful of each other. So there was a lot of organizational learning.

At the beginning of my senior year in high school, which was the fall of 1968, I was working part time at the Orchard Park Country Club. I worked in the men's locker room shining shoes, and as a locker room attendant. In the wintertime I went upstairs in the clubhouse and was a dishwasher. I wasn't a great high school student, and I knew that I really needed to decide what I was going to do with myself. There was not much of a future working in a minimum wage job at the country club. The Vietnam War was in full swing, and I had a draft card and a lottery number. So I started working with my guidance counselor and talking to my parents. My mother started reading about career opportunities and she had this idea that if I went into a business program, I would always be able to get a job. I didn't really know what I wanted to do, and she knew that. A four-year college with my grades was not an option, so I started looking at two-year colleges.

One day, I went to the guidance office, and I got out a stack of catalogs for three or four nearby colleges that people had told me about, and I took them to study hall to look over. I had the Alfred State College book, and I was paging through it. And there in the middle of the book was this little section called "Agricultural Business." In a way, the rest is history, because that started me down a path that has continued to this day. I looked at the curriculum, and it looked pretty interesting. People were encouraging me to study business, and all of my social network and my mentors and all of the things I really liked in life came from my 4-H agricultural background. I thought, wouldn't this be a pretty good if I could combine these things? So I took the Alfred catalog to my guidance counselor, and told her I wanted to pursue this. Like I said, my grades weren't very good. But I worked very hard as a senior to get my grades up and to write a good application. In early spring of 1969, I was accepted at Alfred.

Going to college, I knew if I wanted to get into extension work, I would have to have a bachelor's degree. Extension work was always in the back of my mind. But most importantly, I figured that if I took an agribusiness program, I would always be able to get a job, that there would be a market for those skills. That was always my plan B.

All during my freshman year, I thought about what do I do after graduating from Alfred. That year went pretty fast, and then it was decision-making time again. I decided that summer that I really wanted to go to Cornell. Getting in was not a sure thing, because they said you needed a 3.0, and I didn't quite have that. I probably never worked harder in school than that fall, and I made the dean's list. So now, good things were becoming possible.

My advisor at Alfred was an interesting guy. He was head of Alfred's agribusiness program, and his name was Walter Wheatgraf. He was a dry lecturer, but he was a bright guy who really cared about his students. My plan was to go to Cornell, and to be a 4-H agent. And the agribusiness part of this was so that I would always have a backup. So I applied to Cornell's farm business management program in the Department of Agricultural Economics. I thought I had good enough grades to get in, but nothing was guaranteed. As a backup, I applied to Ohio State, and I got accepted. There were a handful of us at Alfred who were trying to get into Cornell, and every day that spring we would see each other and say, "Did you hear anything from Cornell?"

One Saturday morning in May, I was getting ready to participate in the college livestock-showing contest, and the mail came. I got a postcard from Cornell, and it said, "Thank you so much for your interest in Cornell University. Since we haven't heard from you, we assume you have made other plans. We wish you luck in your future endeavors." I began to hyperventilate. After all my hard work to get into Cornell, they were going to give my spot to someone else. My advisor, Mr. Wheatgraf, was at the show, and I went up to him and showed him the postcard, and my hand was shaking. "Don't worry about it," he said. "Just come in on Monday, and we'll call Cornell and get it straightened out." I was very upset but he was remarkably calm. He knew Leonard Fedema, who was the director of admissions for the College of Agriculture at Cornell. He called him up while I was sitting in his office, and found out that the letter had been sent five weeks earlier. I never received it. They promised to send me another one right away. I was always grateful for Mr. Wheatgraf's intervention. So finally I was going to Cornell.

My experience at Cornell was incredible in many ways. Alfred was pretty conservative, and Cornell—all kinds of stuff was going on. You couldn't walk into Willard Straight Hall, the student union, without somebody handing you a leaflet about one cause or another, and there were war protests going on. I lived in a cooperative house with a whole bunch of people who had nothing to do with agriculture.

I remember the first day of my first class at Cornell. It was taught in Warren Hall by Professor Stan Warren. He was the son of George Warren, the person the building was named after. Stan was at the end of his career. I was taking his farm appraisal course, and I didn't know who he was, but he had a presence that was just incredible. I remember, we all were sitting in class downstairs in the building we're in here today, and he said, "We're going out on a farm, and we're going to appraise it this afternoon." He's telling us a little bit about farm appraisal, and he had a piece of orange field tile. He was talking about the importance of land improvements to the value of a farm. And he said, "Okay, next Monday, your appraisal of the farm we see this afternoon will be due." I remember the sinking feeling I had at that point. I thought I had missed two or three prerequisite courses. I thought, how am I ever going to appraise this farm? But I ended up doing fine, and that was probably one of the best courses—if not the best—that I ever took.

Cornell was exciting. It was a big place, so it was a little bit lonely at first. But I made friends, and there was a lot going on. There were rock concerts with Jethro Tull and Jim Croce and Paul Simon, and it just was a cool place to be. And it was a hard place to be, because the work was difficult. I had to work hard for everything I achieved at Cornell. And I was not a farm kid. That does not mean so much today, but it meant a lot then. One of my potential opportunities in agribusiness was agricultural lending. In that profession, they really felt that if you weren't a farm kid, you couldn't relate; you couldn't talk to farmers. So I took a year off and worked on a dairy farm. I got a 4-H summer assistant job in Penn Yan, in Yates County, with a guy by the name of Clarence Tallman. He was a 4-H agent there. When the summer was over, I took a leave of absence, and I found a farm in Yates County, a fifty-cow dairy owned by Howard Travis. He hired me and I worked there for the fall. I wanted a break from school. But I also wanted to make sure I had farm experience so I didn't jeopardize my chances of working in agriculture.

In the spring semester I came back to Cornell and I worked at a couple of jobs in Collegetown. Then the next summer I was a 4-H summer assistant in Cattaraugus County. I did a little bit of ag work on the side—some field crops work with Dan Hudson, who was the field crop agent at the time—and answered some home-gardening questions. Then came my senior year. I was taking advanced farm management with Professor George Casler, who is an emeritus professor now. It was spring, and we were on a field trip, and he said, "Well, what are you going to do after college?" And I said, "I want to be a 4-H agent." I was applying for 4-H jobs at the time. He said, "If you want to go into Extension, why don't you look at an extension farm business management job? You're certainly qualified by your education to do that." I didn't really give what he said a lot of consideration at the time.

The job market was horrendous when I graduated in the spring of 1975. It was terrible. Extension jobs came up at random, and you just applied. I had been applying all spring my senior year, but I went home without a job. I ended up working as a horticultural summer assistant in the Erie County Extension office. I was interested in horticulture as well as 4-H, because I had done some extension horticultural work the previous summer.

When the summer was over, my girlfriend Mimi Ansbro, who is now my wife, went to St. Louis. She was a hotel major, and she went to St. Louis to work for Marriott. So I spent most of the winter out there working as a waiter, and then came back and worked another summer with 4-H in Erie County. They had a 4-H position open. They needed an assistant before they filled the position, so I started doing that. I did that temporary job for three or four months, and then they were ready to interview for the position. I did not do very well in the interview, so I didn't get the job. Beforehand, myself and everybody else thought that it was a slam dunk. And actually, it probably turned out for the better, because it was my home county. It would have been convenient, but it may not have been the best thing for expanding my horizons. And after a few years, they eliminated the position anyway due to funding problems. So then I went back to doing extension horticultural work in Erie County. I just kept working for Extension as long as I could, and applied for a few jobs outside of Extension, but I really was pinning my hopes on an extension position.

In the fall of '75, I applied for three jobs: a 4-H position in Monroe County, which was a city-type 4-H position; a 4-H position in Delaware County; and an ag position in Cortland County. I got interviews for all three, all in the same month. Monroe wasn't interested in me. They were dying to have me in Delaware County, and I was dying to go to Cortland County. Delaware County was too rural for me. But the location in Cortland, and the fact that it was a commercial ag job, were both extremely appealing to me. I spent many prior years thinking I would be a 4-H agent, but now for a variety of reasons agricultural extension work was more appealing.

I was one of five candidates for the Cortland County job, and I was the first one they interviewed. While I was driving home to Buffalo, they were on the phone to my mother with a job offer, which I immediately accepted. When I finally got the president of the board on the phone to formally offer me the job, he said, "We're really impressed with your experience and interest in Extension." In the preceding year, I kept working on my package of experiences that I would bring to the table, and in the end, between working with the extension field crop guy in Cattaraugus County and working on the horticulture questions in Erie County, and having a farm management degree and working on a farm, when I finally had the opportunity to tell people why I wanted to work in Extension, and that I had all these experiences, it all came together.

The main reason why I really wanted to work in Extension was because it's a very people-oriented organization. Especially when I was younger, I was a very social person. I think the other attraction was that the horticultural part of it was a lot like consulting. The idea of having knowledge that was valuable to people was extremely compelling to me. I could become an expert, and that would be valuable to other people: not only in a question-answering sense, but also, later, in a teaching sense. I could convey knowledge in a way that would help people's business or lives. I guess the other intangible thing was that I looked at those 4-H guys and the ag agents in Erie County, and thought, boy, these guys love their jobs, and they're good at them. They're very proud of what they do. And it's not a high-pressure business environment. It's an environment that is enjoyable—every day.

So in November of '75, I became what the farmers in Cortland County used to call the "assistant county agent." I think the actual title was staff associate. Carl Crispell was the agricultural program leader. There were six extension agents at the time in the Cortland extension office: two ag agents, two 4-H agents, and two home economists. And they were all highly visible in the community.

The job descriptions that I worked under during the ten years I worked for Extension in Cortland County were fairly specific. When I came in, field crop work was in the job description, along with some dairy work, and some farm management work. Every extension office gets horticulture questions, and I already done that for two summers. So Carl was happy to give that to me. I had taken agronomy and soil science and botany and other plant science courses, but I was never trained as a crop and soil science expert. I was trained in farm management. But one of the things about an Alfred education is, they had trimesters, and you took a lot of courses. So even though I wasn't an agronomy major I had taken enough courses to get by. I became a quick study in field crop production, and I liked it. The only thing I really had to hang my hat on in field crops going into the job was a couple of courses, and doing some test plots with Dan Hudson in Cattaraugus County. But during the interview, I sold that for everything it was worth.

The work I did in field crops included soil testing, and making fertilizer recommendations and lime recommendations based on soil tests. I worked with the ASCS office, because they were doing cost sharing with farmers for lime. So all of those tests would come through me, and I'd have to make the recommendations. We would do winter meetings on the latest crop production technologies, herbicides, and seed varieties. And I always had test plots out in the field. I worked closely with the field crop faculty at Cornell. Russ Hahn was a great mentor and friend. He's the extension weed scientist for field crops. I also had a huge commitment to write newsletters. I wrote two news articles a month, and never realized until later how powerful that was, how much that shaped my reputation in terms of farmers' view of me. They knew me better than I knew them. They had read what I wrote, they had seen the pictures I had taken and read the captions. There are still people in Cortland County who regard me highly, because of being on the radio every other week, our newsletters, and being a very visible leader in the ag community.

Farmers had tremendous confidence in our system. They had great confidence that if we had the information they were looking for, it was good information, and that if we had an answer to their question, it was an answer they could trust. I think also, because I had personal relationships with these people, they had a sense that I would do my best, that I would try my darnedest to help with the question at hand, and that if I had information on my test plots in my newsletter, that it was information that they should know and pay attention to. Not everybody, obviously, but most people.

So the first four years I was a staff associate. Then later, Carl Crispell left, and I became the ag program leader. Carl was wonderful. He knew all the farmers, and he was very practical. He could sit down with a piece of paper and figure out a budget in half an hour—and something that made sense. It might not have been something that a professor would have done. Maybe it would not have been as thorough or academic. But it was what somebody could pick up and use. It made sense to them, and was practical for their situation. Those were the skills that he taught me. He taught me how to read soil test reports. He taught me how to make fertilizer recommendations. He taught me how to do farm business summaries, analysis, and budgeting. All of this was superimposed over what I already knew; I came in with a fairly strong knowledge base on the financial side.

My experience working in Cortland County during these years was shaped by what was going on in agriculture at the time. I was there during a period where a dairy farmer would say, "We're going to add on." I think there were two or three farms that were 500 cows, and one of them was owned by Cornell. Now we've got farms with 500 cows or more all over the state. But back then there was a countryside filled with these fifty-, sixty-, seventy-cow barns. And most of the early years I was working in Cortland County, the milk price wasn't too bad. We would help design barn additions, and people would say, "We're going to put a twenty-cow or thirty-cow addition on the end of this barn, and this is going to be the last one. We'll be as big as we ever need to get." That's what they would say. Well, you look around now, that seems remarkably far-fetched, that people really could have believed that, because by comparison the dairies are so large now.

I became very interested in milk marketing, because there were many, many milk co-ops, and they were all competing with each other. There were independent companies, and they were competing with the co-ops, and the smaller farms were being discriminated against because they were too small to have their milk picked up economically. So there was a lot of turmoil, and I became very interested in that whole topic of how we market milk. For our newsletter, I did interviews with all the handlers that bought Cortland County milk. I learned a lot about the milk-marketing business, and about milk co-ops in the process, to try to shed some light on how farmers had to work together in the future to assure their markets. It was an important issue for farmers at the time.

Carl did a lot of business analysis with farmers, and he taught me to do it as well. I did a lot of farm summaries, keeping records for our system here at Cornell, but also to help the farmer with ratios and one-on-one to manage the business, and to think about being profitable. At that time, we did a lot of work with people who were in the middle—people who really needed to make more money, wanted to become more profitable in order to stay in farming. We spent a lot of time on those farms.

Cortland County was a big dairy county, and while I was there, we had three years in a row during the late seventies where the milk price went up, big time, at a time when those of us who were watching, who knew something about what was going on, were really concerned about what that was going to do to the glut of milk and the amount of surplus that the government was buying. The government was buying a huge amount of surplus milk, and the price support system was being manipulated. Instead of being a balancing process, the price support system became a political process. Senators who wanted to get reelected just voted to increase the milk price through the price support program. So it was a three-year heyday of growth and expansion. Farmers bought new Harvestore silos and a lot of expensive equipment. They were having a great time. But the subsidies got so big that the government had to say stop. Milk prices went down and it really got rocky in the early to mid-eighties, and a lot of people went out of business. Farm lenders, who socialized with their clients, were now hated by their clients. It was part of the mid-eighties era of farm stress.

You ask how we facilitate change in Extension. In every one of the stages of my work in Cortland County during the ten years I was there, I would have answered that question almost the same way. You sit at a kitchen table with the farm family, and you look at their numbers. You look at their finances, you look at their production data. You look at the land and the resources that they have for production. And then you talk to them about their options, what their reasonable options are. And when they say to you, "We want to bring our son into this business," then sometimes you have to say, "This business isn't big enough to support you. It will never be big enough to support you and your son and his wife, and their family." It just isn't that hard to assemble all those pieces of information. You have to get the facts. You have to find out what they made last year, even if all you have is a tax return, and look at the number of acres, look at what the production facilities are, look at what the milk price is, and say, "Can you really make it with this set of resources?" So, on an individual basis, you facilitate change by helping people identify their choices, and getting them to tell you what they think some of their options are. And then you analyze the options. That's what you do as a farm business management educator.

The other thing that I would say about my time in Cortland County is that I worked doggedly to know as many of the farmers as I could possibly know, and visit them on their farms, even on the weekends, and know where their farm was. To me, the underpinning of my work and my relationships with all those people was knowing who they were, and where they were located, and what kind of a farm they had. A couple of friends I would have lunch with were artificial inseminators. Occasionally I would ride with those guys to get out on farms more, because they knew some of the farmers I didn't know. Carl and those guys really helped me, and when I left, I bet I knew two-thirds of the farms in the whole county. And there were three hundred. You might ask, "Well, why is that important?" I think it says something about why Extension is important. One of the ways farmers saw Extension as valuable is that they knew the county agents. They knew the people who had the link to the land-grant system. And the agents went to farm dinners and events with them, like the annual Holstein Association banquet. They were a part of—we were a part of—that agricultural community.

The closeness to those Cortland County farmers that I developed had its upsides and its downsides. The guy before me, Ira Blixt, who worked with Carl Crispell, was a very strong leader. Very strong. He was really big on farm tours. He took farmers on extension tours all over the east coast. After twenty years of this, he was running out of places to take people. But he had established the tradition. And then after I got there, we started flying on the tours. And so we got really close to the people when we took them on tours. And actually, it got a little bit controversial, because the farmers who didn't have the wherewithal to come on the tours were critical of the people who had the resources to go.

One of the things that happened to me during the later part of my career in Cortland County was at an ag program committee meeting. Every year we did program planning, where we asked committee members, "What do you want to see from us? What do we need to do?" One evening at one of these meetings, I asked, "What should I be doing? I've got some new project ideas, I think we can go here, I think we can go there. I think agriculture really needs to move in this direction." And one of the guys sat there, and he said, "You know, I don't really know what you ought to be doing. But the important thing to me is that you're there if I have a question." Well that really deflated me, because I was thinking in terms of going somewhere educationally, and he wasn't. He was thinking in terms of staying where he was. He was thinking, "No, I probably won't go to your next workshop. But if I have a question, I'll call you on the phone, and you can answer it for me, and I'll go along my merry way."

Isn't that interesting? What do you do in response to that kind of view? You go back to the drawing board, and you circle the wagons, and you say to yourself, "Well, look, agriculture still needs to move forward, and so I need to influence this somehow." Fortunately, not all the farmers in Cortland County were like this guy. But it was conversations like these that made me think about moving on, because at that point, I said, "I need to do more. I need to make a bigger contribution." Sitting in the office waiting for that guy to call me is not enough. That's not enough influence. And a lot of it is about influence—maybe altruistic influence, because most of us want to make the world a better place. It's about influence and making a difference, and causing something to happen. And what this guy says to me—"We just want to know you're at the end of the telephone if we have a question"—sort of defeats the whole purpose.

After I was in Cortland County for about eight years, I was fortunate enough to apply for and get a sabbatical. So I went to Cornell and got my master of professional studies degree (MPS). I worked on milk-marketing issues. Olin Forker, who was department chair at the time, and Bob Milligan were the major and minor members of my committee. After I finished the MPS, I went back to the county, knowing I would eventually change jobs, that it really was time to move on. I went to Cornell to get a master's degree to move ahead in my career. I was looking at everything. I was looking outside Extension, inside Extension. It so happened that Extension had a three-year soft money project, called the Dairy Farm Audit Program. That was a whole-farm business analysis program to intensively work with farmers who needed to change for the future. It was heavily centered around management skills. It was organizing, it was business control, it was thinking like a manager. And that was very exciting to me. I applied and was offered the job. So in November of '85, I left my job in Cortland County and came to campus.

I enjoyed the Dairy Farm Audit Program very much. But after two years, I needed to get on a different track. I came to Cornell on a soft money job because the job was really exciting, but then it was time to go the next step in my career. In the Department of Agricultural Economics at that time, the only people who were doing anything on farm labor and human resource management were two emeritus professors: Brian Howe and Art Bratton. And as

273

they got further and further into retirement, they worked less and less time on human resource issues. So Bob Milligan went to the dean of the College of Agriculture, Dave Call, and they had discussions about how to fill the labor education need in an environment where farms were getting bigger, and it wasn't just family labor anymore. Increasingly farmers had to recruit and train and motivate and do all these things with hired employees. Dean Call created the extension associate position in human resource management that I ended up being hired for. The position evolved into the senior extension associate position I hold today. In a day and age where people change jobs every five years, I have made a career in Extension for reasons that were established very early in my life, and that's a pretty powerful thing.

So, with that as setting the stage, the first practice story I want to tell took place over a five- or six-year period of time during those early years after I came to Cornell in 1985. A program called PRO-DAIRY was being born at the same time, and Bob was the director. As far as Bob was concerned, what he and I did together in human resource management and what PRO-DAIRY did in regards to dairy management were not separate. They were hand in glove with each other. Bob and those of us who were county farm management agents had spent time doing business analysis, crunching numbers, and helping farmers keep good records, and learn how to interpret those records. After a dozen years of this, Bob engaged in a discussion with many of us. He said, "You know, we've been crunching these numbers with farmers for ten years, and some of these businesses never really improve. We probably can't crunch the numbers any better than we are now. So maybe there's something more to improving the management of a farm, especially a growing one, than keeping and analyzing good financial records."

We started to go to the management literature and look at things like planning and organizing and directing and leading, and all those things that you learn in an MBA program. And we said, "Okay, how do we bring those things to the dairy farmers of the state to improve dairy productivity and profitability?" And so that moved us from what I call traditional farm business management education, which is all about keeping books and analyzing the finances, to management education, which is about directing people and leading and empowering them.

After PRO-DAIRY was up and running for four, five, six years, it was copied all over the country. It was really a landmark program, and Bob Milligan's leadership made it happen. It became the dairy extension program in the state. It had a group of faculty and a group of agents in the field, and they hired seven or eight senior extension associates and extension associates to work specifically on this program with the agents in the field, and directly with the farmers. There was extra money to really beef up the extension education effort. It was state legislative money that passed through the New York State Department of Agriculture and Markets. What I did in those early years was very much related to what was going on in PRO-DAIRY. We did it together, essentially, even though my position has always been housed in this department, and I have never technically been an employee of PRO-DAIRY.

Back at that time, we were thinking, "How do we take all the business education we had previously done and add management education? Can we do it, and will the farmers go for it?" There was a guy over in Cornell's College of Industrial and Labor Relations (ILR) by the name of Bill Frank. And one of the things that happened at the time was that we went to Bill and Craig McCallister, who were doing ILR extension programs in many places in the state, including Buffalo. They were training front-line managers at the General Motors plant in Buffalo. Those managers routinely were sent to management training.

At the time, Guy Hutt was working in PRO-DAIRY with Bob and me. Guy was also a grad student, and he was instrumental in directing us to management education resources for the PRO-DAIRY program. We developed human resource management extension programs, and we did it as a trio. Bob sent Guy and me, at Bill Franks's invitation, out to Buffalo to sit in on the training for front-line supervisors from General Motors. And we came back and we said, "You know, if you put these guys in flannel work shirts and bib overalls and work shoes, the front-line supervisors at GM aren't a whole lot different than farmers." This group of GM supervisors had senses of humor, they cared about their work, they were very articulate about their work, and when they sat down, they had a notebook in front of them to train them in management. When they walked in the door, they knew that they were there for management training. And we said to ourselves, "We can do this." It's going to take a while for a farmer to walk in the door and say, "Ah, now I'm learning leadership skills today. Now I'm learning communication skills today." But we were convinced that we could do it, and that started us on a remarkably exciting path.

Bob provided very strong leadership to move PRO-DAIRY forward. Guy Hutt, our third member, was taking business courses in ILR, and in Cornell's Johnson School of Management. Guy and I took one ILR course together. So we were immersed in this whole question of what do we teach, and how do we teach it. In 1990, we embarked on three years of seminars called Managing Farm Personnel in the Nineties. What we learned from our ILR colleagues was they needed the notebook, and it needed to look impressive. It had to have worksheets and exercises, and mini-lectures, and all of the things that modern management education has.

So we did these seminars for three years running, and we tweaked them each year. We tried for repeat participants every year, and we didn't always achieve that. We always lost a bunch and got a bunch more who were new. We thought it was a continuing process, but the farmers thought, "I did it, so I've been there, and I've done it.' And even that was a learning experience for us. We started out in two locations in the state, Batavia and Schenectady, and then by the third year, we were down to one location, because of poor attendance.

One of the people who attended in western New York was a farmer by the name of Willard DeGolyer, who owns Table Rock farm. This was a two-day seminar, and people came and stayed overnight. Willard tells the story of going home so fired up after the seminar that he told his wife, "We have to plan and we have to have a mission statement, and we have to have goals and we have to plan for the next ten years, and we really need to take this business somewhere new." And she looked at him and said, "Look, I've got five kids that I'm trying to raise here. I'm trying to get through the day. I can't think about the next ten years." But Willard took it all to heart. He had a lot of help from farm credit consultants and others, but this set of seminars really fired him up.

Also at the time, I was setting up a farmer panel for the seminar, because farmers like to hear from their peers. They like to hear other farmers' success stories. I was setting up a

275

panel of people who set goals and who had a mission and a vision for their business, because that's what we were teaching. And I had a heck of a time finding a farmer with a mission statement, because this was all new.

The punch line that I'm coming to is this. About five or six or seven years after Willard DeGolyer attended his first workshop seminar with us, Bob Milligan and I were invited out to a big program in Wisconsin, entitled Personnel Management on the Farm. It was a big three-day conference, with 150 people there, some of the best managers in the upper Midwest. Bob and I were asked to talk about the things we always talked about: motivation and leadership and conflict management and communication. And unbeknownst to us, Willard DeGoyer was invited to be a farmer speaker. He and another farmer were invited to go first, and they spent the better part of the first morning talking about their own farm businesses. We had not worked closely with Willard in the years immediately prior to the Wisconsin meeting, so we weren't sure what he had been up to or what he would say.

Willard got up and did a great slideshow. He had pictures of his farm. He had his mission statement, he had his goals, he had his training program, and he had his employee hand-book. He had the package. And six or seven years earlier, I couldn't find anybody who had the package. And not only did he have the package, his neighbors had the package, and the people who the farm credit consultants were working with had the package. And it started the agricultural industry down a road of improving farm management practices that helped these farmers grow their businesses and personally grow as managers. It appeared to have a huge impact on their success. Now, I'm not going to say that we did it all, because we didn't do follow-up consulting and some of those kinds of things. But we created the paradigm. We created a new paradigm. We created in their minds a vision of what their businesses could be. And there were many Willard DeGolyers.

That trip to Wisconsin, watching Willard's presentation, taught me that if you want to evaluate your work on an annual basis, you're only going to see so much progress, for two reasons. One is, a year might not be a long enough period of time. Secondly, if Willard DeGolyer never tells you what he did, based on what you taught him, and you don't get to see him at a conference somewhere, you might never know.

So that's my first story. It was the first time in my career that I really began to develop a historical perspective, and a tremendous sense that I indeed had a career, and that it had a path, and that I was accumulating something along the way in terms of—I don't know if *legacy* is too strong of a word, but there was some kind of historical presence and accumula-tion of benefits to New York agriculture. Then it got to be in other states, because what hap-pened with PRO-DAIRY was being picked up by Extension in many other states. We got invited all over the country to do this work. That was another thing that Bob Milligan as my mentor always encouraged, that if you were going to have a career here, you needed to develop a national reputation. Bob and I, for a time, developed that national reputation together.

I think that it would be easy to make the case that in our farm management work, we were continuing the work of George Warren. He was the founder of Cornell's farm manage-ment program back in the early 1900s. They spent a lot of time counting everything in those early days: counting acres and cows, and creating ratios, etc. But if you go back and read

George Warren's farm management book, he talks about the human dimension. He talks about labor, to a certain extent. So I think that there are elements of what we were trying to do in his early work. On the other hand, George Warren was not dealing with five-million-dollar businesses with a layered organizational structure, with highly technical training, recruiting the best people, and so on. He talked about things we are now talking about, but we have really added modern business school management instruction.

Our Managing Farm Personnel in the Nineties seminars were mainly targeted at a cutting-edge group of farmers. We had a lot of dairy farmers, but we also had vegetable growers, greenhouse producers, and fruit growers. They were charged $150 to come for two days. That was a lot of money. People weren't accustomed to spending that kind of money, especially for extension seminars. We really hit at the high end. In the PRO-DAIRY program at the same time, we were training the agents to train the more middle group of farmers. So those farmers were getting this kind of training as well, but they were getting it through a more traditional county or regional-level training program.

In those early days, I developed a seminar that I still teach on recruiting and selecting the best employees, and how to hire the best employees. I've now taught that recruitment and selection seminar for fifteen years, although I have changed it a little. I developed it when Bernie Erven from Ohio State was here on sabbatical. He actually was kind of our fourth team member our very first year. I had done a little bit of teaching before, and we were all picking topics, and I picked that topic, and Bernie helped me prepare. I went to management textbooks, and I looked at what other people were doing. As I developed it, I would go down the hall and talk to Bernie and talk to Bob. The very hardest part of that was figuring out the activities, because we also changed our teaching paradigm, and our teaching model, from a lecture format to an active learning format to get people involved. So we had to have lots of activities.

It was Merrill Ewert, a faculty member in the Department of Education, who inspired us to change our teaching paradigm. He spent a lot of time with us back then. He told us that his research showed that people didn't have the attention span for lectures, and that if people were actively involved in their own education, they would learn more and retain more. The key to it all was to have activities where they would learn. The other key to it all was to lower your expectations in terms of how much material you thought you should plow through. That was the biggest challenge for many of us. It's easy to stand up and lecture, but it's a whole different role to stand up and facilitate. I've been doing it now for fifteen years, and its incredibly exciting and exhilarating. It's still a lot of work, because you are always asking yourself, "Do I have the right set of activities? Am I teaching this the right way?" And you're constantly looking at your evaluations to see if it's working.

One experience from doing these workshops stands out. We were teaching in Schenectady during our second year of Managing Farm Personnel in the Nineties, and all the participants had come in and we were having lunch. I was sitting next to a woman who is a farm wife from southern Vermont, and we were talking about all kinds of things. She said that her latest recruiting method was to use the services of the Labor Department: ad-writing resources, job-posting resources, and interviewing resources. I was really, really impressed with that, because I knew those resources existed, and that farmers generally gave them very little attention, or credence, or credibility. So I turned to her, and I asked, "How did you come to pursue that as a way to recruit good people?" And not only had she done it, but she'd been successful: that's where all her employees were coming from. She said to me, "Well, I learned it here last year." And I was the guy who was teaching in front of the room when she learned it. So that's one thing that sticks in my mind. It goes back to what I said about Willard DeGolyer: if I never sat down next to that lady at lunch, I would never have known that she actually used some of the information I presented. So one of the challenging things about this work is that you don't always know what someone has done as a result of what you've taught them. And now that I think about it, there's probably a gazillion examples of that very thing, because I've now talked to thousands of people in seminars and workshops.

In our workshops with ag businesses, the number of employees they generally have would be ten employees up to fifty or sixty, and sometimes bigger, depending upon what we're doing. In the fruit and vegetable business, you might have five or ten year-round employees, including family members, and then you go up to fifty or sixty when you're picking apples or harvesting vegetables. On our large dairy farms, I think ten to fifty would be a pretty good figure, because we now have gotten to a point where when we expand dairy businesses, we don't just expand it on one site. Because of manure and land resources, you get to a certain point, and then it's time to start a new business elsewhere. So it's the same farm, it's just a different site. The interesting thing about it is these guys grow from modest-sized farms, and they're still family farms, most of the ones who have gotten big and are successful. They've really excelled at their profession. But many weren't necessarily excelling in productivity, profitability, and management the way they could have as an industry. That's why PRO-DAIRY started.

Our management workshops have addressed business planning, leadership, conflict management and communication, performance appraisal and performance management, training, recruitment and selection, and motivation. In leadership, we've taught the Blanchard situational leadership concepts. We also teach something with six leadership styles, where they take a little test, and they get to see what their predominant and less dominant leadership styles are. Then we get them to think about what that means when they go home to work with their employees, and how to not overuse their more dominant leadership styles, and how to use the less dominant ones more. When we teach leadership, we teach it in terms of relationships with their employees. We also teach a model with four conflict management styles. Typically, the conflicts in farm businesses are interpersonal conflicts within the business. It's when somebody doesn't get along with somebody else. It also can be a conflict between family members over issues that are really important to the people who are involved. The way we teach it is to get the manager to think about how he deals with conflict. They take a test to analyze their conflict styles, and then we role-play, and set up situations.

The next story I want to tell builds on many of the things I've already said. It has to do with the land-grant system, and how I feel about the land-grant system. After the three-year era of Managing Farm Personnel in the Nineties was over, I got a call one day from Joanne Gruttadorio over in the Department of Plant Science, and she said, "Tom, I have somebody here from the Golf Course Superintendents Association of America (GCSAA), and they're looking for some human resource information." So Joanne put this woman on the phone, and the woman said, "We have a certification program, and we have five or six sections in our certification program. A lot of it has to do with soils and grass and turf, and so on. But the last section is on human resource management, and we don't have good materials for them to read and study before they take the test. We really want to shore up that part of our program." So I asked a bunch of questions, and she said, "Well, we really would like a textbook." I cited about four or five different textbooks, and I said, "Well, you could use this book, but the problem with it is that it doesn't have this, and it doesn't have this. And then this other one has way too much of this, and not enough of that." Then off the cuff, half in jest, I said, "You know, you should have guys like us write the book for you." And there was a long pause, and she said, "Well, you know, we've been thinking about that."

To make a long story short, we wrote the book. The title is *Human Resources Management for Golf Course Superintendents*, and it was published in '96. It took Bob Milligan and me three years to write. It was one of the hardest things I'd ever done. We interviewed golf course superintendents, and we had focus groups so that we could learn about the industry. The whole time we were writing the book, we had as our goal to become seminar speakers for the Golf Course Superintendents Association of America. Every year for their annual conference they have 20,000 people that go to a southern city, like Orlando or San Diego. Superintendents choose from seventy or eighty seminars on all kinds of topics. So when our book was done, we were asked to put together a seminar. It introduced us to one of the most advanced, sophisticated professional improvement programs we'd ever been involved in, and it really raised the bar for us as educators to be able to teach what that group wanted, and to be able to teach to the high standards of the Association. The seminar we did was called Managing People for Peak Performance and Job Satisfaction. And if you took time to look through our book, you would see that it is built on all our previous work.

So we wrote the book and it was introduced, and the next year we were invited to do this two-day seminar, and we billed it as being based on the book. We'd been doing this kind of teaching for ten or eleven years. The first time we went to the superintendents' conference was when we were getting ready to sign the contract for the book, and then the next time we went there, it was to teach the seminar and to publicize the book. Golf course superintendents are very talented people; they're very advanced, more advanced than some of the farmers we deal with. Golf course superintendents, by the nature of their job, are highly accountable, there's high turnover, and they're under a lot of pressure to perform. So they take their management education very seriously. It was exciting to be there with 20,000 people in a big convention center in Las Vegas. It was just exhilarating.

The punch line of this story has to do with the land-grant system. All of the seminar speakers—and there were seventy or eighty of us—were invited to have lunch together. So you'd be teaching your all-day seminar, and when it was time for lunch, you went to the seminar speakers' lounge for a lovely, served lunch. You got to sit there with all the other seminar speakers. And when I walked in the room and sat there and ate lunch, I got two really strong impressions. One is that I was in really terrific company, the company of some really capable people, because if you weren't a capable seminar instructor, you just wouldn't be invited. But the other impression I had was really interesting. We sat down to lunch, and we introduced ourselves to the other people at our table, and this is how it went. You introduce yourself to Joe, and he says, "Hi, I'm Joe. I'm the turfgrass entomologist at Rutgers University." And the next guy says, "I'm the turfgrass pathologist at Clemson." And the next guy says, "I'm the turf science professor at Texas A&M." Now, all the speakers weren't from the land-grant system. Half of them were from businesses, others were consultants, etc. But a third to half of the people in that room were some of the best turf scientists and extension educators in the whole country. They were all there to educate golf course superintendents.

That was an "aha" moment in my career, because I go to work every day in my little compartment within the land-grant system, and all of a sudden, I find myself at lunch with all these other land-grant professionals, looking at how remarkably powerful our system is, just in the field of turf management on golf courses. It made me realize that this is a really huge deal, that this is something that taxpayers don't know: the impact their federal tax dollars for Extension, Smith-Lever, and Hatch have, and how much good it does—locally and nationally—for our various audiences.

I'm also very involved with my colleagues who do human resource management work nationally. There aren't very many of us who do human resource management in agriculture and horticulture—maybe a dozen or so people. It's a small group, but it's a terrific group. We're a little family.

In addition to workshops and teaching, I conduct some applied research. I publish papers for the common practitioner to pick up and read, and also for my professional colleagues. Now, it's just once every two or three years that I crank out a study, but nonetheless, there's always been some applied research component of my job, a scholarship component. Again, Bob Milligan has encouraged me to build a strong vita, because even though I'm not a tenure-track professor, I've moved from extension associate to senior extension associate, and have advanced my career along the way. Bob retired last year, so I'm now taking much more of my own initiative. Most of the research we did was applied research, surveying human resource practices and things of that nature. Nobody else has much of an interest in human resource research now that Bob is gone.

It's worth mentioning that in our work, we're not taking the research-based knowledge of the tenured faculty in this department and transferring it out. I think the reason for that is that HR is kind of a fringe area, or a new, developing area of farm management. So there isn't a research base for it in the department. If I want to find a research base, I need to go to ILR, or to Cornell's Johnson School of Management.

In recent years, a whole new dimension of my work has emerged. We have had an increasing number of Hispanic farmworkers in New York, so in recent years I've begun to apply my work in HR to the Hispanic workers. I want to talk about how that came about. In '98, I was invited to do the Managing People for Peak Performance two-day workshop for golf course superintendents in three places in the country: Boston, Baltimore, and Orlando. Each time I would get halfway through this seminar, not even halfway through, and I'd have people coming up to me and say, "You know, this is really good stuff, Tom, but can you tell us how this relates to our new workforce, the Latinos? We've got Mexicans working for us now, we've got Guatemalans working for us now." And I came back from that trip, and said, "I don't have good answers to these questions. And I don't think these questions are going to stop." And then, at the same time, we got to looking at what was going on in our dairy industry. At that time there were probably two dozen farms that had Hispanic workers, and it seemed like that might just be the beginning.

So I took a sabbatical, and I went down to the Hotel School where they were teaching about multicultural issues in business, and they introduced me to some of the research in this area. I decided to survey all the dairy farm employers I could find who had Hispanic workers, to try to figure out what were the issues and what was going on. I developed a survey questionnaire, and administered it myself, over the phone, because I personally knew the people I was interviewing. It took forty minutes to an hour with each manager. I did twenty interviews with a specific set of questions. That started the information-gathering process relating to Hispanic workers. I found out that there was a whole set of issues that were unique to this workforce, including language, culture, community acceptance, transportation, law enforcement, and illegal aliens. So I decided to roll up my sleeves and put some effort into that area. I immersed myself in Hispanic workforce issues. I remember after about two years of that saying to somebody, "I'm not getting a lot of traction with the various audiences who should be interested in this stuff." I also remember saying, "I think I'm ahead of them. I may be way out ahead of them." I also remember saying things like, "I feel like a missionary. I see things that farmers may not see for five years until there's a problem, or until something doesn't go right, or until something gets stuck."

My interest in Hispanic workforce issues led to a golf course superintendent workshop called Managing a Multicultural Workforce. I teach that same workshop to every agriculture and horticulture audience that is involved with the Hispanic workforce now. I also teamed up with Dave Grusenmeyer here, and two guys from Penn State. We put together a conference called Managing the Hispanic Workforce. We've done two sets of them now, two years apart. The first set we did in New York and Pennsylvania. Two years after that we did another set, and now we're getting ready to do our third set of conferences on that topic. It's interesting that a lot of what I learned in setting up the conferences for Managing Farm Personnel in the Nineties is what has gone into structuring these new conferences. My question the first time around was, "Can we teach farmers human resource management?" Now we're asking, "Can we teach farmers how to manage the Hispanic workforce?' I went into it with a lot of confidence, because I thought that we could have a successful conference. I thought people would come, and we had almost 100 people at every one of these conferences—100 people at each site, with four different sites. We tend to get a lot of dairy farmers because in this state, that's who's here. But we also get fruit, vegetable, and horticultural managers.

For the big conferences that we do, like Managing the Hispanic Workforce, we get sponsors. We are on the agenda as speakers, but we also bring in the best nationally known speakers we can find. We go to Farm Credit, and we go to the trade organizations and ask for money to bring in the speakers, to pay their honorariums, and to pay their travel expenses. Then we charge everybody $170 for the notebook and for a spot in the conference. It's self-supporting, as long as you can buy into the fact that asking for sponsorships for the speakers is part of being self-supporting.

The Managing the Hispanic Workforce conferences have been successful, and I think we're having a real impact. My philosophy going into this is based on what I learned in Managing Farm Personnel in the Nineties. If we show the managers the path, and give them the tools, they will go down the path. And that has been our experience here, that farmers are learning the concepts of managing a Hispanic workforce, especially cultural differences, and taking it to heart.

I want to tell a story relating to the Hispanic workforce. I was doing the Managing the Hispanic Workforce work for a year or two, and one day there was a problem out in Perry, New York, in Wyoming County. I can't remember how I got wind of it, but people were talking about it, and there were news reports. Apparently, the problem had to do with the Mexican workers and the police. In Perry, there are a lot of large dairy farms. A number of them had Mexican workers, and they didn't have housing on the farm. So the farmers rented some upstairs apartments on the main street of little downtown Perry, and that's where the Mexicans lived. One night, outside of a Perry bar, a guy was stabbed. He made his way back into the bar, bleeding, and told the police that he was stabbed by a Mexican or Puerto Rican–looking person. He was taken to the hospital and patched up, and it turns out he was okay. He recovered.

What happened next was that the local sheriff and the Perry Village police force raided the upstairs apartments where the Mexicans lived, and according to the farmers, did something that might be referred to as an "NYPD Blue raid"—barging into the apartments, looking for suspects. The early word from the farm community was that they broke down doors, and it was racial profiling and police brutality. According to the police, they went to the first apartment with guns drawn, and they did it because they did not know what they were going to find behind closed doors. Both the sheriff and the police department were telling the same story: they needed to protect the safety of the police. They got to one apartment, and the guy let them in, and he knew some English, so they went to the next apartment. At the third apartment, two guys ran in and locked the door. That immediately resulted in the door being broken down. When it all calmed down, they found the workers were illegal and deported them.

The farmers were really upset about this. One of the town justices was a farmer, and he resigned his job and told the media that he couldn't work with the police and the town anymore. And that created a huge amount of press. The media found other farmers, and the farmers just made the police look terrible. The police were in an uproar. They felt they were simply using their power to do their job, and were very angry that they were being portrayed by the farmers as racial profilers who were guilty of police brutality.

I read a couple of the newspaper articles one of my farmer friends sent me, and about a week later, I got a call from Bruce Tillapaugh, who is a county agent in Wyoming County. He said, "Tom, one of our farmers who's involved in all of this has been a long-time extension supporter, and he asked me if there isn't something Extension could do to work on this situation. The people in the community are all upset, and the farmers are all upset, and the police have circled the wagons and are very defensive." I had just gotten into working on this issue of managing a Hispanic workforce, and now I'm faced with a real-world crisis, and a specific invitation that Extension get involved. Initially I thought that nothing had prepared me for this. On the other hand, one of my friends who is a dairy farm wife in Cortland who I was telling about this said, "Well, in another respect, you've been preparing for this your whole career." In retrospect, I think she was right. But at the time, I wondered if there was a place for me there. In the end, I did think we did some good, and I learned a lot.

Let me tell you what happened. My colleague Dave Grusenmeyer has worked with me on the multicultural workforce issues. He and I huddled up after Bruce's call. I told him, "They want us to come out and talk to some people." Then I got on the phone to some farm leaders that I knew out there, and one of them was John Noble, who I've known for a while, and have a great respect for. He is a very distinguished dairy leader in the state. I got on the phone with him—he had some workers involved in this as well—and I said, "Look, we've been invited to come out. Bruce Tillapaugh is setting up this meeting, and Dave and I are going to come and facilitate a discussion. We're going to get the farmers together, and we're going to let them talk about how they feel about this. Then we're thinking of getting the police together and having some of kind of exchange. But the last thing we need is a shouting match." Before we got there, one had already erupted at a town meeting. So John said to me, "Tom, don't have the whole group of farmers meet with the police. The police will be out-numbered. Just have a small group of farmers meet with them." And that turned out to be an excellent piece of advice.

So we went there, and we had all these farmers, plus a town supervisor and some other officials. They all vented, without the police there, and said what their concerns were about how the police conducted themselves. The farmers were in a tough spot. By the time we got there, the community members had made up their mind that the farmers were the problem, because they were bringing in illegal workers. We had flip chart sheets all over the walls with their concerns. We brought in the police after we had met for an hour and a half. Most of the group went home, but the designated leaders of the farm group met, and had what I thought was an extremely level-headed discussion. No acting out, no hostility, genuine concern over what the police's protocols were, what could happen in the future.

One of the things that stuck in my mind was the police saying to the farmers, "If you're asking us to look the other way, we're not going to do it." It was very important for the farm-ers to understand that, and to think about that, and they backtracked and said, "Oh, no, we're not asking for that. But you can call us if there's a problem with our employees, you can get us on the phone. Employees can carry the farm business card with them, so there's some connectedness, especially if people can't speak English." So they came to some understand-ing. There was still some real concern that the police had not acted as professionally as they could have. The case was never solved, and everyone moved on.

We left, and things calmed down, and there was more respect, and everybody in the situation was a little more careful. Dave and I were out there for another meeting two months ago, and we actually met with some of the leaders, as sort of a recap. Things really did calm down, and people really did make a bigger effort to work together. The county sheriff is an elected position, and the guy who was involved with this is no longer in that position. Now the reason I'm telling you this story is that in one respect, it was a very, very good thing that we were asked to go there, because Dave and I are leading a statewide educational program on managing the Hispanic workforce, and community acceptance is going to be a huge issue. The only reason it's not now, in the minds of the farmers, is because they have so many things to worry about, including language and culture and building a multicultural team. They have so much to worry about *inside* that business that they can't think *outside* the business unless something like this happens. One of the things that I've been thinking about since that day is how do we educate around community acceptance issues, because they're inevitable. In fruit and vegetables over the last thirty years we've had community-related incidents, now that Hispanic workers are arriving in New York's all-white rural dairy communities. So I left there saying, "We need to think about community acceptance." And I have been thinking about it ever since.

I wrote a grant for federal Smith-Lever funds last fall that was just accepted. We're going to take dairy farm leaders who have Hispanic workers to Mexico for an immersion experience, so that they can come back and be ambassadors for their industry, and for their communities on behalf of their workers. We're going to have an academic component. There will be study discussions and papers to read. Participants will be required to give a presentation when they return, either to a group of their peers, or to a community group, to foster understanding about what is happening in the dairy industry regarding Hispanic workers. It's a three-year program, and this is not an original idea. They've done this at the University of Northern Iowa. There are a couple of anthropologists out there who we've been in contact with who've had great success with this. They've had an even more urgent set of issues, because in Iowa meatpacking towns, there are zero Hispanic workers one day, and a year later, there's a thousand. So this is a model that's worked there and has worked in the mushroom-growing area in southern Pennsylvania, and we're going to try it.

In our foray into teaching management education and trying to get people to change what they do when they manage, we have tried all kinds of things. We did "To Do" lists, and we provided a lot of very basic personal management techniques that we were trying to get people to adopt so that they would change their behavior. If you're asking somebody to keep a "To Do" list, you don't just ask them to put on there what they're going to do in their job that day. You're trying to get them to organize everything, to reorganize themselves and learn some things about themselves so they change how they behave and how they get things done, whether it's doing things personally or professionally in their business. The thing that I think is unique about management education is that it's different from the educators and the researchers and the extension people who teach technical things, who teach operational things.

Let me give you a specific example. Robin Bellinder is a professor in the Department of Horticulture here at Cornell. Let's say hypothetically that she goes out and does her work with vegetable growers and she finds out that there is a herbicide-resistant weed. She goes out and surveys the situation and says, "Oh, we've got these weeds and they're herbicide resistant." So she goes over to her test plots in the summertime and she does some experiments, and she says, "Okay, here are the weeds that are resistant, and now I've got a new set of herbicides that the farmers need to use, and my test plot work showed that these three herbicides will take care of the resistance problems." And she goes into her meetings with the farmers all across the state and rolls out these recommendations for new herbicides. Then the farmers purchase the herbicides and start using them in their crop program. And if the farmers don't do that, they're going to lose money.

It is much, much harder to convince somebody that if they turn over a position on their farm two or three times in a year, or even once in two years, that it's going to cost them money. And even if you convince them that it's going to cost them money, then you have to convince them to go to school on how to interview, how to recruit, how to select the best person for the job, how to do a trial period, and how to do a whole set of things that they don't feel comfortable with. That requires personal change—a lot more personal change than changing the herbicide on your order sheet. Much more personal change than that. Leadership skills, conflict management in a business, all of the things that we teach and have taught when we're talking about management education are much more about difficult behavioral change than they are in some technical areas, because the subject matter has a more emotional piece to it.

Any one of us that teaches management will tell you that when farmers go to conferences, you can fill the room when you're talking about new technology. You can fill the room when you're talking about a technical problem that needs to be solved on the farm. They'll all show up, you'll have 300 people. And then when you start to talk about management, and you have a competing session, they'll all get up and go to the other technical thing down the hall. I had that happen on Long Island. There were 300 arborists and landscapers in the room, and George Hudler, a Cornell plant pathologist, was talking about a beech tree disease. There wasn't an empty chair in the room almost. I came on to talk about managing Hispanic employees after that, and three-quarters of the people got up and left. I think that happened because these folks almost always get into the arborist business or the landscaping business or the dairy business or the apple business because they like the work. They like the hands-on part of whatever it is they're producing. People don't come to us and say, "I got into this because I like to plan and control and organize and lead and motivate and communicate." Nobody ever says that. They got into it because of the production aspects that they were interested in, and then found out they had to run a business, and they had to lead people.

To be successful in management education in Extension, you need to set up the expectation that this is yet another important part of running a business. And you have to use active teaching methods. The way we do our seminars and workshops, we don't just stand in front of the room and talk at people. The best educational seminar that Bob Milligan and I ever conducted was a two-day workshop for the Golf Course Superintendents Association of America, entitled "Managing People for Peak Performance." We taught it for five or six years. One of the reasons why it was so good, even though it was a grueling two days for everybody, was that every fifteen or twenty minutes we changed our teaching methods. First we had the introduction, then we had the workbook exercise, then we had the mini-lecture, then we had the video, then we had another mini-lecture, then we had a self-disclosure exercise (a series of questions people answered about themselves). In that two-day experience, there was no more than twenty minutes of lecture in any part. It was always group discussions, problem-solving exercises, or case studies. One of the key things we learned is that there is no way you can lecture on this. It has to be experiential. I think that's why we've been successful.

The longer I do this, the greater sense I get about what all of those career extension people before me were trying to tell me about what extension education is. I finally think I understand, or at least I understand as it relates to my world and my work. What they were trying to tell me is that you can't think of this work in terms of "what I did this year." My annual report goes to the dean and the department chair every year, and I can tell them what the activities were, and I can update my vita with what I wrote and what I did and where, what my seminars were, and it looks pretty impressive. But when you're talking about having an impact on the state of New York, or on agricultural and horticultural industries in the Northeast, it's not one year. It's a lot of years, a lot of perspective, and a lot of trial and error. It's learning from mistakes, and learning how to do it better, and learning how to have an even greater impact than you had the last time. It's surveying the landscape and seeing where is the opportunity, who are the people to get involved, who is the audience, and how do we finance it. How do we get it all together so we hit a home run?

I think it's a long-term investment. Part of my responsibility is to provide leadership for the farm management agents out in the counties and regions of the state. Indeed, if it is a long-term investment, then you should have people around with a historical perspective who have enough experience to grow the profession and grow the educational program that you're talking about at any point in time. In this state now, we've turned over many of the extension educator positions, and now the county officials say, "Well, why do we need this position?" When you have somebody in that job for two years or three years, and they leave, and you get another one and another one and another one, maybe it's no surprise that people say, "We're not getting the bang for our buck." Because maybe we didn't pay enough for that person to be there in the first place, and maybe we didn't pick the right one. Now the stakes for how much we pay and who we pick get really high, because not everybody cares about extension work, and there aren't that many mentors. If you do care about this work, you have to survive this system. You have to address the budget crunches, you have to endure the changes in administration, you have to deal with "We've been marching this way for seven years. Now we're going to march this other way."

You ask me what all this has to do with the land-grant mission. Well what is the land-grant mission? To me, it's to educate individuals and community members to improve their lives and their communities. That's almost paraphrased from the Cornell Cooperative Extension mission statement. It's about getting people to learn and change their behavior to improve their lives. It was born out of an agrarian society, where teaching agriculture and home economics and 4-H were all a part of rural communities. The people who did that work operated within the fabric of the community, helping in many ways to improve the community. Now society has modernized and changed and added technology in ways people never imagined. Yet we're still doing many of the same things. We're still carrying out the land-grant mission, because in a global economy, we need a competitive agriculture, we need a modern agriculture, we need an agriculture that will feed large populations of people. We need an agriculture that will use technology and will create safe and healthy food products. My job is to help farmers do that with their farm management and their human resource management, and to do it in a way that they can be successful.

I think my work is an example of how the land-grant system provides service to the agricultural industry. But we have to be careful how we define service, and how we define education. There is a framework where you could loosely define service to include education. But if we're making a distinction between the two, then I would say what we're doing is intended from the very beginning, explicitly, to be education and not service. Service to me is when someone comes to you and says, "I want you to help me write my employee handbook." The distinction for me is that if it's education instead of service, the individual is very involved in learning about himself or herself and very involved in looking at how he or she wants to behave in the workplace with the people they supervise. That can be a very powerful educational experience. And so I think that service is like consulting, like providing something. It has a connotation of providing something for a fee, as opposed to education being teaching a person to fish. It's something that a person does internally: they change themselves, and they own it.

There has been a service versus education conversation for the entire thirty years I've been in this system. And the way that conversation goes is, "We need to make sure we're doing less service and more education." I think that faculty members who engage in these conversations are saying that, and I think extension administration—even though they've sort of gone back and forth—has said that a lot, often in the context of budgets and in justifying our existence to our funders. There's always been this concern that if we take away the service component, education may not be able to stand on its own, that people won't value the education part of what they're getting as much as they value the service. I think that that makes us afraid to make hard decisions about service. I would go back to this trip to Mexico I'm planning. The service in this is huge—hiring interpreters, setting up meals and hotels and logistics and tour guides. That's a huge service. But I have to provide all that service to get them to the education table.

I have an interesting dilemma at the moment. There is a tremendous feeling out in the agricultural and horticultural industries that because we have a Hispanic workforce that has come here to work and support their families back home, our labor problems are solved. There is a feeling among employers that we have now gotten a quick and relatively inexpensive fix to what has been historically a really difficult problem: finding good people. I have felt lately they think they need me less. Now I can list the issues I think farmers should be thinking about, but they're not coming to me and asking about them. I feel alone sometimes, in the sense that if human resource management education in New York agriculture is going to go forward, one of the few people who is going to make that happen is me.

One of the things that's happening in this state right now is there is a war raging between the farm labor advocates and the Farm Bureau over overtime pay and collective bargaining. Currently farm employers are exempt from both. There is this gut reaction—this huge, historical, gut reaction in the farm community—that overtime pay and collective bargaining laws the way they are today have to remain, or farmers will perish. Farmers sometimes think if they lose that battle, it'll just be awful. They have a hard time seeing the future on this issue. I don't know how to give them the bad news that eventually they are probably going to lose. Not that I think that they should just give up. But I really think that they should think about where they're going, and what is the future on those two issues, and ask themselves if it's worth the price they're paying to fight this battle. I'm concerned that the more agriculture opposes overtime pay and collective bargaining the worse the industry looks to the public. Perhaps there is a middle ground.

287

I've struggled with this for a number of years, and I have to be very careful whose mind I try to open on this issue. If there's no huge consequence that prevents you from doing your job in the future, then you can be bold, and step up. It's much easier to sit at somebody's kitchen table, when the senior generation clearly needs to give up some ownership and some authority to the younger generation, and be bold in that situation. But you can't be bold in every situation. And so I haven't quite figured out always how to give bad news. But I think we do give bad news sometimes, and we shock people sometimes, and we make enemies sometimes. You have to stand for something in this business. You just have to be careful about the politics, and about the venue. And I think you also need to very clearly know what your support base is.

I've devoted my career to New York agriculture and horticulture. And now I have a national context within which I work as well. Although I don't have all the evidence that I wish I had that I've helped people, that people have learned something from me that they can really use, I do have lots of evidence. I have evaluations that say, "Every golf course superintendent should take this seminar." These guys come up to you after the seminar, and they shake your hand and say, "Thank you very much." So there are outward signs that you're hitting the mark, and that good management is going to lead to professional successes and organizational successes, and industry-wide successes.

More and more people up and down this hallway sit around here and we ask ourselves, "What's the direction of agriculture in New York?" Like the folks in the New York State Department of Ag and Markets, we're constantly looking at this entity as an industry, and we're looking at where the industry as a whole is going. So when you start to think about it in that regard, you have to think about economic development in the state of New York—rural economic development and the well-being of communities. And it's not until a community loses half the dairy farms or half the apple farms that people start to say, "Are we losing something more than $20 million of apple income. Are people moving away? Is land vacant? Is the productivity of the resources in this community less than it was before?" I think there are societal and community benefits that are spillovers.

People are asking why we need people like me—professionals who are funded by their tax dollars—to address agricultural management and business issues. They think these issues can be addressed better or cheaper by private consultants. Well, some of them can be. But the standard response to that is that we're impartial. There are people out there who challenge our impartiality from time to time, but we're not selling a product per se, and a lot of the consultants, especially on farms and in landscaping businesses, are selling a product, and some of these consulting services come along with the product. So there is a bias there. We're not selling a product. We're not associated with a profit motive.

I live in Cortland, and I live outside of town. There's a dairy farm across the road from me. There are field crops all around my property. My family and I like that community, and we want to see farmers survive in it. We want to see the landscape businesses do well. We don't have any fruit farms where I live, but I think New Yorkers would say they want to see the apple industry recover from a very difficult financial time, and still be able to drive on Route 104 near Lake Ontario and drive through orchards. I personally don't want the landscapes of New York all to be Blockbuster video stores and Applebee's restaurants and

Comfort Inns. That open space is something that's really valuable. As our 7,000 dairy farms in this state diminish, we need to replace them with something that is equally acceptable to us. And so, to the extent that I can, I want to help keep people in business, doing what they're good at, doing what they like to do. Not all of them will make it, and maybe that's not such a bad thing. But to evolve to a state that still is producing food, and has landscapes that are valuable and attractive to all of us, is what keeps me going.

There are some things that give me hope. We just had a farm business management extension retreat, and I'm surrounded by a group of people who still love what they do, and are good at what they do, and care about what they do, and who also have hope. I spent two years scrambling for money to pay part of my salary, especially Smith-Lever money, and I was pretty down about that. I think it would be bad if we had a whole organization of people who were feeling that way. I don't think we do. I think that people do get down when they're hit with a financial challenge that they can't get out of in a short period of time. But, having said that, I think people find ways to draw support to find their way out. After all, many of us have been here a long time. I think that after a point, you say, "I don't want to finish my career somewhere else. I want to finish it here, and I'm going to find a way."

I just found out the other day that my five-year reappointment was approved, and funding is looking better. I have a whole bunch of projects that I'm just dying to dig into, including community acceptance of Hispanic workers, these trips to Mexico, and leadership-building issues. I don't want to spend a lot of time fretting about the system. I want to spend my time thinking about the exciting things that are ahead. I think I have had a long and successful career, and I still have a lot I want to accomplish.

A Sense of Communion

A Profile of Anu Rangarajan

Senior Extension Associate, Department of Horticulture, Cornell University

During the summers while she was growing up in Detroit, Anu Rangarajan took care of her family's yard and garden and gave her mother a rose every day. In this two-part profile, she tells us how she has integrated her love for plants and people—especially the people who grow our food—in developing her life work as an educator. What we see in her stories and experiences is an academic professional with a remarkable commitment to building respectful, collaborative relationships between university experts, farmers, and community members. The main practice story she tells about her work of organizing the Cornell Organic Advisory Council, which grew into the Northeast Organic Network (NEON), gives us an instructive glimpse into the roles and contributions of a public scholar and educational organizer who seeks to have, as she puts it, "a sense of communion where you can be at Cornell but still be in partnership with growers." Her profile leaves us with the impression that she is achieving what she is seeking. But we also learn that as an engaged faculty member who works from a position of humility about her knowledge and expertise—and who prioritizes public relationships over academic publishing—her experience in the research university context has sometimes been painful and difficult.

Part One
Interview conducted by Scott Peters, February 2, 2002

I'm a faculty member in the Department of Horticulture with a 60 percent Extension, 40 percent research split. I work on fresh market vegetables. My official title is Statewide Specialist for Fresh Market Vegetable Production. I started here in 1996, with a focus on cultural practices and sustainability of vegetable systems in New York State. I focus on ways of establishing plants in the field, including fertility requirements, the selection of varieties, and the design of the fields for insect and pest management. I don't focus on insects and pests directly, but on the quality and productivity of the crop. That's my window for looking at the system. All my work is related to actually growing crops in the field.

My position has had a long history. One of my predecessors, Phil Mingus, was in it over twenty years and had a very strong connection to the commercial vegetable industry. Since then, three people have held the position for relatively brief periods. This has led to challenges because, after Phil left, there's not been long-term continuity in the job. The identity of the position in the field has been lost a bit.

What I'm passionate about are relationships. I'm passionate about change and growth and personal development. Agriculture is a means to achieve that end for me. I interact with farmers. The person who tills the soil has an appeal to me. That's why I do what I do. I also like to work with people who are perceived as being disconnected from the city, even though I grew up in Detroit.

My parents emigrated to the U.S. from India when I was one month old. My father was brought to this country by Detroit General Hospital as an emergency room physician. Because the hospital's generosity allowed him and my mother to come here, he never left the city and always worked with Medicare and Medicaid recipients. We grew up with an ethic of working with the poor and the underprivileged. My siblings and I all feel cursed with a strong sense of social responsibility. We joke about it because all of us now have careers in public service.

Growing up in Detroit was great. It's got secrets that people don't see from the outside. I enjoyed the tension and diversity between the African American, white, Greek, and Hispanic populations that all lived there. For me, it was great to be an immigrant. We lived within the city limits until I was about eight, and then moved to the suburbs. I worked in my father's office downtown until I was probably sixteen or seventeen. I was programmed to follow in his footsteps, to move into his practice in the city and continue his work. I didn't do it.

The whole time I was growing up, I had a vegetable garden. My mother would give me the seeds, and I would experiment. I accepted it as a chore, but it never was one. It was just something I did. I loved it. I took care of the yard and garden and gave her a rose every day. When I went to college at the University of Michigan, I started in premed, but couldn't stand the students. They were in it for the money, and I got discouraged by that. I never seriously considered horticulture as an opportunity until I took a class in practical botany. The class had a lab twice a week for four hours. I went out to the university's botanic gardens and I had four hours there just playing with plants. I had greenhouse space, and made wine and yogurt. We did things that I had felt very connected to as a child. It nurtured me and sent me down a different road.

I quit college, dropped out, and moved home. It was an immigrant's nightmare—to have their eldest daughter quit college. My parents freaked. I got a job at a greenhouse for nine months, which put me on the track for horticulture.

I grew up in an urban place, but it was where I discovered horticulture. I never, ever considered that I could actually farm, nor had I heard of horticulture as a science, until I got the job in the greenhouse. They told me about the land-grant system. I found out about Michigan State University (MSU). I had no idea what a land-grant was and had never heard of 4-H. They said, "Why aren't you going into the Horticulture Department at Michigan State?" I said, "I didn't know there was such a thing!" I applied and got accepted.

MSU was racially diverse, which struck me right away. There was such a strong vibrant black community. That was a really important to me. I felt more at home there. As an undergraduate, I got involved with research. Then I interned in California working on poinsettias. The greenhouse where I had originally been employed took me back every time I came home, so I maintained a long-term relationship with them. They hired me after I graduated. I was a grower with them for a year until I decided to go back to school and get a master's degree.

My relationship with faculty at MSU was really collegial. I had a couple of mentors there. One faculty member in horticulture kept pushing me to consider graduate school. Every time I would talk to him, that's what he'd bring up. When I decided to go, I called him and he got me an assistantship at the University of Wisconsin with one phone call.

I did a master's in horticulture at Wisconsin studying greenhouse production. I was into floriculture for the aesthetic part of it. I really enjoyed that, and in fact now I think, "Why did I ever change?" Others in my lab were working on "Spuds in Space," a NASA project. A friend made a casual comment that really struck me: "Why grow flowers when people can't eat?" It was a pivotal moment in my life. It rocked me. I started to feel, frankly, that it was foolish to invest in the production of food in space when we couldn't feed people on the planet. I chose to focus on vegetable crops for my Ph.D. I focused on a project about women in international development, and home gardens as an economic tool to satisfy family nutrition and provide cash income. So I went from "Spuds in Space" all the way to the other extreme: poor women in developing areas!

For my Ph.D., I went back to MSU. My mentor at Wisconsin told me he didn't think that women had what it took to do a Ph.D. He flat out said he just didn't think women had staying power. They have kids and they quit. To my face! So I knew that wasn't a place for me to stay. It also put fire under my feet to get a Ph.D. Several years later, at a professional meeting, he told me that he hoped that Wisconsin would fill his position when he retired with somebody like me. I felt like I got him back.

I approached the Horticulture Department chair at Michigan State saying that I was looking for a place to do a Ph.D. He wrote to me and said that he had money and would like to take me on. He invited me to design my own project. I studied the potential to improve amaranth's nutritional quality for iron. It's a tropical grain that's also eaten as a leafy green. Iron is a primary nutritional deficiency of women in the developing world. I picked amaranth as a crop because nobody worked on it and it was a poor person's crop. I selected it based upon who grew it (women in home gardens) and how it was marketed (locally). The ultimate target of the work for me was women. My objective was to work on a crop that could make money and improve the personal health of women and their families.

I designed the project after a vacation I took between the master's and Ph.D. I did a walkabout through Central America, where I met with some researchers at a nutrition center in Guatemala. I spent time walking on coffee farms and indigenous gardens, and that's how I came back wanting to study amaranth and iron. The goal was to answer the question, "Can we actually breed a green for improved iron nutritional quality?"

I assessed iron bioavailability in a very broad range of amaranth germplasm from the plant collection in Ames, Iowa. I selected lines based on their common use as greens in tropical areas. I screened about eighty different types and found three that represented fairly diverse iron bioavailability. Then I fed the lines to rats to verify the nutritional differences in an animal model. I think the reality is that a plant-breeding approach for improvement on this particular trait will be challenging, since there is not a broad range in genetic variation.

The department I did my Ph.D. in was really focused on horticultural systems and on practical science-based recommendations on how to grow crops better. There were people involved with international development but very few making the intersection with the social sciences, putting context around the work. The questions they were asking were fairly basic. They were also doing some applied agricultural research.

My graduate work was unique. Nobody else in my department designed their own Ph.D. They walked into a project. What was unique for me is that I had that freedom. It's unusual in horticulture to hear, "Whatever you want to do, here's the money, here's the lab, go for it!" I had a different experience than other people, but I also felt very isolated. I didn't have people to talk to or a big lab group focused on one area of inquiry. The people I talked to were human and animal nutritionists—people who didn't think about horticulture. Within horticulture at the time there were very few people talking about the nutritional value of our crops. When I defended my dissertation people said, "Wow, this is really different." It was! It wasn't within the mold of what people would do in that department. The fact that I took a plant and talked about it as a food, not just looking at it as a crop, was really different. There were people who had the improved economic status of farmers in mind as a goal. But efficiency and cost of production would be it, not necessarily the relationships needed to make change happen.

In the middle of the Ph.D., I went to the Philippines and worked for Winrock International. I did not want to graduate from a Ph.D. program with no experience in international agriculture, especially since my research was totally focused on working with women in developing areas. I wanted an experience that would enable me to say that I'd done something internationally. At that time, that was my dream: to be able to work internationally on vegetables. There used to be this wonderful internship program through the Midwestern University Consortium for International Agriculture (MUCIA) that placed students all over the world. I was in the last group. Richard Harwood, an agroecologist at Michigan State, was on my committee and had worked at Winrock. When I applied for the internship, he got me in to Winrock.

My job was to analyze and identify ways that Winrock could support the institutional capacity and professional development of Filipino nonprofit organizations working in sustainable agriculture and natural resource management, to help these organizations be more competitive and viable. I interviewed executive directors and studied their methods of operating their nongovernment organizations (NGOs). I directly interviewed thirty-five people and collected survey information from another seventy. I then compiled a report of strategies that Winrock could use to make these organizations more viable. The experience gave me a transparent view into how international organizations like Winrock are good at playing the system, compared to small nonprofit NGOs on the ground that are good at making real change, but have little sense of how to play the system. Winrock called itself an NGO, but functioned like an international development agency. It really opened my eyes to the differences in institutions, their roles and how they function. I spent four months doing this work. It has affected me profoundly to this day.

From 1994 to 96, I was a postdoc at Ohio State, although I didn't defend my Ph.D. dissertation until 1995. At OSU I worked half time doing a project on potatoes that were being bred for resistance to Colorado potato beetle. For the other half, I got funded through the Great Lakes Protection Fund and a USDA Sustainable Agriculture Research and Education (SARE) grant to do organizational development with a group called the Innovative Farmers of Ohio. My job was to help them develop ways to improve self-monitoring for water quality and soil erosion through whole-farm planning. The overall project looked at how growers make decisions about farm management to reduce their environmental impact.

I had the position description for a job at Cornell on my desk for about eight months before I applied. I didn't think I was qualified for it. It sounded like it was more than I had under my belt. My mentor in Horticulture at the time made me apply. He just sat me down and said, "You are going to do this and do it now!" I FedExed everything the day before it was due, even though I was sure that I was not qualified for the job. My Ph.D. was on women and the nutrition of vegetable crops, and my postdoc involved working with dairy farmers whose backs were up against the wall, trying to help them make a transition.

I got the interview, and it went really well. Before the interview, I called the executive director of the New York State Vegetable Growers Association and said, "I'm a candidate for this job, and I want to get a sense of the lay of the landscape." She gave me the names of all the extension educators with vegetable responsibilities in the state. I called them and said, "If I were in this position, what would you expect from me and how do you feel about it?" They opened right up. They went on and on. They couldn't believe I'd called. They were honest about their perceptions of Cornell, the institution. I actually built my interview presentation on their comments. I said, "This is what the people in the field say about Cornell. This is what I think is happening and why I think it's happening." The extension educators felt there was no continuity in the position. They felt that people at the academic level went around them all the time to work with farmers rather than involving them in the learning process. They felt there wasn't long-term thinking, and that marketing was weak. They said they never felt heard.

Talking with the educators was a way of informing myself on what to expect. Before I came here I remember rehearsing my presentation with my mentor at OSU, and he said, "You called them?" And I said, "Yeah, why wouldn't I?" He said that was strategic. He said, "If you were interviewing and you called me to ask more about it, I would be flattered and think you were serious." But the fact of the matter was, I was just freaked! I was going to interview for a job in a state with a huge vegetable industry. I wanted them to give me clues. What are the issues? What are the areas of focus? I learned later that it really biased the department towards me, which was not at all my intention. I think they were biased towards me because I had asked what they thought. This experience helped me realize the importance of this position. It's an integrator for a lot of different people's interests.

When I was offered the position, I couldn't believe it. It blew me out of the water. I've only ever interviewed for one job in my whole life, and it was this one. The funny thing is, I had told my OSU mentor all along, "This is my dream job, because I get to grow stuff!" Fundamentally, that's what tied me as a child to horticulture. It felt right and it meant working with a diversity of farmers. I had worked with organic farmers before at Michigan State as a graduate student. I also worked on a Kellogg project called the Michigan Integrated Food and Farming Systems Initiative, where I was part of the design team. I had come to understand that whatever your philosophical bent is in agriculture, your bottom line is often the same. You just have different tools at your disposal.

My primary audience as a fresh market vegetable specialist is people that work in the vegetable industry. The more I study it, the less I feel I know. It's big. New York State used to be the largest vegetable producer in the country, serving the eastern seaboard. We had a huge industry of seed producers and a processing infrastructure. Now there's a vibrant fresh market industry growing many of the main crops people consume. It's holding its own. Other parts of the industry, like processing vegetables, seem to be slipping as that industry moves either south or west or out of the country. There's a skew and divide in the size of farms. There are a lot of really big farms in western New York, a smaller segment of medium-sized farms, and then a ton of small ones.

I started the job here at Cornell in August of 1996. I visited all the extension educators. They took me out to farms in their area. I spent the first two months on the road meeting people, trying to figure out how to focus my work. There was no end to the opportunities. I didn't want to work on anything that only suited large farms. I tried to identify areas that addressed issues of sustainability and could be adapted by all farms, or, if anything, by small farms rather than large. When I asked farmers what they're really struggling with, they'd always say marketing. They never said production. They were trying to make a living and they could grow tons of stuff, but they had nowhere to go with it. There was a mismatch between farmers' interests in marketing and the faculty's focus on productivity. This mismatch has always been there. An older professor in the department says we're missing the mark. We're addressing some needs, but the bottom line is our impact on these people. I struggle with it. The way we choose to work isn't necessarily the way we need to be working right now.

The whole first year, I tried to keep my research broad. I had a technician who kept things going. I learned more about growing vegetables. I had to build a knowledge base. I spent time in the field watching and visiting, reading everything I could. I hadn't had that opportunity before. In a Ph.D. you focus on one project. Now I had to focus on eight projects at the same time. I did a lot of reading, and even more talking to growers, getting to know what it was that made their farms tick.

After a year, I started getting some small grants from grower organizations where we focused on questions related to, say, corn production, or particular problems in peppers. I was trying to think about ways to reduce chemical and fertilizer inputs and enhance profitability. That's always the window, the lens. I ended up working with compost. Could compost be something that commercial vegetable growers could use profitably? We tried to build value by looking at disease suppressiveness and nutrient values of compost to their systems and assign long-term economic benefits.

There were people that had ideas they wanted to test, and I would take them on. I was so eager when I first got here. I would do anything! People started saying, "Let's just call Anu. She'll do it. She does everything. We've got this thing that's happening. Would you be interested in trying to help us figure it out?" I went down the road with some ideas, and some of the wild ones I tossed. The field research that I do focuses in on dealing with specific production problems. I generate research material and information that is relevant to grower questions and problems. I have been presenting at ten to fifteen conventional grower meetings every winter since I got to Cornell. I get invitations from all over the country. But I haven't distilled all of that into any research publications, which I still have to do.

Sometimes my project choices were driven by farmers I like and my relationships with them. I probably shouldn't have done it that way, but I really valued these good relationships with people. I wanted to help them solve their problems. There's a series of people's faces in my mind when I think of the farmers of New York. When I have a new idea, I consider what these people would think about it. That would help me to direct myself. I still feel like I'm wandering. When it comes to commercial agriculture, the things we choose to do versus the things that need to happen are still far apart.

In 1997, Cornell hosted a meeting of organic farmers in New York to come talk about organic agriculture. I attended it, and what struck me was that it was obvious this had happened before, and it was completely meaningless to the farmers. They felt like once again they're coming to Cornell to say, "Pay attention to us!" And Cornell would say, "Thanks for coming," and never respond. It bothered me because these people have a philosophy they choose to live by, and they're trying to make a living. There are fewer of them and they don't have large amounts of acreage, but they deserved attention. I thought, "What's the point of this?" We can come up with all these lists of things that people have done at Cornell that they think are relevant to organic farms, but the fact is they're not.

So the year after that meeting, I created the Cornell Organic Advisory Council. I invited key farmers and faculty members on campus across all departments who had some interest in organic agriculture to meet together and to design a research and extension agenda. That group provided a way to reflect on an idea and to focus its objectives. It generated mass amounts of support from the growers, which later resulted in letters of support for project proposals.

I wanted the Cornell Organic Advisory Council to have a mission. It wasn't going to be that once-a-year meeting where people got together and bitched about what wasn't happening. We had the first meeting in December of '97 and we've had it every December since then. The first year we put together our objectives. The second year we designed a research and extension list and tried to identify support grants.

At the Advisory Council meetings, I was both the facilitator and organizer. I did it all. I wanted a strategic way to spread information to people in the community as well as to share things about Cornell with those communities. At the initial stage, we invited people from several regions of the state based upon on how the Northeast Organic Farming Association of New York (NOFA NY) set up its regional districts. Our goal was to have a couple of representatives from each of those areas participate, and then go back and share with their regional groups. Brian Caldwell, an extension agent, and Steve Gilman, a farmer, were cochairs. They helped facilitate the meetings. Steve could say things to farmers that I never could, like, "Shut up, you're going off topic!" Any of them could say things to each other or their peers that I couldn't, based upon trust and the negative view of Cornell as being disconnected from their community.

Early meetings had a lot of back and forth. It was disheartening because there were some growers who were angrily saying, "Why do you want me here? You never pay me." It took a while to diffuse that by talking, by being consistent, by coming back to them and saying, "We still want to hear what you are thinking. Because you don't agree with us, doesn't mean we don't need to hear it." We developed relationships with others in the community who actually could talk to particular people and help to diffuse the tension. We'll never get past Cornell "the institution" with some people. One of my objectives is that this should be about Cornell "the individuals." Cornell has all these other objectives and agendas that are more visible than organic agriculture, but it doesn't mean that Cornell itself is not interested in organic. The growers' objective should be to work with the people that have their ear, and we should help them work with us better.

The advisory committee met once a year. Between meetings we talked with people. I worked with a leadership team. We tried to support researchers who had ideas that they wanted to get funded. In 1999 we got an anonymous donation to the Department of Horticulture of $50,000 to support organic agriculture activity. We made the decision that we would issue a call for proposals across the campus for anything related to organic agriculture with the stipulation that you'd have to partner with somebody in the field. Those stupid little grants did more to get a new group of people involved than anything else we'd ever done. It did more than having an advisory council. The growers saw it, too. Once we got grants submitted, the growers volunteered and were enthused about being on the review panel. They volunteered their farms as research sites. The partnerships started to emerge.

The Organic Advisory Council helped develop projects. Growers had observed what they believed to be lower pest pressure on their organic farms compared to conventional farms. I'm now part of a research team that's trying to verify this observation. We're doing an intensive survey of five conventional and five organic farms. We're looking at all aspects of the farm system—soil quality, organic matter, insects and pests, field boundaries, and the yield and quality of two crops. We have research plots on the farms. Our goal is to design testable hypotheses for disciplinary sciences. It's a groovy role for me, as a statewide specialist for fresh market production. It means that I'm investigating a farm system to generate a series of questions that I can ask my plant pathologist to figure out instead of having to figure it out myself. I can help direct their work more specifically.

In the middle of all this, I was doing work to develop a sense and respect for and collegiality with growers. My conversations were about listening. Some of them just want to be heard, and they would go off on stuff. Organic growers are not afraid to throw punches; I've taken a lot from them. I've developed a thick skin. I'll take them for Cornell if I have to. I'll say, "Remember, we do biotechnology here. No matter what you say that will never change. So you can either focus on the fact that we do that, or you can focus on those of us who are trying to understand how your system works. The choice is yours." I really tried to engage them in more productive dialogue.

By '98 or '99, we started to develop a concept we called the Northeast Organic Network (NEON). The Cornell Organic Advisory Council helped set up the vision for it. In 2000, we submitted a proposal to organize NEON to USDA, but it wasn't funded. It did, however, provide important connections to individuals outside of Cornell. In 2001 we applied again, and this time we were funded. I'm the principal investigator (PI).

No one thought NEON could happen. What it represents is a chance to demonstrate a whole new model of doing Extension with nonprofits engaged in organic agriculture. My goal is to demonstrate an extension and research program for organic agriculture that does not exist within institutional boundaries, that harnesses the best resources in the region and takes advantage of the indigenous knowledge that we already have among organizations that work with farmers. We have people who do different things as equals. I want to be able to take that at the end of two years and present it to all the deans and directors of all the land-grants in the Northeast and say, "Support us, this is a worthwhile endeavor."

We have $1.2 million from USDA for a two-and-a-half-year project. We had asked for $4.5 million. When they offered us less, we thought, "We'll take what you give us." We're still doing almost everything we said we would. The money is going towards labor. We have three regional coordinators based at nonprofits. We're supporting a senior research associate in Cornell's Department of Crop and Soil Sciences with a long history of doing interesting work with weeds. We're also hiring a project coordinator/director who will work day to day with me as well as help achieve this giant mission to organize a feasible network.

The actual NEON core team is probably twelve people. There are three nonprofits, and they have three staff people, so that would be six all together. There are six faculty members at three different institutions: the University of Maine, the Connecticut Agricultural Experiment Station, and Cornell. We tried to pick people who are already involved and help build that network. The other thing about NEON is that almost all of us are nontenured faculty. We're idiots for doing this, but we're all committed to it.

I don't think anyone else at Cornell could have pulled it off. In fact, it was our CALS research office that really encouraged me to pursue this type of large regional project. I had relationships that I brought with me which helped put NEON together. While we're involving research faculty in NEON, I've often had to take the role where I tell them they're out of line by saying, "I'm sorry, that's not relevant to this project," or "If you want to do that basic science, you'll have to do it elsewhere." Otherwise, it would be easy for people to be driven by only academic agendas.

NEON has two functional objectives or outcomes to achieve. One is to design a network to look at the way land-grant universities communicate with community organizations and how those organizations perceive us, even among this group that already supports organic. There are ways of thinking that become barriers to collaboration. As a group, we're all really equal. But, it's easy for Cornell to take all of the credit. My job becomes the trickiest in fostering an environment where all of us are valued in the same way, and all of our voices are heard. So one objective is to demonstrate a network that would require minimal input to effectively serve organic agriculture in the Northeast.

The second objective is to examine the productivity and profitability of established organic farms in the Northeast. We're sitting on all these markets, yet these farms hit a ceiling of profitability based on their marketing structures. How can we help improve that bottom line and profitability after studying organic systems? There are marketing, enterprise, and farm-planning components that are closely related to our understanding of biological systems. We focus on soil management, insect management, and crop rotation planning as three integrating components, then tie each of those practices to economics. We hope to end up with a way to assess decision making on organic farms and create tools for other organic farmers. We're focused on established farms, not on farms that are transitioning. We think it's great if farmers transition, but this project is meant to enhance the profitability and the sustainability of established organic farms.

We did a really interesting exercise on designing an effective crop rotation, which is a fundamental management strategy to make an organic system work. We engaged a group of twelve expert farmers from the Northeast, nominated by their peers. They met for three days and designed the framework of a rotation planning tool. The gelling of the group was interesting, the way that they talked to each other, the way they took ownership of this thing, the way they struggled with it. What these organic farmers did was to pull together and build on each other. They shared with each other how they manage rotations on their farms. They stuck with it. At the end of it they said, "Give us a manual and then we'll take it on the road. We'll teach it." I'm hoping to learn from this ways to engage conventional farmers in a more empowered approach to learning. Conventional farmers still use Cooperative Extension, journal articles, and newsletters. They've had the ear of land-grants for so long, it's a comfortable, but not necessarily "action-oriented" relationship.

In NEON, I'll be doing in-depth survey work with soils and crop productivity, and I'll be just one of a group of researchers. I'll also have a technician trying to understand how these systems work. My other role is the project leader. I've hired an evaluator who's familiar with agriculture. She's done evaluation work for the Kellogg Foundation and other groups. A colleague asked, "Why are you spending that much money on evaluation?" And I said, "What's the point of doing this if we don't learn how to do it better?" What is it that I do or say from within this very well-endowed institution that makes it harder for a nonprofit to be heard? We live in a bubble that affects the way we relate to people. I know I'll have a real hard time arguing my approach, but I'll do my best. I'm just thinking about the sense of desperation in agriculture as a whole. We just can't keep doing it the same way.

Facilitator is the word I would use to describe my role in how this thing happened, but that's not in my job description, which is part of my struggle. I keep my research component completely separate from this stuff, because the organizing I do in the grower community requires a whole different set of skills. This is all in my face right now because I don't fit the mold that I think this university wants for faculty. But I'm doing what I really believe in, which I think is going to have more meaning for change in the long run. As part of the process, what I end up understanding is how people learn and the ways you can shape that environment. It means I don't generate a whole bunch of publications on some miniscule thing that goes in a journal and sits on a shelf. This is what Cornell wants, and I've always known that. I've always been a rebel who's not willing to conform.

NEON is about doing systems research. But it's also about conflict resolution and problem solving to harness diversity. There's a power in people who think differently. I want to publish what I learn about *how* we learn. I don't want to publish *what* we learned. I'm more interested in the bigger piece. I am, more than anything, a magnifying glass. I'm scrutinizing every relationship or interaction that happens to try and get a better sense of how we're growing into a brain trust.

I'm in the process of submitting my reappointment package, and a lot of what I've been doing doesn't really fit the institution's expectations. I don't publish in a thousand journals. Nothing has been published yet from the work that I'm most interested in, because it's all been discovery. I'm still in the process of discovering. NEON is just starting. We're finally at the place where we're doing systems research. What I learn in working on organic systems I'll be able to translate and manipulate to enhance the long-term sustainability of conventional systems. That's the core of it. I've only done one experiment on organic farms. I did fifty on conventional farms. I am by no means turning my back on the people I work with, but I see this as a great opportunity to learn from organic systems.

I feel like I'm in the driver's seat of something big that I can sink my teeth into now. Yet not everything has worked from either an organizing or a research perspective. I separate the two in my mind. I've tried to do too many things in both senses. On the organizing side, I've been trying to balance these multiple roles. I'd like to clear my plate and focus. I have enough people to do the work from day to day. I'm finally going to be in the role of driving versus scrambling all the time. When you're scrambling you don't have the moments for reflection that you need to feel like you've made meaningful change. Everything's about, "Okay, I've got this down, I'll put it aside . . . Now where was I?" It's been this sense of panic that I don't know what it is that the institution wants me to do, so I feel I've got to do everything because I don't know who's looking at me.

In terms of my reappointment, the main message I get from Cornell is that I haven't published enough. I get that over and over again. I can't change that now. That's what I've done. It ends up making me feel that all I have done has no weight or value. It's made me consider long and hard about what I will do if I don't get reappointed. It's really made me open up my mind to that, because I do believe in what I do here. I just hope that the perception of what I do is something that fits this mission. I have a 60 percent Extension, 40 percent research split. That's a tough one because people say that means 100 percent of both. It feels like a hazing process, and part of me rebels. As a child I had to deal with a whole lot of racism, and so I partly react from a place that's a bit more rebellious when I am asked to conform to rules or fit a mold instead of being encouraged to create my own path. I celebrate diversity, in person and approach. I don't feel like this place cherishes or cultivates these differences as assets. There is no way in this system to evaluate and reward someone like me. So I rebel against it, maybe because I'm not white and have never belonged anywhere I've been, maybe because I'm a woman in a male-dominated field. I know fully what I was supposed to do. I didn't do it. So I've been eating my own cake, I guess.

I don't think of myself as a scholar. I've never considered myself a scholar. I don't think that will ever be part of my language. I don't think I'm wired that way. I didn't commit to this job or this field to become a scholar. *Scholar* to me speaks of ivory tower; it speaks of separation. It doesn't speak at all of what I want to do. I'm an *educator*. I consider myself an educator, 100 percent. I don't want to aspire to be a scholar. It's not a word that I care for. I guess I should because I'm supposed to be doing that here at Cornell, but on a personal level I find it distancing. It places you on the outside of what you work on.

As an educator, I'm trying to help people change by creating knowledge for change. Robert Chambers talked about theorists versus practitioners. I was really struck by that. I felt, "Okay, I know where I fit!" Yet I walk this line where I have to flip-flop between sides. My Ph.D. was embedded in a new science which wasn't established. I wasn't part of a bigger lab group that was pushing the boundaries. I was doing something no one had ever done before—alone. One thing I wanted to do when I first started here, but didn't, was to create a mentor group composed of growers. I would look to them, instead of my academic colleagues, for guidance—especially since my position is focused on integrating Extension and research. I didn't do it because it wasn't part of the common practice. Instead, I put together a mentoring committee of faculty. They know how to survive the system, but they don't necessarily give you a sense of meaning.

I think a lot about the land-grant mission. I often check myself against what I perceive that to be. For me, the mission means working with groups that have been underrepresented in the traditional educational scheme. Cornell hasn't made itself democratic and widely available with respect to organic growers. The land-grant system as a whole hasn't done that. What I envision will happen if I get reappointed is that I'll become the poster child for Cornell's Organic Program. It's already happened. I got a letter from a person who wrote to the governor, who then gave the letter to the commissioner of agriculture. It said, "Talk to Anu." Suddenly there's somebody at Cornell that this group can talk to. I'm glad to serve that role, but it has to have meaning; it has to function.

On a personal level, I'm still insecure with my role at Cornell. I'm motivated often to do things that I shouldn't do. This insecurity means I continue to put myself out there for everyone. I'm being unreasonable in attending to needs rather than being willing to make the hard decisions to not do something, such as, "I really appreciate that you're struggling with this, but I can't help you on it." I have an unwillingness to compromise those things when I need to. My worry about reappointment is tied to people who do not necessarily value extension work. As much as they want to, they have a concept of what they think Cornell should be, and it's more Ivy League than I ever care to be.

My colleagues and everyone I've met give me hope, though. There are people in this department that I hope I can be like when I grow up. There are people that have the love and respect of the group of farmers they support. I hope that I can have that some day, that same kind of relationship where everyone calls me by my first name (they can't pronounce the last!). I hope to have a sense of communion where you can be at Cornell but still be in partnership with growers. In this department, we do it. I don't know if we get recognized for it, but I feel like we express the land-grant mission more clearly than most of the departments on this campus. People talk about Cornell being disconnected from farmers, but our department doesn't feel that way.

Part Two

Interview conducted by Allison Jack, March 3, 2005

The 2002 interview with Scott rocked me a little bit. When Scott asked me during the previous interview if I considered myself a scholar, he couldn't believe I said, "No, not at all, I consider myself 100 percent an educator." He said, "What do you mean 'no'?" It's because I didn't have the language to think about what I do. But I do now. I think I'm a scholar and an expert with what I do. The Organic Advisory Council meeting the other day was an example. It went so well! I've learned to appreciate that there are other models of leadership and thinking about development, action, and change. I don't know about the theory, and I don't care about the theory. Maybe that's the problem.

I always associate being a scholar with being theoretical, but the truth is there are scholarly practitioners and scholarly theorists. I'm the practitioner who can tell you the how, but not necessarily always the why in terms of why it works. I know intuitively that it does. Scott interviewing me made me reflect. Our challenge is putting the language and the value system around being an educator and a scholar at the same time. Forget pay. I don't think that we've built the capacity to be able to reward people on a personal level for good work. It's one of our downfalls at the university, having such a hierarchical system. It doesn't allow creative leadership or creativity to emerge. It can happen, but it's harder.

In the 2002 interview, I had said that I was looking forward to being in the driver's seat of the NEON project because I wouldn't have to be scrambling around all the time and I would have more time for reflection. It didn't happen! I was still overextended all the time. NEON was supposed to be 25 percent of my time. I wasn't paid by it, but I had said I would devote that much time to it. At the beginning of the project, I did. Here's an interesting place where things intersected. I had to put together my reappointment packet in the midst of NEON. At the very beginning of the project, I was really engaged and did a lot of team-building work. We were all working together. Then I had to step back to do the packet. That pulled me away from NEON, but things went on. The summer came and it got a little crazy because I had not stepped down from my field program to make more time to devote to NEON

I ended up being reappointed, but during the process I got some very negative feedback. When that happened, I lost interest in my work. It took me a while personally to recover. I lost interest in everything I did. I had to resolve issues of shame and disappointment and of a sense loss about my future. What did this mean for me as a person? We all wrap ourselves into our jobs in a way that is so profound. I didn't realize how much of my job I had tied to who I am and my meaning in the world. It took a lot to disentangle that. In many ways I'm more of an adult, of a mature person as a result of the reappointment experience, because it helped me realize this is just a job. My life is very full. The casualty in some ways was NEON, because I became disengaged in everything. The group understood what was going down. The project is over now, and the end of the story is that there are a lot of good things coming out of it anyway.

The whole issue of being in the driver's seat did change for me during the grant. I wanted NEON to have shared leadership, but that ended up frustrating some of the members. They wanted a strong leader, someone who's setting deadlines. But I felt that if this is to serve organic agriculture, our power and our sense of control has to be decentralized. I felt that way, but didn't articulate it. We didn't have an agreement. We could have had discussions around it. They all still deferred to me as the leader, but I was comfortable with the ambiguity and tension. They weren't. I would say, "Let's wrestle with this, let this float. We don't have to say, 'This is the way it is.'" Some got critical of me on parts of the project. They thought I wasn't strong enough in my leadership. Others said, "It's just the nurturing and caring way you move this project that has made it so successful." Others said, "This could have done so much more if you had only pushed it harder."

Through the whole NEON project I came to appreciate my skills as a facilitator. I have a better sense of how to read people's personalities and relationships, and the differing abilities of people to develop trust. I wish I had these skills at the start of NEON. For example, there were bristly personalities I had to manage throughout the project, to not totally derail the group. I would step in and try to bring the group back together. Particular individuals always wanted to suggest that "the land-grants are bad." I had a history with some of these individuals, and valued their brilliance and vision. Maybe it was a bad decision, because it wasn't always helpful to the group. But I stuck with it. Towards the end of NEON, others took on leadership roles and wrote a grant to try to get us additional funding for the next phase, but were not successful. I thought a change of leadership was a way to deal with ownership. I have no need to be the person in charge. I just happened to be the one who knew everyone when we wrote the proposal for NEON.

I recently attended a leadership training in California that really expanded my thinking on group dynamics. Whenever something new comes at us, we can either respond with wonder or by freaking out. When you're in that defensive position, it's called "the grip." You have to be able to recognize when you're in the grip when you're in a team. One NEON member brought some experience to the table and made suggestions early on that we didn't hear. If we'd listened harder, we would have learned some important lessons. She suggested things like partnership agreements on how we make decisions and resolve conflict. We thought, "I don't know why you think that's a big deal." But it was a big deal. All of us from the land-grant universities said, "We're not getting into bed together. We're just trying to do a freaking project!" It was really the issue around the mind-set of your institution. In a nonprofit, everything is about partnership and developing collaborative agreements. In the land-grant university, it's about being an individual. Collaborative agreements in the university environment are mostly about your personal responsibility for your individual piece of the pie. You don't worry about writing down these other things. You don't commit to open, honest, trust-building activity and communication. This touchy-feely stuff that we all make fun of is the meat of making successful collaborations. Looking back, that NEON member we didn't listen to was right.

In the 2002 interview I mentioned that some organic growers have trouble getting past Cornell "the institution." One grower put forth great ideas at an Organic Advisory Council meeting, but it was still like throwing arrows instead of saying, "How can we do this together?" It's all in the delivery. Some people are good at delivery. There's the issue of how the group functions and how you go forward. This grower had been to the group in the past and then hadn't attended for a long time. He then came forward with a research proposal. He sent his vision electronically and said, "I still think that Cornell is not going to be willing to do this." I wrote him back and said, "Just like farmers who have limited resources, so do the people who work in this institution. What you ask would take a whole lot of energy, and a lot of personal, professional, monetary, and creative resources." I think farmers don't understand that this institution is a herd of cats, not a herd of cows. We don't walk in the same line and head to the milk house. We go everywhere. He assumes that we have a *single* mission, but that is not who we are. There are individuals who might take up that mission, but we're not a nonprofit with a single mission or a clear set of areas where we have competitive strength. *We are a collection of missions*, and that's the hard part for growers to understand.

Over the course of NEON, I saw some growers change their idea of what Cornell is as a land-grant and what it could be. The amount of enthusiasm, trust, and energy coming from the growers who were involved is different. They were pleased, excited, and ready to lobby. I have a call list. They're ready to go to bat for anything. It's just a small group of twenty-three farmers that we had a lot of interaction with. It grows from there. Conventional farmers tend to go to Extension and get what they need. There's a history. There's always this issue of science-based information and what we can extend. With conventional agriculture it's easy to extend fertilizer and pesticide recommendations. They're bullets; you're extending bullets. I can give you the bullet and you can apply it. It's different with organic growers. We're not trained to do systems-type recommendations or a systems analysis with organic growers. I'm simplifying it grossly because there are systems components in conventional agriculture, but most of the time, it's those bullet type of interventions that farmers are looking for.

The emphasis on the systems-based approach is definitely compatible with and applicable to conventional systems. We're seeing that with nutrient management on organic farms, and the emergence of certain nutrient balances on soils that are well managed. That's intriguing. Organic growers are leading the way when we look at soil quality and measures of biological activity and tilth. We see this on 1,500-acre organic farms that don't use a lot of compost and other added amendments. They are doing specific crop rotations. So it can't be "us versus them." It's got to be us learning from each other. What makes me unique to people before me in this position is that I don't draw a line between the two. I see organic and conventional approaches as two ways of operating. You can have whatever philosophy you want, I don't care. The bottom line of my job is to help you be more successful. We have to learn from each other and work together. Size and scale shouldn't matter. Management matters. How are we tending the resources that have been given to us? It's soil and water and quality of life.

What has been really interesting the last couple of years is that conventional vegetable growers have been grumbling that all of the Cornell staff are working on organic. They're saying, "Everyone at Cornell is talking about organic and small farms." But "everyone" is basically just me! It's about a balance of resources in my mind. Organic farms represent not even 1 percent of the acreage in New York, and not even 1 percent of the growers. So why put so much energy into it? If I were willing to represent just the majority of New York's production as a statewide specialist, then I would be working with fresh market cabbage, onions, and sweet corn. That's where the volume is; that's where the industry is. Yet I think what

305

organic systems have to offer will have more impact on conventional farming than anything I could do relative to fertilizers, pesticides, and cultivar choice.

In the last year the "us versus them" mentality has changed a little, because I think that conventional growers are looking at organic as a marketing opportunity. It's not a challenge to their way of life; it's an opportunity. We have wholesale-processing growers now looking at organic. Last year, there were five different conventional growers that each put in 100 acres of organic vegetables. Before that our largest organic farm was 100 acres. Suddenly, in one week, you have five people doing that much. These are really good conventional farmers, real leaders. We also have stronger grower leadership in organic where people are talking production agriculture. You meet people with language in a common place. Common language around how we grow stuff makes everyone jibe. People are in this because they love to be working the land. From there you can start to talk about bigger and bigger things. But, that's where you start: with growing.

NEON's role in all this is indirect. It will be more apparent in two years because we're coming out with tools that will leverage this change. One piece is the summary of pest management products and strategies by crop. That's an incredible piece of work that is going to lay open how you deal with the most challenging insect and disease problems on organic vegetable crops. As soon as people start to read this and get a sense of it, they're going to say, "OK, this is not as threatening as I thought it was." Another piece is on crop rotation planning, what rotational sequences you need to think about and for what reason. That piece will be good for any system, but it's most important in organic. Finally, we have a case study piece that lays out the intersection across weeds, pests, insects, disease, yield, and community. How do exemplary organic farms function? We studied really mature farms. Farmers shared with us how they think and work in organic and how they have been leaders in the development of the industry. Those stories will help people put it all together. I think in two years, we'll start to see the effects of NEON.

NEON has played a role in the maturation of organic growers as part of a research community. We brought all the right people together in the same room and had what I've come to call "crucial conversations." I've learned that term, it's not my term. They're conversations that lay things open and are sometimes difficult. We had some conversations about the future of organic in the Northeast, and the future of wholesale, and the fact that globalization is going to kill it. What does it mean for these people in this room? How do we respond? How similar is this story to every conventional farmer who has ever lived here? Then suddenly the line starts to disappear, because you're dealing with these larger social forces that you don't have control over. The conversations blurred the lines and made this group realize they have power. They can help other people in decision making, and they have skills that they need to use and teach to keep this industry alive. They recognized some shared responsibility for the next generation.

In NEON, we asked farmers hard questions. I would poke. We all did. We said, "What do you mean by that?" We even poked at the question, "What does it mean to be an excellent organic farmer?" It was difficult for farmers to wrap their heads around that. It's the sense of management, holism, right livelihood. These are all pieces that implicate values that are close to the core. It's a part of the dilemma with the growth of organic: "Can we maintain these values and have the industry expand?" It challenges their identities. Before, they could afford to be "us versus them." They can't afford that now, not with Whole Foods, not with Wegman's, not with California. It was an easy group to ask the difficult questions. They knew each other. They were the old-timers. They're the ones that were doing organic twenty years ago. They have a long history. NEON could not be replicated easily with another group of people. We had a really special group.

The farmers absolutely would not have had these conversations if it weren't for NEON. They wouldn't have taken the time. They would've been in social environments or having fun, but they wouldn't be asked to deal with questions like "What are the things that are constraining your success? What are the things that worry you? What needs to happen next?" Those are the kinds of conversations they need to have more of, and that's what they enjoyed. They also came to appreciate how messy research is. They would see how we would talk about something and say, "We don't know how to do this!" Systems research? We bat this word around like it means something! Try to put it on the ground and do it! *You* try to publish that data and stay at a university! Nobody gets it. What does it mean?

Our nonprofit partners watched us struggle with the question "How do we want to do this big study?" They realized that organic research is an evolutionary process, and that decisions are made along the way, all the time, that affect the final product. If we'd had more time and money, we could have done more. We did the rotation piece well. The nutrient budgeting piece has provided one of the biggest learning moments that happened in NEON.

A researcher challenged farmers to think about what they are doing, and they didn't like it, which is part of resistance to change. The grower attitude has been, "We're doing the right thing. *We're* the ones on the moral high ground. You can't tell me that plowing in too much vetch is going to cause a nitrogen problem." That piece was captured in a set of case studies we wrote. We would say, "Look, every year you're adding x tons of compost like you're taking a prescription drug. Why are you doing that? How's that different than a conventional mindset?" That's an example of the great conversations we would have. The growers would say, "Yikes, that's not what my intention was!" But in the flurry of everything, they didn't think about it. When people read the cases we wrote, it forces them to step back and consider why and how they do what they do. Research questions emerge out of this. Our goal was to generate a series of testable hypotheses. We summarized quite a few research questions that we generated in different ways.

We engaged farmers in different ways with some really interesting methods. I defended these methods even though nobody else from universities in the project believed in them. For example, one nonprofit proposed a participatory method that I knew could be quite powerful. Others said, "This sounds really dumb, and I can't believe we're going to spend all this money on it." But I said, "No, this puts farmers front and center. They have to resolve the problems and tell us in detail what it is they do, how they do it, and why they do it. It will end up creating more accurate information for us to build upon." The focus was on how organic farmers plan crop rotations. The process is called DACUM: Develop a Curriculum. It's being pioneered out of Ohio State. It's a way of modeling expertise. It's traditionally used to deal with developing curriculum. For example, how would you create a curriculum for horticulture students? You would interview some successful horticulturists. They would say, "These are the skills I need to do my job, these are the tasks I have to do, and these are the duties within those tasks." Usually DACUM is used to describe management decisions in more controlled environments: for example, managing a type of business or a nuclear reactor. We applied it—for the first time—to managing a biological system. We asked farmers: How do you use your skills, observations, and knowledge to make the right decision, and to adjust the decision to optimize an organic crop rotation?

We used a nomination process to identify our expert farmers from across the region. Sixty-three people's names came in. We whittled it down to twenty-four and looked for diversity. The challenge we had was finding women. We only found one. But we did get people from several different states, all vegetable growers. We flew them in to a farmer's great big old house, who agreed to host us. It was twelve farmers, three facilitators, and three researchers—me and two others. As part of the process, the researchers couldn't say anything, because we weren't the experts. We were strictly flies on the wall. We put these twelve growers in a room, and basically put their brains through the machine and extracted information, through a highly facilitated process.

The document that summarized the process was titled "Manage Crop Rotations." If you open it to the centerfold, the growers came up with the key tasks in doing a rotation, and within that, how it is done. The goal was to provide enough detail so that someone else could evaluate their own organic crop rotation and improve it. They fleshed out rotation goals that were important in organic farming. How do they classify crops? How do you look at the field and adapt your cropping plan to the field characteristics? One thing that came up is how important where the barn is relative to how they plan rotations. I had never even thought about that! You put crops that you need to get to the barn quickly close to the barn. All this knowledge was captured through this process in three days! What was remarkable about it was how we were able to do it. It includes examples of incredibly complicated four-year, seven-year, and eight-year rotations. Our goal was to clarify how farmers manage their systems of rotation in order for researchers to ask more accurate questions. While it was designed for researchers, now farmers want it.

The document was agreed upon through a democratic process. If something bothered them, they talked about why. There was a certain amount of tension and creative energy around it. They argued over everything. They had to have consensus about the order and the words and the terms that were used. If they didn't agree, they'd have to say, "That's OK, I accept it" before the group moved on. We would go 8:00 am to 10:00 pm, all day, with awesome food breaks. They would hang out. It was a great community. They got to be close to each other and to us. I would every now and then ask a question, because someone would allude to something, and then they'd pass over it. I would want to make sure that they got back to it, because it was good. By the end of their time together, the twelve growers were saying, "Oh my God, this is incredible!" They'd never been put into a place where they were asked to think so hard and learn from each other.

The success of this method has changed the minds of some of the people who pooh-poohed it. There was resistance at the beginning. Even some of the nonprofits thought it was dumb. They didn't want to do it. They said, "I hate this expert systems stuff!" Now they're like, "Wow, DACUM! We want to do it for *this*, and we want to do it for *that*." Others asked, "Why do we have to do it like this. Can't we just do focus groups?" But I knew we needed more than a focus group to create a framework from which we could hang research. *This grounds our research in reality.* If a systems approach is what we are advocating in NEON, it's essential to ask the right questions. This process helped us understand the system. The growers have a lot of ownership of this document. They took it on the road. Growers did public presentations with the collaborators on the project in a variety of venues. They shared the information. At the final evaluation they said, "I don't care what Anu does, but she's gotta get this out. Forget about solving the rest of it, she's gotta get this out! It would be such a shame if we did this piece of work and it got lost. It happens so often. Don't let it happen!" They were moved by it and grateful that we asked.

The success of the DACUM process was a big contrast to another piece of NEON, where we developed case studies of exemplary organic farms. Instead of having the farmers get together and do something intensive, like DACUM, they were isolated. We interacted with them individually. When we put the DACUM and case study farmers in the same room together, there was an incredible difference! The farmers from DACUM were together, saying, "Come on, let's go! Change can happen!" They were ready for action. They had an *ethic*. The other farmers, the case study farmers, were saying, "OK, so what is this about?" For me it was a big lesson about how we affected their engagement. If you're going to do anything with farmers, the first thing you do is you make them work really hard to get them on board. It's not enough to just do a meeting. You ask—you *demand*—that they unload and tell you what they know on whatever topic. Do it! Because then they will understand the value of the team. They come forward and they stay engaged.

I don't know many other people who could have run the NEON project. It was a diverse herd of people. Everyone has told me, "Anu, there was no one else on this team that could have led it." There are times when I shift into the role of the expert talking to farmers. They look to me for that, saying, "What do you think?" I'll go there, but I certainly don't walk through the world with that assumption. I take the role of facilitator, and then I will step outside of that role to be an expert. I quickly return because of the importance of being a facilitator, the one who's helping lead through the subtleties. The trick in a university position is knowing when and how you walk back and forth. I don't know anyone else here who could have done it in our college.

I serve as the director of Cornell's Small Farms Program, and I've been hosting trainings on facilitation skills. Agricultural extension workers need training in facilitation. One of the key pieces of work we're doing is helping our extension educators build farmer discussion groups. Our hidden agenda is developing leadership by having farmers engage and value each other. We let leadership emerge. I hire professional facilitators to provide the training, but I have a very heavy hand in the design of the day. I say, "These are the things we have to cover and this is the process I want you to use. I want to do a maximum of forty minutes of lecture and then I want forty minutes of practice time where these educators are using these skills." The educators get so much out of it. They're engaged all of the way through it.

If you ask me how I learned to do facilitation, I'd say maybe it was a way of coping with the sense that I wasn't the academic others thought I should be. I'm going very personal here.

Maybe it was coping with a need to have relationships with people I don't understand and who don't understand me. I don't look the part here; I'm not the white man. I'm in a role that is not common for an Indian woman. Some of it is a survival skill. I just read a paper about sharing leadership from a feminist perspective and how this process is scholarly. It blew my socks off. It argues for the need to use this type of model for democratic processes, for making really fundamental change to how we value and grow.

When I was in college I started out in premed and I quit and went to work in a greenhouse. My family struggled. When I went back to school in horticulture, I was so happy to be working with plants. That's when I started to emerge as a bit of a joker. I felt my spirit was freed. I had finally let go of this shackle of feeling, as an Indian person, that I had to be an engineer or a doctor. During my Ph.D. work, I came to value that everyone is an expert in the place that they are. The arrogance of the academy, thinking it knows better, is why we aren't as effective as we could be. I trusted that everyone's an expert, and for me, that was the truth. It set a limit on the things I was willing to do as far as science. I was not going to go molecular. I wanted to be at the interface of how people manage their environment. In my position, I struggled when I felt I had to have agendas and get people together to achieve goals. That was a real kicker coming here and doing "expert" extension presentations.

It was in working with the organic community that I developed my skills. I knew you couldn't use the same approach. The nature of trying to effect change in the organic community affected me. I look at it like a big water balloon. When I push on it here, it goes "blob" around me. OK, what does that mean? It's all reflective. Everything you do pushes back at you. So I back up and push over here and see what happens.

I do all these talks and extension presentations where I'm the talking head. I can do them really well, but they always feel a bit flat. Who cares how to grow pumpkins of a certain variety? I hate to say that; it's important, but at the same time, what difference is it going to make in ten years? My work with the organic community is about laying out a longer-term vision.

Facilitation gives me an opportunity to interact with people and involve people in a different way. Beyond that, I've been looking, learning, and watching. I'm doing this training for agricultural professionals in Extension, from the Natural Resources Conservation Service (NRCS) and from the university. There are twenty-two people, and it's funded by SARE. We have three sets of intensive four-day workshops. Our goal is to give them the basics of how you deal with organic agriculture. My hidden agenda (I always have a hidden agenda) is to build a cadre of people who keep each other going, who support organic agriculture. We need support. By them knowing each other and colleagues around the region in their own states who also think and learn and have struggled in the same way, they will be more successful in sustaining a northeast effort. That's my agenda. I want some new people on board.

I have a new grant. I'm excited about it because it's with some economists and sociologists. The goal of the project is to examine the possibility of using an economic model called "cluster analysis" to enhance the sustainability and viability of small farms. We hope to figure out how and where we as educators and researchers can work with groups of farmers more effectively, instead of simply with individual farmers. You want to develop cohesion in the group, so their success is dependent on all of their success as opposed to an individual pitted against another individual. I prefer the whole. We want to create competitive cooperation, not cooperative competitiveness. They don't have to be a cooperative. They don't have to sign any documents. I want them to cooperate enough to keep each other excited, but competitive enough that they continue to innovate and evolve. We're going to ask questions relative to developing an identifiable cluster of farms and businesses. What can we learn about how they organize themselves? Is it based upon location, commodity (like apples), or social identity (like women or ethnic minorities)? What happens when you engage these different groups of people? How do they think and develop as a cluster? I'm looking forward to trying to do it. I'm not the lead. It will be interesting to go and foray there because it will force more thinking in this area of what does it really mean to create long-term change.

In the 2002 interview, I said that I wanted to bring the finished NEON project to the dean in my college and to the deans at other land-grant institutions as an alternative model of Extension. After the painful reappointment experience I had, I have to say that it isn't that important to me to affect the system any more. I had big visions. I was really ready to put on a suit and have conversations with deans at land-grant institutions, some of whom had already come to me saying, "What can we do with this NEON thing to really help us get our act together?" It could still happen. We can lead by example.

Recently the dean of my college sent out a letter requesting stakeholders to contact the their state representatives because of cuts to the SUNY system in the governor's budget. In the letter she wrote, "There are all of these important applied research and extension programs." Then she had a bulleted list, including Dairy, Horticulture, and "Small Farms and Organics." I said, "That's me! I've got my own bullet!"

Now, I think if my job is lost here, it wouldn't be a bad thing. I used to think there was nothing else I could do. Now I think, "Hell, I would play my accordion and farm, and be every bit as happy." That's where we fail our students, and we fail in our way of looking at our world. The work that we do has to be nested in a real healthy lifestyle and outlook. I'm not saying I'm there! I'm not making any claims about how I live, because I think I'm still pretty screwed up with the things I do. I take on too much and am not able to finish it all. We used to value downtime. Other cultures value it. I don't know why we don't. We're the richest country in the world! If there's anyone that has idleness as a luxury, it's us! Yet we don't bring that into the way we live, and being idle is so important! Conversation, reflection, time to chat, the sense of a place, being personable—all those things are important, too.

In my position here at Cornell, I have the ability to do and make a kind of change that I wouldn't be able to do in other positions. I have so many resources at my disposal here! I can get a car and go anywhere I want, anytime! I was recruited and had the opportunity to apply to three other positions since I started here. I didn't go because New York's a big state. I'm grooving on the fact that there is real agriculture here. Other institutions never struck me as being as intense. That's what this place offers. You've got this intense community and industry of agriculture. You've got people here who are incredible at what they do. You don't have to know the answers, but you do have to be comfortable with that sense of mystery and relish it.

PART 3

Learning from Profiles and Practice Stories

Lessons

The practitioner profiles published in part 2 of this book are highly complex texts. They include views and opinions about a wide range of issues. Much more importantly, they are richly and densely storied. They include life stories, practice stories, and larger institutional and cultural stories. Some of these stories are relatively long and detailed, while others are quite brief and sketchy.

In reading these profiles, we're faced with the dual challenge of figuring out not only *what* but also *how* we might learn from them. How are we to interpret, analyze, and make sense of the views and stories they contain? What lessons should we draw from them?

Instead of answering these questions on our own, we would prefer to pull up some chairs and pursue them with a circle of readers. Our preference isn't an indication of our laziness as interpreters and analysts. Rather, it's an indication of our judgment that the best way to learn from practitioner profiles is with others, in collective, face-to-face discussion and reflection. There are two main reasons why this is so. First, by their very nature as storied texts profiles are open to many different interpretations. Each reader will read them differently, depending on her or his standpoint, worldview, values, biases, interests, experience, theoretical lens, and analytical tools and skills. Given this reality, when individuals interpret profiles by themselves, they are likely to miss a great deal of what can be discovered in them. Second, the collective experience of interpreting practitioners' stories of their work and life experiences can be powerful and transformative on several levels. It can help to illuminate previously obscured avenues of thought and action. It can provoke an open discussion of people's self-interests, motivations, purposes, values, ideals, and commitments. And it can help to build or strengthen public relationships among people who hope to be or already are working together.

Setting aside our preference for collective reflection and discussion, in this chapter we offer our own interpretation of the profiles in this book. We present what we have learned from them as lessons that challenge and enlarge our understanding of the nature, meaning, significance, and value of higher education's public purposes and work, in and for a democratic society. Our aim in this chapter—and in this book as a whole—is to contribute to a new thread in the conversation about the public purposes and work question in American higher education. In pursuing this aim, we shift the focus of attention away from normative traditions and types, and from theoretical debates about what academic professionals could, should, or should not do as participants in the public work of democracy. Instead, we focus on an appreciative interpretation of practice stories about what they already have done and are doing as they step off their campuses and become engaged in civic life.

Before we move on, we want to acknowledge that what we provide in this chapter is inescapably partial and selective. We don't attempt to conduct a full, fine-grained, micro-level analysis of any of the profiles in this book, let alone all of them. And instead of attempting to discuss all of the lessons we have learned from the profiles, we have chosen to focus only on what we see as some of the most important positive and instructive lessons. We have done this despite—and in seeming contradiction to—the suggestion we offered at the end of chapter 3, to read these profiles with a critical as well as appreciate eye.

There are two main reasons why we have chosen in this chapter to conduct an appreciative rather than critical reading of the profiles. First, the identities of the people we interviewed have not been hidden by the use of pseudonyms. These are real people who have granted us permission to publish deeply personal accounts of their life stories, and their public work and experiences. They have *entrusted* us with their stories. In doing so, they have given us an ethical obligation to treat them with respect. It is of course possible to be both respectful and critical at the same time. We have tried to do so in collective, face-to-face discussions we have had with those we profiled. We hope to do so again. But being critical here, when they can't answer us back, was something we were not willing to do.[1]

The second reason why we limit ourselves to the positive in this chapter is strategic. As we mentioned in the introduction, we have deliberately taken a prophetic, imaginative approach to our discussion of the public purposes and work question in American higher education. In reading the profiles, we therefore focus our analytical attention on positive, hopeful possibilities. This doesn't mean that there are no negative lessons to be drawn from the profiles, or that the practitioners we interviewed and profiled are beyond criticism. It's simply a reflection of our practical theory that there is a lot more going on in academic professionals' civic engagement work than many people presume, that much of it is positive, and that appreciative readings of stories of such work can inspire positive change at least as much as—or perhaps even more than—critical readings.[2]

There is one more thing we want to acknowledge here. All of the academic professionals who are profiled in this book are or were affiliated with a college that is part of a land-grant university—the College of Agriculture and Life Sciences at Cornell University. Land-grant colleges of agriculture have been widely celebrated as exemplars of the public service mission in American higher education. They have also been sharply criticized as being culturally, economically, and environmentally oppressive and destructive instruments of elite corporate interests. It is not our purpose in this chapter and book to celebrate or criticize these colleges. Rather, it is to illuminate and interpret positive dimensions of higher education's roles in the public work of democracy that we believe have all too often been glossed over or missed altogether.[3]

First, a Meta-Lesson

We begin with a meta-lesson, inspired by a brief passage from Frank Rossi's profile (chapter 12). Frank is a tenured associate professor in the Department of Horticulture at Cornell University who specializes in turfgrass science, a field that includes the study of the production and maintenance of grasses for recreational, aesthetic, and other uses. He tells us that he felt disillusioned when he was pursuing his Ph.D. "I was disillusioned with becoming an academic in the turf area," he recalls. "I think maybe deep down, I always felt like it really isn't that important. I'd like to contribute to society in a meaningful way, and can I do that with grass? Well, turned out I could."

There are two reasons why this passage is significant. First, it's surprising. It's surprising because it challenges our presumptions. Like Frank when he was pursuing his Ph.D., most people would likely presume that academic professionals in highly technical disciplines like turfgrass science not only don't but *can't* contribute to society in a meaningful way—specifically when "meaningful way" includes contributions to the public work of democracy. Frank's profile provokes us to rethink this presumption. It provokes us to imagine that people like him not only *can* contribute to the public work of democracy, but *already do*.

The second reason the brief passage is significant is because it compels us to look for stories. When Frank tells us that he learned that he *could* contribute to society in a meaningful way "with grass," we're not just surprised. We're curious. We're also a little skeptical. We want to know *how* he has contributed, and we want to see for ourselves whether—and if so, in what ways—his contributions can be interpreted as being meaningful. To find out, we could ask Frank for an explanation. We could ask him to give us his theory about how his contributions have been meaningful. But it would be much better if we were to ask him to give us an example. To see what he means when he says that it turned out that he *could* contribute to society in a meaningful way "with grass," we need more than an explanation or a theory that *tells* us how he contributes. We need an example that *shows* us. In short, we need a *story*.

We asked Frank and all of the other academic professionals who are profiled in this book for stories of their public work and experiences. With the brief passage from Frank's profile in mind, we draw a key meta-lesson from our reading of the stories they told us: *Academic professionals can make meaningful contributions to the public work of democracy with grass—or winter squash varieties (Molly Jahn), or gardens (Marcia Eames-Sheavly), or weeds (Antonio DiTommaso), or any number of ordinary things.*

This may seem like a small lesson, or one that goes without saying. But it's neither. It's huge, and it's not at all obvious. Rather than going without saying, it goes without being recognized, appreciated, or understood.

In conversations about higher education's public purposes and work, the spotlight is typically turned on scientists and engineers who construct and produce knowledge, theory, and/or technical innovations that can be used to cure diseases, create jobs, fight climate change, and the like. It's also often placed on faculty members in the humanities and social sciences who study social issues and then write and speak about them as experts and critics for general public audiences. Meanwhile, the civic engagement work of people like Frank Rossi, Molly Jahn, Tom Maloney, Marcia Eames-Sheavly, and all of the other academic professionals who are profiled in this book is routinely overlooked. When we ignore what people like them are doing as participants in civic life, however, we're missing a great deal of the action. The action we're missing isn't necessarily having a direct and immediate impact on the economy. It isn't playing out in the national media, on the national stage. It's playing out in everyday places—like golf courses, in Frank's case. And it's playing out in subtle ways that are cultural and political in nature, as academic professionals in fields that include but also reach well beyond the humanities and social sciences establish face-to-face relationships with their nonuniversity partners and engage with them in the public work of democracy.

There are several reasons why people like Frank are being overlooked in the conversation about higher education's public purposes and work. It's partly a reflection of the privileging of economics, social criticism, and responsive service in our understanding of what counts as a public purpose. It's partly a consequence of the presumptions people make about the work that academic professionals like Frank do. It's also a reflection of the prevailing view of democracy—of what it is, whom it involves, and when and where it's practiced. The prevailing view is that democracy is system of government: that it's a thing rather than an activity, something we *have* rather than something we *do*. When people do think of democracy as an activity, they mainly think of voting, volunteer community service, or political campaigns. They think of politicians, lobbyists, and special interest groups engaged in policymaking. They don't think of academic professionals in turfgrass science.[4]

We need to take a broader view of what democracy is and when, where, how, and by whom it's practiced if we are to understand the public purposes and work of academic professionals like Frank Rossi. We need to see democracy as a way of life—as a philosophy of social relations. We need to see it as public work that engages people in developing and exercising agency and power in everyday settings as they seek to understand and address technical and social problems, stand for and further key normative ideals and values, and deliberate about and take action to pursue their self-interests, their common interests, and larger public interests. And despite Stanley Fish's claim that democracy "is a political not an educational project," we need to see that it is both a political *and* an educational project, one that is being taken up by academic professionals like the ones who are profiled in this book.[5]

As President Truman's Commission on Higher Education declared, "The first and most essential charge upon higher education is that at all its levels and in all its fields of specialization it shall be the carrier of democratic values, ideals, and processes." It's quite likely that many people will view this charge as a feel-good platitude that wasn't meant to be taken seriously. But the profiles in this book help us to see that some academic professionals *have* taken it seriously. More importantly, they help us to see some of the ordinary, everyday ways and places it is being embraced and enacted. They enable us to see some of the dilemmas and challenges academic professionals face as they strive "to deploy technical expertise and judgment not only skillfully but also for public-regarding ends and in a public-regarding way."[6]

With our meta-lesson in mind, we divide the rest of the lessons we draw from our reading of the profiles into two sections. First, we name and discuss a set of lessons about the *nature* of higher education's public purposes and work. By "nature," we are referring to what such purposes are and how they are pursued. We then move on to identify a few key lessons about the *meaning, significance, and value* of higher education's public purposes and work: in other words, the ways and reasons such purposes and work matter.

Here we'd like to add a brief note about the methods we used in conducting our readings, analysis, and interpretations. We chose not to "code" the profiles, as scholars often do when they work with qualitative interview data. We also chose not to use any special software to organize our data, or to facilitate a process of "content analysis" or other technical analytical methods. Rather, following one of the key principles of narrative inquiry, we focused our attention on stories, without trying to segment them, categorize them, or isolate them from their larger context. In line with this approach, we focused our attention on reading and rereading each profile as one complete narrative, and on identifying and trying to make sense of the smaller stories we found in each profile. We wrote many notes from multiple readings of the profiles about what we found to be illuminating, troubling, or provocative, particularly with respect to the debate about higher education's public purposes and work. We looked across the profiles for patterns and for exceptions to patterns. And we chose not to try to force the academic professionals we interviewed into specific normative traditions and types.

To put all this more succinctly, our method was to read and reread the profiles many, many times to see what we might learn from them. We immersed ourselves in them for many months, coming back to them again and again to test earlier insights and lessons, always finding new ones in the process. Because our main interest was to illuminate and understand what academic professionals have done and experienced rather than what they believe or think, we attended closely to the action verbs we found in their stories. And as we have already noted, we approached our readings with an appreciative rather than critical eye. Our method, in short, was to read and listen closely and deeply to the stories those we interviewed told us, and to open our minds to learning from them.

Lessons about the Nature of Higher Education's Public Purposes and Work

In their profiles, the academic professionals we interviewed *story* their lives and work, and their contexts and situations. They narrate themselves and others as characters who act and react in purposeful ways. In doing so, they are not just telling stories and spouting their views and opinions. They are teaching us what their public purposes are, and what it takes and involves to pursue them with others in off-campus civic life.

Four Key Activities
Before trying to make sense of the public purposes these academic professionals speak of, we focus first on what we see them doing in the stories they told. In order to see them as

actors in their stories, as we read and reread the profiles we identified the action verbs they used. We asked ourselves the following questions: In their stories, what verbs do these academic professionals use to characterize their work and roles? In what ways and to what degree might we interpret the things we see them doing as being "public" in nature? We also asked ourselves another question: What verbs do these academic professionals use in characterizing the actions, work, and roles of the people they engage with?

Reading and rereading the profiles with these questions in mind, we found four main kinds of activities that are particularly public in nature:

- Going out and being present
- Becoming an insider
- Making "I" "we"
- Leapfrogging back and forth

These four kinds of work are not a linear sequence. Rather, they are a complicated set of simultaneous, looped, and overlapping activities. "It's all a big dance," Paula Horrigan says in her profile. As we have come to understand it, the dance is not always graceful. It can be awkward. It goes in fits and stops, sometimes over long periods of time. And while it's often productive in both a public and academic sense, it's also filled with dilemmas, ambiguities, and contradictions.

Before we move on, we want to note that most of the academic professionals we interviewed also speak about providing information, extending and applying knowledge and expertise, or transferring technologies. While we find these activities in nearly every profile, we don't include them among the four main kinds of work we see academic professionals doing their practice stories. By not including them, we're not implying that they're not important. We're simply focusing on other activities that are frequently overlooked, even though they are critically important components of academic professionals' civic engagement work.

Going Out and Being Present

"I have to find out what I should be doing," Marvin Pritts recalls saying to himself during his first year on the faculty at Cornell. Marvin is a professor in the Department of Horticulture who specializes in berry crops. Instead of only looking to his colleagues in his department for guidance, he asked community-based extension educators for their views (following a historical tradition, Marvin refers to them as "agents"). "What are some of the problems out there?" he remembers asking them at a campus-based in-service. "What might someone like me be working on?" People gave him their opinions, and he took notes and thought about the things they suggested. But he did more than this. "During my first year," Marvin tells us in his profile,

> I visited 179 farms. I called up extension agents and said, "I'm a new guy. Do you have any berry growers you'd be willing to take me out and visit with?" Everybody said yes. We'd set a time, and I'd go out and visit four or five farms. I got to visit a huge part of the state.

Anu Rangarajan, one of Marvin's departmental colleagues who specializes in fresh market vegetable production, speaks of her first year on the job in much the same way. "I started the job here at Cornell in August of 1996," she recalls. "I visited all the extension educators. They took me out to farms in their area. I spent the first two months on the road meeting people, trying to figure out how to focus my work. There was no end to the opportunities."

Anu actually began interacting with community-based extension educators before she interviewed for her job. She tells us what she did to prepare for her interview:

> I called the executive director of the New York State Vegetable Growers Association and said, "I'm a candidate for this job, and I want to get a sense of the lay of the landscape." She gave me the names of all the extension educators in the state. I called them and said, "If I were in this position, what would you expect from me, and what do you feel about it?" They opened right up. They went on and on. They couldn't believe I'd called.

Marvin and Anu both hold academic appointments with formal extension responsibilities. It's not surprising that we find them speaking of going out beyond the Cornell campus to speak with people around the state about their issues. But we also find faculty members who don't have such appointments going out into communities around the state. For example, Tom Lyson, a professor in Cornell's Department of Development Sociology, tells how he approached his work as a member of the advisory committee for the Farming Alternatives Program soon after he arrived at Cornell. "We met with groups out in the state," he recalls. "You just go out into the state and start talking with farmers. Go into rural communities and the issues are all there. They just pop up at you."

While going out into the state can be a means of identifying issues to work on by having them just "pop up at you," one of the things we learned from the profiles is that it can also require something more active: *listening.* "As much as possible whenever you interact with people," Frank Rossi says, "the first thing you need to do is to listen to what they have to say." With Frank's point in mind, we can see that Tom's comment about "talking with farmers" shouldn't be taken to mean talking *to* or *at* them. "Talking with" includes asking people questions and listening to what they have to say. While all of the academic professionals we interviewed do this in person in their practice stories, they also tell us that they do it over the phone. "It's all just common sense—keeping channels open," Molly Jahn tells us in her profile. "I get on the phone and I talk to people, and I say, 'Here's what we know and what we can do, what do you think? How do we fit? From where you sit, what do things look like? What are your problems?'"

Molly is a plant geneticist who was a professor in Cornell's Department of Plant Breeding and Genetics at the time we interviewed her. Early on in her profile, she tells a brief story about how she learned about what farmers in New York were doing to deal with powdery mildew disease in pumpkins. "We happened by accident to hear an extension person telling us about how they make aerial applications of a horrible fungicide to control this disease," she recalls. "We had no idea people were out applying carcinogens aerially to control it. And we thought, 'Why don't we put powdery mildew resistance in pumpkins?' So we did it. And the variety we bred is now in seed catalogs."

Molly goes on to explain that the issue about how farmers were dealing with powdery mildew disease "came to our attention because we talk to people, especially farmers." She continues:

I live out in a little town called Lansing. I never aimed at an academic background, so my peer group is not the people who have the same job as me. The people that I run into—my neighbors, people I go to church with, and a guy that sells vegetables up at the top of my hill—they're people who tell me things like, "Goll-darnit, these pumpkins have rotten handles!" If there's a major disease problem that accounts for 60 percent of their production costs, and I have the solution sitting on my shelf, well that's not a very hard one to figure out, is it?

We want to note a few more things Molly says about her work before we interpret what she and the others are telling us in these excerpts from their profiles. In reflecting on her experience of being on a panel with people from the organic agriculture community who were deeply critical and suspicious of Cornell, Molly said the following:

People have a lot of attitudes that don't necessarily serve them well. I can understand where they come from, but I think it's our job to go out and be available to provide alternative information. We don't have to convert people or anything like that. But I think it is where participation is important in reaching the end point we set our eyes on. I think we need to go out and be present, and if that means me, then it's me, or one of the guys on our team.

The main practice story Molly tells us in her profile is about how she organized the Public Seed Initiative (PSI). We opened this book by briefly telling the story of the birth of PSI. Listen to one of the things Molly said in her profile while she was telling this story:

PSI reflects our priority of working on things that are relevant to the public. Unfortunately, the priority in academics often has been, "I want to work on a disease that's interesting to me, and I'm going to make up a story about why you should care." It's not that it's untrue, but if you step back and state it objectively based on actual importance in agriculture, chances are that wouldn't be the disease you'd pick. But you pick it because you really love this particular category of organism, and then you write the story around it. In general, we haven't done business that way in my program, at least not very much. We have maybe a little bit here and there focused on extra-interesting pathogens just because they're interesting. But again, it's been an intersection; the conversation doesn't start one place or the other. What we pick to move forward with are places we see opportunity on both sides. And there's no shortage of opportunity.

Borrowing a phrase from Molly, what we see these academic professionals speaking about in these excerpts from their profiles is the activity of *going out and being present*. We might be tempted to gloss over these passages, thinking that the activity they are speaking about isn't that important, or that it's significance is simple and obvious. But the more we read and reread the profiles, the more we saw this activity as both more important and more complicated than we initially understood it to be. It represents a key lesson about what the pursuit of public purposes in the academic profession can involve and require.

What Marvin, Anu, Tom, Frank, and Molly are teaching us in these passages from their profiles is that going out and being present isn't a simple, one-time activity. It isn't a passive activity. And it isn't optional, volunteer service that stands apart from their "real" work as academic professionals. It's a complex, ongoing, active, and nonoptional component of their professional work as scientists, scholars, and educators. It's about entering the public sphere. It's about asking good questions and listening, two underappreciated skills that run counter to the presumption that all academics do when they interact with the public is answer questions and talk to or at people. These skills enable academic professionals to "see opportunity on both sides," as Molly puts it. But Molly and the others we profiled don't just "see" opportunities; they strategically move forward with them, both for and with their nonacademic partners. In short, one of the key things we learn from their practice stories is that going out and being present is not a distraction from their core academic work of research and teaching. It's a critical step in the ongoing process of configuring their research and teaching in ways that combine public and academic interests. When we understand it as such, we see that the nature of this activity is deeply and richly public.

Becoming an Insider

Paula Horrigan tells a story in her profile about a participatory community design project she helped to organize in the North Side neighborhood of Binghamton, New York. The project was the centerpiece of an upper-level undergraduate course in Cornell's Department of Landscape Architecture that combined service-learning with action research. Binghamton is about fifty miles away from the Cornell campus. Prior to their participation in the project, neither Paula nor her students knew much about the town. In telling the story of what she and her students did and experienced, Paula said the following: "You have to become an insider."

We noted this line while we were looking for action verbs in Paula's profile. After we noted it, we began to discover passages about the activity of *becoming an insider* in many of the other profiles. We began to see it as one of the key activities the work of pursuing public purposes in the academic profession can involve and require. Like the first activity we identified, of going out and being present, becoming an insider is more important and more complicated than we initially understood it to be.

Paula recounts that she and Cheryl Doble, a colleague from Syracuse University, received a grant to work in one of twelve economically distressed communities in New York State that were part of something called the Quality Communities Initiative (QCI). Binghamton was one of the twelve communities. After Paula and Cheryl received their grant, they met with staff in the Mayor's Office in Binghamton to explore the possibility of a partnership with the city. "As a result of these initial meetings," Paula says,

> the city connected us to a community group called the Communities of Shalom. This is a consortium of leaders from the churches in the North Side neighborhood. They had just been going through a training called the "Shalom Community," a national program of the Methodist Church that trains community leaders to understand community needs and undertake grassroots planning. So these folks from the North Side had been going through the Shalom training, and they were beginning to identify and develop a vision statement and mission for their neighborhood. They were at this pivotal moment in their work. There was a group of them. We connected with them and told them who we were. We told them that we would be interested in helping them shape some of their community visions and do a participatory planning and design process with them. And they were very receptive.

Paula goes on to recall an experience that helped her understand why the North Side group was receptive:

It's funny because we just did this presentation last week at the QCI conference in Albany with two of the folks from the North Side Shalom group. I interviewed them a few weeks ago, just reflecting on some of the process, and one of the things that the Methodist minister, Gary Doupe, said was that initially they were a little skeptical of us. But when we said that we were interested in working *with* them instead of *on* them, they realized that that was really important. They were really scoping us out. They didn't want to work with somebody who was going to work *on* them. But *with* them was different. They recognized that there was a sympathy we shared, a way of thinking about how to undertake a project that was consistent with what they had been doing with Shalom.

As Paula continues her story about the Binghamton project, she begins to recount some of the things it involved:

We shaped a process working with the North Side Shalom group over the duration of the semester. A lot of the terms for that process were very much set by them, like where the meetings were going to happen. We had a lot of community meetings. They always had to include dinners. They were held at area churches, so that they were not associated with any one specific place. They were basically a sharing of food and dialogue. They were always on Sunday nights. The churches made sure that people got there.

When she tells us what her students were doing in the project, we hear her name the activity of becoming an insider:

The students were helping to manage the group. They were developing ways of working that would be participatory. If you do something, it has to be participatory. It's got to engage people. They've got to see the knowledge disclosed *through* the learning process. You're not here to just *tell* them, you're here to *invent* ways that knowledge gets *disclosed*. And it's also for you to see differently, because you can't see those dimensions of the community from the outside. You have to become an insider.

We learn several things from these brief excerpts from Paula's profile about the activity or work of becoming an insider. We learn that it begins with the very first interaction she has with the North Side Shalom group. To this group, Paula and Cheryl are academic outsiders. But when they tell Gary and others in the group that they are interested in working *with* rather than *on* them, they position themselves and their students as insiders. They are *already working to become insiders*, even as they have their first conversation with members of the North Side Shalom group. We also learn that becoming an insider requires going out and being present—in this case, at Sunday evening dinners in neighborhood churches.

We learn more than this from these excerpts. We also learn that becoming an insider is key to the process of learning and knowing—not only for Paula's and Cheryl's students, and not only for themselves, but also for neighborhood residents. Here we see that becoming an insider is work that community members do, too. Neighborhood residents have to become insiders in the process of disclosing and working with knowledge, a process that is central to the participatory planning work that Paula teaches and promotes. This kind of planning doesn't position Paula and her students as tellers of knowledge; it positions everyone—including neighborhood residents—as discoverers of knowledge, as partners and insiders in a process they "invent" together to disclose knowledge. It positions everyone as insiders who are working together to know the history, dynamics, and social and material resources of the neighborhood, and the options for what could be done to improve it. It also positions everyone as insiders who are working to create a vision of what *should* be done to improve the neighborhood.

In democratic societies that take self-rule seriously, the kind of knowing it takes to decide what *should* be done about a public issue at the local level can't be imposed from the outside. It has to be disclosed, discovered, and created by insiders. As we learn from Paula's practice story, this kind of knowing not only occurs in and through deliberation and dialogue; it occurs in and through productive public work—making something that has both public and academic value. "You make to know," Paula tells us. "That is the revelation. That to me is the integration of theory and practice. The practice is the making, and we theorize *through* the making. In the making we are revealing knowledge." In her practice story, Paula, Cheryl, their students, and members of the North Side neighborhood all become insiders who "make to know." They invent ways of disclosing knowledge, and together they create a vision of what could and should be.

As Paula narrates the story of the Shalom group, she does not position herself as a technocratic outside expert who tells a passive and needy group of "clients" or "customers" what they should do, or fixes their problems for them. She also does not position herself and her students as "helpers" who are *only* there to "serve" neighborhood residents (they are serving, in a way, but that's not all they're doing). In other words, the action verbs she uses do not position her and her students as service intellectuals who work from a neutral stance, limiting their contributions to providing options for what could be done and avoiding becoming involved in deciding what should be done. Her practice story positions her and her students as insiders who are engaged with neighborhood residents in all four dimensions of the public work of democracy: naming and setting a problem or a positive goal; identifying options for what can be done; deciding what should be done; and taking action to create things of public value. In her practice story, we see Paula working in ways that are consistent with the action research / public scholarship / educational organizing tradition in American higher education. We see her taking up multiple roles as critic and leader as well as a servant, with all the many dilemmas and challenges such roles involve.

We also see the activity of becoming an insider in other profiles. We see it in great detail in Ken Reardon's profile. Ken's practice story is about how he and a group of students and local merchants organized an action research project aimed at saving a public market in New York City called the Essex Street Market. His profile is filled with insights about becoming an insider that parallel Paula's in many ways. For example, we not only see Ken and his students becoming insiders in the public work of saving the Essex Street Market; we also see the merchants at the market becoming insiders in the work of planning.

In other profiles, we find different dimensions of the activity of becoming an insider. For example, listen to how Antonio DiTommaso describes himself in his profile:

> People ask if I consider myself a spokesman for scientists. I answer, "In the true sense, probably not." I'm a scientist in terms of my degrees, but I consider myself an individual, a person, and a part of the whole community. I never set myself up as somebody special. I'm like that with my students. I consider myself one of them.

Here we see that becoming an insider can involve an internal process of determining one's identity; it can involve the way academic professionals think of who they are in relation to others. We see an additional dimension of the activity from Antonio in a brief passage in his profile where he is reflecting on his interactions with growers in New York State:

> One of the things I've noticed is that your educational title does make a difference to some of these growers. They'll listen to you. They'll listen to you even more if you start speaking their language. Don't speak above or below their heads. Don't treat them as though they might not know anything, or use terminology or jargon that we might use in science. I think that's a skill some of the extension folks here at Cornell have. Some of them have gone out to farmer groups for twenty or thirty years. I sit there and absorb all the stories of their work and how they interact with growers—how they put to rest some of their fears, how they address growers to get information. This is a real skill. Growers appreciate that, even if they may disagree with something you said.

What Antonio is teaching us here is that becoming an insider can involve both learning and unlearning a language. Antonio becomes an insider by changing the way he speaks: by learning to speak the language of the people he interacts with, and by learning not to speak academic jargon. We also see another dimension of becoming an insider when he tells us how he sits and absorbs stories from "extension folks." Here we see that Antonio is not only becoming an insider with a community of growers; he's also becoming an insider with a community of extension professionals. And once again, we see the ways the activity of becoming an insider is integrated with the activity of going out and being present.

Marvin Pritts helps us to see yet another dimension of becoming an insider in the following passage from his profile:

> The other thing I've done, I don't know if it's a hindrance or a help because I haven't "tooted" it a lot, but my wife started a pick-your-own strawberry operation about three years ago. It's not on a huge commercial scale, but she does it, and it's a significant amount of cash flow. I wouldn't say we're making money, because of high costs, but a lot of money comes in. The important thing is that we're actually *doing* it. We're putting things into practice, and I know for a lot of extension educators, it gives them more credibility and trustworthiness because they're actually doing it themselves. It's not anything I stand up and say much about, but there's a network of people that know, and I think that adds some credibility. It's one thing to suggest ideas to people, but it's another thing to put them into practice yourself, and put your own money and time at risk.

As we previously noted about the activity of going out and being present, we may well be tempted to gloss over passages such as this one about becoming an insider. But in such passages we learn important lessons about how academic professionals become insiders, and how the activity can be valuable. In the passage quoted above Marvin teaches us that one of the ways he becomes an insider is through his wife's work of growing strawberries (we assume Marvin participates in this in some way). How is this useful, and why should it be noted? Marvin suggests an answer: because it builds credibility and trustworthiness, two things that are essential for his participation in the public work of democracy. By not only suggesting ideas but putting them into practice himself, Marvin moves from being an outsider with respect to the problems and experiences of berry growers to becoming an insider. This changes his relationship with growers in profound ways.

In Frank Rossi's profile, we see how Marvin's approach to the activity of becoming an insider can be combined with the language issue Antonio spoke about. "I would say the key to my success in working with people," Frank tell us,

> whether they're a golf course superintendent, athletic field manager, a homeowner, a landscaper, whoever they are, is that I speak their language. I pushed a lawnmower for days on end. I can take a small engine apart and rebuild it. I know just about everything I need to know with regard to the practical aspects of my area. I've been doing it all my life.

With a background that included mowing lawns and working in the turf industry, Frank didn't have to work to become an insider: he already was. In the way he tells his practice story, we see that when he speaks of the turf industry he often uses the word "we." While this reflects the insider reality of his life experience and work, it also reflects a strategic decision he made about how to construct his identity after he had in effect become an outsider by becoming a professor. He tells us at one point in his profile that he realized the only way he "could ever make a difference was to change the turf industry from the inside." Here Frank isn't speaking of the industry changing from the inside all by itself; he's speaking of how he needs and intends to be an insider in order to facilitate and contribute to a process of change.

We want to note one more dimension of becoming an insider that we find in the profiles. Marcia Eames-Sheavly tells a practice story about her work in a community garden project at an elementary school in a small town called Freeville that her oldest son was attending. Listen as she tells us how she decided to position herself in this work:

> You have to understand that in a small rural community, a "Cornell person," as they're called, they're maybe not trusted much. So I really put myself in the role of Jake's and Will's mother in this project, and approached it as a parent. I really didn't want to step in and start telling the teachers, "Here's how this is going to be done."

Here we see that for academic professionals, becoming an insider can involve putting themselves in the role of a parent. Reading this, Antonio's words echo in our minds: "I consider myself an individual, a person, and a part of the whole community. I never set myself up as somebody special. I'm like that with my students. I consider myself one of them." In considering themselves "a part of the whole community," academic professionals open themselves to the work of becoming an insider. They open themselves to being not only a "Cornell person," an outside expert who is above so-called "ordinary" people, but also to being a citizen. Not a citizen in the legal sense of the term, but a citizen in the sense of an active participant in the process of self-rule, and an equal in the public work of democracy.

There are many, many passages in each of the profiles in this book where we can discover and learn lessons about the activity of becoming an insider. This activity is much richer and more complicated than we could ever have imagined before we constructed and read these profiles. And it deeply challenges one of the key presumptions people make about academic work. As many people see them, academics are outsiders. They stand off to the side, apart from the public sphere, and from the workings of the private sector. While some see academic professionals' identity and position as outsiders as a problem or fault, others see it as a necessity. Many people think that being an outsider enables distance, which allegedly protects objectivity. They think that a disinterested, objective, outsider stance helps scholars and educators avoid the cardinal sin of "going native." They think that it helps them function as trustworthy experts and effective critics.

There are some important truths in these views about the value of being an outsider. But the profiles in this book show us different truths. They show us that in some contexts, becoming an insider can facilitate academic professionals' credibility and trustworthiness. They show us that academics who become insiders can enhance rather than damage their ability to function as critics, leaders, and servants. They also teach us that becoming an insider doesn't require academic professionals to abandon their identity and position as outsiders. Rather, it requires them to hold their identities as insiders and outsiders in tension. It requires them to embrace the contradiction of being both.

Making "I" "We"

Because we were interested in learning about their own roles in the public work of democracy, we asked each of the academic professionals we profiled to speak in the first person. We wanted to hear the word "I" while they were telling their practice stories. Most had no problem doing so. But Marcia Eames-Sheavly resisted telling her story this way. It's a good thing she did. By resisting she taught us an important lesson.

Marcia's official position at Cornell is senior extension associate in the Department of Horticulture. Her work is focused on youth development and garden-based learning. As we mentioned above, the practice story Marcia tells in her profile is about a community garden project at an elementary school one of her sons was attending in the small town of Freeville, New York. During her interview, she started out using the word "we" to name the actors in her story. It was unclear exactly who "we" were. The word obscured her own roles and contributions. When she was pressed to say what *she* as opposed to "we" did in the project, here's how she responded:

> What I did was . . . You know, I have a hard time saying "I." In a community-based project, you want it to be *we*. So at the same time that I was initiating this and moving it forward, it was very important that "I" be a "we." What I did was bring up the idea and suggest a process. I said, "If you like these ideas, then we need to think about these things. We can't just get out the rototiller. We want to talk with people to make sure that people are on board, that there's a sense of ownership. We can't over plan." I organized this effort, but I kept pulling in people at various points along the way to own it, to move it forward in their own fashion.

This passage from Marcia's profile helps us to see a third activity the academic professionals we interviewed speak about doing when they engage in the public work of democracy. Paraphrasing Marcia, we name this activity *making "I" "we."* While going out and being present and becoming an insider are key activities the academic professionals we interviewed speak about in their practice stories, making "I" "we" is absolutely essential. *This is the most important lesson the academic professionals we interviewed teach us in their practice stories.*

Marcia has a great deal to teach us about the activity of making "I" "we." "This may not sound earth shattering," she says at one point in her profile, but often when people do a community-based project, they'll just *do* it. I spent a year *not* doing it, trying to think of everybody that needed to know or needed to be involved. With this kind of project, it's almost like we think in terms of efficiency. But for this type of job, I think of making it as *in*efficient as possible, because you want to pull in so many people. It's almost like a backward way of thinking. Instead of making a straight line to the garden, you want to think of all the different people that you can pull in. It may make it a little bit unwieldy at first, but it's a way of making sure that everyone is involved.

To speed things along, to be efficient, we could paraphrase and summarize the main practice story Marcia tells in her profile. But like Marcia, sometimes we need make things as inefficient as possible. So listen now as we pause to let Marcia tell her story without us interrupting her:

I remember it was from September to April that we spent planning all the facets of the garden. I wasn't so much wrapped up with what plants were going to go into it as I was wanting it to be really, really well-organized. I was more at the helm with the "who" part. I was asking, "Who are we going to involve? Who will be doing the maintenance for this program? Who needs to know? How do we get people excited about it? How do we guarantee that people are going to care for this, that it won't be vandalized, that people are going to own it? How do we create excitement among the students?" When someone got excited and said, "I'd like to do that, I'd like to be the one to communicate with the teachers, I'd like to be the one that helps organize the planting day", then I very quickly shifted out of that role.

Let me tell you about how this garden came about, and I think that will help you understand what I'm talking about. To the committee, I said, "You know, we could easily do this ourselves. We could do this ourselves. We could go out on a Saturday morning. The garden is small, we could do it easily. But let's think of how to be as inefficient as we possibly can. How can we involve so many people with this, that people will feel that it's their garden?"

And so we planned a big bed-building day. We decided to have square raised beds. That's not an ideal children's garden design, but we knew that we could maintain it. I felt that in this case, for this site, it's not going to be what we know as ideal and having hiding places and water and all sorts of children friendly things. We wanted to make a garden that would last and be well maintained. The other parent and I came up with a very simple design for beds that would be built. This was another place where someone said, "Let me take care of getting all the materials together for the beds." And someone else said, "And I will be the one that has the tools." And so on and so forth.

We asked the school to send a note home to every child in the elementary grades, saying that we're having a big bed building and we want everyone there. We invited all the children. I remember asking the McDonalds and the Dunkin Donuts to contribute food. I sent a notice to the police and fire departments, letting them know we were doing this and please join us. I think I even sent a note to all the service groups, like the Rotary. Imagine taking this simple garden and making it into a three-ring circus! We wanted everyone in town there.

So, on a Saturday morning there were 120 people that showed up in the rain. It was a day just like this in April, in the 40's and raining. Tons of children. The school principal was there, and the groundskeeper. We mixed soil and compost in the parking lot and a couple hundred yards away we had people building the beds. I invited someone from the Department of Horticulture at Cornell to come and just be an extra, to oversee the whole thing. I knew I would be so wrapped up and involved that I might not see the forest for the trees.

And so, we built the beds. We mixed the soil. Rather than take a backhoe and put the soil into the garden, which would take about five minutes, we lined all 120 people up from the parking lot to the beds and they passed the soil in fifty small buckets for an hour and a half. And, the kids all year would point to the spot where they dumped the soil from their buckets and say, "That's mine! That's my spot! I did that!"

Because we had 120 people there, 120 people owned that garden that day. It was a very, very simple bed structure, but a heck of a lot of people made it. The principal, she was just circulating and talking to people, and there were people in the school bringing out coffee and sandwiches and donuts to the people who were working all morning.

When we left, we had done this really incredible community thing. And I had initiated this whole process and organized it. But, I realized later that summer that my deep seated goal of wanting to disappear, of not wanting to be seen as a foreman, came true when someone came up to me and said, "Did you see what they did here?" And my inner reaction was, "They?!?" She said, "Come here, I want to show you something," and brought me over to this garden, which was in full bloom and was just extraordinary.

She said, "Look what they did," and then explained this whole process to me. "There was this day, and all these people came together in the community and they created this thing, and it's amazing. And my child was the one that put the footing in, right there!" I stood there talking to her and I realized that it's a community thing. It isn't identified as one person's project, which was really important to me. Everyone, everyone owned it. It was an incredible thing, and I look back on that as being an ideal experience, because we moved away and it's still thriving.

As sweet and romantic as it is, we are not embarrassed to say that we love this story. We don't love it only or mainly because it helps us understand, in an intellectual sense, the political nature of the activity of making "I" "we." We love it because it makes us *feel*, in an emotional and cultural sense, the meaning and significance of making "I" "we." What we feel when we read the story seems true—not just factually true, but ethically and culturally true. As small as the story is in the scheme of things, in a world of poverty and war and suffering, it still feels hugely important. It may not, in Marcia's words, be "earth shattering," but it is nonetheless powerful and instructive.

Reading and reflecting on Marcia's story, we return to a key line from President Truman's Commission on Higher Education: "The first and most essential charge upon higher education is that at all its levels and in all its fields of specialization it shall be the carrier of democratic values, ideals, and processes." In light of this charge, the most important lesson we can learn from Marcia's story is simply this: making "I" "we" in a community garden project in Freeville, New York, is one of the ways academic professionals can function as carriers of democratic values, ideals, and processes. This is what it can look like and what it can involve when academic professionals from one of higher education's "fields of specialization" take their "first and most essential charge" seriously.

We could easily miss this lesson. We could easily gloss over Marcia's story, thinking that it's not that important, that it's merely a sweet story about the volunteer work of a mother at her son's school that teaches us little about the work of an academic professional, of a faculty member in the Department of Horticulture at Cornell University. But we would be wrong to see it this way. It's true that Marcia chose to put herself in the *insider* role of "Jake's and Will's mother" in the Freeville project. But when we read the whole of her profile, we see that she held this role in tension with her *outsider* role as a Cornell faculty member. And we see that her story does indeed offer us lessons about the work of academic professionals who are engaged in civic life.

We can see this in the following passages from Marcia's profile, where she reflects on her work and experience:

> I would say—and this is my experience, maybe other people would say something else—but here at Cornell it seems to me that there's a lot of ego and a lot of authority and a lot of expertise. But in community projects, you have to think of a way to get yourself out of it, like how do you pull back your person? How do you quickly become a member of a greater team and gently be moving a movement forward in a way that people don't realize you're doing it? That for me is the goal. What are all the ways that you can get people to step in and own it? You can still be the catalyst, the organizer, the coordinator that's moving it forward. But if somebody asks whose project is this, and everyone points at you, that's not the goal for me.

> What is the goal? It's to have *this* group that is doing this, and *this other group* that is in charge of fund-raising, and *these teachers* excited about this butterfly garden. In the process, you begin to step back and watch things happen, or be gently moving them along, but not so flat-out yourself that you're doing everything. I think that our model in the university is often that we have to be in the limelight, and we have to get credit for it, and we have to be the experts. This—what I have described—is like a totally different way of thinking about these things.

It is indeed. But this different way of thinking doesn't mean that academic professionals should *abandon* their academic expertise. What it requires them to do is reposition and combine it with other kinds of expertise. "The kinds of skills I would say are necessary to achieve a project like this," Marcia says,

> include recognizing different abilities in people, and that there is a role for everyone—understanding the need for creating ownership, and understanding the need for creating a sense of identity around a project. Certainly, there's a whole group of folks who need skills in planting, in knowing what plants need, what plants are going to thrive, and the full kind of horticultural skills arena. There are two pots of skills: one around horticulture, and one around organizing. . . . Even though it's a garden, the horticultural knowledge is probably the least of the worry. We know you have to work with the soil and find a right site and all that business. But I think the real challenges are moving this giant body of people forward and helping people to see how critical it is to move slowly, to involve others and to think of everyone that ought to be involved, to ask people's opinion. The whole process of moving a group of people forward is challenging—and also, understanding that not everybody's going to buy in all at once.

Here we catch a glimpse of what it can look like and mean for academic professionals to put into practice the pledge William Sullivan says that civic professionals make: "to deploy technical expertise and judgment not only skillfully but also for public-regarding ends and in a public-regarding way." Here we also see that Marcia's story is not merely that of a mother volunteering in her children's school. It is also a story of a civic professional at work. And it is a story of a civic professional learning and growing as a professional, in and through her experience in the public work of democracy. "Everything that I do in this job with respect to youth development," Marcia tells us in the latter part of her profile,

> hangs on the framework of that one volunteer effort. People will ask me, "How would you suggest doing this?" And you know how you have a map in your head, this conceptual framework that you hang theory on? It all gets tucked there. *Everything for me gets hung on the conceptual framework of this one community project.* For me that's so important because it's not just something I've read about. It's not just something I've dabbled in or that I've witnessed. To be in there, in the thick of it, is a much more meaningful way than, here in Extension, telling people statewide how you go about this. Well, *I know how to go about it.* That's why, although it was a volunteer thing, it's just so deep in my heart as such a formative experience. It's the thing on which everything sits for me.

We have learned a great deal from Marcia's profile about the work of making "I" "we." There is something to learn about this activity in every one of the profiles in this book. In Dan Decker's profile, we learn that it is central to the project of transforming the way wildlife management is conducted. We learn about how tough it can be from Frank Rossi's stories of "taking bullets" from environmental and turf industry groups in response to his efforts to get these groups to move from I to we. Fundamentally, Frank's work as an "expert in the middle" is all about making "I" "we," even though he tells us in the first paragraph of his profile that his job is to "externalize or extend information" from the university to the public. Frank's own summary of his job description leaves out most of his civic engagement work. We found this pattern in other profiles. As Anu Rangarajan notes in her profile after she tells us how she spent a lot of time making "I" "we" in a project she was engaged in, "that's not in my job description."

While making "I" "we" may not be in Anu's job description, or in that of any of the other academic professionals we profiled in this book, *it's in their practice stories.* It's another way of naming a critically important aspect of their work that is rarely recognized and named: the work of organizing, of establishing working public relationships. In such relationships, academic professionals are not merely helping and serving and informing, and people beyond the academy are not merely being helped or served or informed. Nor are people beyond the academy merely telling the university about their needs and problems so the university can address and fix them. Rather, they are taking their place as full participants in the public work of democracy alongside civic-minded academic professionals who do the same.

Leapfrogging Back and Forth

Going out and being present, becoming an insider, and making "I" "we" are public activities. They situate academic professionals in public settings, relationships, and work. Of course, academic professionals who choose to be directly engaged in civic life are not situated entirely or only in public. They are also situated in academic institutions, disciplines, fields, and positions. Speaking metaphorically, they have one foot in the public sphere and one foot in the academy. This important but rather precarious stance gives rise to a fourth activity we find the academic professionals speaking about in their practice stories. Quoting a line from John Sipple's profile, we refer to this activity as *leapfrogging back and forth*.

When we interviewed John Sipple, he was an untenured assistant professor in the Department of Education at Cornell University. Utilizing theoretical and methodological tools and approaches from sociology, he was building a research program focused on the responses of public school districts to changes in state and federal policy. The main practice story he tells in his profile is about documenting and analyzing how schools in New York State were responding to the implementation of new learning and graduation standards that had been established by the Board of Regents and the state legislature. His research involved visits to schools in five different school districts and interviews with over 100 teachers and administrators. It was funded by a small grant from the Educational Finance Research Consortium, a policy analysis venture between the New York State Board of Education, the Board of Regents, academic professionals, and policymakers.[7]

In his profile, John tells us that the goal of the consortium, which is funded by the state legislature, is to enable more informed decision-making about education policy by improving the flow of information to policymakers and policy implementers. He tells us that the government staff and academic professionals who set up the consortium in the 1990s faced a difficult challenge:

> They all got together to try to figure out a way that research could be sponsored in a fairly autonomous way, meaning it would be separated from the State Education Department, and yet somewhat be connected to the State Education Department people. So there's this interesting tension of trying to solicit studies that would be relevant to the agenda in the State Education Department and the Board of Regents, but also autonomous from the State Education Department so that they wouldn't be viewed as reflecting the company line. They're actually fairly sophisticated in how they think about this. And of course the academics, this is where they come from, where all their work is reportedly independent and not biased per se by specific political agendas.

As an untenured assistant professor in a research university, John had a strong interest in establishing a productive research program that would enable him to contribute to conversations about theoretical issues in his academic field. But as he tells us, he and the other scholars who were conducting studies for the consortium also had another interest. "Our interest as scholars," John says,

> was to have a chance to impact practice. It was a way to contribute to the conversation that was taking place in the state around the raising of standards, around pushing kids and teachers and administrators to higher levels of performance. And as I recall we all welcomed the opportunity to interact with state policymakers, and to be able to do what we do and have them actually use it in a small way. There were no guarantees it was going to shape practice, but we would contribute to the conversation.

Here John is situating himself as a member of a group of academic professionals who seek to have one foot in their academic institutions and disciplines and one foot in the public sphere. As John puts it in the above passage from his profile, he and the other scholars who received funding from the consortium welcomed the opportunity "to be able to do what we do and have them [i.e., state policymakers] actually use it in a small way." For scholars who are employed in tenure-track positions at research universities, "what we do" mainly means conduct research and write articles for academic journals. But the opportunity from the consortium required John to do more than this. It carried an extra obligation or requirement to write what he alternately refers to as "technical reports" and "condition studies" for a nonacademic audience of policymakers. As we learn when John goes on to tell and reflect on his practice story, this turned out to be more difficult—and more political—than he originally thought it would be.

In essence, John's decision as an untenured assistant professor to accept money from the consortium meant that he would have to deliver on dual obligations—one for the academic world, which expected him to publish peer-reviewed articles, and another for a group in the public sphere, which expected him to inform decision making about public policies related to education. Pursuing these dual obligations had a big impact on his work as a scholar. It required him to do a lot of what he called "leapfrogging." Part of the leapfrogging was between qualitative and quantitative research methods. But there was another kind of leapfrogging that was more important and difficult. In John's words, "There was also a leapfrogging back and forth between the scholarly and the policy world." The leapfrogging John is speaking about here was largely related to the challenge of meeting his dual—and simultaneous—obligations of writing separate papers for distinctly different audiences from the same study. "That's been an interesting struggle," he says,

> to try to take a document that was formatted for the consortium, that was also being constrained by their timeline, taking those manuscripts, the technical reports we give to the state, and then altering them, revising them, enriching them both from the analytic standpoint and from the theoretical standpoint. We inserted theory, inserted lit reviews into these things, leapfrogging back to the scholarly literature. I had to do these academic papers, because I would never survive here on just these technical reports to the consortium.

We catch of glimpse of what made this struggle "interesting" in a brief story that highlights the political nature of his leapfrogging in the consortium-funded project. The story has to do with the response he received from the first draft of his first technical report. "We submitted the initial report," John recalls,

> with big, huge letters: "DRAFT." And within two days, there were these fairly forceful emails being zipped around, which we were then copied on, saying that something had gone awry with our initial report that we had sent to the consortium, this draft report. I'm not sure the word *dangerous* was used, but essentially the emails insinuated that this study is dangerous. They said, "What is going on with this study? What agenda do they have? What are they trying to do? This could have potential ramifications down the road." We got these emails, and I remember it being on a Friday afternoon, and I'm thinking, "Oh God, what'd I write? What'd I do?"

> What happened was, I had included a literature review, as if I was presenting this paper at a conference to an academic body. I reviewed the existing literature, and discussed what we know about how school districts respond to state policy, how we know that they rebuff or they rebuke policy. It's exceedingly hard for state policy to infiltrate through a district shell and work its way

into the classroom. I reviewed that. Well, that got interpreted by these policymakers that these policies in New York State are never going to work, that we're wasting all this money. Now it was just a lit review, so we had that disconnect. Also, as with most any research study, at the very end of the paper, in the last paragraph, I raised some concerns and questions for future research. I forget the comment I made, but I lived to regret it. It was something about how the worth and value of the new state standards are being called into question, which was roughly based on some of the comments from our interviewees. And that just scared and then horrified some of the people who read this. And this got up to the highest echelons of the State Ed Department, and the people were in a tizzy.

We got word of this, and we said, "Wait a minute. We're not out to get anybody here. This is just a lit review. We posed a question at the end. Okay, we'll take the question out, we'll take the last sentence out, fine, because it's just a thought-provoking question. It's not a substantive part of the study." I tell this story because it's how I began to learn what pressures practitioners were under, and what role research could play in their jobs. We then altered some of the lit review, toning down some of the language a little bit, making it clear that these were studies from other states, because I had no intention of saying this is what's going on in New York State. And I believe I took out the last line of the paper.

John went on to explain that before the technical reports or condition studies scholars write for the consortium go up on the consortium's web site and are disseminated,

they go through a revision process to address all the comments readers have made about them. So we revised our paper and completed more of our analyses. It was fairly sketchy at the early draft stage. We learned to take out some of the conjectures, some of the interpretation. What we learned, what we were told explicitly, and what I then began to understand in a much better way, was that the role of these condition studies is to provide information to the state, and then let the state interpret what it really means. They said, "Don't interpret this for us. Let us interpret it." That final paragraph we wrote was our interpretation, and so we took out our interpretation. Now, to their credit, they never pressured us to change any of our findings. They never pressured us to change any text. They never pressured us to hide anything. They said, "Just present it, and let us interpret it."

In terms of academic work, you can't get away with that. You have to interpret what you find in light of theory, and in light of previous empirical literature. Here, you just present your findings, and let others interpret them. So I learned how the game was going to be played, and I began to understand the phenomenal pressure the State Department of Education and the Board of Regents were under. I guess I hadn't really thought about it. I wasn't thinking they were just goof-balls up there, immune from pressure and immune from politics. I just hadn't really thought about it, which was my fault.

In reflecting on his work with the consortium, John says that the tensions that emerged between scholars, policymakers, teachers, and administrators are healthy. "But I think what I've learned," he goes on to tell us,

is that these people have jobs, they have lives, they operate in an exceedingly politicized environment, and research can play a role in helping them do their work. But research can also make their lives quite miserable. I think as academics we need to understand that. Not that it censors our work, but if I truly want to be party to and contribute to a conversation about practice, I have to understand the constraints practitioners are under. That's an important understanding, and I'm still trying to make sense of how that actually impacts my work.

As we asked ourselves what we might learn from John's emphasis on leapfrogging, we thought about the dilemma of the relation of democracy and expertise. We thought about the pledge civic professionals are supposed to make to deploy their technical expertise and judgment not only skillfully but also for public-regarding ends and in a public-regarding way. And we thought about one of the things President Truman's Commission on Higher Education wrote in its final report: "The democratic way of life can endure only as private careers and social obligations are made to mesh, as personal ambition is reconciled with public responsibility." In thinking about these things, we came to see leapfrogging back and forth as an essential activity in the public work of an academic professional who seeks to navigate the relation of democracy and expertise in a public-regarding way—a way that meshes both personal ambition and public responsibility. Before we conducted our interviews, we knew this in abstract, theoretical terms as something that "should" be. Through detailed and richly drawn practice stories, we now know it in tangible terms as something that is.[8]

Tom Maloney helps us to see one of the public dimensions of leapfrogging back and forth that we should take special note of. Tom is a senior extension associate in Cornell's Department of Applied Economics and Management. He focuses his work on human resource management in agricultural and horticultural enterprises. As a non-tenure-line faculty member, he spends most of his time developing and providing seminars and workshops for managers. Near the end of his profile, he says that his work

is an example of how the land-grant system provides service to the agricultural industry. But we have to be careful how we define service, and how we define education. There is a framework where you could loosely define service to include education. But if we're making a distinction between the two, then I would say what we're doing is intended from the very beginning, explicitly, to be education and not service. Service to me is when someone comes to you and says, "I want you to help me write my employee handbook." The distinction for me is that if it's education instead of service, the individual is very involved in learning about himself or herself and very involved in looking at how he or she wants to behave in the workplace with the people they supervise. That can be a very powerful educational experience. And so I think that service is like consulting, like providing something. It has a connotation of providing something for a fee, as opposed to education being teaching a person to fish. It's something that a person does internally: they change themselves, and they own it.

There has been a service versus education conversation for the entire thirty years I've been in this system. And the way that conversation goes is, "We need to make sure we're doing less service and more education." I think that faculty members who engage in these conversations are saying that, and I think extension administration—even though they've sort of gone back and forth—has said that a lot, often in the context of budgets and in justifying our existence to our funders. There's always been this concern that if we take away the service component, education may not be able to stand on its own, that people won't value the education part of what they're getting as much as they value the service. I think that that makes us afraid to make hard decisions about service.

The conversation on service versus education that Tom speaks about in this passage is important. There is an uneasy tension between these two activities, particularly when one believes—as Tom does—that the intention of those who established the land-grant system was to provide education instead of service. Despite his personal views on the matter, his experience has taught him that he needs to offer both. In his profile, he tells us that he has to provide people with a variety of services in order "to get them to the education table." In other words, he has to leapfrog back and forth between service and education.

Like the other three activities we have named in this chapter, we find the activity of leapfrogging back and forth in every one of the profiles in this book. Reflecting the situational dynamics of context and the diversity of academic professionals' political interests and commitments, the activity looks different in each profile. To be "public-regarding" in John Sipple's situation, he had to function as a service intellectual who provides research findings and lets others interpret what they mean and what if anything should be done with them. That's what the "public" in his situation asked for. In other situations, such as Dan Decker's and Frank Rossi's, to be public-regarding includes functioning not only as a servant, but also as a critic and leader. The leapfrogging back and forth in their practice stories is not only between the public world and the academy, but also between the roles they take up and perform as critic, leader, and servant.

In summary, leapfrogging back and forth has many dimensions and takes many forms. It can be between the academic and public worlds. It can be between service and education. It can be between education and research, between being an outsider and being an insider, between practice and theory, between functioning as an expert and functioning as a facilitator, between being "Jake's and Will's mother" and being a "Cornell person," between the "compartmentalized structure" of the university that Molly Jahn speaks of and the interrelated whole of the community or the food system. And more.

Public Purposes

The activities of going out and being present, becoming an insider, making "I" "we," and leapfrogging back and forth are not ends in themselves. They are means to an end. To make sense of them, we need to see them in relation to the public purposes they are meant to advance.

There are passages in most of the profiles in this book where the academic professionals we interviewed directly state what their public purposes are. Let's look at a few examples. Here is Marvin Pritts telling us what his main role is, which he ties to a public purpose:

> I see my role as trying to identify some key areas of research that I can work in that will not only help growers with some immediate problems, but maybe push their thinking a little bit in terms of issues that might involve sustainability, and get them thinking a little bit broader than how they thought in the past. I do this because I feel not only a commitment to them, but a commitment to society, to people who pay my salary, to New York State residents. My work should not be focused exclusively on the grower community. I have an obligation to the greater part of society, too, and if I can help growers produce high-quality fruit in a way that is more environmentally sustainable, everybody wins.

Here is Paula Horrigan describing her goals, which we see as public purposes:

> My goals are to create wonderful and meaningful places *with* communities, to reinvigorate the relationship between people and their places and empower them through that process. Another goal is to empower my students to recognize that their work has the potential to change the world. They can be leaders in that respect. I want to motivate them at that level so that their work is situated in a meaningful way. I want to connect them at that place where they can embrace the spectrum of power that they can have in helping to motivate the relationships between people and places that are empowering to people and sustaining. I want the education experience to set up an opportunity for them to engage at that level, so that they can see that their work has ethics and values associated with it. When they make a place, it goes out into the world. Our field is about making space that directly impacts relationships. I want them to be accountable and sensitive to that and responsible to it, and combine that with all their other motivations—poetry, art, or whatever. Those things aren't exclusive of one another. That's what motivates me with my students.

What Marvin and Paula are telling us in these passage lines up with several components of the official mission statement for Cornell's College of Agriculture and Life Sciences: advancing a productive and sustainable agriculture, promoting a wise stewardship of the environment, supporting a safe, secure food supply, fostering economic vitality, facilitating individual and community health and well-being, and pursuing scholarship that addresses social issues. Importantly, when we read their profiles, we learn that Marvin and Paula don't just pursue their public purposes through the typical academic means of writing articles and teaching in classrooms. They also pursue them off-campus through the four activities we named and described above. They pursue them in face-to-face interactions with their non-academic partners as they engage with them in all four components of the public work of democracy.[9]

With John Sipple as the only exception, the public purposes the academic professionals we interviewed speak about go well beyond informing people's decision-making with research findings. They also include purposes that reflect an proactive agenda for social change that is meant to advance specific values, interests, purposes, and ends. This is most dramatically evident in Ken Reardon's and Tom Lyson's profiles, both of which feature political organizing from an explicitly nonneutral position. But it's also evident in more subtle ways in other profiles. For example, we learn from Tom Maloney that his work is aimed at changing the way agricultural and horticultural businesses are managed. His public purpose is not only to help businesses to make more money. It's also to help them deal in ethical ways with difficult issues of difference and diversity. We learn that Dan Decker's whole career has been devoted to changing the way wildlife management is understood and conducted, in ways that are meant to advance civic and ecological purposes. We learn from Molly Jahn that her work is not just about breeding new varieties of plants to help farmers make more money. It's also about changing people's practices and attitudes to advance sustainability. And we learn from Frank Rossi that he *can* contribute to society in a meaningful way "with grass" by pursuing public purposes that are not only technical and economic but also richly civic. We want to take a moment now to look at Frank's profile to see what we might learn from it about the nature of the public purposes he pursues.

Frank tells us in the first paragraph of his profile that his "primary responsibility" as an associate professor and extension specialist of turfgrass science is to "externalize or extend information" from Cornell and other universities to the "citizens of New York State." He tells us that he does "a lot of transfer-of-technology kind of work," and that what appeals to him is "problem-solving work" that utilizes "rigorous science." And he says that he "absolutely love(s) learning new things that are important to my industry, including environmental issues, management issues on golf courses, unique things on sports fields, and innovations in lawns."

Reading the opening paragraph of his profile, we might guess that Frank works out of the service intellectual tradition. This would seem like a safe bet, given the language he uses to describe his primary responsibility and work, and his location in a land-grant college of agriculture. The prevailing view of the extension and "outreach" work of land-grant colleges of agriculture is that such work is responsive, apolitical service. As a service intellectual, we would assume that the only public purpose Frank pursues is that of helping people pursue their own freely chosen ends. We would assume that the way he pursues this purpose is to provide people with information, technologies, and technical assistance from a neutral stance of unbiased and disinterested objectivity.

As we discover when we read beyond the first paragraph, our initial impression of Frank and our assumptions about the nature of his public purposes and work turn out to be wrong. Listen to him as he gives us a general description of what he did when he began his academic career as an environmental education specialist at Michigan State University:

> When I was working at Michigan State, I became a highly visible member of their turf extension program. I was outspoken. I was in everybody's face about environmental issues. I was engaged in the environmental debate with advocacy groups and regulators and legislators. That's where I got my reputation for working in these kinds of situations, for my willingness to get in there, into that debate.

He remembers observing environmental advocacy groups in Michigan:

> I was watching what these advocacy groups were doing. They took an offensive approach. They were saying to the turf industry, "We don't even want to talk to you. We don't like what you're doing with chemicals. We're going to pass laws so you can't use them. We're not going to discuss it. We're going to go to our legislators. We're going to start a grassroots movement and get laws passed. And then these regulators are going to regulate you, and you're going to have to change what you're doing."

Frank tells us that his observation of advocacy groups influenced his view of what his job was. In his words, it was to "go in and take them off their offensive approach." He tells us how he tried to do this:

> I went to the environmental advocates and said, "Look, if you want to change the turf industry, your law-based approach will do that. But long term, it's going to make it adversarial. You're going to come to a place where you just can't regulate anymore, and you're going to need some cooperation. And you need to understand why they're doing what they're doing. They're not addicted to spraying chemicals. They're doing it because right now it's the only technology they've got to provide the products people want. This is not a viable long-term strategy. You need to think about their end of this deal."

339

But taking environmental advocates off of their offensive approach wasn't the only thing Frank viewed as his job. He also thought it was his job to challenge the "defensive mode" the turf industry was working out of, in response to what the environmental advocates were doing. "I said to the turf industry," Frank recalls,

> You need to knock it off, spending $100,000 a year fighting advocacy groups in the legislature, and open a dialogue with them so they can understand what motivates you. Because right now they think what motivates you is killing stuff—killing insects and killing weeds. They think that ultimately, you're killing them. They view what you're doing as damaging to their health. They don't see the recreational benefit, the quality-of-life benefit, the environmental benefits that might come from having a well-maintained turf. And we've got to do a better job with it.

Frank goes on to say more about his approach to advocacy groups in Michigan:

> I was willing to go in there and say to the advocacy groups, "You know what? I can't defend some of the things we do in the turf industry. I can't defend them. I know some of the things are problematic. I know some of the things could be wrong. We're missing a lot of data about health effects, and these guys are lacking alternatives. They have to produce this product, and this is the only way they know how to do it right now. They're a generation of guys who were trained in managing turf a certain way, and they'll fight before they give in to what you're trying to make them do." I said to them, "I think we can change it. Let's work together on this. Let's do a project with zero pesticide use. Let's do a project on reducing fertilizer use. If you have some money, I'll lend the expertise. If you don't have money I'll just give you some advice, and we can get moving along." At the same time, I went to the industry and said, "Look, we need to really start moving towards the way these people are talking, or we're going to get regulated back to the Stone Age." And it was hard for them to hear that, too.

After Frank gave us this general recounting of his early work and experience, we asked him for a specific example of his work at Cornell. He gave us a brief practice story about a project he was still in the midst of conducting with Jennifer Grant, one of his colleagues at Cornell. The project began with a highly visible experiment devoted to testing nonchemical approaches to pest and weed control on a prestigious Long Island golf course at Bethpage State Park. Frank tells us his motivation for the project: "Laws are being passed to ban pesticide use, and there's very little understanding in the legislature, in the industry, or among advocacy groups about what would be the real impacts on the ground of not being able to use pesticides."

In telling his practice story, Frank situates himself as an "expert in the middle" who is "taking bullets" from "both sides" in the battle over how pests and weeds are being controlled on golf courses. The two sides are the golf course industry and environmental advocacy groups. When we asked him to reflect on his roles and work in the Bethpage experiment and other projects, Frank said the following:

> You ask what my main role is. I think it's to be the expert in the middle. That's my role. And to convey information in a way that effects change, that helps people make change themselves. In this job, we're in the middle. I'm not uncomfortable in that spot. I think the groups I work with all have valid points, and I think it's my job to be in the middle. That's my job because I get state dollars. I'm supposed to be the most knowledgeable guy in turf in New York State. This is an area

that I'm an expert in. And I'm not in anybody's pocket. I'm completely objective. I have no hidden agenda. That's my job. I don't know *why* it's my job, I just think it's my job. I think that was what the people who set up the extension service would have wanted it to evolve to.

Here we see that for Frank, taking up the role of the expert in the middle is linked to the pursuit of a public purpose that is about change. But in reading what he says here, we also wonder whether it's really true that he is "completely objective." This claim is hard to square with what he told us when we asked him if he considers his work as an expert in the middle to be "political" in nature. "I almost entirely stay on the technical end of things in my work," he told us.

And politics—you know, I just stay away from that. But I imagine if you probed me about it, you might find that I am absolutely pushing (in the environmental arena, anyway) the turf industry to be more responsible. But at the same time, I'm pushing the environmental groups by saying, "If you want the industry to be more responsible, stop bashing them, and let's work together." I don't know if that's political, or if I'm just leveraging my technical expertise. I guess I don't view either of those positions as espousing political or ethical feelings or opinions. I think that's a slippery slope for us. The way I look at it, I guess it's political if you think about it with a small *p*. I immediately think of politics as taking a stand on things. But I feel like what I'm doing is facilitating the discussion. A lot of times in my field, you can't even get these people to talk to each other. So one of the things I have to do is find a way to facilitate that discussion. Now, some people might say I'm beholden to science. I think that puts us in a good, neutral position. If I state my ethical or political feelings, then I think that undermines every-thing. It's the combination of technical knowledge and practical experience that allows us to facilitate the discussion.

This is not what we would expect to hear from someone who is "completely objective." Rather, it's what we would expect from someone who is biased in favor of making specific kinds of changes in the way interested groups are behaving. While Frank tells us that he "almost entirely" stays on the technical end of things, the passages we quoted above are not about the technical end of things. They are about the civic end of things. The civic end, as Frank recognizes, is *normative*; it's political in a small letter p sense. His work on the civic end of things involves "pushing" both the turf industry and environmental groups to change how they work and interact with each other in ways that are meant to advance a public purpose that is economic, political, cultural, and environmental in nature. But as Frank says, he doesn't "push" these groups by stating his personal ethical or political feelings. Rather, he "pushes" them by raising questions about and pointing out the implications of these groups' views and behaviors. He does not do this from a neutral stance that is "com-pletely objective." He does it from a biased position that reflects his embrace of a specific public purpose.

In reading the stories he tells of his civic engagement work and experiences as an aca-demic professional, we come to see Frank as an educator who is challenging people to think about the implications of their actions. "One of the things that I have a real innate ability to do," he tells us, "is to get people to think about what they are doing. That ultimately is what the goal is." He tells us that he is especially committed to the goal of getting turf profession-als "to question every single practice they're using."

For example, when they make a decision to use a chemical for a pest, are they chronically using that product because there's an environmental problem at that particular site where there's not good air movement, and it's conducive to creating the pest problem? If that's the case, why don't they fix the inherent problem rather than choosing the technology as the short-term fix? Now, that's not to say that careful, thoughtful use of water, fertilizer, and pesticides is problematic! Careful, thoughtful use of antibiotics, it's not problematic, right? But we've become a society where we don't think about it. We just want to move on to the next technology.

That's the kind of thing I want them thinking about. I want them thinking about efficiency. Gas prices are going up. They use a lot of nonrenewable resources. Are there ways you can stop mowing certain areas? Are there ways you can minimize the amount of water you're using? Are there ways that you can be more efficient with your labor resources? I'm always curious, I'm always thinking. I want *them* to be thinking. If we're thinking, it's going to keep getting better. I tell my students, "Your job, in the time people take to read what you write, listen to what you say, or see what you do, is to get them to *think* about what they're doing."

Near the end of his profile, Frank situates the main public purpose he pursues in his civic engagement work within the land-grant extension system. "I think the founders of the land-grant extension system," he says,

wanted the system to help farmers produce cheap food. Well, the fact is, we've got cheap food. But we still have people concerned about human-managed landscapes. Now, I don't manage food crops. The landscapes that I manage are in urban and suburban environments. And people are concerned—it's not so much that they want cheap food as that they want clean water and clean air, and they want to recreate, which is important. That's where we come in. Recreation has become an even more important part of our society than it might have been years ago. People want to make sure what they do to get those recreational services provided doesn't affect their health in other ways. That's the place for me.

What is Frank telling us here? He's telling us that the place for him is inside the public work of democracy. As a critic and leader as well as servant, he pursues a public purpose that is not mainly or only guided and measured by a narrowly cast, short-term economic bottom-line, but by a broad set of long-term economic, political, cultural, and ethical values, interests, ideals, and ends.

Lessons about the Meaning, Significance, and Value of Higher Education's Public Purposes and Work

Our final task in this chapter is to draw lessons from our reading of the profiles that are published in this book about the meaning, significance, and value of higher education's public purposes and work, in and for a democratic society. In taking up this task, we return to the passage we quoted at the beginning of this chapter from Frank Rossi's profile:

I was disillusioned with becoming an academic in the turf area. I think maybe deep down, I always felt like it really isn't that important. I'd like to contribute to society in a meaningful way, and can I do that with grass? Well, turned out I could.

Listen to Frank as he recalls when and how he lost his sense of disillusionment:

> When I got the job at Michigan State, I got to work in this environmental area, which put me right in the middle of the discussion. I had to go and meet with advocacy groups. I had to go and meet with legislators. I had to go and meet with regulators, and I had to work in a traditional land-grant industry model as well. And I learned early on that a lot of people cared a lot about what I was doing. There were regulations, there were people who had to enforce those regulations, there were people who were pushing for those regulations who were genuinely concerned about their health and well-being, the quality of their water, and then there was a turf industry that was mindful of the whole thing going on, but in the end, they're judged by the product that they put on the ground. It really appealed to me to be in that situation. I was no longer disillusioned. I saw that there was real value to what I did, and everything that I did to get into that place, I could use.

What we learn from reading Frank's profile is that the "real value" of his work—and its "real" meaning and significance—is about both product and process. It's not only to be measured by the impact on the economy of the tangible things he produces, extends, disseminates, applies, or teaches as a specialist in turfgrass science. It's also to be found in the impact on democracy of the intangible things he contributes as a participant in public work—one who tries to deploy his technical expertise and judgment not only skillfully but also for public-regarding ends and in a public-regarding way. And we learn one more thing from Frank's profile. We learn that as a "leapfrogging" academic professional with one foot in the academy and one foot in the public sphere, the "real value" of his civic engagement work is not only public in nature, but also academic. It's a means for him to learn and grow as an academic professional in ways that help him contribute something of value to his academic field and institution as well as the publics he interacts with.

While Frank is in many ways unique, these lessons are not unique to Frank. We find them in all of the other profiles in this book. With respect to the land-grant system, they show us that there is more going on in faculty members' civic engagement work than we knew, and that what is going on is much more relational and has a much more powerful and richly developed political meaning and value than most people would likely presume. Our lessons not only challenge the prevailing rhetoric in the land-grant system; they also challenge, complicate, and enlarge the prevailing understanding of the meaning, significance, and value of higher education's public purposes and work. Contrary to Stanley Fish's claim, they show us that democracy is an educational as well as political project, and that even specialists in turfgrass science can—and in Frank's case, do—contribute to it.

There are many, many passages in the profiles that help us to discover and understand the nuances and intricacies of these lessons. We'll take a moment now to look at just a few of them.

Our main leapfrogging academic professional, John Sipple, helps us to see how the value of higher education's public purposes and work can be both public and academic in nature. In his profile, he notes that leapfrogging between the public sphere and the academy is both inefficient and time-consuming. "But I'm also absolutely convinced," he goes on to say, that because I kept interacting with the policy community and practitioners in the field, in terms of my data collection and in various forms of survey and casework, right now when I sit down to my work in 2004, I can produce better-quality work than I would have been able to produce had I not engaged in that activity. My CV doesn't look nearly as impressive as it would otherwise, but I think where I am right now, the quality of work I can do, my understanding of what has gone on in New York State has been so enriched that I don't regret what I did. I think if I had sat with that initial survey and tried to work for several years off that, I would not be where I am today in terms of the sophistication of how I understand what's going on in New York State. So I think I'm a better scholar for having done this, and I think my work in the long term—well at least my productivity over the next six years—will be much richer and much better for having made the decisions I made that day. It may not be at Cornell; we'll find out. But I think these next x number of years will be more productive for those decisions I made. And I have a much greater appreciation of how to interact with the policymaking community—a much greater appreciation— although I still have not figured out in any great sense how to go out and help actual school districts.

John's work in the long run likely will be at Cornell. He received tenure and was promoted to associate professor in 2005. His public engagement work turned out to be valuable not only for the publics he interacts with, but also for his peers in his academic institution and field.

As we have already noted in the section on making "I" "we," Marcia Eames-Sheavly also speaks in her profile of the academic value of her civic engagement work. We see this when she tells us that everything she does with respect to youth development hangs on what she learned from her engagement in the Freeville garden project. Marcia also speaks of the public value of the project, and her roles in and contributions to it:

In terms of what I think we accomplished in this project, we showed people that if we all work together toward a common vision, we can do something extraordinary. Something extraordinary in this case may not seem like much—a small garden. But for a community of folks who were feeling that they couldn't achieve or maybe hadn't had a success in a while, it was a really big deal. Also, we learned that many hands make light work. Often I'll see that people will get involved in a community project and they want to run the show. But if you want it to last, that's probably not the best approach.

Some of the key contributions I would say I made were balancing the need for organization with understanding plant needs. It was huge; I don't know how to sum that up. It wouldn't be there, there would not be a garden, if I hadn't been involved. So the garden itself could be a key contribution. It enlivens the school landscape. It's a gathering point. It's beautiful. Kids love it. There are birds that visit the garden. I mean the garden itself is a key contribution. But the sense that "we can" is a key contribution, too, that people feel that they can achieve something.

What Marcia is telling us here helps us to see the meaning and value of both product and process. The garden is tangible, and its value is tangible. But the public work process that created it holds intangible value. It helped give people a sense of "we can," of showing them what they can accomplish when they work together toward a common vision. In other words, it helped bring life to the ideal and practice of everyday democracy. That is one of the ways Marcia's work can—and we think should—be judged to be meaningful and valuable.

So far in this chapter we have not quoted anything from Ken Reardon's profile. When we interviewed him, Ken was an associate professor in Cornell's Department of City and Regional Planning. While that department is in the College of Art, Architecture, and Planning, his position was partly funded by the College of Agriculture and Life Sciences. In his profile, Ken tells a lengthy practice story from his work at the beginning of his academic career that was about an action research project in the Lower East Side of New York City that was focused on saving the Essex Street Market. Ken's reflections on his experience illuminate the significance of higher education's public purposes and work in ways that are hard to summarize. Because the lessons are *in* his stories and his own meaning-making reflections on them, we need to keep the stories whole and let Ken tell and reflect on them in his own voice.

In his profile, Ken reflects on the meaning of the Essex Street Market project:

So we participated in a joint effort that saved fifty small businesses serving the city's poorest residents. We helped save an institution that somehow managed to generate three hundred better-than-living-wage jobs. We managed to save one of the few democratic public spaces in New York, where immigrants from a variety of cultures, often coming from very repressive environments, where they weren't allowed to even think about the culture of others—that was viewed as a disloyalty—could learn about the remarkable diversity of America in this space, and learn about the ways and means and language and cultural symbols and resources of other peoples. We helped create a coalition of merchants with their local religious communities that hadn't existed before. And in the end, we also brought in a local development corporation, which was run by radical young Puerto Ricans, called Pueblo Nuevo. Never would these people have gotten to know each other.

We also brought together two universities, Cornell and Pratt, which even though they had strong community-planning histories, hadn't done a lot of work together. That was a really good thing. They had some technical skills that we didn't have. We had some other skills that I don't think they had. And that was quite nice. I think we demonstrated the possibility for respectful community-university collaboration on a critical economic development issue.

The last thing is that I think it was transformative for many of the students. They realized through the project that doing this kind of research for folks like the ethnic merchants, who were being squeezed out of our economy, and in some ways our political life, that working with them was an enormously powerful experience. One of the students early on said, "No one works harder than these people. In my education I've been told that if you work hard, you'll get ahead. We have a liberal mayor, a liberal governor, a president who says he cares about entrepreneurship and business and the American dream. These folks really embody that. They came to America to participate in that, and they're getting screwed." I think the students felt real satisfaction in trying to help extend to these ethnic merchants the kind of opportunities they and their family had.

The other thing that was remarkable was that many of the students' families had histories in the Lower East Side. And the project gave a way for them to connect with their grandparents and great-uncles, and learn the story of their own family's journey. For example, a young woman, her name is Alena Tepper, who ended up working as a buyer at Macy's, her father met her mother while working in a rag business across the street from Essex Street. Her grandparents actually bought a stand in Essex Street back in the thirties, and yet that had never been taught to her, this period in her own neighborhood's history. The family's effort to move ahead had largely left behind these really powerful stories of how they made it in America. The fact that Alena worked on this project gave her a chance to talk to her grandmother about difficult and challenging issues that helped her better understand the making of America in a way that I think most students can't appreciate.

Ken continues his meaning-making reflections by telling a story about what happened when his students gave a presentation about their work back on the Cornell campus:

When they came back to campus, the students were so excited about the project. They wanted to show other faculty and fellow students how meaningful this part of their experience was. So they organized a presentation of their project on campus. In the College of Human Ecology, about thirty faculty came, and forty or fifty students came. They were packed in the faculty lounge. The students were in the middle of the presentation, and Dean Jerry Zigler, who is now retired but still teaches, was leaning over so far in his chair during the presentation listening to every word, that about halfway through, his knee gave out and he fell, almost on the floor, disrupting things a bit. Anyway, afterwards I went over to him and said, "You seemed really riveted by this." And then he told me the story of his own family. His grandfather had sold potatoes on Delancey Street, and as Jew, that was the best job he could get. He said that he knew about the importance of these kinds of markets, and that as the dean of this college, he was never prouder that his students were making a contribution by trying to guarantee that this pathway to a better life wasn't closed.

Ken tells another story we need to listen to, one that happened while he was a professor of planning at the University of Illinois, more than a decade after his involvement in the Essex Street Market project. Alan Ruhalter, a butcher who shows up as a character in this story, was the president of the Essex Street Merchants Association during the time when Ken and his students were working on the Essex Street Market project. "Several years ago," Ken begins, in classic storytelling mode,

I had the chance to go back to the Lower East Side to attend a national planning conference in Brooklyn. They asked me if I would do a tour of the Lower East Side. Thirty people signed up, we went on the train, we got off, we went to Ratner's, we went to Gus's Pickles, we went to the Henry Street Settlement House, we went to the Jewish Daily Forward Building. Everything was going great. We're a block away from Essex Street and my wife Kathleen, who was with me at the conference, said, "You know, if anyone sees you in this neighborhood and you don't go to the market, they're going to be really mad at you." I had been in Illinois for more than ten years by then, and it just didn't occur to me that I should go. So anyway, I took the whole group one block out of the way to the Essex Street Market. And of course, it looked drop-dead beautiful, and my heart just raced. I went in, and there's Alan Ruhalter, coming out of a refrigerator with half a side of beef, just like I saw him when we first met. He threw the goddamn cow on the ground, came over and gave me a huge bear hug, and asked me if I got tenure yet. I said yes. He said, "Where are the kiddies?" And I said, "Well, I have some people outside." He said, "Bring them in!" And I brought the whole thirty-person walking tour in. And then Alan Ruhalter regaled them for thirty minutes about how the merchants working with these local churches and this radical group of Puerto Ricans, with the help of the students from Cornell, had saved their market, and how grateful they were. Then he took us on a tour of the market, and every merchant that I knew came and showed me all their goods. It was one of those days where I thought it was a pretty good thing to be a teacher of planning.

In drawing lessons from his experience in the Essex Street Market project, Ken gives us more to learn from and think about. "I don't think anything we did in the Essex Street project was rocket science," he tells us.

There were some basic problem-solving and research techniques that many of us in our own lives use, but not in an intentional and organized fashion. I guess one of the qualities I have is to remind people that they know more than they think they know, particularly poor and working-class people, who are told every day that they're where they are in their station in life because they don't have something that someone else has, and that's why they're poor, and that's why they're working class. So I think the first lesson from this story is about the importance of helping people appreciate the richness of their own experience and knowledge and commitment and passion, and to value that. I think that's really done well in the participatory action research field. So I think bringing to people that appreciation and giving them some sense of the techniques that are available that extend their own thoughtful commonsense approach to problem solving, I think that's one lesson.

The second lesson has to do with the biggest obstacle we have in changing the socioeconomic landscape: the notion that trend is destiny, that there's nothing you can do. I think part of what I do well is to tell the stories from other places where I've been privileged to work, in order to remind people that many of these things that they take for granted as immutable and unchangeable structures are only the inventions of mere men and women, and that thoughtful men and women can change them. So I think it's bringing out those stories through storytelling. I think that has a value.

Think about when people have been moved into action. Often it's been because of the wisdom of the community or culture that has been shared with them in the form of a story. Being able to share the experiences of other successful communities that have turned things around, through sort of storytelling, I think that's an important thing. In the Irish tradition, there is the *seanchaí*, who is the keeper of village wisdom, who is the storyteller, and it's often tales of heroic accomplishments by very common people. It seems to me that that's probably helped the Irish survive through very tough times. The African American community has the same kind of thing—the role of the elder storyteller.

The third lesson is about organizing principles. I know something about an undervalued profession called community organizing, which is a rigorous approach to addressing issues of power and inequality. And I've had training and experience participatory action research (PAR), which is, in many ways, the people's science. Other than that, nothing that I think I've learned is that unique. And I think all these things are teachable and learnable by anyone who has a heartbeat left. It isn't rocket science.

We read what Ken is telling us in these passages from his profile, and what we want to say, quite simply and directly, is *yes*. *Yes* to the truths we find in them—the truths about what students and others can learn by engaging in public work; the truths about people's experience and knowledge and commitment and passion; the truths about the notion that trend is not destiny; the truths about the wisdom of a community or people or culture that is brought out through storytelling; the truths about the changes that storytelling can help to make happen; the truths about rocket science and common sense; and the truths about what academic professionals not only might or could or should do as participants in the public work of democracy, but already have done and are doing.

347

To us, Ken's stories and reflections, and those of all of the other academic professionals we profiled for this book, are powerful and compelling. They teach and show us a great deal about the meaning and value of higher education's public purposes and work, in and for a democratic society. We want to remember what we have learned from and discovered in them. We want to know—better, more deeply, and with a critical as well as an appreciative eye—how to name the lessons we draw from them. Most importantly, we want to discuss and consider what we have found in these profiles with others who have read them, too.

So we're back now where we began in this chapter. After laying out our own interpretation and analysis—incompletely, with so much of what we have learned left out—we're ready to pull up some chairs and ask our readers: What did you find and learn?

Conclusion

In the introduction, we pointed out that the issue of higher education's public purposes and work is not a simple, settled, and empirically documented fact. Rather, it is a complex normative and political question about which there continues to be debate and disagreement. Most important for this book is the specific question of whether academic professionals should be engaged off their campuses in the public work of democracy, and if so, what public purposes they should pursue, what roles they should play, and what contributions they should make.

As we demonstrated in chapter 1, there are four distinct normative traditions in the American academic profession that represent general answers to this question. But as we argued in chapters 2 and 3, we need more than general answers if we are to improve our understanding of higher education's public purposes and work, in and for a democratic society. We need to question the four normative traditions we identified, and the practical theories upon which they are based. Just as importantly, we need to listen to and learn from richly drawn, first-person stories of what academic professionals have been doing and experiencing as they step off their campuses and become engaged in civic life. Such stories can provide us with answers to the public purposes and work question that are specific to the contingencies of context, and the values, interests, and ends academic professionals seek to stand for and pursue in their academic and public work. They can shift our attention from what could or should be to what already has been and is. In doing so, they can help us avoid two unproductive traps: becoming stuck in cycles of abstract theoretical and philosophical hairsplitting, and becoming polarized in contentious debates over which normative tradition is "correct," and what—in general rather than context-specific terms—academic professionals should do as participants in civic life.

Constructed from the transcripts of narrative interviews, the twelve practitioner profiles in part 2 of this book contain a wealth of first-person stories about the civic engagement work and experiences of faculty members from Cornell University's College of Agriculture and Life Sciences. We drew a set of positive lessons from our own deliberately appreciative reading of these profiles in chapter 16. Our lessons challenge our presumptions about and enlarge our understanding of the public purposes and work of academic professionals in land-grant colleges of agriculture. There is more going on than we might presume in the stories these academic professionals tell of their "outreach" and "extension" work. While these stories show us that these academic professionals take up a responsive servant role in their civic engagement work—a role that is tied to their academic expertise and involves attempts to be neutral, unbiased, and objective—they also show us how and why many of them take up additional roles as proactive critics, leaders, and change agents that reflect their nonneutral political and cultural biases, interests, identities, and values.

While the profiles in this book and the lessons we draw from them have a particular relevance in land-grant colleges of agriculture, they also apply across the whole of American higher education. Academic professionals in every institutional type—from community colleges to private research universities—can learn from provocative stories that illuminate how others have answered the public purposes and work question. The profiles also carry a specific kind of relevance that has to do with the ways people understand the meaning and significance of the "land-grant mission." For example, the American Association of State Colleges and Universities (AASCU) launched the American Democracy Project in 2003 as a means of strengthening the civic mission, work, and impacts of its 430 member institutions. While many AASCU members see their institutions as "stewards of place," one president of an AASCU university has referred to AASCU institutions as "land-grants for the 21st century." The profiles in this book and the lessons we draw from them can be used to influence how AASCU members understand the "land-grant" mission and how it connects with the "stewards of place" ethic. The prevailing view in academic literatures, official institutional rhetoric, and informal culture characterizes the land-grant mission (in both historical and contemporary contexts) as being about apolitical and responsive "public service," the meaning and value of which is mainly if not entirely technical and economic rather than political and cultural in nature. It positions academic professionals as service intellectuals, and the land-grant system as *the* historical exemplar of the so-called service ideal in American higher education. By illuminating the proactive, nonneutral political and cultural change agent roles that land-grant faculty members take up in their civic engagement work, our profiles and the lessons we draw from them challenge the trustworthiness of this view.[1]

As we finish this book, we have a new appreciation of the positive roles and contributions academic professionals have taken up in and made to the public work of democracy. We have a strong sense that there is a potential for much greater contribution and impact, and that advances are being made as many people and institutions join an emerging civic engagement movement in American higher education. But we also believe that academic professionals' engagement in civic life often has problematic dimensions and impacts that are not well recognized, and that need to be critically examined and challenged. And we have serious worries about the future of democratic varieties of civic engagement—in the land-grant system and beyond—that require reciprocal, long-term public relationships between academic professionals and their external partners.

With all this in mind, in the remainder of this brief concluding chapter we look to the future as something to be collectively envisioned and shaped in a way that affirms the "first and most essential charge" that President Truman's Commission on Higher Education proclaimed for higher education in 1948: "that at all its levels and in all its fields of specialization it shall be the carrier of democratic values, ideals, and processes."[2] In light of this charge, we are mindful of something Ken Reardon said in his profile:

> There really is very little understanding that the current wave of community-university partnerships is as much a resurrection project for the university—a renewal project for universities' hearts, minds, souls, pedagogy, and intellectual life—as it is just helping the poor.

The resurrection project Ken is speaking about in this passage involves the reclaiming of higher education's "first and most essential charge." This charge is not just to the university as an institution. It's also to scholars, scientists, engineers, artists, and educators as democratic, civic-minded, publicly engaged professionals. In our view, a project aimed at renewing universities' hearts, minds, souls, pedagogy, and intellectual life will not amount to much if it fails to include a companion project that explicitly aims to strengthen the civic nature and meaning of the academic profession. This companion project, borrowing language that William Sullivan has usefully developed, is to reconstruct a civic professionalism in the academic profession. The aim of reconstruction in the professions, Sullivan writes, is "both to better understand the intrinsic purposes of the professional enterprise and to suggest the lines along which the enterprise needs to move if it is to reclaim those purposes more vigorously and coherently."[3]

Civic professionalism in higher education comes in many forms. Academic professionals can and do work for public-regarding ends in public-regarding ways in campus-based laboratories, classrooms, archives, libraries, workshops, and studios. A pluralist approach to the project of reconstructing civic professionalism would affirm and seek to strengthen all of its many varieties—including the variety we have been focusing on in this book, which is expressed through direct, face-to-face, off-campus engagement in the public work of democracy.

In concluding this book, we want to name and briefly discuss three things we can and must do to improve, support, and defend this particular variety of civic professionalism in American higher education at this critical historical moment. First, we need to take an organizing approach to change. Second, we need to engage in collective reflection and inquiry that is both appreciative and critical. And third, we need to work from a hopeful, prophetic stance that focuses on the pursuit of unrealized ideals and potential. These three things are closely interrelated. They reflect our practical theory about the way things are and the way things should be, and how the gap between them not only can, but also should be narrowed.

An Organizing Approach

The faculty members we interviewed and profiled for this book are remarkably positive people. But when we asked them how well they think their off-campus civic engagement work is understood, valued, and supported, and where they see things heading in the future, many were quite pessimistic. Drawing on their own experience and/or the experiences of those they know as evidence, many of them claimed that such work is not often understood, valued, or supported by their peers or by administrative leaders. In explaining why, they pointed to a variety of internal and external barriers and disincentives, including a lack of rewards, a lack of interest, an unwillingness to expend the level and kind of energy and time it takes to be engaged in public work, the erosion of public funding, the decline (in both numbers and political power) of rural and agricultural constituencies, hiring patterns in their departments that reflect a privileging of the research university norm of civic detachment, and the growing attraction of "big science" initiatives in genomics and other areas of study that make working in local communities look trivial and outdated.

This is a bleak picture. If it is real rather than imagined, and if nothing is done to change it, the end result seems obvious. As Frank Rossi tells us in his profile, reflecting on the future of the land-grant system's public engagement mission, "the whole thing is going to go away. People just aren't going to see the value."

In light of the pessimistic view of the future we heard from Frank and others—and often feel ourselves—we need to listen to something Nick Jordan told us. Jordan is a professor in the Department of Agronomy and Plant Genetics at the University of Minnesota. We interviewed him several years ago for a previous book we were working on. When we asked him about what he is up against as a publicly engaged scholar, he said that "the most important challenge is that there is a rapid decline in public support for what we're doing. It's just very clear that we're not getting an adequate base of financial support for what we do here." He went on to speak of a "managed decline" in his college, the official name of which is the College of Food, Agricultural, and Natural Resource Sciences. In his view, this decline is partly a result of the "obsolescent story" he says his college communicates to the public about agriculture, and the college's role in supporting it. "The obsolescent story," he says, "is that agriculture is about the production of commodities in an industrial mode, and that's all it's about. It's not about public health, it's not about environmental quality, and it's not about rural communities."[4]

Jordan has been working with many of his colleagues to challenge and change this story. In reflecting on his experience, he offers us a glimmer of hope. "I'm hopeful," he says,

> that we're developing what I think is an increasingly powerful and compelling case against current industrialized agriculture. This case is rapidly expanding beyond the traditional sustainability concerns of environmental quality and rural community well-being to issues such as public health, children's health, and environmental quality that are compelling to a much larger group of people. I think that we are coming to connect our notions of how we should function differently as an agriculture college to a broader movement about how universities in general should function differently as engaged civic institutions.

In order to understand the significance of what Jordan is saying here, we need to relate it to something William Sullivan has written. Sullivan writes that it is "far from clear" whether professionals in a variety of fields "will be able to sustain their social importance without re-engaging the public over the value of their work to the society at large." If the professions are to have a future, he goes on to say, "they may need to rest their case on the basis of a civic rather than a wholly technical understanding of what it is that professionals are about."[5]

What Sullivan tells us professionals "may" need to do, Nick Jordan is already doing with his colleagues in Minnesota. Jordan and his colleagues are making and resting their case about the value of their work in a land-grant college of agriculture on a civic rather than wholly technical understanding of their roles and work as academic professionals. From this we see that reconstructing civic professionalism in the academic profession is partly an intellectual and educational project. But a sober assessment of realities of power and interests teaches us that it is not only an intellectual and educational project. It is also a political project that requires an organizing approach to change, both within and beyond the academy. The kind of organizing we have in mind is practical, educational, developmental, democratic, and productive. It is an expression of a democratic populist politics—a politics that is not about mobilizing people for protests but tapping people's self-interests and talents, and developing and exercising leadership, relational power, and civic agency. It borrows and builds on lessons from organizing traditions of the American civil rights movement and the Industrial Areas Foundation (IAF).[6]

Pursuing this kind of organizing in the academy is a difficult and time-consuming challenge that cuts against the grain of technocratic tendencies that are especially pronounced in research universities, as well as more general tendencies in higher education toward one-way service delivery and civic detachment. But we know it is possible, because we know people who are doing it. Nick Jordan is one of them. He and several of his colleagues from the University of Minnesota have taken an organizing approach in their academic and public work on issues of agricultural sustainability. Another one of the practitioners of this kind of organizing in American higher education is Maria Avila, a former IAF organizer who is now the director of the Center for Community Based Learning at Occidental College in Los Angeles. Together with her academic and community partners, she is crafting an approach to civic engagement that can be adapted to fit other settings and situations. Many, many others are taking an organizing approach in their institutions and communities through civic education and service-learning initiatives, collaborative initiatives in the arts and humanities, and community-based research.[7]

Collective Reflection and Inquiry, Appreciative and Critical

In line with an organizing approach that is educative and developmental, that seeks to build and exercise leadership, relational power, and civic agency rather than simply mobilizing people for protests, the project of reconstructing civic professionalism in the academic profession must include robust forms of collective reflection and inquiry that are both appreciative and critical in nature. Participants in such reflection and inquiry would attend to the two main elements of the reconstruction project that William Sullivan notes, "both to better understand the intrinsic purposes of the professional enterprise and to suggest the lines along which the enterprise needs to move if it is to reclaim those purposes more vigorously and coherently." But because the nature of the reconstruction project is political as well as intellectual and educational, participants in collective reflection and inquiry have to do more than "suggest" lines of movement; they have to act on them as well.[8]

353

There are many tools available to help us design and facilitate processes of collective, action-oriented reflection and inquiry. Unsurprisingly, we favor processes that are centered on stories. Stories and storytelling can be powerful sources of collective learning about the public purposes and work of the "professional enterprise" in higher education, and the lines along which we need to move in our efforts to reclaim, support, and strengthen them. In finding stories to learn from, we have tried to follow the spirit of the organizing philosophy that civil rights leader Ella Baker promoted: find people who are already working, learn from them, and help them move into positions of leadership. In our case, those who are "already working" are people who are deeply engaged in the public work of democracy not only as "private" citizens, but also as academic professionals.[9]

In this book we limit ourselves to appreciative inquiry and analysis, for the strategic and ethical reasons named in chapter 16. At the risk of stating the obvious, we want to say a few words about why collective reflection and inquiry aimed at reconstructing civic professionalism in the academy must be critical as well as appreciative.

First, while we found a lot to appreciate in the practice stories the academic professionals we interviewed told us, we also noted that their civic engagement work and experiences involve significant tensions, conflicts, dilemmas, ambiguities, and contradictions. By no means do we think that they all dealt with these challenges in ways that are beyond criticism. Many of them have expressed doubts about their own work and that of their colleagues. For example, as we mentioned in the abstract we wrote for Tom Lyson's profile some of the people we asked to review it were deeply troubled by the way he relates his work and experiences. They were also highly critical of the way he worked when he was a Cornell faculty member. As an outspoken critic of industrial agriculture—and at times, his own academic institution and discipline—Tom ruffled many feathers. In light of this, we should ask: How did others view his work? How well did he play the role of social critic? What were the consequences of the ways he took up his role as a critic, particularly with respect to his college's relationships with its various stakeholders and funders, and its work on sustainability? And what about what we see him saying and doing in the practice story he tells in his profile about fighting against school consolidation in Freeville, New York? How well did he negotiate the dilemma of the relation of expertise and democracy in that project? How well did he recognize and navigate the tensions between his identity as an academic professional and his identity as a resident of Freeville? Tom's profile is not the only one that provokes critical questions such as these. There are troubling things to be found in all of the profiles in this book that should be examined with a critical eye. For collective, action-oriented reflection and inquiry to be effective, such questions must be raised and addressed.

A second reason why collective reflection and inquiry must be critical as well as appreciative is that civic professionalism is not merely a matter of individual choice. It requires support, legitimacy, and what amounts to a social compact within specific institutional settings, and between institutions in the larger society. It can be enabled or disabled by people's attitudes, behaviors, and presumptions, and by forces of power and interests that act with or against it. Narrow technical, instrumental, and economic views of the professional enterprise can corrupt or block a broader civic conception of professionalism. When such forces show up in a particular context, they must be examined critically.

Third, collective reflection and inquiry that is action-oriented requires the development and testing of practical theories about the way things are and the way things should be, and how the gap between them can and should be narrowed. The development of effective practical theories requires critical reflection and inquiry about not only people's conceptual frameworks, but also their experiences. (The latter is one reason why we see a value in stories.) Without critical reflection that highlights the tension between the world as it is and the world as it should be, we run the risk of developing practical theories that reflect a romantic and ineffective idealism or a pessimistic and hopeless realism.[10]

A Prophetic Stance

Finally, if we are to live in the tension between the world as it is and the world as it should be with a sense of hope for the future, we must take a prophetic stance that enables us to focus our attention on the pursuit of unrealized ideals and potential that are worth fighting and working for. Approached from a prophetic stance, the intellectual and political project of reconstructing civic professionalism in the American academy calls on us to reclaim a set of ideals and values related not only to higher education's public purposes, but also to the public philosophy we embrace for our nation and world, and our local and global sense of civic and ecological agency and responsibility.

We are mindful here of something the moral philosopher Alasdair MacIntyre has written:

> I can only answer the question, "What am I to do?" if I can answer the question "Of what story or stories do I find myself a part?" We enter human society, that is, with one or more imputed characters—roles into which we have been drafted—and we have to learn what they are in order to be able to understand how others respond to us and how our responses to them are apt to be construed.[11]

What MacIntyre says makes a lot of sense to us. People (including academic professionals) do find themselves a part of stories that draft them into roles and influence how they answer the question, "What am I to do?" But they don't just passively find themselves a part of stories that are not of their own choosing, and that draft them into predetermined roles they have no say about. They also do two other things: they actively situate (rather than "find") themselves in stories they choose to play particular kinds of roles in, and they restory the stories they find themselves a part of. These two things are expressions of civic and moral agency. They guide and shape how people answer the question, "What am I to do?"

The ways the academic professionals we interviewed answer the public purposes and work question in American higher education are not simply a function of the stories they "find" themselves a part of. They are also a function of the stories they choose to be a part of. This is one of the marks of a civic professional who is not simply "serving" others, but working with them for public-regarding ends and in public-regarding ways.

Let's listen for a moment to Tom Maloney. "People are asking," he tells us near the end of his profile, why we need people like me—professionals who are funded by their tax dollars—to address agricultural management and business issues. They think these issues can be addressed better or cheaper by private consultants. Well, some of them can be. But the standard response to that is that we're impartial. There are people out there who challenge our impartiality from time to time, but we're not selling a product per se, and a lot of the consultants, especially on farms and in landscaping businesses, are selling a product, and some of these consulting services come along with the product. So there is a bias there. We're not selling a product. We're not associated with a profit motive.

Here we see Tom speaking from a story he finds himself a part of: the familiar land-grant mission story of responsive and impartial service. But as Tom continues, he situates himself in another story. "I live in Cortland, and I live outside of town," he says.

There's a dairy farm across the road from me. There are field crops all around my property. My family and I like that community, and we want to see farmers survive in it. We want to see the landscape businesses do well. We don't have any fruit farms where I live, but I think New Yorkers would say they want to see the apple industry recover from a very difficult financial time, and still be able to drive on Route 104 near Lake Ontario and drive through orchards. I personally don't want the landscapes of New York all to be Blockbuster video stores and Applebee's restaurants and Comfort Inns. That open space is something that's really valuable. As our 7,000 dairy farms in this state diminish, we need to replace them with something that is equally acceptable to us. And so, to the extent that I can, I want to help keep people in business, doing what they're good at, doing what they like to do. Not all of them will make it, and maybe that's not such a bad thing. But to evolve to a state that still is producing food, and has landscapes that are valuable and attractive to all of us, is what keeps me going.

Here we see a story that is rich with public meaning, and with the tension between the world as it is and the world as it should be. From a prophetic stance, Tom chooses to situate himself as an actor in this story. In doing so, we see that he is not only or merely working as an impartial servant. He is working as a critic and leader as well. Reading what he says here, and what he and the others we interviewed say in their practice stories, we see elements of civic professionalism—not perfectly rendered, but present nonetheless, and already under reconstruction. We see in their stories the prophetic words of President Truman's Commission on Higher Education: that higher education's "task is not merely to meet the demands of the present but to alter those demands if necessary, so as to keep them always suited to democratic ideals. Perhaps its most important role is to serve as an instrument of social transition, and its responsibilities are defined in terms of the kind of civilization society hopes to build."[12]

Mindful of the temptations and dangers of a technocratic hubris in academia that corrupts democratic ideals, we've been heartened to find and learn from academic professionals who not only have a deep sense of humility about their own expertise, but also a profound respect for the knowledge, expertise, and wisdom of people from all walks of life. "During my Ph.D. work," Anu Rangarajan tells us in her profile, "I came to value that everyone is an expert in the place that they are. The arrogance of the academy, thinking it knows better, is why we aren't as effective as we could be." Moving forward with the project of reconstructing a democratic-minded civic professionalism in the academy, we would be well advised to remember Anu's words.

Notes

Foreword

1. "Solving the College Crisis" *US News and World Report* Special Issue on America's Best Colleges, September 2009.
2. Bernard Crick in his great 1962 dissenting work, *In Defense of Politics* called politics "a great and civilizing activity" that emphasized negotiation and engagement of diverse views and interests. Drawing on Aristotle and Hannah Arendt, Crick argued that politics is about plurality, not similarity. Aristotle (and following him Arendt) had proposed that an emphasis on the "unity" of the political community destroyed its defining quality. He contrasted politics with military alliance, based on "similarity" of aim. In this vein, Crick defended politics against a list of forces which he saw as obliterating recognition of plurality. Its "enemies" included nationalism, technology, and mass democracy, as well as partisans of conservative, liberal, and socialist ideologies.
3. Josiah Ober, *Democracy and Knowledge: Innovation and Learning in Classical Athens* (Princeton: Princeton University Press, 2009), p. 1.
4. Donna Shalala, "Mandate for a New Century," October 31, 1989, University of Illinois, David Dodds Henry Lectures, http://www.uic.edu/depts/oaa/ddh/ddhlectures/Lec11.pdf.
5. See Harry C. Boyte, "The Struggle Against Positivism," *Academe* August 2000.
6. Thomas Bender, *Intellect and Public Life: Essays on the Social History of Academic Intellectuals in the United States* (Baltimore, MD: Johns Hopkins University Press, 1993).
7. Jürgen Habermas, *Between Facts and Norms: Contributions to a Discourse Theory of Law and Democracy* (Cambridge: MIT Press, 1992).

Introduction and Overview

1. For a historical perspective on and provocative exploration of the social and environmental issues related to the seed industry, see Jack R. Kloppenburg, *First the Seed: The Political Economy of Plant Biotechnology,* 2nd ed. (Madison: University of Wisconsin Press, 2005).

2. For more on the Public Seed Initiative, visit www.plbr.cornell.edu/psi.

3. *Higher Education for American Democracy: A Report of the President's Commission on Higher Education* (New York: Harper & Brothers, 1948). For critiques of the commission's work, see Gail Kennedy, ed., *Education for Democracy: The Debate over the Report of the President's Commission on Higher Education* (Boston: D.C. Heath, 1952).

4. President's Commission on Higher Education, *Report,* 2, 6.

5. Ibid., 2.

6. Ibid., 8, 11, 14.

7. Ibid., 12, 13. The commission's celebration of reason and its negative characterization of "emotion" in this passage from its report reflects a normative theory of citizenship and deliberative work in democratic politics that has recently been challenged. Instead of viewing emotion as something that should be put aside in favor of reason, scholars are now viewing it as an essential dimension of democratic citizenship that must be interwoven with reason. For examples of works on this theme, see Martha C. Nussbaum, *Upheavals of Thought: The Intelligence of Emotions* (New York: Cambridge University Press, 2001); George E. Marcus, *The Sentimental Citizen: Emotion in Democratic Politics* (University Park: Pennsylvania State University Press, 2002); Sharon R. Krause, *Civil Passions: Moral Sentiment and Democratic Deliberation* (Princeton, N.J.: Princeton University Press, 2008); and Frank Fischer, *Democracy and Expertise: Reorienting Policy Inquiry* (New York: Oxford University Press, 2009).

8. President's Commission on Higher Education, *Report,* 10.

9. Ibid., 48.

10. Ibid., 97, 100. The commission's view of the deficiencies of the college graduate and its call for an education that attends to more than technical training was influenced in part by the Harvard report on general education, *General Education in a Free Society: Report of the Harvard Committee* (Cambridge: The University, 1945).

11. President's Commission on Higher Education, *Report,* 102, 6.

12. *Presidents' Declaration on the Civic Responsibility of Higher Education* (Providence: Campus Compact, 1999).

13. On the commercialization trend, see S. Slaughter and L.L. Leslie, *Academic Capitalism: Politics, Policies, and the Entrepreneurial University* (Baltimore: Johns Hopkins University Press, 1997); D. Bok, *Universities in the Marketplace: The Commercialization of Higher Education* (Princeton, N.J.: Princeton University Press, 2003); D.G. Stein, ed., *Buying In or Selling Out? The Commercialization of the American Research University* (New Brunswick, N.J.: Rutgers University Press, 2004); F. Newman, L. Couturier, and J. Scurry, *The Future of Higher Education: Rhetoric, Reality, and the Risks of the Market* (San Francisco: Jossey-Bass, 2004); R.L. Geiger, *Knowledge and Money: Research Universities*

and the Paradox of the Marketplace (Stanford, Calif.: Stanford University Press, 2004); and Burton A. Weisbrod, Jeffrey P. Ballou, and Evelyn D. Asch, *Mission and Money: Understanding the University* (New York: Cambridge University Press, 2008).

14. Examples of works in this thread of the conversation include Thomas Ehrlich, ed., *Civic Responsibility and Higher Education* (Westport, Conn.: Oryx Press, 2000); Barbara Jacoby and Associates, *Building Partnerships for Service-Learning* (San Francisco: Jossey-Bass, 2003); Anne Colby, Thomas Ehrlich, Elizabeth Beaumont, and Jason Stephens, *Educating Citizens: Preparing America's Undergraduates for Lives of Moral and Civic Responsibility* (San Francisco: Jossey-Bass, 2003); Anne Colby, Elizabeth Beaumont, Thomas Ehrlich, and Josh Corngold, *Educating for Democracy: Preparing Undergraduates for Responsible Political Engagement* (San Francisco: Jossey-Bass, 2007); Lee Benson, Ira Harkavy, and John Puckett, *Dewey's Dream: Universities and Democracies in an Age of Education Reform* (Philadelphia: Temple University Press, 2007); and Barbara Jacoby and Associates, *Civic Engagement in Higher Education: Concepts and Practices* (San Francisco: Jossey-Bass, 2009).

15. Examples of works in this thread of the conversation include Russell Jacoby, *The Last Intellectuals: American Culture in the Age of Academe* (New York: Noonday Press, 1987); Zygmunt Bauman, *Legislators and Interpreters: On Modernity, Post-Modernity, and Intellectuals* (Ithaca, N.Y.: Cornell University Press, 1987); Carl Boggs, *Intellectuals and the Crisis of Modernity* (Albany, N.Y.: SUNY Press, 1993); Edward W. Said, *Representations of the Intellectual* (New York: Vintage Books, 1994); Ron Eyerman, *Between Culture and Politics: Intellectuals in Modern Society* (Cambridge, Mass.: Polity Press, 1994); Leon Fink, S.T. Leonard, and D.M. Reid, eds., *Intellectuals and Public Life: Between Radicalism and Reform* (Ithaca, N.Y.: Cornell University Press, 1996); Jeffrey C. Goldfarb, *Civility and Subversion: The Intellectual in Democratic Society* (New York: Cambridge University Press, 1998); Richard A. Posner, *Public Intellectuals: A Study of Decline* (Cambridge: Harvard University Press, 2001); Michael Walzer, *The Company of Critics: Social Criticism and Political Commitment in the Twentieth Century* (New York: Basic Books, 2002); Arthur M. Melzer, Jerry Weinberger, and M. Richard Zinman, eds., *The Public Intellectual: Between Philosophy and Politics* (Lanham, Md.: Rowman & Littlefield, 2003); Alan Wolfe, *An Intellectual in Public* (Ann Arbor: University of Michigan Press, 2003); and Amitai Etzioni and Alyssa Bowditch, eds., *Public Intellectuals: An Endangered Species?* (Lanham, Md.: Rowman & Littlefield, 2006).

16. Stanley Fish, *Save the World on Your Own Time* (New York: Oxford University Press, 2008), 71, 72. The views and positions Fish articulates in his book are remarkably consistent with those that Max Weber laid out in his classic essay "Science as a Vocation," which was originally published in 1919. Weber's essay is included in *From Max Weber: Essays in Sociology*, edited by H.H. Gerth and C. Wright Mills (New York: Routledge, 1948).

17. President's Commission on Higher Education, *Report*, 6.

18. Harry C. Boyte, *Everyday Politics: Reconnecting Citizens and Public Life* (Philadelphia: University of Pennsylvania Press, 2004), 5. On politics as the work of citizens in everyday settings, also see David Mathews, *Politics for People: Finding a Responsible Public Voice*, 2nd ed. (Urbana: University of Illinois Press, 1999), and Harry C. Boyte, *The Citizen Solution: How You Can Make a Difference* (St. Paul: Minnesota Historical Society Press, 2008).

19. Steven Brint, *In an Age of Experts: The Changing Role of Professionals in Politics and Public Life* (Princeton, N.J.: Princeton University Press, 1994); William M. Sullivan, "Engaging the Civic Option: A New Academic Professionalism?" *Campus Compact Reader* (Summer 2003), 10; Thomas Bender, *Intellect and Public Life* (Baltimore: Johns Hopkins University Press, 1993), 128. On civic professionalism, also see William M. Sullivan, *Work and Integrity: The Crisis and Promise of Professionalism in America* (San Francisco: Jossey-Bass, 2005).

20. Our approach to developing and using practitioner profiles is inspired by John Forester's work. For examples, see *The Deliberative Practitioner: Encouraging Participatory Planning Processes* (Cambridge: MIT Press, 1999) and *Dealing with Differences: Dramas of Mediating Public Disputes* (New York: Oxford University Press, 2009).

21. Kurt Lewin, a social psychologist who served on the faculties of both Cornell University and MIT, has been credited with saying: "Nothing is as practical as a good theory." See Davydd J. Greenwood and Morten Levin, *Introduction to Action Research: Social Research for Social Change*, 2nd ed (Thousand Oaks, Calif.: Sage Publications, 2007), 18. The "practical theory" phrase was used as the title of an intellectual biography of Kurt Lewin. See Alfred J. Marrow, *The Practical Theorist: The Life and Work of Kurt Lewin* (New York: Basic Books, 1969).

Chapter One. Answering the Public Purposes and Work Question

1. Richard Hofstadter, "The Revolution in Higher Education," in *Paths of American Thought*, edited by A.M. Schlesinger Jr. and M. White (Boston: Houghton Mifflin, 1963), 287, 288. On the academic revolution, see R.F. Butts, *The College Charts Its Course: Historical Conceptions and Current Proposals* (New York: McGraw-Hill, 1939); L.R. Veysey, *The Emergence of the American University* (Chicago: University of Chicago Press, 1965); and C. Jencks and D. Riesman, *The Academic Revolution* (Garden City, N.Y.: Doubleday, 1968).

2. Thomas Haskell, *Objectivity Is Not Neutrality: Explanatory Schemes in History* (Baltimore: Johns Hopkins University Press, 1998), 184. On the history of the struggle for academic freedom, see R. Hofstadter and W.P. Metzger, *The Development of Academic Freedom in the United States* (New York: Columbia University Press, 1955). On collegial autonomy and self-governance in the academic profession, see P.G. Altbach, "Problems and Possibilities: The US Academic Profession," in *The Academic Profession: The Professoriate in Crisis*, edited by P.G. Altbach and M.J. Finkelstein (New York: Garland Publishing, 1997); and R.O. Berdahl and T.R. McConnell, "Autonomy and Accountability in American Higher Education," in *American Higher Education in the Twenty-first Century: Social, Political, and Economic Challenges*, edited by P.G. Altbach, R.O. Berdahl, and P.J. Gumport (Baltimore: Johns Hopkins University Press, 1999).

3. American Association of University Professors (AAUP), "Report of the Committee on Academic Freedom and Tenure," in *American Higher Education: A Documentary History*, edited by R. Hofstadter and W. Smith, vol. 2 (Chicago: University of Chicago Press, 1961), 862.

4. Ibid., 864, 865.

5. Ibid., 865.

6. Ibid., 868.

7. Ibid., 870, 871.

8. Ibid, 874, 875.

9. Mark C. Smith, *Social Science in the Crucible: The American Debate over Objectivity and Purpose, 1918–1941* (Durham, N.C.: Duke University Press, 1994), 6.

10. Many scholars have sharply (and persuasively) critiqued the philosophical, epistemological, and political groundings of the service intellectual tradition, particularly in the discipline of sociology. See, for example, Robert W. Friedrichs, *A Sociology of Sociology* (New York: Free Press, 1970).

11. For discussions of Lundberg's life and work, see Alfred de Grazia, Rollo Handy, E.C. Harwood, and Paul Kurtz, eds., *The Behavioral Sciences: Essays in Honor of George A. Lundberg* (Great Barrington, Mass.: Behavioral Research Council, 1968).

12. George A. Lundberg, *Can Science Save Us?* 2nd ed. (New York: David McKay, 1961), 1, 2.

13. Ibid., 2, 15, 78.

14. Ibid., 16, 29.

15. Ibid., 19, 59–60.

16. Ibid., 38.

17. Ibid.

18. Ibid., 40.

19. Ibid., 33, 35.

20. Ibid., 35–57.

21. Ibid., 57, 58.

22. While the so-called Chicago school of sociology was not monolithic in its normative views, it did have a dominant service intellectual character during the 1920s. See T.V. Smith and L.D. White, eds., *Chicago: An Experiment in Social Research* (Chicago: University of Chicago Press, 1929), M. Bulmer, *The Chicago School of Sociology: Institutionalization, Diversity, and the Role of Social Research* (Chicago: University of Chicago Press, 1984), and Martyn Hammersley, *The Dilemma of Qualitative Method: Herbert Blumer and the Chicago Tradition* (New York: Routledge, 1909). For what amounts to a contemporary defense of the service intellectual tradition in the social science methods literature, see Martyn Hammersley, *The Politics of Social Research* (Thousand Oaks, Calif.: Sage Publications, 1995).

23. See Weber, "Science as a Vocation"; and Fish, *Save the World.*

24. For an account of Albion Small's life and work, see Vernon K. Dibble, *The Legacy of Albion Small* (Chicago: University of Chicago Press, 1975).

25. Albion W. Small, "Scholarship and Social Agitation," *American Journal of Sociology* 1, no. 5 (1896), 564. Small's views about the nature and purposes of sociology represent an interesting attempt to maintain reformist elements of the discipline even as its practitioners adopted "scientific" methods and epistemologies. For studies of the tensions and problems the shift from so-called classical to scientific forms of sociology raised during the late nineteenth and early twentieth centuries, see Mary O. Furner, *Advocacy and Objectivity: A Crisis in the Professionalization of American Social Science, 1865–1905*

(Lexington: University Press of Kentucky, 1975); and Hammersley, *The Dilemma of Qualitative Method.*

26. Small, "Scholarship and Social Agitation," 565.

27. Ibid., 566, 567.

28. Ibid., 567, 569.

29. Ibid., 569.

30. Ibid., 569, 570, 576–77.

31. Ibid., 581. It must be noted that Small later rejected his view that the scholar should function as a social agitator. In a book published in 1905, he declared that "the sociologist's business is not to agitate, but to investigate. He will do his best work in the end upon concrete questions, by provisionally not working upon them at all. Thus in the present instance there is work enough for many sociologists, in determining typical relations of the leading social interests, without leaving the field of scientific investigation to enlist in the fighting ranks of any particular social class." Albion W. Small, *General Sociology: An Exposition of the Main Development in Sociological Theory from Spencer to Ratzenhofer* (Chicago: University of Chicago Press, 1905), 303.

32. Small, "Scholarship and Social Agitation," 581–82. This passage from Small's article reveals an earlier purposivist dimension of the sociological work of the University of Chicago. During the development of the so-called Chicago school during the 1920s, this dimension was placed in tension with—and ultimately was eclipsed by—the service intellectual tradition. See Bulmer, *Chicago School of Sociology.*

33. Small, "Scholarship and Social Agitation," 582.

34. AAUP, "Academic Freedom and Tenure," 870–71.

35. Posner, *Public Intellectuals*, 25. There is a growing literature on the public intellectual tradition. See, for example, Jacoby, *The Last Intellectuals*; Said, *Representations of the Intellectual*; Fink, Leonard, and Reid, *Intellectuals and Public Life*; Leon Fink, *Progressive Intellectuals and the Dilemmas of Democratic Commitment* (Cambridge: Harvard University Press, 1997); Walzer, *The Company of Critics*; Melzer, Weinberger, and Zinman, *The Public Intellectual*; Etzioni and Bowditch, *Public Intellectuals*; and John Louis Recchiuti, *Civic Engagement: Social Science and Progressive-Era Reform in New York City* (Philadelphia: University of Pennsylvania Press, 2007). On the inherently subjective nature of conceptions of "the public interest," see Charles E. Lindblom and David K. Cohen, *Usable Knowledge: Social Science and Social Problem Solving* (New Haven: Yale University Press, 1979).

36. Amy Gutmann, *Democratic Education*, rev. ed. (Princeton, N.J.: Princeton University Press, 1999), 174, 188, 175.

37. Ibid., 179.

38. C. Wright Mills, *The Sociological Imagination* (New York: Oxford University Press, 1959), 195. For a study of Mills's life and work, see Daniel Geary, *Radical Ambition: C. Wright Mills, the Left, and American Social Thought* (Berkeley: University of California Press, 2009). A new collection of Mills's writings has recently been published. See John H. Summers, ed., *The Politics of Truth: Selected Writings of C. Wright Mills* (New York: Oxford University Press, 2008).

39. Mills, *The Sociological Imagianation*, 4, 5, 6, 7, 8.

40. Ibid., 11, 13.

41. Ibid., 21, 84, 21.

42. Ibid., 74, 33.

43. Ibid., 56, 55.

44. Ibid., 74, 75.

45. Ibid., 100, 101, 55, 102, 76, 102.

46. Ibid., 178, 179.

47. Ibid., 179, 180, 181.

48. Ibid., 183.

49. Ibid., 184, 185–86.

50. Ibid., 186.

51. Ibid., 187–88.

52. Ibid., 189, 191, 191–92. Interestingly, in a footnote on page 189, Mills claims that those who practice abstracted empiricism as their sole activity "cannot perform a liberating educational role."

53. Evan Thomas, "Obama's Nobel Headache," *Newsweek,* April 6, 2009, 24. There are literally thousands of examples of books that academic professionals like Krugman have written throughout the history of American higher education.

54. Mills, *The Sociological Imagination*, 192.

55. Small, "Scholarship and Social Agitation," 581. For an excellent and important study of how scholars enacted Small's vision in the Progressive Era, see Recchiuti, *Civic Engagement*. For a contemporary critique of Mills position rejecting close and direct engagement in civic life on the part of social scientists, see Michael Burawoy, "Open Letter to C. Wright Mills," in *Practising Public Scholarship: Experiences and Possibilities beyond the Academy*, edited by Katharyne Mitchell (West Sussex, UK: Wiley-Blackwell, 2008). It should be noted here that Mills's own work took him beyond the restrictive range he articulated in the appendix of *The Sociological Imagination*. He was, for example, deeply and directly engaged in off-campus work with labor unions. See Geary, *Radical Ambition*.

56. There is a large and growing literature about this second purposivist tradition. For a few examples, see the following: on action research and participatory action research, see Greenwood and Levin, *Introduction to Action Research*; and Peter Reason and Hilary Bradbury, eds., *The SAGE Handbook of Action Research: Participative Inquiry and Practice*, 2nd ed. (Thousand Oaks, Calif.: Sage Publications, 2007); on community-based research, see Kerry J. Strand, Nicholas Cutforth, Randy Stoecker, Sam Marullo, and Patrick Donohue, *Community-Based Research and Higher Education: Principles and Practices* (San Francisco: Jossey-Bass, 2003), Meredith Minkler and Nina Wallerstein, eds., *Community-Based Participatory Research for Health* (San Francisco: Jossey-Bass, 2003), and Barbara A. Israel, Eugenia Eng, Amy J. Schulz, and Edith A. Parker, eds., *Methods in Community-Based Participatory Research for Health* (San Francisco: Jossey-Bass, 2005); on emancipatory research, see Brian Fay, *Critical Social Science: Liberation and Its Limits* (Ithaca, N.Y.: Cornell University Press, 1987), Patti Lather, *Getting Smart: Feminist Research and Pedagogy with/in the Postmodern* (New York: Routledge, 1991), and Andrew Gitlin,

ed., *Power and Method: Political Activism and Educational Research* (New York: Routledge, 1994); on activist research, see Charles. F. Hale, ed., *Engaging Contradictions: Theory, Politics, and Methods of Activist Scholarship* (Berkeley: University of California Press, 2008); on the scholarship of engagement and engaged scholarship, see Kelly Ward, *Faculty Service Roles and the Scholarship of Engagement*, ASHE-ERIC Higher Education Report, vol. 29, no. 5 (San Francisco: Jossey-Bass, 2003), Andrew H. Van de Ven, *Engaged Scholarship: A Guide for Organizational and Social Research* (New York: Oxford University Press, 2007), and Dan W. Butin, *Rethinking Service Learning: Embracing the Scholarship of Engagement within Higher Education* (Sterling, Va.: Stylus Publishing, 2008); on public scholarship, see Scott J. Peters, Nicholas R. Jordan, Margaret Adamek, and Theodore R. Alter, eds., *Engaging Campus and Community: The Practice of Public Scholarship in the State and Land-Grant University System* (Dayton, Ohio: Kettering Foundation Press, 2005), and Rosa A. Eberly and Jeremy Cohen, eds., *A Laboratory for Public Scholarship and Democracy* (San Francisco: Jossey-Bass, 2006).

57. Greenwood and Levin, *Introduction to Action Research*, 3.

58. Our view of public scholarship is drawn from our own work. See Peters et al., *Engaging Campus and Community*, and Scott J. Peters, "Reconstructing a Democratic Tradition of Public Scholarship in the Land-Grant System," in *Agent of Democracy: Higher Education and the HEX Journey*, edited by David W. Brown and Deborah Witte (Dayton, Ohio: Kettering Foundation Press, 2008), 121–48.

59. Our view of educational organizing draws from both the American civic rights movement of the 1950s and 1960s and the Industrial Areas Foundation (IAF). For the educational organizing tradition in the civil rights movement, see Charles M. Payne, *I've Got the Light of Freedom: The Organizing Tradition and the Mississippi Freedom Struggle* (Berkeley: University of California Press, 1995, 2007); and Barbara Ransby, *Ella Baker and the Black Freedom Movement: A Radical Democratic Vision* (Chapel Hill: University of North Carolina Press, 2003). For the educational organizing tradition in the IAF, see Mary Beth Rogers, *Cold Anger: A Story of Faith and Power Politics* (Denton: University of North Texas Press, 1990); Mark R. Warren, *Dry Bones Rattling: Community Building to Revitalize American Democracy* (Princeton, N.J.: Princeton University Press, 2001); and Edward T. Chambers, *Roots for Radicals: Organizing for Power, Action, and Justice* (New York: Continuum, 2003). There is a little-known tradition of educational organizing in the extension work of the national land-grant university system. See Scott J. Peters, "Rousing the People on the Land: The Roots of an Educational Organizing Tradition in Extension Work," *Journal of Extension* 40, no. 3 (2002), online at http://www.joe.org/joe/2002june/a1.php.; and Scott J. Peters, "Citizens Developing a Voice at the Table: A Story of Educational Organizing in Contemporary Extension Work," *Journal of Extension.* 40, no. 4 (2002), online at http://www.joe.org/joe/2002june/a1.php.

60. There is no published history of the democratic variety of the purposivist AR/PS/EO tradition in the land-grant system. However, a technocratic variety of this tradition is indirectly documented in several works in the field of agricultural history, including David D. Danbom, *The Resisted Revolution: Urban America and the Industrialization of*

Agriculture, 1900–1930 (Ames: Iowa State University Press, 1979); Alan I. Marcus, *Agricultural Science and the Quest for Legitimacy* (Ames, Iowa: State University Press, 1985); Kathleen Jellison, *Entitled to Power: Farm Women and Technology, 1913–1963* (Chapel Hill: University of North Carolina Press, 1993); Mary Neth, *Preserving the Family Farm: Women, Community, and the Foundations of Agribusiness in the Midwest, 1900–1940* (Baltimore: Johns Hopkins University Press, 1995); Ronald R. Kline, *Consumers in the Country: Technology and Social Change in Rural America* (Baltimore: Johns Hopkins University Press, 2000); and Deborah Fitzgerald, *Every Farm a Factory: The Industrial Ideal in American Agriculture* (New Haven: Yale University Press, 2003).

61. On the history of the land-grant system, see especially F.B. Mumford, *The Land Grant College Movement* (Columbia: University of Missouri Agricultural Experiment Station, 1940); Earle D. Ross, *Democracy's College: The Land-Grant Movement in the Formative Stage* (Ames: Iowa State College Press, 1942); Edward Danforth Eddy Jr., *Colleges for Our Land and Time: The Land-Grant Idea in American Education* (New York: Harper & Brothers, 1957); Joseph Bailey Edmond, *The Magnificent Charter: The Origin and Role of the Morrill Land-Grant Colleges and Universities* (Hicksville, N.Y.: Exposition Press, 1978); and Roger L. Williams, *The Origins of Federal Support for Higher Education: George W. Atherton and the Land-Grant College Movement* (University Park: Pennsylvania State University Press, 1991). On the land-grant mission, see James T. Bonnen, "The Land-Grant Idea and the Evolving Outreach University," in *University-Community Collaborations for the Twenty-first Century: Outreach Scholarship for Youth and Families*, edited by Richard M. Lerner and Lou Anna K. Simon (New York: Garland Publishing, 1998), 25–70.

62. On the establishment of new disciplines in land-grant colleges of agriculture, see Margaret W. Rossiter, "The Organization of the Agricultural Sciences," in *The Organization of Knowledge in Modern America, 1860–1920*, edited by A. Oleson and J. Voss (Baltimore: Johns Hopkins University Press, 1979). For profiles of contemporary extension educators who view themselves as teachers, organizers, and change agents, see Scott J. Peters and Margo Hittleman, *We Grow People: Profiles of Extension Educators, Cornell University Cooperative Extension, New York City* (Ithaca, N.Y.: Cornell University, 2003); and Scott J. Peters, Daniel J. O'Connell, Theodore R. Alter, and Allison L.H. Jack, *Catalyzing Change: Profiles of Cornell Cooperative Extension Educators from Greene, Tompkins, and Erie Counties, New York* (Ithaca, N.Y.: Cornell University, 2006). These publications are available as pdf downloads at www.communityuniversityengagement.org.

63. For accounts of Liberty Hyde Bailey's life and work, see A.D. Rodgers, *Liberty Hyde Bailey: A Story of American Plant Sciences* (Princeton, N.J.: Princeton University Press, 1949); and P. Dorf, *Liberty Hyde Bailey: An Informal Biography* (Ithaca, N.Y.: Cornell University Press, 1956). For a selection of Bailey's writings, see Zachary Michael Jack, ed., *Liberty Hyde Bailey: Essential Agrarian and Environmental Writings* (Ithaca, N.Y.: Cornell University Press, 2008). For interpretations of Bailey's civic, educational, and environmental work and views, see Scott J. Peters and Paul A. Morgan, "The Country Life Commission: Reconsidering a Milestone in American Agricultural History," *Agricultural History* 78, no. 3 (2004), 289–316; Scott J. Peters, "Every Farmer Should Be Awakened: Liberty Hyde Bailey's Vision of Agricultural Extension Work," *Agricultural History* 80, no. 2 (2006), 190–219;

Paul A. Morgan and Scott J. Peters, "The Foundations of Planetary Agrarianism: Thomas Berry and Liberty Hyde Bailey," *Journal of Agricultural and Environmental Ethics* 19, no. 5 (2006), 443–68; and Ben A. Minteer, *The Landscape of Reform: Civic Pragmatism and Environmental Thought in America* (Cambridge: MIT Press, 2006).

64. Liberty Hyde Bailey, *The Agricultural Status* (East Lansing: Michigan Agricultural College, 1897), 14; Liberty Hyde Bailey, *The College of Agriculture and the State* (Ithaca, N.Y.: New York State College of Agriculture, 1909), 1; Liberty Hyde Bailey, "The Better Preparation of Men for College and Station Work," in *Proceedings of the Twenty-third Annual Convention of the Association of American Agricultural Colleges and Experiment Stations*, edited by A.C. True and W.H. Beal (Washington, D.C.: Government Printing Office, 1910), 25–26.

65. Liberty Hyde Bailey, "The Outlook for the College of Agriculture," in *Addresses at the Dedication of the Buildings of the New York State College of Agriculture* (Ithaca, N.Y.: Cornell University, 1907), 37–38.

66. Ibid., 40, 37.

67. Bailey, *College of Agriculture*, 11, 11–12.

68. Kenyon L. Butterfield, "The Morrill Act Institutions and the New Epoch," in *Proceedings of the Thirty-first Annual Convention of the American Agricultural Colleges and Experiment Stations, November 14–16, 1917*, edited by J. L. Hills (Washington, D.C.: Government Printing Office, 1918), 54.

69. Ibid., 55.

70. Ibid.

71. On the founding and history of the Cooperative Extension system, see Alfred C. True, *A History of Agricultural Extension Work in the United States, 1785–1923* (Washington D.C.: United States Department of Agriculture, 1928); E.S. Brunner and E.H. Pao Yang, *Rural America and the Extension Service: A History and Critique of the Cooperative Agricultural and Home Economics Extension Service* (New York: Teachers College Press, 1949); Roy V. Scott, *The Reluctant Farmer: The Rise of Agricultural Extension to 1914* (Urbana: University of Illinois Press, 1970); and Wayne D. Rasmussen, *Taking the University to the People: Seventy-five Years of Cooperative Extension* (Ames: Iowa State University Press, 1989).

72. Smith-Lever Act quoted in True, *History of Agricultural Extension*, 195.

73. C.B. Smith and M.C. Wilson, *The Agricultural Extension System of the United States* (New York, NY: John Wiley & Sons, 1930), 1.

74. Ibid., 1–2, 2, 5. It is interesting to note how frequently the word *spiritual* was used in much of the early literature on cooperative extension. This is rarely directly attached to religion, but it is also never fully explained or developed. It may have been meant to refer to the sense of *connectedness* that participation in cooperative community work can often produce, of being a useful and needed part of a larger whole. Reflecting this idea, Smith and Wilson wrote on page 130 of their book that people not only experience great satisfaction from helping their own communities, but that they also "grow mentally and spiritually as they acquire and give."

75. Ibid., 12, 42.

76. Ibid., 20.

77. Ibid., 21. The use of the phrase "farmers and their wives" suggests that all farmers during this time were men. This was not the case. According to USDA statistics, in 1920 there were more than 260,000 farms in the United States that were being operated by women. See William A. Lloyd, *County Agricultural Agent Work under the Smith-Lever Act, 1914–1924* (Washington, D.C.: USDA, 1926), 50.

78. Smith and Wilson, *Agricultural Extension System*, 24.

79. Ibid., 132.

80. Ibid., 132, 138.

81. Ibid., 157, 182, 229.

82. Ibid., 66–67.

83. Ibid., 194, 131.

84. Gertrude Humphreys, "Building a Long-Time Home-Economics Program," *Extension Service Review* 2, no. 9 (1934), 134.

85. As of this writing, we could not find any published studies of the origins and evolution of the AR/PS/EO tradition in the land-grant system. In our own research, we have uncovered hundreds of books and articles that offer evidence of the presence of this tradition during the decades before the Second World War. These include Liberty Hyde Bailey, *The Holy Earth* (New York: Charles Scribner's Sons, 1915); Kenyon L. Butterfield, *The Farmer and the New Day* (New York: Macmillan, 1920); Alfred G. Arvold, *The Little Country Theater* (New York: Macmillan, 1922); Mary Mims, *The Awakening Community* (New York: Macmillan, 1932); Marjorie Patten, *The Arts Workshop of Rural America: A Study of the Rural Arts Program of the Agricultural Extension System* (New York: Columbia University Press, 1937); and Robert Gard, *Grassroots Theater: A Search for Regional Arts in America* (Madison: University of Wisconsin Press, 1955). As the latter of these works suggest, the democratic tradition included a strong cultural dimension that utilized the arts as a means of civic development. For a brief account of this dimension and a fuller treatment of the conflicting narratives about the land-grant mission, see Scott J. Peters, *Changing the Story about Higher Education's Public Purposes and Work: Land-Grants, Liberty, and the Little Country Theater* (Ann Arbor, Mich.: Imagining America, 2007).

86. Fish, *Save the World*, 8, 12–13.

87. Ibid., 99, 66, 67.

88. Ibid., 71, 72.

89. As previously mentioned, Weber's essay "Science as a Vocation" is included in Gerth and Mills, *From Max Weber*. Abraham Flexner, *Universities: American, English, German* (New York: Oxford University Press, 1930), 6.

90. Walter Lippmann, "The Scholar in a Troubled World," in *The Essential Lippmann: A Political Philosophy for Liberal Democracy*, edited by C. Rossiter and J. Lare (New York: Random House, 1963), 509–10.

91. Ibid., 510, 511.

92. Ibid., 515.

93. Ibid.

94. Arthur T. Hadley, "The Relation between Higher Education and the Welfare of the Country," in *Thirty-Third Annual Report of the Secretary of the Connecticut Board of Agriculture, 1899* (Hartford, Conn.: The Case, Lockwood & Brainard Company, 1901), 29.

Chapter Two. Questioning the Answers

1. On the philosophical dimensions of educators' roles in a democratic society, see John Dewey, *Democracy and Education* (New York: The Free Press, 1916). Dewey addresses the issue of higher education's roles in a democratic society in many of his writings, including *The Educational Situation* (Chicago: University of Chicago Press, 1902), *The Public and Its Problems* (New York: Henry Holt and Company, 1927), and *Freedom and Culture* (Buffalo: Prometheus Books, 1989). For reviews and critiques of Dewey's ideas about democracy and education, see Robert B. Westbrook, *John Dewey and American Democracy* (Ithaca: Cornell University Press, 1991), William R. Caspary, *Dewey on Democracy* (Ithaca: Cornell University Press, 2000), and Lee Benson, Ira Harkavy, and John Puckett, *Dewey's Dream: Universities and Democracies in an Age of Education Reform* (Philadelphia: Temple University Press, 2007).

2. See Michael J. Sandel, *Democracy's Discontent: America in Search of a Public Philosophy* (Cambridge: Harvard University Press, 1996). Many scholars have sharply critiqued Sandel's ideas and views. See, for example, Anita L. Allen and Milton C. Regan Jr., eds., *Debating Democracy's Discontent: Essays on American Politics, Law, and Public Philosophy* (New York: Oxford University Press, 1998).

3. There are quite literally thousands of studies, books, and articles in many academic fields that question the central assumptions and implications of the service intellectual tradition. Among the most useful of these works for us are Friedrichs, *A Sociology of Sociology*; Richard J. Bernstein, *Beyond Objectivism and Relativism: Science, Hermeneutics, and Praxis* (Philadelphia: University of Pennsylvania Press, 1983); Hans-George Gadamer, *Truth and Method*, 2nd ed. (New York: Continuum, 1989); Michel Foucault, *The Order of Things: An Archeology of the Human Sciences* (New York: Random House, 1970); Lindblom and Cohen, *Usable Knowledge*; and Sandra Harding, "After the Neutrality Ideal: Science, Politics, and 'Strong Objectivity,'" *Social Research* 59, no. 30 (1992), pp. 567–87. For an extended examination of the "legislative" role academics are supposed to play in deciding what is "true," see Bauman, *Legislators and Interpreters*.

4. For good introductions to Antonio Gramsci's views about intellectuals and politics, see David Forgacs, ed., *The Antonio Gramsci Reader: Selected Writings, 1916–1935* (New York: NYU Press, 2000), and Fink, Leonard, and Reid, *Intellectuals and Public Life*. For Foucault's views about the oppressive nature of what he refers to as the "human" sciences," see *The Order of Things* and *Power/Knowledge* (New York: Pantheon, 1980). For Habermas's views, see *Knowledge and Human Interests*, 2nd ed. (London: Heinemann, 1972); *The Theory of Communicative Action*, vol. 1: *Reason and the Rationalization of Society* (Boston: Beacon Press, 1984); and *The Structural Transformation of the Public Sphere* (Cambridge: MIT Press, 1989). For Frank Fischer's views, see *Technocracy and the Politics of Expertise* (Newbury Park, Calif.: Sage Publications, 1990); *Citizens, Experts, and the Environment: The Politics of Local Knowledge* (Durham, N.C.: Duke University Press, 2000); and *Democracy and Expertise*.

5. The "detached attachment" phrase is from Arthur M. Melzer, "What Is an Intellectual?" in Melzer, Weinberger, and Zinman, *The Public Intellectual*, 4.

6. See Sandel, *Democracy's Discontent,* for a discussion of the formative politics of civic republicanism.

7. Mills, *The Sociological Imagination,* 192.

8. On the issue of objectivity and trustworthiness in academic work, see Nancy Tuana and Sandra Morgen, eds., *Engendering Rationalities* (Albany: SUNY Press, 2001).

9. Fish, *Save the World,* 71.

10. Flexner, *Universities,* 15; Lippmann, "Scholar in Troubled World," 510.

Chapter Three. Developing and Using Practitioner Profiles

1. Our approach to constructing and using practitioner profiles is guided by the pioneering work and wise counsel of John Forester, a professor in the Department of City and Regional Planning at Cornell University. Examples of his work with practitioner profiles include *The Deliberative Practitioner;* "Exploring Urban Practice in a Democratising Society: Opportunities, Techniques and Challenges," *Development Southern Africa* 23, no. 5 (2006), 569–86; "Policy Analysis as Critical Listening," in *The Oxford Handbook of Public Policy,* edited by M. Moran, M. Rein, and R.E. Goodin (New York: Oxford University Press, 2006); and *Dealing with Differences.* Our approach to conducting narrative interviews is also inspired and guided by Susan E. Chase, "Taking Narrative Seriously: Consequences for Method and Theory in Interview Studies," in *Interpreting Experience: The Narrative Study of Lives,* edited by R. Josselson and A. Lieblich (Thousand Oaks, Calif.: Sage Publications, 1995); and Irving Seidman, *Interviewing as Qualitative Research: A Guide for Researchers in Education and the Social Sciences,* 3rd ed. (New York: Teachers College Press, 2006).

2. These steps are laid out in much greater detail on the following web site: courses.cit. cornell.edu/practicestories.

3. On "interpretivist" research, see Paul Rabinow and William M. Sullivan, eds., *Interpretive Social Science: A Second Look* (Berkeley: University of California Press, 1987); Michael J. Crotty, *The Foundations of Social Research: Meaning and Perspective in the Research Process* (Thousand Oaks, Calif.: Sage Publications, 1998); Joan W. Scott and Debra Keates, eds., *Schools of Thought: Twenty-five Years of Interpretive Social Science* (Princeton, N.J.: Princeton University Press, 2001); and Bent Flyvbjerg, *Making Social Science Matter: Why Social Inquiry Fails and How It Can Succeed Again* (New York: Cambridge University Press, 2001). There is a vast and growing literature on narrative inquiry in a wide range of academic disciplines and fields. The best introduction to this literature is D. Jean Clandinin, ed., *Handbook of Narrative Inquiry: Mapping a Methodology* (Thousand Oaks, Calif.: Sage Publications, 2007). Also see Mary Jo Maynes, Jennifer L. Pierce, and Barbara Laslett, *Telling Stories: The Use of Personal Narratives in the Social Sciences and History* (Ithaca, N.Y.: Cornell University Press, 2008). For a discussion of the nature and meaning of "truth" in narrative inquiry, see Personal Narratives Group, "Truths," in *Interpreting Women's Lives* (Bloomington: Indiana University Press, 1989).

4. On the idea and theory of "narrative strategies" and storytelling and talk as a form of social action, see Susan E. Chase, *Ambiguous Empowerment: The Work Narratives of Women School Superintendents* (Amherst: University of Massachusetts Press, 1995).

5. William Cronon, "A Place for Stories: Nature, History, and Narrative," *Journal of American History* 78, no. 4 (1992), 1374.

6. Statistics from "Cornell Facts," accessed on May 13, 2009 at www.cornell.edu/about/facts/cornell_facts2008–09.pdf. For more about Cornell, see Morris Bishop, *A History of Cornell* (Ithaca, N.Y.: Cornell University Press, 1962).

7. Statistics from "Cornell University College of Agriculture and Life Sciences, Facts and Figures," at www.cals.cornell.edu/cals/public/comm/pubs/upload/CALS-Facts-and-Figures-05–06.pdf. For a history of CALS, see Gould P. Colman, *Education and Agriculture: A History of the New York State College of Agriculture at Cornell University* (Ithaca, N.Y.: Cornell University, 1963).

8. Hunter R. Rawlings III, "State of the University Address," delivered June 9, 2001, at http://www.news.cornell.edu/http://www.news.corne/campus/stateofuniv01.html.

9. The Charles F. Kettering Foundation is not a grant-making foundation. It is a research foundation that is focused on the question of how to make democracy work as it should. It has a special interest in higher education. It supported our previous project on public scholarship in the land-grant system, and published the book reporting our findings. See Peters et al., *Engaging Campus and Community*. For details about the Kettering Foundation's work, go to www.kettering.org.

Chapter Ten. Is It Your Problem, or Is It a Social Problem?

1. For an appreciative review of Tom's life and work, see Gilbert W. Gillespie Jr., "Thomas A. Lyson: A Biographical Note," *Agriculture and Human Values* (2009) 26:15–19.

Chapter Sixteen. Lessons

1. Here we are mindful of the ways researchers have often deceived and betrayed the trust of those who have agreed to participate in their studies. For a provocative look at this pattern in the social sciences, see Thomas Newkirk, "Seduction and Betrayal in Qualitative Research," in *Ethics and Representation in Qualitative Studies of Literacy*, edited by Peter Mortensen and Gesa E. Kirsch (Urbana, Ill.: National Council of Teachers of English, 1996), 3–16.

2. Our practical theory and our sense of the importance of taking a prophetic, appreciative approach in our research are influenced by Sara Lawrence-Lightfoot and Jessica Hoffman Davis, *The Art and Science of Portraiture* (San Francisco: Jossey-Bass, 1997).

3. For uncritical celebratory views of land-grant colleges of agriculture, see Edmond, *The Magnificent Charter*; Patricia H. Crosson, *Public Service in Higher Education: Practices and Priorities* (Washington, D.C.: Association for the Study of Higher Education, 1983); Rasmussen, *University to the People*; National Research Council, *Colleges of Agriculture at the Land-Grant Universities: Public Service and Public Policy* (Washington, D.C.: National Academy Press, 1996); John R. Campbell, *Reclaiming a Lost Heritage: Land-Grant and Other Higher Education Initiatives for the Twenty-first Century* (East Lansing: Michigan State University Press, 1998); and Ward, *Faculty Service Roles*. For critical views of land-grant colleges of agriculture, see Jim Hightower, *Hard Tomatoes, Hard Times*

(Cambridge, Mass.: Schenkman Publishing, 1978); and Wendell Berry, *The Unsettling of America: Culture and Agriculture*, 3rd ed. (San Francisco: Sierra Club Books, 1996). Leading examples of other critical views include Danbom, *The Resisted Revolution*; Marcus, *Agricultural Science*; Jellison, *Entitled to Power*; Neth, *Preserving the Family Farm*; Kline, *Consumers in the Country*; and Fitzgerald, *Every Farm a Factory*.

4. On the idea of democracy as something we do rather than something we have, see Frances Moore Lappé, *Democracy's Edge: Choosing to Save Our Country by Bringing Democracy Back to Life* (San Francisco: Jossey-Bass, 2006).

5. Fish, *Save the World*.

6. President's Commission on Higher Education, *Report*, 102; Sullivan, "Engaging the Civic Option," 10. On the history and theory of civic (or democratic) professionalism, see Sullivan, *Work and Integrity*, and Albert W. Dzur, *Democratic Professionalism: Citizen Participation and the Reconstruction of Professional Ethics, Identity, and Practice* (University Park: Pennsylvania State University Press, 2008).

7. For more about the Educational Finance Research Consortium, go to www.albany.edu/edfin/index.html.

8. President's Commission on Higher Education, *Report*, 10.

9. For the full statement of the college's mission, go to http://www.cals.cornell.edu/cals/about/vision.cfm.

Conclusion

1. Our reference to AASCU member institutions as "stewards of place" and "land-grants for the 21st century" is based on email correspondence with George Mehaffy, AASCU's vice president for Academic Leadership and Change, on July 26, 2009. The prevailing view of the land-grant mission we characterize here can be found in many sources. See especially Edmond, *The Magnificent Charter*; Crosson, *Public Service*; Rasmussen, *Taking the University to the People*; National Research Council, *Colleges of Agriculture*; Campbell, *Reclaiming a Lost Heritage*; and Ward, *Faculty Service Roles*.

2. President's Commission on Higher Education, *Report*, 102.

3. Sullivan, *Work and Integrity*, 180.

4. We interviewed Nick Jordan in 2001 and 2002. The previous book we are referring to is Peters et al., *Engaging Campus and Community*.

5. William M. Sullivan, "What Is Left of Professionalism after Managed Care?" *Hastings Center Report* 29, no. 2 (1999), 6.

6. On the organizing tradition in the civil rights movement, see Payne, *I've Got the Light*. For the organizing tradition in the IAF, see Rogers, *Cold Anger*; Warren, *Dry Bones Rattling*; and Chambers, *Roots for Radicals*.

7. On the organizing Nick Jordan and his colleagues have been doing in Minnesota, see Nicholas Jordan et al., "Building a Knowledge Network for Sustainable Weed Management: An Experiment in Public Scholarship," and Scott Peters and Karen Lehman, "Organizing for Public Scholarship in Southeast Minnesota," both of which are published in Peters et al., *Engaging Campus and Community*. For an overview of the organizing

approach Maria Avila and her colleagues are using at Occidental, see Maria Avila, "Community Organizing Practices in Academia: A Model, and Stories of Partnerships," forthcoming in *Journal of Higher Education Outreach and Engagement* 14, no. 2 (2010). For examples of organizing approaches in civic education, service learning, the arts and humanities, and community-based research, see Ehrlich, *Civic Responsibility*; Jacoby and Associates, *Building Partnerships*; Colby et al., *Educating Citizens*; Strand et al., *Community-Based Research*; Minkler and Wallerstein, *Community-Based Participatory Research*; Israel et al., *Methods*; Colby et al., *Educating for Democracy*; Benson, Harkavy, and Puckett, *Dewey's Dream*; and Jacoby and Associates, *Civic Engagement*.

8. Sullivan, *Work and Integrity*, 180.

9. For examples of models and tools for collective, action-oriented reflection and inquiry, see especially John N. Bray, Joyce Lee, Linda L. Smith, and Lyle Yorks, *Collaborative Inquiry in Practice: Action, Reflection, and Making Meaning* (Thousand Oaks, Calif.: Sage Publications, 2000); Michael Reynolds and Russ Vince, eds., *Organizing Reflection* (Burlington, Vt.: Ashgate Publishers, 2004); Reason and Bradbury, *SAGE Handbook*; and Varun Vidyarthi and Patricia A. Wilson, *Development from Within: Facilitating Collective Reflection for Sustainable Change* (Herndon, Va.: Apex Foundation, 2008). Ella Baker was one of the most important leaders in the American civil rights movement of the 1950s and 1960s. For discussions of her work, see Payne, *I've Got the Light*; Mary Field Belenky, Lynne A. Bond, and Jacqueline S. Weinstock, *A Tradition That Has No Name: Nurturing the Development of People, Families, and Communities* (New York: Basic Books, 1997); and Ransby, *Ella Baker*.

10. On the importance of holding the tension between the world as it is and the world as it should be in the practice of organizing, see Chambers, *Roots for Radicals*.

11. Alasdair MacIntyre, *After Virtue: A Study in Moral Theory* (Notre Dame, Ind.: University of Notre Dame Press, 1981/1984), 216.

12. President's Commission on Higher Education, *Report*, 6.

Bibliography

Allen, A.L., and M.C. Regan, Jr., eds. 1998. *Debating Democracy's Discontent: Essays on American Politics, Law, and Public Philosophy*. New York: Oxford University Press.

Altbach, P.G. 1997. "Problems and Possibilities: The US Academic Profession." In *The Academic Profession: The Professoriate in Crisis*, edited by P.G. Altbach and M.J. Finkelstein. New York: Garland Publishing.

American Association of University Professors. 1961. "Report of the Committee on Academic Freedom and Tenure." In *American Higher Education: A Documentary History*, vol. 2, edited by R. Hofstadter and W. Smith. Chicago: University of Chicago Press.

Arvold, A.G. 1922. *The Little Country Theater*. New York: Macmillan.

Bailey, L.H. 1897. *The Agricultural Status*. East Lansing: Michigan Agricultural College.

———. 1907. "The Outlook for the College of Agriculture." In *Addresses at the Dedication of the Buildings of the New York State College of Agriculture*. Ithaca, N.Y.: Cornell University.

———. 1909. *The College of Agriculture and the State*. Ithaca, N.Y.: New York State College of Agriculture.

———. 1910. "The Better Preparation of Men for College and Station Work." In *Proceedings of the Twenty-Third Annual Convention of the Association of American Agricultural Colleges and Experiment Stations*, edited by A.C. True and W.H. Beal. Washington, D.C.: Government Printing Office.

———. 1915. *The Holy Earth*. New York: Charles Scribner's Sons.

Bauman, Z. 1987. *Legislators and Interpreters: On Modernity, Post-Modernity, and Intellectuals*. Ithaca, N.Y.: Cornell University Press.

Bender, T. 1993. *Intellect and Public Life*. Baltimore: Johns Hopkins University Press.

Benson, L., I. Harkavy, and J. Puckett. 2007. *Dewey's Dream: Universities and Democracies in an Age of Education Reform.* Philadelphia: Temple University Press.

Berdahl, R.O., and T.R. McConnell. 1999. "Autonomy and Accountability in American Higher Education." In *American Higher Education in the Twenty-first Century: Social, Political, and Economic Challenges,* edited by P.G. Altbach, R.O. Berdahl, and P.J. Gumport. Baltimore: Johns Hopkins University Press.

Bernstein, R.J. 1983. *Beyond Objectivism and Relativism: Science, Hermeneutics, and Praxis.* Philadelphia: University of Pennsylvania Press.

Berry, W. 1996. *The Unsettling of America: Culture and Agriculture.* 3rd ed. San Francisco: Sierra Club Books.

Bishop, M. 1962. *A History of Cornell.* Ithaca, N.Y.: Cornell University Press.

Boggs, C. 1993. *Intellectuals and the Crisis of Modernity.* Albany, N.Y.: SUNY Press.

Bok, D. 2003. *Universities in the Marketplace: The Commercialization of Higher Education.* Princeton, N.J.: Princeton University Press.

Bonnen, J.T. 1998. "The Land-Grant Idea and the Evolving Outreach University." In *University-Community Collaborations for the Twenty-first Century: Outreach Scholarship for Youth and Families,* edited by R.M. Lerner and L.A.K. Simon. New York: Garland Publishing.

Boyte, H.C. 2004. *Everyday Politics: Reconnecting Citizens and Public Life.* Philadelphia: University of Pennsylvania Press.

———. 2008. *The Citizen Solution: How You Can Make a Difference.* St. Paul: Minnesota Historical Society Press.

Brint, S. 1994. *In an Age of Experts: The Changing Role of Professionals in Politics and Public Life.* Princeton, N.J.: Princeton University Press.

Brunner, E.S. and E.H.P. Yang. 1949. *Rural America and the Extension Service: A History and Critique of the Cooperative Agricultural and Home Economics Extension Service.* New York: Teachers College Press.

Bulmer, M. 1984. *The Chicago School of Sociology: Institutionalization, Diversity, and the Role of Social Research.* Chicago: University of Chicago Press.

Burawoy, M. 2008. "Open Letter to C. Wright Mills." In *Practising Public Scholarship: Experiences and Possibilities Beyond the Academy,* edited by K. Mitchell. West Sussex, U.K.: Wiley-Blackwell.

Butin, D.W. 2008. *Rethinking Service Learning: Embracing the Scholarship of Engagement within Higher Education.* Sterling, Va.: Stylus Publishing.

Butterfield, K.L. 1918. "The Morrill Act Institutions and the New Epoch." In *Proceedings of the Thirty-first Annual Convention of the American Agricultural Colleges and Experiment Stations, November 14–16, 1917,* edited by J.L. Hills. Washington, D.C.: Government Printing Office.

———. 1920. *The Farmer and the New Day.* New York: Macmillan.

Butts, R.F. 1939. *The College Charts Its Course: Historical Conceptions and Current Proposals.* New York: McGraw-Hill.

Campbell, J.R. 1998. *Reclaiming a Lost Heritage: Land-Grant and Other Higher Education Initiatives for the Twenty-first Century.* East Lansing: Michigan State University Press.

Caspary, W.R. 2000. *Dewey on Democracy*. Ithaca: Cornell University Press.

Chambers, E.T. 2003. *Roots for Radicals: Organizing for Power, Action, and Justice*. New York: Continuum.

Chase, S.E. 1995. *Ambiguous Empowerment: The Work Narratives of Women School Superintendents*. Amherst: University of Massachusetts Press.

———. 1995. "Taking Narrative Seriously: Consequences for Method and Theory in Interview Studies." In *Interpreting Experience: The Narrative Study of Lives*, edited by R. Josselson and A. Lieblich. Thousand Oaks, Calif.: Sage Publications.

Clandinin, D.J., ed. 2007. *Handbook of Narrative Inquiry: Mapping a Methodology*. Thousand Oaks, Calif.: Sage Publications.

Colby, A., E. Beaumont, T. Ehrlich, and J. Corngold. 2007. *Educating for Democracy: Preparing Undergraduates for Responsible Political Engagement*. San Francisco: Jossey-Bass.

Colby, A., T. Ehrlich, E. Beaumont, and J. Stephens. 2003. *Educating Citizens: Preparing America's Undergraduates for Lives of Moral and Civic Responsibility*. San Francisco: Jossey-Bass.

Colman, G.P. 1963. *Education and Agriculture: A History of the New York State College of Agriculture at Cornell University*. Ithaca, N.Y.: Cornell University.

Cronon, W. 1992. "A Place for Stories: Nature, History, and Narrative." *Journal of American History* 78, no. 4, pp. 1347–76.

Crosson, P.H. 1983. *Public Service in Higher Education: Practices and Priorities*. Washington, D.C.: Association for the Study of Higher Education.

Crotty, M.J. 1998. *The Foundations of Social Research: Meaning and Perspective in the Research Process*. Thousand Oaks, Calif.: Sage Publications.

Danbom, D.D. 1979. *The Resisted Revolution: Urban America and the Industrialization of Agriculture, 1900–1930*. Ames: Iowa State University Press.

Dewey, J. 1902. *The Educational Situation*. Chicago: University of Chicago Press.

———. 1916. *Democracy and Education*. New York: The Free Press.

———. 1927. *The Public and Its Problems*. New York: Henry Holt and Company.

———. 1989. *Freedom and Culture*. Buffalo: Prometheus Books.

Dibble, V.K. 1975. *The Legacy of Albion Small*. Chicago: University of Chicago Press.

Dorf, P. 1956. *Liberty Hyde Bailey: An Informal Biography*. Ithaca, N.Y.: Cornell University Press.

Dzur, A.W. 2008. *Democratic Professionalism: Citizen Participation and the Reconstruction of Professional Ethics, Identity, and Practice*. University Park: Pennsylvania State University Press.

Eberly, R.A., and J. Cohen, eds. 2006. *A Laboratory for Public Scholarship and Democracy*. San Francisco: Jossey-Bass.

Eddy, E.D. 1957. *Colleges for Our Land and Time: The Land-Grant Idea in American Education*. New York: Harper & Brothers.

Edmond, J.B. 1978. *The Magnificent Charter: The Origin and Role of the Morrill Land-Grant Colleges and Universities*. Hicksville, N.Y.: Exposition Press.

Ehrlich T., ed. 2000. *Civic Responsibility and Higher Education*. Westport, Conn.: Oryx Press.

Etzioni, A., and A. Bowditch. 2006. *Public Intellectuals: An Endangered Species?* Lanham, Md.: Rowman & Littlefield.

Eyerman, R. 1994. *Between Culture and Politics: Intellectuals in Modern Society.* Cambridge, Mass.: Polity Press.

Fay, B. 1987. *Critical Social Science: Liberation and Its Limits.* Ithaca, N.Y.: Cornell University Press.

Fink, L. 1997. *Progressive Intellectuals and the Dilemmas of Democratic Commitment.* Cambridge, Mass.: Harvard University Press.

Fink, L., S.T. Leonard, and D.M. Reid, eds. 1996. *Intellectuals and Public Life: Between Radicalism and Reform.* Ithaca, N.Y.: Cornell University Press.

Fischer, F. 1990. *Technocracy and the Politics of Expertise.* Newbury Park, Calif.: Sage Publications.

———. 2000. *Citizens, Experts, and the Environment: The Politics of Local Knowledge.* Durham, N.C.: Duke University Press.

———. 2009. *Democracy and Expertise: Reorienting Policy Inquiry.* New York: Oxford University Press.

Fish, S. 2008. *Save the World on Your Own Time.* New York: Oxford University Press.

Fitzgerald, D. 2003. *Every Farm a Factory: The Industrial Ideal in American Agriculture.* New Haven: Yale University Press.

Flexner, A. 1930. *Universities: American, English, German.* New York: Oxford University Press.

Flyvbjerg, B. 2001. *Making Social Science Matter: Why Social Inquiry Fails and How It Can Succeed Again.* New York: Cambridge University Press.

Forester, J. 1999. *The Deliberative Practitioner: Encouraging Participatory Planning Processes.* Cambridge: MIT Press.

———. 2006a. "Exploring Urban Practice in a Democratising Society: Opportunities, Techniques and Challenges." *Development Southern Africa* 23, no. 5: 569–86.

———. 2006b. "Policy Analysis as Critical Listening." In *The Oxford Handbook of Public Policy,* edited by M. Moran, M. Rein, and R.E. Goodin. New York: Oxford University Press.

———. 2009. *Dealing with Differences: Dramas of Mediating Public Disputes.* New York: Oxford University Press.

Forgacs, D., ed. 2000. *The Antonio Gramsci Reader: Selected Writings, 1916–1935.* New York: NYU Press.

Foucault, M. 1970. *The Order of Things: An Archeology of the Human Sciences.* New York: Random House.

———. 1980. *Power/Knowledge.* New York: Pantheon, 1980.

Friedrichs, R.W. 1970. *A Sociology of Sociology.* New York: Free Press.

Furner, M.O. 1975. *Advocacy and Objectivity: A Crisis in the Professionalization of American Social Science, 1865–1905.* Lexington: University Press of Kentucky.

Gadamer, H.G. 1989. *Truth and Method.* 2nd ed. New York: Continuum.

Gard, R. 1955. *Grassroots Theater: A Search for Regional Arts in America.* Madison: University of Wisconsin Press.

Geary, D. 2009. *Radical Ambition: C. Wright Mills, the Left, and American Social Thought.* Berkeley: University of California Press.

Geiger, R.L. 2004. *Knowledge and Money: Research Universities and the Paradox of the Marketplace.* Stanford, Calif.: Stanford University Press.

General Education in a Free Society: Report of the Harvard Committee. 1945. Cambridge: The University.

Gitlin, A., ed. 1994. *Power and Method: Political Activism and Educational Research.* New York: Routledge.

Goldfarb, J.C. 1998. *Civility and Subversion: The Intellectual in Democratic Society.* New York: Cambridge University Press.

Grazia, A., R. Handy, E.C. Harwood, and P. Kurtz, eds. 1968. *The Behavioral Sciences: Essays in Honor of George A. Lundberg.* Great Barrington, Mass.: Behavioral Research Council.

Greenwood, D.J., and M. Levin. 2007. *Introduction to Action Research: Social Research for Social Change.* 2nd ed. Thousand Oaks, Calif.: Sage Publications.

Gutmann, A. 1999. *Democratic Education.* Rev. ed. Princeton, N.J.: Princeton University Press.

Habermas, J. 1972. *Knowledge and Human Interests.* 2nd ed. London: Heinemann.

———. 1984. *The Theory of Communicative Action.* Vol. 1: *Reason and the Rationalization of Society.* Boston: Beacon Press.

———. 1989. *The Structural Transformation of the Public Sphere.* Cambridge: MIT Press.

Hadley, A.T. 1901. "The Relation Between Higher Education and the Welfare of the Country." In *Thirty-Third Annual Report of the Secretary of the Connecticut Board of Agriculture, 1899.* Hartford, Conn.: Case, Lockwood & Brainard Company.

Hale, C.F., ed. 2008. *Engaging Contradictions: Theory, Politics, and Methods of Activist Scholarship.* Berkeley: University of California Press.

Hammersley, M. 1989. *The Dilemma of Qualitative Method: Herbert Blumer and the Chicago Tradition.* New York: Routledge.

———. 1995. *The Politics of Social Research.* Thousand Oaks, Calif.: Sage Publications.

Harding, S. 1992, "After the Neutrality Ideal: Science, Politics, and 'Strong Objectivity,'" *Social Research* 59, no. 30, pp. 567–87.

Haskell, T. 1998. *Objectivity Is Not Neutrality: Explanatory Schemes in History.* Baltimore: Johns Hopkins University Press.

Higher Education for American Democracy: A Report of the President's Commission on Higher Education. New York: Harper & Brothers, 1948.

Hightower, J. 1978. *Hard Tomatoes, Hard Times.* Cambridge, Mass.: Schenkman Publishing.

Hofstadter, R. 1963. "The Revolution in Higher Education." In *Paths of American Thought,* edited by A.M. Schlesinger, Jr. and M. White. Boston: Houghton Mifflin.

Hofstadter, R. and W.P. Metzger. 1955. *The Development of Academic Freedom in the United States.* New York: Columbia University Press.

Humphreys, G. 1934. "Building a Long-Time Home-Economics Program." *Extension Service Review* Vol. 2 No. 9, p. 134.

Israel, B.A., E. Eng, A.J. Schulz, and E.A. Parker, eds. 2005. *Methods in Community-Based Participatory Research for Health.* San Francisco: Jossey-Bass.

Jack, Z.M., ed. 2008. *Liberty Hyde Bailey: Essential Agrarian and Environmental Writings.* Ithaca, N.Y.: Cornell University Press.

Jacoby, B., and Associates. 2003. *Building Partnerships for Service-Learning.* San Francisco: Jossey-Bass.

————. 2009. *Civic Engagement in Higher Education: Concepts and Practices.* San Francisco: Jossey-Bass.

Jacoby, R. 1987. *The Last Intellectuals: American Culture in the Age of Academe.* New York: Noonday Press.

Jellison, K. 1993. *Entitled to Power: Farm Women and Technology, 1913–1963.* Chapel Hill: University of North Carolina Press.

Jencks, C., and D. Riesman. 1968. *The Academic Revolution.* Garden City, N.Y.: Doubleday.

Kennedy, G., ed. 1952. *Education for Democracy: The Debate over the Report of the President's Commission on Higher Education.* Boston: D.C. Heath.

Kline, R.R. 2000. *Consumers in the Country: Technology and Social Change in Rural America.* Baltimore: Johns Hopkins University Press.

Kloppenburg, J.R. 2005. *First the Seed: The Political Economy of Plant Biotechnology.* 2nd ed. Madison: University of Wisconsin Press.

Krause, S.R. 2008. *Civil Passions: Moral Sentiment and Democratic Deliberation.* Princeton, N.J.: Princeton University Press.

Lappé, F.M. 2006. *Democracy's Edge: Choosing to Save Our Country by Bringing Democracy Back to Life.* San Francisco: Jossey-Bass.

Lather, P. 1991. *Getting Smart: Feminist Research and Pedagogy with/in the Postmodern.* New York: Routledge.

Lawrence-Lightfoot, S., and J.H. Davis. 1997. *The Art and Science of Portraiture.* San Francisco: Jossey-Bass.

Lindblom, C.E., and D.K. Cohen. 1979. *Usable Knowledge: Social Science and Social Problem Solving.* New Haven: Yale University Press.

Lippmann, W. 1963. "The Scholar in a Troubled World." In *The Essential Lippmann: A Political Philosophy for Liberal Democracy,* edited by C. Rossiter and J. Lare. New York: Random House.

Lloyd, W.A. 1926. *County Agricultural Agent Work under the Smith-Lever Act, 1914–1924.* Washington, D.C.: USDA.

Lundberg, G.A. 1961. *Can Science Save Us?* 2nd ed. New York: David McKay.

Marcus, A.I. 1985. *Agricultural Science and the Quest for Legitimacy.* Ames, Iowa: State University Press.

Marcus, G.E. 2002. *The Sentimental Citizen: Emotion in Democratic Politics.* University Park: Pennsylvania State University Press.

Marrow, A.J. 1969. *The Practical Theorist: The Life and Work of Kurt Lewin.* New York: Basic Books.

Mathews, D. 1999. *Politics for People: Finding a Responsible Public Voice.* 2nd ed. Urbana: University of Illinois Press.

Maynes, M.J., J.L. Pierce, and B. Laslett. 2008. *Telling Stories: The Use of Personal Narratives in the Social Sciences and History.* Ithaca, N.Y.: Cornell University Press.

Melzer, A.M. 2003. "What Is an Intellectual?" In *The Public Intellectual: Between Philosophy and Politics,* edited by A.M. Melzer, J. Weinberger, and M.R. Zinman. Lanham, Md.: Rowman & Littlefield.

Melzer, A.M., J. Weinberger, and M.R. Zinman, eds. 2003. *The Public Intellectual: Between Philosophy and Politics.* Lanham, Md.: Rowman & Littlefield.

Mills, C.W. 1959. *The Sociological Imagination.* New York: Oxford University Press.

Mims, M. 1932. *The Awakening Community.* New York: Macmillan.

Minkler, M., and N. Wallerstein, eds. 2003. *Community-Based Participatory Research for Health.* San Francisco: Jossey-Bass.

Minteer, B.A. 2006. *The Landscape of Reform: Civic Pragmatism and Environmental Thought in America.* Cambridge: MIT Press.

Morgan, P.A., and S.J. Peters. 2006. "The Foundations of Planetary Agrarianism: Thomas Berry and Liberty Hyde Bailey." *Journal of Agricultural and Environmental Ethics* 19, no. 5, pp. 443–68.

Mumford, F.B. 1940. *The Land Grant College Movement.* Columbia: University of Missouri Agricultural Experiment Station.

National Research Council. 1996. *Colleges of Agriculture at the Land-Grant Universities: Public Service and Public Policy.* Washington, D.C.: National Academy Press.

Neth, M. 1995. *Preserving the Family Farm: Women, Community, and the Foundations of Agribusiness in the Midwest, 1900–1940.* Baltimore: Johns Hopkins University Press.

Newkirk, T. 1996. "Seduction and Betrayal in Qualitative Research." In *Ethics and Representation in Qualitative Studies of Literacy,* edited by P. Mortensen and G.E. Kirsch. Urbana, Ill.: National Council of Teachers of English.

Newman, F., L. Couturier, and J. Scurry. 2004. *The Future of Higher Education: Rhetoric, Reality, and the Risks of the Market.* San Francisco: Jossey-Bass.

Nussbaum, M.C. 2001. *Upheavals of Thought: The Intelligence of Emotions.* New York: Cambridge University Press.

Patten, M. 1937. *The Arts Workshop of Rural America: A Study of the Rural Arts Program of the Agricultural Extension System.* New York: Columbia University Press.

Payne, C.M. 2007. *I've Got the Light of Freedom: The Organizing Tradition and the Mississippi Freedom Struggle.* Berkeley: University of California Press.

Personal Narratives Group. 1980. "Truths." In *Interpreting Women's Lives.* Bloomington: Indiana University Press.

Peters, S.J. 2002a. "Citizens Developing a Voice at the Table: A Story of Educational Organizing in Contemporary Extension Work." *Journal of Extension* 40, no. 4.

———. 2002b. "Rousing the People on the Land: The Roots of an Educational Organizing Tradition in Extension Work." *Journal of Extension* 40, no. 3.

———. 2006. "Every Farmer Should Be Awakened: Liberty Hyde Bailey's Vision of Agricultural Extension Work." *Agricultural History* 80, no. 2, pp. 190–219.

———. 2007. *Changing the Story about Higher Education's Public Purposes and Work: Land-Grants, Liberty, and the Little Country Theater.* Ann Arbor, Mich.: Imagining America.

———. 2008. "Reconstructing a Democratic Tradition of Public Scholarship in the Land-Grant System." In *Agent of Democracy: Higher Education and the HEX Journey,* edited by D.W. Brown and D. Witte. Dayton, Ohio: Kettering Foundation Press.

Peters, S.J., and M. Hittleman, eds. 2003. *We Grow People: Profiles of Extension Educators, Cornell University Cooperative Extension, New York City.* Ithaca, N.Y.: Cornell University.

Peters, S.J., and P.A. Morgan. 2004. "The Country Life Commission: Reconsidering a Milestone in American agricultural history." *Agricultural History* 78, no. 3, pp. 289–316.

Peters, S.J., N.R. Jordan, M. Adamek, and T.R. Alter, eds. 2005. *Engaging Campus and Community: The Practice of Public Scholarship in the State and Land-Grant University System.* Dayton, Ohio: Kettering Foundation Press.

Peters, S.J., D.J. O'Connell, T.R. Alter, and A.L.H Jack, eds. 2006. *Catalyzing Change: Profiles of Cornell Cooperative Extension Educators from Greene, Tompkins, and Erie Counties, New York.* Ithaca, N.Y.: Cornell University.

Posner, R.A. 2001. *Public Intellectuals: A Study of Decline.* Cambridge: Harvard University Press.

Presidents' Declaration on the Civic Responsibility of Higher Education. 1999. Providence: Campus Compact.

Rabinow, P., and W.M. Sullivan, eds. 1987. *Interpretive Social Science: A Second Look.* Berkeley: University of California Press.

Ransby, B. 2003. *Ella Baker and the Black Freedom Movement: A Radical Democratic Vision.* Chapel Hill: University of North Carolina Press.

Rasmussen, W.D. 1989. *Taking the University to the People: Seventy-Five Years of Cooperative Extension.* Ames: Iowa State University Press.

Reason, P., and H. Bradbury, eds. 2007. *The Sage Handbook of Action Research: Participative Inquiry and Practice.* 2nd ed. Thousand Oaks, Calif.: Sage Publications.

Recchiuti, J.L. 2007. *Civic Engagement: Social Science and Progressive-Era Reform in New York City.* Philadelphia: University of Pennsylvania Press.

Rodgers, A.D. 1949. *Liberty Hyde Bailey: A Story of American Plant Sciences.* Princeton, N.J.: Princeton University Press.

Rogers, M.B. 1990. *Cold Anger: A Story of Faith and Power Politics.* Denton: University of North Texas Press.

Ross, E.D. 1942. *Democracy's College: The Land-Grant Movement in the Formative Stage.* Ames: Iowa State College Press.

Rossiter, M.W. 1979. "The Organization of the Agricultural Sciences." In *The Organization of Knowledge in Modern America, 1860–1920,* edited by A. Oleson and J. Voss. Baltimore: Johns Hopkins University Press.

Said, E.W. 1994. *Representations of the Intellectual.* New York: Vintage Books.

Sandel, M.J. 1996. *Democracy's Discontent: America in Search of a Public Philosophy.* Cambridge: Harvard University Press.

Scott, J.W., and D. Keates, eds. 2001. *Schools of Thought: Twenty-Five Years of Interpretive Social Science.* Princeton, N.J.: Princeton University Press.

Scott, R.V. 1970. *The Reluctant Farmer: The Rise of Agricultural Extension to 1914.* Urbana: University of Illinois Press.

Seidman, I. 2006. *Interviewing as Qualitative Research: A Guide for Researchers in Education and the Social Sciences.* 3rd ed. New York: Teachers College Press.

Slaughter, S., and L.L. Leslie. 1997. *Academic Capitalism: Politics, Policies, and the Entrepreneurial University.* Baltimore: Johns Hopkins University Press.

Small, A.W. 1905. *General Sociology: An Exposition of the Main Development in Sociological Theory from Spencer to Ratzenhofer.* Chicago, IL: University of Chicago Press.

———. 1986. "Scholarship and Social Agitation." *American Journal of Sociology* 1, no. 5.

Smith, C.B., and M.C. Wilson. 1930. *The Agricultural Extension System of the United States.* New York: John Wiley & Sons.

Smith, M.C. 1994. *Social Science in the Crucible: The American Debate over Objectivity and Purpose, 1918–1941.* Durham, N.C.: Duke University Press.

Smith, T.V., and L.D. White, eds. 1929. *Chicago: An Experiment in Social Research.* Chicago: University of Chicago Press.

Stein, D.G., ed. 2004. *Buying In or Selling Out? The Commercialization of the American Research University.* New Brunswick, N.J.: Rutgers University Press.

Strand, K.J., N. Cutforth, R. Stoecker, S. Marullo, and P. Donohue. 2003. *Community-Based Research and Higher Education: Principles and Practices.* San Francisco: Jossey-Bass.

Sullivan, W.M. 1999. "What Is Left of Professionalism after Managed Care?" *Hastings Center Report* 29, no. 2, pp. 7–13.

———. 2003. "Engaging the Civic Option: A New Academic Professionalism?" *Campus Compact Reader* (summer). Providence, R.I.: Campus Compact.

———. 2005. *Work and Integrity: The Crisis and Promise of Professionalism in America.* San Francisco: Jossey-Bass.

Summers, J.H., ed. 2008. *The Politics of Truth: Selected Writings of C. Wright Mills.* New York: Oxford University Press.

Thomas, E. 2009. "Obama's Nobel Headache." *Newsweek,* April 6.

True, A.C. 1928. *A History of Agricultural Extension Work in the United States, 1785–1923.* Washington D.C.: United States Department of Agriculture.

Tuana, N. and S. Morgen, eds. 2001. *Engendering Rationalities.* Albany: SUNY Press.

Van de Ven, A.H. 2007. *Engaged Scholarship: A Guide for Organizational and Social Research.* New York: Oxford University Press.

Veysey, L.R. 1965. *The Emergence of the American University.* Chicago: University of Chicago Press.

Walzer, M. 2002. *The Company of Critics: Social Criticism and Political Commitment in the Twentieth Century.* New York: Basic Books.

Ward, K. 2003. *Faculty Service Roles and the Scholarship of Engagement.* ASHE-ERIC Higher Education Report, vol. 29, no. 5. San Francisco: Jossey-Bass.

Warren, M.R. 2001. *Dry Bones Rattling: Community Building to Revitalize American Democracy.* Princeton, N.J.: Princeton University Press.

Weber, M. 1948. "Science as a Vocation." In *From Max Weber: Essays in Sociology,* edited by H.H. Gerth and C.W. Mills. New York: Routledge.

Weisbrod, B.A., J.P. Ballou, and E.D. Asch. 2008. *Mission and Money: Understanding the University.* New York: Cambridge University Press.

Westbrook, R.B. 1991. *John Dewey and American Democracy.* Ithaca: Cornell University Press.

Williams, R.L. 1991. *The Origins of Federal Support for Higher Education: George W. Atherton and the Land-Grant College Movement.* University Park: Pennsylvania State University Press.

Wolfe, A. 2003. *An Intellectual in Public.* Ann Arbor: University of Michigan Press.

Index

AASCU. *See* American Association of State Colleges and Universities

AAUP. *See* American Association of University Professors (AAUP)

abstracted empiricism, 363n52

academia. *See* academic institutions; academic professionals; civic life; higher education; politics; science

academic freedom: ideas and, 32; lessons, 256–57; Lundberg on, 26, 27; public intellectual tradition and, 56; "Report of the Committee on Academic Freedom and Tenure," 20–21, 23–24, 26, 31, 32; tyranny and, 22–23, 32, 55–57, 59; using, 256

academic institutions, 21, 46; AR/PS/EO and, 60; civic life and, 22, 332, 333; cultural norms and, xvii; democracy advanced by, 9, 22; economics and, 8; mission of, 8; teaching styles of, 137. *See also* land-grant system

academic professionals, 96: academic calling for, 21–22; active, 37, 322; AR/PS/EO tradition and, 38, 23–24, 46, 57, 58–60; civic engagement of, 56, 57; civic forms of work, 351–52; civic life off-campus of, xii–xiii, xviii–xix, 3, 7, 10, 11–14, 37–38, 47–48, 50–51; and civic work of, 19–20, 24, 33, 37, 47, 317–18, 333, 349–51; commercialized

education and, 8–9; conflicts and tensions and, 96, 354; at Cornell, 3, 68, 142, 148, 177, 202, 224; defined, 15, 21–23, 320; democracy and expertise of, 64, 66, 151, 318–19, 331; "detached attachment" and, 56, 57, 58; Educational Finance Research Consortium and, 333; evolution of, 65–66, 69; extension's unique, 46; identity of, 11, 27–28, 31, 326, 327–28, 331–32; as insiders, 326–28, 332; knowledge and, 22, 27, 28, 31, 53–54; land-grant system and, 30, 40, 316; as listeners, 321–22; in New York State, 68; normative anti-tradition and, 61–62, 349; as organic intellectuals, 57, 59; politics and, 31, 57; public intellectual tradition and, 32, 52–55; purposive, 28, 37; "Report of the Committee on Academic Freedom and Tenure," and, 20–21; role of, 15, 21–22, 47, 49, 56–57, 61, 96–97; social function of, 21–22, 24; in technical fields, 213, 317; types of, 34, 37, 46. *See also* interviewed academic professionals by specific name (listed under practitioner profiles); academic institutions; Cooperative Extension System; outreach; public intellectual tradition

access, xvi, 9–10, 134, 152, 172, 182, 252, 261

Access Versus Excellence, xv

383

385